The Life and Times of
VLADIMIR JABOTINSKY

FIGHTER AND PROPHET

The Last Years

JOSEPH B. SCHECHTMAN

Eshel
Books

ACKNOWLEDGMENTS

Even more than the first volume of Vladimir Jabotinsky's biography, this second, concluding volume owes its completion largely to the encouragement, help, and cooperation extended by several institutions and scores of individuals. Considerations of space make it impossible to thank each and every one of them by name. Many are mentioned either in the text or in the bibliographical notes at the end of the book. It would, however, be unfair not to single out at least a few of those whose assistance was particularly outstanding; and, although all errors of fact and judgment are exclusively the author's own, he should like to acknowledge with sincere gratitude their share in the preparation of the book.

Mrs. T. E. Jabotinsky-Kopp, Jabotinsky's sister, generously contributed personal reminiscences and abundant correspondence. Dr. Oskar K. Rabinowicz and Messrs. Joseph Klarman, Shmuel Katz, and David Sivan went over the entire text of this volume, offering invaluable suggestions, supplying additional material, and checking sources. Messrs. Menachem Begin and Yaakov Meridor read and commented on the chapters dealing with Jabotinsky as "The Father of the Jewish Armed Resistance," while Dr. Aba Achimeir rendered a similar service in regard to the chapter "The Father of the Jewish Resistance." M. Grossman read and discussed with the author the chapters "Between Opposition and Independence" and "The Big Split," and David Ben Gurion did the same in regard to the chapter "The Abortive Ben Gurion Romance." Adolph Gourevitch and Serge Galperin assisted materially in the preparation of the sub-chapters on Jabotinsky as novelist and linguist.

The author did not feel competent to cope adequately with two essential topics of this volume, and he is sincerely grateful to Mordehai

Katz who contributed the chapter "The Father of the Betar," and to Adolph Gourevitch for contributing the chapter "Jabotinsky and the Hebrew Language."

The Jabotinsky Institute (Tel Aviv), the Central Zionist Archives (Jerusalem), the Editorial Board of the *History of the Hagana* (Tel Aviv), and the Zionist Archives and Library (New York) were as cooperative and helpful in providing documentation for this volume as they were in regard to the first volume. To the heads of these institutions—Dr. J. Paamoni, Dr. A. Bein, Yehuda Slutzky, and Mrs. Sylvia Landress—as well as to their respective staffs, this biography is very much indebted.

The Jabotinsky Biography Committee, composed of outstanding leaders of Jewish public opinion, gave precious moral backing to the preparation and publication of the biography in its entirety. Mr. Leo Wolfson, Chairman of its Board of Directors, continued taking active interest in all questions connected with this work.

The extensive preparatory work for this volume, especially for the English edition, was made possible by the grants of the World Executive of the Herut-Revisionist Organization and of the Jewish Agency Executive, as well as by conributions of the following persons and institutions: American Friends of the Alliance Israelite Universelle; S. Frimerman (Toronto); Fraternidad Bene Berit (Caracas); A. Gurvitch; Dr. R. Hecht (Haifa); S. Korner; L. Kronik (Montreal); Mrs. A. Levi; H. Michelson (London); Netzivut Betar (Peru); C. Pickel; Dr. O. Rabinowicz; E. Reifer; A. Schnur (Bogota); O. Shainhouse (Toronto); Sociedad Union Israelita del Peru (Lima); J. Spector; M. Sperber; S. Wang; M. Weinberg; M. Yardney.

The Spanish edition contains the names of persons and institutions who have contributed to its preparation and publication.

Special acknowledgment is due to Mrs. Katie Kaplan, Haifa, who, as editor, was eminently instrumental in the preparation of this volume in its present shape.

And, just as in the first volume, special mention must be made of the invaluable assistance offered from the very beginning by the author's wife whose help he cannot ever adequately acknowledge.

J. B. S.

CONTENTS

ILLUSTRATIONS

The following illustrations appear as a group after page 256.

INTRODUCTION

INTRODUCTION

Reviews of the first volume of *The Vladimir Jabotinsky Story* were numerous and almost without exception extremely favorable. It seems reasonable to suppose that at least a contributing factor to this friendly reception was the fact that the period (1880-1923) dealt with in that first part belongs to the not so distant past. The controversies which loomed so large at that time are now viewed in a different, more detached perspective; and most of its main personages are no longer among the living.

The present volume covers the last seventeen years (1923-1940) of Jabotinsky's life. These years are still a living part of the annals of our generation. Many were personally involved in the battles whose storm center was Jabotinsky—they see their own lifetime through him. And, at one time or another, many hated or loved him, attacked or fervently revered him. Embers of relatively recent passions are still smoldering, and, though no effort was spared in this biography to avoid political or personal bias, criticism and resentment from one or another quarter is probably unavoidable: this seems to be a "professional risk" inherent in any attempt to reconstruct the life of so dynamic and controversial a figure as Jabotinsky was. Almost every review, however favorable, contained the challenging remark: "We eagerly look forward to the second volume of this work, which will deal with the most controversial period of Jabotinsky's life."

It took about three years to prepare this second volume. Now, at publication, the author would like to outline a few fundamental methodological considerations which, he feels, are mandatory for every biographer.

1. To write the history of a man, or the history of an epoch—these are essentially two distinct undertakings, differing both in name and technique. It was probably because Plutarch renounced the one, and Carlyle the other, that each of them was able to achieve his respective task in so masterly a manner. This biography is *not* a history of the Zionist or Revisionist movement of the Jabotinsky era. It is first and last the life story of the man. But an integrated biography of a man of Jabotinsky's stature and range of interests cannot be adequately written without outlining the factual historical background of his time. The interrelation between the personal and historical ingredients is, however, very delicate. If either assumes ascendancy, the biography lacks in balance: the background may overshadow the subject; take direction in defiance of the overall structure; convert the whole into history first and biography second; offer too much of the "times" and not enough of the "man," so that even if the "man" is there, he is somehow lost in the abundance of historical detail. This would be something like giving *Hamlet* without the Dane. Or, on the other hand, the subject may stand lonely and forlorn, without the proper setting of time and place. The biographer's task is to establish and maintain the proper proportion, so that the total product remains more important than either of the contributing partners.

This biographer is not in a position to judge whether, and to what extent, he has succeeded in following this precept. It is possible that in some instances the background is overemphasized, and in others—played down. The intention was always to present a well-substantiated, integral picture, to see to it that the book should contain not even a breath of windy speculation, not an ounce of rhetorical fat, and scarcely a shred of information that is not fully necessary to the understanding of the complex personality whose story is being told here.

2. The prime duty of the biographer is to set down the indisputable facts, so far as the facts are available or discoverable. In this book, all the data are recorded facts that can be easily checked. Annotations and footnotes are admittedly annoying to almost everyone except professional historians and researchers. However, a biographer, if he is to play fair with his readers, can hardly dispense with the most painstaking specification of the sources he has used. The preparation of this book demanded a tremendous amount of patient sifting through acres of controversial ground where facts and legend have lain closely

commingled for decades, separating the probable from the impossible, the truth from mere fancy. Far more work has gone into this book than is visible on the immediate surface.

A contemporary biographer, unlike his earlier predecessors, is seldom in a position to encompass fully the mountains of material at his disposal, and is forced to melt them down to sizeable volume. This biographer was unable to lend himself to the multi-volumed treatment of the Nicolay and Hay *Life of Abraham Lincoln* (ten volumes), or the W. F. Monypenny and G. E. Buckle *The Life of Benjamin Disraeli* (six volumes published within a decade). He was compelled to leave unmentioned or unquoted many of Jabotinsky's speeches, articles and letters that he would very much have liked to include in part or as a whole; and he had to decide which sentences or paragraphs would shed more significant light on Jabotinsky's life.

Particularly difficult were such decisions in regard to Jabotinsky's letters. A biographer seeking to give a picture of a life as full as Jabotinsky's, must perforce follow the subject's manner and tempo; he is, therefore, naturally eager to make the most extensive use of the subject's correspondence and private papers, and can never let that subject speak too much for himself. For, in truth, a man always explains himself better than anyone can do it for him; even when he is mistaken, or tries to conceal his true feelings and intentions, he unwittingly reveals himself. This is particularly true in regard to such a master of the *art épistolaire* as was Jabotinsky, and it was often painful to forego quoting *in extenso* scores of the thousands of letters written in half a dozen languages.

This biographer was also forced to omit many minor—and sometimes not so minor—figures and events. If all could be told, it would take a far more extensive study than the two volumes to which he has had to limit himself. Therefore, synthesis and strict verbal economy have had to replace prolixity; rigid selection imposed itself.

At the same time, it was mandatory to see to it that as little as possible of the truly essential was sacrificed. The narrative follows Jabotinsky's last seventeen years year by year, item by item, examining his thoughts and words and actions for significant clues.

3. A biography must cling throughout to the framework of historical truth, to avoid retouching any detail, adjusting a date or an event to fit a preconceived purpose, even though, because of structural or stylistical considerations, the author may see fit to leave one or

another unmentioned. A biographer who tries to twist or pervert actual events in order to produce what he deems to be a convenient version, defeats his own purpose.

Historical truth is not the servant of the biographer, but his master. No biography can be better than its research. The product of a wide, penetrating, honest research, with all its recurrent themes of conflict and accomplishment, has to be woven through the entirety of the life story, creating an overall, perceivable pattern into which the parts can be fitted to make an organic whole.

Others may perhaps in time come to paint portraits of Jabotinsky in their own style, more expressive and imaginative, more critical or assertive. The prerequisite for all such interpretative studies is, however, the sturdy platform of pragmatically established incontrovertible particulars which this book purports to offer.

Of course, the biographer may—and should—be as imaginative as he pleases in the manner in which he collates the material. But he may not imagine the material. He has to read himself into the time and into the life he is writing; but then he must also beware of re-creating that life in his own image. He is entitled to judge the facts but not to sit in judgment, refraining from hindsight and after-thoughts: Truman rightly said in his autobiography that "any school-boy's afterthought is worth more than the forethought of greatest statesmen." And, finally, he must respect the dead, but he has to tell the truth as he sees it.

Ultimately, a biographer paints a picture which emerges in his mind after close and intense study of the material as a whole, and he can only paint it from *his* angle, from *his* time, and *his* relation-ship to the time and life he seeks to recapture. A mere chronicler, limiting himself to piling up the known facts, would confront the reader not with a palpable and breathing individual, but a card index, a calendar, a date book, a figure of *papier-mâché*.

4. The noted English writer Giles Lytton Strachey spoke of the biographical art as "the most delicate and humane of all the branches of the art of writing." It is delicate because the biographer seeks to blow the breath of life into the inert and fragmentary material which survives an individual's passage on earth. It is humane because such an effort is inevitably a selective and refining process. What a biographer must learn to look for, is not only what happened in the given life but also what everything that happened meant to the sub-

ject. He must strive to discover the life behind the facts. An adequate biography must meet three essential demands. It has to tell enough about its subject to make him real; to tell it well enough to make him interesting; and to tell it thoughtfully enough to make him important.

The biographer's responsibility is great inded. He is largely responsible for the image in which the man he is writing about will be seen by future generations, which did not know the man and will judge him mainly, if not exclusively, on the basis of the record preserved by his biography. In Jabotinsky's *Samson,* the Levite Machbonai ben Shuni says to the Nazarite : "One thing will stand out for all eternity : the thing I, the Levite Machbonai, set down as the truth . . . the things I preserve in prayers and set down on bits of skin, and people will call them the truth. All else is mere smoke." And indeed, Samson's life and deeds have been transferred to posterity by his unknown "biographer."

5. The introduction to the first volume of *The Vladimir Jabotinsky Story* stressed that "this biography is not an act of hero worship, however great the writer's respect and admiration for Jabotinsky's person and achievements." This statement fully applies to the present volume.

There is undoubtedly in the masses a deep longing for a hero, who gives them blessed relief from their daily lives, which are all too frequently composites of one petty thing after another. Hemmed in by their narrow horizons, they yearn to hear the hero's voice, clear and confident, releasing them, telling them where to go and why. The timid and the bored hanker for a hero to bow before and follow blindly. The danger of hero worship is implicit in the human need for heroes.

And this is a great danger indeed. The immediate and unavoidable result of a hero-worshipping biography is that it turns its subject into an object of unbounded adulation, invested with putative attributes to supplement or explain his real ones, enshrouded, and concealed, in a misty cloud of myth. He is always right—never wrong; no hint of blemish is permitted.

Such a picture of Jabotinsky would be neither whole nor real and would be unfair to him. He deserves better of history than this, and he needs no superlatives—which, in the words of H. G. Wells, are "the language of immaturity"—to make his life story both dramatic and significant.

In a letter dated June 4, 1956, Professor Joseph Klausner praised the first volume of this biography for "its blend of objectivity and profound admiration." "A biography," he wrote, "cannot be good if it has no love for its subject, but that love should not be blind. Your affection [for Jabotinsky] is an open-eyed love. You should be complimented . . . for not avoiding to mention the mistakes of the great man and the shortcomings of some of his less essential actions. Your book is therefore unique in its truthfulness and comprehensiveness among the writings about Jabotinsky."

This volume is an attempt to live up to that standard.

JOSEPH B. SCHECHTMAN.

New York City
1959

To My Wife and Collaborator

1

TWILIGHT AND COMEBACK

ONE

FROM LETTERS TO ACTION

1. *Poet and Publisher*

"A LOAD HAS fallen from my shoulders," wrote Jabotinsky from Berlin to his mother and sister on January 21, 1923, confirming the news of his having left the Zionist Organization. "I am genuinely happy . . . no responsibilities; and no more need to lie. I shall be able to devote myself to my own affairs and start getting rich." Three days later, he added: "Today I am going to London . . . together with Ania I shall decide what our plans are to be . . . I am well—and it feels good to be a free man."

These were brave and cheerful words. They were also undoubtedly a true reflection of the psychological relief that came as a climax to the termination of a tense and frustrating situation. But there can hardly be any doubt that, alongside this genuine spiritual elation, there were mundane cares weighing heavily on Jabotinsky's mind. He had abandoned a well-paid position on the Zionist Executive, which had been his sole source of income for about two yearse. In February, he also resigned from the Board of Directors of the *Keren ha' Yessod*. He had a wife and son to support; he also contributed to the budget of his mother and sister in Palestine, and of his nephew studying in Switzerland. In his letters to Palestine he made light of these worries and spoke of "getting rich." In fact, the problem he faced was simply not to founder financially, and to secure a modest living for the family. Journalism was practically out of the question as a major source of income: there was no Russian-language press in the free world; of the Anglo-Jewish publications, only the London *Jewish Chronicle* would occasionally publish an article of his; and at that time he had not yet become fluent in Yiddish.

But side by side with journalism and politics, literature and publishing had always held a strong appeal for Jabotinsky, and to these he willingly, even eagerly, used to turn whenever the opportunity presented itself. (See Vol. I, pp. 145, 171.) And when he left the Zionist Executive, he did so with the firm intention of concentrating on these fields. "No more politics for me," he told Dr. S. Perlman. "When Dr. Weizmann retires—or is forced to retire—he will have a hobby: chemistry. My hobby is literature. I am fundamentally a *Stubenhocker* (homebird), and people are always dragging me into politics." [2]

In fact, he had never abandoned his literary activities. When, in Berlin in September, 1923, he received the nineteenth volume of the Hebrew literary almanac *Hatqufa* containing twenty pages (four cantos) of his translation of Dante's *Divine Comedy*, he was "as happy as a child." "I have been reading this translation all morning—and as God is my witness, I understood every word of it," he reported in light vein to his sister.[3] In the same year, a tastefully printed Hebrew booklet (with vowel signs) *Targumim* (Translations), appeared in Berlin, containing translations of poems by Edgar Allan Poe, Gabriele d'Annunzio, Joséphin Soulari, Omar Khayyam, and Edmond Rostand. As far as this writer was able to ascertain, this was the first attempt in modern Hebrew poetry at versification based on the Sefardic pronunciation. Up to that time, all Hebrew poets, including Chaim Nachman Bialik, Saul Tchernikowsky, Zalman Schneur, and Jacob Kahan, had written poetry adapted to the *Ashkenazi* pronunciation of the Hebrew language.

Targumim appeared as "copyright by S. D. Salzman," who owned the publishing house *Hasefer* (The Book). Determined this time to realize the dream he had cherished in Jerusalem in 1919 (see Vol. I, pp. 301-302) Jabotinsky joined forces with Salzman in order to build up *Hasefer* into a joint stock company with sufficient funds for the publication of textbooks for Hebrew schools, as well as novels and poetry. With the help of a group of London friends, they succeeded in raising several thousand pounds as the initial capital. Jabotinsky was appointed editor-in-chief.[4]

Hasefer concentrated on literature intended to serve the needs of Hebrew schools. Jabotinsky's notebooks for 1923 contain an ambitious two-year program of publications. In the field of school manuals, it provided for twenty-four elementary books on general and Jewish subjects (with vowel signs), as well as for geographical and zoological atlases. To further the study of everyday Hebrew, eight pocket-books of self-instruction were scheduled—for Russian, English, French, German, Italian, Spanish, Polish, and Yiddish—and sixteen dictionaries (two in each of those languages). In the field of children's literature, the program envisaged the translation of one hundred of the most popular novels by Jules Verne, Bret Harte, Rider Haggard, Zane Grey, Conan Doyle, Mayne Reid, as well as abridged translations from the works of Walter Scott, Charles Dickens, Alexandre Dumas, and James Fenimore Cooper. The list included such classics as *Uncle Tom's Cabin, Don Quixote, Robinson Crusoe, Gulliver's Travels,* as well as selected tales of all nations. Jabotinsky held very definite views on children's literature. "The topics must be adventure, travel, and the like," he wrote to his sister. "No stories of school life, no sentimental stories, no moralizing literature. This stuff I will not publish. It is a matter of principle with me." [5] He contended that a pedagogue must strive to develop the child's imagination before his intellect. The modern school makes pupils prematurely "knowledge-able," over-rationalistic, cold, slaves of reality. To counteract this trend, literature for children must instill in its readers, as provision for their journey through life, vividness of imagination, love of adventure, warmheartedness; books of this kind are bound to enrich their vision so that when they grow up, they will dream "royal dreams" and have the daring to do great things.

Hasefer published only two books of this category: Conan Doyle's Sherlock Holmes stories and *The Prisoner of Zenda* by Anthony Hope; the purpose was to give the pupil of a Hebrew school interesting light reading matter, thus sparing him the necessity of looking for it in a foreign language library. "You will *not* be pleased by these publications," Jabotinsky wrote to S. D. Salzman; "in general appearance and paper, they look like French novels in yellow covers, without *nekudot* [vowel signs]—but I want to accustom the [Hebrew] reading public to a cheap book—the shilling book." [6] *Hasefer* also published the *Kol Bo la Talmid,* a 288-page schoolboy's pocket almanac, which contained a wealth of topics and information never before supplied by Hebrew pedagogues to their pupils. Jabotinsky himself contributed five chapters: on Jewish organizations, Sefardic pronunciation, the Zion Mule Corps, the Jewish Legion, as well as on table manners (*Shulkhan Arukh*)—how to behave and how not to behave when eating—(with illustrations by Maxa Nordau).

Hasefer's most important publication was, however, the *Hebrew Geographical Atlas,* which was edited by Jabotinsky in cooperation with Dr. S. Perlman. The *Atlas* represented a new venture in Hebrew publishing. It was intended not only for children, but also for adults, with special emphasis on the location of Jewish communities throughout the world, their numerical strength, economic, political, and cultural status. Nor was the general purpose of a geographic atlas neglected. In addition to maps of the most important regions, ample information was given about the salient features of the individual countries : population, occupational structure, industry, and trade. The *Atlas* filled a long-felt need in Hebrew educational literature. It was welcomed by qualified reviewers as "an unexpected realization of a dream of both teachers and pupils of geography," as an attempt which "must be pronounced successful in practically every respect"; its publishers were "to be congratulated by all friends of Hebrew education on their capital work, which may with confidence be acclaimed as the pride of Hebrew pedagogical literature." [7]

This writer was privileged to collaborate in the preparation of the *Atlas* by supplying statistical and demographic data, and he knows how much diligence and work Jabotinsky devoted to every detail of the publication. He loved his work for *Hasefer* and cherished the hope of transferring the entire undertaking to Palestine and settling there himself. On the occasion of his sister's birthday he wrote : "Every year I feel ever more strong how senseless it is that we are always apart on family occasions. But now I am toiling away in order to organize the business [*Hasefer*] in Palestine. Never in my life have I worked so hard." [8]

All these plans did not materialize. In the spring of 1924, *Hasefer* was temporarily transferred from Berlin to Paris. For some time, its offices were located in Jabotinsky's three-room apartment on 71, rue de la Tombe Issoire : the dining room was assigned to Dr. Perlmann and two clerical assistants; Jabotinsky worked in the adjoining room. [9] In 1926, the offices were transferred to 99, rue de Rome. [10] But by that time Jabotinsky was again deep in political work. The *Hasefer* venture petered out. Its most valuable and lasting achievement remained the *Atlas* which was widely used in the Hebrew schools throughout the world.

Ten years after publication, the entire edition was sold out and the need for a new printing was felt everywhere. But the plates of the

28

maps were in the possession of the Leipzig firm of H. Wagner and
E. Debes that had engraved them, and Leipzig was in Hitler-ruled
Germany, which to Jabotinsky was morally untouchable. In March,
1935, he wrote from Chicago:[11] "No matter how painful it is, I must
categorically refuse to publish a new edition [of the *Atlas*] . . . I
can have nothing to do with this book. Even if Wagner were to be
able to transfer the engraved plates to Holland or any other county—
the money [from the sale of the new edition] would come to him,
i.e. where it shouldn't. This is particularly inadmissible (*for me*) now,
when his [Wagner's] homeland is so obviously becoming the enemy
of the entire world, and every penny will be used for bullets." Later,
he tentatively consented to cede his copyright to the Zionist Organization in Germany—stipulating that he personally would not receive,
either directly or indirectly, any profit from the publication. In 1936,
Dr. Georg Karesky contacted Wagner and Debes, who agreed to
reprint five thousand copies for the modest remuneration of ten
thousand Marks (twenty-five hundred dollars) and promised to try
to obtain official permission to replace the "Made in Germany" label
by any other at the discretion of the Zionist Organization. A complete
report on the tentative agreement was sent to Jabotinsky with the
request that he give his final approval.

The reply was long in coming. When it did come, it contained a
somewhat embarrassed but firm "No." Apologizing for the trouble
he was causing his friends in Germany, Jabotinsky stated that after
having thought over the project afresh, he had come to the conclusion
that it was "neither proper nor justifiable." This conclusion was sustained by Professor Alexander M. Kulischer, the Supreme Judge of
the New Zionist Organization, to whom he submitted the matter.[12]

2. Back in the Harness

As could easily have been foreseen, Jabotinsky's status of a "free man"
and his aloofness from active Zionist politics did not last long. In
October, 1923, two young Russian-Jewish refugees, A. Davisski and
L. Czeskis, visited Jabotinsky at the Heindrich boarding house at
Kurfürstendamm 42. They were members of a youth group which,
aroused by anti-Semitic slogans *Juden heraus!* that were then being
openly voiced in the German capital, was looking for action. They
asked Jabotinsky to attend a meeting of this group and to discuss

plans for the future with them. After some hesitation, Jabotinsky agreed. It was his first direct contact with the youth after his resignation from the Zionist Executive.

About a dozen young people were present. Jabotinsky spoke briefly and rather inconclusively: "I may try again. I have been deeply disappointed in our youth, but have not lost faith in it." No decisions were taken at this first meeting. The young people agreed to meet again. At the second meeting they decided to form a "League of Zionist Activists" with its office at Kurfürstendamm 149. Jabotinsky liked their spirit, but remained aloof. He had little faith in the ability of this youth group to achieve tangible results. But he provided them with a list of names and addresses of several friends and sympathizers in Vienna, Riga, Bulgaria, Greece, and Palestine.[13] He himself, however, stuck to his determination to remain "just a writer," to limit his public activities to the Russian Zionist weekly *Rasswyet,* with which he had become associated in July, 1923, and which was his sole mouthpiece. In an address delivered on October 14, 1923, before the American Jewish Congress in New York, Israel Zangwill, describing the nadir reached by the Zionist Movement, said with bitterness: "Jabotinsky nearly touched the true war-standard of service, but even he now edits a paper in Berlin." [14]

It was, however, just this "paper in Berlin" that was indirectly instrumental in putting Jabotinsky back into Zionist political harness. In the fall of 1923, the *Rasswyet's* financial position became critical. The increasing cost of printing, mailing, etc., could not be met by subscriptions and the few advertisements. To save the paper, Jabotinsky agreed to undertake a lecture tour in the Baltic countries (Lithuania, Latvia, Esthonia), where the traditions of Russian Zionism were still very much alive, where the name of Jabotinsky meant a good deal, and where he could lecture in Russian or Hebrew. The first lecture on "Activism and Zionism" was to have been delivered in Hebrew on November 9 in Lithuania's capital, Kaunas, among whose Jewish community the knowledge of the Hebrew language was widespread. Jabotinsky's manager, Israel M. Span, cabled, however, from Kaunas, that everybody he met insisted that the lecture be delivered in Yiddish. Informed of this demand, Jabotinsky calmly said: "Please wire Span that I will speak in Hebrew,—or let him cancel the lecture."

Very few people came to meet Jabotinsky on November 7 at the

Kaunas railway station. A small group of local Jewish *intelligentsia* attended the reception which was arranged for him at the home of his host, Dr. M. Schwartz. His lecture, on the other hand, attracted a large audience, which gave him an enthusiastic ovation. The next day, he was besieged by countless visitors from whom his secretary tried desperately to protect him. One of the visitors, a pupil of the famous Slobodka Yeshiva, was particularly insistent upon seeing Jabotinsky. Asked what his problem was, he confided: "I want to marry Weizmann's daughter and all I want of Jabotinsky is that he act as my *shadchen;* he is the only one who could persuade Weizmann." Told about the request, Jabotinsky said amusedly: "I would love to oblige the young man; the only trouble is that Weizmann has no daughter. . . . "[15]

After Kaunas, where his ideas were accepted by a small but valuable group of Zionist intellectuals headed by Reuven Rubinstein, Abraham Idelson, and Moshe de Shalit, Jabotinsky visited two other Lithuanian towns, Poneves and Shauli. He then turned toward Latvia's capital, Riga. At the railway station he was warmly greeted by a large crowd. He was acclaimed with particular enthusiasm by the Zionist Academic Corps, *Hasmonaea*. It was this student group that actually broke Jabotinsky's determination to stick to political "enlightenment," and keep aloof from organized political activities. In an article, "The Hasmonaea of Riga," published in 1926, Jabotinsky briefly told the story of his "conversion":[16]

In October or November [it was in November], 1923, a gentleman came to Riga and delivered a lecture on [Zionist] activism. The next day, *Hasmonaea* invited him to a meeting at its club, and squarely put to him the question: "And what now? You have no right to preach such views and to stir up young people if you don't intend to call them to action. You either keep quiet, or organize a party." This sounded logical, and their guest belonged to that brand of people, unpopular in Israel, who do believe in logic. Later, after midnight, the guest and *Hasmonaea* rose and gave each other a solemn pledge to roll up their sleeves and straighten out the Zionist movement.

The high-school youth of Riga organized a group under the name of *Histadrut ha'Noar ha'Zioni ha'Activisti al Shem Joseph Trumpeldor* (Organization of Zionist Activist Youth in the name of Joseph Trumpeldor), headed by Aaron Propes. Jabotinsky also visited Dvinsk, Ludze, Rezekne, and Lepaya in Latvia, Tallin and Tartu in Esthonia, and Memel, Lithuania (where he spoke in German). The reaction of the official and semi-official Zionist circles to Jabotinsky's lecture tour was a mixture of annoyance and concern. The New York *Tog* complained that Jabotinsky was "attacking Zionism and painting a black picture of the situation in the Zionist movement." [17] The New York weekly *Dos Yiddische Folk,* the official organ of the American Zionist Organization, wrote: "Just at this time Jabotinsky has to come to the fore with his extremist demands . . . again to give the world the wrong notion that we [Zionists] intend to dominate the Arabs of Palestine by force of arms, thus offering our enemies a new weapon against us." The *Jewish Morning Journal* in New York, *Di Zeit* in London, and *Die Jüdische Rundschau* in Berlin reacted similarly, describing Jabotinsky's lecture tour as a campaign "against the sacred fundamentals of the Zionist movement," as a venture bound to harm "the progressing reconciliation with the Arabs," the Keren ha'Yessod drive, etc.[18]

If anything, these attacks only strengthened Jabotinsky's determination to "roll up his sleeves." After his return from his lecture tour he wrote to Dr. Paul Diamant in Vienna:

The day before yesterday I returned from my tour through the *Randstaaten.* My impression is unexpectedly good. There is really a new youth, new in that they are longing for discipline and smartening-up. . . . This impression has sealed my fate. I have decided to turn from mere writing to action, i.e., to take the necessary steps in order to create some kind of movement out of activists who are now scattered all over the world.

On February 13, 1924, he wrote to Eliahu Ben Horin:

When I was in Lithuania and Latvia, I saw a young generation that is worth believing in. I will try to organize them for the cause, if I will have enough strength to do so.

It took Jabotinsky some time to decide about this "if." After his return to Berlin, he initiated several closed meetings of the *Rasswyet* editorial group in an effort to formulate its program. In March, 1924, a series of articles, under the common heading *Our Platform,* started appearing in *Rasswyet.*[19] Written by Jabotinsky, Dr. J. Brutzkus, S. Gepstein, I. Klinov, Dr. S. Perlman, I. Rosov, J. Schechtman, and I. Trivus, they touched upon all major aspects of Zionist political, economic, and organizational problems. In his article "Political

32

Offensive," Jabotinsky enumerated the fundamental points of this platform : the goal of Zionism—a Jewish State; the territory of the State—both sides of the Jordan; the method—mass colonization; the financial system—national loan. These four points could not be realized without international sanction. The immediate task of Zionism was, therefore, a sustained political offensive, coupled with the militarization of the Jewish youth in Palestine and in the Diaspora. On December 14, 1923, Jabotinsky wrote to Dr. Jacob I. Hoffman, one of the spiritual leaders of the *Hasmonaea* :[20] "Yesterday, we established an office here [in Berlin] to deal with organizational questions." Simultaneously, several Zionist leaders in various countries received a memorandum on the stationery of the *Ligue Pour la Révision de la Politique Sioniste, Bureau Provisoire d'Organisation,* containing a critical analysis of the political position of the Zionist cause and a concise program of action along the lines of *Our Platform.* Its authors felt confident that many Zionists the world over would sympathize with their views and announced that in December, 1924, they proposed to hold the first conference of the League.

The response was not uniform. As Jabotinsky put it : "the youth responded well, the 'notables'—poorly." Among the latter, particularly disappointing was Israel Zangwill's reaction : "He [Zangwill] sympathizes, but has no faith. 'Political Zionism is dead, and even you will be unable to revive it,' he writes; instead, he advises me to devote myself to the 'Jewish Republic (sic!) in the Crimea. . . . ' Zangwill is in general not a man who could fit in with us. To him, the fate of the [Zionist] movement is always contingent upon the attitude of today's parish constable." [21] Meir Grossman's attitude was also rather lukewarm at that time : "Grossman approves of our platform but confesses that he lacks enthusiasm." [22]

In the meantime, however, Jabotinsky's original plans for the organization of a new movement underwent a drastic change. Early in 1924, his personal affairs forced him to leave Berlin and settle in Paris. "Where our temporary center will now be located—in Berlin or in Paris—will be clarified in the course of this month," he wrote on January 3. By the end of the month he admitted that his change of domicile—"imposed by personal considerations, because bread is a necessity—had indeed delayed the progress of the cause. It had, among other things, disrupted the activities of the [Berlin] office, which had practically ceased to function. . . . I am not a pessimist,

33

but I see that apathy is stronger than the 'divine discontent.' " [23] The Berlin office was later reorganized and Jabotinsky was again hopeful about the prospects of a conference in December.

These hopes did not materialize. The Berlin group of Russian Zionists which centered around the *Rasswyet* disintegrated—some went to Palestine, others to Paris. The *Rasswyet* succumbed to its financial troubles, and the last issue appeared on May 15, 1924. Jabotinsky admitted that " the center in Berlin is no center. In June I will transfer both the office and the *Rasswyet* to Paris, if there'll be any money. I am again undertaking a lecture tour for this purpose. . . . The conference will apparently not be convened *now*." [24]

In May, 1924, Jabotinsky left Paris to undertake the lecture tour that was intended to finance the establishment of the new office and the revival of the *Rasswyet*. He visited Germany, Austria and Czechoslovakia, where the academic youth proved to be particularly responsive to his appeal. Especially heartening was the response of the Vienna Student Corps, *Unitas*. Arthur Koestler, then a member of *Unitas*, recalls in his *Arrow in the Blue* :

At the end of three discussion meetings, we rallied unconditionally to the banner of the Activist opposition. Jabotinsky was elected Honorary *Bursch* of the *Corps*, a distinction which had been previously only bestowed on Herzl and Nordau—and a gold badge was ordered. [25]

With this gold badge, encased in a velvet box, I traveled one May day in 1924 to the frontier station of Lundenburg—in high spirits and third class, accompanied by "Puttl," the Falstaffian old boy and terror of the Pan-Germanists. . . . On the crowded platform of the frontier station, we recognized Jabotinsky from his photographs as he emerged from the Austrian customs with a volume of Dante in Italian under his arm. I had the gruesome task of accosting him, welcoming him to Austria, and pinning the badge on his lapel under the goggling eyes of customs officials and travelers. . . . He took the whole thing with good grace and acknowledged the honor with a few courteous words.

Jabotinsky later confessed to Koestler that "he had rarely been so embarrassed in all his life."

In Vienna, Jabotinsky's conference in the *Kursaal*, the largest concert hall in Austria's capital, was a "remarkable event." He felt relaxed and happy in the company of carefree Viennese school youth and gladly particpated in their informal gatherings. At an evening spent in a *Kneipe* with a group of students from Russia, he matched

"immaterial whether or not we say 'Jewish State.'" A bright young
student, Albert Starasselsky, while defending Jabotinsky's viewpoint,
suggested that the Conference endorse the formula used by Sir
Herbert Samuel in his address at the London Opera House on
November 2, 1919, where he spoke of a "self-governing commonwealth under the auspices of an established Jewish majority."[30]
Jabotinsky accepted this suggestion and it was made the basis of the
new movement's program: "The aim of Zionism is the gradual
transformation of Palestine (Trans Jordan included) into a Jewish
Commonwealth, that is into a self-governing Commonwealth under
the auspices of an established Jewish majority. Any other interpretation of Zionism, especially the White Paper of 1922, must be
considered invalid."

Other main points of the program submitted by Jabotinsky were
in conformity with the views and demands formulated in his earlier
Rasswyet articles.

Much attention was paid to the problem of independent political
action on the part of the new movement. Jabotinsky put this question
clearly in his pre-Conference article: should the movement undertake independent action, or should it limit itself to influencing the
policy of the Zionist Organization? "Both lines of conduct," he
said, "are equally *possible*. . . . If we consider this question coolly,
its *pro* and *con* appear to be equally weighty." He himself
considered independence a "lesser evil," but this, he insisted, was his
own opinion: "the Conference will decide."[31] The decision was
that "The Union of Zionist Revisionists is an integral part of the
Zionist World Organization, but it reserves to itself the right of
independent propaganda in Jewish and non-Jewish circles."

The Conference elected a Central Committee of twelve members;
most of them lived in Paris, which was chosen as the Committee's seat.
Jabotinsky was elected President.

4. *Canossa*

The first problems the new Central Committee had to face, was
whether the Revisionist Union should participate in the forthcoming
Zionist Congress and put up candidates for the elections.
The obvious and possibly the only likely candidate was Jabotinsky. His colleagues on the Central Committee were eager to seize

drink for drink with every one of the participants. On the way to
his hotel late in the night, they organized a "one legged race" along
the *Ring*. When one of the students outdistanced him, Jabotinsky
said admiringly: "You are the first one to outrun me." But when
the enthusiastic youngsters tried—in typical Russian fashion—to lift
him up and swing him, he resisted violently and angrily, and when
they failed to release him, struck several of them hard: "My body is
tabu; I can't stand being touched," he later apologetically explained.[26]

Jabotinsky returned from his lecture tour tired, though encouraged.
But the basic question as to whether he was actually going to launch
an organized movement remained unanswered. His personal affairs
were still very much unsettled and this, of course, contributed to his
uncertainty. He frankly discussed this state of affairs in a letter to
one of his early followers, Abraham Recanati from Salonica, who
bluntly queried: "Is it your genuine intention to do something, or
is all this [articles and speeches] nothing but fine words?"

"That is a question," Jabotinsky answered on September 15,
"which I have often asked myself. There are now some fifty groups
of adherents, from Canada to Harbin in Manchuria, but there is
no center. The center we established in Berlin disintegrated for the
sad and simple reason that those who headed it were Russian refugees.
poor, tired, never sure of how they were going to feed their children
tomorrow, or where they were going to be in a fortnight. I am myself
after all nothing but a refugee. Since I had resigned from the Zionist
Executive, I haven't spent a whole month in any one city. I am
writing you about all these details as an introduction to a dilemma
I am now determined to break: if I succeed in arranging my affairs
in such a way as to be able to live somewhere for one year steadily,
I will establish a central bureau, try to revive the *Rasswyet* and
organize a movement; if not—I will send a circular letter to all our
friends stating plainly and bluntly that life has beaten me, that I am
renouncing all Jewish political activity. All this will be decided during
the month of October; please have patience until then, and believe
me that I am not a man to arouse enthusiasm which I do not intend
to bring to fruition; I will go to the very end, or I will not move at all."

Jabotinsky kept his promise that "all this will be decided" during
the month of October. On October 29, 1924, he sent a circular from
Paris to a number of people announcing the establishment in that
city of "an office for the organization of all existing opposition groups

and for the creation of new groups." He asked all the addressees to get in touch with this office, to which he "promised close and constant cooperation."

The response was encouraging. Organized groups of adherents sprang up in Palestine, England, Austria, Germany, France, Poland, Danzig, Bessarabia, Latvia, Bulgaria, and Greece. *Yevreyski Glas* in Sofia, *Pro-Israel* in Salonica, and *Poilen-Erez Israel* in Warsaw became the local mouthpieces for the new Jabotinsky movement. On December 25, 1924, the *Rasswyet* resumed publication in Paris. For some time, its "editorial offices" were housed in the attic of Jabotinsky's apartment at 71, rue de la Tombe Issoire. An unpaid young lady who volunteered for work and operated a rented Russian typewriter, constituted the "clerical staff." During the first six months Jabotinsky edited the paper singlehanded; later, Michael Y. Berchin, a veteran Russian journalist on the staff of P. N. Miliukov's Russian emigrée daily *Posledniya Novosti,* became co-editor. Neither Berchin nor any of the contributors received a salary or honorarium. A devoted circle of friends and admirers (among them were Zionists who did not fully share Jabotinsky's views) took care of the paper's modest budget. Its circulation was growing: the first issue sold one thousand copies, the tenth twenty-five hundred.[27]

The problem of oral propaganda proved to be more complicated. In Jewish Communist circles, as well as in those of the Jewish Socialist *Bund,* feeling against Jabotinsky and his views was already so violent that for about seven months (from July, 1924, to February, 1925) every public meeting addressed by him in Paris was the scene of well-planned heckling and disturbance, strongly reminiscent of what he had had to face in London in 1916, while campaigning for the Jewish Legion. The counter measure used was also similar to that employed in 1916: young supporters of Jabotinsky organized a "self defense" composed mainly of members of the Student Corps, *Barissia.* The showdown took place at Jabotinsky's lecture held on the second floor of the Café Odeon: when the usual riot had started, the troublemakers were soundly thrashed and kicked rather roughly downstairs. There were no more disturbances at Jabotinsky's meetings.[28]

3 *The Die Is Cast*

"Alea jacta est," Jabotinsky announced with mock p writer on November 6, 1924: "I am again in the going to do my damndest to launch a truly Herzlia foundation conference of this movement, so often p time take place not later than next spring. You The name of the movement was the object of live the Paris group that was in charge of the prepa suggestions were offered: "Activists," the *"R* "And why not 'Revisionists?'" timidly asked zealots, Y. Yeivine.[29] Jabotinsky liked the sug his concept of the mission he was about to u program and tactics of the Zionist Organiza the new situation.

The first conference of the new moveme as the "Conference of the League of Zionist at the Café de Pantheon in the very heart center of the Paris intellectuals. The par Zionist stalwarts of Russian origin: the b Tiomkin, Israel Trivus, Michael Berchin They were surrounded by a crowd of en who arrived from abroad, Jabotinsky v Jacob Weinshal, the sole delegate fr in-arms, Meir Grossman, who came fr from Salonica whom he regarded Jewry; and Aaron Propes, represen

It is hardly necessary to say th dominated the Conference. But i he met with considerable oppositi

In an article, "Political Tasks in the *Rasswyet* on April 19, 19 to proclaim aloud and clearly" t ment of a Jewish State. But voiced doubts as to the tacti Trivus said: "I, too, am for the *words.* . . . Why should away even friends." Meir (

this opportunity for Jabotinsky to present the Revisionist program to the Congress.

However, Jabotinsky was strongly opposed to this course. On June 4, 1925, he wrote from Paris: "Personally, I am most reluctant to go [to the Congress]. . . . This would mean rejoining the Zionist Organization. Should our [Revisionist] Union develop well, I would be able to do things which a member of the Zionist Organization—in my honest opinion—has no right to do. It is hardly worth while binding myself in the future for the sake of one (useless) speech at the Congress, before five hundred heads of *Stimmvieh* [unthinking herd of voters]."[32] His colleagues on the Revisionist Central Committee argued that according to the Constitution of the World Zionist Organization it was sufficient to acquire a *shekel* to qualify as a member of good standing. Jabotinsky insisted however that the nature of the problem was not a legalistic one. In his opinion, what mattered was "*my* own notion about what is being required from a member of the [Zionist] Organization, and what I myself would demand of every member if I were the Tsar."[33]

Overruling Jabotinsky's objections, the Central Committee decided that he had to head the Revisionist list in the Congress elections in Palestine. He yielded to this decision partly because, as he wrote to a friend, he "did not want to put his foot down"; such an attitude "would have created a certain coolness in our relationship at the very outset of our cooperation." [34] Another major factor was his concern lest the World Zionist Organization lose its control over its most valuable political instrument—the Jewish Agency. As early as 1923, Dr. Weizmann had begun negotiations with a group of wealthy and influential non-Zionist Jewish leaders headed by Louis Marshall and Felix Warburg, with a view to securing their participation in the Jewish Agency on a fifty-fifty basis. Such an "extended" Jewish Agency was expected to provide financial aid to the construction work in Palestine and prestige to the Jewish Agency.

Jabotinsky was fiercely opposed to this scheme. To him it was tantamount to giving up the sovereignty of the democratically elected Zionist Congress, making its decisions in all matters of Zionist policy and work dependent on the approval of a self-appointed group of non-Zionist financial potentates. He deemed it the elementary duty of every Zionist patriot not to let such a scheme pass. The Zionist Congress was the only forum from which it could be combatted.

There was no other way than to be present himself, barring the way to what he considered the destruction of Herzl's heritage. He recognized the compelling logic of the situation. But he was not happy about it : "I will go [to the Congress] probably as almost the sole delegate of the formidable Revisionist Party and will make a fool of myself."

At the Fourteenth Zionist Congress in Vienna, Jabotinsky was indeed the sole Revisionist elected in his party capacity. He was, however, joined by three more delegates from Palestine, Salonica, and Sofia. They formed a group of four, which, according to the Congress rules, entitled them to a speaker of their own in the general discussion. Jabotinsky was allotted thirty minutes for his speech.

A New Palestine correspondent reported that "everyone had been waiting for three days to hear" Jabotinsky's address. When his turn came, "the corridors, usually the scene of much traffic, are deserted to a man. The great Saal fills to capacity. The continuous restless shifting in the uncomfortable seats stops as if by magic." [35]

Strategically considered, the speech was a surprise. It stirred the Congress largely because of its tactics. Instead of immediately and directly attacking as was expected the official Zionist policy, Jabotinsky devoted the first half of his address to stating his definitions and developing his positive program. Even the correspondent of the official organ of the Zionist Executive, the London New Judea, could not help admitting the "vigor" of this part of the speech : "He recites facts and figures. He is an activist and logical to the very end, betraying the influence of French rather than British politics. He impresses the Congress not with his sentiments, not with his opinions, but with his knowledge and the manner [in which] he presents the facts." [36] The Congress listened to this part of the speech with unusual stillness. Weitzmann's followers, who expected personal criticism, found Jabotinsky's sachlich (matter-of-fact) approach puzzling, even disappointing and they kept quiet. The official Congress Protokoll lists only seven interruptions from the floor during this period, mostly when Jabotinsky started speaking of the land problem and the colonization finances. He was not even halfway through his address when the thirty minutes allotted to him expired. He calmly requested the Chairman to ask the Congress whether he could be permitted to continue. Amidst excited exclamations of both consent and opposition, Rabbi Meyer Berlin, who presided, put the request to a vote. It was granted by a large majority. Angered by this manifestation of sympathetic interest for Jabotinsky's ideas, some overzealous partisans of Weizmann tried to invalidate the vote and indignantly accused the Chair (which had been taken over by Nachum Sokolov) of violating the rules of Congress. Particularly incensed were the Labor groups. A second vote was taken, and by an overwhelming majority of assenting votes (including that of Weizmann) Jabotinsky was allotted another thirty minutes. "After some more noisy attempts to protest," reported a *New Palestine* correspondent, "the protesters settled down to enjoy the perfection of form and the fascination of manner which make the address a masterpiece of oratorical art, though delivered in German, which ranks third or fourth in Jabotinsky's list of languages." [37]

It was in this second part of the address that Jabotinsky attacked. But by this time the Congress was so fascinated and the opponents so subdued that not more than five interruptions are listed in the official *Protokoll*. Louis Lipsky, by no means a friend or supporter of Jabotinsky, recalled: "When he . . . launched into a grand criticism of Zionist policy—satiric, courteous, denunciatory—he was like the Angry Conscience of the movement. He poured acid on open wounds. He reminded us of the goal and made us ashamed of the results." [38] Another leading American delegate, Abraham Goldberg, stressed that the strongest point of the speech was Jabotinsky's indirect question to the Zionist administration: "If not my program, what have you to offer?" Goldberg admitted that "none of the exponents of the administration answered this cardinal point. The administration still owes an answer more convincing than the mere negation of Jabotinsky's program. . . . Everyone, not only Jabotinsky, asks what is the plan of the administration. . . . The ovation given him was clearly a demonstration voicing the dissatisfaction of the Congress with England, and perhaps with the Weizmann policies which lately brought about some appreciable setbacks." [39] Ludwig Lewisohn had the same impression: "His [Jabotinsky's] brilliant oration was listened to with a mixture of fascination and fear. Through him the Congress found a vent for its own inner restlessness, its disquiet."[40]

At the end of the address, the Congress gave Jabotinsky a rousing ovation.

In its contents, the address was a masterful presentation of the program formulated at the recent Revisionist world conference in Paris. Particularly impressive was the concluding part of the speech.

41

Referring to Weizmann's project to make non-Zionists co-masters of the Jewish Agency and to his own recent attempt to leave the Zionist Organization, Jabotinsky concluded his speech by a powerful and moving peroration :[41]

I stand here in Canossa. Four (!) years ago I, like many emigrants, believed that I should leave my fatherland in the hope of being able to fight for it better from the outside. I stand before you as a *Baal Teshuva*, penitent. This Congress can agree or disagree with me—this is of no importance; with you I have a common language; but with the others [non-Zionists] I have nothing to talk about. The Congress is sovereign— that's why I am here. Don't drive patriots away from the Zionist movement. It is possible that at a Congress which is no longer sovereign we will not meet many figures who now face each other at this Congress.

In this writer's opinion, Jabotinsky's Vienna speech was by far the best of all his addresses to the Congress both in content and delivery. Abraham Goldberg, a leading American Zionist and journalist, and a keen observer at the Zionist Congresses, gave a penetrating description of how Jabotinsky spoke at the Fourteenth Congress :[42]

He has a "different," refreshing quality. When one hears him after the other speakers, one has the feeling of emerging from mossy thick-grown woods into green, sunlit fields offering far horizons. . . . Jabotinsky is no casuist. He is simplicity itself. Whatever he believes, he pronounces with the utmost earnestness and beauty. He speaks beautifully: not for the effect, though such may be the impression, but because a sense for the aesthetic is part of his innermost being and personality. . . . His oratory shines with a carefree assurance, a confidence in his own nature, and rare fearlessness. It savors of a normal life. He speaks like the child of a people living normally. So will speak some of the Jews of tomorrow. Jabotinsky presages the morrow. When he speaks, he stands upright and inflexible, reminding one of the rock-hewn Jews of former days who spoke frankly and unmistakably to their rulers. He uses his voice only, modulating it according to the content. It is a forceful instrument.

In the general debate that followed, several speakers referred to Jabotinsky's address, mostly critically. Dr. Shmaryahu Levin accused him of preaching a "mechanistic" philosophy of Zionism and of intending to "send soldiers to Palestine before we have Jews there." [42a] Jean Fischer (Belgium) argued that Jabotinsky had no right to criticize the Executive's policy, since he was equally responsible for the acceptance of Churchill's White Paper of 1922. Referring to Jabotinsky's demand for a colonization regime in Palestine, Dr. Weizmann agreed that it would have been justified if the Zionists had had to colonize Rhodesia; but, he argued, Palestine is no Rhodesia, but a sensitive world nerve, located in the midst of an Arab world. Recalling that during World War I he had assisted Jabotinsky in establishing the Jewish Legion [Jabotinsky joined the delegates in applauding this statement], Dr. Weizmann stated that at the present time he considered the demand for a Legion "not only useless but even harmful. The key to the [present] situation is to be found on a different level: we have to open up the Near East to Jewish initiative, in genuine friendship and cooperation with the Arabs." [43]

A characteristic incident occurred when, at the thirteenth meeting of the Congress, the chairman, Leo Motzkin, called upon Jabotinsky to take the floor on behalf of the Revisionist group for a statement on their attitude toward the new Zionist Executive: loud applause broke out in the gallery. Dr. Shmaryahu Levin angrily protested against this demonstration, and demanded that "the public must be excluded while Mr. Jabotinsky makes his statement." The chairman dismissed this motion. Before Jabotinsky could start speaking, Weizmann rose and asked how large the group was on whose behalf he wished to make the announcement. "Four, of whom two are Palestinians," retorted Jabotinsky curtly. When the chairman added that a group of four delegates was entitled to a statement, Weizmann interrupted saying: "I don't oppose it." Turning to Weizmann, Leo Motzkin declared: "You have no right to oppose. Only the Congress is entitled to do so." [44] The statement, read by Jabotinsky in Hebrew and later in German, sharply criticized the political passivity of the Zionist Executive and its lack of program in the economic field coupled with the neglect of the security of Palestine Jewry; it maintained that the Executive's tactics were "gravely endangering the sovereignty of the Zionist Organization." Therefore, the Revisionist delegates "will vote against the motion of confidence for the Executive." [45]

Jabotinsky was deeply disgusted by what he saw at the Congress: "It was the most hideous show of its kind; by God, except for my speech, there wasn't a single decent moment in the whole performance," he wrote to a friend.[46]

5. *In the Field*

In October-November, 1925, Jabotinsky undertook an extensive lecture tour of Germany, Lithuania, Latvia, Bessarabia, Bukovina, Old Rumania, Czechoslovakia, and Austria. Altogether, he visited fifteen towns. But, he wrote on December 4, his lecture tour had been "interrupted by the generous gesture of Lord Plumer who refused to grant me Palestinian citizenship; I remained suspended in mid-air in Rumania, with a quasi-passport [the so-called Nansen passport, which in another letter he angrily described as "a shameful scrap of paper issued in Berlin"] which was expiring on November 30. I hurried back [to Paris], but because I was four hours late, I was stopped at the Swiss border on December 1." He was forced to wait at Innsbruck, the capital of the Austrian Tyrol, until the matter was straightened out.

In the course of Jabotinsky's tour, the attitude of the official Zionist bodies in individual countries was not uniform. In Berlin they proclaimed a boycott of his lecture. In Vienna, on the other hand, all the Zionist leaders attended as guests at the Revisionist Conference. In Cernauti (the capital of Bukovina), the leaders of the local Zionist organization also participated in all functions in Jabotinsky's honor. He was even invited to address the Bukovina conference of the Keren ha'Yessod and received a vote of thanks from this body.[47] The Bucharest correspondent of the Berlin *Jüdische Rundschau*—a paper strongly opposed to Jabotinsky and to everything he stood for— described his Rumanian tour as an outstanding success [48] and admitted that:

Jabotinsky's oratory has stirred up the somewhat sluggish Zionist conscience of Rumanian Jewry. . . . The political perspectives that he outlined in his program did not fail to make a deep impression on the Jewish masses in this country. . . . The good that Jabotinsky's visit has done will begin to make itself felt later, and on General Zionism in particular: the General Zionists will awaken from their sleep and begin once again to think of political matters. And this perhaps will not be the least part of the service that Jabotinsky will have rendered: that he has shaken his adversaries into wakefulness, and forced them to think.

Jabotinsky himself was not blinded by his oratorical successes, and his appraisal of the strength of the Revisionist branches he visited or created was a very cautious one: "We do have a movement, but I wouldn't call it a strong one. Many people are applauding my lectures, but they are still afraid to join us." For some reason he was particularly skeptical about the impact of his visit to the Jewish community of Chisinau, the capital of former Bessarabia, where Russian-Jewish traditions were still very strong. "I was least successful in Bessarabia. I've lost contact with Russian Jewry, by God, I have. In Chisinau, I was met by a crowd of six thousand Jews, but they were silent; the mood was that of cold curiosity. Coolness prevailed also during my lecture." [49]

THE FIRST BATTLE FOR AMERICA

1. *Lonely Landing*

BY THE END of 1925, Jabotinsky felt that the Revisionist movement he had launched in the spring of the same year was taking firm root in most European countries. "In Europe we are making headway," he wrote in a private letter. "I am not an optimist, but I am pretty sure that if we had money, we'd sweep the floor with the whole moldy bunch of them within six months." [1] In Palestine, the movement started to assert itself slowly but vigorously. But America was completely untouched by Jabotinsky's ideas.

In January, 1926, the noted lecture bureau of Sol Hurok in New York (Universal Artists, Incorporated) invited Jabotinsky to deliver a series of lectures in the United States. The Central Committee of the Revisionist World Union thought that this lecture tour could be utilized for the purposes of laying the foundation for an American Revisionist organization. No such organization, not even a nucleus, was then in existence. The only person with whom the Revisionist Headquarters in Paris had been in correspondence was Israel Posnansky, a young man who for months had been unsuccessfully trying to establish a Revisionist group in New York. It was to him that the Central Committee cabled to meet Jabotinsky who was to arrive on the *S.S. France.* [2]

The *Jewish Daily News Bulletin* charitably reported that he "was met at the pier by representatives of the American group of Zionist Revisionists, as well as a number of American Zionists." [3] In fact, Posnansky alone was at the pier on that cold and snowy morning of January 27. Jabotinsky, however, was not at all put out by this modest reception. Noticing, on the way to the hotel, that Posnansky felt badly

46

about being the only one to greet the guest, he said soothingly : "Never mind, don't take it to heart. I wouldn't have been able to discuss our problems with them anyway. On the contrary, I am pleased that I now have the opportunity to talk first to one of our own people and to acquaint myself with the situation here and to decide what we are to do." That very evening, in his hotel room, he again met with Posnansky and with his old comrade from the Self-Defense and Acre Prison days, Elias Ginsburg. They decided to utilize Jabotinsky's lectures for Revisionist organizational activities, to distribute thousands of "application forms," and to invite Herman Bernstein, a distinguished Anglo-Yiddish journalist and editor of the *Jewish Daily News Bulletin,* to act as Chairman at the first lecture in New York.

The lecture took place on January 31 at the Manhattan Opera House before an audience of two thousand persons. Presenting his program, Jabotinsky concentrated on the demands for protective tariffs for Palestine industry and state land for Jewish colonization, with the immediate goal of fifty thousand immigrants yearly. He vigorously opposed the plan of extending the Jewish Agency to include non-Zionists, and severely criticized the sponsors of the idea of Jewish colonization in Soviet Russia.[4]

The original contract with the lecture bureau provided for twenty lectures, for which Jabotinsky was to receive eight hundred pounds (about four thousand dollars). But, apparently influenced by the unfriendly attitude of official Zionist circles, Hurok reduced the scheduled program to ten lectures, and accordingly halved the fee. "As I was not in a position to enforce the implementation of the contract in full, I had to yield," complained Jabotinsky.[5] After his appearance in New York, he spoke in Chicago, Philadelphia, Detroit, Montreal, and Toronto, attracting large audiences and provoking lively discussions. "My tour is all right," he wrote to his mother and sister. "I am being paid regularly. The audiences are applauding and the attitude of the press is good." [6] And, indeed, the reaction of the press was on the whole favorable, both with regard to Jabotinsky himself and to his ideas.

In the *Tog,* S. Rosenfeld pointed out that the "bogey man" stories about Jabotinsky the "destroyer" who "aims to annihilate" all Zionist achievements and leaders, had been disproven by his first lecture in New York. "Now that we have heard Jabotinsky," he continued, "we know, at first hand, what his opinions on various Zionist problems

are. . . . The most loyal Zionists could endorse most of his demands."
The article concluded : "What does Jabotinsky want? He wants more
attention to facts, and less fear of consequences." [7] Abe Goldberg,
one of the pillars of the American Zionist administration, said in the
Yiddish organ, *Dos Yiddische Folk* (March 5), that Jabotinsky and
his movement had "put up a program; we may be displeased with this
or not, but one thing is certain : they see clearly the duty of Zionism
—to create in a short time, say in twenty years, a Jewish majority in
Palestine. I sympathize with Revisionism because it has vision, because
it has a program, and because it is not afraid to criticize sharply and
openly." *Far'n Folk,* the official organ of the *Hitachdut* (non-Marxian
Zionist labor group) wrote in a similar vein : "If Jabotinsky succeeds
in dispelling the indifference of the masses and helping them to grasp
the cardinal points in Zionist problems, he will fulfil an important
cultural mission for the Zionist cause." [8] The comment of the Jewish
press in Canada was on similar lines.

2. *Discreet Wooing*

The attitude of the American Zionist Administration was very significant. The President of the Zionist Organization of America (ZOA),
Louis Lipsky, was then in London, but several influential members
and officials of his administration (Abe Goldberg, Maurice Samuel,
Joseph Brainin, Mayer Weisgal) were privately wooing Jabotinsky,
maintaining a frequent and friendly contact with him, professing to
be fully or "up to 99 per cent" in agreement with his ideas. Some tried
to dissuade him from establishing an independent Revisionist organization in the United States : they assured him that the forthcoming
Convention of the Zionist Organization of America would endorse
"99 per cent" of his program anyway, which would certainly be
preferable to the emergence of a small organization of his own. An
editorial published in the official organ of the ZOA argued that in fact
there was not much difference between the views of Jabotinsky and
those of the General Zionists : [9]

The group of which Mr. Jabotinsky is the head—very small in numbers
—is part and parcel of the general Zionist grouping in the Zionist
Organization. The Revisionists may be said to belong to *our* party. They
are merely a dissenting group that wants to impress upon the action of
the movement the quality of their own views, but they do not form, in

any real sense, a party as the term has been used in Zionist affairs hereto-fore. . . . If you take all the views of Mr. Jabotinsky together . . . some of them good, some of them unacceptable . . . all of them in fact not in principle at variance with the prevailing views in any of the existing parties or groups. But, Mr. Jabotinsky gives his program a characteristic nuance. He sings the same song in a higher key—with only slight variations.

It was in this spirit that the Zionist press and officialdom started acting toward Jabotinsky after the cold-shouldering of the first few weeks. When his pamphlet *Revisionism—The Essentials of its Program* was translated into English, it was Maurice Samuel who edited the translation; *The New Palestine* hospitably published it in two issues "on the basis of free discussion." [10] *The Jewish Daily News Bulletin* reprinted it in full, giving their ten thousand subscribers an opportunity to get acquainted with Jabotinsky's views.[11]

This display of friendliness and cooperation looked rather suspicious to some of Jabotinsky's faithful adherents, who warned him not to put much trust in promises to "conquer" the official Zionist Organization of America for his program; their advice was to concentrate on building an independent Revisionist party. They saw the motivation for the wooing of Jabotinsky in the impotent hatred of the American Zionist officialdom for Weizmann's plan of introducing non-Zionists into the Jewish Agency. Some of the officials candidly explained that, being bound by their positions, they could not attack this plan openly, but would be happy if Jabotinsky could block it.[12]

Nobody made a secret of these conversations and plans. Rumors that Jabotinsky had "conquered" the Zionist movement in America were widespread, and considerably slowed down the work for the establishment of the Revisionist organization.

The attitude of the great Jewish philanthropist Nathan Strauss was very friendly and, in the early stages, very promising. His "warmth of feeling toward V. Jabotinsky" was particularly stressed by Bernard G. Richards, who had known Strauss long and intimately. "Always a fighter, Mr. Strauss admired the aggressive spirit within our [Zionist] ranks, and Mr. Jabotinsky's achievements in connection with the formation and operation of the Jewish Legion continued to elicit his profound admiration." This attitude was about to produce what Richards cautiously calls "substantial assurances of sympathy with his [Jabotinsky's] ideas." This writer remembers Jabotinsky's report to the Revisionist headquarters in Paris stating that a check for the very substantial sum of twenty-five thousand dollars was definitely promised to him. But this promise somehow became known in certain Zionist circles, and heavy pressure was put on Strauss to withdraw his support. As Richards puts it: "differences of opinion arose and between peaceful friends who were afraid of a military unit and Mr. Strauss' advanced age . . . the pending cooperation did not come through." [13]

3. End of an Idyll

It took Jabotinsky almost two months to realize the true meaning and value of the discreet cordiality displayed by official Zionist circles. At a Revisionist gathering, on March 21, he scoffed at this attitude as that of *gruess mich nicht Unter den Linden*. "While they do not hesitate to express approval of our program in private, they avoid public identification with me. What have I done to deserve this treatment? Would I not bestow on them at least as much honor as they do on me?" [14]

The end of the idyllic period in the relationship between the Administration leaders and Jabotinsky was confirmed by Louis Lipsky after his return from London. It was "unfortunate," he said, "that certain discussions which have taken place in connection with the reorganization of the Zionist center have coincided with Mr. Jabotinsky's stay in this country and that rumors were set afloat connecting Mr. Jabotinsky with these discussions. . . . I regret that the courtesies extended by us to Mr. Jabotinsky have in some quarters been construed as an endorsement of his program. . . . I can very well imagine that we could adopt one or two points emphasized by the Revisionists; even the demand for Jewish military units in view of recent events in Palestine may receive justification which until now it did not have." But, Lipsky insisted, Jabotinsky and his movement "do not indicate a new direction for the Zionist movement to take." [15]

The break with Jabotinsky was clear-cut. It found expression in several characteristic episodes. At an early stage of Jabotinsky's activities, Joseph Brainin, the son of the well-known Hebrew-Yiddish writer Reuben Brainin, agreed to serve as chairman of the New York Revisionist group; but, recalled I. Posnansky, "his days as chairman were numbered; he was soon informed by 111 Fifth Avenue (he was on their payroll) that he must immediately sever his relations with the Revisionists, otherwise. . . . It goes without saying that he obeyed. . . . " (The office of the ZOA was at 111 Fifth Avenue at that time.) Another instance quoted by Posnansky is no less indicative of the changed "climate": a group of members of the Downtown New York Zion District had recommended that Jabotinsky deliver a lecture in their Center; at a special meeting called to decide upon this suggestion, a veteran Zionist and member of the Executive Committee, Mr. Askenazy, exclaimed: "I do not wish to be branded as the man in whose district Jabotinsky spoke." [16]

With a view to disparaging Jabotinsky as a disloyal and destructive force in Zionism, rumors were spread that he was opposed to the five million dollar United Palestine Appeal which was being conducted in the United States. Denying these rumors, Jabotinsky stated through the Jewish Telegraphic Agency that if he were not bound by his contract with Hurok's lecture bureau, which did not permit him to appear on any other platform, he would gladly have taken an active part in the campaign. "Regardless of any criticism I may have against certain activities of the World Zionist Executive, I am always pleased to see as many Jews as possible going to Palestine, and as much money as possible collected for Palestine purposes." When his commitments toward Hurok expired, Jabotinsky wrote to the leaders of the campaign offering his collaboration. For two weeks there was no answer. Then he was offered an audience in some obscure township: "Though I myself once published an Atlas, I never heard of such a place," Jabotinsky ironically commented.[17]

4. Capturing the "Sons of Zion"

The anti-Jabotinsky trend was considerably accentuated by a new spectacular development. In their early contacts with him, several ZOA leaders advised Jabotinsky to cultivate individual districts and constituent bodies of the ZOA. He took this advice seriously and succeeded in "capturing" the "Order of the Sons of Zion."

Established in 1909 as a mutual aid society, the Order had gradually developed into a dynamic and constructive Zionist body with a membership of five thousand. In the field of practical work for Palestine, it had founded the Judea Industrial Corporation which, in turn, established the Judea Insurance Company. In the first year of its existence the latter had written $1,265,000 worth of insurance. Most of it was invested in first mortgages in Palestine. In 1926, "Judea" had three branches in Palestine and two in Egypt. The Order also founded the Palestine Exhibition and Fair Corporation, which arranged two exhibitions—in 1925 and 1926. In the political field "Sons of Zion" had more than once demonstrated independence of mind and bold initiative.[18] The Order's Executive was impressed by Jabotinsky's crusade for Greater Zionism. They invited him to their plenary session, and after a thorough discussion, decided to "endorse the principles of the League of Zionist Revisionists." The President was to appoint a committee to "work out the propaganda plans for that purpose." Jabotinsky, who intended to leave the United States on April 10, was prevailed upon to prolong his stay. He was enrolled as a member of the Order.[19]

At a banquet given for Jabotinsky by the "Sons of Zion," Herman Bernstein criticized what he termed "the silent boycott of the Zionist press" against Jabotinsky. "It is a mistake to believe that a gifted publicist cannot be entrusted with the affairs of statemanship. . . . Herzl was a publicist, Nordau was a publicist, and, one may say that, in a broader sense, Moses, the Jewish Law-giver, was a publicist, who put the Jewish people on the pages of mankind's history." Judge Jacob S. Strahl, President of the Judea Industrial Corporation, stressed that the "Sons of Zion," who were the first to endorse the *Keren ha'Yessod* in America, "felt that it was its duty to come out openly" for Jabotinsky's cause. Dr. Herman Koerner, President of the famous Viennese *Hakoah* Sport Club, which was then being enthusiastically greeted in the United States, declared: "I am capitulating to Jabotinsky. We will join his ranks with banners flying." [20] In a letter to a friend, Jabotinsky wrote: "I am satisfied with my political work here. Of course, I do not expect to conquer the Zionist Organization [in America] *this* year, but I hope to leave behind a solid Revisionist stronghold." [21]

This spectacular success was a most unwelcome surprise to the American Zionist leaders. A frontal attack was launched against the "Sons of Zion" Executive. Abe Goldberg, First Vice President of the Order, issued a statement publicly disassociating himself from its action. Referring to his previous pro-Revisionist utterances, he stressed that he did not "mean to imply that he was opposed to all the planks of the Revisionist program" and that "as a matter of fact, in public print, he had expressed approval of some of the principles of Revisionism." But, he insisted, "it is inconceivable to me that the 'Order of the Sons of Zion,' an integral part of the ZOA and subject to the policies adopted by the Zionist Conventions, should embark on an independent policy." [22] Special emissaries were dispatched to all the "Sons of Zion" Camps to induce them to protest against the action of their Executive. Taking an active part in the crusade against Jabotinsky's program were two noted representatives of the Palestine Labor movement, David Remez and Abraham Harzfeld. They had come to the States several months previously for a fund-raising campaign, which by that time was already finished; but they remained in the country and were specifically attacking Jabotinsky's demand for agrarian reform that included expropriation of uncultivated lands owned by Arab *effendis* (landlords). These lands, they insisted, must be bought from the *efféndis* with money collected by world Jewry. Jabotinsky had to do a lot of explaining in defense of his program against the attacks by Palestinian delegates who claimed to speak from experience and with authority. He visited scores of the Order's camps, presenting his program and answering questions. During this campaign, he participated in six, seven, sometimes eight meetings every week. This effort paid off. Before the Seventeenth National "Sons of Zion" Convention, scheduled for June 20 to 21, he already knew that the majority of the camps stood firmly behind his program and were ready to back the Order's Executive. [23]

For this Convention, held at Long Branch, New Jersey, the Zionist administration mobilized all its forces : Louis Lipsky, Abe Goldberg, Dr. Shimon Bernstein, David Remez, Abraham Harzfeld, Joseph Barondes (one of the founders of the Order), etc. Its proceedings were centered on the endorsement of Jabotinsky's program by the Order's Executive. [24] Louis Lipsky contended in his address that by doing so, the Executive had acted contrary to the spirit and letter of the agreement between the Order and the Zionist Organization, according to which on matters of general policy only joint action, through the regularly elected bodies of the Zionist movement in America, was to be effective. Certain aspects of Jabotinsky's propaganda were, in his view, harmful to the Zionist cause. Harzfeld and Remez argued against the two basic points of the Jabotinsky program—the Jewish Legion and agrarian reform.

Unlike other speakers, Jabotinsky did not limit himself to discussing the controversial issue of the Order's attitude toward him and his program. He devoted a great part of his address to the general activities of the "Sons of Zion" and paid special tribute to their attempts to tap one stream of Jewish financial energy—Jewish savings—for the rebuilding of Palestine. Both the Judea Insurance Company and the Near East Exhibition, he said, were of paramount importance. Turning to the question of his program and actions, Jabotinsky stressed that when he and his friends had started their propaganda, they did it bearing in mind "the safety and entirety of the Zionist Organization" : "As a loyal member of the World Zionist Organization . . . I greet you, another loyal part of the World Zionist Organization." The main feature of Zionist loyalty, he said, was that "in acting, we act as one." That is why, he explained, he could not follow any advice "to go and reprimand the British Government instead of striking at the Zionists." He concluded :

I have no right to appear before the British Government. May I boast that in this country of America, many American papers would be open to me and I could achieve greater results by conducting my propaganda in an English newspaper. May I mention to you that in London the same thing applies to the English press, where I could express our views. But no one will ever point out any article on Revisionism written by me or any of my associates outside the Jewish press. It is the Executive of the Zionist Congress that has to deal with the British Government.

There is another loyalty: loyalty of expression. If you have certain doubts that perhaps the leadership of the Zionist Organization is not what it ought to be, it would be unfair to the movement and the Executive to withhold your criticism, and then spring it upon them at the Congress. . . . There is loyalty to leaders and loyalty to a movement. Stick to that real loyalty which can be compressed into one word, *Emes*.

In the heated debate that followed the first addresses, Louis Lipsky and Abe Goldberg openly threatened that the Order would be expelled from the ZOA if the Convention did not repudiate the action of the Executive. Lipsky refused to "enter into a discussion here with Jabotinsky on the Revisionist program" but stated that he was "opposed to this program and to the kind of propaganda carried on to further it."

In his concluding speech Jabotinsky, in turn, refused to discuss the question as to whether he had always been fair in his polemic attacks against his opponents. "I may be a tactless writer, or altogether a bad

54

man; what does it matter? What if the teacher has an unpleasant voice? The question is whether his teachings are right."

He expressed his conviction that the forthcoming ZOA Convention in Buffalo "will never agree to execute Mr. Lipsky's 'divorce' threat just because a part of the delegates favor a program which, as Mr. Goldberg said, is 99 per cent *kosher*. It is for you to say whether you think this program right or wrong. If you think it wrong, I will go away without rancor, alone as I came. But if you think it right, do not believe those who say that your connection with me will ruin the Order. So far nothing that I have ever been connected with has gone to ruin."

After Jabotinsky's address, the resolution approving the stand of the Executive was passed by a vote of 90 to 35, and a purely pro-Revisionist Executive was nominated. Jabotinsky was elected honorary Executive member. "Overwhelming victory," he cabled to S. Jacobi.

5. *The Aftermath*

At the Annual Convention of the ZOA in Buffalo, June 27 to 28, there was no mention whatsoever of the professed intention to adopt a "99 per cent Revisionist program" and thus "to steal Jupiter's thunder." [25] The "Order of the Sons of Zion" demanded that Jabotinsky be invited to address the Convention. The ZOA Executive turned down this demand. The "Sons of Zion," therefore, had little interest in the Convention, and of the seventy delegates, to which it was entitled, only forty-one appeared.[26] Nor was any serious attempt made to implement the threat to expel the Order from the ZOA. A motion to this effect was introduced, but was never put to the vote. Instead, a very weak and evasive compromise formula was adopted. In the discussion, those ZOA leaders who only a few months before had been busily wooing Jabotinsky and now considered the endorsement of his program as subversive activity, were put in a rather embarrassing position by one of the younger Order delegates, Elias Ginsburg. Replying to a violent attack by Maurice Samuel, Ginsburg recalled that Samuel had only recently "negotiated with Mr. Jabotinsky and had helped to edit the pamphlet which had been issued by the League of Zionist Revisionists." It was, therefore, "incomprehensible that Mr. Samuel could declare that the action of the Order was subversive." Obviously embarrassed by this imputation which reflected upon their loyalty to the official administration, some of those who had been involved in those compromising contacts with Jabotinsky tried, to extricate themselves. "On a point of personal privilege," Maurice Samuel "objected to the term 'negotiations' "; he, "like many of his colleagues, had gladly invited Mr. Jabotinsky to present his views at frequent personal interviews"—nothing more. He furthermore denied the "allegation that he had helped to edit the pamphlet mentioned. . . . He had been requested by Mr. Jabotinsky to correct the English of the pamphlet and had gladly done so. . . . He would have done the same for a member of the *Agudat Israel.*" Abe Goldberg "also deprecated the allusion to negotiations. . . . Like Mr. Samuel, he had been a party to several private conversations [with Jabotinsky] and regarded the use of the word 'negotiations' in this connection as ridiculous." [27]

Jabotinsky's involuntary absence from the Buffalo Convention was widely discussed in Zionist circles. Speaking at a farewell dinner prior to his departure for Europe, he said : "At Long Branch we defeated Mr. Lipsky in his presence. He was invited to attend the 'Order of the Sons of Zion' Convention, was given the floor whenever he asked for it, and was seen lobbying until three o'clock in the morning. This is partly the reason why the Revisionist victory at Long Branch was so convincing : it was won in the face of the opponent's main forces. Buffalo was quite a different thing. It was decided not to invite me to the Convention of the Zionist Organization of America. Mr. Lipsky prefers to fight me in my absence." [28]

This was also the opinion of leading Zionist publicists. Shlomo Dingol said in *Der Tog* : "If the Zionist Executive had maintained its former high level, it would have considered it a privilege and a duty to invite Jabotinsky and let him explain his views." He concluded that "though the Revisionists were defeated at the Convention, they emerged as moral victors." [29] Dr. Samuel Margoshes wrote in the same paper : "Everyone felt that were it not for the controversy over Revisionism, the Convention would have been monotonous and lifeless. The shadow of Jabotinsky hovering over Buffalo furnished the Convention with material for the first lively conflict in American Zionism since Cleveland." [30] In another article, Dr. Margoshes said : "The spirit of Revisionism broke through the fence surrounding the Buffalo Convention, though the main spokesman of this movement remained in New York, because this was the wish of the people who were afraid of his presence and influence." [31] Very unfriendly, in contrast, were Jacob Fishman's "Convention Impressions" in the *New Palestine* : "Neither Jabotinsky nor the 'Sons of Zion' had many adherents here. . . . Personally, I wish Jabotinsky had attended this Convention; he would then have had the opportunity of learning that some of his principles are very unpopular." [32]

Jabotinsky returned to Europe on the *S.S. Minnetonka* in mid-July, after almost five and a half months spent in America. It was with mixed feelings that he evaluated the results achieved : "I am satisfied with my American trip. The 'Sons of Zion' are an important conquest, but the situation in the entire American Zionist Organization is such that three more months of work would have been likely to change everything. . . . But," he ruefully confessed, "I did not succeed in making money—not for myself, not for the *Hasefer*, nor for the [Revisionist] Central Committee, nor the *Rasswyet*. Not because there was no possibility of making money, but because I just don't know how." [33]

PALESTINE : 1926

1. *The Balm of Gilead*

Hᴉs ᴍᴏᴛʜᴇʀ and sister were repeatedly urging Jabotinsky to settle in, or at least to visit, Palestine, which he had not seen since October, 1922. They were particularly eager—and so was he—to have a family reunion for his son Eri's *Bar Mitzvah* in December, 1923. There was, however, no money for such a trip. On the eve of the *Bar Mitzvah*, Jabotinsky wrote from Paris: "Without you, it will be a sad celebration." But he still hoped to be able to be with them for Passover, 1924.[1] This hope, too, did not materialize. It was not until October, 1926, that he was able to go.

The immediate cause of Jabotinsky's visit in October, 1926, was, as in 1922, the illness of his mother. In order to "finance" his trip, he undertook to revise the scenario of a film he had prepared for the Jewish National Fund, on the basis of a personal review of the latest developments of the Zionist constructive work in Palestine, in particular in the *kibbutzim* (communal settlements). The Board of Directors of the Fund welcomed this suggestion. But, even at that early stage, animosity against Jabotinsky in certain leftist circles was so strong that, anticipating trouble, he felt compelled to write to a friend in Palestine asking him to investigate which *kibbutz* he could visit without incurring the risk of meeting with hostile reception.[2] Fortunately, these apprehensions proved to be unwarranted. When, upon his arrival, Jabotinsky started touring the *kibbutzim* and *kvutzot* of the Emek (Valley of Ezdrelon), familiarizing himself with their progress, he was received courteously, often with friendship. In a few weeks he submitted to the Jewish National Fund the revised version for a scenario called *Balm of Gilead: A Galilean Romance*.

In the Jabotinsky Institute this writer had the opportunity of perusing the original handwritten English text of the scenario.[3] He is also familiar with the synopsis of a novel on the same subject, which Jabotinsky contemplated writing in 1940.[4] The gist of both is as follows :

The story begins in Tiberias in about 1912. The main characters are Amnon and Tamar—he the son of a doctor from Russia, she the daughter of a *Sefardi* family of Cabalists, long established in Palestine. The boy's hobby is botany, especially flowers and their scents; the girl is of a rather practical disposition. There is a childhood romance between them, with Amnon taking it seriously, and Tamar remaining more aloof. Tamar leaves the country to live with a rich uncle at Trieste. Before parting, Amnon hands her an ancient medallion with a flower in it called *"The Balm of Gilead."* He had received it from an old Transjordan Sheikh, Okba-El-Eldjuni, who assured him that "its scent is a charm—give it to that friend whom you wish never to forget you."

From this point, the story runs in two parallel threads—hers in pre-war and war-time Trieste, his in Palestine. During the years spent in Trieste, Tamar seems to have forgotten both Palestine and Amnon. They never write to each other. She wanders through life with empty hands and a hungry heart. The only steadying force in her existence is her great-uncle, Marco Granada, who warns her "never to marry a man who wears ready-made clothes, who feeds on things made for him by others." Amnon, in a war-stricken Palestine, untouched by any specific political trend, concentrates all his longings on one vision : to build *Gancori,* a perfume factory on the shores of the Lake Tiberias. After the war, he goes to Paris to study chemistry, establishes his factory as a cooperative venture, but fails to build it up as a sound undertaking.

Eventually, Tamar returns to Galilee. Before her departure, the great-uncle gives her a sealed envelope, not to be opened until she needs it. Back home, she learns that Amnon's perfume factory is on the verge of bankruptcy. She opens the medallion and is overwhelmed by the magic scent of the Balm of Gilead. In the envelope she finds a substantial check. Meeting Amnon on a night trip on the lake, she rejoins and marries him. Marco Granada's check solves the factory's financial problems, and the Balm of Gilead provides Amnon with that specific, original scent that had been missing until then.

Other characters include Lieutenant Semedor (Trumpeldor), who arrives with a shabby bag and, when asked "What do you want to be?", answers: "workman—or teacher—or lawyer—or soldier—whatever the country may need—I have no tastes—I am just a wheel;" Robert McGregor, the young British Governor of Tiberias, who finds that "the (Arab) natives are all right," but the Jews are "a damn difficult lot" with the "mentality of conquerors"; a French perfume expert; *chalutzim* and watchmen. The Jewish National Fund figures in the script prominently but discreetly, without undue cheap propaganda.

The leftish *Hapoel Hatzair* severely criticized the Board of Directors of the Jewish National Fund for having entrusted Jabotinsky with preparing the script; the scenario remained for ever buried in the Fund's archives. Its leadership, however, denied that it was criticism of the labor wing that had caused the abandonment of the project: Shalom Schwarz, who investigated the matter, was told by a spokesman of the Fund that the main reason was the high cost of producing the film which the Board of Directors of the *Keren ha' Yessod* refused to share with the JNF.[5] This explanation might be substantially correct. However, apart from this practical consideration, there was in the script very little to endear it to the then dominant trend in Zionist thought and action. Its central figure, Amnon, was not a *Kibbutznik,* and his dream was not an agricultural communal settlement, but a factory producing perfume for export, at that time a most unorthodox and unpopular venture. Amnon's first attempts failed: the perfume samples sent to Paris were found unattractive. The factory needed better, more modern installations to be able to compete on the world market. But Amnon had no money to invest. Looking at the JNF's Blue Box in his office, he commented: "Poor little Box, you gave me the land on which my factory stands, you can do no more." On his way to Jerusalem, where he expected to obtain funds from other Zionist institutions, he met Jewish workmen draining swamps—without tents to sleep in, suffering from malaria—and he decided: "I have no right to ask for even a penny." Amnon's problem was solved not by national institutions, but by a silent foreign investor—Tamar's great-uncle.

All these features of the script, which reflected Jabotinsky's matured outlook on Palestine's economy and prospects, were undoubtedly at great variance with the then dominant emphasis on agriculture as against industry, and collective economy as against private initiative.

2. Forty Thousand Listeners

Jabotinsky arrived in Jaffa on the *S.S. Lotos* on October 3, 1926. When the Arab leaders learned of his impending arrival, the militant *Falastin* strongly attacked him as the promoter of "aggressive Zionism." The paper stressed that while Weizmann had chosen a moderate and cautious policy, Jabotinsky was opposed to this line and claimed that, while trying to deceive the Arabs, such a policy was also deceiving the Jews.[6]

The attitude of Palestine Jewry was not uniform. For the first time Jabotinsky had come to the country not in his personal capacity, but as the leader of a faction in Zionism. This accentuated the animosity on the part of the leftist Zionist groups. But this animosity seems to have only slightly affected the feelings of the average Palestine Jew. The *Yishuv* at large was glad to see Jabotinsky back, to greet him and to listen to him. The non-party Hebrew press devoted much space to his arrival. *Doar Hayom* (September 9) published an enthusiastic article of welcome by Ben Baruch (Shalom Schwarz). *Palestine Weekly* (October 8, 1926) wrote editorially :

The arrival of Vladimir Jabotinsky in Palestine this week has created a stir not only in the circles of the Revisionist Organization, but also in the Jewish community as a whole. . . . To our knowledge, there are thousands of Jews in this country whose ideas naturally tend in the direction indicated by Mr. Jabotinsky, but who have not found their feet as yet as far as a definite and positive system of work is concerned. It needs the prestige and the fiery eloquence of Mr. Jabotinsky himself to convince them of both the wisdom and the feasibility of the Revisionist program.

The non-party weekly, *Yishuv*, said that "Jabotinsky . . . returns to Eretz Israel triumphantly." The influential *Haaretz* was more critical of the Revisionists as a party than of Jabotinsky personally.[7]

When, on the morning of October 3, the Jews of Tel Aviv had learned of the arrival of the *Lotos*, almost everybody, young and old, rushed to Jaffa harbor to meet and greet the guest, according to the Palestine correspondent of the *Haint*. "It would not be an exaggeration to say," he wrote, "that he was given a 'royal' reception. . . . Thousands applauded him enthusiastically." On his way from the harbor "women and girls threw flowers from the balconies. Most of the houses were adorned with blue-white banners. Cries of 'Long Live Jabotinsky!' accompanied him all the way." [8] When he reviewed the *Brit Trumpeldor* groups in Allenby Street, thousands gathered to listen to his short address, reported the *Palestine Weekly* (October 19). Jabotinsky called for internal discipline and protection of the working Jew, the Hebrew language and all the Jewish achievements in Palestine. His public appearances attracted exceptionally large audiences. In Tel Aviv, he spoke twice within three days. The first meeting (October 17) at the *Beit Am* was attended by ten thousand people; the second (October 19) at the *Maccabi* Sport ground, by six thousand. For the first time in Palestine, a loud-speaker was used to broadcast the lecture.[9] His address in the Revisionist Club, *Hashachar,* was listened to by an unusually large audience. The crowded hall was besieged by many hundreds who could not gain admission.

Equally enthusiastic was the reception in Jerusalem. Met in Motza, two and one half miles from the city, by personal and party friends, he was escorted to the central part of Jerusalem by a cavalcade of cars and bicycles. Large crowds lined the Jaffa Road. The police had to stop all traffic. When Jabotinsky's car appeared, thousands of people spontaneously intoned *Hatiqva*. He was greeted by the president of the Jewish Community Council.[10] The *Palestine Weekly* (October 22) gave a glowing report of "Jabotinsky's Great Speech in Jerusalem."

In "red Haifa," dominated by an extremely well-organized and powerful branch of the Labor party, where the Revisionist group was very small, tension ran high prior to Jabotinsky's arrival. "From early September," recalls Nahum Levin, "there were rumors of an impending visit of Vladimir Jabotinsky. Opponents, sympathizers and adherents eagerly awaited his appearance. . . . Many 'eyewitnesses' 'saw' and 'heard' him in Jerusalem, the *Emek, Petach Tiqvah* and other places long before he actually reached the shores of Palestine. Excitement hung in the air." [11] A few days before Jabotinsky's arrival, Jacob Pat, the commander of the *Haganah* in Haifa, summoned Nahum Levin, together with two other *Haganah* members (all three were at that time not associated with the Revisionist party) and told them that since there was danger of an Arab attempt to assassinate Jabotinsky, they had been appointed his bodyguards. They had to be on duty twenty-four hours a day, eight hours each. As weapons, they received one big revolver. Jabotinsky was not aware of this arrangement.

Measures were taken to reduce the danger. The public were informed that Jabotinsky would arrive on October 20 at the central railway station, and crowds began to stream in that direction. But a selected group of party and personal friends met him at the Carmel railway station, about four and a third miles from Haifa. From there, he was to proceed by car.[12] Dr. Joseph Paamoni, who was in charge of the reception, somehow managed to procure a luxurious limousine, which he richly adorned with roses. When the group approached the car, Jabotinsky asked: "For whom is this?"—"For you, of course." —"For me? Never! Couldn't we get a taxi? Or else, please remove all these trimmings." When they arrived in Haifa and were warmly greeted by the crowd, which had in the meantime returned from the central station, Jabotinsky apologetically said to Paamoni: "I hope you are not offended. You see, young man, even if the roses were meant as a mark of admiration, there must still remain some difference between the President of a political party and a popular cabaret singer. . . ."[13] Next day, about two thousand people came to hear Jabotinsky—the largest gathering ever arranged in Haifa. He addressed them from the steps of the Haifa Technical Institute. A force of fifty policemen was dispatched to maintain order, but, though the great majority of the audience were strongly opposed to Jabotinsky's views, not a single interruption occurred. He kept the crowd standing in the open-air, spellbound for several hours.[14]

The correspondent of the *Yiddishe Zeitung* (Kaunas) reported that "never before has Palestine seen such huge meetings." The *Rasswyet* correspondent estimated the number of people who had heard Jabotinsky during his 1926 visit at forty thousand, about one fourth of the Jewish population of the country at the time.[15]

3. Security Problems and Arab Contacts

In his speeches, Jabotinsky developed the entire Revisionist program, which does not need to be expounded in this biography. In the political field, the *Yishuv* was by that time more than before receptive to the basic trends of Jabotinsky's ideas. The Herbert Samuel fixation, against which he had been fighting since 1922, was thoroughly destroyed in Palestine Jewry. Disappointment in both British and official Zionist policy was strong and growing. Jabotinsky's opponents claimed that his program appealed only to the "discontented" in Zionism. Referring to this argument, he said in a speech at the Revisionist Club : "This is certainly true. Because there is now in the Zionist movement only one group that is satisfied with everything—the members of the Zionist Executive." He also accepted as true the opponents' claim that he and his party did not contribute anything "new" to the Zionist ideology. "This is so because we are actually fighting for the old Herzlian concept, against the *galut* tendencies which now dominate the Zionist movement." [16]

The policy of the Mandatory administration made the *Yishuv* particularly responsive to Jabotinsky's concept of security. Yielding to the British taxpayers' demand for economies, the administration had drastically reduced the British garrison in Palestine. Side by side with the mixed Arab-Jewish police force, the Trans Jordan Frontier Force was created—a military unit whose task was to defend the borders of the Mandatory territory. To all intents and purposes, it was an Arab force, from which Jews were virtually excluded. The entire Hebrew press protested vehemently against this discrimination, as did a meeting of Jewish ex-legionaries. The Revisionists issued a proclamation demanding the re-establishment of the Jewish Legion. This appeal found considerable sympathy in the Jewish community. The Palestine correspondent of the *Jewish Morning Journal* wrote on March 11 : "Although hitherto all the papers were opposed to Jabotinsky's idea of creating a Jewish Legion, they all now agree that since the Government has established a separate Arab Legion, permission should be given for the creation of a separate Jewish Legion to preserve peace and order in the country." Nevertheless, no clear decision along these lines was taken by the representative bodies of Palestine Jewry in the course of the six months that followed. Two weeks after his arrival, Jabotinsky was invited by the Presidium of the *Vaad Leumi* to take part in the *Vaad's* session devoted to the question of defense of the *Yishuv* in connection with the establishment of the Trans Jordan Frontier Force. It was largely under his and Itzhak Ben Zvi's influence that the *Vaad Leumi,* on October 22, overwhelmingly voted to demand from the Palestine Government the establishment of a purely Jewish military unit within the Trans Jordan Frontier Force; there were only two dissenting votes.[17]

One of the few opponents of the demand for a Jewish military force, Chaim Kalvarisky, argued during the debate that an amicable understanding between Jews and Arabs would secure peaceful relations and make defense arrangements unnecessary. Replying to this argument, Jabotinsky said : "I, too, want peace, Mr. Kalvarisky. But what can we offer the Arabs? I had the very interesting experience of being approached by a group of Arabs. They wrote : 'You are the only one among the Zionists who has no intention of fooling us and who understands that the Arab is a patriot and not a prostitute (who can be bought).' I asked them : 'What could we offer you (as a concession)?' and their answer was : 'Do not demand (Jewish) mass immigration.' " But since the only thing the Zionists cannot renounce is mass immigration, "there is no place for the illusion of peace," Jabotinsky maintained.

Jabotinsky's contacts with the Arabs, which he mentioned in his *Vaad Leumi* speech, culminated in an encounter with a thirty-six-year old brilliant Egyptian intellectual, Dr. Mahmoud Azmi. Born and educated in Cairo, Azmi received the degree of Doctor of Law in 1912 from the University of Paris, and from 1917 to 1937 owned or edited a number of Egyptian dailies. He was a frequent visitor to Palestine and, while maintaining friendly relations with Jewish intellectuals, had considerable influence in Arab circles. In an attempt to find some basis for Arab-Jewish understanding, Jabotinsky met Azmi on November 7, 1926, in the house of a mutual friend.[18] He was not alone at this meeting. He was accompanied by Michael Aleinikov, an outstanding spokesman for the official Zionist policy on the Arab question; architect Samuel Rosov (the son of the noted Zionist leader, Israel Rosov), at that time a very young man, was present as a "silent observer." According to Rosov's recollection, the discussion, conducted in French, was opened by Aleinikov, who endeavoured to soften Azmi's opposition to Zionism by stressing the financial and cultural benefits the Arab population was deriving from the Jewish penetration into Palestine. Jabotinsky's approach was different. Emphasizing that he was speaking on behalf of a group strongly opposed to the official Zionist line, he said he refused to believe that a proud people like the Arabs, with a great past, would ever agree to sell their country for money or even for the prospect of being imbued with a higher, European, culture. Every people possesses and cherishes a culture of its own, created and developed in

65

accordance with its own needs and tastes, and not superimposed by others. He did not deny that Jewish immigration was bound to convert the Arabs of Palestine into a minority; nor did he attempt to minimize the fact that in this respect there did exist a local political conflict of interests between Arabs and Jews. He insisted, however, that the problem must be viewed from a broader and more constructive viewpoint. He reminded Dr. Azmi of the vast, empty spaces owned by the newly created independent Arab states, while little Palestine was the only spot on earth where the homeless Jewish people could build a homeland. There was place within the framework of a regenerated Middle East for a Jewish commonwealth, whose emergence would be a source of progress for the entire population of that area.

Rosov recalls Dr. Azmi's reaction to the two different presentations of the Zionist case : neither of them changed his negative attitude toward Zionism, but he particularly thanked Jabotinsky for having spoken so frankly; he appreciated and respected an opponent who stated his aims honestly and believed in their justness, without trying to disguise their true nature.* [19]

As strongly politically minded as he was, Jabotinsky did not neglect the economic problems of the Zionist colonization effort. He actively participated in a special session of the Revisionist Economic Council, where he endorsed Dr. Eugene Soskin's system of intensive agriculture as the most suitable for the rural sector of the Palestine economy. Furthering of industry was, in his view, connected with the *Totzeret Haaretz la'Golah* scheme for the distribution of Palestine products in the countries of the Diaspora, along the lines of the American "Order of the Sons of Zion" (see Chapter Two). He also participated in the Council's discussion on ways and means of rationalizing Palestine's Jewish economy. He visited the Near East Fair and the *Totzeret Haaretz* Museum in Tel Aviv, which were organized by the monthly periodical *Miskhar ve'Taasiah* (Trade and

* In the winter of 1954, when Dr. Azmi was Egypt's chief delegate to the United Nations, this writer informed him that he knew of the meeting with Jabotinsky, but before utilizing this information for the Jabotinsky biography, " would like in all frankness to inquire whether, in view of the present strained relations between Egypt and Israel, the publication of this item would not cause you any inconvenience." This letter was mailed on November 1 and must have reached the addressee on November 2; on November 3, Dr. Azmi collapsed at the meeting of the United Nations Security Council while delivering Egypt's reply to the Israeli charge in connection with the seizure of the Israeli freighter *Bat Galim* in the Suez Canal. He died a little more than an hour later. (*The New York Times*, November 4, 1954.)

Industry) headed by young and dynamic Revisionists, Alexander M. Evzerov and Abraham I. Idelson. He stressed that both institutions were essential for the development of Palestine industry : the Fair as a link between producer and consumer, and the Museum as a source of scientific factual data and guidance as to methods for future progress. With the leaders of the Manufacturers' Association (Arieh Shenkar, Dr. Moses, Zew Gluskin, and others) he discussed the problems of Jewish industry in Palestine. Replying to their grievances, he insisted that no piecemeal reforms, but only the establishment of a "colonization regime" could satisfy the needs of the country's economic development. He also received delegations of Palestine Jewish artisans who reported on the desperate situation in the trade and complained of insufficient support on the part of the Zionist ruling bodies. One of the delegations expressed readiness to participate in the constructive Revisionist economic work in Palestine.[20]

The five weeks of Jabotinsky's sojourn in Palestine had been crammed with speechmaking, banquets, closed meetings with party friends and leaders of various organizations. He also spent a good deal of time with his sister and mother. His mother had recovered sufficiently to attend the banquets arranged in the "Palatin" hotel and at Israel Rosov's house, and was understandably happy to see her son feted. Jabotinsky was, however, not in a festive mood, and he said so outspokenly at a banquet in Jerusalem. He reminded the guests that he had been refused permission to hold a conference in the amphi-theater of the Hebrew University, that his friends were being discriminated against, that the leaders of the *Yishuv* did not support his plans—and concluded by saying that should he again fail in his attempt to induce the Zionist movement to change its policy, he would remind himself that he was also a poet and a novelist and would devote himself entirely to literature.[21]

The meeting with Achad Haam, who had settled in Palestine in 1922 was an unforgettable experience. Together with the entire Zionist intelligentsia, Jabotinsky owed much to this original and courageous Zionist thinker, whose teachings played a considerable role in the formation of his own Zionist concept. Later, however, their ways parted. Achad Haam strongly disapproved of Jabotinsky's struggle for the Jewish Legion. Opponents of Jabotinsky's main thesis that a Jewish majority in Palestine was the prerequisite to a Zionist solution of the Jewish problem asserted that this thesis was in contradiction to Achad Haam's concept of a "spiritual center" which could be created without a Jewish majority in Palestine.

This alleged contradiction, however, in no way affected their personal relationship. Yohanan Pograbinsky, Achad Haam's private secretary, testifies that his great teacher had been always deeply interested in Jabotinsky and his activities and spoke of him with affection.[22] "Jabotinsky is my friend. Though there are *now* no close relations between us, we are still friends, and so it shall remain." When Jabotinsky arrived in Palestine, Achad Haam expressed a wish to see him. They met at Achad Haam's home (three months before the latter's death) and had a long heart-to-heart talk. At one point, Jabotinsky mentioned Achad Haam's rejection of the principles of a Jewish majority in Palestine as the central aim of Zionism, and his belief that it was not the quantity but the quality that counted, that fifty thousand Jews brought up in the spirit of Eretz Israel Judaism were of greater value than fifteen million Diaspora Jews. "And to me," Jabotinsky declared emphatically, "three million Jews (in Palestine) without Hebrew education are more important than a tiny group of Hebrew-educated Jews in your 'spiritual center.' I say so not because I don't value quality, but because I believe that if there will be a Jewish majority in Eretz Israel, they will, in the final analysis, be brought up in the spirit of Judaism: great quantity will thus be converted into great quality." Achad Haam vigorously denied that he was "against a Jewish majority" in Palestine, and insisted that he was one of the first to stress that a "spiritual center" was unthinkable without a Jewish majority in Eretz Israel. He asked Pograbinsky to find a passage to this effect in the collection of his writings, *Al Parashat Drakhim* (At the Crossroads) and send it to Jabotinsky.[23] Such a passage does indeed appear on pages 64 to 65 of the second volume, in the speech *Shalosh Madregot* (Three Steps), and was quoted by Jabotinsky five years later, at the Seventeenth Zionist Congress in Zurich.[24]

FOUR

INNER ZIONIST BATTLES

1. *The White Guest*

ON his return journey from Palestine, Jabotinsky was glad to be able to pay a "debt of honor" that he had involuntarily contracted the previous year when passport trouble had forced him to interrupt his lecture tour and to forego the scheduled visits to Greece and Bulgaria, centers of *Sefardic* Jewry. He first went to Salonica where he spoke in Ladino on what he saw in Palestine. The Chief Rabbinate and the Jewish Community Council officially participated in the reception held for him by the local Revisionist organization.[1] His next destination was Bulgaria. While in Sofia, he sprained his left foot and, as he had a long journey before him, the doctor decided to put the foot in plaster. It was only after his arrival in Berlin that he was able to remove the dressing.[2]

While in Germany, he delivered sixteen lectures in fourteen cities. During his stay in Berlin, he had the satisfaction of winning Richard Lichtheim over to the Revisionist party. This "conversion" did not come suddenly. Jabotinsky had been "working on" Lichtheim from afar for some time. On August 28, he wrote to him: "Our convictions are identical, and always have been so. If there are some small differences, they can be straightened out. If it is I who am the obstacle—please believe me—I have no pretentions, nor do I consider myself the A-1 candidate for our paltry crown. . . . My dear old man, it is worth your while to bank on us, even if we are right now half paralyzed by poverty. That won't last. . . . I am ashamed to try to influence you by propaganda. But I beg you to earnestly consider my request. Join us, openly with *éclat,* and everything will work out beautifully." It was, however, not until Jabotinsky came to Berlin that Lichtheim finally made up his mind.

When Jabotinsky informed his colleagues on the Paris Central Committee of Lichtheim's joining and expressed the hope of greeting him at the forthcoming Second Revisionist World Conference, the fiery brothers Tiomkin balked at the idea: "Have you already forgotten that at the January, 1923, session of the Actions Committee he joined the crowd of your detractors and attackers and was among those responsible for your resignation? [See Vol. I, p. 428]. And now you are ready to receive him with open arms. Or are you perhaps going to offer him a leading position in the movement?" Jabotinsky listened to this tirade with studied amazement: "Was Lichtheim ever disloyal to me? I don't remember. I only keep in mind that he is an exceptionally gifted man, a sincere and thinking Zionist, and that his Zionist credo had always been in keeping with mine. And that's good enough, as far as I am concerned. And I definitely do intend to offer him any responsible position he might be ready to accept." This writer vividly remembers the bewildered expressions on the faces of the two Revisionist stalwarts.

Lichtheim did come to the World Conference, held in Paris, December 26 to 30, 1926. Following Jabotinsky's lead, the delegates received him warmly. Moreover, he was elected—together with Vladimir Tiomkin and Meir Grossman—Vice President of the Revisionist World Union; Jabotinsky was reelected President. Eager to give Lichtheim a position of responsibility, he induced the Conference to transfer the Union's headquarters from Paris to Berlin and to put Lichtheim in charge of the central office.[3]

At this Conference, Jabotinsky appeared in a new role. In May, 1925, when the first Conference met, the Zionist world was in a mood of unbounded jubilation: the Hebrew University was solemnly inaugurated, immigration was on the increase. In his opening speech, in which he ruthlessly debunked this inflated optimism, Jabotinsky admitted that by doing so he was "coming to a wedding clad in mourning." Mourning clothes "symbolize the Black Guest, who does not believe in this wedding: the bridegroom is sick, there is no love, the entire celebration is self-deception. Such a guest usually gets thrown out; the trouble is that this 'guest' is right." [4] Three months later, he acknowledged the nickname "Cassandra" (mythical princess of Troy who possessed the gift of prophecy and predicted defeat, but was not believed), given to him by opponents. Within a year, his devastating analysis proved to be alarmingly correct. In 1926, the number of immigrants decreased by twenty thousand as against the previous year, while almost seven thousand left Palestine. Unemployment in the country was growing. Deep gloom replaced the rosy optimism of the previous year. Jabotinsky was able to state: "Cassandra proved to be right all along the line: about immigration, industry, land and security. . . . People are very angry with Cassandra." [5]

It was at that psychological juncture that Jabotinsky revealed himself as "The White Guest," bringing the Zionist world a message of faith and confidence. In his opening speech at the Second Conference he said: "The task of our Conference is to make every effort to combat the fog of pessimism—just as at the first Conference we fought against the fog of optimism. At that time we were the Black Guest, now we are the White Guest." [6] Not the Jewish people, but the mandatory regime, he insisted, was responsible for the crisis in Palestine. [7]

The Jews have proved themselves to be first-class colonizers. In all her colonial experience, Great Britain has never witnessed such splendid colonizing achievements. It is not the Jewish people but the British regime, with its agrarian, industrial, and political system, that has failed. It is not a regime suitable for a country which is being colonized. . . .

[On the other hand] the Zionist Executive has been conducting an opportunist policy, neither pressing, nor being able to stand up for, the just demands of the Jews. It has been addressing itself with demands, petitions, and appeals to various individuals, whereas the Government of Palestine is controlled not by those individuals but by British public opinion. Nowadays politics is democratic. It addresses itself to the masses. It is the appeal of one people to another. It is to British public opinion that appeal should be made. The main difficulty lies in the attitude of the Zionist leaders toward the non-Jewish world. . . . Theirs is a typical ghetto mentality, which regards all non-Jews as *Goyim*, as enemies. With such a mentality nothing can be achieved. It is time that the Jewish people began to have confidence in the *Goyim*. The *Goyim* have not produced only Hamans; they have also produced great idealists who have given their blood for the cause of humanity. I say *'morenu we rabenu ha'Goy* [our teacher and mentor, the Gentile]. We must collaborate with the non-Jewish world. We must begin to explain to British public opinion what the Jewish desiderata are. Being repeatedly told that everything is all right in Palestine, British public opinion naturally believes that the Jews are satisfied, and that the people they have to reckon with are the

71

discontended Arabs. This must and can be changed. The present crisis is not the crisis of Zionism or Jewry, but of a political system. Nothing is lost, and much can be achieved by a powerful political offensive."

The Conference endorsed Jabotinsky's analysis and prognosis.

2. *Mixed Feelings*

The two years preceding and following the Vienna Congress witnessed considerable and promising progress of the young Jabotinsky movement. The official Zionist camp was, on the other hand, in a mood of depression : the immigration wave of 1925 was petering out, the finances of the Executive were in a disastrous state, and the negotiations about the much vaunted—and embattled—"extended" Jewish Agency were languishing. In the light of this situation, Jabotinsky was for some time inclined to believe that his party might be called upon to assume the actual leadership of the World Zionist Organization at the forthcoming Fifteenth Zionist Congress. He viewed this prospect with an odd mixture of expectation and apprehension. His personal letters contain several references to this subject.

In September, 1925, he wrote : "In the coming months we will make every effort to convert activism into a strong party and to take over [the Zionist Executive] at the Fifteenth Congress. I consider this quite possible." A Revisionist-controlled Executive, he pledged in another letter, would "completely reverse the present 'rough-neck' [*khamskoye*] attitude toward the opposition. We would introduce the opposition leaders to cabinet ministers or members of Parliament, so that in the event of a change [in the Zionist leadership] the Zionist Organization would not find itself cut off from the [British] Government and Parliament." [8] Three months later he predicted : [9] "At the next Congress we will be strong, and possibly victorious." He "feared that next August we might be put into harness." Explaining later why he was "afraid" of such a prospect, he wrote in March, 1927 : "Our fate at the [Fifteenth] Congress depends not on us but on what happens with the ["extended"] Agency. If it succeeds, or if there is at least a hope for its success, nobody will listen to us; if it fails or is delayed, we will be running the serious risk of a triumph—of a premature victory that would find us unprepared, with every chance of failure within the next year or so." He therefore argued that

72

"chasing after numerical strength at the Fifteenth Congress" was vitiating the movement's prospects. His contention was that it was possible to build "a good new organization" within the next three years, even without formally leaving the World Zionist Organization. It would be sufficient "just not to be too eager to come to the fore." But if the movement has "to hurry, to look for allies . . . it cannot be looking after the party's interests." "All this," Jabotinsky complained, "is terribly slovenly. I will wait until the Congress. If, as is quite possible, we get our ears boxed there, I will insist on a complete change of course." Two months later, Jabotinsky came to the definite conclusion that "this Congress isn't worth a penny. I don't see why we should break our necks to have our delegates elected. But our people want it. Let's try. During this spring, our chances have become much weaker; but we will see." [10]

"We will see" did not mean "wait and see." The last part of May and almost the entire month of June, Jabotinsky spent on the road, actively participating in the electoral campaign in the countries of Central and Eastern Europe. Purely personal reasons forced him to interrupt the lecture tour: Mrs. Jabotinsky had to undergo an appendicitis operation, and his "financial affairs had taken a catastrophic turn. I don't feel like explaining, and there is no need to do so. Who trusts me, will believe that if I had had the slightest possibility, I would have continued the tour. Even so, I don't know how I will get out of this jam. . . . No more journeys for me. I will do what I can by writing articles." Replying to protestations that without his direct participation the party's effort would be disastrously handicapped, Jabotinsky remonstrated that there was no Revisionist group in the world which would not at least twice a year ask for a visit and a lecture of his; all the Revisionist papers were clamoring for articles from him, and when he did not comply, the paper's failure was laid at his door. "What kind of a party is it that depends on one man's omnipresence? In this respect, I am not going to be in the picture any more. Next year, I will simply go nowhere. If we are a movement, this movement will grow without my constant journeying as a traveling salesman. If we are just a bluff, we deserve nothing better." [11]

With the Congress drawing nearer, Jabotinsky's reluctance to take an active part in its deliberations was markedly increasing. "I am in no mood to go to Basle. I find the idea even more repulsive than going to the Vienna Zionist Congress two years ago. . . . Least of all am I now in a mood to fight for a [Revisionist-dominated Zionist] Executive, when success would mean inheriting a cart that is hopelessly stuck in the mud." [12] Shortly before the Congress, while admitting that "we will have to be in Basle," he approved of Lichtheim's suggestion "to behave there in a very restrained manner, without holding big speeches." "But," he added, "according to the Congress' standing orders, we are not even entitled to sit on the committees. So what are we going to do there? . . . Most probably, we will haunt the movies." [13]

3. *The Fifteenth Congress*

At the Congress, Jabotinsky headed a Revisionist faction of nine, representing 8,436 voters. In comparison with the four-man strong representation at the Vienna Congress, this was quite a respectable advance. But it was, of course, a far cry from "taking over." Jabotinsky had to rely not so much on the numerical strength of his own delegation as on a certain sympathy for his ideas among non-Revisionist delegates—and again on the influence of his own "big speech," which, as usual, was the focal point of the Congress.[14]

He began with a sober analysis of the nature of the crisis Palestine was then facing.

During the preceding seven years, seventy-two thousand Jews had arrived in Eretz Israel, an average of ten thousand a year. The Arab population of Western Palestine numbered three quarters of a million, and being a primitive and polygamic race, they would within a generation number one million souls. Of what significance could be under these circumstances an annual immigration of ten thousand? And still, under those conditions, Palestine was unable to absorb even those ten thousand Jews per year. There were eight thousand unemployed in the country.

A real solution to the unemployment problem, Jabotinsky told them, was not public works which would be only of temporary help, and not agricultural colonization; that was too slow a process. The answer lay in the development of industry. Jewish industry had made considerable progress in recent years, and in the opinion of prominent industrialists there were further possibilities—but under certain conditions only: the Government must create the necessary prerequisites for industrial development. This had not been the case up to then: the Palestine Government had only grudgingly made some minor concessions to industry.

Jabotinsky then devoted a few realistic remarks to the problem of security in Palestine. He reminded the Congress that there were actually hardly any British troops in the country: only forty-five Englishmen had remaineed in the police force, and thirty-one in the Frontier Force. In the latter, there were only thirty-seven Jews (mostly bandsmen) as compared with seven hundred non-Jewish natives, and in the police there were only two hundred and twelve Jews as against thirteen hundred non-Jewish natives. "I ask every honest-thinking man whether this situation is satisfactory"—in a country where one has always to reckon with the ever-present possibility of conflicts.

"I don't believe," said Jabotinsky, "in a policy of aggression, which I am always being accused of. Such a policy can be entertained only if one has material power. Since our strength is of a moral nature, there can naturally be no question of an aggressive policy." Experience had proved, he went on to say, that great results can be achieved by moral pressure. But these possibilities were being paralyzed by recurrent statements by Zionist leaders that "the political situation in Palestine is satisfactory." The highest representative of the Zionist Executive had declared in Boston, in the presence of the foreign press and consuls: "The political situation in Palestine is sufficiently good to permit a yearly immigration of twenty-five thousand Jews—if only we had the money!" And Jabotinsky asked: "What can the 'man in the street,' the average Englishman, say to that, even if he is our best friend? He is bound to say to himself: We, the English, have done everything, but these Shylocks, these stingy Jews, they are the guilty ones—they did not give the money." Jabotinsky admitted that the Jewish people had of course not contributed the twenty-five million pounds called for in the first *Keren ha'Yessod* manifesto, of which he himself was one of the signatories, and thus had not fulfilled the duty toward Palestine. "But as to the seventy-two thousand immigrants—surely there is still some proportion in this world." Greece resettled a million refugees from Turkey at a cost of fifteen million pounds (about seventy-two million dollars). Of course, colonization in Palestine was bound to be much more expensive than in Greece—three, four times more expensive, but certainly not twenty times more expensive.

Jabotinsky scathingly criticized the official Zionist line of always exonerating the British Mandatory Power from guilt and reproaching the Jewish people with not having done enough. This policy was eliminating any chance of improving the political situation of Zionism. The leaders of Zionism had a fixed pattern of their own. Their political impressionism, their political color-blindness, was deeply rooted in ,their mentality. It would have been, therefore, useless to demand a radical change of attitude, policy, and tactics toward the Mandatory Power, while simultaneously entrusting the implementation of this new line to the same leaders.

Firmly opposing the surrender of 50 per cent of the control of the Jewish Agency to non-Zionists, Jabotinsky offered a constructive alternative to the official scheme of an "extended" Agency: non-Zionists—whose participation in the Agency was being sought—must be given the possibility of cooperating in the economic field, leaving all political matters to the Zionist Organization. This bi-cameral system would best serve the purpose and the interests of both sides. And as long as there was a politically sovereign Zionist Congress, all Zionists would have a Court of Appeal, before which they could appear with their complaints and demands. The inevitable party strife in the Zionist movement would still be a struggle between brothers. Jabotinsky concluded with a call for faith:

We firmly believe in the Jewish State and in the strength of our just cause. We also believe in England . . . in the English people and its public opinion. It is the Court of Appeal before which we can plead our just cause. . . . We believe in the honesty of our non-Zionist partner and we believe in England's honesty. We have no confidence only in a few individuals. That, however, the Congress can change!

Jabotinsky, who was never inclined to brag of his oratorical performances, wrote to his sister: "My speech was an even greater success than my address in Vienna two years ago." [15] The Congress correspondent of the official New Judea (London) reported: "Dazzling oration that of Jabotinsky. Fine analysis of the political situation. Well put together, eloquently delivered." The address was, however, in the correspondent's opinion, "marred by irrelevant illustrations and a parading of subtlety . . . transparently mischievous.

Congress impressed if not convinced." [16] Very similar was the judgement of the *New Palestine* correspondent: "Jabotinsky's speech was followed with an enthusiastic ovation, in which many American delegates joined. It was generally admitted, however, that the applause which greeted Jabotinsky's address was a tribute to his fine oratory rather than to the logic and power of his political arguments." [17]

In striking contrast with his pre-Congress attitude, Jabotinsky returned from Basle in a confident and cheerful frame of mind. To his friends in London, he wrote: "I am well pleased with the Congress," [18] and to his sister: "I consider the Congress a moral victory for us. This is not just my personal opinion—it is shared by all delegates. The political resolutions were copied from Revisionist manifestos, only slightly censored. Our representatives in all committees have made an excellent impression." [18]

This optimistic balance-sheet of Revisionist achievements must be taken with a grain of salt. It is true that the political demands voted by Congress closely resembled those formulated by Jabotinsky. But their implementation was entrusted to an Executive headed by Weizmann, who frankly admitted that he did not believe in the possibility of changing the political conditions in Palestine. Nor did the opposition succeed in its efforts to prevent the formal adoption of the "extended" Agency scheme by the Fifteenth Congress, and to leave its final ratification to the forthcoming Sixteenth Congress. It was with bitter restraint that Jabotinsky stated in the name of the Revisionist delegation that they "fully maintain their absolute opposition to any attempt to share the political functions [of the Jewish Agency] with non-Zionist elements . . . we will fight it with all the honest means at our disposal in the conviction that this struggle will render impossible the implementation of the proposed scheme." [20]

At the Fifteenth Congress, the Revisionists had, for the first time, obtained representation on the Actions Committee. According to Jabotinsky's own evidence, he had "firmly asked his colleagues once and for all to excuse him from this office." "I am always sorry for those friends who accepted it," he added. [21]

The last quarter of 1927, and the first half of 1928, were largely devoted to the struggle for the reform of the Hebrew University in Jerusalem, which had been solemnly inaugurated in May, 1925, in the presence of numerous Zionist and British dignitaries. This celebration revived a more than a decade old controversy between Jabotinsky and Weizmann (See Vol. I. pp. 187-194). The inauguration on Mount Scopus implemented Weizmann's original concept of a research institute for postgraduates. Jabotinsky—in 1925, as in 1914 —insisted that world Jewry and Palestine were badly in need of, not a research institute for scholars, but a regular undergraduate school for Jewish students barred by the *numerus clausus* from entering European universities. He angrily denounced the "travesty of a university" established in Jerusalem, as well as the costly and misleading pomp of the ceremony. "I do not deny that research institutes are useful. Yet one thing is clear and incontestable : a research institute is not a university and cannot be called one. . . . Because a university is a school for students and not a laboratory for scholars." The elaborate pageantry of the inauguration ceremony reminded him of the *panem et circenses* technique of the Roman Caesars, who fed the hungry people with circus performances. He denied that budgetary limitations precluded the creation of a "genuine" university : some of the best run universities in Germany, from which scores of students had been graduated, were functioning on budgets similar to that of the Hebrew University and, some, maintained by smaller states, on much smaller budgets.[22]

In the early spring of 1928, a petition movement, inspired by Jabotinsky, was launched among Jewish university youth in Europe. It proved to be both dynamic and successful. The demand to transform the research institute into a "university for students" found understanding and support in all European university centers. "Our 'action' for the reform of the Hebrew University is a success," wrote Jabotinsky to S. Jacobi. "Students' meetings and petitions have been organized all over Europe. The [University's] Board of Governors issued a statement that 'because of the Revisionist propaganda' they announce that the question is already under consideration, 'with due attention to the situation of Jewish students in Palestine and in the Diaspora.' " [23] Six weeks later, the Board of Governors and the Academic Council decided to open the doors of the University to undergraduates, candidates for degrees in the liberal arts and sciences.[24]

Jabotinsky was exceedingly pleased with this promising achievement. The interests and needs of Jewish college youth had always been particularly dear to him, and he was proud that it was from among them that, like Herzl thirty years earlier, he found his most ardent and devoted followers. He was nominated *Ehrenbursch* (honorary member) by almost every existing student corporation. In 1927, all student corporations in Vienna arranged a joint solemn *Kommers* (revelry) for him. Its participants remember Jabotinsky's speech as an exceptionally brilliant masterpiece. He spoke separately of every student group in Vienna (*Kadimah, Unitas, Ivria, Lebanonia, Hasmonaea, Bar Giora, Emunah, Maccabaea, Bar Kochba, Zephirah*), giving a thoughtful interpretation of the meaning of each name.[25] He was a convinced partisan of all the elaborate ritual of the corporations, including the highly controversial custom of dueling. When the instructor of the *Unitas* said that he intended to do away with "all the ceremonial inherited from the German corporations," Jabotinsky strenuously objected: "You can abolish everything—the caps, the ribbons, the colors, heavy drinking, the songs, everything. But not the sword. You are going to keep the sword. Swordfighting is not a German invention, it belonged to our forefathers. The Torah and the sword were both handed down to us from Heaven."[26]

4. *Jabotinsky: Typist*

Simultaneously with the Fifteenth Congress a plenary session of the Central Committee of the Revisionist World Union took place. At this session, Jabotinsky resigned as President of the Union, arguing that one person should not hold this position for longer than two years. Vladimir Tiomkin was elected President, with Jabotinsky, Lichtheim and Grossman as Vice Presidents. Another important change was caused by Lichtheim's refusal to continue managing the World Union's Berlin headquarters, with which he had been entrusted eight months previously.[27] No steady budget was available for the functioning of this Head Office, and Lichtheim, with his orderly German mentality, was organically incapable of conducting it on a "from-hand-to-mouth" basis. There was no other alternative but to transfer the office back to Paris. Jabotinsky again assumed personal responsibility for its functioning. It was a heavy burden, and he accepted it in addition to the responsibility of securing the budget of the *Rasswyet*. In October, 1927, he dejectedly reported to Dr. Jacob Hoffman: "Not only is the paper foundering, but personally, I am, too. My I.O.U's are in the hands of the printers. I am twisting and turning like a bankrupt, and borrowing from everybody. There are no more sources to borrow from." [28]

The party treasury was empty. There was no money to rent an office and to engage a skeleton staff. When Jabotinsky returned to Paris, he was forced to act as his own secretary and typist. This writer offered to take care of the office, but Jabotinsky, characteristically enough, at first refused : " This is a full-time job and there isn't a penny to pay you. I know that you are as much of a beggar as I am; you have to earn a living and you can't afford doing this work unpaid." It was only after much wrangling that he accepted the argument that it was after all not the first time that we were starting something without a budget. "There never was a steady budget and what there was, was never enough. But we somehow always survived and the work was done. Why not try it again? Lichtheim could not work in this fashion, but we, Russian emigrés and professional vagabonds, we would manage." Laughing and cursing with a relish in his expressive Russian, Jabotinsky agreed.

It was certainly the queerest Head Office of a world movement. Its "premises" consisted of a corner of Jabotinsky's crowded desk in the study of his five-room apartment at No. 4, rue Marié Davy. There was no telephone. To make or receive a call, one of us had to run down (and then up!) five flights of stairs to the janitor's lodge. This writer's exalted position was that of "Secretary General." Since he was completely ignorant of the art of typing, he dictated letters and circulars to Jabotinsky, who acted as typist, using, slowly and cautiously, two fingers. There was no regular filing system. But in Jabotinsky's notebook for that period can be found a full registry of every letter and circular dispatched by this makeshift office, with the date, the name of addressee, and often a summary of the contents under heading *lettres parties*. When the rather meager results of a day's work were ready for mailing, there always arose the agonizing question : do we possess enough money for stamps? If this problem was solved satisfactorily—often by digging into Jabotinsky's personal funds—one of us happily ran to the post office, six blocks away (Jabotinsky insisted on taking turns, and carefuly kept the count), to buy the necessary stamps. We never had stamps in stock for another day. To send a telegram was a major, sometimes insoluble problem. But petty worries of this kind never affected Jabotinsky's mood. He was invariably cheerful and confident, laughing, telling stories, making plans. He seemed happy sharing with the "Secretary General" the prosaic clerical office tasks.

Eventually, little by little, things began to improve. Some money began to arrive—always too little and too late, but still enabling us to pay modest salaries and to move out of Jabotinsky's private apartment. In January, 1928, we rented, together with the *Rasswyet*, a two-room office at 12, rue Blanche, on the sixth floor of a residential building : without an elevator, without a toilet, and, at the beginning, without a telephone. Jabotinsky was relieved of his typist's position and was replaced, as he used to joke, by "one-fourth of a girl" : she worked for the office half a day, three times a week. "We are working almost without staff," wrote Jabotinsky to the Central Committee of the Palestine Revisionist Organization. "When Schechtman or the office girl has the flu, the entire work of the world movement comes to a standstill." [29]

The tiny office space was not all we shared with the *Rasswyet*. In addition to being "Secretary General" of the Revisionist World Union, this writer had to assume the function of *Rasswyet's* managing editor as well, and held this position until his departure for Warsaw in 1932. Throughout this entire five-year period, Jabotinsky's writings were the mainstay of this leading Revisionist weekly. He wrote for the *Rasswyet* willingly and easily, and never complained of the heavy load of articles (signed and anonymous), novels (*Samson, The Five*), and editorials he was expected to supply. He was also exceptionally easy to work with. Completely devoid of petty author-pride, he did not consider his writings sacred. At an early stage of his editorship, this writer hesitated to make even minor changes and corrections in Jabotinsky's articles. On one occasion, he decided to phone the author and to submit to him a few suggestions about such changes. After having patiently listened for several minutes, Jabotinsky first burst into an affectionate salvo of fearful Russian curses—an art in which he excelled—and then explained : "Listen, Yosif Borisovitch, let's make it clear once and for all. There must be fair distribution of work and responsibility. I undertook to write this article—and I did. Here my role ends. You have undertaken to be managing editor, and it is your damned duty to edit this—and any other—article. Don't try to pass the buck. Don't bother me with 'suggestions.' Do whatever you deem right with my article, and I promise solemnly never to question your decisions. This is my way of working with people :

either I trust a man—then he is sole boss in the sphere assigned to him —or I don't—then I would oppose giving him this responsibility. So far, I do trust you. Should I change my mind, I will let you know. In the meantime, please forget my telephone number for this kind of inquiry. Is it a deal?"

It was. There wasn't of course much that the humble managing editor was ever tempted to "correct" in Jabotinsky's articles. But whenever I did so, I did not even once have to explain these changes to the author. Minor contributors used to give me much more trouble.

And this was not only my privilege. The same pattern was applied to every editor whom Jabotinsky knew and trusted. In 1931, Albert Starasselski established in Cairo a French-language weekly *La Voix Juive*, obtained from Jabotinsky the permission to translate and print every article of his which appeared in other languages and, somewhat shyly, asked for authority to eliminate or soften certain sentences, which might be resented in a Moslem country. The answer was: "Please don't hesitate to make any changes you deem necessary; there will never be any objection on my part." [30] When, in 1938, Joseph Klarman, the editor of the Revisionist weekly *Unser Welt* in Warsaw, apologized for not having published two articles contributed by Jabotinsky because, in his view, they were likely to provoke undesirable friction with the Polish Government circles, Jabotinsky's anwser was: "You are the editor and sole judge of whether an article of mine shall or shall not be published; so far as I am concerned, you have *carte blanche*." [31]

2

IN AND OUT OF PALESTINE

SETTLING IN THE HOMELAND

1. *Breaking the Visa Barrier*

B Y the middle of 1927, Jabotinsky's financial affairs seemed to be improving for the first time since 1923. "I now have a firm agreement with the [New York] *Morgen Journal* and the [Warsaw] *Haint*, which secures me a regular monthly income of two hundred and twenty dollars," he wrote to a friend.[1] With these earnings as a basis, plus an income from occasional lectures, he was able to live in Paris modestly, but comfortably.

But it was just at that time that he "positively and definitely decided to settle in Palestine." The intention was to establish himself—in association with his wife's brother, Eliahu M. Galperin, in Haifa or Tel Aviv as a practicing lawyer. He knew that in order to be able to practice law he would have to pass an examination in Palestine, but was confident that he would not need to invest much time and effort in preparation: "Three-quarters of the stuff I know—I studied the Ottoman Codes in Constantinople [in 1909—1910]—and the ordinances of the Palestinian Government I not only know but despise as well." [2] His intention was to come to Palestine in the late autumn of 1927, and to pass the examinations in January, 1928, so that he could serve his articles as from that time.[3] In July, 1927, he had already applied for a Palestine visa.[4]

But by October, 1927, he had begun to hesitate:[5] "Under the present circumstances, I am not ready to rely on [local] Palestine earnings. Everybody says that the money situation there is going to get even worse, and the first one not to be paid is bound to be the lawyer, in particular the kind that would feel awkward about going to court in order to recover his fees. . . . No, this plan will have to be abandoned for the time being, though I am increasingly keen on the idea of passing my law examinations."

Apparently, in order not to have to rely on local income, Jabotinsky accepted the proposal of the Judea Industrial Corporation of the State of New York, founded by the "Order of the Sons of Zion" (see chapter two) to become Vice President, Managing Director, and Treasurer of the Judea Insurance Company in Palestine. The contract was signed in Paris on September 7, 1928, and was valid for a period of two years commencing from September 15. The salary was five hundred dollars per month. Clause nine of the agreement stipulated that Jabotinsky "was at liberty, outside of his office hours . . . to pursue his journalistic, literary, and public activities, whether connected with material gains or otherwise." He had to leave for Palestine not later than September 15, 1928, "subject to the visa being grated before this time." Apparently anticipating difficulties, the agreement provided that "any delay in the granting of the visa shall not invalidate the present agreement."

And difficulties did arise. When "Judea" approached the Immigration Department of the Palestine Government with the request to grant a visa to its Jerusalem Director, the Department demanded a written undertaking that during his term of office Jabotinsky would not engage in any political activities. This demand provoked an indignant reaction. Judge Strahl, President of the New York "Judea," cabled to the Company's representative in Jerusalem : "The Company takes exception to [Palestine] authorities asking our Director for any assurance of the kind. The Company authorizes you to insist that the visa be granted immediately."

In ' Palestine, *Davar,* the official organ of the Socialist Labor Federation, strongly condemned the Administration's attempt to bar a man because of his political views. *Haaretz* ridiculed the Government's apprehensions that Jabotinsky could endanger the existing state of affairs in Palestine. If Jabotinsky did represent a danger for anybody, said the paper, it was perhaps for the Zionist Executive, not the British regime in the country; no detractor of the Palestine Administration, intent on discrediting it, could have suggested a worse move than this refusal to grant a visa to Jabotinsky. The Tel Aviv municipal council unanimously declared that it saw "in the withholding of a visa for Vladimir Jabotinsky, one of the finest sons and defenders of the Jewish people, a blunt and most outrageous

86

expression of the policy of the Immigration Department, which violates our fundamental rights in the country." The Council demanded that the visa be granted immediately. Colonel Frederic H. Kisch, the political representative of the Jewish Agency in Jerusalem, also interceded with the Palestine authorities. Jabotinsky himself went to London, where he enlisted the aid of Colonel Wedgwood and William Ormsby-Gore (then Under Secretary of State for the Colonies). According to his own report, "the Palestine Administration received a box on the ear and sent the visa by cable."

On September 21, the visa was granted—unconditionally. Jabotinsky embarked from Marseille on September 29, and landed in Jaffa on October 5, 1928.

The Palestine Administration, however, did not miss a second opportunity to commit a *faux pas*. When Jabotinsky arrived and sent for his luggage, he discovered that the trunk containing books and documents had been ransacked by the police, and that a file of personal letters from Ormsby-Gore, Colonel Wedgwood, Colonel Kisch, and others, had been thoroughly searched. Informed of this new outrage, Colonel Kisch wrote an indignant letter to E. Mills, Assistant Chief Secretary to the Palestine Government. The latter answered that he himself was utterly shocked and disturbed by this administrative arbitrariness, and that an investigation would be made to establish who was responsible for this move.[6] When no results of this investigation were forthcoming, Colonel Wedgwood, on November 27, 1928, and again on March 29, 1929, asked the Secretary of State for the Colonies in the House of Commons whether the search of Jabotinsky's luggage and correspondence was made by special order from Jerusalem or on the initiative of the customs authorities. Leopold S. Amery answered on behalf of the Government that the examination of Jabotinsky's luggage "was undertaken in accordance with the general practice which has since been terminated." He denied the allegation that the Palestine immigration authorities had photographed correspondence or made extracts from letters found in Jabotinsky's luggage during this routine examination.[7]

The announcement of Jabotinsky's arrival provoked venomous comments in the nationalistic Arab press. *Falastin* wrote on September 21, 1928: "One can easily imagine what this extremist is likely to do to incite the Jews against the Arabs and the English." When Jabotinsky settled in Jerusalem, the same paper wrote, on October 9, that he did so, "not only as the Director of 'Judea,' but also in order to assume the leadership of the Revisionist party and, as an orator and publicist, to participate in the anti-Arab campaign." *Sout Shaab* (October 26) described Jabotinsky as a "notorious revolutionary Zionist leader who, in a speech made in Germany, called upon the Jewish youth to enroll in a Jewish Army which would liberate Palestine from the Arabs."

This time the attitude of the leftist Zionist groups was also aggressively hostile. In a letter to I. Klinov, who had been trying to explain that this hostility was due to Jabotinsky's own aggressiveness, he wrote:[8] "You are wrong. It is not we who 'started it,' but they. I arrived in Palestine early in October. Until the first of December I had no paper and was absolutely silent. But still, the *Davar* kept attacking us, and me personally, every week, almost every day." The animosity was not limited to press attacks only. On October 13, in Tel Aviv, Jabotinsky delivered his first public address at a review of *Brit Trumpeldor* detachments from all parts of the country. Two *Betar* officers came to escort him from Allenby Street, where he was staying, to King George Street, where the review was to take place. They went on foot. The route was jammed by a dense and violently antagonistic crowd shouting: "Militarists! Generals!" Many spat at them. The two *Betarim* tried to protect Jabotinsky with their bodies, but one spittle reached him. Jabotinsky walked slowly and calmly, with his head high.[9] After the review, a procession through the streets took place. Before the *Betarim* started moving, Jabotinsky instructed them:[10] "If they throw stones at you—don't pay any attention. If they insult you—don't answer. But should anybody try to bar your way—do whatever your commander orders." There was no attempt to bar the way.

The non-Socialist sector of the community, on the contrary, received Jabotinsky very cordially. His political friends had intended to arrange a formal reception for him, with a procession of cars, an orchestra, and a parade of the *Brit Trumpeldor* youth, but he asked them to abstain from any pomp. Only a small group of his closest associates and personal friends met him at Jaffa port. In Tel Aviv, where he stayed for two days, he was officially welcomed by delegations of the municipality and of the local *Kehila,* as well as by representatives of non-leftist Zionist parties. In Jerusalem, he attended the Jewish ex-soldiers' parade on Armistice Day. The parade, recalled Norman Bentwich, was "memorable for his [Jabotinsky's] reception as the parade marched through the Jewish quarters to the cemetery on Mount Scopus. He was in mufti and did not wear his medals, but carried a hatchet stick, perhaps to symbolize that he would bury the hatchet in the cemetery." *Doar Hayom* (October 12) published an article by Ben Baruch (Shalom Schwarz) entitled "This is Jabotinsky's Hour." Stressing the utter seriousness of the situation in Palestine and the complete inaction of the official Zionist administration, the author said that it was not an accident that Jabotinsky had returned to the country just at this desperate moment; the entire *Yishuv* would enthusiastically follow him if he would now state his program before the *Vaad Leumi*.

What prompted Jabotinsky to leave Paris and settle in Palestine where, he knew only too well, he was going to have a much harder time? Was it a compelling sentiment for the Holy Land or a feeling of Zionist duty, his usual pattern of living-up to his convictions, of practicing whatever he preached to others?

Fundamentally, Jabotinsky's Zionism was not of a romantic or sentimental brand. A few months after his arrival in the country, he told a group of friends gathered at the house of Eliahu Berlin, that he was not sure whether he would be able to become acclimatized, and stressed: "My attitude to Eretz Israel is in no way based on romanticism. My Zionism is neither romantic nor sentimental; perhaps this is the reason for the estrangement between myself and the majority [of the Zionist movement]." Told that this was an over-statement, Jabotinsky insisted that it was not so, and that this attitude was "not new" to him; it was his "companion" since the early days of his Zionist activity.[12] Later, trying in his *Autobiography* to interpret his unhesitating anti-Uganda vote at the Sixth Zionist Congress, he wrote: "At that time I had no romantic love for Palestine, and I am not sure whether I have it even now." In his post-Congress polemics with the territorialist tendencies, he emphatic-ally stressed (1905):[13] "Our belief in Palestine is not a blind, half-mystical sentiment, but the result of a dispassionate study of the entire essence of our history and our movement. . . . Our link with Zion is to us not only an ineradicably powerful instinct, but also a solid, legitimate conclusion from strictly positive thinking."*

* In this, as in many other respects, Jabotinsky's approach was in line with that of Max Nordau. At the Fourth Zionist Congress Nordau said: " Why did we become Zionists? Perhaps because of a mystical yearning for Zion? Of that, most of us are free.

But this "link with Zion" seems to have been much more than a purely rationalistic concept. Even in the above quoted early anti-territorialist pamphlet, after having formulated his positivist *profession de foi*, Jabotinsky added: "And having said all this, I freely confess that I still really *believe* [in Eretz Israel]. The more I think, the more firmly I believe. It is with me not even a belief, but something different. Do you 'believe' that February will be followed by March? You *know* it, because it cannot be otherwise. Equally incontestable for me is the conviction that because of irresistible elementary processes, our people will gather in our homeland Palestine and that my children or grandchildren will go to the polls there."

Jabotinsky's attitude to Palestine was not based on pure rationalism; nor did it have its roots in religious or traditional romanticism. His love for the country was *amor politicus*. He was deeply, though unostentatiously, attached to Palestine, first and foremost because he saw in it the future homeland of his people, the country, which his people would some day call its own, which would belong to the Jews. This concept of "belonging" played an outstanding role in his inner world. When he came to settle in Palestine in 1928, he said to himself: "*Reb Yid*, you are now at home. Here at last you are going to build a house of your own, and your years of wandering are over." [14] Later, when banned by the British, he felt even more strongly the deep personal significance of having a country. One of the *Betar* leaders recalls that when, in 1931, Jabotinsky heard the song *Kinneret* by Rachel, he asked: "What appeals to you particularly in this song?" The answer was: "The possessive pronoun *sheli* [mine]." "Right." And Jabotinsky went on elaborating the profound and wonderful meaning of the word *mine* for the soul and mind of both Jews and Jewry. [15] With his usual self-restraint in all personal matters, he carefully abstained from manifesting his feelings on his exile. Only rarely would he give vent to a pent-up sadness and bitterness. During one of his visits to Poland (1938), he asked a young *Betari,* who was acting as his aide-de-camp, what his dearest desire

We became Zionists because the plight of the Jewish people grips our hearts, because we see with the gravest concern that the logic of conditions must inevitably lead to a swift deterioration of this plight, indeed to sudden violent catastrophies "(*Zionistische Schriften,* p. 108). Still more bluntly he disassociated himself from Zionist mysticism before a Paris audience in 1914: "I nurture the hope some day to see in Palestine a new Jewish national life. Otherwise I would have had an archaeological interest in that country" (*Die Welt,* April 3, 1914).

was. "I would like to go to Eretz Israel," was the answer. "I too," said Jabotinsky with a somewhat bitter smile.[16] A year later, another *Betari*—a Palestinian who was the acting editor of the Revisionist weekly *Tribuna Narodowa* in Krakow, asked to be relieved of his duty and allowed to return home: "It is difficult for me to sit here. I am homesick." "I shall never forget Jabotinsky's reply," he later recalled: "Homesick? Longing for home? Don't you think that for me, too, it is hard to be here? I, too, am longing to be in Eretz!" [17]

2. First Steps

Jabotinsky left for Palestine with great expectations. On September 30, from the S.S. *Com. Ramel* which was carrying him to Jaffa, he sent a batch of letters to several leaders of the Zionist opposition in the United States (the so-called Brandeis-Mack group), who, though sympathizing with many of his views, were reluctant to join the Revisionist party. Among those to whom he wrote were Judge Julian Mack, Judge M. Rosenson, Abraham Tulin, Jacob De Haas, Robert Szold, and Mrs. Irma Lindheim of Hadassah. In these letters he outlined an ambitious scheme of action both in Palestine and in the Zionist world movement.

"Without overestimating the influence which the addition of one single man can exercise in a community, I think that the community called the Palestine *Yishuv* is so small that the influence may in some cases prove noticeable. I feel sure that, within a few months after I settle in Jerusalem, there will be at least some knot of muscle within the *Yishuv*. . . . And so in time there may develop a possibility of a junction between the opposition forces [in the Diaspora] and a healthy nucleus of the *Yishuv*." "I assume," he added, that "I need not assure you that I have in mind no display of 'violence,' either in deed or in word—if such an assurance were needed, it would be useless for me to write to a man who has such an opinion of me." He regretted, of course, that the American opposition was not ready to unite with his party and argued that "it's just the multiplicity of opposition groups which undermines our chances; it creates the impression that we are either diffident or ashamed of each other, and of course weakens our pull." He was, however, ready to accept this state of affairs, provided that "there should be contact and cooperation between the American opposition, our European forces, and

91

Jerusalem. . . . There may be divergence about some niceties of the Revisionist program; but let me hope that this will not stop us from cooperating in what we can and must do together."

In his letter to Judge Mack, Jabotinsky significantly said: "I have a feeling that we both understand each other better than we did years ago. What I want is: a) in politics—a constant, stubborn and quiet stand for every one of our rights and every bit of our due; b) in economics—the gradual elimination of the dole system called *Keren ha'Yessod,* in its present form, to be replaced by a scheme which would make sound commercial credit accessible." It is evident from this that in the economic field Jabotinsky, who in 1921 so strongly rejected and combated Brandeis' economic program, was now essentially endorsing it.*

He arrived in Palestine in a time of great tension. On the eve of the Day of Atonement, September 23, the Jews erected a portable screen at the Wailing Wall to separate the men from the women. Moslem religious authorities protested against this alleged "violation of customary practice and Islamic property rights." A British police officer forcibly removed the screen during the Jewish service, and precipitated an unseemly fracas when some of the worshippers attempted to stop him. This indignity, coming on top of the entire anti-Zionist policy of the Mandatory Administration, provoked great excitement in the *Yishuv* and in the Jewish communities throughout the world. Public opinion expected Jabotinsky to react immediately and strongly to this state of affairs, and was somewhat puzzled by his reticence during the first week following his arrival. The Jerusalem correspondent of the [Warsaw] *Haint* gave eloquent expression to this feeling, in a dispatch headed: "Jabotinsky Is Silent." [18]

*In a conversation with Revisionist leaders in Stanislavov (Poland) in June, 1933, Jabotinsky was asked how it was that in 1921 he had supported Dr. Weizmann in his struggle against Justice Brandeis. "I have no monopoly on wisdom," answered Jabotinsky, "and I have now revised my standpoint." (Interview with Uri Carin, Jerusalem, who was present at this conversation).

When, in 1934, Dr. Oscar Rabinowicz once referred to Brandeis' treatment of the cable sent from Acre (see Vol. I, pp. 362-63), Jabotinsky answered: "I have long ago forgotten this episode." He felt that in matters of an economic nature and Zionist financial policy, Brandeis was fundamentally right. "He has only one *Schonheitsfehler* [aesthetic deficiency], and in this he differs from us—he puts our one per cent of political activities at the bottom of the Zionist agenda, while we put it at the top." (Interview with Dr. Oscar K. Rabinowicz, London).

Jabotinsky broke his silence on October 11. In a letter to Dr. Jacob Thon, Chairman of the *Vaad Leumi*, he insisted that an extraordinary session of this body be convened. The text of the letter appeared in the press. The *Vaad Leumi* met five days later. Analyzing the political situation in Palestine, he insisted that the Zionist cause was now defending the last ditch, and asked: "Will you be able to defend this last ditch?" Referring to the proposal to send a memorandum to the Zionist Executive and demand its intercession, he reminded them that a similar memorandum, signed by David Yellin and Itzhak Ben Zvi, and protesting against the policy of Sir Herbert Samuel, had been dispatched by the *Vaad Leumi* in January, 1923, to the Berlin session of the Zionist Actions Committee, and had been completely disregarded. There was no reason to think that this time the reaction would be different. He was equally sceptical of the proposal to send an *ad hoc* delegation abroad to present the grievances and demands of the *Yishuv*: "What could such a delegation do? It could only pursue one or two specific objectives. What is needed, is a permanent body, which would strive to influence the entire policy of decisive international political factors. . . . If you say 'a,' you have to say 'z.' In London a permanent representation of the *Yishuv* must function alongside that of the Zionist Executive. This would be analogous to the position of the Dominions within the British Empire. There are possibilities of political work both in London and in Geneva. . . . There are forces favourable to us, and we can utilize them."

The *Vaad Leumi* decided to postpone the question of its representation in London and Geneva until the resolutions of the Permanent Mandates Commission of the League of Nations became known. Jabotinsky was disappointed not so much by the procrastinating decision, as by the general mood and attitude of the assembly: "They have lost the quality of feeling offended," he later commented.[19] "The Rabbis and the leftist representatives had made heated speeches, but one felt that behind all this there was no intensity of feeling. They have bouillon instead of blood in their veins. They are resigned to everything, and their spirit no longer reacts."

3. *A Paper of His Own*

Since its inception in 1925, the Revisionist party in Palestine had no press of its own. The daily *Doar Hayom* was friendly, but Jewish public opinion did not take the paper's vacillating views and policies seriously, and its political influence was insignificant.[20]

When Jabotinsky settled in Jerusalem, Zalman White, the publisher of *Doar Hayom*, and its editor, Ittamar Ben Avi, approached him with the request to join their editorial staff. Jabotinsky asked S. Gepstein and A. Evzerov to negotiate on his behalf.[21] On November 22, Jabotinsky reported to this writer: "Today I am signing the agreement to take over the *Doar Hayom*. I am going to be the chief editor, solely responsible for the composition of the editorial staff, etc. The publishers put a monthly lump sum of £175 (about 875 dollars) at my disposal for the staff. The agreement is valid for two years, beginning December 1."

Official Zionist circles in Jerusalem were seriously perturbed by the prospect of Jabotinsky's taking over the *Doar Hayom*. Writing to the London Zionist Executive on November 8, Colonel Kisch quoted Dr. M. Glickson, editor of the semi-official *Haaretz*, to the effect that while the latter "hoped that *Haaretz* would be able to hold its own against the *Doar Hayom* of Mr. Ben Avi, the position would be greatly changed, with the editorship passing into the hands of Mr. Jabotinsky." Five days later, Gershon Agronsky [Agron], then Secretary of the Jerusalem Zionist Executive, informed Louis Lipsky that "if Jabotinsky becomes the editor of the *Doar Hayom* as rumored, *Haaretz* will not be able to stand up against that paper, and it may lead to only one voice being heard from Palestine, the Revisionist voice, with only the feeble *Davar* trying to shout it down."

The first issue under Jabotinsky's editorship appeared on December 2, 1928. It opened with a powerful article "Ani Maamin" (I Believe), in which Jabotinsky stated that he had accepted the paper's editorship not as a personal mission, but on behalf of a movement that was striving for the regeneration of Zionism. He stressed his aversion to the "concept of the overwhelming importance and omnipotence of an individual, which has been lately spreading in Southern Europe [meaning Italian Fascism with its cult of the "Duce"] and among certain Zionist groups, and which was poisoning political moral." He would not promise miracles either as a "leader" or as a journalist, but he had faith in the full realization of the Zionist idea, in the emergence of the Jewish State, for the establishment of which the Jews would work together with the British nation. This was in itself a contribution to the revival of Zionism in the prevailing atmosphere of lack of faith in the future. The new *Doar Hayom* was going to be a fighting paper of those who believe.

And the *Doar Hayom* under Jabotinsky was indeed a fighting paper. It conducted an unrelenting struggle against both the anti-Zionist policy of the British Administration, and against the defeatist policies of the Zionist Executive. Jabotinsky could hardly be described as the actual managing editor of the paper. That he never was, even of the Paris *Rasswyet*. He had no mind and no patience to read, to comment upon, and to correct articles submitted by others. In a private letter he confessed:[22] "Never in my life was I able to 'edit' articles that have already been written; I have always wanted to write articles of my own." Nevertheless, he devoted much time and energy to his work on the *Doar Hayom*, for which he, of course, never received any remuneration. * He succeeded in gathering around the paper a group of outstanding and devoted contributors, both Revisionists and non-Revisionists. Though seasoned journalists, those in charge had no experience in the technical handling of a paper, and when they had to break the pages of the first issue, not one of them had the slightest idea how to do it. They turned to Jabotinsky, who, however, shamefacedly confessed to his own ignorance in this field: "In spite of the fact that in my young days I was simultaneously the editor of several publications [in Constantinople], I don't know the first thing about setting up a paper." [23] But he actively participated in all other branches of the editorial work. Besides political articles, he occasionally contributed delightful semi-belletristic pieces like *Twenty-Four Hours* (reminiscences of the "Moscobia" prison in 1920), or *The Four Cups*, written for the 1929 Passover issue. When one of the collaborators said about the latter: "Is it a *chef d'oeuvre* even according to your standards," Jabotinsky smilingly answered: "Don't forget that I wrote it in between attending to two insurance policies." [24]

* In Jabotinsky's note-books for 1928 a detailed estimate of salaries to be paid to the staff members (five pounds to fifteen pounds) can be found: no salary (or fee for articles) was earmarked for himself.

Friends and opponents alike considered the new *Doar Hayom* a serious and dynamic political organ. While uncompromising in its editorial policies, it was courteous and restrained in form in its polemics with other papers—a pattern strictly supervised by Jabotinsky. On October 10, 1929, he wrote from Paris to S. Gepstein, who acted as his representative in press affairs during his absences, asking him not to permit any renewal of polemics with the Left. "Please don't answer their abuse, or simply quote their abusive articles and add : 'we believe that such a style is now untimely and we will not reply in kind.' . . . Do so, at least for the time being."

Under Jabotinsky's leadership, *Doar Hayom* was growing both in stature and circulation. As early as December 5, 1928, Jabotinsky related : "The paper is pretty successful. Indicative are the sales in Tel Aviv : before we took over, they totalled 1,000—1,200 copies; our first issue sold 1,750, the second—1,850, the third—the same number. . . . Any reminiscence of the odium that used to be connected with the paper has disappeared completely. Even *Davar* has said so." [25] This initial progress proved to be of a lasting nature. Fourteen months later, Jabotinsky—who was not prone to boastful exaggerations—reported to the Revisionist World Executive that "now the paper has the biggest circulation and has become a truly important moral force in the *Yishuv*." [26]

In the summer of 1930, when it became clear that there was little chance of Jabotinsky's returning to Palestine (see Chapter Seven), the publisher Zalman White began demanding that the paper be "returned" to him : he "had given the *Doar Hayom* to Jabotinsky and not to Abba Achimeir or Yeivin," he argued.[27] On the other hand, in Jabotinsky's absence, some of those in charge of the editorial policies were occasionally sinning against the pattern of journalistic self-restraint so carefully laid down by him. On June 12, Jabotinsky wrote to S. Gepstein from Paris : "For God's sake, forbid our contributors all brands of hysteria. 'Strong' words are hysteria; uncontrolled accusations are hysteria." And again on July 10 : "Don't permit hysterics and improvisations [*otsiebiatiny*]."

On June 7, 1930, *Doar Hayom* was—without any explanation—suspended by the Palestine administration. The publisher White used this opportunity to send a plaintive cable to Jabotinsky in Paris : "We learn from official [British] circles that our paper will not be permitted to reappear as long as it will remain under Revisionist control. No license for a new paper will be issued. Our losses are very great. We face ruin. We appeal to you under our gentleman's agreement and beg you to waive the contract as a temporary measure." Jabotinsky succumbed to this whining plea and asked Gepstein to dissolve the contract if he finds it necessary. "We dare not ruin our excellent collaborators or render them jobless." For a short time, the paper *Yerusholaim* appeared instead of *Doar Hayom*. But, ultimately, White had his way. On July 22, 1930, Jabotinsky's name as editor of *Doar Hayom* was removed, and the Revisionist Organization announced that it no longer had any connection with the paper.[28]

4. *"Utilization of Niagara"*

Jabotinsky did not accept the position offered to him by the "Judea" just because it was a well paid job, enabling him to settle in Palestine. His active interest in any attempt to utilize Jewish savings for the rebuilding of Palestine can be traced back to his visit to America in 1926. Speaking at the Convention of the "Sons of Zion," he had stressed the great importance and value of the Judea Insurance Company. After his return to Europe, he published in the *Rasswyet*, under the heading "Utilization of Niagara," a thought-provoking imaginary "conversation" between three delegates to the Zionist Conference in Buffalo who, instead of attending one of its noisy meetings, went to admire Niagara Falls.[29] One of them, whom Jabotinsky obviously chose as his spokesman, observed that of the four main components of "Niagara" of Jewish capital—personal budget, business investment, savings, and philanthropic contributions —only the last one, which is of course the least, was being utilized, though inadequately, for Palestine. The third component, savings, was a wide and promising field. Its most popular form was life insurance; premiums paid by individual Jews throughout the world into the pockets of various insurance companies run into many millions of pounds and with this money, ambitious building projects —railways and harbors and irrigating schemes—had been financed in various countries. In his early days, Herzl dreamed of creating a Palestine insurance company which would gain the confidence of world Jewry, so as to attract at least a portion of so much wealth for constructive purposes. Two years later, Jabotinsky published an article, "Secret of Successful Colonization" in the *New Palestine*, developing similar ideas and stressing that channelling Jewish insurance premiums into Palestine would have "Zionist" value only if they "could be safely and profitably invested in some enterprises of the *Yishuv*." [30]

It is against this background that one must view Jabotinsky's attitude toward his position with the "Judea." He took his duties very seriously. His contract stipulated that, in addition to presiding at meetings of the Board of Directors and of its contemplated National Board of Advisors, he had "to pay special attention to all the propaganda work of the Judea Insurance Company, written as well as oral." In this particular field, he prepared (in French) a seven-page broadcast on the importance and usefulness of life insurance, as well as an instructive and well-documented propaganda leaflet, with the slogan: "Insurance grows with civilization." He also submitted a detailed project for the organization of the "Judea" branch in Egypt, with Colonel Patterson at the head, and paid close attention to the administrative problems of the Jerusalem office. To Jacob Ish Kishor, "Judea's" General Secretary in New York, he wrote on October 18, 1928, that the office was "in a deplorable state," the main short-comings being cash and the actuarial side. But, he stressed, "I am not downhearted." There was "perfect harmony" between him and his co-director Mark Shwarz. Within two weeks, from October 1 to October 16, he wrote thirty-two thousand pounds worth of business, which, he pointed out, was "to Shwarz's credit, not mine." And to this writer he confided:[31] "Between you, me, and the lamppost, this is quite a neglected business, but it is growing by leaps and bounds; it is thoroughly defeating all its thirty overseas competitors, including the Phoenix, and is promising to become a great force. . . . I am very busy here, mostly with the affairs of the 'Judea.' "

In fact, he devoted to these affairs a great part of his time and energy, without permitting his journalistic and other activities to interfere with his duty towards the Company. S. Gepstein, who closely collaborated with him in the *Doar Hayom*, recalls that when he used to visit him in the "Judea" offices, Jabotinsky sternly admonished: "This is office time, which has been sold. I don't want to rob my employers—please go away." Gepstein jokingly offered to produce a written authorization from Mark Shwarz, but received the answer: "No, this would be *protekzia* [pull]—off with you!" When, by the middle of 1930, it became obvious that there was no immediate prospect of his returning to Palestine, Jabotinsky resigned from his position as director of the Palestine branch. He was asked to continue as the Company's director at large, with his seat in Europe, but declined this offer seeing in it a sinecure in disguise.[32]

Both in 1926 and 1928, Jabotinsky was rather sceptical as to the immediate prospects of attracting to Palestine the second stream of the Jewish financial "Niagara"—the dividend-seeking investment capital: "capitalists consider the risk too great, and the prospects, at best, too small." In order to overcome this handicap, the Palestinian enterprises "must make investment attractive; they must 'make good.' "[33] "Making good," he explained, did not only mean producing a good commodity. An essential prerequisite was to secure markets for these products, to make inroads into the first stream of the Jewish "Niagara"—the "living expenses" of the Diaspora Jew; to make him include Palestine products in his day-by-day purchases of food, clothing, furniture, books or luxury items. The slogan *Totzeret ha'Aretz la'Gola* (Jewish Palestine products for the Diaspora), Jabotinsky insisted, must become a major item in Zionist propaganda. As a "sample" of such propaganda, which must be built not only on sentiment for Palestine, but has to appeal to all possible human urges, feelings, and inhibitions, he himself contributed a witty "literary advertisement in rhyme" for the popular Carmel wines:

> Are you shy and dumb as salesman?
> Have a Carmel *Koss*:
> It will make you brave in facing
> Customer and boss.
> Are you seasick on the ocean?
> Have a Carmel cup:
> What's all force of storm and thunder
> When a man's full up?
> Are you poor: then have a Carmel,
> Carmel red or white:
> Who are Vanderbilt and Rothschild
> To a man that's tight?
> Are you timid with the ladies?
> Have a Carmel quick:
> Charm is heady, wit is ready
> When the tongue is thick.

I am sick on calmest waters;
Shy with men and with their daughters;
Not a franc is mine:
Aren't I therefore, acting rightly,
In my drinking, daily, nightly,
Always Carmel wine?

Summing up his concept of the "financial relationship between Palestine and the Diaspora," Jabotinsky insisted that this relationship "cannot be based on charity. It must be built on two foundations: the first—the Diaspora keeps its savings in Palestine; the second— Palestine produces, the Diaspora buys." Faithful to this concept, he served "Judea" in his professional capacity. But he was also doing his very best to serve both the production of Palestine commodities and their marketing among Diaspora Jewry. It was in this conjuncture that one must view his consistent advocacy of the interests of the Palestine Jewish industry at the Zionist Congresses, and his extolling of the Jewish merchant as the carrier of Palestine products into the world.

In a speech delivered at the Manufacturers' Conference that followed the 1929 Palestine Fair,,[34] he paid special tribute to its "real organizers"—to the group of young men of the *Mischar v'Taassia* (Trade and Industry) monthly. These men (Alexander Evserov, Abraham Idelson, Solomon Jaffe—all of them Revisionists) "were among the first in this country who believed in the future of the factory; at a time when every so-called serious-minded man laughed at the possibility of any industry in this our 'purely agricultural' country, they blazoned the word 'industry' on their flag."

As one of the Directors of the Palestine Exhibition and Fairs Company, established by the "Sons of Zion," on whose grounds the Fair took place, he was proud to be able to say that the founders of this Company "were also among the first believers" in industry in Palestine and "because of their faith, they laid out these grounds and erected these pavilions."

He particularly welcomed the fact that a "class which we have been taught almost to despise, that strong and important element, the Jewish merchant . . . now comes into its own in Zionism."

5. *Personal Problems*

Jabotinsky left for Palestine alone. On the eve of his landing in Jaffa, he wrote to a friend:[35] "Ania has remained in Paris. Next January, after the [Third World] Conference of our party in Vienna, I hope to bring her here. Eri [who at that time was a student at the Ecole Centrale] will, of course, remain in Paris."

The question of Mrs. Jabotinsky's following her husband to Palestine presented a problem in more than one respect. She had never liked the idea of settling there. In the spring of 1919, when Jabotinsky asked her to join him in Jerusalem together with Eri, she insisted on his returning to London. In a series of letters, he patiently explained that such a suggestion was simply impractical:[36] "I am now earning my livelihood here and I can't come to London. . . . The Russian newspapers I used to work for, have been suppressed, so that for the time being I *have* to live here. . . . I would be glad to spend a year or more in a big city instead of living in my tent, but you know very well that I havn't a chance of making a living in England. . . . Of course, I don't intend to *compel* you to come. If for some reason you feel that it would be more sensible to stay in London for the time being, please don't feel embarrassed: everything will be taken care of. . . . I am longing for both of you very much and I think that you do, too—not only Eri, but you as well. However, if this is inconvenient for you, don't do anything against your will. . . . If you have any plans that don't include me—you know my convictions, and I am not going to stand in your way."

Mrs. Jabotinsky and Eri did come to Palestine in 1919, and stayed there for over a year. It was an exciting and, on the whole, a happy period. Life was, however, far from being easy and comfortable for a woman and a housewife with limited means at her disposal. Mrs. Jabotinsky preserved rather gloomy memories of the countless petty cares of life, primitive accommodation, and household and other troubles. According to the testimony of relatives, who at that time lived in close contact with the Jabotinsky family, she was reluctant to repeat the experience of 1919—1920 in 1928. She argued that, should it become necessary to abandon her modest but cosy Paris apartment in the rue Marié Davy, she would be ready to do so only if their existence in Jerusalem could be of a "good middle-class" pattern; if Jabotinsky would drastically cut down his endless traveling; and if she could have a normal well-functioning household.[37]

Another essential consideration was her health. On November 1, 1928, she wrote to Jabotinsky from Paris that she would, of course, join him in Palestine, "but I don't know how I would stand Jerusalem now; my blood pressure has risen again, and I feel tired and irritable." This consideration strongly impressed Jabotinsky. On December 13, he wrote to S. Jacobi: "Ania's blood pressure has gone up considerably —and I wonder whether it would be advisable to bring her to Jerusalem with its eight hundred meter altitude."

Jabotinsky's hope that his wife would accompany him to Palestine after the Vienna conference did not materialize. Early in 1929, he returned to Jerusalem alone. It was, however, decided that the entire family would definitely settle in Jerusalem in the Fall of that year. The Paris apartment was given up, and the furniture and personal belongings packed in crates and stored in a warehouse.[38] The outbreak of the riots in August, 1929, upset this plan, and it was not until the end of November, 1929, when Jabotinsky decided to return to Palestine "for a fortnight and for a fortnight only," that Mrs. Jabotinsky accompanied him. "We are leaving for Palestine on November 26. Ania is also going, otherwise she would worry," he wrote.[39] After a short stay in the country, Mrs. Jabotinsky was to spend a few weeks visiting her mother in Constantsa (Rumania) and then return to Paris. But, as Jabotinsky wrote to Raphael Rosov, "this visit reconciled Ania with Palestine, and from now on everything will be much easier. You personally, and the Rosov family, are 75 per cent responsible for that. Thank you." [40]

In Jerusalem, Jabotinsky lived alone. His sister, Mrs. Jabotinsky-Kopp, had moved to Tel Aviv. Left to himself, Jabotinsky lived in Jerusalem as a bachelor, simply and frugally. He rented a room in a six room apartment of Meyer Rubin at 46 Rehov ha'Anglim, across the way from the Hadassah Hospital, for which he paid six pounds (thirty dollars) per month. In comparison with the then prevailing rentals in the country, this was an unusually high price, and Rubin, who knew Jabotinsky from Odessa and was a fervent Revisionist, asked for much less. But Jabotinsky insisted that he would be "cheating" his landlord by paying a lower price. He took breakfast in his room, and lunch and dinner in various restaurants. Rubin, a deeply religious man, recalls that Jabotinsky usually worked very late in his room, smoking innumerable cigarettes (and often taking "Kalmine" pills to alleviate violent headaches), but the very first Saturday he spent with the Rubin family, he volunteered a firm promise that there would be no *Chillul Shabbat* (violation of the Sabbath) on his part: "No smoking, and my typewriter will be resting as well;" and he observed this pledge faithfully. While at home, he kept mostly to himself, receiving few visitors.[41] On the whole, he disliked Jerusalem's "human climate." In June, 1929, he wrote in *Rasswyet*:[42] "Jerusalem is as yet a miserable provincial town, without cultural life, without inner cohesion. The various communities—the 'English,' the 'Russians,' the 'Germans'—are isolated from one another. The overwhelming majority among them haven't even any interest in the *Vaad Leumi*. Everybody is discontented. A great and interesting center has degenerated into an obscure hole. It would take a lot of shaking to wake them up." In Tel Aviv, which he visited frequently, he usually stayed with his sister (3, Balfour Street), but Israel Rosov's house was his "headquarters." Rubin, who had the opportunity of observing Jabotinsky in everyday life, recalls that behind his usual outward cheerfulness, there was a distinct undertone of loneliness and even sadness, of longing for his family.

The abortive attempt of the Palestine Administration to demand that Jabotinsky abstain from Zionist political activity as condition to granting him a resident visa, had a painful personal aftermath.

The *Haaretz* saw fit to publish articles alleging that Jabotinsky had submitted to this demand. Incensed by this unwarranted slur on Jabotinsky's integrity, a group of his friends proclaimed a boycott of the paper. Several leading Hebrew writers—headed by Chaim Nachman Bialik, whose poetry Jabotinsky had translated into Russian, and Joshua Ravnitzky, his first Hebrew teacher—who had kept silent when *Haaretz* printed the defamatory articles, published an indignant protest against the boycott.[43]

Jabotinsky was deeply hurt by this. He broke off personal relations with all the signatories of the protest, and refused to accept the explanations that some of them tried to offer. Particularly bitter was he against Ravnitzky, from whom he had not expected this kind of attitude. A letter Ravnitzky sent him, had at first remained unanswered. But several months later, on June 14, 1929, he decided to reply: "After all, I cannot forget my childhood, when you taught

103

me our language [Hebrew], and opened to me the world in which and for which I live." It was, however, not a conciliatory reply.

This is a farewell letter. . . . You offended me in a way which an honest man cannot forgive. . . . A venal journalist spread a rumor through his paper that I, too, had sold my soul for money: that I had signed a contract providing me with a highly-paid job, that for such a price I had consented to renounce political work—and that, as the setting for such a vileness, I had chosen Eretz Israel. . . . This journalist, a friend of yours, repeated this slander twice, though in the meantime it had been refuted from New York, and though every Jew and every Arab and every Englishman in the country knew that the [Palestine] Government had demanded this concession from me and that I had refused. *Against this* slander you raised no protest. But when some of my young friends revolted against this calumny, and appealed to the Jewish public to boycott those who had spread this aspersion against a man who never in his life had sold his beliefs—you hastily girded your loins and—together with Bialik, who forgot what a decent man should not have forgotten, and with [Alter] Druyanov, who is as faithful to his friends as you are, published a protest against those who were trying to defend me.

"Don't answer this letter," Jabotinsky concluded. "My secretary had been instructed not to show me any of your letters and to return them to you."

This was not, however, the last word in the Jabotinsky-Ravnitzky relationship. Six years later, during the Arlosoroff affair (see Chapter Ten), Ravnitzky belonged to the circle of distinguished Palestine leaders who stood up against the combined effort of the Palestine Administration and the leftist parties to hang Stavsky. Jabotinsky was deeply moved by this courageous stand and wrote to Ravnitzky from Warsaw: "It is the second time that your voice reaches me in defense of our friends. When I first heard it, I wanted to hold out my hand to you, to offer to make peace and to renew our friendship, born several decades ago. For a long time I have been suffering from the separation from the man who taught me the first words of our language."

TWO JOURNEYS TO EUROPE

1. *Vienna*

FOR a man of Jabotinsky's mode of life, "settling" in a country was by no means synonymous with staying there for long, uninterruptedly. On the local Palestine scene, he was director of "Judea," chief-editor of *Doar Hayom,* and vigorous proponent of Revisionist ideas in the *Yishuv.* Yet at the same time he was also the head of a world-wide Revisionist Union and a leading figure in the world Zionist movement. In these latter capacities, he was bound to absent himself often, and for long periods, from his Palestine domicile.

He arrived in the country on October 5, 1928. By the middle of December, he was already on his way to Europe, to attend the Third Revisionist World Conference in Vienna (December 28 to 31). Afterward he spent a few weeks in Warsaw and Paris, and it was not before the end of January, 1929, that he returned to Palestine. At the end of July, he again left the country for the Sixteenth Zionist Congress at Zurich. He was absent the whole of August, September, October, and November, returning only in December. Both journeys to Europe were of considerable significance in Jabotinsky's political career.

Seventy delegates representing eighteen countries attended the Vienna Conference. Jabotinsky's opening address lasted two hours. The next day he presented a program of political activities of the Revisionist Union. In a closing address he summed up the work and achievements of the Conference.[1]

On the basis of his personal experience in Palestine, he charged that the country at present was being administered in a manner contrary to the interests of the ultimate aims of the Zionist movement, and that :

under its present leadership, the Zionist movement is also being conducted in a manner contrary to the interests of the ultimate aim of Zionism. In recent years, official Zionist leaders have given up the idea of a Jewish State in Palestine. They are busily whitewashing and justifying the British anti-Zionist regime. Their economic policy is hopelessly planless.

Particularly strong was Jabotinsky's indictment of the official Zionist policy of introducing non-Zionists into the Jewish Agency as full-fledged partners. The implementation of such a scheme, he charged, would put an end to the sovereignty of the World Zionist Congress created by Herzl, and of the democratic national Jewish renaissance movement. The Revisionists would fight this suicidal policy relentlessly. They would, however, not leave the Zionist Organization should this "extended" Jewish Agency come into existence, but would continue the struggle for the restoration of the sovereignty of Congress. "To be or not to be," was the problem the Zionist movement is facing. Appealing to Zionist patriots outside the Revisionist ranks, Jabotinsky exclaimed: "You, my Zionist brother, save your Zionism! Save the Zionist Congress! Guard the greatest of our national treasures!"

Outlining a program for independent Revisionist political action, Jabotinsky stressed that it was not his intention to usurp the prerogatives of the Zionist Executive; but it was the right and the duty of the Revisionist movement to continue, through its own channels, a campaign of enlightenment of public opinion in the British Empire and throughout the civilized world. In line with the stand he had taken in the *Vaad Leumi*, Jabotinsky expounded his concept of independent political action by the *Yishuv*. He also insisted on a wide autonomy for the Palestine branch of the Revisionist world movement.

The Conference went along with most of Jabotinsky's ideas and proposals. There were, however, some areas of dissent, which had developed long before the Conference met.

There had been a long-standing controversy on the question of independent Revisionist political action. Jabotinsky and most of the Paris members of the Revisionist leadership advocated a far-reaching program in this field. Meir Grossman and Richard Lichtheim argued that the Second Revisionist World Conference had stipulated that political activities of the Union have to be conducted in such a way

106

as to "safeguard the justified prerogatives of the Zionist Executive in regard to outside political affairs." They, therefore, insisted that no political action beyond enlightenment of public opinion be undertaken. This tactical controversy became acute after Jabotinsky's ten-days visit to London in April, 1928, where he renewed his political connections: "I mobilized Wedgwood and Kenworthy [both members of Parliament] for a campaign against the 'Arab Parliament. . . .' I also went to Amery [then Under-Secretary of State for the Colonies] and asked: 'What have you against me?' He swore that he had nothing against me and it was agreed that we would send him material on our activities addressed to him as 'Under Secretary of State for the Colonies.' At a dinner which Wedgwood arranged [for me] at the House of Commons I was made much of by Mr. and Mrs. Snowden [Philip Snowden was, together with Wedgwood and Ramsay Mac-Donald, the organizer of the Palestine Mandate Society which was disseminating pro-Zionist information in England] and I have made friends with Arnold Bennet. My former Colonel of the Twentieth London Battalion is now Sir Asheton Pownall, Under Secretary of State for Labor." [2] Informed by friends that the Zionist Executive was resentful of his contacts with British Government circles, he scornfully answered: "It is none of their business. It was Amery himself who summoned me—I have his letter to this effect—and all of them (including Amery) are old acquaintances of mine." [3] According to a Jewish Telegraphic Agency dispatch, "after hearing Mr. Jabotinsky's views, Mr. Amery declared that he would give his attention to the demands of the opposition." [4] In a personal letter, Jabotinsky reported that he had asked Amery point blank: "Is it true that in certain circles we are considered enemies of England? Amery's reply was, 'Nothing of the kind.' " [5]

At the Vienna Conference, where the question of independent political activities was thoroughly discussed, the disagreement lay more in the emphasis than in the substance. The spokesman for the "extreme" wing urged the immediate adoption of a far-reaching program for economic and political action fully independent of the Zionist Executive, while those advocating a more moderate course insisted on a slower and more wary pace. Jabotinsky had no difficulty in getting the Conference to accept a middle course: to seek the realization of a program of activity which would not interfere with the prerogatives of the Zionist Executive.

Where he really met with determined opposition, was on the question of independent political action of the organized Palestine Jewish community. He had advocated such action in the *Vaad Leumi* and hoped to have it endorsed by the Conference. In this he failed. The *Rasswyet* correspondent in Vienna reported that, "taking into account the radical mood of a section of the younger delegates, Jabotinsky's viewpoint might have been victorious if it would have come to a vote; but Jabotinsky and the leading group responsible for the Conference were on the whole against creating a mental attitude of victors and vanquished." [6] Jabotinsky himself confirmed this approach in a letter to Palestine : though he could have mustered a numerical majority for his resolution, "it would have meant mortifying Grossman, Lichtheim, Soskin, Klinov, and the London friends." [7]

No decision on the controversial issue was taken by the Conference. On the question of the status of the Revisionist Organization in Palestine, a compromise resolution was adopted giving it limited autonomy in all local problems, including the question of protection of the rights, interests, and security of Palestine Jewry.

The Conference also devoted considerable attention to Wedgwood's "Seventh Dominion" plan, which this imaginative and courageous Labour M.P. had formulated in a book published early in 1928.[8] The gist of this scheme was that the upbuilding of Palestine was not solely the "business of the Jews," but was England's business as well. England must actively cooperate in the establishment of a Jewish majority in that country. Before such majority is established, no experiments with ideas of Parliamentariarism should be made : the country must be administered under a Crown Colony Rule. Afterward, it must be converted into a Jewish Dominion—the seventh Dominion within the British Commonwealth of Nations.

Wedgwood's scheme appealed strongly to Jabotinsky. In a letter, which he requested be kept confidential, he told the author that his book was "more than brilliant and clever—it is a service to both causes, the British and the Zionist." He particularly appreciated its main idea—"to make the British official directly responsible for the success of Jewish colonization." This closely corresponded with Jabotinsky's basic demand for a "colonizing regime." The "Dominion" concept gained his unreserved approval : "Had we today even a 99 per cent majority in Palestine, I , the extremist, would still fight every idea of independence and would insist on keeping within the British Empire." He told Wedgwood squarely that he "liked the slogan and should not be averse to submitting it to the Revisionist League for acceptance." This would soon make it "a household term in all Zionist discussions," for, he added, "whatever their voting power, Revisionists had proved their great efficacy as channels for the spreading of new ideas. That might give you—supposing that you want it—a very lively backing within the Zionist movement." [9] Wedgwood was amenable to this suggestion, and the Vienna Conference resolved that there was "no contradiction" between the idea of a Jewish Palestine and an eventual Dominion status within a British Commonwealth of Nations; every Revisionist was free individually to join the Palestine Dominion League.[10] In May, 1929, when a Seventh Dominion League was constituted in Jerusalem, Jabotinsky accepted its chairmanship.[11]

On the whole, Jabotinsky had every reason to be satisfied with the Vienna Conference. There were, however, moments when he felt hurt by the opposition that some of his views and proposals met with. This writer who, together with Klinov, occupied a room in the same hotel where Jabotinsky was staying, recalls the night when, at about three a.m., we were awakened by a gentle knock at the door. "Who is there?"—"It's me, Jabotinsky." He entered wearing a dressing gown, embarrassed, and apparently unhappy. "Sorry to have disturbed you, but I just couldn't fall asleep, and I feel miserable. Why is it that even here, at a conference of the movement I have created, there is so little understanding for my views, so much opposition even among my closest friends and collaborators? Is it really my destiny to carry alone, always to be a lone wolf? Why is everybody against me?" These complaints, though undoubtedly sincere, sounded to Klinov and myself both unjustified and preposterous. We told him firmly and kindly that he was being ungrateful, that rarely had a man enjoyed such deep loyalty and affection on the part of his followers and colleagues; that this outburst of his was nothing but the same kind of "impressionism," which he had been fighting so strenuously in Zionist politics; and that he should go to bed and get some sleep. Jabotinsky took this admonition well, in sporting spirit. "Maybe you are right; maybe I am just overtired." We escorted him to his room. At the door, he turned to us and said: "Thank you, and don't tell anybody; we do have a wonderful movement."

109

It was in this spirit that, after the Conference, he wrote to Gepstein: "It was simply wonderful. Many excellent forces, first-class youth, interest on the part of the press." [12] He did not ignore the existence of far-reaching differences of opinion among the delegates, but he was not at all dismayed by them. In his concluding address he developed what he called "the philosophy of our struggle:" [13]

There has been a lot of fighting at this Conference. But we can pride ourselves on this, for such fights teach us where the evolution of a united movement lies. Not in uniformity. . . . I hope we will have fights at all our Conferences. We want to be able to state freely and openly what we hold to be right. And then we will reach accord, as we have always done up to now. Within a movement bound by a common aim, there is no such thing as "victory" for any single group. Level out your differences! Somewhere in the middle lies the truth.

2. *Zurich*

Jabotinsky's departure to the Sixteenth Zionist Congress in Zurich, to which he had been elected as one of the delegates from Palestine, was preceded by a dramatic clash at a session of the *Assefat ha'Nivharim* (July 3). On the agenda of the meeting was the election of six representatives of Palestine Jewry to the non-Zionist part of the "extended" Jewish Agency. Firmly opposed to the entire scheme, Jabotinsky insisted that Palestine Jewry as a community had no right to send delegates to a Jewish Agency, whose "extension" had not as yet been ratified by the Zionist Congress. When the session opened, Jabotinsky sharply protested against this item on the agenda and called the proposed election procedure a "presidium swindle." To this, Dr. Jacob Thon, who was presiding, replied that Jabotinsky "ought to be ashamed of himself." Feeling ran high in the Assembly and tumultuous scenes occurred. The labor wing, one hundred strong, angrily accused the twelve Jabotinsky-led Revisionist delegates of obstructionist tactics and attacked them bodily. Some of the Labor delegates wrested Jabotinsky's cane, with which he was alleged to have been making threatening gestures.[13a] The arrival of a well-trained group of *Betar* instructors, who surrounded Jabotinsky, prevented attempts to attack him physically. But some of his eleven comrades took a severe beating.

Jabotinsky was deeply shocked by this scene, which he vividly described in the article "Hatred" in the Warsaw *Haint* (September 26, 1929):

In a Jewish gathering, in a purely Jewish city, I have seen *people being beaten*. Not "people fighting each other": people being beaten! Four, six, ten men attacking one man, right before my eyes. . . . Somebody comes up from behind a man sitting in his place completely unprepared for the assault, seizes him by the hair with both hands and starts beating the back of his head against the sharp edge of the chair. A moment later, eight men attack another man, catch hold of his arms and legs and hurl him through the crowd towards the door; on the way, the crowd beat him and kick him (I saw it myself). Outside the building he falls unconscious on the pavement and is left lying there. A man of over seventy, one of the first *Biluim*, known throughout Eretz Israel, received blows on both shoulders.

What struck Jabotinsky particularly, were the faces of the attackers : "such an expression of inhuman hatred I have not seen even in Russia, even among the Arabs during the pogrom days in Jerusalem . . . a bitter hatred, a blind urge to hit, to tear, to pull to pieces." "A great part of this hatred," wrote Jabotinsky, "is directed against my own humble person. Physically, they have as yet not touched me, though there is no guarantee for the future. For the time being, they only shout two words : the one is *buz* (shame), the other is my name. A piquant combination, particularly in Eretz Israel." Years later, he still remembered with a shudder how "a hundred pairs of eyes, eyes belonging to the best youth that our people have possessed since the days of Bar Kochba, look at you with a deep and almost inhuman hatred and boo: 'Down with him! He deserves the fate of De Haan [who had been murdered in 1921]! Break his bones!' And he asked himself : "What was your sin at that time? You attempted, together with a handful of friends . . . to defend the sovereignty of Herzl's organization (you believed at that time that it still merited the crown of sovereignty), to combat the silly and harmful idea which is regretted today even by its greatest adherents of yesterday. And the best of Jewish youth responded with hatred." [14]

The session was interrupted. When it was resumed the next morning, Jabotinsky demanded that election of Jewish Agency representatives be removed from the agenda. By a majority of 72 to 26 (the twelve Revisionists were joined by fourteen other delegates), the Assembly decided to proceed with the election. Jabotinsky then re-stated his unalterable opposition to the extension of the Jewish Agency, and to the election of Palestine delegates under existing circumstances, and left the session together with his eleven colleagues.

Jabotinsky was very reluctant to attend the Congress. "It is going to be so disgusting that I would be glad not to be there," he wrote to a friend. "But I will have to," he admitted.[15]

He left Palestine in a strange and perturbed mood, which five years later he described as follows: "While on the boat, I was all of a sudden struck by the thought: What is it? Why do I, an old Zionist, get this odd feeling of relief—when I leave Erez Israel for a while? (I did not know as yet that it was going to be such a long absence). What is it that I have suddenly become so joyful and carefree; that I say to myself: Thank God, now—at least for a few weeks—I am not going to see angry faces and wolfish sidelong glances; and read no poisonous and hateful articles. Is this supposed to be the feeling with which a man sails from his homeland? And for the first time I realized that, just as in the times of Ezra and Nehemia, we are fated to build the Temple in an atmosphere of hatred."[16]

At the outset, Jabotinsky refused to speak at this Congress. At a caucus of the twenty-one strong Revisionist delegation, elected by eighteen thousand voters, he argued: "There is no sense in making speeches. Our program is known. All it will amount to, will be an oratorical performance. Who needs it? Who needs this platform appearance, all these efforts, to create an impression, and all these theatrical effects?"[17] Nevertheless, he yielded to the decision of the delegation which designated him as its main speaker. His address dealt with the very essentials of the problems facing the Zionist movement. He started with the definition of the basic ideas of Zionist terminology.[18]

"What is the Jewish National Home? It is 'a national State, a State with a predominant Jewish majority, where the will of the Jewish people will determine the forms and ways of collective life.' What is Palestine? 'It is an area, whose essential geographical characteristic is that the Jordan River flows not along its frontier, but through the middle of it.' " What is the meaning of Zionism? Zionism aims at the "actual solution to the political, economic and cultural tragedy of many millions of Jews. Its purpose is, therefore, not only to create a [Jewish] majority in Palestine, but to create living space

112

for millions on both sides of the Jordan." A "Charter" or a "Mandate" implies " an obligation on the part of the civilized world, and also on the part of a great nation not simply to 'favor' us, not only to 'treat us friendly,' but a solemn pledge to establish in Palestine a colonizing regime, so that the entire administrative system would be so organised as to prepare and develop the land on both sides of the Jordan for the absorption of great masses of colonists. . . ."

"Everybody now knows what four years ago, or even two years ago, was perhaps not yet fully realized: *this* problem will not be solved through fund-raising. The true Zionist upbuilding of the country will be achieved not through national money collections, but through the free mobilization of individual capital. And it is an established fact that free capital goes only where political conditions permit."

The Zionist Executive, Jabotinsky charged, was systematically deprecating all the grievances of the *Yishuv* against the Mandatory Government, and was "indulging in a bacchanal of *Zidduk ha'Din*" (apology of the Government).

Jabotinsky dismissed the hope that new possibilities had been opened for the cause of Zionism by the emergence of a Labor Government in London: "Let us not deceive ourselves. The friendliest British Government cannot be more Catholic than the Pope; it cannot give more than is being demanded of it. If you again content yourselves with making paper manifestations and reelect the same leadership, you will fritter away the new opportunities just as you frittered away similar opportunities four years ago, and the change in English parliamentary history will not benefit us in any way."

Attacking the Executive for its handling of the Jewish Agency problem, Jabotinsky insisted that nothing had been done to safeguard Zionist interests and that the sovereignty of the Congress had been flouted on every occasion. The elementary principle of Zionism—democracy—had been violated in the composition of the extended Jewish Agency: why had America received forty-four seats on the Jewish Agency Council whereas Poland, with a Jewish population almost as large had received only thirteen? "So clear, so blatant: we are not concerned with the size of the population; we only want the *Gevirim*. But the Jew of today is not the same as he was thirty years ago. He is proud, he has awareness, he is a citizen. . . . A tiny piece of paper, the shekel, has revolutionized the Jewish soul." The shekel

113

gave every Jew, whether rich or poor, an equal right to determine the fate of the Jewish people. This was the meaning of Zionist democracy. The extended Jewish Agency deprives the shekel of its moral value.

Jabotinsky concluded his address with an impressive reminder: "Today, at the crossroads—for tomorrow we vote, and many of you will say 'yes' with a heavy heart—I announce, not only on behalf of the eighteen thousand Zionists who sent our delegation to this Congress, but in the name of conscience, in the name of the naive, pure faith of our youth and the faith of our fathers, in the name of everything for which you and I once fought together—in the name of all these I announce, before God and history, our final conclusion: *non possumus*!"

The Congress listened to Jabotinsky's address in deep and tense silence. The official Congress minutes listed but eight interruptions, of which only five were hostile. Hostile interpolations came mostly from the Labor delegates and became particularly violent when Jabotinsky was speaking on Zionist democracy. But on the whole, the address made a strong impression. The *New Palestine* wrote: "It was generally agreed that Mr. Jabotinsky's address, delivered in German, was one of the finest oratorical efforts of the Congress; and when it was concluded, even many who opposed his views applauded him." [19] In the influential French language monthly *Revue de Genève* (October, 1929), José Jehuda wrote: "Jabotinsky's mastery of word comes from his mastery of thought. His clear, precise sentences are full of restrained vigor. He restores the lost meaning of terms, he quotes facts and draws conclusions from them."

Jabotinsky's contribution to the Congress deliberations was not limited to one speech. [20] Before the resolutions on the extended Jewish Agency were put to the vote, he rose to ask the Congress Presidium as well as the Political Committee, whether, according to the proposed constitution of the Jewish Agency, the forthcoming Congress would still be sovereign in its decisions concerning the budget and political matters. The answer given by Morris Rothenberg on behalf of the Political Committee (to which Weizmann expressed his assent by nodding) was that as long as the provisional agreement with the non-Zionists, which was to last for three years, was in existence, the constitution of the Jewish Agency would bind the Congress as well. The resolutions of the next Zionist Congress would also have to be approved by the Council of the Jewish Agency. This answer clinched it. Even those among the Revisionist Congress delegation who had originally disagreed with Jabotinsky's unyielding stand with regard to the extended Agency and, though opposed to Weizmann's scheme, favored Revisionist participation in the Agency's Council in order to pursue there an opposition course, agreed to make unanimous the decision to refuse the seats on the Council to which the Revisionists were entitled.

One of the highlights of the Congress was a special session devoted to Hebrew cultural work in the Diaspora. Jabotinsky was among the six speakers of this session. He reminded the Congress of the great struggle for the Hebraization of the Diaspora which started sixteen years ago. Fully realizing the difficulties of the goal and the insufficiency of the results achieved, he, however, now as then, was opposed to any compromise in this field.

At the nineteenth session of the Congress, Jabotinsky introduced a motion that the interests of "*Sefardic,* Yemenite, and other Oriental Jews be taken into consideration" in the selection of new colonists. Asked by the Chairman whether he intended "to introduce the proportional principle," Jabotinsky answered: "There is a difference between [the principle of] proportion which, of course, cannot be demanded, and disproportion, to which, I am sure, the entire Congress will be opposed." While the *Sefardic* Jews comprised approximately one-third of Palestine's Jewish population, among the ten thousand settlers in the Zionist colonies only seventy-eight were Sefardim. Jabotinsky asked that his motion be accepted unanimously, which the Congress did.

On the whole, Jabotinsky was highly satisfied with the job done at the Congress. "To me," he said in a personal letter, "this is the first Congress since 1903, that I don't regret having attended and having tried to achieve something." [21] In another letter, written in lighter, somewhat self-deprecating vein, he wrote: "For some reason, we have highly impressed everybody at the Congress, and our adversaries, one after the other, kept buttonholing me and asserting that in the Congress lobby 'everybody' was saying how much we were needed. . . . I don't understand anything in all this, but apparently it is a fact: our operetta was a hit, though in my view it had neither catchy tunes nor an original libretto. But there is no arguing with success." [22]

SEVEN

THE BATTLE OF THE SHAW COMMISSION

1. *In Absentia*

WHEN Jabotinsky left Palestine late in July, 1929, the political atmosphere in the country was heavy and explosive. The Arabs were working themselves into a fury of recrimination and accusation over the Wailing Wall controversy. The British Administration was watching the growing Arab militancy with a passively, almost friendly eye. The *Yishuv* was tense, apprehensive, and practically leaderless: the responsible heads of the Palestine Zionist Executive and of the *Vaad Leumi* were in Zurich, where the session of the Sixteenth Zionist Congress opened on July 28.

After a series of minor skirmishes, the Arab mob on August 23 invaded the New City of Jerusalem and began to massacre Jews. The assault spread to Hebron, Safed, and several Jewish colonies. The riots resulted in 133 Jewish deaths and 116 reported Arab deaths, many of them the result of police and military actions.

The new Colonial Secretary, Lord Passfield, appointed a commission to "inquire into the immediate causes" of the riots and to "make recommendation as to the steps necessary to avoid a recurrence." [1] Headed by Sir Walter Shaw, the Commission (usually referred to as the "Shaw Commission") arrived in Palestine late in October, 1929, and returned to London on January 4, 1930. It heard evidence submitted by the Palestine Government, the Arab Executive Committee, and the Executive of the Jewish Agency.

It was largely with a view to testifying before the Commission that Jabotinsky decided to return to Palestine in November, 1929. When his intention became known, a group of party and personal friends in Lithuania wired him, drawing his attention to Arab threats and

116

begging him to forego the journey. In a short letter, dated November 18, he thanked the signatories for their solicitude on his behalf, but assured them that he personally was not running any danger. He added that, "as a matter of principle, it is inadmissable to renounce the import into Palestine of goods which the Arabs dislike—otherwise we would have to renounce everything." Nevertheless, when he arrived in Palestine, a non-partisan group of twenty-six constituted itself as his bodyguard. [2]

Jabotinsky had weighty reasons for wanting to be heard by the Shaw Commission. One of them was the manner in which his name was referred to—in absentia—before the Commission.

On the third day of deliberations, Major Alan Saunders, Acting Commissioner of the Police and Prisons Department, volunteered the following information : "Jabotinsky was here [in Palestine] in 1920, and was sentenced to fifteen years imprisonment and deported; he came back in November, 1928. I cannot say if he came previous to that." [3] That was all the Commission learned about Jabotinsky. For about two months none of the witnesses representing the Zionist Executive made the slightest attempt at contradicting or correcting this testimony. When he returned to Palestine late in November, Jabotinsky felt very bitter about this attitude. In a letter to Solomon Horowitz, who was the Executive's adviser to Sir Boyd Merriman, the Gentile legal counsel representing the Zionist cause, he wrote : "I protest most indignantly that he [Merriman] was advised or allowed to let pass the Saunders reference to me without any reply." In addition to its legal and factual mendaciousness, it was, Jabotinsky stressed, "most unwise to leave the Commission under the impression that a party in Zionism [the Revisionist Party] is headed by a man, whose only characteristic is a sentence of penal servitude. . . . Are you a part to all this ?" "I simply want to know in order to decide whether I can shake hands with you again." [4] Simultaneously Jabotinsky also wrote to Merriman himself, giving a correct version of the legal aspect of the matter.

This direct approach helped. On December 12, Sir Boyd Merriman told the Commission that he had "received a personal letter from Mr. Jabotinsky whose attention has only recently been drawn to this [Saunders statement], and naturally he felt a little hurt about it." Merriman promised him to "take the earliest opportunity of bringing the matter to the notice of the Commission." In doing so, he stated that the sentence against Jabotinsky" had been quashed by the Army Council. . . . Being a sentence of a Military Court, it was quashed not on appeal but for lack of evidence. . . . The Army Council was the only body which can quash such a sentence." Sir Boyd added that now that he had been allowed to state that in public, he hoped "that the same publicity will be given to it as to the earlier statement [by Saunders] and then no injustice will be done." [5]

The second item on the Commission's agenda that directly involved Jabotinsky was the role his paper *Doar Hayom* had played during the tense and explosive weeks preceding the outbreak of the pogrom. [6] *Doar Hayom* had insistently warned against the impending danger. On August 1, Issaia Braude of the Provincial Zionist Executive in Jerusalem (together with Sigfried Hoofien and Solomon Horowitz, was at that time in charge of current Zionist affairs) approached representatives of the three Hebrew dailies—*Haaretz, Davar* and *Doar Hayom*—appealing to them "to have patience and to avoid all incitement of the people." According to the Commission's report, *Haaretz* "responded in small measure" to this appeal; the *Doar Hayom* "continued to publish intemperate articles;" and articles appearing in the *Davar* during the first fortnight of August also contained passages which, Braude admitted in evidence, were "not helpful to the Government" and of an "exciting" character. [7]

It was, however, Jabotinsky's *Doar Hayom* alone that the provisional Zionist Executive chose as scapegoat. They felt, as Braude later (December 10) told the Commission, that the *Doar Hayom* was "trying to force the hand of the Zionist Executive through articles calling for action regarding the Wailing Wall." Since Jabotinsky, the chief editor of the paper, was at that time at the Zionist Congress, Hoofien cabled him on August 5 :

Doar Hayom ignores all action of the Zionist Congress in regard to the Wailing Wall and is calling for revolt and violence. Although the public is not influenced thereby, there is excitement among the youth, which might lead to incidents without being of any practical utility. I ask that you cable them [the editors of *Doar Hayom*] to change their attitude; otherwise the responsibility is theirs and yours.

In reply to this appeal, Jabotinsky cabled on August 6 : "Communicating with *Doar Hayom*." According to Braude, Jabotinsky "instructed the *Doar Hayom* editors to abate their agitation." "This they did," he continued, in an article on August 7, "in that they renounced violence."

The Counsel for the Government, Kenelm Preedy, prodded Hoofien to explain whether the word "revolt" used in his cable meant "revolt against the Zionist Executive or against the [local Palestine] Jewish institutions." Hoofien's answer was: "I used an ambiguous expression, leaving it for Mr. Jabotinsky to read it as he might." This evasive reply did not satisfy Preedy: "That may be very useful from your point of view," he said, "but what about Mr. Jabotinsky? This cable is addressed to him, and he had to form some conclusion on it. What conclusion did you intend he should form?" Pushed to the wall, the witness for the Zionist Executive gave the following elaborate explanation: "I intended him to form in general the following conclusion—as he knows me and as he knows I am a man who is moderate in expression—if I go to the length of using a strong expression, it is time that he should appeal to his people to use more moderate language in his paper, which is what we wished to attain."

Preedy then asked a second embarrassing question: "What do you mean by the word 'revolt'? Revolt against the Palestine Zionist Executive or against the Government?" Hoofien tried once more to avoid a straight answer by saying: "Whatever he [Jabotinsky] liked." Preedy again did not let him get away with this evasion: "Well, which was it in fact? Did you treat it as a revolt against the Government or the Palestine Zionist Executive?" Hoofien was forced to be frank:

I treated it, first of all, as a revolt against the Palestine Zionist Executive; but the article to which I referred was written in such a tone that if things had been allowed to go on in that way, in the long run people might be excited by pulling things concerning this Wailing Wall matter which the Government would have to prevent; and if they were going to do things which the Government felt it their duty to prevent, then naturally such an attitude might be called revolt.

To which Preedy meaningfully said: "Whatever Mr. Jabotinsky thought, I understand it now."

When Jabotinsky received Hoofien's alarming cable in Zurich, making him responsible for *Doar Hayom's* articles and their eventual results, he had no knowledge of either the contents or the tone of the incriminating articles. Later, he firmly assumed full responsibility for the paper's attitude during his absence. Replying in the *Doar Hayom*

119

of February 7, 1930, to the accusation that it had incited Jewish public opinion, Jabotinsky insisted that the paper had merely been doing its duty by giving expression at a critical moment to what the Jews really felt and thought: to their indignation at being continually insulted and deprived of their rights at the Wailing Wall.

Another attempt to put the resposibility at Jabotinsky's door for "provoking" Arab violence was made in connection with the "march to the Wailing Wall," on August 15. This demonstration was organized by a group of Jewish youth with the permission of Harry Luke, the Acting High Commissioner, as a protest both against the Arab claims to the Wailing Wall and the British officials who were opposed to the policy of the Jewish National Home. The demonstration raised the Zionist flag and sang *Hatiqva*. The Commission of Inquiry asserted that this demonstration was "more than any other single incident, an immediate cause of the [anti-Jewish] outbreak," and Jabotinsky's political opponents claimed that it was the *Brit Trumpeldor* organization which he headed that had been responsible for it.

"I must say to my great regret that it [the Wailing Wall demonstration] was not organized by the *Brit Trumpeldor*," stated Jabotinsky in the *Doar Hayom*.[8] And in that, he was fully upheld by the authoritative evidence submitted to the Commission by both British and Jewish responsible authorities, who were anything but friendly to this organization. Major Alan Saunders stated firmly that "it was not a [*Brit*] *Trumpeldor* demonstration, though they may have been members of the [*Brit*] *Trumpeldor* as well." Similarly, Hoofien, while admitting the possibility that among the Jerusalem demonstrators there might have been a number of people who also belonged to the *Trumpeldor* Organization, stated that this has been denied by the heads of this organization.[9] As far as Jabotinsky was concerned, he deeply regretted that the Jerusalem demonstration had not been organized by the *Brit Trumpeldor,* because, as he insisted in a letter to a friend, it "was a psychological and practical necessity; and if I believed for a moment that *that* was the cause of the outbreak, I should heartily congratulate the promoter(s). . . . It is the main thing in all strategy to force the enemy to attack before he is ready. A year later it would have been infinitely worse."[10] Elaborating on this argument in the *Doar Hayom*, Jabotinsky wrote that the demonstration was "at that time a necessary, a useful and a fine thing. It was necessary because an unbearable atmosphere had been created in which it appeared that the Jews had given up everything, so that someone had to get up and say: 'Thus far and no further!' The argument that the Arabs should not have been stirred up, is a heritage of the ghetto. In Palestine we are not just tolerated guests, and in order to show this, the demonstration was necessary. It made a great impression even abroad, in the countries of the *galut*."

One more aspect of the Jewish cause, as presented to the Inquiry Commission, deeply affected Jabotinsky. It was—as he put it—the "attempt to divide Zionists into good ones and bad ones," the bad ones being the party he headed.[11]

At one of the first sessions of the Commission (October 31, 1929), Reginald Silley, one of the counsels for the Arab Executive, referred to the noted Revisionist Dr. Wolfgang von Weisl as a "Zionist leader." Sir Boyd Merriman, the counsel for the Zionist Executive, immediately corrected him "He [v. Weisl] is the opposite: he is a Revisionist." "An anti-Zionist?" inquired Silley. "A Revisionist," Sir Boyd repeated. When Silley said that this distinction seemed to him to be a "refinement," the answer was: "It is not a refinement. I will define it later, but he is a Revisionist." [12]

This attempt to imply that being a Revisionist was the "opposite" of being a Zionist, provoked an indignant reaction in the *Yishuv*. Sir Boyd, who was, of course, innocent of any knowledge of internal Zionist problems, apparently made this remark on the basis of previous briefing by official Zionist leaders. Realizing the blunder, they asked him to correct it. Six days later, on November 4, Sir Boyd loyally stated that his previous remark "in the sense it was made, was inaccurate because the Revisionists are not officially Zionist [!], but they are Zionists . . . they have the same Zionist ideas." [13] Writing in *Doar Hayom* (November 20), Jabotinsky graciously accepted Sir Boyd's rather lame but well-intended self-correction and confirmed that there was no difference between Zionists as far as the ultimate goal of Zionism was concerned. He later added that he attached no blame to Sir Boyd for the original misrepresentation; the full responsibility for it lay with the Zionist Executive.

On the whole, Jabotinsky was deeply disappointed by the conduct of the Jewish case before the Commission. In a letter to Meir Grossman, written from Jerusalem on December 12, 1929, he said: "Situation here: rotten. Instead of an attack on the regime, our case before the Commission has been converted into a sort of apologia,

121

justifying our existence—just like the old *Abwehr des Antisemitismus*. This is the main line; the main sideline—drowning the Revisionists and the *Doar Hayom*. The Executive produced the cable Hoofien sent me to Zurich, which contains the words '*Doar Hayom* is inciting to *revolt* and *acts of violence*'; and this is dated long *before* the trouble had started, so unless the Commission are angels, they will say that the real revolt and violence came through Jewish initiative. The rumor is that Merriman would have preferred to 'hang the Government,' but Kisch and Company prevailed upon him with the argument that it would only irritate the officials with whom they [Kisch and Company] would still have to work in the future. However it may be, instead of a *cause célèbre* we have the petty, inglorious business of trying to prove that Jews do not use Christian blood or steal horses."

2. *Testimony*

Jabotinsky had no illusions as to what the Jewish cause could expect from the Shaw Commission. That was not the parliamentary commission he had demanded. Soon after its appointment, he wrote in the *Rasswyet* :[14] "Everybody in England knows that the Commission has been set up with the sole view to whitewashing the Palestine Administration, and they will whitewash it." But he firmly believed that the Jewish case must be presented even to this obviously biased body in a frank and forceful manner, and that such a presentation was likely to have a great influence on British public opinion.

The Zionist Executive did not include Jabotinsky in the list of witnesses who were to appear before the Commission. This omission caused considerable indignation in the *Yishuv*. The General Zionists added their protest to that of the Revisionists. They sent a special delegation to Jerusalem demanding that Jabotinsky be called as witness. In the strongly anti-Revisionist *Davar*, M. Beilinson indignantly wrote (January 2, 1930) that the Inquiry Commission had left Palestine "with the impression that Jabotinsky was some kind of pogrom hero, whom [the Jews] do not dare to exhibit." The question was also raised at a closed meeting of the *Vaad Leumi*, of which Jabotinsky was still a member. The general mood was strongly in favor of taking energetic steps to secure Jabotinsky's appearance before the Commission. The representatives of the Labor parties skillfully obviated a decision to this effect by proposing that the Executive be requested to summon representatives of every Zionist party, an obvious impossibility. Jabotinsky asked the *Vaad Leumi* not to worry about him : he would find the proper ways and means to protect his rights.[15]

On December 20, Jabotinsky wrote to the chairman of the Commission asking to be invited to give testimony in a public session of the Commission.[16] He gave as the reason for his request the fact that his name had been repeatedly mentioned to the Commission in such a way as to create a distorted impression about his influence on the Jewish community during the period preceding the outbreak of the riots; the same applied to the *Doar Hayom* and the *Brit Trumpeldor (Betar)*. On the other hand, "the ideal of Palestine as a Jewish State— the very foundation of my political creed—has been interpreted as contradictory to the Mandate and directed against the non-Jewish population of that country." In his testimony, Jabotinsky wrote, he intended to prove that the idea of a Jewish State with a Jewish majority was, and always had been, the goal of the founders of Zionism (Pinsker, Herzl, Achad Haam, and others), as well as the underlying intention of the Balfour Declaration; and that its implementation would in no way affect the welfare of the population of the country as a whole. He also intended to refute all accusations against the *Betar* and the *Doar Hayom,* and to prove that the sole cause of the pogrom was the policy of the Palestine Administration. The Commission proved to be more fair than the official Zionist bodies. In its final *Report* it explained that "as his [Jabotinsky's] name had been mentioned on several occasions in the course of our proceedings, we agreed to hear him although he had not been called as a witness by the Palestine Zionist Executive." However, since his application was not made until a few days before the Commission's departure, they "were unable to hear him in Jerusalem and his evidence was to be given before us [the Commission] in London in private." [17]

Jabotinsky prepared his evidence very carefully. He testified on January 24 and then gave considerable attention to checking and correcting the shorthand minutes. He also submitted an additional memorandum on the land question in Palestine. Since the evidence was given *in camera,* no full text of the testimony and of the following cross-examination was ever published. The Commission was, however, fair enough to reproduce in its final *Report* several extensive extracts from the evidence, which give an adequate notion of some of its highlights.[18]

The object of the Revisionist movement he represented, Jabotinsky told the Commission, was "to revise certain conceptions of Zionist policy."

When we started our movement in 1925, the official point of view as expressed by Dr. Weizmann and his associates was this: the business of Zionism can be completed and achieved simply by the process of the Jews pouring money and energy into Palestine, and it ought not to matter at all what the attitude of the [Mandatory] Government was, provided that the Government was a decent European Administration. We [Revisionists] demanded the revision of this point of view, saying that large-scale colonization cannot be conducted independently of a Government, that it is a Government enterprise by its nature, and can only be complete if the Government supports it by legislative and administrative action.

Developing this thesis, Jabotinsky explained that there is in Eastern Europe a large area extending over several countries which he described as "a zone of incurable anti-Semitism." This zone was overcrowded with Jews, one half of whom had to be evacuated within the next two generations. Palestine was the only country to which many of them could be directed. He maintained that the Palestine Government ought "actively to promote Jewish colonization with a view, of course, to establishing a Jewish majority" as the prerequisite of the establishment of a Jewish State.

Defining the term "Jewish State," Jabotinsky said:

It does not necessarily mean being independent in the sense of having the right to declare war on anybody, but what it means is first of all a majority of Jewish people in Palestine, so that under a democratic rule the Jewish point of view should always prevail, and secondly, that measure of self-Government which for instance the State of Nebraska possesses. That would satisfy me completely as long as it is a local self-Government, enough to conduct our own affairs, and so long as there is a Jewish majority in the country.

His conception of future political development in Palestine, Jabotinsky argued, was the only logical interpretation of the policy embodied in the Balfour Declaration. By numerous quotations from

124

speeches and official documents he established that, though he and his party were now described as "extremists" by the General Zionists, the policy he advocated was in fact based on the spoken and written word of Zionist leaders, whose ultimate aim was identical with his own, though their immediate methods for the attainment of that end were different.

Jabotinsky's own impression was that all this had been "of course, love's labor lost." "The Commission," he wrote to his friends on February 7, 1930, "is almost unanimously against Zionism, and the report will be a most venomous one." He was also outspoken in his criticism of the Zionist Executive's conduct of the Jewish case before the Commission. At a press conference in London, he said that Palestine Jewry expected that "definite light would be thrown on the anti-Zionist character and activities of the Palestine bureaucracy and political regime which led the Arabs to believe that England had withdrawn from her original intentions. . . . Instead of unmasking the regime, the Jewish case was conducted in a spirit of apologia. . . ."[19] I do not think their report will be decisive. . . . But it will do a lot of harm."

3. Exile

On December 23, 1929, two days before his departure from Palestine, Jabotinsky spoke in Tel Aviv before six thousand people.[20] He subjected the policy of the Zionist Executive to devastating criticism and decried its continuing in office. He warned against concessions to the Arabs which lead nowhere, and presented a clearly defined program of demands to be submitted to the Mandatory Power.

The speech was reproduced next day almost in full in *Doar Hayom*. On December 25, Jabotinsky left for Europe and South Africa, where he continued his crusade against both the British regime in Palestine and the official Zionist policy.

Some time after his departure, officials of the Palestine Government had a "friendly talk" with Jabotinsky's political associates and plainly hinted that his return to Palestine would be most unwelcome: his speeches and articles had been causing excitement and angering the Arabs.[21] The Colonial Office informed Jabotinsky personally that the High Commissioner had been displeased with his speech. The answer was: if the speech contained something unlawful, the Palestine

Government should arraign the orator or the paper that published the speech before a court of law.[22] The Government did not take recourse to either of these legal steps. There was obviously little hope of obtaining a conviction even in a Palestine court. The speech was anything but inciting. The very moderate *Haaretz* later (September 17, 1931) bluntly said that "it would not make a single hair fall from anybody's head."

Nevertheless, when Jabotinsky, after a few months' stay abroad, wanted to resume his work in Jerusalem, the Palestine administration refused to honor the reentry visa which had been issued to him prior to his departure. The High Commissioner, Sir John Robert Chancellor, asked by the Colonial Office, whether he had any objections to Jabotinsky's return, answered in the affirmative. "I understand that Amery is trying to get the *ukas* cancelled, but it's doubtful whether he'll succeed," Jabotinsky wrote from Cape Town on May 10. Three weeks later, he learned that "correspondence about my [return] visa is still going on between [Colonial Secretary, Lord] Passfield and Chancellor." [23] But the opinion of "the man on the spot" prevailed. The return visa was cancelled. As Jabotinsky was already a "permanent resident" of Palestine since 1928, this measure was actually tantamount to the banishment of a person who had already settled there and had been officially recognized as a resident.

There can be hardly any doubt that this banishment was an attempt to satisfy the wishes of both Arab nationalist agitators and anti-Zionist English politicians. As early as September, 1929, the Arab Executive demanded from the Palestine Government that Jabotinsky be prevented from reentering Palestine.[24] On March 29, 1930, the English edition of *Falastin* again claimed that he should be forbidden to return since he was propagating the establishment of a Jewish State. In the paper's view, this was contrary to the Balfour Declaration and to the Palestine Mandate, and was likely to disturb peace in the country. On February 5, 1930, the anti-Zionist M.P., Colonel Howard-Bury, asked the Secretary of State for the Colonies in the House of Commons whether his attention had been drawn to "an extremely inflammatory speech delivered by Jabotinsky in Tel Aviv on December 23; and why steps were not taken under the Seditious Offences Ordinance with regard to this speech." Dr. Drummond Shiels, Under Secretary of State for the Colonies in the Labor Government, replied that he had seen a report on the speech and

126

that he agreed that "it would be generally advantageous if both Jews and Arabs would talk more calmly on these matters." [25] In reply to Jabotinsky's bitter complaint about the manner in which he was treated in the House, L. S. Amery regretted that he was absent when Howard-Bury's interpolation was dealt with, and that "there was apparently no one on the spot who knew enough about your record to put in a supplementary bringing out of the facts." He, however, sent "a line to Dr. Shiels to put him wise in case questions get asked again, and will see if any other opportunity arises to correct any unfair insinuation that may be made against you." [26]

This "line" apparently did produce some results. Simultaneously with Colonel Howard Bury, another anti-Zionist M.P., Captain E. N. Bennet, asked the Secretary of State for the Colonies whether he was aware that in 1920, after having been amnestied, Jabotinsky "was deported under the distinct understanding that he was not to return to Palestine." The answer to this question, given by Dr. Drummond Shiels on March 17, was to the effect that he was "not aware that Mr. Jabotinsky ever entered into an understanding referred to." Then the following characteristic exchange of remarks developed: Captain E. N. Bennet: "Is it not a fact that a person deported from Palestine or any other country is *ipso facto* debarred from returning as and when he likes?" Colonel Wedgwood: "Was he deported?" Ormsby-Gore: "Is it not a fact that the sentence [against Jabotinsky] was quashed and never ought to have been passed, and the Honorable Member's suggestion is, therefore, without foundation?" [27]

The Palestine Government let it be known unofficially that a reentry visa would eventually be granted if Jabotinsky would undertake to abstain from "certain activities." The entire Hebrew press of June 13, 1930, was outraged by this demand. *Davar*, a fierce opponent of Jabotinsky, qualified it as an attempt to reduce Palestine Jews to a status of second-rate citizens who are deprived of such rights as are being enjoyed by other inhabitants of the country. *Haaretz* branded the Government's action as amounting to outright expulsion and as capitulation to Arab demands. *Yerushalayim,* (which then replaced the suspended *Doar Hayom*) called it "unheard of."

In an article by Dr. Wolfgang von Weisl, *Yerushalayim* expressed the hope that the Zionist Executive would react to the ban on Jabotinsky as to an occurrence of general Jewish significance. [28] Jabotinsky most outspokenly expressed regret that such a suggestion had been made in his paper. "Revisionists must not lift a finger in this matter," he wrote to S. Gepstein.[29] In another letter (undated) to a small circle of friends, he stated: "As to my exclusion from Palestine, I have nothing to say. Immoral acts of cynicism and ingratitude are beneath comment. And I urgently request all Revisionists to abstain from any action in this respect. The quarrel of the Jews with this replica of Plehve's regime is too deep for personal issues." When he learned that Professor Selig Brodetsky had written to the Zionist Executive in London, suggesting that appropriate steps be taken to redress the injustice, he officially asked the Revisionist World Headquarters in London on July 1 not to cooperate with the Zionist Executive in this matter. While expressing his appreciation of Professor Brodetsky's initiative, he insisted that the Zionist Executive was "hardly the appropriate agent for an intervention of this kind," and continued: "The prejudice against Revisionism and against me personally which has been so deeply instilled in official British circles, and of which my exclusion is only the natural outcome, is largely due to many utterances or omissions for which the Zionist Executive is unfortunately responsible, either through its agents or itself." The letter contained a selected list of such "utterances or omissions" during the years 1925 to 1928, and went on:

Other instances could be quoted, but this is enough to show how much the attitudes of the Zionist Executive and of its agents have themselves contributed toward discrediting Revisionism and myself in the eyes of the authorities both in England and Palestine, and toward making these authorities consider us and me not as elements of the Zionist family, but rather as Ishmaels of which Zionists washed their hands ("a thorn in their flesh" was the expression used by Sir Walter Shaw, during my interrogation, to describe the Zionist Executive's attitude toward us).

Under these conditions, I have no assurance that any intervention by the Zionist Executive on my behalf would be made in accordance with either the interests or the dignity of the [Revisionist] Union and its President.

Indicative of the reputation which had been insiduously created around Jabotinsky's name in non-Jewish circles, is the episode described to this writer by Advocate Max Seligman, whom Jabotinsky had asked to substitute for him during his absence as Managing Director of the "Judea." Seligman approached the American Consul General in Jerusalem and, stressing the fact that Jabotinsky was the representative of an American firm, requested the Consul's intercession with the Palestine authorities. The first reaction to this request was the question: "Isn't Mr. Jabotinsky a notorious Communist?"[30]

The *Vaad Leumi* sent a letter to the High Commissioner demanding the revocation of the ban on Jabotinsky's return to the country. This intercession was unsuccessful. Moreover, the Jaffa District Commissioner prohibited a meeting called to protest against the banishment of Jabotinsky.[31] Jabotinsky himself addressed a letter to the British Colonial Office demanding the unconditional repeal of the Palestine Government's order cancelling his return to Palestine; he urged his reinstatement as a permanent resident of Palestine, free to engage in any form of activity not prohibited by law. When no reply was forthcoming, he consulted legal experts with a view to a possible suit against Sir John Chancellor, High Commissioner for Palestine, and Lord Passfield, British Colonial Secretary, for harming his interests in declining to grant him a return visa.[32] The experts' advice was discouraging: the expulsion order had been put into effect by an administrative act which could not be reviewed, and was not subject to investigation.

This situation continued for about a year and a half. During this period, considerable changes occurred both in London and in Jerusalem: Lord Passfield was succeeded in the Colonial Office by J. H. Thomas, who was considered an openminded man, and Under-Secretary Drummond Shiels was replaced by Sir Robert Hamilton and Malcolm MacDonald, who also passed as unprejudiced toward Zionism and Zionists. In the Palestine Administration, Sir Arthur Wauchope succeeded Sir John Chancellor as High Commissioner—a new man who was not bound by a decision taken before his term of office. It seemed that the time was propitious for a revision. Colonel Wedgwood, therefore, on September 16, 1931, asked the Colonial Secretary in the House of Commons:[33] "Is the Right Honorable Gentleman aware that Lieutenant Jabotinsky fought for us in the war and was decorated, and that he has been excluded from Palestine solely because of the Arab massacres?"

Answering Wedgwood's interpolation, the new Colonial Secretary dryly said that "the question as to what should be the attitude to those who fought in the war will have to be considered in relationship to their present attitude." He was confident that his predecessor, Lord Passfield, who was "always anxious to preserve what is called freedom of speech, arrived at this decision [to refuse the visa] in the best interests of Palestine and in the best interests of everybody." Thomas himself had consulted the High Commissioner [Wauchope] and "saw no reason for a change of decision" in the Jabotinsky matter.

Late in 1933, rumors were being spread in Warsaw that Jabotinsky was seeking Polish citizenship and would appear in the next elections for Polish Sejm, heading a Revisionist list. Jabotinsky categorically denied this allegation. Revealing that the French Government had offered him citizenship rights, he stated that he had declined this offer "since he desires only Palestine citizenship, which he hopes to secure soon." Until that time he preferred to remain stateless, holder of the Nansen, League of Nations, passport.[34] In April 1934, the Jewish Telegraphic Agency reported from Jerusalem that the High Commissioner, Sir Arthur Wauchope, had cabled the Colonial Office that he had no objection to the granting of a Palestine visa to Jabotinsky. There was speculation that this alleged change of heart was the result of a "personal appeal" by Jabotinsky to King George V, "pointing out his military services in Gallipoli (!) and in Palestine under Allenby, and asking the King to intercede and grant him permission to reside in Palestine." [35] This speculation was, of course, unfounded. It derived from a misinterpretation of the "individual petition," which Jabotinsky had sent to King George "as one of the initiators of the petition movement" that had been launched in 1933—1934 by the Revisionist organization (see Chapter Eleven). There was nothing personal in this application (and certainly no reference to his military services); it was similar to those sent by tens of thousands of other petitioners. Jabotinsky wrote to his sister from Warsaw on April 21, 1934 : "Of my 'admission' to Palestine, I know only from the press; I did not receive any communication. I have never troubled anybody about a visa. In my petition to the King I did not ask for a visa for myself, but requested an appropriate change of the immigration legislation." Arab nationalist leaders manifested strong indignation in connection with the rumors of Jabotinsky's readmission to Palestine, and the Jerusalem paper Al Jamia al Islamia warned that the Arabs were planning to stage a demonstration if Jabotinsky were allowed to enter Palestine.[36]

Rumors about Jabotinsky's pending admission to Palestine nevertheless persisted. When he arrived in New York at the end of January, 1935, he was surprised to learn that word had been received that he was no longer to be debarred from Palestine. He was unable to say whether the rumor was correct, and whether he would return to Palestine for a visit. That, he said, depended on the "business requirements" of the Revisionist organization. For several months to come, he apparently toyed with the idea of attempting to obtain a visa for a short visit. On May 27, 1935, he wrote from Warsaw to G. Bonfeld: "I have been thinking a good deal of paying a flying visit to Palestine, at least for a month. I swore that I would not apply for a visa; what is worse, it could be refused. But I still give it much thought. I feel that I could find out a lot, and also be helpful in many respects." Later, on June 25, he guardedly wrote to Dr. I. Freulich, the head of the *Betar* in Palestine: "Very secret: there's a possibility that in mid-summer I might come to Palestine for a few days." This writer was unable to find any direct evidence as to whether Jabotinsky did or did not apply for a visa at that time. From a passing remark in a letter (dated July 19, 1935) to S. Jacobi, "We are going to exploit to the full the refusal to grant me a visa," it may be inferred that an application had been made and refused.

In the fall of 1935, Jabotinsky met Sir Arthur Wauchope in London—on the latter's initiative—in the house of Lord Melchett [Sir Alfred Mond]. In the course of the conversation, Wauchope asked why he had never seen Jabotinsky in Palestine, and received the answer: "Does not your Excellency know that I was refused admission?" To this Wauchope is reported to have said: "When you wish to come, please let me know, I shall gladly arrange the matter. I shall be glad to meet you in Jerusalem." [37] Nothing came of this seemingly generous offer. Whether because Sir Arthur simply did not live up to his promise, or because his good intentions were frustrated by the Colonial Office, but Jabotinsky's return to Palestine proved to be as impossible after their encounter as it had been before.

4. *Last Experiment*

Jabotinsky was acutely aware of the fact that the August pogrom had precipitated a profound crisis in the attitude of world Jewry toward the Mandatory Power. In a series of articles published in October and December, 1929,[38] he frankly admitted: "It is certainly not a secret that nine-tenths of Zionists are now revising their stand in regard to England." They felt that Great Britain had become a

131

"tired" Empire, vegetating in a twilight atmosphere, and that time had come for a "parting of the ways." Jabotinsky did not discard such a possibility *in limine*. If those premises were true, the conclusion had to be accepted regretfully, but unhesitatingly. Orientation was not a "tabu," he insisted, and could be revised. Jewry's alliance with England "was not concluded for ever." But he denied that the premises were correct, and warned against "impressionism" in politics. "Conclusions of major importance can be reached only on the basis of an experiment that has been properly carried through. Our experiment with England was not made correctly and was not carried out to the end. . . . Notwithstanding all the disappointments, England always will be our friend; she will keep her word." He realized that, in the prevailing Jewish bitterness, this stand—"faith in England"—was bound to be highly unpopular; "but we are not going to renounce it : a political orientation must be built on common sense and not on impressionist moods." He firmly believed that a determined political offensive was able to change Great Britain's Palestine policy.

Anti-British feeling had been rising steadily during the two-year period between the Sixteenth and Seventeenth Zionist Congresses. It was a period of an almost unbroken chain of grave political setbacks for the Zionist cause, which reached a climax on October 20, 1930, when the British Government issued a statement of policy, known as the "Passfield White Paper." [39] This document announced the establishment of a Legislative Council in Palestine, flatly declared that there was no more land available for Jewish colonization, and stressed the need for a more stringently controlled immigration. The official Zionist leadership was not consulted before the issue of this White Paper. This was too much even for Weizmann. Simultaneously with the publication of the White Paper, he announced his resignation as President of the Zionist Organization and the Jewish Agency. Felix M. Warburg and Lord Melchett of the Jewish Agency Council followed suit.

All these developments shocked Jewish public opinion even more strongly and profoundly than did the August 1929 pogrom. The disappointment with British policy induced many to proclaim the slogan *Los von England* (Away from England), and to demand a change of the Mandatory Power. This time, too, Jabotinsky, a determined critic of long standing of the British regime in Palestine,

132

refused to join in the popular clamor. In his opening speech at the Fourth Revisionist World Conference in Prague (August, 1930), he gave eloquent expression to well-founded Jewish grievances against the Palestine Administration, which, he said, was now being called the "Hebron Government" in the same sense in which the Czarist regime in Russia used to be called the "Kishinev Government." He admitted that "under certain circumstances the presence of the British Mandatory Power in Palestine might be more harmful to the Zionist cause than its absence. . . . One of the most dangerous aspects of the present situation is the notion, which is widespread in England, that the Zionists wish Palestine to be under British control under *all* circumstances. This misleading notion must be eradicated." He nevertheless strongly opposed the demand that the Palestine Mandate be transferred at that stage from England to some other power. "It is true," he said, "that distrust of England is now prevalent among world Jewry, but we must keep calm and make a *last experiment* with England, which will have to determine whether or not she is willing to cooperate with the Jews in creating a Jewish majority. The time may come when England will lose every moral right to remain in Palestine. Should this misfortune occur, the Jewish people will not remain alone in Palestine." But for the time being it could not be claimed that the "experiment with England" had been carried out fully and expertly to the very end, for the Zionist leadership which had been responsible for its proper handling had failed pitifully. "England is less to be blamed for her present policy than the official Zionist Executive, because the latter always claimed that all was well, and never demanded adequate protection from the British Government. . . . This policy of the Zionist Executive must now be declared bankrupt and largely reponsible for many recent events." [40]

The Conference unanimously endorsed the "last experiment" concept. Most of its 122 delegates, who came from twenty countries, were looking forward to a hard but promising election campaign at the forthcoming Seventeenth Zionist Congress.

5. *South African Safari*

Four weeks after appearing before the Shaw Commission, Jabotinsky, accompanied by his wife, left by boat for, as he jokingly called it, "a month-long South African safari of Revisionist enlightenment." Such an expedition was badly needed and long overdue. In the staunchly Zionist South African Jewish community the ignorance of and prejudice against Jabotinsky and his ideas were staggering. When the wife of a prominent Jewish M.P. heard of his intention to visit the country, she said: "But surely this man will not be allowed to enter South Africa." Asked why, she answered: "You know, of course, that he is a Bolshevik. . . ." [41] There were also apprehensions that he would harm the Keren ha'Yessod fund-raising campaign.* To an inquiry whether he would be ready to lend his support to it, the reply was in the affirmative. He stressed, however, that he expected the organizers of the campaign to maintain a neutral attitude in the inner-Zionist strife and neither defend the Zionist Executive nor attack Revisionism. The conditions were not accepted, and Jabotinsky's support was not solicited. Indicative of his own mood on the eve of departure was the concluding part of a speech delivered by him at a farewell banquet in London. He hoped, Jabotinsky said, that Revisionism would succeed in fulfilling its duty in the Zionist Organization; but should it prove impossible, the Revisionists would be forced to look for better and more effective ways to serve the ideas of Herzl.[42]

Before leaving, Jabotinsky wrote to a friend: "I am going to South Africa, and it would be an exaggeration to say that I am enchanted by this prospect. Nevertheless, seventeen days of *far niente* is after all something positive." [43] He arrived in Cape Town rested and in good form and was met on board the ship by the leaders of the Jewish community. At the reception organized for him in the Zionist Hall, he warned that he was bringing with him "not peace, but the sword": "After their return from South Africa, Mr. [Nachum] Sokolov and Mr. [Alexander] Goldstein delightedly reported that peace and calm reigned in the Zionist ranks of that country, that there was no discontent, that full harmony prevailed. I am afraid that this idyll has now come to an end. I for one will do my very best to end it. I want a struggle for ideas and opinions to develop in South Africa, and I want one of the ideas to emerge victorious." [44]

* As a matter of fact, Jabotinsky postponed his trip to South Africa from February 7 to February 21, because the Zionist Executive maintained that his political campaign would have an unfavourable effect on the *Keren ha'Yessod* campaign in that country. (*J.D.N.B.*, February 27, 1930.)

There can hardly be any doubt that he succeeded in disturbing the spiritual complacency of South African Jewry. In a series of stirring lectures and speeches throughout the country (and in Rhodesia), he brought home to them for the first time the basic problems of Zionist thought and action. He could hardly claim that his ideas "emerged victorious" to the extent of "conquering" the Jewish community, but the response was friendly and encouraging. A "History of South African Zionism" sponsored by the official Zionist Federation of South Africa, stresses that:[45]

although not in agreement with the views held, the Federation extended a cordial welcome to Jabotinsky as "the redoubtable champion of the Zionist cause." And the Jewish masses throughout the country came in their thousands to hear him speak. He was an orator who held them spellbound. The fire that burned through his speeches and the eloquence of his silences, not less than the eloquence of his words and gestures, had an almost electric effect on his audience. . . . Among large sections of South African Jewry, he succeeded in arousing a sense of acute uneasiness and distrust of the (official) Zionist organization.

At one of the banquets held in his honor, Jabotinsky said that he and his wife were deeply grateful for "the atmosphere of friendliness and homeliness with which they had been surrounded; an atmosphere which had not been paralleled in any of the other communities they had ever visited." It was a privilege for him "to have fought so clean a fight with opponents so ready to accept a challenge on real issues and so proud to avow their points of agreement and disagreement. May your children be like you, perhaps better than you, in regard to Zionism, good comradeship, and loyalty to Jewry." [46]

Jabotinsky was deeply impressed by South Africa—its vastness, vitality, and promise. Travelling to Bulawayo and to the Victoria Falls he said: "If the Jewish people had been given such a country with an Administration favoring colonization—what would the Jews not have achieved in forty years." [47] After his return to Europe, he devoted two extensive, well-documented articles to South Africa's struggle for independence and to her Boer population in the *Posledniya Norosti* of Paris.[48] He met with the Prime Minister of the Union of South Africa, General Herzog, several Cabinet Ministers, and many Members of Parliament. He was particularly happy to see General Smuts again, whom he had known in London during World War I as a member of the British War Cabinet. In his *History of the Jewish Legion* he called Smuts one of the world's last knights, and "hero of two nations."

Politically, the South African trip was a noteworthy achievement. But financially it turned out to be a failure. Jabotinsky bitterly complained in letters to friends that the same people who had insistently cabled "come," had not made any serious effort to make the fundraising a success, or organize his lecture tour efficiently. They "shouldn't have let me come, knowing that the trip was bound to be a fiasco financially. . . . I get coldly mad whenever I think of it." [49]

3

ON TWO FRONTS

EIGHT

BETWEEN OPPOSITION AND INDEPENDENCE

1. *Bonus Pater Familias*

JABOTINSKY displayed little enthusiasm for active Revisionist participation in the elections to the forthcoming (Seventeenth) Zionist Congress. At a plenary session of the Revisionist World Executive in London (June, 1930), he admitted that his party was likely to register noticeable gains in the Congress elections. "But," he asked, "what for? Is it in our interest now, late in 1930, to 'conquer' the Zionist Executive? The Zionist political positions have been so undermined that even Moses would have been unable to repair them within two years. . . . My feeling is that under the present circumstances it does not pay to strive for power." Of the two possible courses—a full-steam Congress campaign or studied indifference—he favored the second.[1] From Poland, where he was on a two-month lecture tour (which was gradually assuming the character of a pre-Congress campaign), he wrote:[2] "Many will vote for us. Our Congress delegation will be an impressive one. Some groups near to us might be tempted to hand over 'power' to us, but in the final analysis they would not dare to do so. . . . The [Zionist] Executive will again be either a Weizmann executive, or—simply for lack of personalities—some concoction like Ussishkin, Sokolov, Greenbaum. I don't know which is worse, and I don't care."

Of much greater interest and concern to him was the problem of the Revisionist Union's relationship with the Zionist Organization. His original concept of the movement he founded was that it would be completely independent. But he yielded to the prevailing opinion of its co-founders that Revisionism had to be an opposition party within the general framework of the Zionist Organization, striving for the acceptance of its program by the parent body, and for decisive influence in that body's governing organs. It was to this task that he had faithfully devoted the bulk of his time and energy since 1925. Intermittently, he would give vent to his doubts as to the wisdom of this course. In October, 1926, he published in the *Rasswyet* a thought-provoking "Talk with the Devil," signed "Altalena," in which he reported how an "Envoy of the Devil" had been tempting him to forego the futile exercise of merely preaching ideas and criticising the Zionist Organization, and concentrate on independent economic and political work. "I have a hundred objections to each of his arguments," Jabotinsky cautiously commented, "but the matter is not at all simple —and is worth thinking over." [3]

He was quietly thinking it over for several years, and a conviction was ripening in his mind that independent constructive activities in all fields of the Zionist effort, and not opposition within the Zionist organization, was the only proper and dignified course to follow. He was confident that self-assertion was bound ultimately to result in full-scale independence, without hurting the feelings or convictions of those who insisted on the closest links with the Zionist Organization. He therefore refused to be hurried by those Revisionist circles which, having endorsed his "separatist" line, were pressing for drastic action.

This was the gist of his reply [March, 1928] to a message from the Central Committee of the Revisionist Party in Palestine, advocating secession from the World Zionist Organization.[4] Personally he was in full agreement with this demand. But, he insisted, "this is not the feeling of all Revisionists today : not even of one half of them. . . . In a year's time, this mood may change : but now any emphasis on the 'away from the Zionist Organization' principle would provoke a split and the secession of important colleagues. I do not consider this to be the right way. If we really succeeded in creating a party composed of people with an identical spiritual tonality, we have to wait until this specific party soul has evolved sufficiently to make it ripe for certain eventualities."

This letter—one of the many he had written on the subject—can be considered as characteristic of Jabotinsky's fundamental attitude. For many years the unity of the movement had been to him *suprema lex*. His was the approach of a *bonus pater familias*, whose paramount duty was to preserve and build up the patrimony of his movement. He had been trying, with boundless patience, to bring to a common denominator the divergent tendencies in Revisionism : first and fore-most the conflicting trends advocating, on the one hand full independence of the movement from the World Zionist Organization, and on the other hand, continued attempts to "conquer" this organiza-tion. His own position in this fateful issue was clear : he was for independence. But he was keenly aware of the fact that a great part of the movement and—what was even more important—of the leadership and the "noncoms" felt differently. With his tremendous personal authority among the rank and file, he could possibly have overcome this resistance and led the movement in his own direction. But he was not ready to use this weapon. Those firmly opposed to this course were men of courage and integrity. He knew that they would not yield to this kind of majorization but would either leave the movement or withdraw from active work.

Jabotinsky was determined not to bring things to such a point. While fully maintaining his own diagnosis and prognosis, he compromised for years with those who held a different opinion, trying to explain such compromises to those who were growing more and more insistent on immediate action and blaming him for his "delaying tactics." In his profuse personal correspondence, he time and again patiently explained his alleged dilly-dallying, asking for understanding of the paramount necessity to maintain the unity of the movement. He refused to force events artificially. Firmly believing in the soundness of his policy, he was confident that life's logic would demonstrate the inevitability of a fully independent Revisionist movement. He was therefore ready to wait. He pleaded with both his followers and his opponents within the party not to precipitate events and was always willing and eager to temporize, to respect his colleagues' sensibilities.

He therefore refrained from raising the issue of the party's independence at the Second (Paris, December, 1926) and Third (Vienna, December, 1928) Revisionist World Conferences. Shortly before the Third Conference was to convene, he reassured this writer that "there is not going to be any clash on my part with Grossman [one of his main opponents on this question] either in Vienna, or afterward, even if the Central Committee were to be transferred [from Paris, where it was under this writer's management] to London [where Grossman resided]. In my opinion, he [Grossman] is wrong; but I would rather make every concession than permit a split or a

quarrel." [5] He was ready to make these concessions in all organizational matters and formal pronouncements of the party. His own
attitude, however, remained unshaken. On May 30, 1929, he wrote
to this writer: "I cannot remain in opposition to anybody, and I
don't understand those who can. I know that the party is growing,
and this is a great achievement of yours and Grossman's. But if this
party is such as you describe it, if even the [inclusion of a non-Zionist
'fifty' into the] Agency will not induce it to see itself as the successor
to the Zionist Organization, then I am afraid that here, too, I am as
much of a stranger as in the Zionist Organization." Nevertheless, he
promised: "Don't be afraid of a conflict at the [forthcoming Fourth
Revisionist World] Conference; if I see that the more important of
our colleagues are in favor of the old course, I won't fight."

In spite of the far-reaching divergence of views, Jabotinsky wholeheartedly agreed (at the Sixteenth Zionist Congress in Zurich, August,
1929) to the transfer of Revisionist world headquarters to London,
where Grossman and other firm opponents of the idea of Revisionist
independence (Y. M. Machover, Dr. M. Schwarzman, A. Angel, and
others) were in charge. Only the Revisionist press remained in Paris.
"The *Rasswyet*, of course continues here," he reported from Paris.
The *Naier Weg* (a new Revisionist organ in Yiddish) will be published
weekly in Paris. The chief-editor of both is Schechtman; co-editors
for the *Rasswyet*—[Michael] Berchin, for the *Naier Weg*—[Issaiya]
Klinov." [6] Jabotinsky was firmly determined not to upset this
laboriously erected organizational structure. Early in 1930, he wrote
to Jacobi: [7] " . . . I will not let the [Revisionist] Union fall apart. . . .
Should I see that 'secession' [from the Zionist Organization] is going
to lead to the loss of, or even only to passivism on the part of a large
section of the Union or of some of its founders, I would prefer to
yield. It is impossible to start building the party anew—I am too old
for that." Searching for some compromise solution, he carefully
explained that he was "insisting not so much on 'secession' (that's
why the word is put in inverted commas) as on the creation of some
sort of independent concern, such as 'Independent Zionist Organization' or 'Jewish Commonwealth League.' Those of us who want to
remain in the Zionist Organization and continue the struggle to drain
that swamp, could keep on indulging in that sport, could participate
in the [Zionist] Congress elections, and form [Revisionist] factions, at
Congresses provided, of course, they accept the primacy of our

[Revisionist] discipline. This is incoherent, but compromises are always incoherent. . . . So far as I personally am concerned, I shall, of course, 'secede' if we do not conquer the Zionist Organization this time. This does not mean that I shall secede formally. . . . I shall simply demand that my colleagues do not put up my candidacy at the Congress elections, nor expect my support in Congress matters."

At the Fourth Revisionist World Conference (Prague, August, 1930), Jabotinsky unexpectedly initiated a spirited discussion on "independence" at a closed night session on August 15. He argued that there was little chance of "conquering" the World Zionist Organization, because Revisionism is in its essence not only a political party and a *Weltanschauung* [philosophy], but, above all, a "psychological race," a definite inborn mentality, which can hardly be communicated to those who do not possess it inherently. The mission of the Revisionist movement is therefore to look for people of its own "race," to organize them for constructive achievements, and not to waste its energies in attempts to "conquer" a Zionist crowd with a different outlook. Grossman, for his part, saw in this "racial" self-isolation the manifestation of an "inferiority complex." The debate took an impassioned, sometimes acrimonious character. There was, in fact, little valid motive for such a discussion. The prevailing mood at the Conference, even among those who usually advocated moderation in regard to the official Zionist Organization, was already a very belligerent one. Many felt that the night debate provoked by Jabotinsky had hardly contributed to the strengthening of this tendency and had rather sharpened the controversy within the movement.

Jabotinsky himself was, however, satisfied with the proceedings and the results of the Prague gathering. His faith that things were going his way remained unshakable. A few months after Prague, in a letter to a staunch advocate of secession, he explained that he was doing all this manoeuvering only because he wanted to give those internal trends a chance to develop and thus "preserve the unity of the nucleus of the party." He felt that the trend he was interested in was "ripening by itself." Admitting that "delays were harmful," he contended that "a split would have been more disastrous." He would, of course, "ruthlessly revise this strategy" if he had felt that "on some paramount issue there was not even a subconscious unity in that 'nucleus,' so that there was nothing to wait for, nothing to 'ripen!' But I know our movement and I am confident as to how it will evolve." He therefore

143

begged those who felt as he did, to help him by bringing the same sacrifice of forebearance that he was bringing, in the endeavour to adapt "the long-legged to the short-legged." [8]

2. *Inner-Party Struggle*

Dr. Weizmann's utterance at the meeting of the Zionist Actions Committee in Berlin on August 27, 1930, played a considerable role in the intensification of Jabotinsky's insistence on clarifying the Revisionist relationship with the Zionist Organization. Weizmann said: "The Jewish State was never an aim in itself, it was only a means to an end. Nothing is said about the Jewish State in the Basle program, nor in the Balfour Declaration. The essence of Zionism is to create a number of important material foundations, upon which an autonomous, compact, and productive community can be built." [9] This repudiation of the Jewish State aim by the President of the Zionist Organization provoked a great stir in Zionist public opinion. To Jabotinsky it was tantamount to renunciation of the very essence of the Zionist creed. "Even our Zionist world has not as yet seen so disgusting a performance as this session of the Actions Committee," he wrote to Dr. Eugene Soskin.[10] "I have now decided, as a mere publicist, to start direct and open propaganda for an independent Zionist Organization. For Heaven's sake, consider the situation. What are we counting on? It is not Weizmann that bothers me . . . it is the entire Zionist crowd, which is afraid to oust him in a moment of most vehement indignation." Pursuing this line, he urged that the Revisionist members resign from the Actions Committee "unless its next session takes steps amounting to a rejection of Weizmann's Berlin speech. . . . Everything must be prepared for the eventuality that we may be compelled to leave the forthcoming Seventeenth Zionist Congress and continue as the Constituent Assembly of the Independent Zionist Organization." [11]

In this he met with determined opposition on the part of the London branch of the Revisionist World Executive which, since August, 1929, was in charge of the entire central machinery of the world movement. It thoroughly disagreed with the line urged by Jabotinsky and used its authority in the direction of a policy contrary to that advocated by him. Jabotinsky felt that his opinions and wishes were being systematically disregarded by his London colleagues, and repeatedly complained of this state of affairs to Machover. The latter, though a "Londoner" by conviction, was an old friend whom Jabotinsky considered capable of exercising a conciliatory influence.

He wrote in one of the letters (from Paris): "I am compelled to speak of myself. I am in a very difficult predicament. People have the impression (I was told so in Poland, too) that I am now 'in disgrace,' and that the policy, which the movement is conducting, is in open disregard of my point of view. I consider my capability for work—and even, if you will pardon me, my prestige—as elements of the Revisionist assets. Both are being undermined." And in another letter: "I don't believe in my 'leadership' and don't want it. I truly and deeply love to work with men who have a will and mind of their own, and to forge a common line of action on the basis of mutual concessions. But it is quite a different matter to feel that my views (and not only mine) are simply being disregarded." [12]

For a time, the showdown between Jabotinsky (backed by the Paris members of the Revisionist World Executive) and the London group (Grossman—Machover—Angel, backed by Lichtheim, Soskin, and Stricker) was averted by both sides accepting Lichtheim's proposal to postpone the question of Revisionist post-Congress strategy until after the Congress elections. But Jabotinsky insisted that this issue had to be taken up *before* the Congress convened. On March 10, 1931, he wrote to Machover:

I have for years been toiling hard in the distasteful harness of "opposition." To me, the Seventeenth Congress is, for objective reasons, the last experiment, and should it, too, miscarry, I shall not agree to remain as a minority in the Zionist Organization. . . . This is irrevocable. . . . Please find some compromise. If there is none, I think we should no longer fool the people. I am not at all delighted at the prospect of going to Congress for two weeks of mud-slinging, and ending up with a split in our own ranks . . . .

I don't think that anybody could accuse me of inventing problems, of dragooning people into accepting my views. But when I demand that a certain issue be *put on the agenda* now regardless of the *outcome*, this must be done. . . . I am compelled to insist that the question what we will do in case we are unsuccessful at the Congress, should be discussed by the leadership—confidentially of course—during the next few days; if we find a formula for agreement, well and good. If not, we will consider ways and means of bringing about a painless separation.

145

The Grossman—Lichtheim group, however, assumed a rather belligerent stand in regard to Jabotinsky's position and was unwilling to temporize. In a long letter to Lichtheim, dated March 20, Jabotinsky tried to assess the new situation soberly :

I accepted *your* suggestion to postpone the issue until after the elections, but now you yourself are dropping it, and Grossman wants a *Kraftprobe.* . . . He writes to me—"I want to fight it out, to force the issue." He says that the system of conciliating or bridging dissensions in our midst is no good; it's got to be either his line, or the other. . . . Very well, only to me *Kraftprobe* is not *Parteirat* nor a Conference. I have not the slightest interest in exploring which side has a majority, though I am perfectly sure that the majority would follow me. What interests me is one question only: can we find a compromise? As long as I believed that there was a desire on both sides to find a compromise, I went on playing a game which I hate and detest (yelling all over Poland that we must go to Congress and conquer the Z.O.—all against my innermost convictions). But now it looks as if a portion of our most influential members reject the compromise idea on principle. That means that, whatever the "majority," a certain minority will have to secede. If so, I don't care a damn for staging such a bit of *Nachass* in the form of a solemn gathering, *Parteirat* or Conference; even less for an oratorical duel with Grossman whose polemic style I don't admire. *Das kann ich haben naher und billiger* (*This* I can have closer and cheaper). If there is to be a break in any case, I prefer that it should start at once, and that I at least be spared the expenditure of energy, and the wear and tear of a Congress campaign. . . .

There's no need to tell you how bitter it is for me to see Revisionism break up, but I prefer to go the right way with half the movement, or a third, or even a dozen people than finish my Zionist days as the "opposition" to a crowd of spiritual bastards calling themselves the Z.O., a crowd I coldly and infinitely despise. Sorry, but there you are.

A few days later, he wrote to both Lichtheim and Machover that he and other Paris members of the Revisionist World Executive had accepted Grossman's proposal to hold a plenary session of the Executive on April 5 and 6 half-way between London and Paris, in the small seaport town of Boulogne on the English Channel.[18]

According to this writer's recollection, the Boulogne meeting—at least in its initial stages—was anything but harmonious. Most of its deliberations belong to the history of the Revisionist movement. For the purposes of this biography, it is sufficient to state that, after a long and acrimonious discussion, Jabotinsky had his way in the main

146

controversial issue. An agreement was reached and signed, stipulating, among other things, that should the forthcoming Seventeenth Zionist Congress fail to adopt a resolution proclaiming the Jewish majority in Palestine as the aim of Zionism, the Revisionist World Executive as a whole undertakes to propose the secession of the Revisionist Union from the Zionist Organization.[14]

Having secured the post-Congress clause, which he considered morally and politically mandatory, Jabotinsky unreservedly threw himself into the election campaign for the Congress. The Boulogne meeting ended on April 6, and by April 15 he was in Danzig, and spent the five weeks that followed in hectic electioneering all over Eastern and Central Europe. The outcome of the elections was very satisfactory for his party. While at the Sixteenth Congress the Revisionits had twenty-one delegates, representing eighteen thousand votes, they came to the Seventeenth with a delegation of fifty-two, which represented 55,848 Zionists, and with 21 per cent of the entire Congress, appeared as the third-strongest faction. Particularly encouraging were the results among the Jewish masses of Poland, where his list obtained 29,985 votes as against 4,229 in 1929. Introducing an autobiographical note in his attempt to appraise "The Meaning of the Congress Election," Jabotinsky confessed that the Zionist voters in Poland had given him "a lesson, a reminder, a piece of wisdom : during the long years of struggle for the regeneration of Zionism, I had almost completely lost faith in the Jewish masses; one [Congress] election after another—1925, 1927, 1929—proved to me that it was useless to speak to them. I see now that I was wrong. I am glad to acknowledge my mistake. Of course, what happened in the Polish elections is by far not enough to save Zionism. But it is proof that the gulf between the 'psychological races,' about which I wrote recently, is not at all so wide, that the average Jew still possesses common sense, logic, courage to acknowledge a mistake and to demand a radical change." [15]

3. The Seventeenth Congress

As usual, Jabotinsky's address was eagerly awaited by delegates and guests. It constituted the highlight of the Congress. Unlike his speeches at the previous Congresses, which covered a wide variety of subjects, this one was devoted largely to the necessity of clarifying and openly stating the *Endziel* (ultimate goal) of Zionism.[16] This aim, he said,

147

had been "generally expressed in three different terms: a Home guaranteed by public law (as formulated in the Basle Program), National Home, and Jewish State." None of them, Jabotinsky insisted, possessed the necessary precision. The first:

has no legal standing, and therefore admits of various interpretations . . . it was adopted [by the First Zionist Congress in 1897] for the very reason that it was nebulous, and could be expected not to irritate the Sultan of Turkey. The term "National Home" is also not clear. This is apparent from the many arguments about its exact significance. It, too, has no legal tradition. The expression "State" is the most precise of them all. But even the word "State" has various meanings in political usage. It is never quiet clear whether it designates complete independence or not. France is a State within the meaning of complete independence. But Illinois or Kentucky are states, too, and yet merely parts of a State. As to the idea of majority the word State does not give a reply either. South Africa, for example, is the State of the Boers and the British, and yet these do not form the majority of the population. . . . The essence of the term "Jewish State" is determined by the following two factors:

(1) An ethnic majority of the Jewish element in the population of the land; and (2) self-Government. This second factor is rather elastic. If we had today a Jewish country with a preponderantly Jewish population, but occupied by another power, we could certainly combat this power, but Zionism would not exist. For the Jews of that country would be in the same position as many normal nations already living in their own country. . . . But one factor is not elastic. It exists or it does not, and that is—numerical majority. . . .

A National Home is a country in which the people whose National Home it is, constitute the majority of the population. This is not the ultimate aim of Zionism. One million Jews would suffice today to create a majority in Palestine. This, however, is not the limit of our hopes. We want a Home for all the suffering Jews, and nobody can predict how many Jews there will be who will suffer during the next few generations. But the immediate aim of the practical Zionist effort must be the creation of a majority. . . .

I may be asked why we have to proclaim our interpretation aloud. It must be stated, because it is the only legal basis for our demand for large-scale immigration. My friends and my opponents keep looking in vain for a passage in the Mandate which specifically mentions our right to large-scale and rapid immigration. Our adversaries are making use of this. The only legal basis for our right to demand mass immigration is that the expression "National Home" means Jewish majority. I would advise you not to renounce that basis, for the enemies of Zionism assert that a minority could also create a National Home, and that a small immigration would suffice for it. If you want a legal basis for large-scale immigration, you must insist on this interpretation.

The second reason is that the *elan* of the Zionist movement has decreased. This is apparent in all countries. There are few new adherents to pure Zionism: Zionism has lost its spell over the Jewish soul. There are parties that have filled this gap with other things, things which may be good in themselves, but are not Zionism. Purely Zionist enthusiasm is in danger of disappearing, and we must proclaim that the aim of Zionism is in reality the solution of the Jewish problem and the creation of what is called the Jewish State.

And another thing: truth has a purifying effect. Are we not all tired, are we not all nauseated by the eternal evasion? It has became a political necessity to clean the atmosphere, and this can be done by telling the truth. Why should we allow the term "Jewish State" to be called extremism? The Albanians have their State, the Bulgarians have their State; a State is, after all, the normal condition of a people. If the Jewish State were in existence today, nobody would say that it is abnormal. And if we want to normalize our existence, who dare to call it extremism —and are we ourselves expected to say so? . . .

But there is also another question, that of the area of the territory to be colonized. . . . My formula may be subject to alteration; instead of "on both sides of the Jordan," you may say "the historic frontiers at the time of King David," or "at the time of the twelve tribes," or "colonization in the whole of the mandated territory"—but the formula must deal with both sides of a certain river. However, do not modify the other part of this formula; simply say: majority. The resolution reads as follows:

The aim of Zionism, expressed in the terms "Jewish State," "National Home," or "a Homestead guaranteed by public law," is the creation of a Jewish majority in Palestine on both sides of the Jordan.

In conclusion, Jabotinsky said, he felt the urge to voice "an optimistic confession of faith." Everyone is deeply shocked by England's anti-Zionist policy. The main poser is: how could such state of affairs have come about? Was it "fated to be so and would it have come to this even with better methods [of Zionist policy] and under better [Zionist] leadership? Could it be that nothing could have helped us because fate and the objective factors of world politics wanted it so? Or could our own errors have been responsible?"

Of these two conceptions, one is deeply pessimistic: if it were true that the best of methods would have been of no avail, every hope is lost. But

149

if we can assert that even under present circumstances better methods would have produced better results, then there is some hope left. The real optimists are those of us who say: our policy is responsible for it [the present state of affairs]. It is this policy, expressed in innumerable speeches, that has convinced the British people that the political situation is satisfactory. What we now want is to embark on a new and final experiment, but with different methods. I think I am entitled to say, perhaps on behalf of the whole of Congress, that the Jewish attitude in these questions is unshakably optimistic.

Before the Jews admit that the whole world is against us, that one of the greatest among the civilized nations is devoid of honesty, that even the Lord has averted His face from us—before we say that, it would be more honest to say *Ashamti, bagad'ti* (I have sinned, I have betrayed) and to change our methods and our system. . . . And as naively as those who foregathered in Basle many years ago when I was still a boy, so naively do I now believe in the honesty of the world and the power of a just cause: I believe that great problems are decided by the powerful influence of moral pressure, and that the Jewish people is a tremendous factor of moral pressure. Accept it or not—it is my, and our, Confession of Faith: *Ani maamin* (I believe!).

Jabotinsky's address once again made a strong impression on the Congress. His demand for a clear and definite statement that a Jewish majority in a Jewish State was the aim of Zionism was rendered particularly timely when, during the Congress, Weizmann found it necessary to say, in an interview granted to the director of the Jewish Telegraphic Agency: "I have no understanding of, and no sympathy for a Jewish majority in Palestine." [17] Robert Stricker read this statement out to the Congress.[18] It created a deep impression amongst all groups, and it was Chaim Arlosoroff of the Labor wing who demanded of Weizmann an authoritative explanation of this interview which, he said, "if correctly quoted, is in its essence wrong and politically harmful." [19] The explanation given by Weizmann was dealt with in the Political Committee of the Congress, on whose behalf Nachum Goldmann submitted to the *plenum* the following resolution: "The Congress regrets the views expressed by Weizmann in his interview with the J.T.A., and regards his reply to the interpolation as unsatisfactory." [20] This resolution amounted to a vote of no confidence on a major ideological-political issue. Its acceptance by a substantial majority precluded Weizmann's reelection to the Presidency of the World Zionist Organization.

Dr. Weizmann took his defeat manfully. Always appreciative of good sportsmanship, Jabotinsky sent Mrs. Weizmann an affectionate short note (in Russian), the original of which this writer saw in the Weizmann Archives at Rehovot: "You and Chaim Yevserovitch behaved bravely. I am proud of my old friends." For some reason the Weizmanns felt hurt by this friendly note and Mrs. Weizmann wrote back: "Thanks for the condolences: we are not dead yet." [21]

According to parliamentary tradition and sound political logic, Dr. Weizmann's defeat should have brought in its wake a) the acceptance of Jabotinsky's resolution and b) his election as the new President of the Zionist Organization. This was, curiously enough, the conclusion reached by Weizmann himself and by some of his main supporters. In an exclusive interview granted to Jacob Landau, the director of the Jewish Telegraphic Agency, Dr. Weizmann praised Jabotinsky as a man of great ability and quality, who had the courage of his convictions. "I hope," Weizmann said, "that Jabotinsky will be my successor. Because, at any rate, he is an open opponent and I prefer him to some of the others who declare themselves to be my friends, but are ready to stab me in the back." [22] * In fact, on one occasion he said that much to Jabotinsky himself. On July 3, during a speech by Stephen Wise, who fiercely attacked Weizmann's policy, the latter walked over to Jabotinsky who was sitting in the first row of the Congress hall, and sat down at his side. Joseph Klarman, who was Jabotinsky's neighbor on the other side, recalls Weizmann's suggestion that Jabotinsky use his influence with Wise and induce him to withdraw some of his sharper expressions. To this Jabotinsky answered: "Dr. Wise is not a member of our [Revisionist] delegation. His speech was not inspired by me, although he undoubtedly gave expression to feelings which were shared by all of us while listening to your defense of England. Of course, the tone of his speech was sharp, and its form and manner were different from those acceptable to me. In my view, facts are more powerful than the strongest attack. But apparently Rabbi Wise feels differently. I regret it, but I am not responsible for him." After a somewhat awkward pause, Weizmann said: "I believe that *you are now the only one* in the Zionist move-

* This part of the interview was, however, not published at the time. Jacob Landau later disclosed that when he submitted the full text of the interview to Weizmann for approval, the latter crossed out these few lines as could still be seen in the original in Landau's possession. The story of this interview was told in Jacob Landau's "Iberlebungen un Bagegenishen", *Der Tag,* October 13, 1951.

ment qualified to become President of the World Zionist Organization." "Thanks for the compliment," was the answer; "I regret I am unable to reciprocate." [23]

The view that it was Jabotinsky who should replace Weizmann was also held by David Eder, who headed the English delegation to Congress and was a staunch supporter of Weizmann. According to his biographer, "Eder took the view that, Dr. Weizmann having been defeated, the Opposition—in other words Jabotinsky and his friends—should come in. . . . His advice was not accepted. . . . The Congress closed with Dr. Weizmann out of the office, it closed nevertheless, without having committed itself to any change of policy or, indeed, to any clear policy at all." [24]

In fact, by a roll-call majority of 121 against 57, the Congress decided not to put Jabotinsky's resolution to the vote, thus implicitly refusing to take any stand.[25] This decision provoked a violent reaction among the delegates and the guests. According to the official *Protokoll*, it was followed by "tumultuous applause and violent cries of 'shame.' "

Grossman tried to make a statement on behalf of the Revisionist delegation, but the Labor wing refused to give him a hearing and shouted him down by singing Hebrew songs and *Hatiqva,* thus forcing all the delegates to stand up (Jabotinsky and the Mizrachi leader Heshel Farbstein were the only ones to remain seated). Chairman Motzkin entreated the Labor delegates to stop the disturbance, reminding them that this is "a Zionist Congress." "This is not a Zionist Congress any longer," heatedly retorted Dr. Oscar Rabinowicz, a Revisionist delegate from Czechoslovakia. Holding on to Rabinowicz's shoulder and supported by the six-footer Joseph Klarman from Poland, Jabotinsky climbed upon a chair and exclaimed: "This is *not* a Zionist Congress any more," took his delegate card out of his pocket, tore it to shreds, and scattered the pieces among the labor delegates. His opponents lunged menacingly toward him, while other delegates and Revisionist youth formed a protective chain around him. At two fifteen a.m. the Congress broke up in disorder, Jabotinsky being borne shoulder high by his followers. Stephen Wise later called this episode "the most dramatic scene of the Congress." [26] Next day, the Revisionist delegates returned to the Congress hall, with the exception of Jabotinsky himself, who until the very end of Congress, did not attend its sessions again.

Then arose the question of electing a new leadership of the World

Zionist Organization. There were strong expectations in the Congress lobbies that, with Weizmann and his policy defeated, Jabotinsky would be the natural candidate for the presidency. These expectations proved to be wrong. The forces that had brought about Weizmann's downfall, were not ready to draw the consequences from the situation created by their action. It was not Jabotinsky but Nachum Sokolov who emerged as Weizmann's successor.

Evidence as to Jabotinsky's personal stand in regard to the prospect of his being elected to the Presidency of the Zionist Organization is contradictory. Abraham Tulin, one of the leaders of the American delegation, who was very friendly with Jabotinsky, asserts that the latter "fell victim to his ingrained passion for absolute logic. . . . He reasoned logically that with Weizmann's fall, he, Jabotinsky, as leader of the opposition, should be called to take the helm. I spent many hours in an effort to convince him that his logic wouldn't work in the situation as it actually was and tried to persuade him to accept a place or places on the Executive and someone else's nominal leadership until the next Congress. Jabotinsky, however, was adamant: it was to be the leadership or nothing. . . ." [27] Ignaz Schwarzbard gives a different picture. As Chairman of the World Union of General Zionists, he had a number of discussions with Jabotinsky on the situation which had been created: "I remember my conversation with Jabotinsky at that time. He viewed the situation soberly, and not for a moment did he entertain the idea that the plan to push him for the Presidency would come off." [28]

This writer's personal recollection bears out Schwarzbard's testimony. Nor did Meir Grossman ever hear from Jabotinsky that presidency of the Zionist Organization was his goal at the Congress. [29] He was, of course, firmly convinced that after Weizmann's removal, he was "logically" the indicated President of the Zionist Organization. But he did not try to prevent the Revisionist delegation from securing by their fifty-one votes (Jabotinsky himself did not vote) Sokolov's election. Their reasons for doing so were correctly interpreted by Weizmann: [30] "It was, I think, the feeling of my opponents that pliability of Sokolov would make it easier for them to give the movement the direction they had in mind." Oscar Rabinowicz, who was the Revisionist representative on the Standing Committee, asked Jabotinsky for his guidance with regard to the stand he should take on the question of the new Executive. The answer was:

153

"Do not discuss personalities, press for a statement of policy." When Sokolov was nominated, Rabinowicz again asked for instructions, and the answer again was: "Press for a program to be submitted by Sokolov to Congress, only then will we be ready to state our position." [31]

4. *The Calais Compromise*

Shortly after the Congress, Jabotinsky published a statement in which he said: "From the moment when Congress rejected the Jewish State resolution and I tore up my delegate card, I did not enter the meeting hall." Stressing that "the Revisionist position at this Congress had been firm and sound," he insisted that the time had come for the Revisionists to decide what was to be done now. "We all agree that the political activities of the Revisionist Union must continue on the basis of full independence, and the issue before us is whether we have to convert the Union into a New Zionist Organzation." A special issue of the *Rasswyet* appeared on August 30, devoted exclusively to the question of secession from the Zionist Organization. Most of the articles, although signed by Z. Tiomkin, M. Berchin and others, had been written by Jabotinsky. When this writer suggested that he would forego this privilege and tackle the topic assigned to him by himself, Jabotinsky asked: "What's wrong about signing an article written by me?" The answer was a quotation from a French poet: *"Mon verre n'est pas grand, mais je bois dans mon verre"* (My glass is not big, but I drink from my glass). "Go on and drink," Jabotinsky smilingly approved.

However, his mood in the months immediately following the Congress was anything but cheerful. His stand met with determined and ever stiffening resistance on the part of some of his colleagues on the Revisionist World Executive. In the hope of lessening the tension, Jabotinsky even resorted to the unusual step of taking a "leave of absence" as President of the Revisionist World Union. Evoking Homer's *Iliad,* a *Jewish Chronicle* editorial writer was reminded of "Achilles, who for the time being still slumbers in his tent." [32] The Revisionist Head Office in the meantime remained in London under the control of Grossman. Jabotinsky expected that his temporary retirement "would help both camps to reach an agreement." This experiment failed to produce the expected results. In a very official letter, addressed to "Mr. M. Grossman, Vice President U.Z.R.," Jabotinsky wrote on September 6, 1931: "I beg to state that. . . . I am resuming from today my functions as President of the Union." The purpose of this change of mind, he explained, was "to prevent the debate about our connection with the Zionist Organization from degenerating into strife and a split." He was distressed to see that this debate was being conducted in quite a contrary spirit, "culminating in direct suggestions to speed up the split, and make certain persons and groups leave the Union, while no effort is being made, it seems, to counteract such disruptive aberrations. Under these conditions, it is the duty of the President to step in and remind all concerned that the object of the present debate is to attain unity." He warned, however, that this aim was not identical with the "upholding of the *status quo* which, as everybody must see, is no longer conducive to unity."

In the correspondence he had been conducting with the leading opponents of his views, Jabotinsky made ample use of the *argumentum ad hominem*. We read in a letter to Lichtheim:[33] "I cherished the hope that friends like you and Grossman, whom I had followed for years against my own political conscience, would now give *me* a couple of years' credit and follow me, and see whether my way is not perhaps the right one. I am sorry that this credit has been refused." And in a letter to Israel Rosov:[34] "There is one thing I resent. I have for so many years followed my colleagues, honestly doing my job that I did not believe in and disliked—the conquest of the Zionist Organization. What I now ask is that they should follow me for two or three years, honestly doing what they dislike, and then we shall see what the sum total is; but they refuse. They prefer to lose me rather than make such an experiment, or they are ready to go away themselves. I will remember this experience." These personal approaches, which in the past used to be very effective, somehow fell flat in this particular case.

There was, of course, the unanimous decision of the April meeting at Boulogne, to propose secesssion should the Zionist Congress reject a Jewish State resolution. In a letter to Machover, Jabotinsky tried to "collect" on this undertaking and asked for suggestions, "in what form the Boulogne agreement should be carried out." But he apparently realized that it would be unpractical to demand his full "pound of flesh" on the basis of Boulogne. He therefore stressed that

he "would particularly appreciate suggestions in the nature of an
Ausgleich (compromise)." [35] And he almost frantically sought such a
compromise. This internal conflict, he wrote to Litchtheim, "may
prove to be the beginning of the end of my work and my career as a
public figure," and finished on a personal note: "whatever may
happen, I shall never forget our association and the joy and pride I
took in it." [36] Mentioning in a letter to Israel Rosov that he had
dispatched a long epistle to Grossman, he assured him that "no
'whispering' will divorce me from him personally: should anybody
tell me something unworthy about him or about you, I would simply
refuse to believe it." [37] Nevertheless, "whisperings" about a personal
conflict between Grossman and Jabotinsky continued unabated.

On September 3, 1931, Grossman published a statement categorically denying "sensational reports" on "the controversy which is
proceeding within the Revisionist Union regarding our future
relations with the Zionist Organization." The concluding part of the
statement read: "I particularly desire to say that there is no truth
in any suggestion that Mr. Jabotinsky has been kept from effective
leadership of the party. No single member of the Executive
Committee has called into question Mr. Jabotinsky's position as
leader, nor is there any personal animosity or rivalry on the part of
any of the Executive Committee." [38]

It would be tedious, and irrelevant for the purpose of this
biography, to record all the preparatory stages of the plenary session
of the Revisionist World Executive, which met on September 28 and
29, this time at Calais, another small French seaport on the Straits
of Dover, half-way between Paris and London. The discussion was,
as at Boulogne, tense, and at different stages plainly acrimonious.
More than once it seemed that no agreement was possible. Finally,
however, as the official communiqué put it, "complete unanimity was
reached on all outstanding questions." It was agreed that at the
forthcoming Revisionist World Conference, members of the Executive
would advocate "a homogeneous Union of Zionist Revisionists,"
whose members shall "accept the program of the Union and be subject
to the Union's discipline." "A section of the membership will be non-
Shekel payers," and thus not members of the World Zionist Organization. On the other hand, it was agreed that the question of establishing
the "Independent Zionist Organization" should not be raised. [39]

In articles, private correspondence, and personal conversations,

Jabotinsky unreservedly praised the outcome of the Calais meeting.[40] He insisted, that it was dictated by the very "logic of life" and that no other conclusions could have been reached without a split. As against this, zealots of complete and immediate secession of the Revisionist movement from the Zionist Organization denied that the Calais agreement signified any real progress in the direction they and Jabotinsky had advocated, and bitterly criticized his yielding to the "moderates," claiming that Jabotinsky's prestige among the youth had suffered considerably because of his "inconsistency." Jabotinsky's letters to one of the most outspoken critics of his strategy, contain a spirited defense of the Calais decisions as an important step in the right direction:[41] "It is as yet *not* the New Zionist Organization, but the (Revisionist) Union is no longer a part of the Zionist Organization, and it would be ridiculous to deny that this is a step forward. Insofar as there will be shekel payers in our midst, their Zonist activities will be carried on not on behalf of the Union as such, but in the name of the 'Revisionist delegation in the Actions Committee.' This is a concession to us; in return, there are concessions to 'them.' *These* concessions are embarrassing; but it would have been even more embarrassing to split the Union, whose members think identically on *all* problems. . . . I will never give up my approach of a *bonus pater familias* [in the Russian original: *'careful baleboss'*], who refuses to forsake valuables as long as there is a possibility of preserving them without *shmad*. As long as I see a moral possibility of concessions, which will preserve our machinery intact, I am opposed to the system of no concessions. Such a system has to be applied only when one intends to get rid of the other partner. If you intend to keep him, you cannot act in this manner. . . . I know," he humbly admitted, "that my prestige has dwindled. When I was about to leave for Congress, I knew that I was bound to bury my good name in Basle. Since I consider my prestige an essential part of the party stock, I regret it. Should I not succeed in settling our party affairs, I will admit my inadequacy and become a private in the ranks. For the time being, all I wanted was that the [Revisionist] Union should become independent. This I did achieve. If because of this my prestige has dwindled even more, then the crux of the matter is to be sought not in my action, but in the fact that there comes a time even for an Aristide when the people just get tired of him, and every step he takes, no matter how reasonable, annoys everybody."

NINE

THE BIG SPLIT

1. *Mend or End*

THE Calais agreement was concluded by Jabotinsky and his opponents as an expedient way out of an internal party conflict. The gist of it was that a Revisionist, while subject to the World Union's discipline, was free to belong or not to belong to the Zionist Organization. This looked like a convenient and logical settlement of an internal Revisionist controversy. Its authors, however, overlooked, or underestimated, the possible reaction of the official leadership of the Zionist Organization. On December 7, 1931, the Zionist Executive published a strongly worded statement to the effect that "membership in the Zionist Organization . . . is incompatible with membership of an outside body requiring acceptance of a discipline which may conflict with and take precedence over the duty of allegiance to the Zionist Organization." It vaguely but meaningfully referred to "the consequences which would have to follow upon the realization of the Calais resolutions." [1] The stern attitude of the Zionist Executive was bluntly formulated by one of its members, the late Dr. Chaim Arlosoroff. Speaking before the *Assefat Hanivcharim*, he described these resolutions as a "declaration of split loyalties . . . nothing short of secession," and concluded: "To the Revisionists it means a clear alternative of mending or ending." [2]

This alternative revived and accentuated the post-Calais controversy in leading Revisionist circles. Shortly after Dr. Arlosoroff's ultimatum, those of Jabotinsky's followers and colleagues who were dead set against any prospect of "ending," started their offensive. At the national conference of the Palestinian Revisionists, the "moderates" refused to participate in the newly elected Central

Committee because the Conference ratified the Calais agreement. Commenting on this move, Jabotinsky wrote to one of the "moderates": "I have declared a hundred times that to demand that the [Revisionist] Union remain a part of the Zionist Organization, means to invite me to leave the Union." [3] He was even more disturbed when, two months later, he received a letter from Lichtheim bluntly demanding the abrogation of the Calais agreement; all the efforts of the Revisionist Union were to be concentrated on gaining control of the Zionist Organization.

Characteristically enough, Jabotinsky did not reject such a demand *in limine*. Instead, in a long letter, he queried several points which he wanted answered in order to "understand rightly" Lichtheim's stand. The first question was: is the goal of gaining control of the Zionist Organization "limited or unlimited in time?" Some friends, he explained, expected him to make one more attempt in this direction, and to concentrate all the energies of the movement on "conquering" the forthcoming Eighteenth Zionist Congress with the proviso that "should this attempt fail, then *schluss*, and we shall all build a New Zionist Organization." "Theoretically speaking," he added, "this time limit could be prolonged, until the Nineteenth Congress, or for five years, and so on. . . . I am not talking of the number of years, I am merely asking: in *your* concept, does this business have any time limit within sight." The second question was not less direct: what does "conquering" mean? "Does it imply obtaining the majority of seats in the Zionist Executive? Or is a fifty-fifty ratio sufficient? Or just a few seats? Or is it a matter of program? If the latter, which points of the Revisionist program should be considered as *conditio sine qua non*?" With regard to the Calais agreement, Jabotinsky reminded Lichtheim that its abrogation "would render illegal our claim to independent political action" and asked: "Do you think that such political activity should still be continued despite our remaining in the Zionist Organization, or should it be stopped?"

Jabotinsky begged Lichtheim to believe that he was "not putting these queries as a kind of veiled polemic," but with the sincere intention of "grasping the ultimate trend" of the latter's thoughts: "just imagine that we are having a friendly chat and that I am asking all this *viva voce*." [4]

2. One to Four

It was in this strained atmosphere that Jabotinsky opened the Fifth Revisionist World Conference on August 28, 1932. His inaugural address was devoted to major political problems of Zionism. Reflecting the growing anti-British trend in the Revisionist ranks, he did not mince words in castigating the anti-Zionist policy of the Mandatory Power.[5]

The Balfour Declaration is degenerating into an anti-Zionist document. Jerusalem is becoming the center of the pan-Islamic movement. In Jewish eyes, England's policy has deprived her of the right to continue as Mandatory; she is gradually losing this right in the eyes of the world as well. . . . Some people still hope that England will be compelled to change her policy radically.Others are convinced that out alliance with England has come to an end. The present Mandate had become unlawful, and this has to be stated before the public opinion of the world.

As a manifestation of this "away from England" trend, the Conference decided "to transfer the seat of the Revisionist World Executive from London to Geneva by February 1, 1933, at the latest, until which time three [out of the five] members of the Executive will have taken up permanent residence in Geneva."[6] Jabotinsky was supposed to be among the three Geneva members. This, of course, implied the continuation and expansion of independent Revisionist political activity. The Conference decided that after the transfer to Geneva, a "vast Jewish Petition Movement" was to be initiated, and a Political Office of the Executive was to be established in Palestine.

At the Conference there was—for the first time since the emergence of the Revisionist movement—considerable open opposition to Jabotinsky's middle-of-the-road policy of compromise with those advocating the continuation of the Revisionist ties with the Zionist Organization. Spokesmen of this group demanded a complete break and accused Jabotinsky of acting contrary to his own convictions. "While trying to preserve the unity of the [Revisionist] movement, Jabotinsky is sacrificing the very idea of Revisionism," declared Eliahu Ben Horin. "You have proclaimed the slogan 'back to Herzl,' we beg you now to proclaim 'back to Jabotinsky.' "[7]

Jabotinsky remained unmoved by these exhortations. He firmly defended the Calais compromise, and dissociated himself from those, to whom secession from the Zionist Organization had become an article of faith. "At the last Congress I tore up my delegate card, but not the shekel of Herzl. It is possible that I might again acquire a shekel if Revisionist shekelpayers would succeed in wiping out the ignominy of the last Congress." [8]

The Conference endorsed the Calais agreement by eighty-two votes to twenty-four. The "noes" came mostly from the ranks of the "extremists." [9] The formation of a new Executive proved to be a complicated and delicate task. In an article published eight months after the Vienna Conference, Jabotinsky admitted that it had come about "after protracted and difficult negotiations, in which my colleagues constituted one side and I—the other." [10] Finally, an agreement was reached on the most controversial issue of the primacy of Revisionist discipline. Evidence in regard to the exact wording and meaning of this agreement is contradictory. In an article published in April, 1933, Robert Stricker asserted that "a great majority of the Conference and the entire Executive rejected Jabotinsky's demands [of primacy] and he had to withdraw his proposal." [11] Jabotinsky, on the other hand, insisted that "in Vienna I had honestly believed that the entire complex of the adopted resolutions about 'primacy' meant for my colleagues—as well as for me—the recognition of the 'primacy' principle; being sure of it, I had willingly made a concession—and did not demand that the *word* primacy be explicitly mentioned, to the extent that my colleagues considered it inconvenient." [12] This statement finds confirmation in the contemporary Jewish press, which reported that the primacy postulate was endorsed unanimously, though not in the form of a specific resolution but as an entry in the official minutes of the Conference. [13] The accuracy of this latter report was at that time not denied by the Grossman-led Revisionist Head Office in London.

At least two groups—the twenty-five strong "Club of Revisionist —Maximalists," headed by Abba Achimeir, and the forty or so "Activists," headed by Dr. Wolfgang von Weisl, advocated a dictatorial regime in the Revisionist movement; the President had to be invested with full authority.

Jabotinsky himself categorically, even scornfully, rejected all such suggestions : [14]

The question of dictatorship could have been considered a dead duck simply because there is no dictator in evidence: the candidate whom the advocates of this idea had in mind, explained to them that this role is both beyond his strength and not to his taste. Unfortunately, however, the issue is much deeper than that. In the world of today, in particular among the younger generation, the dream of a dictator has become epidemic. I use this opportunity to state once more that I am an implacable enemy of this dream. I believe in the ideological patrimony of the nineteenth century, the century of Garibaldi and Lincoln, Gladstone and Hugo. . . . Today's ideological fashion is: a human being is in his essence dishonest and stupid, and he should not therefore be given the right to govern himself; freedom leads to perdition, equality is a lie, society needs leaders, orders, and a stick. . . . I don't want this kind of creed; better not live at all than to live under such a system.

The overwhelming majority of the Conference enthusiastically applauded this *profession de foi*.

Jabotinsky apparently felt that fundamentally, he had had his way in the major political and tactical issues and that there was full harmony between him and his former opponents. He gave expression to this belief in his typical *grand seigneur* manner by submitting to the Conference a list of names for the Executive which, in addition to himself as the President, comprised M. Grossman, Y. Machover, Robert Stricker, and E. Soskin, all four of whom had a record of having been firmly opposed to his policy. He did not include in this new Executive any of his former Paris colleagues, who either shared his views or were unhesitatingly loyal to him personally. He was under no compulsion to take recourse to such a composition of the Executive: the Conference would have endorsed any slate submitted by him. It was on his part a gesture of supreme personal confidence in his colleagues. He implicitly trusted them not to use their majority of four to one to impede his freedom of action.

It was largely this feeling of having behind him a strong and apparently united movement, that prompted him to bring about a major change in his journalistic position in the Yiddish press.

Since 1926, Jabotinsky had been a constant and prominent contributor to the daily *Haint* in Warsaw. In Poland, which was Jabotinsky's main stronghold, and all over Eastern Europe, the *Haint* was considered *the* Zionist mouthpiece. For six years, all his articles on vital probems of Jewry and Zionism appeared in this paper uncensored. But the paper's editorial policies were inalterably opposed to everything Jabotinsky stood for,* and on the local Polish scene the *Haint* was a rabidly anti-Revisionist organ.

By 1932, Jabotinsky had had enough of this incongruous state of affairs. He realized that his articles, widely read and appreciated by East European Jewry, had been actually strengthening the position and circulation of a paper in which he had no say and no influence whatsoever; and he felt entitled to an arrangement that would secure some measure of editorial fair play in regard to his views and his movement. He therefore insisted that a Revisionist publicist of standing be coopted to the *Haint's* editorial board as his personal representative, to safeguard his rights and interests. This writer was suggested as that representative.

Those in control of the *Haint* rejected Jabotinsky's demand. They refused to have—as they called it—a "politcom" (political commissar). As the historian of the *Haint* puts it, they were "even ready to print articles by I. Schechtman, who, incidentally, has in any case been publishing his articles in the *Haint* from time to time, but not to invite him to be a permanent collaborator with a voice in matters of editorial policy." [15] Jabotinsky then broke with the *Haint*, and reached an agreement with another leading Yiddish daily, the *Moment*, which was only too eager to secure his permanent collaboration. Not being associated with any Zionist party, the *Moment* readily agreed to have on its editorial board a leading Revisionist journalist who, incidentally, had also been an occasional contributor to the paper before. In the fall of 1932, I moved to Warsaw, and Jabotinsky began his association with the *Moment*. He did so against determined opposition on the part of many leading Revisionists in Poland, who cited the paper's non-Zionist record and resented his "divorce" from the staunchly Zionist *Haint*. But Jabotinsky was confident that he would succeed in "Zionising" his new journalistic mouthpiece, and he proved to be right. The *Moment* became a militant Zionist organ.

---

* In a recent study devoted to the history of the Yiddish Press in Warsaw, Chaim Finkelstein, one of the pillars of the *Haint*, asserts that the paper's editors had refused to publish some of Jabotinsky's articles and had heavily censored some other articles ("Haint" by Chaim Finkelstein in *Fun Noentn Ovar* [From the Recent Past], Vol. II, New York, 1956, p. 132). This is incorrect. Jabotinsky, who readily permitted editors of Revisionist publications to make changes in his articles, was unbending in regard to articles written for non-Revisionist papers: the inviolability of their contents was a condition *sine qua non* for his collaboration. He repeatedly stressed that in this respect he had never had any trouble with the *Haint*.

This new departure was destined to play a very important role in Jabotinsky's subsequent journalistic and political battles.

3. *The Priority Dilemma*

The apparent unanimity of views and intentions, on which Jabotinsky based his optimistic appraisal of the Vienna Conference, was very soon put to a hard test by the Executive of the Zionist Organization. The endorsement of the Calais resolutions by the Conference and the announced scheme of far-reaching independent political activity prompted the Zionist Executive (on September 30, 1932) to deprive the Revisionist Movement of its status as a "Separate Union." Revisionist attempts at establishing independent political contacts with governments were also actively interfered with. When E. Soskin was received in audience by the Polish Foreign Minister, he was arraigned before the Zionist Congress Court for "infringing the prerogatives of the Zionist Executive." [16]

The intrinsic conflict of two disciplines—the Zionist and the Revisionist—was thus again brought into focus. Jabotinsky insisted that it was no longer a purely ideological controversy. As he saw it, the Revisionist movement, which had decided upon a major political offensive of its own, had now to decide which discipline had priority as far as Revisionists were concerned. He demanded that the primacy of Revisionist discipline be proclaimed in unambiguous terms; any lack of clarity was bound to frustrate and impede independent Revisionist political action.

Jabotinsky's four colleagues on the Executive, together with many other leading Revisionists, did not share this attitude. In their opinion, Revisionist political activities could well be conducted without causing an open and irremediable clash with official Zionist discipline; and they saw in Jabotinsky's insistence on decreeing the primacy of Revisionist discipline a deliberate attempt to stage an artificial conflict, intended to result in the Revisionist secession from the Zionist Organization. This was, they argued, his long-cherished intention; he had been unable to implement it because the overwhelming majority of Revisionists wanted to remain in the Zionist Organization; now he was trying to achieve his goal in a roundabout way.

The disagreement within the Executive was growing more and more intense and irreconcilable. Resistance to Jabotinsky's stand was stiffening. As Jabotinsky later revealed, at least two of his colleagues stated that, in their interpretation, the Vienna resolutions did not imply the primacy of Revisionist discipline; when Jabotinsky appealed to the other two, they sided with the first two. The conclusion he drew from this state of affairs was that the formation of this Executive in Vienna had been apparently based on a most regretful misunderstanding; it was formed on the premise that there was identity of views between the President of the Union and the members of the Executive. Since this proved not to be the case, the body as such did not reflect the wishes of the Conference, which, as he put it, certainly had not intended to create "a majority of four and a minority of one." The reaction of his colleagues to this argument was, that, should he decide to resign as President, the majority of the Executive would continue in office without him.[17] The situation was becoming unbearable. Jabotinsky felt increasingly isolated, one against four in a body, of which he was the President, his authority challenged, his leadership defied. Probably for the first time since the emergence of the Revisionist movement, he began to doubt whether there was a common language between him and his colleagues, a congenial spiritual climate. He was growing more and more uneasy and impatient with their opposition, increasingly eager to assert his leadership. Late in December, 1932, he wrote to his old friend Israel Rosov : "An end must be put to all this. . . . The time has apparently come when there must be a single, principal controller in the movement, a 'leader,' though I still hate this word. All right, if there must be one, there will be one." [18] A few weeks earlier, he confided to another friend : "I am afraid—for the first time—that a split is unavoidable." [19] In January, 1933, he tried to be cautiously optimistic in this regard :[20] "I still have a sneaking hope that it will be possible to avoid a split;" but, he added, "of course not at the price of further lack of clarity in such questions as primacy, etc." However, three weeks before the Party Council's meeting, he again wrote :[21] "It seems that there is going to be a split at the Party Council at Kattowitz."

The Executive decided to submit all the current controversial problems to a session of the World Party Council to be called at Kattowitz (Poland) in March, 1933. In a letter to this writer marked "private," Jabotinsky very frankly, even bluntly, formulated the main points of the stand he was going to take at that session : "The Calais-Vienna decisions mean that the [Revisionist] Union has become an independent and sovereign body; that its task is the direct implementation of its program; that influencing the Zionist Organization is one of the permissible means insofar as . . . and that the Union's discipline has primacy over any other.

"Persons holding responsible positions in the Union cannot be members of the Zionist Executive or Actions Committee.

"Every trace of a separate organization of shekelpayers for specific shekel purposes is being abolished. It must become *de facto* a department of the [Revisionist] Executive and be absolutely subordinated to it. I don't care how this should be formalized *de jure*.

"Three anti-shekel members are being added to the present Executive.

"If the immediate transfer of the Executive to Geneva is impossible, it must be instantly transferred to Paris.

"In regard to the Eighteenth Zionist Congress, I see three [alternative] possibilities :

1. Full steam, i.e., we are going there in order to conquer the Congress with my fullest help in every form. This is possible only under Draconian conditions: (a) a precise definition of what we mean to achieve *sine quibus non*; (b) if we fail to achieve the *sine quibus non*, we all pledge ourselves, on our word of honor, and in writing, to proclaim the New Zionist Organization on the spot.

2. *A priori* and irrevocably to eschew any form of participation in the Zionist Executive, and to strive only for safeguards of a practical nature, such as certificates, equality in the *Histadrut*, etc. *Es lässt sich besprechen* (about this we could come to an understanding).

3. The third possibility—which I shall suggest to all those who are ready to listen to me—is not to take out shekalim and not have anything to do with this business.

"I am writing all this," the letter concluded, "rather bluntly and without mincing words, and I beg of you, should you pass it [to others], not to do so in my own words, but in an elegant style, because I don't want to vex anybody. But this is what I am thinking; and I am fully prepared for a split."

4. *The Impasse of Kattowitz*

Both camps came to Kattowitz in a very belligerent mood, psychologically prepared for a rift. Jabotinsky's frame of mind can be judged

166

from the letter referred to above. Grossman, too, was ready for the eventuality of a breach. During one of the intermissions, he invited this writer—our friendship dated from 1911—to take a nap in his hotel room. Instead of resting, we started discussing the situation in the party. Grossman was most outspoken about his intentions: "I have had enough of Jabotinsky's constant pressure. This can't go on. He must realize that the movement is able to exist without him. We have built an organizational structure which is largely self-sufficient. I have behind me the entire World Executive with the exception of Jabotinsky himself. I have the support of most of the party's intelligentsia, and I have secured the necessary financial means for constructive work. Jabotinsky has behind him the *Betar,* but, if necessary, we shall create a youth organization of our own. I don't want a split, but I am not afraid of such a prospect." He spoke in a similar spirit to a delegation (Joseph Klarman, Abraham Diamond, and David Hoffer) which came to ask him to accept a compromise solution and not to precipitate a breach. His answer was a firm "no." He asserted that 90 per cent of the movement—even the *Betar*—was behind him and, in case of a split, would follow him and not Jabotinsky. "I am not ready to conduct negotiations with Mr. Jabotinsky," he said. To this, Klarman observed half-jokingly, half-earnestly: "Why do you act so big, Mr. Grossman? Don't you know that *with* Jabotinsky, you are *Grossman* [a big man], and *without* Jabotinsky, you are *Kleinman* [a small man]?" [22]

Lichtheim was even more belligerent. Antagonism toward Jabotinsky among some of Grossman's zealots took a deliberately defiant form. Jacob Kahan, the noted Hebrew poet, one of the leading Revisionists in Poland, and for years a personal friend of Jabotinsky, demonstratively remained seated when, as was customary, the entire Council rose to greet the latter's entrance.

Jabotinsky introduced the discussion by stating that the decisions taken at Calais and Vienna were inadequate to establish the primacy of the Revisionist discipline. He demanded that they be extended and made fool-proof, so as to secure the possibility of independent political actions. He also reasserted his demand that three more members who supported his attitude be added to the present Revisionist Executive. Grossman contended that Jabotinsky was unnecessarily dramatizing the issue. He denied the necessity of extending the Calais and Vienna decisions because, he claimed,

167

Revisionists were actually not hampered in their independent political activities by the discipline of the Zionist Organization. Likewise, he considered the cooptation of new members to the Executive unnecessary, because "Jabotinsky had never been subjected to a hostile majority vote in the Executive." [23]

A lively debate on these and related issues went on for three days. No progress toward a solution was noticeable. Even livelier were the behind-the-scene caucuses and parleys in search of a compromise. They, too, remained fruitless. Jabotinsky realized that among the about forty participants in this session of the Party Council he could not muster a majority for his stand. He was realistic enough not to try to precipitate a showdown by submitting his resolutions to a vote —and to defeat. He insisted that it was against the best Revisionist tradition to solve major party problems by purely numerical majorities and pleaded for an agreed solution by mutual concessions. But Grossman and his colleagues also wisely abstained from submitting any resolution of their own to a vote : they, too—though for different reasons—had no interest in a showdown, being satisfied with the *status quo ante* and content with preserving it. In this respect Jabotinsky was at an obvious strategic disadvantage : his opponents did not have to ask the Council for any reaffirmation of their status, which had been established six months before by a World Conference on Jabotinsky's own proposals. It was up to him to make the move to undo a situation which was of his own making; and this move, he knew, had no chance of success. Both sides manoeuvered warily for some opening which would break the deadlock. By the evening of March 22, it became obvious that all attempts at a solution were of no avail. There was no resolution before the Council upon which it could vote, and the Parteirat was closed without having taken any decision. Dr. S. Lazarowicz, who presided over the meeting, stated *ex presidio* that, accordingly, the former party decisions remained in full force, binding all members of the Revisionist Union.[24]

The session ended in utter confusion. Most of the delegates, irrespective of their attitude during the session, felt depressed and frustrated. They were deeply reluctant to accept the finality of the impasse which, they foresaw, augured badly for the future of the movement. Almost none of them went to their hotel rooms, and agitated, though subdued, afterthought discussion continued unabated in the Kattowitz cafés.

Late at night, a few well-meaning delegates made one more attempt to reconcile the differences. Jabotinsky and other members of the Executive were brought together, and a frantic search for some compromise formula started anew. The attempt failed. Though polite and on the surface friendly, neither was prepared to yield. After an hour of futile arguing, the little informal gathering disbanded. Jabotinsky told his colleagues that under the present circumstances he was not prepared to cooperate with them; the answer was that they would continue the work without him.[25]

Most of the participants went to bed, others still continued a muffled debate in the deserted streets. This writer stayed in the same hotel as two charming ladies, Mrs. Miriam Kahan and Dr. Halina Joz. Both were active Revisionists and personal admirers of Jabotinsky. We were all in a depressed mood and did not feel like going to sleep. After some desultory talk, the ladies suggested that we pay Jabotinsky a visit: "He is certainly not asleep and must feel very unhappy and lonesome. An old friend like you can take the liberty of inviting himself on such an occasion, and perhaps female company would also help to relieve the tension." Their feminine instinct proved to be infallible. Jabotinsky was wide awake and answered the phone immediately; he was sincerely moved by our friendly concern and eagerly asked us to come over at once. We ordered some coffee and sandwiches and spent the rest of the night, until about seven A.M. with him. Then we brought him to the railway station where he took a train for Sosnowice—the next stop on his lecture tour.

This night visit was undoubtedly most welcome to Jabotinsky. There was almost no party shop-talk. The only indirect reference to the unhappy events of the previous days was his repeated mention of utter tiredness and depression. We advised him: "You are badly in need of a long and thorough rest; go to some remote spot on the globe, where there will be no Jews, no Zionists, and no Revisionist. Take a cartload of detective stories with you, and come back refreshed and full of vigour. All the other things will, in the meantime take care of themselves somehow, and you will look at them with different eyes." For some reason, the island of Madeira came up as an ideal retreat, and when the train started moving, one of us half-jokingly called after Jabotinsky, who stood at the window of his compartment: "We are waiting for postcards from Madeira." "O.K.," he answered grinning.

169

This episode is told in some detail because it is indicative of Jabotinsky's frame of mind at this critical juncture. Some of the delegates to the Kattowitz gathering, who had supported Jabotinsky's stand, later claimed that they had been a party to his subsequent decision, or had at least been all along "in the know" regarding what was to come, thus attributing to this decision a premeditated character. This writer takes the liberty of doubting the accuracy of such allegations. It is true that Jabotinsky had been urged by several ardent supporters to dissolve the Executive and to assume full authority as President of the Union. According to the evidence of A. Propes and D. Boyko, he informed a *Betar* delegation, which visited him in Kattowitz, that such suggestions had been submitted to him. The delegation assured Jabotinsky that the *Betar* would unhesitatingly follow his personal leadership, provided it would be coupled with a clear, positive stand with regard to the participation in the forthcoming Zionist Congress. But Jabotinsky stated curtly that he had taken no decision whatsoever on these questions.

This appears to have been the case until the very last moment of his stay in Kattowitz. Throughout all the decades of collaboration with Jabotinsky, this writer never noticed in him the slightest trace of deceit, or hypocrisy, and I feel sure that in the course of that intimate all-night chat, Jabotinsky was not concealing from us any already taken decision to cut the Gordian knot by a bold and radical stroke. Joseph Klarman, who accompanied him from Kattowitz to Sosnowice, testifies that during the journey no mention was made of any such action.[26]

All available evidence indicates that the conclusion which Jabotinsky reached the following day, was his own, and that it came spontaneously. In so acting, he was obviously following the pattern of two previous momentous decisions—that after the liberation from the Acre prison in July, 1920 (see Vol. I, pp. 360-61), and that of January, 1923, when he resigned from the Zionist Executive (Vol. I, pp. 429-30).

5. *The Lodz Manifesto*

The conclusion Jabotinsky reached twenty-four hours after his departure from Kattowitz, was announced from Lodz in a statement published on March 23,: "I, the President of the World Union of

Zionist Revisionists, declare that as from today I am personally assuming the actual direction of the Union, and all matters of the world movement. The activities of the existing central institutions of the world movement are thereby being suspended. . . . I shall publish an appeal to the widest possible circles of the Revisionist and *Betar* movements, to participate in the Eighteenth Zionist Congress." He announced the establishment in Warsaw of a Provisional Secretariat, which would act as a temporary World Executive of the Union; and of a Provisional Commissariat for shekel-paying Revisionists.

Three days later (March 26), an article by Jabotinsky, explaining the reasons for his action, appeared in the *Moment*. The gist of it was: the Kattowitz session of the Party Council "broke up with no decision at all, leaving in its wake despair and hopelessness among the participants. . . . When a gathering ends in such silence, it means that it has to turn to somebody with a *kol dmamah daqah* [a silent request], saying: 'We cannot find a solution, but we appeal to you to find it, and to do it in such a way as to enable us to remain united, to continue working together, and to fulfill what we all are striving for.' "

Every one of us has to answer two questions. First: to whom is that silent request directed? and second: what is that common desire? My well-considered belief in regard to the first question is that the request is directed to the President of the [Revisionist World] Union. He is not merely the chairman of the Executive Committee: he was specifically elected as President of the Union. . . .

The second question is the content of the request. Here, I shall not dare to have any illusions. Whether it suits me or not, all Revisionists—or almost all, with a few exceptions—want to go to the Eighteenth Zionist Congress, and to go in all earnest, not with a view to seceding, and not for the sake of an empty demonstration of our strength.

This is the "mandate" contained in the silent request. I decided to accept the "mandate," and to accept it honestly, irrespective of my personal feelings. I will try to fulfill this silent request honestly and earnestly. . . .

The [Revisionist] Party will have the opportunity of telling me "go" or "stay" through a Revisionist World Conference or a plebiscite.

The formation of a Provisional Secretariat and a Provisional Commissariat to replace the suspended World Executive, took some time to materialize. This writer was largely responsible for the delay.

171

Jabotinsky phoned me from Lodz a few hours after the publication of the statement asking me to assume the administrative responsibility for those two bodies. The answer was a flat "no." This reaction was motivated mainly by the unexpectedness of Jabotinsky's action. Though far from being delighted by this method of solving internal party conflicts, I had to admit that I was unable to offer any alternative way out of the impasse reached at the Kattowitz gathering, other than "Madeira," which was, of course, no solution at all. What startled and hurt most, was the fact of having been faced with a *fait accompli*. My reply to Jabotinsky's offer was therefore not only in the negative, it was also bitter.

After Jabotinsky's return to Warsaw, we had several long and painful talks. He pleaded his cause forcefully and persistently, making abundant use of the *argumentum ad hominem*. He admitted that it was not quite fair to ask a man to assume responsibility for an act about which he had not been consulted, but solemnly pledged that this was "the first and last time," and, come what may, he would not repeat this kind of performance. "And even if I erred, I am entitled to expect you, with whom I shared so many battles, not to desert me at this crucial juncture." The arguments and counterarguments went on for hours, until we both felt that there was nothing more to say. After a short and tense silence, Jabotinsky quietly and sadly said: "Well, *razoshlis nashi dorozhki?*" [Do our paths divide? —a quotation from *The Five*]. A salvo of Russian abuse in the best Jabotinsky style was the answer. He grinned broadly and happily: "Now you are talking! Let's sit down and see what has to be done immediately. Whom would you like to have as your colleagues on the Provisional Secretariat?"

On March 27, Jabotinsky announced the formation of a Provisional Executive Secretariat consisting of J. Schechtman (in charge of the office), D. Mowszowicz and A. Propes.

And so began the most hectic and perhaps the most intimate period of collaboration with Jabotinsky. Most of the waking hours were spent in seeing people, writing articles, letters, memoranda, talking over the telephone with half of the European countries, working out plans for future activities. There were in fact very few hours of sleep. Jabotinsky's capacity for work was amazing and often bewildering. Normally, we used to say "good night" around two, three A.M., and around eight A.M. he was already on the phone: "Where the hell

172

are you? I am up, shaved, had breakfast, and am waiting for you. Hurry up, you lazybones!" The only relaxation he sometimes permitted himself was the "Quotations Game." We were both well-versed in Russian poetry, and used now and then to sit in Jabotinsky's room after midnight and play this game. We were sometimes joined by Joseph Szofman, a young lawyer of the Warsaw Revisionist intelligentsia. There were unwritten rules to the game: each of us would in turn quote the beginning of a verse of Russian poetry, the others had to continue and complete the quotation. To the participants, this was a delightful and stimulating sport: "It is just like taking a shower after a long day's exhausting toil," Jabotinsky used to say.

6. *Revolution or Putsch?*

The four suspended members of the Executive did not take their dismissal lying down. They reacted indignantly, and vigorously.

In a statement published in Warsaw on March 23, Grossman branded Jabotinsky's action as "illegal" and his pledge to lead the movement to the Congress as "only a hypocritical manoeuver." To a *Jewish Chronicle* reporter he said: "Mr. Jabotinsky's dictatorship is only comic. It is a 'putsch' and nothing more." [27] In a joint statement issued in Vienna, Robert Stricker and E. Soskin also spoke of Jabotinsky's "anti-constitutional action." Both expressed confidence that "this adventure by Mr. Jabotinsky to split the Revisionist movement will be repudiated in all serious Revisionist quarters." [28]

In this prediction they proved to be mistaken. Strategically, Jabotinsky's move was a master stroke which made his position almost unassailable. By announcing his decision to head the Revisionist election campaign to the Congress, he actually eliminated the only real disagreement between himself and the Revisionist masses who were longing for a chance to have their cause represented at the Congress. He thus rail-roaded the conflict into a purely personal track: whom does the movement trust and prefer—Jabotinsky or his four colleagues? It became a contest of popularity and affection, a vote for or against Jabotinsky. In this contest he was bound to win overwhelmingly. Three of his opponents (Machover, Lichtheim, Soskin) never enjoyed much personal popularity in the movement; Stricker's influence was largely limited to Central Europe. Grossman was the only one widely known. Years of active and devoted

Revisionist work, journalistic and oratorical ability, and forceful advocacy of his policies, had firmly established his position in the movement, especially among the "officer corps" in various countries. Jabotinsky himself had largely contributed to the strengthening of Grossman's position by praising him highly at every opportunity, and by assiduously building up his reputation as an "organizational wizard." But when confronted by the alternative—Jabotinsky or Grossman—the overwhelming majority of the rank and file of the movement made its choice unhesitatingly. Even those who sincerely liked and respected Grossman, were not ready to back him *against* Jabotinsky. They cared little for the legalistic aspect of the conflict. They chose the most wonderful combination they could have dreamed of : Jabotinsky, whom they worshipped, would lead them in the struggle for the Zionist Congress at which they wanted to be. This combination was unbeatable. Ninety per cent of the rank and file said "yes" enthusiastically.

The attitude of the intelligentsia for whom the legal aspect was not at all irrelevant was more sophisticated. Many of them had been previously canvassed by Grossman or his lieutenants, and had committed themselves to support his stand against Jabotinsky's "separatism"; some were personally loyal to him. In this milieu, though psychologically at an advantage, Jabotinsky had to struggle hard for every individual's mind and soul. He used his personal charm lavishly in this struggle and displayed unexpected astuteness. Many among the intelligentsia of the party were plagued by "split loyalties." They wanted Jabotinsky, and felt committed to Grossman. They were, therefore, pathetically eager to bring about some sort of compromise which would restore unity in the movement. Jabotinsky—sincerely or for tactical considerations—went out of his way to show his willingness, even eagerness, to meet their wishes. He said "yes" to every suggestion to meet Grossman and to discuss peace. Grossman, on the other hand, chose to be stiff and unyielding. He demanded a complete retraction of the Lodz manifesto as a prerequisite to any settlement. These tactics— easily explained by the tension under which he was laboring—undoubtedly cost him the support of many of his original sympathizers, who concluded from this attitude that his was the main responsibility for the perpetuation of the conflict. Jabotinsky profited greatly from this confrontation of his studied cooperativeness with Grossman's belligerency.

Grossman's articles in Jabotinsky's "former paper" *Haint* also contributed to the growing estrangement. In an article "The Danger of 'Putschism' and of the Power of the Fist" (March 26) he wrote: "It is hard for me to grasp how democratic principles can be reconciled with the dictatorship of a single person who changes his coats before the eyes of the world in the same way as an oriental dancer (*Nackttänzerin*) changes her veils. . . . Putschism is like a shot in the dark by a night robber piercing the pipes of an aqueduct."

In the beginning, Jabotinsky was inclined to take Grossman's publicistic attacks with equanimity. On his return to Warsaw, he met the editorial staff of the *Moment*. The editor-in-chief of the paper, old Zvi Prilutzky, expressed indignation at the intemperate *Haint* article. Jabotinsky immediately came to Grossman's defense, describing him as "decent, diligent, and gifted." Prilutzky was amazed: "Only yesterday we had Mr. Grossman here, and he spoke of you disparagingly, saying about you just the contrary of what you have just told us about him." Jabotinsky's smiling reaction was: "I see that Mr. Grossman's opinion of me differs from mine of him. Who knows: perhaps we are both mistaken in our judgements? . . ." [29]

Little by little, he began to wonder whether he was not indeed mistaken, and grew increasingly resentful at the attitude of his former colleagues. His early tolerant attitude began to disappear. His correspondence of this period abounds in increasingly bitter references to their way of fighting: "Grossman and all of them are simply blinded, they are out of their minds; at the beginning I suffered, I wanted to patch up the split, but now I am beginning to get used to it. . . . The real background of their mood, which revealed itself in this conflict, is the plebeianism which is inborn in some of them. . . . The tone of my colleagues and present opponents in this struggle somewhat amazed even me, though I always knew that they are somewhat plebian. I must have annoyed them mightily during all these years to make them spew so much bile—even taking into account their understandable indignation." [30] And one month later: [30a] "I am beginning to doubt whether my colleagues on the Executive Committee *want* peace. It seems to me that as long as there is still a desire to collaborate at some time with someone, one does not speak of him publicly in the way in which my colleagues and their associates speak of me, of the *Betar*, and of all of us." In an intimate letter to a friend, he confessed: [31] "Sometimes I wonder if I have not sinned?

175

There is something strange about me—too much hatred around *me* and because of *me*. I am trying to look into myself, but I see no sin, except one : I might have been too soft with my associates, gave them too much leeway, that's true. I would be glad to devote myself to literature, to retire to my Paris apartment, but I simply have no right to do so. I see *tens of thousands* of people who want to follow me, and their number is growing."

Nine years after Kattowitz, when he was capable of a more detached and understanding approach to this stormy period, Grossman advanced the hypothesis that when disbanding the Executive, Jabotinsky "never anticipated that his action would result in a final split and parting with old friends. He probably thought that his fellow opponents, faced with the danger of a rift, would yield a little and compromise a bit, as he would. They would meet half-way, and everything would be again as before. . . . He failed in his strategy, as the greatest of generals sometimes do." But, Grossman admitted, Jabotinsky's "motivation which called forth his acts . . . was of the highest and the noblest nature." [32]

Jabotinsky's statements and personal letters in the early stages of the post-Kattowitz period, largely bear out this hypothesis. In an interview given on April 16, he expressed confidence that the breach would disappear immediately after the plebiscite, and the Revisionist lists for the Congress election would be united lists containing the names of his former colleagues.[33] The following day he wrote to S. Jacobi that he firmly believed that, after the plebiscite, his colleagues, "though they now swear to the contrary, will gradually get tired of being nuisances. . . ." [34]

The plebiscite took place on April 16. The motion put before all organized Revisionists was :

"Until the Sixth World Conference of the Revisionist Union, all the executive functions of the whole Revisionist movement, the Union as well as the Separate Union, shall be vested in the hands of Vladimir Jabotinsky, President of the Union of the Zionist-Revisionists."

The answer had to be "yes" or "no," by secret vote of all Revisionists from the age of eighteen. The counting of the votes in every locality had to take place publicly. In his capacity as *Rosh Betar,* Jabotinsky issued a proclamation calling on every *Betari* to vote in the plebiscite in accordance with his convictions, without any

176

reference to *Betar* discipline.[35] Over thirty-three thousand Revisionists participated in the plebiscite. Of this number 31,724 (93.8 per cent) answered "yes," and 2,066 (6.2 per cent) answered "no," as to whether they approved of Jabotinsky's action.[36]

Jabotinsky's opponents branded his post-Kattowitz action as a *putsch*, which is a German term applied to every abortive mutiny against a legally established authority. There was a substantial kernel of truth in this accusation. It cannot be denied that *ab initio* Jabotinsky's move had no legal foundation. There was nothing in the Union's constitution to entitle the President to disband a World Executive elected by a World Conference, and to assume its powers. The Lodz manifesto was an extra-legal act, but the term *putsch* was not applicable. The decisive difference between a revolution and a *putsch* is the outcome: a successful insurrection against a legally established authority goes down in history under the honorable title of "revolution"; if it fails, it is described contemptuously as a *putsch*. Jabotinsky's disbanding of the Executive was, no doubt, extra-legal and could easily have degenerated into a *putsch*. But the movement overwhelmingly approved and thus *post factum* legalized it.

After the plebiscite, Jabotinsky felt that his position was both morally and legally unassailable. In his correspondence with party colleagues and friends, he particularly insisted on the fact that his leadership was based on the freely expressed *vox populi*. "Leadership in any movement has to lie with those backed by the majority, especially when it is a more than ten to one majority; that is the only sound legality, and the only sound democracy." [37] And in another letter: [38] "What is it indeed? Was a state of affairs, under which 90 per cent [of Revisionist membership] was represented on the Executive by one single member, and 10 per cent were represented by four, a democratic state of affairs, and was it undemocratic to rebel against it?" And again in another: [39] "Let's not argue whether *putsch* is a good method; but is it possible to deny that I have been fighting for the rights of the majority, i.e. for the fundamentals of democracy?"

The 90 per cent of the movement who answered "yes" to Jabotinsky's bid for leadership did so freely and spontaneously. There has been much loose talk about the "dictatorship" established by his Lodz manifesto. Jabotinsky foresaw that he was going to be accused of dictatorial leanings. The day after the publication of the manifesto he wrote to his old friend Israel Trivus: "I assumed leadership not for the sake of dictatorship but for the sake of compromise." In letters to S. Jacobi there are, it is true, significant attempts to justify the very concept of personal leadership :[40] "As I grow old, I am beginning to agree with the view that the party must be 'led,' even when many things are still not clear to it. . . . As I near old age, I am beginning to believe in the inevitability of personal leadership. . . . One cannot mask leadership; the mask only demoralizes the ministers and teaches them to believe that 'Prime Minister' is just an empty word." It is, however, not less significant that having, after a hard struggle, achieved the position of undisputed leadership, Jabotinsky was most definite in his determination not to make use of it. We read in a letter to Israel Rosov (November 9, 1933): "I cannot imagine any way of working, other than with colleagues; and if tomorrow I will get one vote less than the other fellow, I will, without taking offense, become his aide, or simply a private. You *cannot* believe that in my old age I would betray the principles on which I have been raised, and would become infatuated with leader-worship which I despise to the point of revulsion."

The very term "dictatorship" is by definition inapplicable to Jabotinsky's position in the Revisionist movement. Dictatorship presupposes the dictator's ability to impose his will by force or other irresistible means of pressure. No such or similar means were at Jabotinsky's disposal. The only power he exerted over the masses of his followers was rooted in the deep, almost passionate affection they had for him. He commanded devotion of a fervor inspired by few public figures of our time. To many—possibly to the great majority— of his adherents, disciples, associates, and friends he was not merely a thinker, a leader of, and fighter for, the Jewish people, but primarily their highly personal, emotional possession : a living part of their own spiritual life. Of course, when they joined the Jabotinsky camp, each of them endorsed its program. But concurrently with this—organically connected and yet almost independent—each of them had his own intimate and captivating *romance* with the man Jabotinsky. The character, forms, and evolution of this romance varied with young and old, with those close to him and those more distant, with mere sympathizers and intimate associates : but the romance itself was always present, fascinating and intense, with all the attributes inherent in a real love affair—affection, exclusive demands, unlimited idealization, even jealousy. To every one he was "my Jabotinsky," belonging first and foremost to that person personally. Sometimes, one or another was reluctantly prepared to share "his Jabotinsky" with the national movement as a whole, but never with another individual. The unwritten "minimum program" of almost every one of the countless *Khoveve Jabotinsky* (Lovers of Jabotinsky) throughout the world was: "Jabotinsky belongs to the Jewish Nation and to me." Some were even more extreme and reversed the formula; their claim was: "Jabotinsky belongs to me and to the Jewish Nation."

All this was by no means just naive and slightly ridiculous provincial hero-worship. It went much deeper. In its essence, it represented a moving expression of the unique position Jabotinsky occupied in the movement he had created. To the minds and hearts of many thousands of Jewish men and women, he was the incarnation of everything that was great and lofty and inspiring. They did not merely agree with Jabotinsky, they were deeply in love with him. Each of them felt that his or her personal life had been enriched and beautified by their even distant communion with Jabotinsky; they almost religiously cherished this intimate link and were ready and eager to prove their love and veneration.

This "my Jabotinsky" factor played an enormous role in the movement Jabotinsky had created. In their totality, the tens of thousands of individual "romances" gave a powerful impetus to all actions into which Jabotinsky projected his personality. Each of the "Jabotinsky lovers" responded to his call not merely because he deemed it good and right in itself, or because he obeyed discipline: more often than not, he did so because the call stemmed from his very own Jabotinsky, to whom he was eager to prove by his response the extent and strength of his devotion. The cumulative effect of all these personal *stimuli* was perhaps the most powerful force in the movement created by Jabotinsky. This force erupted with almost elemental vigor in response to the appeal to help him in his newly assumed personal responsibility.

When Jabotinsky returned to Warsaw he was enthusiastically greeted by crowds, thousands strong, both at the railway station and on the way to the hotel. The (very unfriendly) Warsaw correspondent of the London *Jewish Chronicle* reported that on March 25 he saw "several hundred Jews standing outside the hall where Mr. Jabotinsky was delivering a lecture for the first time after becoming dictator. Crowds were unable to get in. Fifty policemen kept order,

179

or rather were unable to prevent the disorder." [41] His opponents distributed proclamations headed "Down with Jewish Hitlerism"; tear bombs were thrown, but the audience responded magnificently to his every word. The Polish Revisionist Executive unanimously voted allegiance to Jabotinsky. Hundreds of telegrams from Polish provincial groups greeted him as the undisputed leader of the movement. Most of the Revisionist organizations in other countries either rallied to his call or declared temporary "neutrality" in the hope of some compromise solution. Only Austria, Stricker's stronghold, and in England, the seat of the Grossman-led World Head Office, the official Revisionist bodies decided to support the "legal Executive." Notwithstanding the split, the first post-Kattowitz months witnessed a spectacular growth of the movement, particularly in Poland.

7. The Final Breach

For some time Jabotinsky persisted in trying to achieve some measure of cooperation between the two camps. Early in May, 1933, he wrote to Dr. Max Bodenheimer: [42] "Even if the time is as yet not ripe for [Revisionist] *internal unity*, we can still be united in our struggle *nach aussen*. This means joint lists for the Congress elections. I suggested it in an interview with the JTA [Jewish Telegraphic Agency]. Grossman rejected it in an interview with the JTA. I would consider this [attitude] as unpatriotic." And a few days later: "Nevertheless, I am now officially approaching my colleagues with the proposal for joint lists."

Nothing came out of the scheme for joint lists. The two groups went to the elections separately. The results largely vindicated Jabotinsky: there were at the Congress forty-six Revisionist delegates as against seven of Grossman's "democratic Revisionists."

The Congress definitely sealed the breach. On August 27, "democratic Revisionists" changed their name to *Judenstaatspartei* (Jewish State Party). On their behalf, Meir Grossman told the Congress that they recognized the sovereignty of the Zionist Organization under all circumstances. "For us," he said, "there is no Calais." [43] In accordance with this stand, the Jewish State Party, from 1933 onward, refrained from any political activity of its own. Jabotinsky later argued that this attitude fully vindicated his contention that without having established the primacy of the

Revisionist discipline all plans for conducting independent Revisionist policy lacked the most essential prerequisite for the implementation. "You must admit," he used to say to his colleagues in Paris, "that I was not so crazy when I started 'dramatizing' the issue of primacy. I felt that behind my former colleagues' opposition to a clear-cut decision to this effect was a lack of real determination to go through with these plans *af al pi ken* (a Hebrew expression meaning 'notwithstanding all obstacles'). And my flair proved to be right. As soon as they got rid of my 'pressure,' they dropped all pretense to Revisionist style political activities like a hot potato." "There is no room in Jewry for such a watery urn," he wrote to A. Abrahams.[44] And again, six years later, on June 24, 1939, he made a witty but merciless *post mortem* on the Jewish State Party, in a letter to Elias Ginsburg: "The Jewish State Party tried to combine two assets: (a) a Revisionist program, (b) the link with the Old Zionist Organization, the flavor of Basle, and the connection with the [Zionist] Funds. . . . Their calculation was similar to that which, in Czarist Russia, used to secure success for converted [Jewish] lawyers: '*Di Kop hot er a Yiddishe—un fort a pravoslavni mit ale Recht.*' [His brains are Jewish—and at the same time he is an orthodox Christian possessing all civic rights]. Such lawyers were very successful, indeed. But in this case, as you see, it just did not work out."

Personal relations with his former colleagues were not uniform. Some of them, having broken with the Revisionist party, were not active in the Jewish State Party either.

Richard Lichtheim was not among its delegates either at the Eighteenth (1933) or the Nineteenth (1935) Congress. Later he left the Jewish State Party altogether and became associated with strongly anti-Revisionist groups. This, however, in no way affected the Jabotinsky-Lichtheim friendship. They saw each other very rarely, since Lichtheim had settled in Palestine, but maintained a lively and affectionate correspondence. Characteristic of this correspondence is Jabotinsky's reply to Lichtheim's letter of January 18, 1937. After a few witty inquiries about the Lichtheim household, he expressed the hope that he would see his correspondent in Europe—"since I have no hope of meeting you in the Holy Land. It would be a nice holiday for me to have a chat. Not necessarily political—there was a time when we could just chat and like it, and I am still the same."

Of a somewhat different character were Jabotinsky's relations with

181

Dr. E. Soskin, whose ties with the Jewish State Party also proved to be loose and shortlived (at the Nineteenth Congress he was still a member of the party's delegation, but when he went on record as favoring partition of Palestine, which his party strongly opposed, he had to resign). Whenever Soskin visited Paris or London, he always came to see Jabotinsky at his office or at his home; but, by tacit agreement, they abstained from talking Zionist politics. A similar understanding became the basis of the continued friendship with Y. M. Machover. They talked about everything that was of mutual interest—books, general politics, law, art, economics—but never about internal Zionist problems.[45] Relations with Robert Stricker remained very cordial. Joseph Fraenkel, one of Stricker's most ardent admirers, editor of a collective work devoted to his memory, states that to Stricker Jabotinsky was "the leader, who combined the best and most ideal characteristics of a Zionist."[46] Jabotinsky, whenever he passed through Vienna—usually on his way to Poland—made a point of visiting Stricker who, in turn, always insisted on seeing him off at the station. In February, 1938, Stricker, together with two other leading members of the Jewish State Party in Austria, came specially to Brünn in Czechoslavakia where Jabotinsky was to deliver a lecture, to discuss "joint action against Partition and for Greater Zionism." Reporting this conversation to the *Nessiut* in London, Jabotinsky was delighted to be able to observe that "Stricker [is] most keen, and quite ready to be kicked out of the Old Zionist Organization." [47] They decided to continue negotiations in Paris. But in March, Austria was occupied and annexed by Hitler Germany, and shortly afterward Stricker was arrested and sent to a concentration camp. He was murdered in 1944. Jabotinsky was deeply concerned about Stricker's plight. He repeatedly tried to intercede on his behalf through the American Embassy in London. He also approached several influential British statesmen. His failure to achieve any results was to him a source of great distress. [48]

More complicated were the relations with Grossman. Their friendship dated back to 1915 when they were both in the forefront of the struggle for the Legion. It started deteriorating from 1931, but in the sphere of politics only. The post-Kattowitz breach created personal antagonism. Touched to the quick by Jabotinsky's cavalier disbanding of the Executive, Grossman was understandably bitter and unbending in his attitude, often unrestrained in his criticism.

Jabotinsky not less understandably resented these attacks. He was, however, most reluctant to permit this conflict to poison a long-standing friendship and made a point of not repaying Grossman's antagonistic attitude in kind. He kept inquiring about Grossman's family and personal affairs, and was overjoyed when, in the fall of 1937, the latter for the first time paid him a visit in the London offices of the New Zionist Organization. Yet, the relationship still remained cool and strained, and it was not until Jabotinsky's untimely passing in 1940, that Grossman found occasions to say all the wonderful things he had undoubtedly always thought. At the memorial meeting in London, he called for a "full portrayal of Jabotinsky's personality : he must be given to the Jewish people with both the light and the shadow, so that the essentials will remain." [49] Ten years later, in a letter to this writer on the occasion of the publication of the first volume of the biography of Jabotinsky, Grossman said: [50] "I would like to take this opportunity of putting an end, once and for all, to the legend that there was a personal quarrel between Jabotinsky and myself. I always recognized him as leader and mentor, and never imagined that I could replace him in any way. We had serious differences on problems of tactics, but never on the principles and aims of political Zionism. We worked in complete harmony for eighteen years, and I regret the fact, especially while reading the biography, that our loyal friendship so abruptly terminated."

THE STRUGGLE FOR A MAN'S LIFE: THE STAVSKY AFFAIR

1. *The Hue and Cry*

JUNE 1933 was a busy and strenuous month for Jabotinsky. The aftereffects of the Kattowitz split and the emergence of Hitler's Third Reich, coupled with the strain of the electoral campaign for the Eighteenth Zionist Congress, put exacting demands on his mind and his working schedule. But, in the second half of June, a new and terrifying development burst upon him, making his load almost unbearable.

On the night of June 16, 1933, Chaim Arlosoroff, head of the Political Department of the Jewish Agency, was murdered by two unknown persons while taking a walk with his wife on the sand dunes outside of Tel Aviv. A prominent labor leader of moderate views, he was a determined adversary of Revisionism, but he had never been connected with any of the violent anti-Revisionist actions which had been so frequent during the preceding year. Nevertheless, general opinion among labor circles in Palestine and abroad immediately suspected a Revisionist hand as responsible for the murder. In this, they found fullest understanding and sympathy on the part of the British administration, which did not even consider it necessary to look elsewhere for the culprits. "This is strange," commented Jabotinsky in a detailed "*Aide Memoir* on the Arlosoroff Murder Case in Tel Aviv," prepared on July 31:

Murders of Jews are a frequent occurrence in Palestine, and so far they have always been connected with the well-known tension between Jews and Arabs .. so that it would have been most natural, in the Arlosoroff

184

case, to look for the murderers among the Arab extremists. . . Yet the suspicions of labor circles at once fell upon the Revisionists, and found expression in open hints in the Press and in public speeches.

In the early hours of June 19, the police made a search in the dwelling of Dr. Abba Achimeir, editor of the Revisionist weekly *Hazit Haam*, and there arrested his fellow-lodger Abraham Stavsky, a Revisionist working man arrived from Poland some three months before. Stavsky was subsequently confronted with Mrs. Arlosoroff who, according to a statement made by the representative of the Colonial Office in the House of Commons on June 22, "identified him as resembling the companion of the man who fired the shot." [1] On July 22, twenty more Revisionists were arrested; one of them, Zvi Rosenblatt, was identified by Mrs. Arlosoroff as the man who fired the shot. Abba Achimeir was accused of instigating the murder. When two Arabs, Abdul Majid and Issa el Abrass, confessed to having committed the crime, they were not believed, and were induced to withdraw their confession. The obstinacy with which the police stuck to the Stavsky-Rosenblatt theory, Jabotinsky insisted, was "a direct result of an extremely powerful propaganda campaign conducted both in Palestine and abroad, which aimed at persuading the public, without even awaiting the results of the trial, that the crime is a Revisionist one." In this he hardly exaggerated. Even the official report of the Mandatory Power to the League of Nations for the year 1934, found it proper to say: [2] "Rightly or wrongly, the crime [Arlosoroff's assassination] is ascribed to Revisionist preachings against what that Party is said to regard as the timorous methods of the Jewish Agency."

For those who did not live during that agonizing summer of 1933, it is difficult, almost impossible, to imagine the dreadful atmosphere of violent animosity that permeated Jewish life all over the world, particularly in Palestine and Poland. A broad anti-Revisionist coalition was formed, which included not only Socialists (*Poalei Zion, Hashomer-Hatzair, Hapoel, Hechalutz,* League for Working Palestine), but also Itzhak Grinbaum's "General Zionist" group, *Al Hamishmar*. Under their combined signatures appeared a statement calling for the wholesale outlawing of the entire Jabotinsky movement. "We declare that the moral responsibility for this brutal assassination falls upon the entire Revisionist Movement which has produced such a murderer. . . . Whoever is still concerned about the fate of Zionism must shake himself clear of the Revisionist past. No intercourse whatever with Revisionism! Let our motto be: 'Expel the Revisionist gangs from Jewish life!' " [3] A leaflet published by the *Hechalutz* was directed against Jabotinsky personally, describing him as a "bloodthirsty beast" and "a man with a dark past." [4]

During the first few weeks immediately following Arlosoroff's assassination, the hue and cry continued unabated. The leftist press was joined by the influential General Zionist daily, *Haint*, a paper in which Jabotinsky had collaborated until 1932. Not a single voice was raised to counteract or restrain this savage onslaught.

2. *Jabotinsky Hits Back*

This writer, who was with Jabotinsky in Poland during those trying times, vividly remembers the latter's attitude in the midst of this raging storm. There was in him a quiet and firm, almost instinctive belief in the innocence of the accused. The entire accusation simply did not make sense to him; he was confident that none of his disciples was capable of such a crazy and vile action. His very first statement on the Arlosoroff case began with the words: "I feel sure that Stavsky is innocent, and it is evident that the investigation has so far produced no proof that has a chance of convincing any unbiased Court of his guilt. We will stand by this innocent man as my generation stood by Mendel Beilis." *

"There are two rules sacred to all civilized humanity," the statement went on: "a man claiming his innocence is considered innocent until a Court has pronounced him guilty (the decent part of humanity sometimes goes even farther, as in the Dreyfus case or in the Sacco-Vanzetti case); and, secondly, even the proven guilt of an individual should never be construed as the guilt of the community to which he belongs. Both these rules should be specially sacred to all Jews, doubly so the second one, the violation of which has always been a poisonous weapon in the hands of anti-semitism."

Then came a powerful indictment of the complacency of the Jewish public in the face of the "new Beilissade":

* Mendel Beilis—a Kiev Jew who, in 1913, was accused by the Czarist authorities of committing a ritual murder on a Christian youth Andrei Yushinsky, but was acquitted by the jury.

186

I accuse a large section of Jewry, in this case, of ignominiously violating both these principles. They see a young Jew in a Palestine prison swearing his innocence, fighting for his life and his honor; they have not yet heard any proof against him, yet they already proclaim him a murderer and push him to the gallows. Moreover, they are charging an entire movement, numbering tens of thousands of adherents, and ten times that number of sympathizers, with moral complicity in the hideous crime. And they do it for the glaringly obvious and ugly motives of party vendetta and vote-catching. With all the authority of a lifetime spent in the service of the Jewish cause, I throw in the face of all that unworthy section of Jewry my cold and bitter contempt.

I know that the vast majority of our people are disgusted at this shameful pogrom and blood libel campaign conducted by Jews against Jews. But I warn them that, by their timid silence, they are contributing to an unprecedented demoralization of our public life; and worse—they are helping the enemies of Jewry and of Zionism to divert the inquiry into Arlosoroff's murder away from the real origins of the crime.

3. *"Cool and Steadfast"*

The reactions of the public are unpredictable, and this forceful statement somehow failed to impress public opinion. Incomparably more staggering was the impact of the article "Cool and Steadfast," which Jabotinsky published in the *Moment* of June 22. Those who disparage the power of "mere words," spoken and written alike, would probably have to revise their attitude in the face of the psychological impact of this single article upon Polish Jewry. "Cool and Steadfast" became a catchword among friends and foes alike.

Jabotinsky found moving words of sorrow and admiration for the victim of the dastardly assassination :

I bow my head in silence and profound respect before this tragic grave. This was a man who served his people and his conscience loyally and honorably; he was exact and responsible in his every undertaking, fair and upright in debate, something very rare in his political camp. . . . Together with my comrades and disciples, I proclaim: May the murder and the foul murderer become anathema and a curse. If he is a stranger, I am not his judge; and if he is a Jew—which I do not believe—he will be accursed, even more accursed than the red madness which has created an atmosphere of violence in Eretz Israel.

187

He called upon his Movement to remain "cool and steadfast" in the face of this unprecedented provocation.

We shall not alter our conduct one iota: there is nothing to change. We shall not give one inch in our war against class hatred and class domination. The instigators will not succeed; their attempt to exploit the blood that has been spilt, will not help them either.

He was particularly bitter against his "former paper," the *Haint* of Warsaw, in which he had prominently collaborated for about six years, and which had turned against him in a most abrupt and vicious way: "Never before have I witnessed so sudden and extreme a change: the very moment one of their associates leaves the paper they become his bitterest ideological opponents and his personal enemies. The most interesting thing is that almost all my Revisionist propaganda was conducted in the pages of this newspaper. . . . And now this paper ceaselessly publishes articles on how dangerous those 'lies' of mine were, and even asserts that these ideas lead—directly or indirectly—to the commission of crimes." What irked him most, was not so much the *Haint* as the reaction of the Jewish public who adopted "such a tolerant attitude toward them and even supported them": "You cannot permit newspapers that exist at your expense, to befoul with the stains of blood libel the portals of a movement to which tens of thousands of Jews in this country belong; a movement in which your closest friends and your children are active. That is anarchy, not tolerance. . . . I say to you today without anger, but calmly and firmly: Put an end to this anarchy!"

There was in the article no direct call to boycott the *Haint* for its "blood libel crusade." But large sections of the Polish Jewish public interpreted this barbed passage as an appeal to stop reading the paper, and very many enthusiastically complied. Six days after the publication of the article, Jabotinsky wrote to a friend in Palestine that "the mood of the [Jewish] masses has sharply turned against the blood exploiters; the best proof is the unprecedented growth of the *Moment's* circulation, and the complete boycott of the *Haint,* even on the part of the ordinary 'man in the street.' " [4a]

"Cool and Steadfast" did much to change the mood of the Jewish masses in Poland, which was at that time, together with Palestine, Jabotinsky's main battlefield. As early as July 9, 1933, Jabotinsky asserted in a letter to the London *Jewish Chronicle* that "here in

Poland things have undergone a considerable change. Hasty verdicts describing Stavsky as murderer have almost entirely disappeared from both the headlines and the small type of the Jewish Press; so has the blood libel against Revisionism and the *Betar*, our youth organization. . . . Here in Poland the libel has broken down; today hardly anyone really believes that Stavsky is guilty. . . . As to the question of Revisionism's 'complicity' in favoring the murder of Jewish patriots, the whole subject has simply dropped out of public discussion. *Sheker en lo raglaim* says a Hebrew text—'Falsehood has no legs to stand upon.' " [5] He voiced the same optimistic view in an earlier personal letter : "I believe in our triumph after all this hue and cry. . . . Stavsky is innocent. . . . Our people are behaving bravely and proudly. My lectures in the provinces are greeted with ovations. *On les aura* (we will get them)."

Events proved that Jabotinsky was rather hasty in this optimistic estimate of the situation among Polish Jewry. Inadvertently or deliberately, he failed to mention the unabated fierceness of his opponents' attacks against him personally. They saw in Jabotinsky the spiritual father and teacher of the Revisionist youth, and it was Jabotinsky first and foremost whom they aimed at and whom they were eager to brand as the man morally and politically responsible for all the evil of which Stavsky was merely one of the manifestations. In an article published in the *Yiddishe Stimme* of Kaunas (No. 1418), David Ben Gurion candidly admitted that he was "less interested in whether Stavsky is the murderer or not, than in Jabotinsky." He described Stavsky as an "active Revisionist, a loyal pupil of his master," who "stands under the supreme and exclusive orders of Vladimir Jabotinsky, as *Rosh Betar*." While acknowledging that the *Rosh Betar* "cannot know in advance everything that these people, under his orders, may do at any moment," he insisted that "in the capacity of Supreme Commander, leader and mentor, he [Jabotinsky] bears above all the general responsibility for the deeds and actions of his *Betarim*."

Jabotinsky preferred to ignore the stark fact that the almost incensed animosity and anger of all those who insisted on Stavsky's guilt found its strongest expression in a bitter hatred toward himself. There was widespread talk of physical violence being planned against him, of "avenging our Arlosoroff," of "paying off the blood debt," and so on. The strongly anti-Revisionist *Haint* bestirred itself to

189

announce that, fearing reprisals, Jabotinsky had canceled his lecture tour in the Polish provinces. Jabotinsky immediately refuted this allegation. "It is not true," he wrote in the *Moment*. "Today I am speaking in Lublin, Saturday—in Novogrudek, Sunday—in Pinsk, Tuesday—in Ostrowice, Thursday—in Pabianice, and the next Saturday—in Brest, home town of Abraham Stavsky." But his friends were seriously alarmed by the rumors. They begged him to be careful, not to walk alone in the streets, in particular in the evenings, and to agree that a bodyguard be assigned to him. Jabotinsky goodnaturedly laughed off all these apprehensions. "Nothing untoward will happen to me," he said. "All this idle talk of beating me up or killing me is just so much letting off steam. And as far as a bodyguard is concerned, I simply cannot see myself walking in the shade of a husky fellow with a gun or a stick. Leave me alone." No amount of persuasion could shake his lighthearted stubborness. Then this writer tried irony : "I see," I said in a *tête-à-tête*, "that you are longing for the crown of martyrdom, the only feature that has been missing in your career. Well, you can have it. Go ahead and have yourself killed. I promise you a most elaborate funeral, with banners, orchestra, flowers, and speeches." This sarcastic sally did the trick. Half-angrily, half-laughingly, Jabotinsky said : "You win, damn you. *C'est le ridicule qui tue*, and I certainly don't want to look as if I were longing for hero-victim rites. Let's have a bodyguard." And so, a husky fellow with the odd name of Kuliawy, was appointed to guard Jabotinsky. The Polish authorities gave him a license to carry a gun, and for some time he followed his "ward" about like a shadow. After a week or two, Jabotinsky resolutely shook him off with profuse thanks, and obvious relief.

If the dire predictions of attempts on his life did not materialize, there was no dearth of vicious attempts to interfere with his public appearances, and to harm him physically.

When he arrived in Brest Litowsk, Stavsky's home town, an incensed mob tried to stone him on his way to the lecture hall. In Kaunas, the capital of Lithuania, where a motley coalition of *Poalei Zion*, *Bund*, *Folkspartei*, and Communists swore to "avenge" Arlosoroff's assassination, two rows of *Betarim* were posted on the stretch leading from the roadway to the entrance to the Summer Theater, the largest hall in town. "When Jabotinsky's car arrived," recalls Eliahu Gleser, "he was greeted with noise and shouts. About thirty meters from the entrance, a large stone smashed the windscreen of his car, sending glass splinters flying all over the place and injuring the driver in the eyes. Jabotinsky decided to walk the remaining few meters, daring a crowd that shouted : Here he is ! Stop him ! Hit him ! Jabotinsky continued walking slowly and composedly, followed by a few associates. Almost at the last moment, the crowd broke through the *Betar* barrier, shouting 'Murderer ! Murderer !' Jabotinsky stopped abruptly, turned to his assailants, and fixing them with a silent stare, made them retreat. They were as if hypnotized; subdued, they let him enter the hall." During the lecture, the incensed crowd outside started throwing stones on the iron roof over the speaker's rostrum, causing a disturbing noise, which unsettled the audience.[6] A similar reception awaited him in Kaunas :[7] "A hail of stones greeted his car, accompanied by shouts of 'assassin' and such like epithets," recalls Mordehai Katz.

4. *The Ordeal of the Eighteenth Congress*

The battle for the Eighteenth Congress was fierce and bitter, particularly in Poland, where Jabotinsky personally headed the Revisionist campaign. Despite unprecedented anti-Revisionist horror propaganda, the Jabotinsky list received 64,370 votes in Poland, as compared with 29,985 in 1931. The total number of world-wide Revisionist votes was 96,818 as compared with 55,848 in 1931. The number of delegates (46) was, however, smaller than at the Seventeenth Congress (52), the reason being a tremendous increase in the overall electoral participation (535,113 votes as against 233,730 in 1931).

Despite all the odds, Jabotinsky was (or professed to be) eager to disprove the contention that he was going to the Congress with the sole intention of demonstrating the futility of any attempt to influence the Zionist Organization, and was not pessimistic about the prospects of the Prague Congress. In a "Congress Program" published in April, 1933, he envisaged the possibility of the Eighteenth Congress doing what the Seventeenth Congress had refused to do : proclaim that the aim of Zionism was the establishment of a Jewish State with a Jewish majority on both sides of the Jordan. He even expected the endorsement of the petition idea, the liquidation of the "extended" Jewish Agency, the condemnation of class warfare in Palestine, and a

demand for the legalization of the Jewish self-defense organization.[8]
As late as July, he wrote about a "Congress of Hope." [9] The fact that
nearly one milion Jews took the shekel was in his eyes a clear proof
of what fervent hopes the Jewish people attached to this Congress.
In a statement published four weeks before the opening of the Eighteenth Congress, he foresaw "various attempts to create a big
Judenstaat front . . . strong enough to elect a *Judenstaatler* Executive.
. . . I do not see why Revisionists, if requested, should not join such
an Executive. . . ." "I know," he said, "that everyone is expecting a
very stormy Congress, but I am not so very sure of that. . . . I should
not be surprised if this Congress proves to be one of the quietest. . . .
No blood-libel attempts will be permitted, of course, but I very much
doubt whether anyone at Prague would seek to engage in that sort
of eloquence."

In all these expectations Jabotinsky proved to be badly mistaken.
The Eighteenth Congress was largely controlled by the Labor wing,
and he freely acknowledged that he had been wrong in his forecast.
On the eve of the official opening of the Congress, he stated that
"the Revisionists are building no great hope on this Congress and
will not be disappointed whatever its results." However, he urged his
colleagues in the Revisionist delegation "to keep order at Congress, to
refrain from all demonstrations . . . not to indulge in any temperamental outbursts: the Congress of 1933 will pave the way to a
Revisionist victory in 1935." [10]

This self-imposed rule of self-restraint was not easy to abide by.
The Prague Congress was a severe ordeal for Jabotinsky. He felt
almost physically affected by the cold, intense hatred and scorn
surrounding him and his forty-five colleagues in the Revisionist delegation. The entire atmosphere was permeated by a deliberate tendency
to isolate and to humiliate the Jabotinsky-led Revisionist faction.
This tendency came into evidence in one of the first matters before
the Congress—the election of a Presidium. It was a time-honored
tradition that *all* parties were to be represented in the Presidium.
This time, however, the Labor group moved that this tradition be
broken. Their spokesman declared that "there is in this hall a Party,
together with which Eretz Israel Labor refuses to sit on the Presidium; this is the Party in which people who are being officially
suspected of organizing the murder of one of our comrades grew up."
By a scant majority of two (151 votes to 149), the Congress accepted

a motion which practically precluded Revisionist representation in the Presidium.[11]

This deliberate discrimination set the tone for the entire Congress. Jabotinsky felt its humiliating intention very acutely. Four years later, in the course of a visit to South Africa, he wrote a lengthy memorandum explaining "How and Why We Left the Zionist Organization," in which he insisted that:

this shameful action of the Eighteenth Zionist Congress should not and will not be forgotten. . . . The whole Revisionist party was deliberately and officially pilloried as organically connected with assassination. . . . The Revisionist wing was pronounced unworthy of sharing in the Presidium, because involved in murder; and this was done in a demonstrative way, under the searchlights of the world's press. This was no longer a disagreement between a majority and a minority on ideological matters: this was a deliberate, organized, unprecedentedly venomous insult inflicted on us by the Congress as such, and, as everybody knows now, for no cause at all.

It was this feeling of outraged justice that largely determined the scope of Jabotinsky's personal participation in the Congress. He was ready to share with his colleagues their bitter isolation at this Congress; he was, however, not prepared to participate actively in the deliberations of such a Congress. Contrary to the traditions of the previous four Congresses, he categorically refused to be the main speaker of the Revisionist delegation : "You can't expect me to figure once more as an attraction in the arena of this mad circus," he told a group of friends who were trying to make him reconsider his decision. The Revisionist delegation had to adapt its strategy to this new situation. In the general debate, the first address, dealing with the political situation of Zionism, was this time delivered not by Jabotinsky but by this writer. As soon as I appeared on the platform, the whole of the Labor delegation demonstratively walked out–a reception which otherwise would have been meted on Jabotinsky. Dr. A. Weinshal (Palestine) and Dr. J. Hoffman (Latvia) dealt with other items on the Congress agenda. Jabotinsky seemed to be highly satisfied with the performance of this team and warmly congratulated the speakers on both the content and the form of their addresses. But everybody knew too well that a general debate without Jabotinsky in the lead lost most of its value and significance, and that Jabotinsky's silence had deprived the Revisionist delegation of its main asset.

Despite constant urging, Jabotinsky's participation in the early stages of the Congress proceedings was limited to an occasional *Zwischenruf*. He broke his attitude of non-cooperation only twice, each time on a major and dramatic issue.

The first time was on August 24, when the painful and explosive question of Jewish reaction to the rabidly anti-Semitic Hitler regime in Germany came up for discussion. Resolutions submitted by the Congress majority were deliberately vague and meaningless, the reason being the fear of jeopardizing the position of German Jewry by proclaiming an open struggle against Nazi Germany. *Rasswyet* (September 21, 1933) reported that when the chairman started reading the official resolutions "in an artificially exalted manner, trying to convey a solemn meaning to commonplace phrases," Jabotinsky, imitating him, began mockingly, with a drawling inflection, to recite in Latin: *"Quousque tandem, Catilina, abutere patientia nostra? . . . "* (See also the official Congress *Protokoll*, p. 202.)

Then Jabotinsky rose to present a different policy. The Presidium had ruled that no speeches and no discussion on the German question would be permitted. Jabotinsky was merely allowed to state that "the trend dominating the political system in Germany" was endangering "the securest foundations of the existence of all Jews the world over" and "must be regarded and treated as the affair not only of German Jews but of the entire Jewish people. It is therefore the duty of world Jewry to react with all means of just defense . . . against this attempt to destroy the Jewish people." The resolution calling for a world-wide Jewish boycott of Germany was not even put to the vote: after the two majority resolutions were accepted by the Congress, the Presidium ruled that no further vote was necessary.[12]

At a press conference, attended by over a hundred correspondents, Jabotinsky next day delivered the speech which was intended for the Congress tribune.[13] He bitterly attacked the Zionist Executive for having turned the German tragedy into small change, by reducing it to a mere request for more certificates from the Palestine Administration, when it could have been used for placing the Jewish problem in its wider aspect before the civilized world, and demanding that it should be solved by giving the Jews a place under the sun. No less scathingly he denounced the reported three million mark "transfer" agreement with the Hitler Government, to allow German Jews to take their money out of Germany in the form of goods; he was confident

194

that Palestine Jewry would boycott German goods imported on the basis of such an agreement.

The second Jabotinsky intervention (August 31) was caused by another painful and explosive issue : the pending trial of Stavsky and Rosenblatt. His contention was that this question belonged to the competence of the Palestine Law Courts and not to a Zionist Congress. "The Zionist Congress must not be turned into a support for the Public Prosecutor in Palestine," he declared on the eve of the Congress. This was, however, exactly what his opponents were determined to achieve. The resolution submitted to the Congress abounded in innuendos obviously directed against Jabotinsky's disciples. It spoke vaguely but significantly of "tendencies that are contrary to the fundamental principles of Jewish ethics, and constitute a danger to the upbuilding of Eretz Israel," and empowered the incoming Actions Committee, at its first session, to appoint a Commission to investigate the allegations against the bearers of such tendencies; the Actions Committee was thereupon empowered to "take all steps which can, in its judgment, serve to eliminate effectively such tendencies, if found to exist, and to eradicate from the Zionist movement any elements who are guilty of or responsible for such tendencies." [14]

The most shocking feature of the situation was the dense cloak of secrecy that enveloped the entire matter. The Presidium (from which the Revisionists were excluded) allowed only such declarations to be read as it regarded "admissible." This was a procedure Jabotinsky could not let pass unopposed. Here a moral issue was involved, and he intervened with his usual vigor. When the Chairman asked whether the Revisionists would agree that their statement be read only in the extract approved by the Presidium, Jabotinsky answered : "No, we don't accept censorship." He demanded an opportunity of speaking to a proposal for a free discussion. Warning the Congress that the issues at stake were vital and explosive, he asked the delegates "not to tolerate a procedure which makes a caricature of the representative body of a people." By a vote of 179 against 79, Jabotinsky's plea was rejected. No discussion was allowed. All he was permitted to do was to read an expurgated statement expressing the profound conviction that all allegations to the effect that there were, in the Zionist movement, elements who denied the fundamental tradition of Jewish ethics which abhors violence, were without any foundation. He insisted that, on the contrary, it was the duty of Congress to investigate the alarming rise of party and class warfare in Palestine which was generating bitterness and leading to manifestations of the law of the fist, as well as to allegations liable to imperil the Zionist cause most gravely; this investigation must be, however, conducted in a way precluding the possibility of intepreting it as indicative of a preconceived attitude toward the judicial trial pending in Palestine.

The majority of the Congress chose to disregard this appeal, and adopted the resolution submitted by the majority of the Actions Committee. Jabotinsky then exclaimed: "To our innocent brothers Achimeir, Stavsky, and Rosenblatt, who are languishing in prison, we send our triple *Tel Hai*." [15]

Jabotinsky never doubted the innocence of the imprisoned youths, not even in the face of seemingly "incontrovertible proof." During the Saturday evening (August 26) plenary session of the Congress, a telegram was handed to the chairman, Leo Motzkin. He read it with a perplexed air, and after a brief whispered consultation with other members of the Presidium, adjourned the session. There was no official announcement about the contents of the telegram, but it soon transpired that it came from Palestine and that the gist of it was that one of the accused, Abba Achimeir, had "confessed to the crime." The left wing was jubilant, the Revisionists perturbed. Jabotinsky, who was late for the meeting and did not know why it had been adjourned, inquired of his friends what had happened and why they were looking so gloomy. Having heard the story of the telegram, he burst out laughing and asked that a caucus of all the Revisionist delegates be convened immediately. To this gathering he said briefly, but firmly: "I guarantee that the telegram is a fake. Do you believe that *I* murdered Dr. Arlosoroff? Achimeir and any other accused have as little to do with this assassination as I have. It is late, and I advise you to get some sleep. And when you wake up in the morning, you will find out that the telegram was a fake. I shall ask Dr. Weinshall (leader of the Revisionist party in Palestine) to make cabled inquiries and you will receive authentic confirmation of what I am now saying."

Jabotinsky's prediction came true. Next day, a telegraphic dementi arrived from Palestine. The entire story proved to be a clumsy provocation.

After one of the Congress sessions, an aggressive-looking group of leftists suddenly surrounded Jabotinsky and his wife in the Congress lobby and one of them jostled Mrs. Jabotinsky. A group of *Betarim*

196

came to the rescue, and a scuffle ensued. The police intervened. But Jabotinsky categorically declared that he was preferring no charges against anybody, and that the entire matter was a "misunderstanding." According to a Jewish Telegraphic Agency dispatch from Prague, a "left-wing Zionist youth named Berkowitsch, of East Galicia, was in police custody after his arrest last night on charges of plotting an attack on V. Jabotinsky." At Jabotinsky's request, this charge, too, was dropped.[16]

There was, of course, no question of Revisionist participation in the Executive elected by the Eighteenth Congress. It was more than ever dominated by the Labor wing.

Jabotinsky was ruthless in his *post mortem* of the Congress. In his judgement, Congress "has failed to do anything it should have done, and committed every absurd error that should have been avoided."

It humiliated our nation before the arrogance of the Third Reich; it broke the united front of the boycott movement. It failed to unmask the anti-Zionist essence of the Mandatory Power's policy which hides under a cloak of verbal benevolence. Worst of all, it offered the world an ugly show of internecine hatred, and it has committed what I do not hesitate to call a crime, by intervening in a matter *sub judice* and pushing to the gallows three young Jews who claim to be innocent, and whom I firmly believe to be innocent.

"Fifty-fifty Zionism," Jabotinsky concluded (alluding to the ratio between Zionists and non-Zionists in the extended Jewish Agency), "has lost the last few shreds of its moral authority. The road before us is free; this is the hour of integral Zionism, and we wish to take full advantage of this historic opportunity." [17] In a personal letter to his sister (September 18) he was more outspoken : "This Congress," he wrote, " *is the best thing that has happened to Revisionism since 1925* [underlined in the original]. The [official] Zionist Organization is *erledigt* [liquidated] for years to come; our path is free, and—though not all have realized it as yet—our popularity has grown tremendously."

5. *Organizing the Defense*

In the midst of these tribulations, Jabotinsky never tired of keeping close contact with the Stavsky case in all its aspects, legal and psychological alike. He prepared several Aide-memoirs (July 7 and 31,

197

August 5, 1933) on the juridical, procedural and political aspects of the case, which were remarkable specimens of lucid and penetrating analysis. They are known to have been extensively utilized by the defense lawyers before and during the trial. He carefully studied, in the Yiddish original, Stavsky's personal letters to his parents in Brest (written late in May, shortly before the Arlosoroff tragedy) regarding them as valuable background material for assessing the young man's mentality and possible intentions.

After receiving the first letter from her son from prison, Mrs. Ita Stavsky was anxious to see Jabotinsky, and implore him not to let her boy become the victim of a false accusation. She asked Menachem Begin, then a young leader of the *Betar* in Brest (the Stavskys and the Begins had been close neighbors in the Twenties) to accompany her to Warsaw and introduce her to Jabotinsky. When they were announced at the Hotel Krakowski where Jabotinsky was staying, he immediately came out to meet them. The mother tried to kiss the hands of the man who had so ardently taken up her son's case, but he prevented this, kissed her hand, and consoled her: most probably, there would be no trial at all; but, should the matter come to court, the best lawyer would be retained to defend Abrasha and return him safely to his mother. The writer, who was also present at this encounter, said: "His accusers will yet pay dearly for this ignominy." "They will," Jabotinsky sternly confirmed. He then apologized for the necessity of breaking up the conversation: "I must finish the article I am writing; it is about your son." Next day, this article appeared in the *Moment* under the title *"A Brivele zu der Mame"* (A letter to Mother). Mrs. Stavsky returned to Brest greatly relieved and encouraged.[18]

Jabotinsky's promise to provide the best defense lawyer turned out to be very difficult to fulfil. On July 23, he worriedly wrote from Paris to Michael Haskel: "An awful thing has happened: the [Jewish] Agency has retained *all* the four leading barristers in Palestine on its side, leaving for the defense only smaller fry who hardly speak English. Weinshal [Dr. Abraham Weinshal, a Haifa lawyer] is bombarding me with requests for Horace Samuel [the noted Anglo-Jewish barrister, former legionnaire]. If not he, it ought to be someone else of real caliber. . . . I think even the Palestine Government could be prevailed upon to admit such lawyers to plead."

Finally Jabotinsky succeeded in securing the services of Horace Samuel who conducted the defense with vigor and dignity and of whose strategy he heartily approved: "Samuel's line of defense was first and foremost attack. . . . The entire British administrative system was on trial." [19]

The organization of the defense also presented a serious financial problem. For a while, this problem was solved thanks to the generous gesture of a single man, who was both wealthy and worthy. On the fifth day after Stavsky's arrest, Jabotinsky received a letter in Warsaw from Michael Haskel, a rich South African Zionist of Lithuanian origin, who had been for some time his admirer and supporter, saying: "Whatever the cost, we must save this young man, simply because he is not guilty. . . . I know that Jewish hands have not shed Arlosoroff's blood. Please see to it that all the necessary measures are taken; everything must be done. And a check is enclosed." [20] It was a very substantial check, and many more followed. On the whole, according to Jabotinsky, about two-thirds of all the expenses caused by the defense of Stavsky and Rosenblatt, came from this source.[21] The remaining third had to be found. Jabotinsky heard that the Rothschild family was convinced of Stavsky's and Rosenblatt's innocence. He therefore tried, in January, 1934, to "arrange for a talk with the Baron's secretary *re* helping us to pay for the defense." A few days later, he reported: "Rothschild has refused. I shall look for other sources." [22] In February, 1934, together with the noted Russian-Jewish lawyer, Henry B. Sliosberg (a non-Zionist), he published an appeal for funds: "The friends of the accused who, until now, have covered the expense necessitated by the organization of the defense, can no longer provide for the purpose. According to an approximate estimate, the amount necessary to ensure the regular function of the defense is about fifteen hundred pounds (seventy-five hundred dollars)." [23] The public response was gratifying. In Jabotinsky's notebooks for 1933 and 1934 minute accounts can be found of every penny spent for the "Stavsky affair."

He attended to all the needs of the defense. At an early stage of the affair, he wrote to M. Haskel: [24] "If I had money, I would first ask Colonel Patterson to go to Palestine for preliminary information and private inquiry (our own people are simply terrorized into silence)." The money was provided and Jabotinsky happily informed his Palestine friends that "Colonel Patterson had kindly agreed to look into the matter engaging our attention just now. Please give him the fullest information possible and consult him about every essential step to be taken. . . . Treat him as you would treat me, without any difference." [25] Later, after Stavsky's acquittal, Jabotinsky gratefully recalled : "Patterson flew to Palestine, reassured our friends and defenders, organized the first investigation and brought to Paris and London the first data, on the basis of which it became possible to plan our further work." [26] Realizing that hostile political pressure could be expected to influence the investigation methods of the Palestine Administration, and thus, indirectly, the verdict of the Court, Jabotinsky endeavored to counteract this pressure. On July 23, he cabled to Colonel Wedgwood : "If you have not turned against me, implore you to believe Stavsky innocent and mass arrests of Revisionists in Palestine obvious bureaucratic crusade against hated party, eventually against myself. Please receive my friend Jacobi and intervene to show that honest men in England are watching." Informing Haskel of this appeal, Jabotinsky added :[27] "Of course, I don't mean that he [Wedgwood] should interfere with the judicial aspects of the business. . . . But the authorities in Palestine should get the impression that their attempts at a purely political catch are arousing suspicion and uneasiness at home [in England]."

6. *Death Sentence—and Vindication*

It took the Palestine Administration almost a year to bring the accused Revisionists to trial. During all this time, Jabotinsky repeatedly subjected to devastating criticism the blatant bias and brazen lawlessness of the Palestine police and administration in dealing with the case. But what galled him most was the attitude of "our Jewish characters," whom he described as "The Jackals" and "The Clams." [28] Everybody knows, he wrote, who the jackals are : "That queer human specimen which, though Jewish, sleeps—dreaming hopefully that Jews will be convicted; they dream of it even though aware of the innocence of the accused, and tremble at the thought of their acquittal." But "even more curious is the clam species. Forgive me, gentlemen of the *Yishuv*, for saying this about you . . . but a base and unscrupulous conspiracy against three Jews is being enacted before your eyes; three Jews of whose innocence you are now convinced; a conspiracy against justice; a conspiracy against Jewish honor. Neither in the Dreyfus case, nor in the Beilis case was the intrigue *so* brazen . . . only clams would permit it to go unchallenged.

In any other country such a murderous libel would have made public conscience rebel, and stern representations would have been made to the Government. . . . But the clams keep mum."

Jabotinsky was only partly right in this wholesale indictment of the *Yishuv*. Little by little, the mood was changing. More and more frequently, voices were being raised in influential circles refuting the charges against the accused. The most weighty among them was the voice of the venerable Chief Rabbi Abraham I. Kook.

When, on May 16, Abba Achimeir was acquitted of "conspiracy to murder," many interpreted this verdict as indicative of the Court's final disposal of the case. But the verdict announced on June 8, while acquitting Zvi Rosenblatt, sentenced Abraham Stavsky to death by hanging.

This writer was in Jabotinsky's study in the *rue Pontoise* when the news arrived. Jabotinsky went ashen. For a moment he was silent, then he said in a low voice : "Never mind, we shall rescue Abrasha. . . . Now, it's up to us again." And to his sister he wrote on June 11 : "I don't doubt that we will save Stavsky." It was in this spirit that he answered the frantic telegram from Stavsky's mother, begging him— "Save my son, he is innocent" : "We shall not rest and not tire in our struggle until we restore the honor and liberty of your son, who is free of any guilt." To Stavsky himself, Jabotinsky cabled : "The Jewish people, the Revisionist Movement, and the *Betar*, bow to the fortitude you have shown, and believe that now, too, your courage will not fail you. We shall continue our struggle to a victorious end and we shall see you free."

Jabotinsky was deeply depressed, and outraged, by the enthusiastic reaction of the leftist circles to the death verdict. This writer remembers him sitting in his study at Revisionist headquarters in Paris, and disgustedly perusing a pile of reports from Palestine :

Just listen, *mon jeune ami* (this was his preferred form of addressing his colleagues), how jubilant they are over the news that a Jew is going to be hanged. . . . Here is a report that in Jerusalem, near the Edison Theatre, groups of *Histadrut* workers were shaking hands, and saying *Mazel Tov* (congratulations) to each other; some of them jested: "Now the Revisionists will have to establish a Stavsky Burial Fund." And in Tel Aviv, bands of the Left tramped the streets singing and uttering congratulatory cries. And in the colony of *Bnei Brak*, a group of *Mapai* members wildly danced a *hora*, shouting "Death to Stavsky!. . . ." My God, what happened to this section of the Jewish community? Are their minds so thoroughly poisoned that they can rejoice at the prospect of a Jew being hanged? And how are we, all of us, going to live with them in the same Zionist movement in the future?

The defense lodged an appeal against Stavsky's death sentence. Jabotinsky spent the major part of the months of June and July in London endeavoring to secure a fair re-trial. He contacted old friends from the Legion days—Wickham Steed of the *Times* and Herbert Sidebotham. Articles inspired by the information supplied by him appeared in the *Manchester Guardian, Evening Standard, Daily Sketch, News Chronicle,* and other papers. Several prominent British political leaders visited the Colonial Office demanding guarantees for an unbiased trial. In the House of Commons, Colonel Wedgwood asked the Secretary of State for the Colonies to see to it "that England shall not risk being found guilty of judicial murder." [29] Stavsky Defense Committees were being organized all over the world. Finally, on July 19, Stavsky was acquitted by the Court of Appeal. In a letter to a friend, Jabotinsky emphasized that this came about "only under heavy pressure from London : Jerusalem was given to understand that should the appeal be rejected, the case would inevitably be transferred to the Privy Council, and there not only would the judgement be reversed, but a big scandal would be stirred up in the process. If the weight of this pressure could be estimated at one hundred poods [a pood equals forty Russian pounds], God is my witness that I have carried at least eighty on my own back; this is the measure of my tiredness." [30]

In a statement after the acquittal, Jabotinsky congratulated the judges on having absolved an innocent man, thus vindicating the fair name of British justice. . . . "We are glad to see in the verdict of the Court a promise that whatever controversy may be pending or will further arise between Zionists and the Mandatory Power will be confined to issues of purely political and administrative character and will not involve apprehension as to the basic character of the social order and impartial justice. . . . We also hope that all efforts will be made to discover the murderer of Dr. Arlosoroff and that no leads now not at the disposal of the authorities will be neglected." [31]*

* The British authorities never discovered Dr. Arlosoroff's murderers. But on July 16, 1955, at a meeting of the Bnei Brit. Lodge in Tel Aviv, to commemorate the twenty-second anniversary of Arlosoroff's death, Yehuda Tennenbaum-Arazi, a staunch member of the *Mapai* party, who, as a police officer, had been closely connected with the police

The judicial and political issues connected with the case having been thus disposed of, Jabotinsky was able to direct his attention to the personal problems facing the two liberated youngsters.

On July 25, he sent Zvi Rosenblatt the following characteristic letter, written in Yiddish because Rosenblatt did not know Hebrew : "Dear friend Rosenblatt, I did not write to you before, as I felt it would not be fitting to congratulate you on your liberation as long as Stavsky was not free. Nor did I write to you when there were rumors that you intended to leave Eretz Israel because of the threats against you. I did not believe that you needed anyone's advice to make you remain where you were. Now, I congratulate you with all my heart. You behaved bravely in the face of grave danger and brought honor to the Movement and to the nation." "The grave danger" to the lives of the acquitted youngsters was, however, far from being over. *Davar,* the paper of the Socialist *Histadrut,* declared on July 22, that Stavsky and Rosenblatt "remain murderers." A *Mapai* manifesto plainly stated that although both had been freed, in the eyes of the Party they remained the murderers of Arlosoroff and his death would be avenged. The Tel Aviv police advised them to leave town as their lives were in danger. Jabotinsky boldly intervened. On July 27, he cabled the High Commissioner, Sir Arthur Wauchope :

Am reliably informed that Police Inspectors Barker and Goffer warned Stavsky and Rosenblatt that their lives are in danger but that Tel Aviv police cannot assume responsibility for them. This unprecedented evasion of obvious police duty to protect people whom the Police admittedly know to be threatened compels me to place on record that I hereby most respectfully submit to your Excellency that the fullest responsibility for safety of those two men rests entirely and unquestionably upon the Mandatory Administration headed by your Excellency.

This challenging cable served its purpose. The Palestine police

---

investigation and the trial in 1933, firmly stated: "Abraham Stavsky did not kill Arlosoroff; Arabs did." He brought abundant factual evidence to bear out this statement (*Jewish Herald*, June 24, July 1, 1955). The Revisionist representatives at the session of the Zionist Actions Committee (August, 1955) demanded that the matter be investigated by a special Commission of the Zionist World Organization: this demand was refused. The *Herut* members of the *Knesset* introduced a similar motion calling for the appointment of a judicial committee to "investigate the circumstances and the accusations in connection with the murder of Dr. Chaim Arlosoroff." This motion was debated on June 7, 1956; it was opposed by the Coalition parties (with the exception of *Hapoel Hamizrachi*) and the Communists and was defeated by a vote of 22 to 48 (*The Jewish Agency's Digest of Press and Events*, June 15, 1956).

stopped pleading that they were incapable of protecting Stavsky and Rosenblatt, and no attempt was made to implement the threats against the two of them.

The financial problems of the youngsters were also of serious concern to Jabotinsky. On August 8 he wrote to S. Jacobi: "Perhaps some fictitious job could be found for them in our Revisionist office, or in the National Labor Organization?" Two weeks later, he mentioned the prospect of a lecture tour for Stavski,[32] and late in September he sent his sister sixteen pounds (about eighty dollars, at that time a bachelor could live modestly in Palestine on forty dollars) for them and promised to guarantee the same amount for six months to come.[33]

Another problem which occupied his mind was the post-liberation behavior of Stavsky. On September 27, he wrote to his sister from Paris that while everybody was praising Rosenblatt's conduct, he was receiving contradictory reports concerning Stavsky. Some said that "Abrasha" was behaving with dignified modesty, others—that he was boastful, bragging, and drunk with his popularity. "I have a rule which I hold sacred: when people speak ill of a man, it means that they are lying. Until such a thing is proven, I will not merely disbelieve, but I will not even take notice." But he was worried about the future development of Stavsky's personality and he wrote to his sister, asking her to convey his message to Stavsky:[34]

I do not know him personally, but from afar my impression is that he is a wholesome man. If I am right, I would like—so far as it is within my *very limited* possibilities—to help him to reach his full potential stature. But the main prerequisite for it is that he should find in himself sufficient tact and strength to *cope with his position.* This is terribly difficult, because the position is a very complicated one. There is a certain "halo" around him. He must realize that such a "halo" is capricious by nature: if Stavsky will forget about it entirely, never refer to it either directly or otherwise, then the halo will consolidate and serve him well with all honest people. Should he, however, show in some way that he himself takes his "halo" seriously, that same "halo" would degenerate into a farce that would liquidate him in the end. I would advise Stavsky to take the following stand: "I am a common soldier. Everything that happened to me, is just an accident, an incident. There is no sense in taking notice of it; its significance is of a public and political nature only. As an individual, I, Abraham Stavsky, am of no consequence: I was a simple woodcutter. I would now like to get some rest, and then again become a woodcutter." Should he take this kind of a stand, he would become not a wood-cutter, but, in time, probably a public figure of some stature. I was glad to hear from B. that Stavsky is behaving in precisely this manner; and if it is so, he does not need my advice. But if it is not so, let Stavsky know that in this case it would be my sad duty to foretell much trouble and little benefit for him. People have written me that he believes in my predictions.

It was with great relief that, a few months later, Jabotinsky reported to his sister from the Revisionist World Conference in Krakow, which both Stavsky and Rosenblatt attended, that he "liked them very much and so did the entire Conference. They behaved modestly and inconspicuously. Good boys."

4

INNER - ZIONISTS BATTLES

ELEVEN

ATTEMPT AT COEXISTENCE

1. *Rue Pontoise*

THOSE WHO forecast that immediately after Kattowitz, or at the latest after the Eighteenth Zionist Congress, Jabotinsky would press for secession from the Zionist Organization, were in for a disappointment. He was not at all keen on a formal break with the parent body at all costs. "For Heaven's sake, please understand that now, when nobody has any doubt about the independence of our (Revisionist) Union, the entire interest for the *Austritt* [secession] has disappeared," he wrote on March 29, 1934, to Dr. J. Hoffman. What was of paramount interest to him was the possibility of conducting independent political activities, and he denied that such activities would be incompatible with belonging to the World Zionist Organization, if that Organization would outlive the artificial and misleading concept of imposed discipline. His own concept of a viable and workable Zionist movement he formulated in an article distributed in March, 1934, by the Jewish Telegraphic Agency.[1]

In this article he flatly rejected the attempts to "endow the Zionist movement with all the dignity of a non-territorial 'State,' " every "citizen" of which "should obey the decisions of its 'Parliament' and 'Government,' the same as does a citizen of, say, Sweden or Holland." Jabotinsky considered such an interpretation "not only premature but totally erroneous"; because "the Zionist movement is only a movement, not a State." It comprises widely and deeply conflicting elements, and it would be "idle and useless to dream that such differences can be settled by statutory paragraphs enjoining 'discipline.' These paragraphs will simply be ignored. The ruling majority may then amuse itself by 'expelling' the mutineers from the Zionist Organiza-

209

tion; but everybody realizes by now that this will bring neither help nor solace." Therefore, ordinary "cold common sense" points to one solution only:

Since comparisons are the fashion, I offer a better one: Zionism is not a "State," but a "family." As long as the children were small, and daddy alive, it kept together without difficulty. Now, there is no longer any sign of a person or a party likely to be recognized as the equivalent of daddy; and the children are grown up, long married, each one with his own line of business. Such a family can only be kept from disbanding by free mutual consent, none of the brothers ever attempting to dominate.

The period following the Eighteenth Zionist Congress must be viewed as an attempt to ascertain whether those in control of the Zionist Organization were ready to accept, or at least to acquiesce in such an arrangement of coexistence, of live and let live. Jabotinsky hoped to be left unmolested and to be able to go on with a broad program of political activity, which he considered vital for the triumph of the Zionist cause.

The organizational foundations for the implementation of this program were laid at the Conference of the Revisionist delegates to the Eighteenth Zionist Congress, which was held in Prague simultaneously with the Congress deliberations. Jabotinsky was in full command of this gathering. But he used his power sparingly. In the long series of decisions made in Prague, only a few were directly influenced by him. In the light of previous experience, they were, however, of considerable significance. It was expressly stated that members of the Revisionist World Union must accept its program and submit to its discipline, and that their "participation in any other political body was subject to the control and veto of the [Revisionist] World Executive." This was a somewhat diluted endorsement of Jabotinsky's pre-Kattowitz demand for the priority of Revisionist discipline. Another essential decision endorsing his Kattowitz and post-Kattowitz stand was that "the seat of the Executive Committee must always be the same as the residence of the President of the Union; the President's resignation leads automatically to the resignation of the entire Executive." [2] The newly-elected Executive Committee consisted of six members; four of them were "Parisians," one lived in Riga (Jacob Hoffman) and one in Warsaw (Joseph Schechtman). Jabotinsky insisted, however, that the entire Executive be concentrated in one place, and form a strong and united working team.

He himself was more than willing and eager to integrate his personal effort into the collective machinery that was to be established. This writer, who had been working with Jabotinsky for many years, had never before seen him so deeply involved in even the minutest details of the movement's organizational and technical activities. After three months spent in provisional makeshift quarters, the offices of the Executive were, in December, 1933, transferred to a somewhat dilapidated but spacious three-story building on 7, rue Pontoise—a small, quiet street in the Latin Quarter of Paris. In its eleven rooms were comfortably lodged the central institutions of the world movement. Jabotinsky closely supervised all the arrangements made in this new residence. His attitude was that of a diligent and eager *pater familias* who was establishing a home for his family for the first time, and who wanted this home to be in good shape, conducive to harmonious living and efficient work on the part of its twenty-five strong personnel. He was as happy as a child in this new role of master of his own house, with all branches of the movement united under the same roof. In a touching article, "Together," he confessed:[3]

I would like to write not only a whole article about it, but a poem—a poem about a silly old Jew who fell in love. . . . The name of my beloved is: the Headquarters of the Revisionist World Union, of the *Betar*, the Tel Hai Fund, "Economic Defense," etc.—Paris, 7, rue Pontoise. . . . All my life I have hated "offices" and office work of any kind; I dragged myself to the office sighing, like a boy going to school. Now, I don't know what has happened to me: I hurry eagerly to the office on rue Pontoise, like a pious Jew to the synagogue; I sit at my desk, run up and down the three flights of stairs—and enjoy it. Enjoy every bit of it, even the worries and the vexations when the office machinery all of a sudden stops working properly. . . . *Reb Yid*, if you come to Paris, do not go to the Louvre, rather come and see us at the Rue Pontoise.

The first manifesto of the new Executive, published on October 18, 1933, announced that, having failed in its endeavour to induce the Eighteenth Zionist Congress to take a course in accordance "both with the will and the interests of Nationalist Jewry," the Revisionist movement was compelled to draw one positive conclusion from the situation thus created: "that it is now incumbent upon the Revisionist Union to assume all those duties which have been rejected by the official Zionist Organization." Among the tasks enumerated in this manifesto, two were singled out as of significance and special urgency. The first was the launching of a "Diaspora-wide petition movement of the Jewish masses" as a means of "pressure of millions addressing their demands to all the governments of the civilized universe." The second was "to unite, and definitely consolidate the defensive campaign of world Jewry" against the Third Reich. To both, Jabotinsky devoted his full and immediate personal attention.

2. *The Petition*

The petition idea had been for at least a decade an essential component of Jabotinsky's political concept. Its origin goes as far back as the fall of 1923, when the editorial nucleus of the Berlin *Rasswyet* met with him to work out the highlights of the program he was to develop during his forthcoming lecture tour in the Baltic States (see Chapter One). "It was a small gathering," Jabotinsky recalled, "seven or eight people altogether, among them the two Tiomkin brothers, the two editors of the *Rasswyet*—Gepstein and Schechtman—Dr. Perlman. . . . . It was, I think, Schechtman who made the following remark : 'Zionism is becoming less and less the concern of the people as such. It is increasingly acquiring the peculiar quality of some kind of 'enterprise,' in which but a few thousand 'directly interested' persons participate. We have to give back to Zionism the quality of a mass urge for Palestine, the character of a Messianic movement.' . . . That is how the idea of a Jewish world petition was born that evening," Jabotinsky recalled in May, 1934.[4]

For years, there was no serious attempt at implementing this idea, although Jabotinsky tried to make it a reality at every critical juncture in the Zionist political situation. Other members of the Revisionist World Executive, in particular those who were in control of the London headquarters since 1929, were, however, far from wholeheartedly endorsing such an action which, they feared, was bound to clash with the political prerogatives of the Zionist Executive and provoke an open conflict. It was only after the Kattowitz split that Jabotinsky was able to revive the petition idea in its full vigor, and make it the hub of the movement's activities. "Our future, the future of Revisionism, hinges on the petition campaign; with its success we stand, and with its failure we fall," he wrote in May, 1934.[5]

This writer was entrusted with the direction of the Executive's "Petition Department." But it was Jabotinsky himself who submitted the entire plan of the campaign and prepared the texts of the four separate forms of the petition, as well as of the richly documented memorandum attached. A description of this plan and of the content of the various petition texts, does not belong within the scope of this biography. It suffices to say that separate petitions were to be addressed respectively to the King of England, the British Parliament, the Prime Minister of State of which the respective petitioners were citizens, and the Parliament of that State. The appeals to the King were introduced by a letter "to His Britannic Majesty," signed by Jabotinsky "as one of the initiators of the [petition] movement," in which he said :

These Petitions speak with the genuine voice of a mass distress whose painful acuteness, almost world-wide range, and utter hopelessness no free Nation can even remotely imagine.

No free Nation, therefore, should refuse to listen to that voice; least of all the Nation directly responsible for that day, sixteen years ago, when Your Majesty's Government proclaimed the British Empire's resolve to assist in rebuilding what, in the guarded language of official documents, they called our National Home in Palestine; what all Jews, all Britishers, and all the world understood to mean re-constituting Palestine as the Jewish State.

The Zionist Executive was quick and outspoken in its denunciation of the petition, stating that it "disapproved of this action and regarded it as harmful to the Zionist Movement and to the interests of the Jewish National Home." The Executive saw in it a breach of Zionist discipline, and instructed all Zionists to "abstain from participation in the petition in any form." Jabotinsky devoted a scathing, largely autobiographical article to this argument of "breach of discipline." [6] He reminded his readers that in 1915, when he first started his campaign for a Jewish Legion, the then Zionist Executive also accused him of a "breach of Zionist discipline" and sent out circulars urging all good Zionists not to touch this heresy with a ten-foot pole. "Of course, I did not pay any attention [to these exhortations], and not I alone. Scores of official Zionists helped me to build up the Legion. . . . And now everyone would agree that it would have been woe to us if we had listened to that twaddle about a veto." Defiantly refusing to be impressed by the "breach of discipline" argument in regard to the petition, he invited every thinking Zionist to do likewise. He had the satisfaction of seeing many non-Revisionist Zionist leaders and groups follow this invitation and openly support the petition, which, by the end of 1934, had been signed by more than six hundred thousand Jews in twenty-four countries.[7]

3. *The Anti-Hitler Crusade*

Next to the petition campaign in urgency, the first manifesto of the new Revisionist Executive singled out the coordination of the world-wide Jewish campaign against the Third Reich. In this field, Jabotinsky already had a well-deserved fighting record, the timing of which must be viewed against the timetable of Hitler's rise to power.

On January 30, 1933, Hitler became Chancellor of the German Republic. The March 5 elections gave the National Socialist Party control of the Reichstag, which on March 23 set aside the Weimar Constitution, leaving virtually dictatorial power in Hitler's hands. On April 7, the first anti-Jewish law was enacted.

In two articles published at the time, Jabotinsky lucidly appraised the global all-Jewish significance of this series of events: "The German anti-Jewish crusade is the most important and serious development in generations of our [Jewish] existence. . . . If Hitler's regime is destined to stay, world Jewry is doomed." It was, he stressed, a global "German-Jewish War," in which the German Jewish community as such was "but a minor detail. . . . The Jewish people finds itself face to face not with a party within the German people, but with the German nation as such, or at least with one half of it. At the March 5 elections Hitler received seventeen million votes, and seventeen million are already no longer a party." [8]

Not content with voicing a challenge to the Nazi regime in the Jewish press, Jabotinsky, on April 28, 1933, delivered an address over the Polish Government-controlled radio in Warsaw on "Hitlerism and Palestine." Speaking in Polish and French, he called for a world-wide boycott of Germany, and for the establishment of a Jewish State in Palestine, as the only adequate answer to the Hitlerite menace. It was the first time that a foreign Jew was allowed to appear on a Polish radio program. For Jabotinsky it was a symbolic gesture demonstrating the community of interests between Poland and Jewry in combatting Hitler's menace to the world. Asked, after his address, to sign his name in the station's Visitors' Book, he did so, quoting the motto of Polish rebels against Czarist domination : "For your freedom and ours."

This first appeal to combat the Third Reich was followed by sixty-nine mass meetings throughout Eastern Europe, which openly called on Jews to boycott German goods.

Jabotinsky's gallant anti-Nazi record did not prevent David Ben Gurion from publishing in the *Davar* (July 7, 1933) a fierce article "J'Accuse," in which he charged him with collaboration with the Hitler regime by criticising his Socialist opponents in Zionism. The article asserted that "just after Hitler's accession to power in Germany, when the persecutions of Jews and Marxists were at their height, Mr. Vladimir Jabotinsky arrived in Berlin and in a public address incited against Marxists and Communists in Zionism and in Palestine."

True to his principle of not answering personal attacks, Jabotinsky, at the time, and for several years to come, refrained from refuting this accusation. But in May, 1938, Joel Pincus, one of the leading Revisionists in South Africa, approached him with a request to clarify for him the factual background of Ben Gurion's 1933 indictment. He argued that it was still being used by the Zionist Socialist parties in their campaign against the Jabotinsky movement; he and his friends wanted to be in a position to offer a well-substantiated factual *dementi*. Reluctantly responding to this request, Jabotinsky stressed in a personal letter to Pincus that he had "taken the trouble of writing all that . . . only because of my great affection for all of you." He then quietly went on to explain that :[9]

1. The active persecution of Jews in Germany started in April, 1933. Before that date there was no question of boycotting Germany.

2. His last visit to Germany was in February, 1933: a lecture arranged months before, as usual.

3. In that address he never "incited against" either Marxists, Socialists or Communists. He probably never even mentioned them.

4. That Ben Gurion himself soon discovered that the report he had trusted was a lie, is shown by the fact that during his negotiations with V. Jabotinsky late in 1934 (see Chapter Thirteen), conducted, as is well known, in a very friendly atmosphere and lasting over a fortnight, he never mentioned that story at all.

"It is only by mere chance," he added, "that I happen to remember when I was in Berlin last, and what I spoke about. You will all go to pieces if you go on shying at every new attack or accusation, including those of four and more years ago. I must earnestly deprecate this mania to accept the defensive in dealing with admitted calumniators."

Personal attacks left Jabotinsky unmoved. But he was deeply annoyed and hurt when informed that, in the early stages of National Socialism, the Palestine Revisionist paper, *Hazit Haam* (to which he was a regular contributor), was allegedly treating this movement with a pronounced slant of sympathetic understanding. The editors of the paper (Joshua Yeivin and Abba Achimeir), he was told, though aware of Hitler's rabid anti-Semitism, saw in National Socialism elements of a genuine movement of national liberation.

This reported attitude was in itself distasteful to Jabotinsky, running, as it did, contrary to everything that was holy to him. But it was also widely used by his opponents as "proof" of the "inherent reactionary and Fascist essence" of the Jabotinsky movement. Deeply upset, he addressed to the editors of the *Hazit Haam* an indignant, unusually stern and even rude letter: [10] " The articles and notices on Hitler and the Hitlerite movement appearing in *Hazit Haam* are to me, and to all of us, like a knife thrust in our backs. I demand an unconditional stop to this outrage. To find in Hitlerism some feature of a 'national liberation' movement, is sheer ignorance. Moreover, under present circumstances, all this babbling is discrediting and paralyzing my work. I demand the complete elimination of all unsavory hysterics of this kind from the columns of *Hazit Haam*; I demand that the paper join, unconditionally and absolutely, not merely our campaign against Hitler Germany, but also our hunting-down of Hitlerism, in the fullest sense of the term. Should *Hazit Haam* publish even a single line which could be interpreted as a new attempt at kow-towing . . . I will demand that its editors be expelled from the party, and will break off personal relations with anyone who, for the sake of a cheap raillery, cuts the ground from under my feet."

In reply to an inquiry from this writer, Abba Achimeir categorically denied that *Hazit Haam* had ever indulged in abetting Hitlerism; he argued that, being almost permanently on the go, Jabotinsky was unable to read the paper regularly, and unfortunately relied on incorrect information eagerly supplied by ill-wishers. [11] The purpose of this biography does not warrant a close investigation of the factual background of this controversy. Irrespective of whether *Hazit Haam's* stand justified Jabotinsky's outburst, the very violence of his reaction can be considered indicative of his state of mind.

Not less strong and uncompromising was Jabotinsky's reaction to the reports that the *Brit Trumpeldor* in the Third Reich was adapting itself to certain features of the Nazi regime. In a letter to the former chairman of the Revisionist party in Germany, he firmly condemned this "policy that runs counter to that of the world *Betar . . .* I do not know what exactly has happened," he continued, "but any flirting with the [Nazi] Government or its representatives and ideas I would consider simply criminal. I understand that one can silently bear *Schweinerei* [hoggishness, dirtiness]; but to adapt oneself to *Schweinerei* is *verboten,* and Hitlerism remains *Schweinerei* in spite of the enthusiasm of millions which impresses our youth so much in a manner similar to that in which Communist enthusiasm impresses other Jews; it is a very cheap and common type of assimilation." [12]

This rebuke was conveyed to the *Betar* leadership in Germany and seems to have considerably sobered their attitude towards Hitlerism as the "movement of millions."

The Hitler regime was fully aware of Jabotinsky's anti-Nazi crusade, and its press repeatedly dealt with this arch-enemy. The *Voelkischer Beobachter* (August 26, 1933) published an article by Alfred Rosenberg about the Prague Zionist Congress. Voicing his indignation at Jabotinsky's boycott demand, Rosenberg regretted that although the Congress majority received this demand *"mit Schrecken"* [with horror], it was not courageous enough to exclude the Jabotinsky-led group [the Revisionists]." Rosenberg later returned to the same subject in his pamphlet *Der Staatsfeindliche Zionismus* (Munich, 1938), in which he referred to Jabotinsky as "the *enfant terrible* of the Zionist Organization" who, "to the horror of the other Elders of Zion, spoke more plainly than they would have liked" (p. 22). *Weltdienst,* a Nazi publication specializing in anti-Jewish propaganda, frequently "quoted" Jabotinsky's anti-German statements that, the paper claimed, "quite openly revealed the plans of his race" (1934, No. 4), "as if they had come straight out of the 'Protocols of the Elders of Zion.'" *Mitteilungen Ueber Die Judenfrage,* a fortnightly publication of the Institute for the Study of the Jewish Question, printed, on December 1, 1938, a fairly extensive fifteen-hundred-word "portrait" of "Vladimir Jabotinsky—Champion of the Policy of Violence and 'Self-Defense,' " by Gerhart Rentner. After a survey of Jabotinsky's Zionist record from his student days, Rentner describes him as "one of the most virulent boycott-mongers against the Third Reich," who "places his organization entirely at the service of this incitement campaign." Another Nazi specialist on the Jewish problem, Wolf Meyer-Christian, also devoted considerable attention to the "New Zionist Preacher of Violence" (as the caption to Jabotinsky's photograph reads) in his book *Die englisch-jüdische Allianz: Werden und Wirken der Kapitalistischen Weltherrschaft* (Berlin-Leipzig, 1942). On the strength of a quotation from the New York Yiddish daily *Forward,* of July 19, 1940, Jabotinsky is described as "the most important exponent of the Jewish ambition to achieve world domination" (p. 78); Jabotinsky's alleged "policy of violence" is illustrated by reference (p. 136) to his article "The Iron Wall: We and the Arabs" in *Rasswyet* (German edition) and to the Revisionist program as formulated in 1925.

At a press conference (August 25), attended by over a hundred correspondents, Jabotinsky announced that since the Congress had evaded the issue, the Revisionist Party was ready to act as the central world body for directing and stimulating the boycott.[13] However, he fully realized the inherent limitations of the role his party was capable of playing. He was aware of the existence of an influential and well-financed "Non-Sectarian Anti-Nazi League to Champion Human Rights" in the United States, which was headed by Samuel Untermeyer and in which several Revisionists (Elias Ginsburg, Israel Posnansky, and others) were active. Eager to avoid any misunderstanding, he cabled Untermeyer from Prague: "Should like to coordinate Revisionist boycott activity with your League. Please instruct your Paris representative accordingly if agreeable." Informing Elias Ginsburg of this cable, he carefully explained that though it was "the firm intention of our new Executive Committee to treat the boycott issue as the chief plank, we, of course, do not claim any hegemony or leadership. . . . I need not add what decisive importance we attach to Mr. Untermeyer's personality and to the League headed by him. It is our fervent wish to coordinate all our activity with this powerful factor."[14] For reasons which do not have to be discussed in this biography, Jabotinsky's fervent wish did not materialize. But he continued his journalistic crusade for a sustained effort to organize and tighten the economic blockade around the Third Reich. Pleading for a realistic and efficient approach to this task, he questioned the adequacy of the purely negative slogan "boycott," meaning "*Don't buy German goods*"; his suggestion was to replace it by a positive and more essential formula of "buying"—buying produce "of more acceptable origin"; this to be accompanied by :

exact descriptions of all articles recommended for purchase, with the addresses and telephone numbers of the shops where these articles are to be found.

A real office for boycott propaganda ought to look and sound exactly like a commercial advertising agency. As to the negative side of the business, the "don't"—there is no need for us to bother : the Third Reich itself is taking care of that. Every Berlin cable in every issue of any daily is quite enough to keep up the proper spirit.

In Jabotinsky's concept, the boycott movement was not a purely, and not even a predominantly, "Jewish business." "Some Gentile friends, who are as eager as we are on combatting the Third Reich menace, seem to be relying on Israel : 'The Jew will do it.' That is a dangerous fallacy. We Jews are not more than 1 per cent of purchasing humanity : it is for the remaining 99 per cent to follow our example if they want the blockade to become decisively efficient." And those 99 per cent have every reason to want the blockade to become efficient and to stop talking of "your Jewish boycott." "Pray, Sir, why 'our boycott?' . . . It is yours, it stands and falls with your attitude, not with ours. . . . There are some Gentile nations who, should Germany win, would feel it down to the last man in the remotest hamlet. . . . Our boycott? Not at all : all together."

In this collective effort, Jabotinsky told the London press, his movement "had assigned to itself a modest but important role : to serve, in the beginning, as a *liaison* organization between the various boycott bodies in different lands." The need for such a connecting world-chain had been felt since the movement started. Three attempts at creating it by means of special "world conferences" had proved unsuccessful : "you cannot form a world organization *ad hoc*, world organizations grow up slowly. Well, we Revisionists are a world-wide organization having grown up gradually through ten years of untiring effort, and now we have decided to place our machinery at the disposal of the anti-Hitler movement." [15]

This machinery was a very modest one. At the Revisionist world headquarters in Paris a "Department for Economic Defense" was established which Jabotinsky had to take over himself since, as he put it in a personal letter, "all the Executive Committee members shrank

219

from saddling themselves with a job which obviously could not be done without a fattish budget." [16] He was, however, fully aware of the inadequacy of the work his department was performing. The main handicaps were lack of financial means and the resulting weakness of the machinery. "So far," he wrote on February 5, 1934, to S. Jacobi, "all the work has been done by an unpaid secretary plus a half-time typist lad." He was sure that "very considerable results could be attained in the boycott line. . . . If I get the money, in a few months' time there will be a recognized Center, a little later a world conference of boycott committees." But, he sadly commented, "it is difficult to make bricks without straw," and, until he could get the necessary minimum budget, he refused "to make any big public gestures (which in itself would be very easy): the Jewish world has had enough of big appeals of this kind, unfollowed by a systematic action." He was, however, not ready to take this enforced "half-activity" lying down and was incessantly looking for new channels for popularizing and activating the anti-Nazi crusade: "Recently, I have been thinking of a filmed speech with diagrams on the boycott subject. Twenty minutes of it would cost some ten thousand francs, every additional language about five thousand francs; I could make it really stirring though quiet in tone, and I am sure it would be a most effective and new way of propaganda for Jew and Gentile alike. But . . . " [17]

The "but" killed the projected filmed boycott speech. However, on January 27, 1934, Jabotinsky recorded (at the *Eclair-Tirage* cinema studio in Paris) a film-lecture, "Let the Jews Immigrate to Palestine." Delivered in Yiddish, it lasted about three-quarters of an hour, and was illustrated with diagrams. "It is, as far as I know, the first experiment with a long film-lecture," Jabotinsky wrote to London; "it is intended for simultaneous circulation on the talking screen in various countries during the petition campaign." [18] In Jabotinsky's view, the tragic situation created by the triumph of Nazism in Germany, called not only for economic retaliation against the Third Reich, but first and foremost for the utilization of this situation as a powerful stimulus for a demand for Jewish mass emigration to Palestine. This decisive aspect of the problem was, he felt, completely disregarded both by the official Zionist leadership and by the international bodies in charge of the refugees from Germany.

4. *Life with Jabotinsky*

The two years (1933-35) of the rue Pontoise era were the first experience of steady and truly organized teamwork between Jabotinsky and a group of colleagues on the Revisionist World Executive. In 1925-26 and 1927-29, when the seat of the Executive was in Paris, there was practically no organized collective machinery for them to work with: for a time, this writer and a typist constituted the entire personnel of the office. The members of the Executive were divided between Paris and London, and joint meetings were infrequent. In the early fall of 1929, the world headquarters were transferred to London, while Jabotinsky and four other Executive members resided in Paris. Of the five members of the Executive elected in August, 1932, Jabotinsky was the only one who lived in Paris, while the headquarters remained in London. This state of affairs lasted until March, 1933, and actually precluded his continued, day-to-day cooperation with the ruling body of the movement. It was not before the end of 1933 that all six of the newly elected members of the Executive were concentrated in Paris, holding regular meetings with the President of the Union, currently discussing its problems and making collective decisions, capable of being implemented by an adequately staffed office.

It has for years been common for the critics of Jabotinsky to represent him as fiercely intolerant of any view that did not conform to the "orthodoxy" of his own opinion, as obstinate in his convictions, and as impervious to the arguments of his co-workers. Yet none of this is confirmed by the record of the rue Pontoise experience. It can be firmly asserted—and hardly anyone could be in better position than this writer to judge it at first hand—that Jabotinsky's attitude toward his colleagues was never domineering. He was easy to work with: loyal to his associates, considerate, and never tried to impose his will by the sheer weight of his great authority. Whenever serious divergences of opinion arose, he always endeavored to keep them from developing into an actual rift. He would patiently and tirelessly argue with the dissenters both at meetings and in private talks. In fact, he preferred to use the person-to-person method of settling differences. Past master in dealing with men and women, young and old, simple and refined, he used his charm, both inborn and studied, as one of his main assets. At such a personal discussion, he would state his views in a quiet, persuasive fashion, without undue emphasis, as if still considering the pros and cons, and would then listen attentively and sympathetically to counter-arguments. There was no hint of condescension in his manner, nor of overbearance or intellectual bludgeoning. The aim always was to convert, never to coerce or suppress. The interlocutor was assumed to be a highly intelligent person, with whom he wished to exchange ideas, to make him a fellow seeker after truth. He knew the subtle art of sugarcoating and was not averse to paying an occasional compliment, whether sincere or only half-meant. As a result, the opponent rarely smarted under the humiliation of defeat, having the thrilling sensation of being a partner to an intellectual achievement which, he was made to feel, was as much his as Jabotinsky's

At meetings of the Executive and of other Revisionist ruling bodies, even when matters of major importance were discussed, he never made use of his position as President and acted only as *primus inter pares*, retaining for himself an equal vote with the others. All decisions were made on the basis of majority opinion, to which he submitted graciously. But even if he was not at all satisfied with the outcome of the vote, he never attempted to reverse it by a threat of resignation. While some of his colleagues more than once offered their resignation because of differences of opinion, he consistently opposed such a course. He insisted that a group of earnest, loyal and responsible men must always be able, through discussion and reasoning, to modify each other's opinions in such a way as to produce a decision acceptable to all of them. As a rule, he avoided putting to the vote any major question on which dissension was very strong. He respected dissent. If no accord could be reached, he would postpone decision on the controversial issue, often allowing an opportunity for action to slip by. Some of his over-zealous partisans reproached him for those delaying tactics, claiming that in some cases he temporized beyond the point of prudence; they urged him to use the club of his personal authority against recalcitrant colleagues. Yet he doggedly refused to heed this counsel and act in a dictatorial manner. In the little world of the rue Pontoise, he always acted as mediator in clashes between persons and groups. He was a natural fighter and a born peacemaker. As a rule, he was polite and kind, and curbed his natural impatience. He was gracious and considerate in debate, outspoken but rarely vindictive. Of course, he was no paragon. He had a sharp wit which could and did hurt. He had strong likes and dislikes and was sometimes cutting in retort. But he was quick to recover balance, always eager to establish harmony in discord, unity in diversity.

He used to spend long hours in the rue Pontoise and became fully integrated into daily office life, doing sometimes routine office work himself. It was not at all a rare sight to find him among the secretarial or technical staff, handling stencils or circulars, or even addressing envelopes and attending to the mailing. No amount of insistence that it was wasteful to use his time for this kind of work was of any avail.

The leading nucleus of the "rue Pontoise crowd," as we came to be called, felt at ease and happy in their daily contact with Jabotinsky. This contact was not limited to office hours only, or to regular meetings of the World Executive. More often than not, Jabotinsky would invite one or another of us for a long walk and an intimate chat outside the office. After almost every meeting of the Executive, however late at night, he suggested an *in corpore* excursion to a coffeehouse in order, as he used to say, "to dispel the fumes of the party shop talk by speaking of normal things." Some of us objected, arguing that it was too late, and that he was too tired and in need of rest. Jabotinsky invariably pooh-poohed these objections: "Who is tired? Me? You are dreaming. What we all need now is relaxation, a spiritual bath of light and spirited conversation. Please, let's go. I am going anyway— you wouldn't let me down and abandon me *mutterseelenallein* [quite lonely, forlorn] at a coffeehouse table, would you?" Of course nobody would. And then we stayed in the *Café de la Coupole* until the small hours, exchanging personal reminiscences, talking literature and poetry, telling jokes, gossiping; politics was banned. Jabotinsky was the most animated among us, fresh and carefree, inexhaustible in suggesting new topics, the first to appreciate a well-told story, willing and eager to take up any challenge, as gay and lighthearted as the youngest in our crowd. Those nightly informal gatherings were to all of us a great and unforgettable experience.

There was also no lack of social intercourse. Whenever time permitted, Jabotinsky gladly accepted an invitation for dinner or tea from those of us who had families and homes. He used to come with Mrs. Jabotinsky, and they were most amiable guests and easy to please. More often, the Jabotinskys themselves used to entertain. Their hospitality was simple and friendly, and men and women of all walks of life used to enjoy the atmosphere of their home: Jews and Gentiles, "Parisians" and people in transit. Some of us used to attend these gatherings frequently; others had the privilege of just dropping in informally.

It would, however, be misleading to give the impression that everything was cloudless and idyllically smooth in our "life with Jabotinsky." He suffered greatly from the often petty personal conflicts, acrimonious mutual criticism, and haggling on the part of some of his colleagues and other leading members of the movement. This aspect of the rue Pontaise picture found abundant expression in his personal correspondence of that period.

Answering a long letter from one of his colleagues which, as he put it, "contained reproaches, and very far-reaching ones," Jabotinsky bluntly wrote: [19]

Dear friend, this *entire* gamut must be ruthlessly eliminated from our music. I reserve for myself the sacred right to make mistakes, and I recognize that every member of the Executive Committee is entitled to the same privilege. If something done by one of us looks like a mistake to another, it can be corrected, and in the process of correcting we can have a *sachlich* [matter of fact] argument. But there can be in our midst no question of recriminations or expressions of displeasure; as far as I personally am concerned, I simply exclude them.

In another letter, he pleaded: [20] "For the love of Allah, let's not cavil about the 'tone,' etc. I am already beginning to turn sour from the tornado of multisided susceptibilities."

Personally, he did not resent criticism and was ready to admit mistakes. What he sternly objected to, was that some of the critics made a mountain out of a molehill and tended to dramatize unduly—often at a distance of thousands of miles—things which were of relatively little significance. In a letter to a young and dynamic Palestinian Revisionist, he wrote: [21] "I don't understand all those 'explosions' caused by trifles and I am mortified by them. . . . My rule is at all times: to endure and not to quarrel. We are laboring under hundreds of inconveniences, *and it is going to be always so.* I beg of all of you, too, not to stamp your feet at every difficulty." And in a letter to another Palestinian leader: [22] "You are probably right in many things —I am a bad tactician: either I tolerate [things] for too long, or I stamp my foot too loudly, and in general I make too many mistakes. But what matters is not me, but the movement, which has long ago outgrown *all* of us."

As a rule, he had almost unlimited patience with his colleagues and fellow-workers. Only very rarely, after a long and painful experience, would he reluctantly come to the conclusion that further cooperation was unbearable. In August, 1934, he wrote to S. Jacobi that the Executive Committee "will have to be reconstructed" since one of its members (elected in Prague on Jabotinsky's own recommendation) presented a "difficult and unpleasant problem. I will never forgive myself for having been so mistaken. . . . The more so now that I realize that everything I knew about him should have convinced me beforehand that we would be unable to understand each other. Never in all my life have I seen a more difficult *mauvais coucheur*." [23] Jabotinsky reached this conclusion not because of any serious ideological or tactical dissensions between them, but solely because of the incompatibility of their very natures, of their respective approach to life and work. "He is not just a man," he wrote half-jokingly, half-seriously to the wife of that colleague, "he is Attila, the Scourge of God. . . . If in the Louvre Museum one single corner is not swept properly, he suffers and longs to set things in order: he is like the emperor of all the worlds who feels himself responsible even for the canals on the planet Mars. I am trying to teach him a little of the philosophy of taking it easy." [24]

The attempt to "teach philosophy" failed. Shimshon Younitchman who, in January, 1935, attended the Sixth Revisionist Conference in Cracow, recalls (in an "autobiographical chapter from an unwritten book") a painful episode of which he was an unwilling witness.[25] Invited by Jabotinsky for a chat in the latter's hotel room, he came at the appointed hour. "But when I opened the door, I saw in the room one of the leaders of the movement. I stepped back, but Jabotinsky turned to me and said : 'Come in and listen—and I want you to remember what you hear.' . . . His voice was calm and controlled, but from the first moment on I sensed the storm which was brewing in him."

I sat down and prepared to listen. The speaker was only one of those present—and he was not Jabotinsky. He spoke slowly, with the confidence and assurance of a man who believes in the truth of every word he is saying. His speech encompassed all the current problems from the most important to the trivial; what the policy should be; the actions and methods of achievements; how the World Executive should be organized; where it should reside, and who its members should be.

He did not omit a single point, either important or petty. And it was his opinion that Jabotinsky must perforce accept his views since— according to him—he was the only one who knew and understood. . . .

He did not give Jabotinsky a chance to utter a word. . . . I sat there lost to all sense of time. The day drew to its close, darkness filled the room, and the man left. And then came the eruption I had been waiting for.

"Did you hear, did you see?" Jabotinsky exclaimed as he paced up and down his room. "I must always listen, I must always smile, I must always agree"—and I can't tell anyone off." And then wryly: "I know the choicest swear words in Russian—but can never use them."

In spite of this painful experience, Jabotinsky not only submitted the name of this particular colleague for reelection, but felt highly satisfied with the proceedings and the outcome of the Cracow Conference. "I had at the Conference unqualified *naches* [joy] and no unpleasantness whatsoever," he wrote to his sister.[26] And, indeed, the Cracow gathering was for him in more than one respect a happy and harmonious affair. Not that there was no open and vigorous criticism of his views and policy on the part of several delegates. We will see in Chapter Thirteen that the pact with Ben Gurion met with determined opposition. There was also a strong "maximalist" trend both in regard to the Mandatory Power and the World Zionist Organization. Its spokesmen accused Jabotinsky of "clinging to England" and demanded full endorsement of the aggressive policies of the extreme activist wing in Palestine; they also insisted on non-participation in the forthcoming Nineteenth Zionist Congress and on the immediate establishment of an Independent Zionist Organization.

Newspaper dispatches tended to dramatize this discussion. They spoke of "deeply rooted differences,' of a "fight" between Jabotinsky and the "extremists," and even asserted that he had "left the Conference in protest" against some of the speakers' utterances.[27] In fact, he took all this criticism philosophically, seeing in it a welcome manifestation of the movement's growing political maturity: "Our Revisionist movement suffers from the lack of a regular opposition. Like any other leader, I make enough errors, and I am also not a youngster any longer : I can stand a slap in the face (of course, only metaphorically speaking)." [28]

5. *L'Art Epistolaire*

It was mostly during the rue Pontoise era that Jabotinsky's immediate collaborators had the opportunity of appraising the full scope and character of his *art épistolaire*.

Thomas Jefferson's biographer relates that when this great President died, at the age of eighty-three, his grandson found twenty-six thousand letters addressed to him and sixteen thousand replies on file, and adds: "To answer these letters was a stupendous task." Jefferson himself used to say that he was "devoured by correspondence."[29]

Jabotinsky died when he was fifty-nine. No full record of his correspondence exists. Unlike the "Sage of Monticello," he never possessed a permanent domicile where his correspondence could have been properly preserved. Thousands of his letters were lost or perished together with their addressees in the great holocaust of European Jewry. Yet it can hardly be doubted that, during his much shorter lifetime, his epistolary record matched, and possibly exceeded, that of Jefferson. The Jabotinsky Institute in Tel Aviv possesses a collection of about six thousand letters written by Jabotinsky. But this is indubitably only a small part of his correspondence. This writer was fortunate to discover many more letters, which had been jealously kept by their addressees, and he is sure that they, too, are but a fraction of the real number of letters still scattered in private hands.

Unlike Jefferson, who used "laborsaving devices and timesaving methods" to cope with his correspondence and invented a polygraph which produced stereotyped missives,[30] Jabotinsky, as a rule, wrote each of his letters by hand. He was reluctant to dictate to a stenotypist. Some of his colleagues at the rue Pontoise insisted that this practice wasted precious time, and that the fact that no carbon copies of his letters were available, often led to regrettable complications. After much persuasion, he yielded to these arguments and one morning dictated a flood of letters to the best stenotypist of the office. In the afternoon, when she put on his desk an impressive stack of neatly typed sheets, he gratefully admired the promptness and precision of her work. But—he later shamefacedly confessed—after having read the letters, he burned them in the grate and rewrote every letter . . . by hand. "Dictated and typed letters sound impersonal and hollow; I don't recognize myself in them," he explained. Once, sending a typewritten letter to a friend, he added a handwritten witty postscript:[31] "I hope that this attempt of mine to dictate letters will teach you, once and for all, that I wasn't born to dictate, or, to be more exact, that the Almighty prescribed for me different ways of making use of secretarial help (but even for that all terms have run out)." He therefore begged us in the office to let him conduct his correspondence "in his own old-fashioned way." The only concession we were able to extort from him was to permit the office to make copies of letters dealing fully or in part with political and party matters, thus giving us the possibility of keeping some record of his mail; but whenever he could, he tried to circumvent this arrangement.

He wrote ten to twenty letters almost every day. The procedure was invariably the same. First, he would prepare the required number of envelopes, and write the names and addresses; then, he would begin writing the letters, one after the other, in a clean, neat, easily legible handwriting. It was a rule with him to answer personally every letter he received, even from the most obscure and humble people. To a closer circle of friends and associates he wrote regularly, frequently, and voluminously, taking up item by item the topics they had dealt with in their letters. He, in turn, reported and commented upon the main events and the problems he was facing, discussing them briefly or in detail, and usually asking for the opinion or advice of the adressee. Sometimes his answers were longer than the letters he had received. Some were little concise treatises on political, moral and personal problems. He wrote easily, with clarity, wit, and precision, and phrases tipped with meaning and beauty rolled happily from his pen. There is a *mot juste,* a pithy maxim, an imaginative idea to be culled from almost every page.

It is an essential characteristic of letters written to private persons, in a more or less intimate style and not for publication, that they disclose many facets of a man's life and personality to which he is either unwilling or unable to give expression in his more deliberately written literary works. Letter-writing is, undoubtedly, an art in itself, and many writers have been more successful in their correspondence than in their other forms of literary production. In their letters they are more vivid, uninhibited by their "audience," and able to express themselves in as "self-uncensored" a form as they choose. Jabotinsky's personality is probably best reflected in his letters. They are the record of his public life, with occasional glimpses into the personal sphere. They contain everything of him—his hopes and disillusionments, his obstinacy and his weaknesses, his foibles and caprices, his inspirations and failures. They are crammed with contradictions—a deeply human mixture of courage and despair. They show him in a maze of activities extending in various directions at the same time, striving to achieve in the few years of his lifetime a truly gigantic multitude of things.

To each of his numerous correspondents he wrote in a highly personal manner. Even though the topics he was dealing with were often the same, he would approach them in an individual way in every particular case, adapted to the personality, mentality, and relationship of the man he was writing to. A close study of Jabotinsky's correspondence reveals a highly developed personal technique, a deep perception of human psychology, and an almost uncanny skill in using alternatively serious and light, logical and humorous, lofty and deliberately commonplace arguments and expressions. He did not hesitate to make ample use of the *argumentum ad hominem*, deftly speculating on human vanity, always accurately choosing the weak spot in his correspondent's armor. Many of the letters are homely, abounding in minor and touching *faits divers* about his immediate family and the larger circle of Mrs. Jabotinsky's relatives.

Jabotinsky admitted that as a rule he preferred writing to personal contact. He was easily tired, and even irked, by the necessity of meeting people. He felt more at ease when *tête-à-tête* with a sheet of paper and his fountain pen, free to arrange his arguments as he thought best, than when he had to face an interlocutor.

He was past master of the *art épistolaire*. In this writer's opinion, he excelled in this art more than in any other form of his literary activity. Some of his letters are little masterpieces, both in content and form.

Those familiar with Jabotinsky's habits and tastes often wondered about his evident enjoyment of the very process of writing. In addition to the daily load of correspondence and articles, he, of his own volition, used to keep detailed minutes of Revisionist committee meetings and Party conferences, and write reports of these conferences for the Revisionist press. No amount of arguing that such chores were not for him and could be easily done by a secretary, was of any avail. Whenever not directly occupied otherwise, he was always scribbling, doodling, or sketching. Some of his sketches reveal considerable ability.

Characteristic of Jabotinsky's personality, as reflected in his correspondence, is his handwriting. It is plain, straight, and easily readable; the letters are uniform, the spaces between the letters and the words are well gauged, and the whole is neatly and simply laid out. There is nothing in his penmanship to suggest an intention to produce something out of the ordinary. His signature is always plainly lettered, without flourish : just an initial and his surname.

THE " ENEMY OF LABOR "

1. *Against "Obstanovotchka"*

FOR THE LAST fifteen years of his life, Jabotinsky was known to wide circles of Jewish public opinion as an inveterate "enemy of labor." This label played an important role in his political career. Its genesis and development deserve close attention.

In Jabotinsky's political record prior to the emergence of Revisionism there was very little to warrant a reputation of such kind. In prewar Russia he was the "darling" of all Zionist parties, including the *Poalei Zion* and *Zeirei Zion*. In wartime Palestine, the *Poalei Zion* (later the *Ahdut ha'Avoda*) were the first ones actively to support his campaign for the Legion and his protest against Dr. Weizmann's early appeasement policy.[1] At the embryonic stage of the Revisionist movement, Jabotinsky apparently counted on the support of some labor leaders : when, in 1923, he compiled a list of persons to whom the first "activist" circulars had to be sent (see chapter One), the names of David Ben Gurion and Itzhak Ben Zvi were included. In 1923-1924, when the *Rasswyet* in Berlin became his mouthpiece, no problems affecting the Zionist labor groups or the social nature of Palestine's upbuilding were raised in the paper's columns. Jabotinsky concentrated on ideological and political matters. He firmly believed that the new trend in Zionism that he was advocating was, by its very nature, equally acceptable to all "Herzlian Zionists," irrespective of party allegiance. He urged his early followers in Salonica "to propagate our principles in their respective circles, whether orthodox or free thinkers, bourgeois or workers, because activism is nothing but an expurgated concept of the Zionist idea, which is equally binding upon the *Mizrachi* or the *Poalei Zion*."[2]

It was in 1925, when the *Rasswyet* was transferred to Paris, that a series of articles began to appear, dealing with the attitude of the "leftist" parties toward the basic problems of Zionism. Jabotinsky found this attitude discouraging. The leadership of the labor groups showed no understanding of or sympathy for the activist political program and demands. They saw in them merely an attempt to divert Zionism from everyday constructive work in Palestine, which, they insisted, was the very core of the Zionist effort. Their main concern was to preserve, and further increase whatever positions Palestine labor had gained; and they were distrustful of any demands which, in their opinion, were likely to jeopardize these positions and prospects. Basically, it was the same attitude Jabotinsky had to struggle against a decade before when he first launched the idea of the Legion. In a "Letter from a Journey," published on June 16, 1915, in *Odesskiya Novosti,* he rebelled against the argument that a distinct pro-Allied orientation and propaganda for the Jewish Legion would endanger the existing Jewish achievements in Palestine :

It is now becoming increasingly clear what [Max] Nordau was afraid of, when he was so distrustful of the demands for petty colonization. He once observed in a private conversation: "The Bible says that a man who had recently built himself a cottage is no longer a good soldier." Nordau feared that the "cottage" would become a *Selbstzweck* [end in itself]: its wallpaper, furniture, featherbeds, the entire *obstanovotchka* [an untranslatable Russian word, meaning roughly "little setting,"] which had been accumulated with so much toil, would gradually become more precious than the ultimate goal . . . a cannon ball chained to our ankles, and a cord tying our hands.

It was the same substitution of *obstanovotchka* for the great ultimate aims of Zionism that, ten years later, provoked Jabotinsky's first criticism of Palestine's organized labor.[3] He was deeply troubled by the hold that the practical colonizing acquisitions had taken on Zionist ideology and the Socialist Zionist parties. This attitude, he felt, had become "the privilege of our left wing . . . here, the future is being supplanted by the interests of today." "Is it really unavoidable?"

Aversion against the influence of *obstanovotchka* on Zionist political parties in Palestine remained an essential and permanent feature of Jabotinsky's Zionist concept. He was firmly convinced that, if they allowed themselves to grow absorbed by everyday worries connected with their economic positions, parties and organizations were bound to become "practical" to the extent of losing their wider political perspective, and measuring any Zionist political action solely by its immediate effect on the safety and prosperity of their immediate economic vested interests. He therefore enjoined his followers in Palestine to avoid the "cannon ball" of *obstanovotchka*, thus keeping themselves free for political action, and independent from Zionist budgetary allocations. And indeed, of all the Palestine Zionist formations, the Revisionist party and its affiliates were the only ones who (with few minor exceptions) possessed no settlements, economic enterprises, or institutions of their own. This enabled them to preserve the integrity of their Zionist ideal and their freedom of action, making them the militant political vanguard of the *Yishuv*. The price they paid for it was, however, very high : they were the real "have-nots" of the Jewish community, and their economic poverty more than once adversely affected their political chances.

In 1925, when Jabotinsky's first critical articles appeared, the only group that possessed strong economic positions in Palestine was organized labor. He strongly advocated the necessity to strengthen the position of the Jewish *Mittelstand*, in particular that of the artisans.[4] Quoting the complaints of the private sector of Palestine's Jewish economy that the lion's share of the Zionist budget was going to the labor organizations, with the result that artisans and small settlers in non-collectivist colonies were being discriminated against, Jabotinsky called for the "straightening out of this inequality." He did not minimize the value of the labor colonization : "There can be no question of destroying or weakening this element." But its tremendous preponderance and the pathetic weakness of the private sector were creating a dangerous situation. The latter were bitter and liable to take recourse to "militant self-organization, which may lead to Fascism; we must not let that happen." Saying a forceful "Basta" to the existing state of affairs, Jabotinsky called for an "equilibrium of Palestine's social elements" and offered a three-point program : 1. Revision of the exaggerated pro-labor items of the Zionist budget; 2. Budgetary support for private enterprise; 3. Special consideration for the artisans.

These articles soon earned Jabotinsky the bitter animosity of the labor leadership. He was branded as the arch-enemy of labor. In a fighting rejoinder, "The Enemy of Labor," he lashed out at his accusers :[5]

There is no common language between myself and the majority of the labor leaders, because I have no check book. Their personal integrity is above suspicion. They need the check book not for themselves, but for their party *obstanovotchka*. I cannot talk to them now about principles when, without even blinking, all they look for is what your hands can offer them. . . .

The ideological enthusiasm of our workers has worn off, and they are now submerged in purely economic interests. . . . Everything else is being sacrificed on this altar. As long as payments are forthcoming, everything is all right. I call this kind of tactics—corruption, and this mentality—collective venality. If *this* is the true, inevitable face for the labor movement in Palestine, then I am, indeed, its enemy.

However, he denied the allegation that he was an "enemy" of the collective sector of the Jewish economy in Palestine: "This is not true. . . . There is no Socialism whatsoever either in the *Kvutzot* or in the *Hamashbir* and *Solel Boneh,* and there never will be. There are simply groups of good people, who wish to build their lives in Palestine on cooperative foundations, and they must be helped. Alongside with them, there are other good people who prefer to settle on the basis of individualistic private economy, and they, too, must be helped, without any consideration for the rhetoric slogans, 'right' or 'left.' "

2. *We, the Bourgeois*

This early phase of Jabotinsky's conflict with the Zionist left parties did not meet with the unqualified approval of some of his colleagues. This writer, for instance, objected to antagonizing the labor groups, in whose midst, he believed, there were valuable prospective converts to Zionist activism, while the middle class was less likely to follow Jabotinsky's lead. Jabotinsky responded:[6] "My dear man, don't delude yourself: though many workers are very tempted to accept our program, our true field is *Mittelstand*. We will never be able to come to terms with people who possess, in addition to Zionism, another ideal [Socialism]."

It would be misleading to interpret Jabotinsky's reference to "middle class" as an endorsement of class distinction in the upbuilding of Palestine. He later took pains to make it clear that "what this term really means to describe is simply the average type of Jew nearing or above the age of thirty, just as the term 'proletariat' in common Zionist parlance simply describes the same average Jew of twenty or thereabouts." He insisted that it was "futile here to speak of classes; everybody knows that, in that harmful and preposterous phraseology fashionable in certain Zionist circles, 'proletarian' wage earners are the sons of the 'bourgeoisie' and the 'bourgeoisie' are their fathers and elder brothers." To him, middle-class settlers were as much pioneers of Palestine's upbuilding as were the workers. The difference was only that they represented a category of pioneers that were "sadly neglected in Zionist practice . . . considerably debarred from sharing in the pioneer work." [7]

For his scathing criticism of the predominance of the Socialist groups in Zionism and his advocacy of the rights of private economy in the upbuilding of Palestine, Jabotinsky has been accused of bourgeois leanings. At that time—and much later—the "bourgeois" label was in Jewish public opinion the worst imaginable *capitis diminutio*. The "proletariat" was considered the class of the future, the only worthy object of admiration, and Socialism—the only lofty ideal, toward which humanity was inexorably moving. The bourgeosie, on the other hand, were viewed as a class that had outlived both its value and its usefulness.

Jabotinsky forcefully challenged this concept. In a defiant article, "We, the Bourgeois," published in May, 1927, he ridiculed the snobish cult of the proletariat as the only protagonist of progress and the sole hope of humanity.* He scolded the bourgeosie for its inferiority complex and spineless readiness—even eagerness—to admit that, as a class, it represented an obsolete and reactionary phenomenon. He reminded them that all the lofty and holy principles of freedom, equality, and brotherhood, now upheld primarily by the classless intelligentsia, were first proclaimed by the bourgeoisie. Instead of being ashamed of the label "bourgeoisie," the intelligentsia must be proud of it : "If there is a class in whose hands the future lies . . . it is we, the bourgeoisie, the enemies of a super police-state, the ideologists of individualism. . . . We don't have to be ashamed, my bourgeois comrades." Not less outspoken than his somewhat surprising endorsement of the "bourgeois" label, was his negation of Socialism : "I never

---

* Ten years later, he wrote in a letter to Ben Gurion, marked "Personal:" "The root of the danger lies, in fact, in the very concept of the 'worker' as the crown of creation, in his exaggerated feeling of 'being chosen,' in his monopolizing the title of 'worker,' of which he alone is worthy, and not I or myriads of other 'non-productive' drones like me." (Letter to Ben Gurion, March 30, 1935.)

belonged to a Socialist party, but there was a time when I believed in Socialism. In an old booklet of mine, written in 1910, I found the following lines : 'I consider the socialization of the means of production an inevitable and desirable result of the social process.' I wouldn't say that now. I don't consider the establishment of a socialist order either desirable or inevitable, or even feasible. . . . Humanity is not moving toward Socialism; it is going in the reverse direction."[8]

This article—in particular the identification of the classless intelligentsia with the bourgeoisie as a class—provoked some discussion in Revisionist circles. This writer pleaded for a "Second Basta" (*Rasswyet,* May 22, 1927)—a stop to acrimonious polemics with the labor movement in Palestine : "In years to come, our way will lie *with* the Jewish labor movement, and not against it." Jabotinsky, editor-in-chief of the *Rasswyet,* did not object to the publication of this article. But he remained unconvinced. When, a year later, he settled in Palestine, his experience with the "left" was anything but encouraging. The labor wing press in Palestine unanimously branded him as servant of bourgeoisie and a reactionary. In *Hapoel Hatzair* (December 21, 1928)), Zvi Lufban called him "doorkeeper of the Bourgeoisie," and A. Tabori in *Kuntres* (of 17. Adar B.) considered even this label too flattering : the bourgeois elements in Zionism, he insisted, were more inclined than the bourgeoisie of any other nation "to meet the wishes of the proletariat through social reforms." Jabotinsky's Revisionism was, however, "the reactionary instrument of a certain sector of the bourgeoisie . . . a Jewish Fascism"; Jabotinsky's intention was to "perpetuate the exploitation of the worker by the employer."

Jabotinsky's correspondence with those of his friends who pleaded with him for a more conciliatory policy, is indicative of his reaction. To I. Klinov he wrote :[9]

Do you earnestly believe that I am attacking the left? It is the left that is waging war against us; I don't know why, but it is obviously something organic. Of course, our social *Einstellung* [attitude] is different: it is neither "left" nor "right," but inexorably colonizing. Still, the discussion could be conducted calmly, if they wouldn't hound us.

In a somewhat different version, the same argument was repeated in a letter to this writer :[10] "I don't understand why you overlook [the fact] that it is they who are our enemies. They hate everything that is ours; if I wouldn't have written 'Basta,' they would have hated

us just the same. To them the problem is clear: the Jewish youth
will be either theirs or ours. The ideological abyss between us is
bottomless; so is the moral abyss; and that is what irritates them most.
The hatred here is an organic one; it is not dependent on our will, and
nothing can be done about it."

A spirited defense of his stand can be found in a letter Jabotinsky
wrote to I. Klinov after the Sixteenth Zionist Congress:[11]

> . . . I would like very much to make peace with them. But to achieve
> this goal, we would have, first, to "give" them something, and second—
> and this is the most important part—to stop "taking away" from them.
> Is this objectively possible? What can we "give" them, if our entire
> thinking is in the direction of abolishing *takzivim* [budgetary allocations],
> of prohibiting strikes, and of equilibrium between the classes—and all
> this in a country, where the predomiant influence is now theirs? We just
> cannot stop "taking away" from them. And it is the youth that we are
> snatching away; if the *Gush Avodah* [the Revisionist labor unit] will
> develop, and this is mandatory, we will take away part of the workers;
> we will deprive them of the glamour, of the role of the knightly vanguard,
> of the title of an *arbiter elegantiarum* in Zionist, democratic and radical
> matters. How can *they* make peace with us? We could, of course, change
> our "tune," argue with them in an academic style, without barbs; this
> would change exactly nothing. They hate us organically and inevitably;
> for them, it is—either they or we.

Jabotinsky regretted that "such a major and serious conflict" was
being "reduced to a few offensive sentences of mine." His "quarel"
with the Socialist parties in Zionism was rooted not in his alleged
"enmity toward labor," but in a deep and far-reaching difference
between their respective concepts of Zionist fulfillment.

The underlying principle of Zionist Socialism was the notion of class
struggle in Palestine. According to this notion, as Jabotinsky formulated it, "every Jewish worker should consider himself an enemy of the
Jewish capitalist even though the latter utilizes this capital to build
another factory, or to purchase a plantation, and employs in his concerns Jewish labor exclusively." To him, this conception was "the
most conspicuous example of a blind absurdity." Classes can exist only
in an already formed and established society, and the class-war theory
(no matter whether it be right or wrong in other countries) cannot
and should not be applied to a country undergoing a period of
colonization. "The *Yishuv's* economy is essentially a new growth, and

every enterprise in the country is still but an experiment; this 'infant' economy cannot yet withstand the clashes involved in class war." On the other hand, the influx of private capital, as long as it employs Jewish labor, is an absolute Zionist necessity since every new enterprise provides employment for a number of new immigrants: "the 'harmony' of national interests resulting from this situation should, consequently, outweigh all other considerations." Of course, in Palestine— as in any other country—the individual interests of the worker are different from those of his employer: the former wants to earn more, the latter to pay less. But, whereas in France or England it is not the concern of the worker whether his employer can "stand" higher wages or not, the case is entirely different in Palestine. There the worker, if he is a Zionist, cannot afford the luxury of undermining an enterprise, nor can the employer impose sub-standard working conditions in his enterprise: in both cases, the scope of colonization possibilities would be narrowed. Any manifestation of "class war"—strikes as well as lock-outs—clashes with the supreme interests of Zionism.

Social conflicts in the process of Zionist upbuilding "must be therefore always settled by compulsory national arbitration," to which all disputes between employers and employees must be submitted; "neutral labor exchanges" must distribute employment among Jewish workers. Jabotinsky admitted that as long as the Arbitration Board was not yet set up, situations might arise in which a strike might be the only means of obtaining just wages and working conditions from a miserly employer and he was confident that his followers would "never forget that there is a solidarity among all wage earners" and not attempt to break such a strike. He proudly recorded that they had never been accused, even by their adversaries, of "undercutting wages established by the practice of the Socialist *Histadrut,* nor of 'breaking' any strikes resulting from disputes that were purely and genuinely industrial." He insisted, however, that this principle could not be applied to strikes motivated by the *Histadrut's* intention to secure full control over the economic life of the *Yishuv.* More than once, such strikes were declared when an employer had hired Revisionist workers who did not wish to join the Socialist *Histadrut,* or obtain work through its employment offices. The purpose of those strikes was to have such workers discharged. Revisionists and *Betarim,* whose removal was demanded, could not be expected not to "break" this kind of strike.[12]

237

3. Cease-Fire—After Effects

In the above quoted letter to I. Klinov, written in August, 1929, Jabotinsky offered a challenging interpretation of what could be called the "psychological strategy" of his political crusades : "All my so-called 'talent' amounts to concentrating my entire brain power on one single point: I locate the main center of evil and formulate that evil so sharply as to make it unforgettable to both friend and foe. In doing so, I do not strive for objective justice. On the contrary, I deliberately bend the stick in one direction : there is no other way of making the stick straight. This is the only publicistic method I am good at." But, he added sadly, "in order not to grieve my friends, I am now avoiding sharp expressions, and not only in this field."

This latter statement was but the beginning of a new line he had decided for some time to follow in his journalistic work and introduce into the Revisionist press. Two months later, he entreated S. Gepstein, who was then responsible for the editorial policy of the *Doar Hayom*, to avoid any polemics with the labor parties. As his main reason for this request, he invoked considerations of "educational" nature :[13] "There are in our midst people who dream of peace with the Laborites. ... And they are good people : Klinov, Schechtman, and *many young people*. Now it is the time to reeducate them. But to achieve this, it is necessary that they should see plainly that it is essentially the other side which is the aggressor—*even if we do not call them names*. Otherwise (if we do) the entire effect will be lost again. I attribute *extraordinary* importance to this reeducation : we shall very soon need full unity in this [Revisionist] party." In an article "We and the Workers," Jabotinsky publicly announced this "new deal" of his, and candidly explained its background and purpose.[14]

Our relations with the labor wing in Zionism have become extremely tense. ... It is asserted that my articles and speeches have played a great role in erecting a wall between us. I don't share this view. There is, of course, no denying that I have quite deliberately contributed to the clarification, even to the "sharpening" of the contradiction between the two ideologies; in my opinion, this contradiction is now objectively inevitable. In regard to the "sharpening" of objective contradictions, I have a firm and long-established view of my own—I believe that there are cases when avoiding "sharpening" means contributing to *deepening* [the controversy], which is much worse. But just now, I will not defend this view of mine. On the contrary: I will suggest an experiment based on a converse pledge; and let's see how it will turn out.

The suggestion was that for the duration of the "experiment," he and those who felt like he did, be "eliminated from the field" and that the floor be given to those who believe in reconciliation with the labor wing. "They want reconciliation: let's honestly help them to carry out this experiment. Very well, I shall keep silent on this question. If, in my capacity as a newspaperman on a permanent job, I have to write about the Zionist labor movement, I will write and speak not with my own voice and express not my own thoughts," but those of the believers. And he frankly explained the reason for this decision: because the "troubled conscience of men whose conscience is very dear to me is at stake. During my five years in the Revisionist camp I came to realize, from experience on many questions . . . how important it is, when you are working with people who really belong to your spiritual 'race,' not to violate a comrade's conscience, to give him and yourself time to realize when a mistake has been made."

For a time, Jabotinsky faithfully abided by this self-imposed journalistic restraint. It remained one-sided. There was no noticeable reciprocity on the part of the labor wing. The accentuated class-struggle ideology of the *Histadrut* led to frequent strikes: both this ideology and its application were contrary to the convictions of Jabotinsky's working class followers. They felt unhappy in the *Histadrut* and favored the establishment of an independent labor group. This proposal was brought before the Fourth Revisionist World Conference (Prague, August, 1930), where Jabotinsky supported it, while many influential delegates strongly opposed it.[15] The majority of the Conference endorsed the principle of an independent labor formation. At least one of the opponents took this decision as sufficient reason to resign from the Revisionist party, claiming that the decision was both ideologically wrong and tactically self-defeating. In a long personal letter, Jabotinsky vigorously defended the fundamental necessity of combatting the *Histadrut,* and the Socialist parties whose instrument it had become.[16] He wrote :

Their disease is an organic one: I call it *Sha'atnez.** Put up two idols in a Temple and it is inevitable that "the second one" will emerge as victor; and the longer this [situation] lasts, all the more. We will yet be witnesses

* A Hebrew term applied to a cloth woven from mixed fibres, half wool, half cotton; the manufacturing and wearing of *Sha'atnez* was strictly forbidden by the Bible.

239

to completely paradoxical susprises . . . They [the labor parties] will be compelled to convert the *Histadrut* into a Jewish-Arab Confederation [of Labor], that is to organize the Arab populace and make it nationally conscious (you certainly know that in the final analysis labor unions always perform this task). And they will clearly have to renounce [the idea of] a Jewish State and Jewish majority [in Palestine]. . . . How can Zionism reconcile itself with *such* a labor wing? How can Zionism evade the obligation to fight it quite openly? In other words: how can one not to demand that the working masses leave this camp and join a sounder one?

The question whether it is necessary, in order to achieve this goal, to begin by creating the nucleus of a new camp, or whether it is better to dig from within, is a trifle . . . . The root of the evil, and the core of the problem, is that in its present form the whole labor movement has no *raison d'etre* in Zionism.

The uncertainty as to whether the *Histadrut* could and should be reformed "from within," or a parallel labor union be founded, did not last long. By May, 1932, Jabotinsky came out for the immediate creation of a full-fledged "second labor organization": "A nucleus is already in existence. If a purely professional Federation of Jewish Labor is established, abnegating class struggle during the process of colonization, many workers will join it." Since the existing *Histadrut* was not ready to become a strictly professional labor union, without a class struggle program, "Zionist workers have no place there." [17] Five months later, describing the Socialist *Histadrut* as the "red *Hakenkreuz*," he said: [18] "If the obese sarcoma called *Histadrut,* which grows daily fatter and fatter on middle-class gifts, will be permitted to go on swelling, it will stifle everything that is still alive in Zionism. . . . A stream of healthy blood is fighting this malignant tumor. . . . A handful of young people, to whom Zionism is everything, and the red banner—a rag (and an alien at that)—are defending their right to serve the Jewish State ideal. For that they get beaten up. . . . The *Histadrut* is not, and is not going to be, the only Jewish labor organization in Palestine. There are other organizations that will also grow."

4. *Yes, To Break*

This anti-*Histadrut* crusade culminated in the article "Yes, To Break!" which was widely—and mostly unfavorably—commented upon in the Zionist press;[19] it accentuated Jabotinsky's reputation as a confirmed "enemy of labor." He was, however, not at all impressed by this adverse reaction: "The word 'to break,' which I have used, is very unpopular. I have, however, long ago noticed (and I am probably not the only one to have noticed it) that when a word suddenly begins to become 'unpopular,' it is often an indication that the *notion* itself is popular, maybe even very popular." He nevertheless stressed that he had "never spoken of breaking the *Histadrut* as such, but of breaking its monopolistic status, its privileged position and its predominant role." [20] He denied any intention of minimizing the role and importance of labor in the upbuilding of Palestine: "It is not honest to say, even in the heat of discussion, that we, who want to break the class monopoly, 'forget' the services rendered by the workers or even by the *Histadrut*. It is not true: we remember. But we remember the total [of the services], not only one side. Not one single thing in Palestine has been created by the workers alone. There are two drops of sweat in every stone, in every tree, in every leaf, and any claim to exclusiveness must and will be broken, as it deserves to be." [21] He also denied that militant anti-Socialism had played a role in his anti-*Histadrut* crusade: "We have no quarrel with the Socialist ideal; I personally happen not to like it. I know, however, many people, old and young, even in my own party, who consider the Socialist system a very good one. Class struggle is something quite different." [22] "The second *Histadrut* must be a non-partisan organization, which is open to all Jewish workers, under one condition only: its method of protecting the workers' interests is—arbitration." [23]

The Fifth Revisionist World Conference (Vienna, August, 1932) decided that a "National *Histadrut*" was to be formed the next year. It was, however, not before the spring of 1934, that the Foundation Conference of the "National Labor Federation" took place in Tel Aviv, to which Jabotinsky sent affectionate greetings and a programmatic message.[24] He remained an ardent admirer of this body later also, when it was struggling hard for its very existence: "The *Oved Leum* (National Labor Federation)," he wrote in May, 1935, "is the most important, the most fruitful, and the most dangerous of all our enterprises in Palestine." [25] It was "dangerous" because it was a challenge to the hegemony of the Socialist *Histadrut* in the field of distribution of labor, and insisted that conflicts between workers and employers be settled not by strikes but by arbitration. The left retaliated against this "violation of class solidarity" by physical attacks on greatly outnumbered Revisionist workers. Jabotinsky felt deeply outraged by this violence and his bitterness against the Socialist *Histadrut* reached its peak. After a particularly brutal attack (early in 1934, in Haifa), he gave a new interpretation to his appeal to "break" the *Histadrut*: "When I first wrote this word, what I had in mind was to break only the monopoly of the *Histadrut,* not the *Histadrut* as such. . . . But now I intend to go a bit further. Now I ask: would it be really so great a sin to think of breaking the *Histadrut* itself?" [26]

He was, however, firmly opposed to any attempt on the part of his followers to retaliate in kind. When reports reached him that Revisionists and *Betarim* were retaliating and attacking leftish clubs and their members, he "most earnestly" appealed "to all who are prepared to heed a request of mine," that, irrespective of who was the first to provoke a conflict, "there should be no more attacks of this kind by Revisionists. The custom of beating up other Jews must remain the 'monopoly' of the red camp, a monopoly which we can with a light heart leave to the *Histadrut,* and to its friends in countries other than Palestine." [27]

5. *Jabotinsky's Social Philosophy*

Jabotinsky's actual views on social problems, on the relationship between labor and capital, can be found in two penetrating essays written in 1931 ("Socialism or Jubilee") and 1936 ("The Social Philosophy of the Old Testament"). His choice of the Bible as the source of inspiration in this field was dictated not by a belief that it was divinely inspired, but, as he put it, by the fact that "the brains that cooperated in the creation of the Old Testament were on the whole excellent brains" and that they were applied to essentially the same problems "which torment modern society—freedom and tyranny, labor and wealth, justice and inequity." He felt that in the majority of cases they had "solved" those problems by forecasting "reasonable and practicable methods of dealing with social sores."

Characteristically enough, the first basic item he singled out in the social legislation of the Bible, was the Sabbath idea (Deutoronomy 5: 13-14; 24: 14-15; 23: 15-16; Leviticus 25: 39-40), which he described as the "source of all the devices ever invented for the protection of the proletariat." To him it signified "that the whole relationship between master and servant is the business of God and King;

that there is no 'iron law' limiting exploitation only by what the have-not can stand without collapsing. . . . It seems that whenever a finger if lifted in labor, an important public function is performed, an act of divine service subject to divine and public control."

The second basic item singled out was what Jabotinsky calls the "Social Tax" principle (Leviticus 19 : 9-10; Deutoronomy 14 : 28-29; 23 : 24-25; Exodus 23 : 10-11) reserving to the gleaners the "edge" of the field and of the vineyard : this, too, is "the source of all modern conceptions of social assistance."

The third and most revolutionary answer to the problem of social injustice is, however, the Bible's "Jubilee Year" principle (Leviticus 25 : 8-10; 23-25; 28). This "sweeping social antidote to the free play of riches and poverty" demands that once in every period of fifty years there shall be proclaimed "freedom in the land"; any family that has been forced by poverty or debts to sell or to mortgage its property shall recover it on the Jubilee day, and every man who, during the period of forty-nine years preceding the Jubilee, has sold himself as slave, shall become free with his children and grandchildren. This "scheme sanctioning and legalizing what amounts to periodical social revolutions," strongly appealed to Jabotinsky.

Yet, he stressed, "this is not Socialism . . . this is the reverse of Socialism" :

The gist of all Socialist theories, whether Marxian or not, is to exclude once and for all any "objective" possibility for any private person or private concern to accumulate wealth, the method of exclusion being so thorough as to make unnecessary any correctives, any measures against abuse or exaggerated wealth. . . .

The Jubilee idea is, on the contrary, essentially and admittedly a corollary to the free play of economic forces; a corrective proposed just because the play of those forces is meant to remain free. The competitive order of the world's economy which causes one man to win and another to lose is here recognized as the normal and permanent foundation of all social activity. Society (or Law, or the State) shall only interfere from time to time as a sort of jobbing gardener who, on each of his far-between visits uses his pruning knife to stop such exaggerated growth of a plant as might endanger the development of its neighbors. . . . It is a system eminently "Liberal" in the essential, the "philosophical," sense of the term. Liberalism is, above all, a creed which prefers repression of evil to prevention of evil, just as it discards the preventive censorship of newspapers, relying on the efficacy of fines which will be imposed if and when a *delit de presse* is committed.   Expressed in terms of social economy, it means letting people trade and build and compete as they like, triumph or fail, accumulate millions or lose their last pennies, provided no one is allowed to go hungry and homeless, and no one need submit to slavery for want of food and home.

A quarter of a century ago, Jabotinsky's views on handling the social sores of modern society came very close to what is now called the concept of a "Welfare State." He saw the State's paramount duty in providing basic social services to its citizens and thus guaranteeing them equality of opportunity. Every citizen must be encouraged to rise above the agreed decent minimum standard of living; but none should be allowed to fall below this minimum.

Economic and social problems did not belong to Jabotinsky's main field of interest. But they were never absent in his crowded intellectual life. On May 5, 1940, shortly before his passing, he wrote to a New York publisher: "I have brought along a Russian manuscript boldly entitled *A Textbook of Political Economy for Beginners*. . . . It would take a year to make my textbook printable, and I am not likely to find the time. . . ."

THE ABORTIVE BEN GURION ROMANCE

1. *The Peace Offer*

IT WAS only natural that Jabotinsky should be in high spirits after the favorable outcome of the Stavsky trial. It was for the first time after many months of hard work and anxiety that he was able to relax with the feeling of a "job well done." He was also fully aware that Stavsky's acquittal and the collapse of the "blood libel" represented a great moral victory for his movement. This victory was accentuated by the bad grace with which the main antagonists, the labor wing, took the failure of their anti-Revisionist crusade. Far from acknowledging defeat, they persisted in calling Stavsky a murderer, claiming that he had been acquitted merely because of some legalistic technicalities; they even intensified their offensive against the Revisionists in Palestine, making violence and physical attacks an everyday occurrence. Greatly outnumbered, the Revisionists fiercely struck back. Violent clashes and acrimonious polemics were almost daily reported by the press, causing acute uneasiness and concern in all responsible Zionist circles.

Tactically, as a party, the Jabotinsky camp was in a rather advantageous position. For the first time, public opinion was inclined to blame not them but their adversaries for this sad state of affairs. There was a strong temptation to make capital out of this favorable conjuncture, to intensify the struggle and to reap its profits. Several of Jabotinsky's colleagues on the Revisionist World Executive urged him to endorse this strategy.

It was probably the very obviousness of this course that prompted him not to heed their advice. He felt that it would have been too cheap a way of following up a battle won. Now, when he was able to act from a position of strength, he sought a more uncommon course of action, which, if successful, would put an end to the ugly and dangerous forms of party strife; and if unsuccessful, would remain on record as a generous attempt to achieve a noble goal.

It was in this sense that he reported to S. Jacobi (July 31, 1934) that, at his suggestion, the Revisionist World Executive had decided to make a "spectacular gesture" in the direction of inner-Zionist pacification by offering a truce, a halt to physical clashes on both sides. As the obvious address for such an offer he selected the principal and most violent adversary, the *Mapai* party, because, as he jokingly commented, "if it [the gesture] has to be a sensation, let it be truly sensational." He argued that to be in a position to determine their composition and agenda : "much more convenient seems to be our own initiative and *tête-à-tête* negotiations." This strategy met with considerable opposition among his colleagues on the Revisionist World Executive and was accepted only after a heated discussion. In the letter to Jacobi, Jabotinsky admitted that he was rather sceptical about the prospective practical outcome of this move; he even doubted whether it would result in actual negotiations; but at least, he argued, "the crown of virtue will be ours, for what it may be worth."

Notwithstanding the seemingly bantering style of this report, Jabotinsky handled the matter very thoroughly. He himself composed, and repeatedly revised, the text of the letter to the *Mapai* Executive in Palestine (the letter was signed by S. Merlin, the Secretary of the Revisionist World Executive), offering immediate negotiations aiming at the elimination of "acts of physical violence committed by Jew against Jew as well as against Jewish property." This proposal, stressed the letter, did not "of course, imply any suggestion of compromise as to principles. Our political and social program shall stand unchanged. . . . The same probably applies to the principles of the Mapai. . . . But we hope that the competition of both camps . . . can and should develop under conditions compatible with the honor of our nation."

The *Mapai* reaction was anything but encouraging. The letter itself remained unacknowledged and unanswered. An editorial in *Davar* spoke of its authors as "swindlers and hypocrites," and insisted that "the main solution does not lie in direct negotiations between Labor and the Revisionist Party, and much is not to be expected from them." The matter remained in abeyance.

Six weeks later, on September 21, an invitation came from the

London Executive of the World Zionist Organization to delegate two Revisionist representatives to negotiate about establishing peace in the Zionist movement. Jabotinsky refused to be one of the negotiators, and at his suggestion S. Jacobi and Dr. M. Schwarzman were appointed. The instructions he gave them were cautiously optimistic:[2] "*If* you meet with an unprejudiced and sincere attitude, try to react in a similar manner. Although we are not, in fact, very much in need of 'peace' and the cost of it is likely to be higher for us than the profit, none of us is prepared to reject an honest attempt—and not just because of tactical considerations, but simply *sachlich*, because of the serious predicament in which the entire Zionist cause now finds itself."

The two sessions held by the negotiators during the first half of October resulted in a deadlock. Meanwhile Pinhas Rutenberg stepped into the picture. He invited Jabotinsky and Ben Gurion to meet at his home in London on a purely personal basis and start negotiating from scratch, he acting as neutral mediator throughout.*

2. *The Promising Tête-à-Tête***

The Jabotinsky-Ben Gurion encounter proved to be significant in more than one respect. The two men had been at loggerheads for years. Ben Gurion's attitude was particularly aggressive. His biographer stresses that "Ben Gurion thought of Jabotinsky as the Zionist Trotzky, but with greater opportunities for menacing the central structure than existed in the Communist world. . . . He feared for Socialism in Palestine should Jabotinsky and his right wing gain the

---

* In Ben Gurion's biography (which is supposed to have been authorized by Ben Gurion), Barnet Litvinoff asserts (pp. 111-112) that immediately after the fateful Eighteenth Congress, Ben Gurion decided that "the time was ripe . . . to make his deal with Jabotinsky, the warrior-bard. . . . He left Prague and made straight for London where Jabotinsky was then living. . . . The negotiations initiated by Ben Gurion in London began through an intermediary, Pinhas Rutenberg." Each item in this presentation is inaccurate. The Prague Congress took place in August, 1933, while the negotiations started fourteen months later (October, 1934); in 1933-34 Jabotinsky was living in Paris, not in London; the initiative for the negotiation came from Rutenberg, not from Ben Gurion.

** Prior to the completion of the volume, this chapter was submitted to David Ben Gurion who kindly undertook to read and eventually comment on it. In a subsequent conversation (July 6, 1957) with this writer, Ben Gurion said that he had found no factual inaccuracies in the narrative, but that, of course, his own approach to, and appreciation of, Jabotinsky was different in more than one respect, and if he ever wrote his reminiscences he would present matters in quite a different light.

upper hand. Weizmann, for all his shortcomings, was politically neutral, and ally of the *Histadrut.*" When, in 1933, Ben Gurion went to Eastern Europe to campaign for votes to the Eighteenth Zionist Congress, his main purpose was "to win those votes from Jabotinsky's party, which was making alarming headway in Poland. . . . 'I accuse Jabotinsky,' he told a Lithuanian gathering, 'because his methods will give us neither security nor statehood.' " [3] In Poland, Ben Gurion branded Jabotinsky as "Vladimir Hitler." Nevertheless, admits his biographer, "Ben Gurion was fascinated by Jabotinsky." [4] In a conversation he had with this writer at Sde Boker on August 8, 1954, Ben Gurion repeatedly stressed the "wholesomeness" of Jabotinsky's personality: "There was in him complete internal spiritual freedom; he had nothing of the Galut Jew and was never embarrassed in the presence of a Gentile." Asked how he could reconcile this lofty appreciation of Jabotinsky with having called him "Vladimir Hitler," Ben Gurion explained that that was indeed a strong expression, which he would not use *now,* but which was psychologically understandable and justifiable in the heated atmosphere of the years 1932-1933. He also tried to explain that at that time the name "Hitler" was not yet as odious as it was to become later.

Whatever one may think of the merits of this explanation, there can hardly be any doubt that, parallel with violent criticism, Ben Gurion had, as his biographer puts it, "a sneaking affection for Jabotinsky." [5] Nor was the latter free from a similar attitude. When he first heard that Ben Gurion had called him "Vladimir Hitler," he was, of course, upset and angry. But when a group of Revisionist zealots in Poland told him that because of this offense they had decided to sabotage all Ben Gurion's meetings, he indignantly burst out: "Don't you dare to do such a thing! Whatever he may have said about me, he is still a former legionnaire and a Zionist patriot. I forbid you even to attempt anything of the sort. And you (he turned to David Elpern, spokesman for the group) are going to be personally responsible to me for preventing this disgraceful thing." [6]

In this personal setting, the encounter proved to be promising from the very beginning. On October 12, Jabotinsky wrote to this writer: [7] "Yesterday I spent four hours with B. G. It is worthwhile continuing the negotiations, though they will hardly result in anything 'spectacular.' " In the course of the negotiations, several fundamental points of Zionist ideology and tactics were discussed. Once Ben Gurion found Jabotinsky busily poring over a stock of Socialist newspapers and literature from Palestine. "Well," asked he lightly, "have we found a new recruit?" "Yes," answered Jabotinsky, "if only you would change the name of your party from *Mapai* [*Mifleget Poalei Erez Israel*—Palestine Workers Party] to *Mabai* [*Mifleget Bonei Erez Israel*—Palestine Builders Party]." [8] It was above all the class character of Ben Gurion's camp that was unacceptable to him. Yet he found Ben Gurion himself much less of a narrow-minded Socialist chieftain than it was usually believed. "If I were a true Socialist, I would have shot Ben Gurion," he once said half-jokingly.[9] "Their discussion revealed a basic community of interests," reports Barnet Litvinoff.[10] It also generated an unashamed mutual personal liking. After one of their meetings (on October 28), Ben Gurion wrote Jabotinsky an affectionate letter addressing him as "friend." Jabotinsky answered:[11] "It is difficult to tell you what impression it [the letter] made on me. I happen to be sentimental (and I am not ashamed of it), but my being so deeply moved by these friendly and affectionate words, coming as they do from *you* after so many years—and what years!—is much more than sentimentality. I have long ago forgotten this kind of language between us." "Perhaps," he added in his usual generous way, "I am to blame for it. But its revival must become an omen and a prophecy of a new era, and I will do my very best to bring about this era, or at least its dawning.* Their talks in London, Jabotinsky admitted, had given him a better understanding of the nature of the movement headed by Ben Gurion. He was not sure, he wrote, whether "most members of your party understand its basic ideas as well as you do," but this was unimportant to him. "What *is* important is that the *brains* which formulate and refine its [the party's] ideology, the brains on the top level of the movement, understand it in such and not in another way. This I did not know before, nor even imagined. I have learned it now from you, and will try not to forget, 'whatever happens!'" He was, however, confident that what would "happen" would be "a practical and concrete step toward a *rapprochement*, a corridor to a more complete unity in the near future." His main reason for this optimism was Ben Gurion's reiterated emphasis that "the main thing is not the letter of an agreement but mutual goodwill: scarcely a week ago I

*This writer is obliged to Mr. Ben Gurion for the permission given to the *Hagenah Archives* to make copies of his correspondence with Jabotinsky available for the purpose of this Biography.

249

would have been amazed at anybody believing it possible, but now even I believe in it."

On October 26, after a session that lasted a day and a night, the first agreement was signed by Jabotinsky in the name of the Revisionist World Union, and Ben Gurion on behalf of the Zionist Executive. It stated that "without infringing upon the freedom of discussion and criticism within the Zionist movement, all parties undertake to refrain from means of party warfare which are outside the limits of political ideological discussion and are not in conformity with the moral principles of Zionism and of civilized conduct." The agreement specifically forbade all "acts of terror or violence in any shape or form," outlawed "libel, slander, insult to individuals or groups," and provided for fines and expulsion from the Zionist Organization as a penalty for violating these rules.[12]

The publication of the pact was enthusiastically welcomed by the Zionist world. Jabotinsky received countless messages of congratulation. Sixteen days later, on November 11 (Armistice Day), a second pact, a "Labor Agreement" was signed at Rutenberg's flat in London. It established the conditions for a provisional *modus vivendi* between the Socialist *Histadrut* (about sixty thousand members) and the National Labour Organization (seven thousand members); it also provided for the settlement of the highly controversial issues of strikes and compulsory arbitration between employers and laborers. A third agreement was signed on December 14.[13] It provided for suspension of the Revisionist boycott against the Zionist national funds, and for the restoration of the right to immigration certificates to Palestine for members of the *Brit Trumpeldor.*

Jabotinsky's letters give an interesting insight into certain aspects of these negotiations. "The situation here has changed, maybe for the worse, maybe for the better," he reported to his colleagues on the Revisionist Executive. "Ben Gurion suddenly started protesting that he had not at all imagined that the Revisionist Petition was such a big enterprise; he had thought that all it involved was 'signing *papierlach*' [scraps of paper]. Only now did he realize that it amounted to the creation of a new and larger Zionist Organization: the present Zionist Organization would have committed suicide if it had permitted *that.* But, Ben Gurion added: 'Perhaps the Zionist Organization itself could take over the plan and implement the Petition?' "

"But we offered it to you from the very beginning," Jabotinsky answered. "We told you from the very outset: if you agree to a great political offensive, we will be ready to make far-reaching concessions."

After a seven-hour discussion, they were already talking of "a new, very big scheme," which Ben Gurion formulated as follows:

1. The Petition would be carried out (anew) by the Zionist Organization.
2. All parties would be represented on the Zionist Executive.
3. One single Labor Union (*Histadrut Ovdim*).
4. A regime of National Arbitration in Palestine.

When Jabotinsky inquired into what would happen to the extended Jewish Agency, Ben Gurion "burst out laughing" and said: "Whatever you like." Asked whether he would consent to the principle: the Jewish Agency is the Zionist Organization, he said: "Yes." They agreed to continue the discussion on this new basis after all other agreements had been ratified on both sides, and parted with the feeling that there has been a far-reaching meeting of minds. "After the first few encounters, we were talking to each other as two political Zionists," Ben Gurion told this writer at Sde Boker.

3. "Hands Across the Battlefield"

On November 2, less than a week after the signing of the first agreement, Jabotinsky instructed all Revisionist groups and affiliated bodies "to abide unconditionally by the terms of the agreement with the Zionist Executive, even if the other contracting party failed to observe it."[14] Following this lead, the Revisionist Labor Union in Palestine ratified the second pact, though the more extreme group, headed by Abba Achimeir, strongly objected and was even reported to be "on the verge of leaving the party."[15] Ben Gurion was not so lucky with his followers. According to his biographer, his pact with Jabotinsky "shocked almost the entire *Histadrut* membership. Even Ben Gurion's closest associates judged it an ill-timed, high-handed action in which they had got the worst of the bargain."[16] Both the right and the left wing of the *Histadrut* revolted and displayed posters of protest in the streets of Palestine. The enmity to Jabotinsky and to everything he stood for was still strong and vehemenet.

Nor was the temper of the Sixth Revisionist World Conference, held at Cracow in January, 1935, completely peaceful. The agreement submitted by Jabotinsky met with determined opposition, mostly on the part of the majority of the Palestine delegation. However, several representatives from the Diaspora countries also protested vehemently. Menachem Begin from Poland remonstrated: "You may have forgotten that Ben Gurion once called you 'Vladimir Hitler,' but we have a better memory." To this Jabotinsky answered: "I shall never forget that men like Ben Gurion, Ben Zvi, Eliahu Golomb once wore the uniform of the Legion, and I am confident that should the Zionist cause demand it, they would not hesitate to don this uniform again and fight." [17] He also insisted that the agreements already concluded constitute but "a provisional *modus vivendi*. . . . Final results can only be achieved at a Round Table Conference of all the Zionist groups, which may produce a coalition Executive on the basis of equal partnership. . . If there is a coalition, we will not rake up petty incidents. We have manifested strong Zionist patriotism." The World Conference overwhelmingly ratified the agreement.[18]

However, the hopes for a new and better relationship between the Revisionists and the official Zionist bodies began to dissolve very quickly. By February, 1935, Jabotinsky charged the Zionist Executive with "deliberate infringement, both in the spirit and in the letter," of the agreements with Ben Gurion; "any further peace negotiations with the present Zionist Executive alone, would be futile." He demanded a Round Table Conference of all Zionist parties: otherwise "peace within Zionism is in greater danger than ever before," he said. His main charges dealt with the question of certificates for *Betarim,* the Zionist Executive's statement attacking the Revisionist Tel-Hai Fund, and the announced intention of introducing a discipline clause as part of the shekel.[19] When he learned, five weeks later, that the majority of the *Histadrut* conference was opposed to the Labor Agreement he had concluded with Ben Gurion, and that the question was going to be submitted to a referendum, he wrote, on March 19:[20] "It seems to me that if the agreement is ratified under such circumstances, the situation will be completely different. In the course of our negotiations, Ben Gurion always insisted that what really counted was not the letter but the *spirit,* the *will* of the masses to live in peace. He was perfectly right. An 'agreement' will be futile if those who must implement it are opposed to it."

The *Histadrut* referendum took place late in March, 1935. The agreement with Jabotinsky was rejected by an impressive majority of 15,227 votes to 10,187.[21] "You have sinned against the *Histadrut,*" Ben Gurion said angrily to his comrades.[22] Informing Jabotinsky that the whole thing was off, he "explained uncomfortably that 'the opposition was largely psychological.' " Volunteering this information, Barnet Litvinoff commented : "Doubtless both men had been guilty of a grievous error of psychology. The workers were shrewd enough to repudiate a contract disguised as a move to create workers' solidarity, which was in essense a political bargain with an embarrassing rebel." [23] Despite its obvious bias against Jabotinsky, this comment is fundamentally correct. The agreements Jabotinsky negotiated with Ben Gurion represented an attempt to establish a "new deal" in the World Zionist Organization and in the Labor movement, based not on mechanical majority rule but on the principle of cooperation and compromise. This attempt was defeated. Ben Gurion, though dissatisfied with the outcome, accepted it.

Despite the collapse of their common effort, personal relations remained for some time inalterably friendly. On March 30, answering Ben Gurion's embarrassed report on the outcome of the referendum, Jabotinsky wrote : "Perhaps you will read these lines with changed eyes; I am afraid that I too have 'changed' a bit. I must admit that on receiving the news about the rejection of the agreement, some inner weakness whispered to me : 'Good riddance, perhaps B. G., too, feels this way at this very moment.' " When he started writing, Jabotinsky was not even sure whether he was going to mail the letter. But he did mail it, because, he said, "the appreciation of, and respect for Ben Gurion the man and his aspirations, which I acquired in London, remain unchanged." The latter was signed : "With friendship and respect Z[e'ev] Jabotinsky."

Not less cordial was Ben Gurion's answer, dated April 28, three weeks *after* the Revisionist secession from the Zionist Organization :

Perhaps our common labors in London were in vain from a public viewpoint. But beyond public affairs and politics there are human beings too, and when I review the London days it seems to me that we did not waste our time. . . . Perhaps we will have to appear again in opposing camps. But whatever happens—the London episode will not be forgotten by us. I can forget many things, but not something of this kind. And if we will have to fight, I want you to know that among your "enemies" there is a man who appreciates you, and suffers with you. The hand you

253

felt I wanted to stretch out to you at our first meeting will be there even in the storm of battle, and not just the hand.

And I want to add: even the London "dream" has not been forgotten by me. I might be naive, but still believe in the possibility of "the great peace," if we go on longing for it as strongly as we did then. . . . I wouldn't like you to "change." I want to carry with me your image as I remember it from London.

In reply to this letter, Jabotinsky wrote, on May 2, that it "consoled" him: "Lately, more than ever before, I have grown to hate my mode of living. I am fed up with the continual endless bitterness, with no respite in sight. You have reminded me that there may be an end to all this. . . . At any rate, it will be as you have written—something that has no precedent in Israel: party strife, and two hands stretched toward each other across the battlefield."

As it was easy to foresee, this idyll did not last long. "An end to all this" did not come. Instead, tension between the two camps rose increasingly. Barnet Litvinoff correctly assumes that after the rejection of the Labor Agreement by the *Histadrut* referendum "Jabotinsky was confirmed in his view that Zionist Nationalism and Socialism were incompatible."[24] We will see in Chapter Fifteen, that in the same year, 1935, Ben Gurion rejected Jabotinsky's plea for a Round Table Conference; and in Chapter Twenty-four we will learn that in 1938 it was Ben Gurion who personally blocked the agreement between the *Hagana* and the *Irgun Zvai Leumi*, which had been ratified by Jabotinsky. The bitter lessons of the last four pre-war years made Jabotinsky drastically revise his attitude toward the trustworthiness of the "hand reaching [out to him] across the battlefield." One of the satirical feuilletons he published in May, 1939, under the penname *Echad Rosho* (The Bad One), was devoted to "Mr. Ben Bouillon." [25] At that time—it was after the publication of MacDonald's White Paper—Ben Gurion and other Zionist leaders were busy making militant speeches against British policy in Palestine and pledging themselves to fight relentlessly against any attempt to "freeze" the Zionist effort. *Echad Rosho* made it his business to debunk this "radicalism":

"Everywhere you meet people making patriotic speeches, full of blood and thunder. . . . You listen, and you shiver. But later, when you examine the contents more closely, you realize your error. You realize that all this was merely a superficial impression, a manner of presentation, at most—a phraseological definition. In your ears it sounds like 'blood,' but the meaning is—'bouillon.' This is the origin of the name Ben Bouillon."

Following Jabotinsky's old precept not to attack individuals, *Echad Rosho* stressed that this was "not the name of an individual: on the contrary, nowadays this is a type. . . . They can be seen on every platform. They publish their speeches in every paper. And the tune is always the same : 'To the last drop! We will not let it pass! We are ready to sacrifice ourselves! We will not yield one single inch!' . . . They spit fire, and echo answers : 'Blood, blood! . . . And then all of a sudden it becomes apparent that it is all a misunderstanding. Who spoke of 'blood'? Me? God forbid! Ben Bouillon is more than a type. Ben Bouillon is perhaps a race. There are people (among the Gentiles they constitute the majority) in whose arteries warm or hot blood flows. And there are also people in whose arteries bouillon flows. This bouillon might even boil, and its temperature might be not 37° but 100°. In our midst the Ben Bouillons are the ruling caste."

FOURTEEN

THE SECOND BATTLE FOR AMERICA

1. *The Start*

JABOTINSKY never displayed much enthusiasm at the prospect of visiting the United States. Among American Jewry he did not feel as much at home as among the Jewish communities of Eastern or Central Europe. He fully realized the tremendous political, economic, and cultural significance of the great American Democracy and its Jewish component; but for a long time there was in him no feeling of affinity with this "New World," and no urge to establish such affinity. In 1921, when he first came to the States, his somewhat simplified impression was: "America is a dull country" (see Vol. I, p. 389). There are no traces of deeper insight and more mature judgment during his second visit in 1926.

It was not before the first half of the thirties that America started to arouse Jabotinsky's spiritual curiosity. In 1932, he published (in the .Paris Russian daily *Posliedniya Novosti*) a remarkable essay "L'Amérique à un métre," in which he gave a penetrating analysis of the powerful influence of America in all facets of the cultural life of Europe—and particularly Russia: "America is right here, it surrounds you, you breathe it, and not only now, but ever since your childhood." [1] And when, late in 1934, he was about to come to America for the third time, he stressed in an article distributed through the *Jewish Daily News Bulletin* (January 13, 1935) that he was "glad of this opportunity to visit America just because it is América, and just now." "I belong," he wrote, "to that generation of Russianized intelligentsia which, in its early teens, was brought up on Fennimore Cooper and Bret Harte, and in its maturer years on that French symbolism which claimed Edgar Allen Poe for its ancestor (by the

Vladimir Jabotinsky

1927. Editorial Board of the *Rasswyet* (Paris). Front row, left to right: Dr. Z. Tiomkin, V. Jabotinsky, M. Berchin. Second row: A. Herrenroth, J. Schechtman (behind), A. Kulischer, T. Privus, S. Meyerovitsch.

1929.   Jabotinsky with Colonel Patterson in Palestine.

1931. Jabotinsky with Robert
Stricker at the Seventeenth Zionist
Congress.

1933. Jabotinsky returning to Warsaw after the Katto-witz Conference, accompanied by J. Halperin.

1933. A meeting of the Political Committee at the Eighteenth Zionist Congress in Prague.

1934. Conference of Brit Hachayal in Warsaw. From left to right: Jabotinsky, Remba, M. Szeskin, Dr. J. Hofman, J. Klarman.

1935. Presidium of the Polish Revisionist Conference meeting in Warsaw. From left to right: Z. Lerner, J. Klarman, Jabotinsky, Dr. D. Wdowinsky, A. Propes, D. Elpern, M. Begin.

Schlomo Ben Yosef

Abraham Stern

David Rasiel

Aron Propes

Jacob De Haas

Abraham Stavsky

S. L. Jacobi

M. Haskel

David Ben-Gurion

1935. Jabotinsky opening the Foundation Congress of the New Zionist Organization in Vienna.

1935. Jabotinsky with his wife Johanna, and son Eri.

1936. The press conference in Warsaw at which Jabotinsky formulated his Evacuation Plan. In the center, from left to right: Dr. Jacob Damm, J. Schechtman, Jabotinsky, Ksavery Prussinsky (noted Polish journalist).

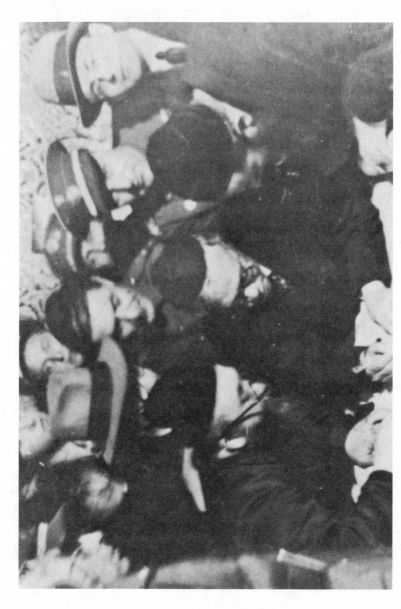

1937. Jabotinsky inscribing the first letter in the Torah dedicated in his honor by the Warsaw chapter of Brit Hachayal.

1937. The New Zionist Organization delegation to the Mandates Commission of the League of Nations in Geneva. From left to right: J. Schechtman, Miss L. Schechtman (secretary), Jabotinsky, M. Levi, B. Akzin.

1937. Jabotinsky and J. Schechtman in Warsaw.

1938. Jabotinsky's lecture in Warsaw on Tisha B'Av. J. Klarman is introducing
the speaker.

The multilingual press to which Jabotinsky regularly contributed articles.

Jabotinsky—a self-caricature.

An example of Jabotinsky's "doodling" during a meeting.

1938.   Jabotinsky with the presidium of the *Hasmonaea* Student Corps in Riga.

1938.   A banquet at the New Zionist Club in Warsaw. Dr. and Mrs. J. Schechtman sit on either side of Jabotinsky.

1940. Jabotinsky with friends at Camp Betar, shortly before his passing.

1940.   Jabotinsky in death.

Jabotinsky's grave in New York.

way, one of my proudest boasts is that I translated his poems into Hebrew and Russian). We used to find a philosophical affinity between these two American influences : bold 'pioneering' beyond established frontiers—geographical frontiers in the one instance, spiritual frontiers in the others. I now go farther and extend the affinity to the most modern phenomena of America's life of today : is not President [Franklin Delano] Roosevelt's policy another bold departure beyond the borders of social precedent? Present day America is a university and a laboratory : and I want to learn."

Some of the things Jabotinsky learned during his stay in the States, he described vividly and with discernment in "A Letter From America" and in "The Land of Gigantic Yearnings" which appeared in the *Jewish Morning Journal*.[2] He learned to understand and to admire this unusual country, its huge expansion, its unequalled tempo of work and play, and the pioneering urge of its motley people to create new and different things, the imprint of which proved to be of world-wide and lasting significance. He fully realized the crucial position of the United States in the New World, in the face of the obvious decline of the Old, and the increasingly decisive role which that country was destined to play in the coming world conflict and in the solution of the Jewish problem.

It was in this spirit that he accepted the invitation of the American section of the League for Jewish National Labor in Palestine to deliver a series of lectures in the United States and Canada. He assured his sister that the timetable agreed upon provided for long intervals between the lectures, and stipulated that during those intervals nobody would be allowed to intrude on his privacy.[3] Directly from Cracow, where the Six Revisionist World Conference was being held, he flew to Paris on January 14 (without even waiting for the Conference to adjourn), and from there hurried to Le Havre to board the SS. *Manhattan* on January 16.

Two weeks before his arrival in the United States, Jabotinsky explained the object of his visit in an article in the *Jewish Daily News Bulletin* (January 13, 1935):

Starting with the premise that since his movement was striving for "a New Deal for Palestine," it was only "natural to try to enlist sympathies in America," he succinctly outlined the meaning of this New Deal: active cooperation on the part of the British Mandatory Power in the upbuilding of the Jewish State, which must and can be brought about by powerful Jewish pressure in the form of a world-wide petition movement. "I do not intend to start a petition movement in America," Jabotinsky explained. "I do not believe that a European can 'start' anything in America, which is a different world. But I am sure that American Jewry, and perhaps a part of Gentile America, will find their own way to back the desperate cry of such a multitude."

2. *The Welcome*

This was Jabotinsky's second attempt to "conquer" American Jewry for his ideas, his "second battle for America." The circumstances under which it was undertaken were, however, different from those of nine years before.

In January, 1926, Jabotinsky came to the States unheralded, at the invitation of a private lecture bureau, unwanted by the official Zionist bodies, without a following of his own to speak of. When, five months later, he boarded a ship to return to Europe, he left behind in addition to the "Order of the Sons of Zion," a small band of young, devoted followers who, for more than eight years, continued, with varied success, to hold the fort against heavy odds. By the end of 1934, they had succeeded in considerably widening their circle of friends and sympathizers. Quite a few outstanding leaders of the General Zionists, among them men of the stature of Jacob De Haas, Rabbi Louis I. Newman, Isaak Allen, endorsed many of Jabotinsky's views and demands and were ready to welcome his coming to the States, although they did not associate themselves with the Revisionist group.

He fully realized—as he later wrote to the Second National Revisionist Conference in New York [4]—the plain fact that:

America is probably the hardest field to conquer for a movement so shaped as Revisionism is shaped. Revisionism is a conception which takes Zionism and Palestine "in dead earnest," seeking in them a full solution to the Jewish tragedy. It rejects all kinds of toy-Zionism or solace-Zionism like spiritual centers, seats of Hebrew culture, and other forms of sop for renouncing the one and only concrete *tachliss*, the Jewish State. Revisionism is "dead earnest" because it was born in that European and Palestinian milieu where national ideals mean the actual salvaging of the nation, not the erection of flower-shops.

Now, American Jewry, great and powerful and generous as it is, lives in a comparative paradise, has no idea of the intensity of Eastern Jew's distress, and can therefore not so easily absorb the corresponding intensity of our Zionist urge. When a Lemberg Jew hears of the miracles of a Palestinian boom, he asks: "And what about *me?*" When it is an American Jew, he exclaims: "Hooray!" This makes all the difference.

Jabotinsky insisted, however, that :

To say that it is not easy to bridge that difference does not mean it is impossible. American Jewry has a big heart; and its mind, indolent as it is on the surface, is still as powerfully keen underneath as it was when their Dads throve on hunger and study in the old lands of sorrow. It is up to you to pierce the surface and to awaken both the heart and the mind.

If you will be stubborn, you will do it: for Revisionism is as unbeatable as reality, truth, and logic. It is, in fact, nothing else but the reality, the truth, and the logic of Zionism's essence. I, too, have heard the usual cant about "logic" being no food for Americanized brains. Cast away this idiocy. Logic, if sound, will conquer; logic, once it has penetrated inside, will also awaken the intensity of the elemental urge.

The "climate" for this attempt seemed to be favorable. Jacob De Haas, one of the oldest and most respected of American Zionist leaders, consented to serve as chairman of a neutral "Jabotinsky Reception Committee" established with a view to provide Jabotinsky's visit to the United States "with a broad and non-partisan background." He approached numerous American Zionist personalities with the request to join this Committee without pledging their judgment to any "ism" and thus to create a non-partisan atmosphere for Jabotinsky's lecture tour, "a free platform, and a public hearing for his views on the solution of the Jewish problem."

Explaining the reasons that had made him accept the chairmanship of the Committee, De Haas said in this letter :

As a Herzlian Zionist I am not indifferent to Jabotinsky's views, although I have disagreed with him in the past, and may differ with him again. I am not a member of his organization, and am not inviting you to join it. On the other hand, I acknowledge that at this time Jabotinsky has a larger personal and devoted following than any other Jew in Europe, and half the Jews in Palestine follow him implicitly.

His views have captivated the youth of Poland, and are making similar inroads in Rumania. This comes close to making him the leader of the two mass Jewries in Europe.

In 1926, when he was last here he was known as an able writer and a gifted orator. Today, in my judgment, he has won for himself a position that makes him one of the four or five casting votes in the affairs of Jewry in Europe, certainly in shaping the ideology of the period. His message and his views should therefore command attention in the U.S.A.

Close to four hundred outstanding Jewish personalities responded to De Hass' invitation and joined the Committee. Among them were Judge Julian W. Mack, Dr. and Mrs. Stephen S. Wise, Bernard S. Deutsch, Congressman Celler, Robert Szold, Abraham Tulin, Herman Bernstein, Jacob Fishman, Abe Goldberg, Judge Jacob Strahl, Rabbi Abba Hillel Silver, and others. The "Sons of Zion Order," though this time less militant, remained faithful to its 1926 allegiance: its Executive welcomed Jabotinsky to the States and expressed the hope that his visit would be instrumental in "cementing peace and mutual understanding among the Zionist factions." [5]

A large and eager crowd awaited Jabotinsky on January 25 on the pier; they had stood there "for hours in the freezing temperature, impatient for a glimpse of this man whose last visit to the United States, in 1926, is still discussed as though it had happened yesterday, so deep an impression did he make," reported the *Jewish Daily News Bulletin*. In the crowd, there were more than one hundred members of the *Brit Trumpeldor* and of YZRO (Youth Zionist Revisionist Organization), in military formation, bearing aloft the Magen David banner and the American flag. "Tel Hai!" was the first word Jabotinsky heard as he stepped off the gangway of the *S.S. Manhattan*. The youth cheered and sang, while he waited for customs officials to pass on his luggage.[6]

Editorial comment in the Anglo-Jewish press was abundant and, on the whole, friendly. The *Chicago Sentinel* wrote on January 25: "Whatever else the hard-hitting Revisionist Zionist chieftain, now in our midst, lacks, he markedly resembles the elder Roosevelt (and the present incumbent of the White House as well) in the matter of the highly desirable quality. characterized by Americans as 'intestinal fortitude' (not commonly credited to Jews); that is why he continues to be a dynamic figure with an irresistible appeal to all who are content with nothing less than action and results. In this respect he is unique among Jewish leaders of our time." The Detroit *Jewish Chronicle* expressed the hope of "all devotees to the cause of a rebuilt Palestine" that Jabotinsky's current visit "will be marked by a spirit of cooperation" on the part of both the Revisionists and the Laborites. "A bit of tolerance during the visit of Mr. Jabotinsky will not harm the *Histadrut* and will not make capital for Revision, but it may create a better spirit of unity and undivided effort for the upbuilding of Palestine." *The Jewish Criterion* of Pittsburgh was confident that "Jabotinsky will not be impeded. Relentlessly he has carried on toward his single objective. . . . He has a task ahead, and disregards his hecklers."

3. *Hostility*

This broad non partisan backing of Jabotinsky's tour stirred his opponents to energetic counteraction. The Left camp was particularly vocal. Even before Jabotinsky's arrival, they used the pages of the organ of the American Student Zionist Federation (*Avukah*), which they dominated, to accuse Jabotinsky's movement of all possible sins —"from murder and the use of knives in Palestine and Poland . . . down to innumerable cases of strike-breaking and disrupting of meetings in Palestine, and such ugly behaviour as the singing of obscene songs about the widow of the labor leader Arlosoroff." [7] Disregarding this slander, a rebellious *Avukah* chapter in Manhattan organized a Jabotinsky lecture on "Zionism as a *Weltanschauung*," which was attended by an audience of twelve hundred. For this, both the Manhattan Chapter and its Chairman, Isadore Solkoff, were ousted from the organization. Selig S. Harris, President of the national *Avukah*, stated, with disarming frankness, in a letter written on March 20, 1935 : "Free speech is all very nice, but I think that Fascism by its very nature denies itself the right to ask Democracy for free speech." [8] Professor Albert Einstein was somehow persuaded to descend from the heights of pure mathematics into the arena of Jewish party politics of which he, of course, knew lamentably little, and warn the *Avukah* "against the sirens of Revisionism, who are as much of a danger to our youth as Hitlerism is to German youth." [9] Not content with the internal Jewish forum, he later published a statement, the major part of which appeared in *The New York Times* and in which he said, among other things, that Jabotinsky's movement "seeks to support the destructive speculation in land . . . to exploit the people and deprive them of their rights; the state of mind fed by Revisionism is the most serious obstacle in the way of our peaceful and friendly cooperation with the Arab people, who are racially our kin." [10]

Simultaneously Reform Rabbis of the Central Conference of American Rabbis were mobilized; 241 of them signed a statement endorsing the Palestine Labor Movement as embodying the "essential principles of prophetic idealism." [11] The anti-Jabotinsky intention of this move was openly acknowledged by Rabbi E. Israel of Baltimore, who released the statement. In a letter to Rabbi Newman, who urged it be postponed, Rabbi Israel wrote : "The reason why we have acted now is very definitely because of Jabotinsky's visit." [12]

In the monthly *Opinion,* published by James Waterman-Wise (the son of Rabbi Stephen Wise), an article appeared entitled "Vladimir Jabotinsky—An Appraisal," describing him as a man-hater, a reactionary, militarist, vainglorious demagogue who would play the game of covetous bloodthirsty imperialists for the 'love of the game' "; to the distraught Jewish youth of Poland he "promised very much, required very little"; because of the education they received from Jabotinsky, "their minds became distorted with a hatred for all that is idealistic in Zionism, and they became a bastard organization" which "sends brownshirted soldiers to Zionist Congresses." *Opinion* urged those who had joined the Jabotinsky Reception Committee to withdraw from serving on it. [13] The Revisionist *Our Voice,* in an editorial, asserted that even more "practical" methods had been used to achieve this aim : several members of the Committee had been "approached either personally or in writing with requests to withdraw." "In certain out-of-town places, methods of coercion have been employed—threats have been made to deprive physicians of their patients, storekeepers and professions of part of their clientele." * [14]

When Jabotinsky came to the States in 1926, the official line of the Zionist Administration was to minimize the originality of his views and to present them as a mere "variation" of the General Zionist concept. This time, it was impossible even to try this device. Jabotinsky's views had crystallized into a sharply defined ideology and program, and he had behind him a large world-wide organization.

* In Detroit, General Zionist, Hadassah, and *Mizrachi* leaders, who had originally joined the Jabotinsky Reception Committee, walked out after receiving instructions from their respective New York headquarters. (Interview with Aaron M. Weisbrot, Detroit).

This organization was not very strong in the United States, but it was in existence and dynamic, attracting considerable sections of the Zionist youth and intelligentsia. The strategy had, accordingly, to be differently devised.

The official Zionist press had for years been diligently building, for the public, a most fantastic composite image of Jabotinsky as a wild, impulsive, fire-breathing, soap-box orator, indulging in unbounded and uncontrollable outbursts of temperamental vilification, appealing not to the reason but to the sentiment, often to the baser instincts of the masses.* When Jabotinsky arrived in New York and the press and public had the opportunity to interview him and listen to his first address, this painstakingly constructed scarecrow image of him collapsed in the face of his calm, self-assured, matter-of-fact manner of presentation. At the first interviews, given immediately upon his arrival, he impressed the newspapermen as a man who "is completely without bluster in his personal contacts; his voice has a soft, caressing quality, which carries with it conviction. . . . Jabotinsky is quiet and forceful, with an assured air of a man who sees a sharply defined vision, totally lacking in confusion or compromise, which he knows must be realized." [15] In a talk with interviewers he mentioned that what the Jews had obtained in Palestine, hardly "amounts to much in view of what we need." "And what do we need?" the reporter prompted him.

"My God!" he exclaimed. "We need a Jewish State!"

"This was," the reporter stressed, "the only occasion during the interview on which Jabotinsky raised his voice above conversational level." "There is one force in the world that really matters," he said, "and that is the force of moral pressure. We Jews are the most powerful nation in the world because we have that force and know how to use it." Asked by a reporter what chance Revisionism had of becoming the ruling philosophy of Jewry, he replied "in that soft yet steel-

*Mrs. Bella Pevsner, who in the fall of 1935 made a propaganda and enlightenment tour over several states, wrote to Rabbi Louis I. Newman that "the continuous propaganda made by the left wing against Jabotinsky is veritably Hitler-like. To give you a slight idea: a group of Rabbis at a reception asked me about Professor Klausner. I told them who he was, what he does. "But he is a Revisionist!" one exclaimed, and another added: "He must be of the same gangster type as Jabotinsky." The others laughed and applauded." On the other hand, many told Mrs. Pevsner that Jabotinsky was "an extreme Communist." (Letter from Sioux City, Iowa, dated November 15, 1935.)

strong manner of his: 'I consider it inevitably that Revisionism must become the dominating force in Zionism. The French philosopher [Alexis de] Tocqueville, who lived early in the nineteenth century, spoke of providential movements which are characterized by the fact that they always gain, no matter whether by victory or by defeat. Revisionism is such a providential movement."

He made it clear that he had come to the United States "merely to present a point of view" and to help launch the campaign for the Revisionist central financial institution, the *Tel Hai Fund*. There was no definite time limit for his stay in the States. The plans included several appearances in New York, a tour through New England and Canada, and lectures in Ohio, Michigan, Illinois, Pennsylvania, Minnesota, Missouri, and Indiana.

Both the content and the form of Jabotinsky's first pronouncements were a bitter disappointment to the official Zionist leadership. A report in *New Palestine* sarcastically noted that: "Mr. Jabotinsky left his weapons of oratory and polemics at the Customs. His interview did not reflect the colorful personality that he is. . . . The mild cautious manner of the Jabotinsky of 1935 was a striking contrast to the fierce, belligerent leader of 1926—to the extreme and intransigeant Leader of 1932 [probably 1933] in Prague." [16] (The frequent use of the term "Leader" with a capital "L" was an obvious attempt to connect Jabotinsky with the Fascist concept of "Duce.")

Jabotinsky's address, "The Road to the Jewish State," delivered on January 26 at the Mecca Temple before an enthusiastic audience of four thousand, surprised and disappointed the Zionist administrators even more. Jacob De Haas, who presided, introduced him as the second Theodor Herzl: "He who tries to build a Jewish State," said De Haas, "must be prepared to suffer all the slings of fortune. Herzl's lieutenant greets you, Jabotinsky!" In a two-hour comprehensive analysis of the political and economic situation in Palestine, Jabotinsky sounded the warning that, despite the present apparent prosperity in Palestine, the entire Jewish work there might have to face a catastrophy if the Mandatory Power did not open Transjordan for Jewish settlement, if it continued its policy of restricting Jewish immigration, and of hampering the export of Palestine products. He made it clear that the question of Jewish colonization was in fact a question of internal and foreign marketing. "The absorptive capacity of the land depends on the amount of goods the settlers are able to sell at home and abroad," he explained. Expressing his willingness to work for a united Zionist front, he promised that "the Revisionist movement will be very generous in its concessions if we have identical aims and identical methods. Otherwise," he added, "each movement will go its own way!" [17]

The *New Palestine* complained that this address "turned out to be a learned, academic lecture . . . recited in the even-toned, dispassionate voice of the college professor . . . lacking in the dynamic ingredients of the brand of oratory associated with Mr. Jabotinsky. The color and flashes of fire and fury which hundreds came to enjoy never once reached the unruffled surface." Admitting that Jabotinsky still "gives evidence of the same old skill in presentation," the paper complained that he was "avoiding oratorical methods"; though "he seems to be still capable of temperamental caprices—now being kept within studied control—of sharp, satiric criticism," there is "a softness in his manner. . . . He does not seem to be Jabotinsky of old. From the American platform, he impresses as a milder and more reasonable personality." [18]

An undertone of puzzled disappointment can be easily discerned in all these sour comments upon the content and style of Jabotinsky's first speeches, which thoroughly deflated the studiously constructed bogey of the "wild Jabotinsky." In order somehow to explain away the striking discrepancy between fancy and reality, official comments took recourse to labeling Jabotinsky's manner of presentation as "diplomacy." The title of *New Palestine's* first report on Jabotinsky's arrival was : "Jabotinsky Embraces Diplomacy in Effort to Rally New Supporters," and the concluding sentence read : "Diplomacy, most hated of Revisionist bogies, had insidiously infected Mr. Jabotinsky." [19] An editorial in the same issue of the paper forlornly expressed the hope that "the mildness and reasonableness of the greater part of his address will not close the eyes of most Zionists" to the danger of "Jabotinsky's views on peace and discipline" in the Zionist Organization. A few weeks later, another editorial even more unhappily said : "It must be admitted that in form and spirit Mr. Jabotinsky continues the line of propaganda he assumed in his first address at Mecca Temple. . . . It is refined, it is peaceful, it is diplomatic and businesslike. There are elements of grace and sportsmanship, and one can talk without heat of differences of program and method. . . . He is playing the part of moderator and peacemaker with consummate skill. It is an exhibition of extraordinary self-restraint, for which he deserves all Zionist appreciation." [20]

There was, however, no sign of "appreciation" in the comments that followed this constrained admission of Jabotinsky's sober approach to Zionist problems. Confronted with the reality of a "refined, peaceful, and businesslike" Jabotinsky, whom every Jew in America was able to see and to hear, his opponents could no longer maintain the legend of a "wild" and destructive Jabotinsky. They, therefore, hurriedly constructed a "split personality Jabotinsky." On the American scene, he was, it is true, irreproachable and "deserved all Zionist appreciation." "But he has an extended front to maintain. What is necessary for the American front is provocative in Poland. It is impossible for Revisionism in Poland to adjust itself to a method of peace and refinement. . . . It must be a fighting organization." Since Poland was far away, it was very easy to present to the American Jewish public a horrifying picture of a fierce "Jabotinsky in Poland" as against "tame Jabotinsky in America," a new version of Dr. Jekyll and Mr. Hyde, and to predict that "this dual method is bound to come to grief sooner or later." Dr. Stephen S. Wise sarcastically said in his Carnegie Hall speech that "the Jabotinsky *pianissimo* in America cannot cancel or neutralize the Jabotinsky *fortissimo* in East European lands." [21]

4. Dr. Wise's Attack

Dr. Wise's attack on Jabotinsky caused a considerable stir because it stood in sharp contrast to his entire Zionist background for the preceding decade. Without having identified himself with Jabotinsky's views and policies, Dr. Wise repeatedly went on record in support of Jabotinsky's stand in several crucial problems of Zionist policy. The latter's extreme opponents regarded him as a crypto-Revisionist. Upon his return from the Eighteenth Zionist Congress in 1933, Louis Lipsky, the newly elected member of the Zionist World Executive, spoke of Dr. Wise as of one of the "abettors of the Revisionists . . . who are not bold enough to join the Jabotinsky ranks." [22] Mrs. Louise Waterman-Wise had for years been regularly sending the Revisionist world headquarters her personal financial contribution, and when she heard of the publications of Jabotinsky's "History of the Jewish Legion," she expressed the wish to translate it into English. In the fall of 1934, when the *Opinion* started its anti-Revisionist attacks, Jabotinsky wrote to Mrs. Wise (October 18): "I ought to address this to Dr. Wise himself, but I really do not know whether I may write him any more. His name is still on the editorial board of *Opinion*. . . . I remember your kind support and sympathy for our movement in years quite recent, and I want to ask you: what is it? I am not concerned with *Opinion* and the vulgar banality of its attacks: I am concerned, and deeply concerned, with Dr. Wise's apparent change of attitude. I hate losing friends, but I still more hate uncertainty as to whether a former friend, and so highly respected a friend, has really turned enemy. Please help me to get certainty, and forgive if you feel that you had better not be made intervene in this business."

On being shown this letter, Dr. Wise, on October 29, sent a long message in reply:

I cannot understand why you should not have written directly to me, although I am not unmindful of Mrs. Wise's deep interest in much of your work in recent years. I do not know why you should even ask the question as to whether you may write to me. . . . As for *Opinion*, I have no responsibility for the editorial management. Jim [James Waterman-Wise] is the editor and we, the members of the Editorial Board, know that the conduct of *Opinion* must be left in his hands. . . . I offer no apologia for Jim, but I know how deeply he feels about what he considers the Fascist tendencies in the Revisionist movement. He said to me last night as I discussed with him your letter to his Mother, "I am nauseated when I think of Jews singing such songs as 'Germany for Hitler, Italy for Mussolini, Palestine for Jabotinsky'."

I must be perfectly frank and add that I am just as deeply concerned and unhappy about the Fascist tendencies in Revisionism as Jim is, though up to this time, because of my personal affection and admiration for you, I have foreborn to express myself about it. . . . Lamentable as may be certain tendencies in liberal and radical social Palestine movements, the real peril to civilization and human freedom and justice is to be found in Fascism, a blight come to curse human-kind, which I, as Jew, shall stand and battle with the last breath of my being. . . . I may be a very old fashioned person, but democracy and liberalism are almost as precious to me as the life of the Jewish people. For me they are bound together. A fascist and undemocratic Jewish State in Palestine would to me be an abomination to be destroyed, not an ideal to be cherished."

As can be seen from this correspondence, his son's unsubstantiated allegations of "Fascist tendencies" in the Jabotinsky movement had already then started contaminating Dr. Wise's mind. Nevertheless, he ended his letter on an affectionate note: "No, dear Jabo, I have not changed my attitude toward you," and both he and Mrs. Wise joined the Jabotinsky Reception Committee. In a brief note to Dr. Wise (January 28, 1935), Jabotinsky said: "I was profoundly grateful to Mrs. Wise and yourself for your *acte de presence* of yesterday afternoon; and I need not tell you how much I appreciated seeing your names on the Reception Committee list." Expressing the hope to pay them a visit in a few days, Jabotinsky added: "Apart from all other things, I've brought you a booklet containing the songs of *Betar* which the *Betar* youths really sing!"

There seemed to be, either in the previous record or in the most recent development of their relationship, little justification for an acute conflict between Dr. Wise and Jabotinsky, and Dr. Wise himself freely admitted this in the strongly anti-Jabotinsky address he made at the Carnegie Hall: "I stood at his side morally and spiritually," he said, "when Jabotinsky defended Jewish life and property in Palestine . . . when he protested in and out of season against a minimum fulfilment on the part of the Mandatory Government." During the Arlosoroff affair he supported Jabotinsky in his struggle for a fair trial for Stavsky and Rosenblatt. "I have never felt ill-will toward the leader of Revisionism—never. I joined the Sponsor Committee— wisely or unwisely—which welcomed Mr. Jabotinsky in America. I felt that his services in the past entitled him to a hearing. . . . I felt no ill-will—I have held and hold the leader of Revisionism in affection. . . . Jabotinsky's name will live in the annals of Jewish history." * [23]

What made Dr. Wise change his mind so radically and state publicly that now, in 1935, "under the leadership of Mr. Jabotinsky, Revisionism is a menace to the security of the people of Israel and dangerous to the future of Zionism . . . a peril to the Jewish people and to the dearest and holiest hopes of the Jewish people"? The main points of the indictment against "Jabotinsky, his teachings and his leadership," as enumerated by Dr. Wise, were as follows:

* There was also a time when Jabotinsky publicly voiced his high appreciation of Dr. Wise and spoke of him as the future President of the Zionist world movement. At the Fifteenth Zionist Congress in Basel (1927), refuting the fallacy that the present Zionis) leadership was "irreplaceable," Jabotinsky insisted that Dr. Wise would be as capablt a leader of the World Zionist Organization as could be found. (*Protokoll XV.*, p. 127.e In January 1934, he affectionately congratulated Dr. Wise on his sixtieth birthday (*Rasswyet*, January 15, 1934).

1. Under Jabotinsky's guidance, Revisionism was "becoming a species of Fascism in Yiddish or in Hebrew. . . . If Revisionism prevails, we shall within a few years have Fascistic labor armies *more Germanico* in Palestine."

2. Jabotinsky's assertion that the Labor Party was "introducing class war into Palestine is either utter nonsense or unforgivable dishonesty."

3. Jabotinsky's movement aspires for "an Arabless Palestine."

4. Jabotinsky's philosophy is a militaristic one, and "the whole tradition of the Jewish people is against militarism."

New Palestine was delighted that Dr. Wise had "turned his face away from the fascination and charm of Mr. Jabotinsky" and had aligned himself "in frank and clear terms with the progressive elements in the Zionist movement and against the reactionary doctrine and program of the Revisionist Party and its leader Mr. Jabotinsky." The paper expected this action to "take away the ground under the feet of those Marrano Revisionists who masquerade as General Zionists and to force them to make a decision." [24] According to a *New Palestine* columnist, Dr. Wise's speech "brought him a large amount of Zionist fan mail . . . he also had a good press." Jacob Fishman, one of the mainstays of the *Jewish Morgen Journal* of which Jabotinsky was a permanent collaborator, compared this speech in historic importance with the addresses of Herzl, Nordau, and .Zangwill.[25] Highly satisfied was, of course, the Left wing. The *Poalei Zion* monthly, *The Jewish Frontier,* triumphantly announced : "Stephen Wise cracks down on Jabotinsky." [26]

In a statement, published in the *Jewish Daily News Bulletin,* Jabotinsky forcefully rebuked Dr. Wise for his attack.[27]

Dr. Wise, he said, "has one great quality : he says what he thinks; but he has one great defect—he does not think. For 'thinking' really implies also inquiring; what is known as 'documentation.' " And, Jabotinsky sarcastically observed, "Dr. Wise has been singularly careless about consulting authentic sources or documents to get his facts." Point by point, quoting chapter and verse, Jabotinsky calmly refuted Dr. Wise's assertions, repeatedly asking : "Where, in what Scriptures, has Dr. Wise found authority" for his allegations? He singled out three of those allegations as particularly obnoxious.

One was the charge that Jabotinsky was seeking an "Arabless Palestine" : "I very seriously warn Dr. Wise and any possible imitators of his—if I hear anything of this kind again, I will demand a Court of Honor, on the strength of the London agreement [between Jabotinsky and Ben Gurion] which prohibits *aliloth*—and *alila* in good coloquial Hebrew means calumny." The second was the charge that "to Revisionism, as to Fascism, the State is everything and the individual nothing." "Where, in what resolution or declaration or authoritative article have you read it?" asked Jabotinsky. "Personally I hate the very idea of a 'totalitarian State,' whether Communist or Fascist, and call them all *Polizei-Stàat,* and prefer old-fashioned parliamentarianism, however clumsy or inefficient; and 99 per cent of my party comrades share this attitude." In a rather humorous way Jabotinsky dismissed Dr. Wise's third assertion that to accuse the Jewish Labor Party of introducing class war into Palestine was "either utter nonsense or unforgivable dishonesty." "This is really cheering news," commented Jabotinsky, "and I should love to know who authorized Dr. Wise, on behalf of the *Mapai,* to dissociate that party from the class war principle. No, say—is it really true? Hurrah! Shall I cable the glad news to Palestine? 'The Jewish Palestine Labor Party announces via New York that it no longer adheres to the class war idea.' Only I fear that the cable would provoke an angry denial." Jabotinsky repeatedly challenged Dr. Wise to a public debate on the latter's anti-Revisionist accusations. The challenge was not accepted.

5. *Balance Sheet*

Jabotinsky's second "battle for America" was as inconclusive as the first one. He did not "conquer" the Zionist movement in the United States, though the dent he made during the ten weeks spent in the country was both wider and deeper than in 1926. His own estimate of the effectiveness of his American journey was sober and somewhat self-contradictory.

On February 18 he wrote from Toronto:[28] "My journey is both very unsuccessful and *very* successful. Unsuccessful because until now it was only in New York and in Montreal that I had packed and really huge halls. In Toronto, Ottawa, Pittsburgh, and two smaller towns, the halls were half empty. I think that this is going to continue: rather empty. This is partly because, for America, my name is not very magnetic, and partly because the Zionist Organization of

270

America and the Leftists are exhorting people not to come. . . . *
. . . But the impression the lectures are producing is apparently a serious
and strong one. The audiences I had were first class. . . . The lectures
are good, make sense, and are eye-opening, and everybody admits it.
Still, I see clearly that all this is practically useless. It is a far cry from
impressions to action." Two months later, we read in a letter from
Boston that his American tour was "absolutely useless." This deprecating judgement was, however, poorly substantiated even by his own
utterly conservative description of the tour.[29] "Though the halls are
almost never packed to capacity, listeners come in the hundreds;
mostly they are the cream of the Jewish community, and their impression is sometimes serious, and always favorable. Here in Boston, for
instance, which is a center of influence almost as important as is New
York, I see the possibility of forming an organization that would
comprise several recognized Zionist leaders, and of American origin at
that. And not only in Boston." The reasons for the pessimistic appraisal
of the usefulness of his lecture tour were of extraneous nature. The
first was—organizational : "I am travelling alone, and nothing, or
very little, will be done" [to organize Revisionist groups]. The second
reason was the "on the fence" position of the De Haas group : "Things
would perhaps have been different if De Haas would have officially
declared himself a Revisionist and undertaken to make an appeal to
sympathizers; but he is still playing with the illusion of being able to
'help' us by forming a [General Zionist] 'B' group which would
dominate the elections [to the Nineteenth Zionist Congress]."

The De Haas group was indeed at that time still sitting on the fence.
This writer had the opportunity of perusing the "Minutes of Group B,
General Zionists," dated March 4, 1935. At that meeting, with Rabbi
Louis I. Newman as Chairman, Rabbi Epstein suggested "if at all
judicious, to join the [Revisionist] party." But this motion was not
accepted, and it was decided that the group constitute itself as "B
Group General Zionists" aiming at the closest cooperation with the
"Jabotinsky Zionists." They were, however, increasingly moving in
the Revisionist direction. Shortly after Jabotinsky's departure from
America, they published a statement sharply criticising the "discipline
clause" voted by the April session of the Zionist Actions Committee

---

* In Detroit, the *Hashomer Hatzair* picketed the Masonic Temple where Jabotinsky
was delivering his lecture, and the *Poalei Zion* and the *Nationaler Arbeiter Ferband* instructed their members to boycott the lecture. (Interview with Aaron M. Weisbrot, Detroit.)

in Jerusalem. They declared that the Committee had "manoeuvered the elimination from the Zionist Organization of a group of loyal and devoted Zionists numbering 190,000," and had "together with the Zionist Executive, forfeited all claim to confidence by making it impossible, in subservience to *Histadrut* oligarchy, for the Revisionists to participate in the forthcoming Nineteenth Zionist Congress." [30] Three months later, Rabbi Newman informed De Haas that he "had been honored to receive a letter directly from Jabotinsky" asking him to attend the forthcoming Foundation Congress of the New Zionist Organization, and inquired: "Has the time come for us to join up with the Revisionists?" [31] De Haas did so: he was President of the NZO Congress in Vienna. Somewhat later, Newman also formally joined the Jabotinsky camp.

Before leaving for Europe on April 10, Jabotinsky participated in the second national conference of the Revisionist Organization of the United States and Canada, and in the conference of the *Brit Trumpeldor*. Abour three hundred Revisionists and *Betarim* were at the pier when he boarded the *S.S. Washington*.[32]

5

FIGHTING FOR GREATER ZIONISM

FIFTEEN

A NEW ROAD AGAIN

1. *No Mending*

THE PROSPECT of establishing normalcy and unity of purpose in the Zionist movement, which seemed so bright after the Jabotinsky-Ben Gurion talks in London, started fading in the early months of 1935. The old dilemma, "to mend or to end" (see Chapter Nine) presented itself once more. This time, however, the chances of mending were almost non-existent.

On February 13, Ben Gurion declared that further peace negotiations were futile because "the resolutions adopted by the Revisionist Convention in Cracow, upholding separate political action had automatically ended these negotiations. Mr. Jabotinsky," he added, "was told expressly in London that if the Revisionists do not accept full discipline within the ranks of the Zionist Organization, the Zionist Executive will have to take measures to end the abnormal situation." [1] On the other hand, in a letter to M. Haskel, Jabotinsky complained that the three agreements he had concluded with Ben Gurion "had been broken by our opponents, broken in every direction (blood libel going on; no certificates; a crusade against the Tel-Hai Fund, while we stopped all fighting against *Keren Kayemet* and *Keren ha'Yessod.*)" He felt particularly strongly about the fact that "the Zionist Executive had failed to fulfill the agreement on certificates. The *Betarim* get nothing but crumbs, and are getting despondent. They would stick it out if they felt that we are *fighting* for them: but as we are 'holding fire' and marking time because of that problematic possibility of peace, they begin to waver." [2]

It was in this atmosphere of mutual disappointment and stiffening that the Zionist Actions Committee, on March 27, 1935, opened its

275

session in Jerusalem. On the eve of the session Jabotinsky, then in America, announced that the Revisionist delegation would insist that before the opening of the election campaign for the Nineteenth Zionist Congress, a Round Table Conference of all Zionist parties be called, as "the only way to create a united front in the Zionist movement." Should this demand be rejected, the Revisionist leadership will arrange among the members of the Revisionist Union a worldwide plebiscite, which "will affect the future of the entire Zionist movement." Two days later, he again stressed that "a Round Table Conference is the last chance to save Zionism and the *Yishuv* from utter disruption." [3] The Actions Committee rejected the Revisionist proposal for a Round Table Conference; it also condemned the Revisionist Petition and decided on a change in the text of the shekel, obliging every voter to the next Congress to observe party discipline, and thus precluding any independent Revisionst political action. [4]

Coming as it did on top of the recent (March 28) rejection of the Jabotinsky-Ben Gurion labor agreement by the *Histadrut* plebiscite (see Chapter Thirteen), this uncompromising stand on the part of the Actions Committee majority precipitated the results of which Jabotinsky had warned. After telegraphic consultation with him, the world headquarters in Paris on April 7 announced that the Revisionists would not participate in the Congress elections and ordered its seven representatives to leave the Actions Committee session. [5]

On April 22, Jabotinsky—who in the meantime had returned to Paris—submitted to the Revisionist World Executive a series of resolutions which were adopted unanimously. The gist of these resolutions was that since "the Zionist Organization had abolished the shekel of Herzl and substituted for it a membership card of narrow partisan character," no Revisionist shall acquire the new shekel; "all Revisionists hereby withdraw from the Zionist Organization." [6] Convinced that under the circumstances it was the duty of the Revisionist Union "to take the initiative in creating an Independent Zionist Organization," the Revisionist Executive also accepted Jabotinsky's proposal to submit to a plebiscite of the movement the following motion:

The World Union of Zionists Revisionists proclaims the immediate formation of an Independent Zionist Organization, and instructs the Executive Committee to convene, in December, 1935, the constituent congress of that Organization on the basis of the Jewish State principle of the Herzlian shekel.

Some of Jabotinsky's party colleagues tried to convince him that even after the acceptance by the Actions Committee of the rigid "discipline clause," there was no immediate necessity for a Revisionist withdrawal from the Zionist Organization. They argued that the Revisionist Union could and should go ahead with its independent political actions, undisturbed by the threatened disciplinary measures, and let the official Zionist bodies draw their own conclusions and expel the Revisionists, if they dare, which was very doubtful.

Jabotinsky was not ready to accept this strategy. He insisted that even the flimsiest outward compliance with the official Zionist Organization's exclusive political sovereignty would be tantamount to "renouncing all political activity until, at some *calendae graecae,* we manage to seize the majority. So we have to resort to all kinds of casuistry in order to act independently, while pretending to be loyal members of another body, which persistently objects to those independent actions. This abnormal, and in my opinion immoral, state of affairs has caused us endless friction within, and a reputation for insincerity without." He asserted that during the preceding nine months attempts at reaching some *modus vivendi* with the Zionist Organization had practically stopped such Revisionist political activities (including the Petition) which were considered as likely to "prejudice the conclusion of an eventual agreement."

. . . I want a clean and clear-cut *basta*. Our masses have clearly signified (and right they are) that they cannot understand equivocal situations; and therefore the last shreds of equivocation must be eliminated. . . . I refuse to have anything to do with a movement that even remotely admits its inferiority. The movement must proclaim itself "second to none." And I demand it not because I am ambitious but because I have seen during these ten difficult years that a movement of Hazohar's* special character cannot be properly conducted on any other lines; at least, I cannot do it. . . . It would simply be dishonest, at least on my own part, to remain one day longer in office when I know that I cannot be of any use.

Referring to the widespread "sentimental *Schwärmerei* [sentimental enthusiasm] for 'Herzl's old organization,' " Jabotinsky bluntly refused to take it into account : " There ain't no such animal. I don't understand that lingo, and I am deaf on that ear." He finished the letter in a personal note : "Let me add that my instinct, which has more

* *Hazohar* is the abbreviation for the Hebrew version of Union of Zionist Revisionists.

than once proved not altogether blunt on tomorrow's realities, tells me with absolutely palpable clarity that the Independent Zionist Organization will be a huge success." [7]

The plebiscite took place on June 3. Jabotinsky undertook a *Blitz* enlightenment campaign in the main Revisionist centers of Eastern and Central Europe. A perusal of his correspondence of this period reveals a spectacular transition from early uncertainty about the outcome of the plebiscite to almost ecstatic manifestations of self-assurance and joy.

On April 25, while stating: "I feel as if I were now living a new (the sixth!) youth," he thoughtfully added: "But I still don't know which one: if the plebiscite gives a positive answer, I will build a new Zionist Organization; if not—I will at last become a writer. I have a real craving to write, I have a hundred books in my head!" [8] But very soon his mood changed radically. Subsequent letters breathe confidence and elation: "Here in Poland the plebiscite will not only give a practically unanimous 'yes,' but also a genuinely enthusiastic 'yes.' In ten days the whole movement has become unrecognizable: no trace of that depression which looked so ominous a fortnight ago—I again see the same cohesion and self-assurance which made me fall in love with our crowd during the Stavsky affair. The same is reported from the places visited by Schechtman." [9] "I am all of a sudden rejuvenated. The month of May when I literally bathed in enthusiasm in Poland, has removed twenty years and eighty per cent of *galut* from me. I have never before seen such enthusiasm. Our youth took the *Austritt* (secession) as if they were at last let out from a cellar into a garden." [10] To Jacob De Haas he wrote: "You saw me leave America disgruntled, tired and depressed. I wish I could show myself to you now: you wouldn't know me. I feel young again. I have had my *bain de jeunesse*: just one month of touring Poland, Lithuania, and Czechoslovakia with the message of the new Zionist Organisation. Out there in America you cannot even remotely imagine the simply incredible intensity of the rejoicing with which our people answered 'yes!' In Warsaw, Vilno, Bialostok, etc., the police had to intervene to keep order in the crowds that waited for their turn to vote in the plebiscite. [11] Hundreds of outsiders inquired as to whether they might be allowed to vote though themselves not Revisionists—which of course we had to refuse, this being a party vote." [12]

Five days before the plebiscite, Jabotinsky published an appeal to all Revisionists to go to the polls and to vote "yes" or "no" with "scrupulous honesty" : not to permit any artificial increase of the number of voters and to safeguard the secrecy of the vote. "Before you deposit your 'yes' or 'no' ballot, think over once more the significance of your answer. Particularly careful thought must be given by those who will vote in the affirmative, for they are taking a great responsibility upon themselves : a new road is full of endless sacrifices, and we will demand of everyone his share of sacrifice up to the last ounce of his strength. Think it over well : make your decision clearly and firmly—and then go to the polls and determine the fate of the Jewish nation." [13]

The plebiscite gave a 167,000 to 3,000 majority for Jabotinsky's proposal to establish a New Zionist Organization.

2. *Why Independence?*

For almost a decade—though with various degrees of emphasis—Jabotinsky had been advocating the abandonment of an opposition status within the official Zionist Organization and the establishment of an Independent (or New) Zionist Organization. What were the considerations that prompted him to implement this policy in the late spring of 1935 ?

He formulated the dilemma he was facing in a letter to his old friend (a non-Revisionist) S. D. Salzman : [14] "One thing is clear to me : it is impossible to drag the matter out any more. I am getting older. There are only three solutions : to conquer the Zionist Organization, or to convert the Revisionist Organization into something very 'wrathful,' or to retire and write novels." In a subsequent article, he was outspoken in voicing his disbelief in the prospect of gaining control of the Zionist Congress "through an electoral victory." [15] "In theory," such prospects did exist, he admitted :

But only in theory; in reality, victory in Zionist elections is almost automatically secured to the party with the biggest war-chest. The shekel has long since lost its original significance as a symbol of allegiance to Zionist ideals. the shekel has actually become a cash fee to buy the franchise—a system unknown even to the most undemocratic constitutions. At the same time that fee is by no means insignificant for the rank and file of an East European Ghetto. Just in those countries where Zionism, in recent years, has become a real mass-movement and Palestine a mass-concern, those masses now live in dire poverty. . . . An inevitable

279

consequence is that a rich party can secure victory over its poorer competitors simply by helping its adherents to get shekalim at a discount or gratis, and I fear no contradiction in stating that this is common practice. By the irony of Jewish realities, Socialism is today by far the richest of all Zionist parties; a result of 15 years' *Keren ha'Yessod* policy, plus a neat little income due to the noble transaction called the German "Transfer" agreement. No other group can ever hope to win under such conditions, no matter what its popularity among the masses.

He, therefore, plainly rejected the strategy of "fighting from within" the Zionist Organization: without a reasonable prospect of victory, "no opposition has any shred of *raison d'être*."

This *negative* conclusion was undoubtedly supplemented and strengthened by a major *positive* strategic consideration. Meir Grossman, who was (both before and after 1935) a strong opponent of the idea of Revisionist secession from the Zionist Organization, gave, in retrospect, a thoughtful interpretation of Jabotinsky's strategy:[16] "He attempted to effect unity in Zionism by force, unity through a split; he sought to gain recognition and leadership through withdrawal and attack. He declared war on the Zionist Organization, not with the aim of destroying Herzl's greatest creation—he was too true a Zionist, and too experienced a politician for this—but in order to compel the moguls of Zionism to stop the game of artificial majorities and force them to come to terms with the opposition. He despaired of Zionist Parliamentarianism, and hoped that a fierce struggle might open the eyes of the people, goad them to revolt and thus force unity and accord."

This interpretation is largely borne out by Jabotinsky's own contemporary pronouncements. In a letter to S. Jacobi (May 12, 1935) we read: "As to the future: I earnestly think that the existence of two Zionist Organizations may prove more conducive to a *modus vivendi* than the former situation. The Zionist Organization will be forced to seek some sort of agreement. . . . I have never been so confident, or so convinced, that we have chosen the best course imaginable, good for us and for Zionism." Three weeks later, in a speech in Vienna, he expressed the "hope that after their separation, the two Zionist Organizations and their followers would come together on a more peaceful and conciliatory basis."[17]

What Jabotinsky really had in mind was, however, something broader and deeper than even the mechanical reunification or cooperation of the "old" and the "new" Zionist Organizations. The vision, which had been ripening in his mind, belonged to quite a different order of values.

The very term "organization," which he was still using—though reluctantly—was rather a misnomer. As he later explained in a statement submitted to the British Colonial Office, the real purpose of the formation he was endeavoring to create was—"to constitute, at first *de facto* and later on *de jure,* that 'Jewish people,' which, though internationally recognized in the Palestine Mandate, still possesses no concrete or tangible legal status." This formation was "not a party nor a combine of parties, but rather the legal framework for evolving, in due course, what might be termed the *Senatus Populusque Judaicus.*" Its nature was that of "an independent organism neither subordinated nor affiliated to any other association pursuing Zionist aims; nor, indeed, intended to be an improved or competing replica of any such association now in existence." These associations, "including the Jewish Agency, as at present constituted, are leagues of ideological 'adherents'; membership depends on some deliberate act of joining, almost invariably expressed in the payment of a monetary contribution." Jabotinsky's own scheme, as it had been crystallizing in his mind in the course of the plebiscite campaign, was fundamentally different. Its basis was : free franchise.[18]

We proclaim that no fees should be paid for the right to vote, and the Herzl shekel will therefore not be sold for money. Our shekel will be given to any adult Jew, who, before entering the voting hall, will sign a short declaration.*

Jabotinsky did not intend to make the Foundation Congress of the new Organization a purely Revisionist affair, and reckoned that it was one of the main tasks of the pre-election campaign "to induce non-Revisionist candidates to stand." But he was not looking for "notables" : "The whole charm of the New Z.O. (this is the provisional term adopted) will be the fact of its being representative of the masses." He hoped "to rope in circles that really have a *specific* interest in Palestine—'specific' in the sense that their *aliya* and establishment is being hampered under the present system."

It was with this broad and lofty concept that Jabotinsky, after the

---

* The formula of the declaration was: "My aim is a Jewish State on both sides of the Jordan, and social justice without class war within Palestine Jewry."

positive outcome of the plebiscite, plunged into the electoral campaign. He himself was indescribably happy and elated. He wrote to a friend in Palestine. "Never have I heard such vigor of response from all parts of the movement." [19]

The elections were scheduled for August. The goal was : one million voters.[20] Jabotinsky wanted that million fervently, with an intensity bordering on superstition. Those who worked with him during the hectic months preceding the Vienna Congress, remember that, at that time, his physician categorically ordered him to give up smoking, lest he lose his voice. Jabotinsky was a heavy smoker and his daily consumption amounted to sixty cigarettes. Complete abstention from tobacco was for him a terrible, almost unbearable ordeal which often affected his capacity for work. He repeatedly voiced the apprehension that he might yield to temptation and resume smoking. But, at this particular period, he suddenly calmed down and came to the office with a serene air : "I have pledged myself not to touch a cigarette, and I know that if I keep my vow, we shall obtain our million votes." He kept his vow (for the rest of his life he never smoked), but the full million he was hoping for did not materialize. On August 31, he admitted that though he had "no exact figures yet, it does not look like a million voters." He was, however, not dismayed : "the figure will be quite respectable all the same." [21] Seven hundred thirteen thousand voters in thirty-two countries came to the polls, as compared with six hundred thirty-five thousand participants in the elections to the Nineteenth Zionist Congress, which convened at Luzern in August, 1935. Of the elected 318 delegates, 278 came to Vienna.

3. The Foundation Congress

The Vienna Congress belongs to Zionist history. Only those aspects of this momentous gathering which bear Jabotinsky's personal imprint and mark a milestone in his spiritual development, will be dealt with in this chapter.

Jacob De Haas, a seasoned and keen observer, who also participated in all the behind-the-scenes caucuses, frankly reported his impressions in letters to Rabbi Louis I. Newman and Justice Louis D. Brandeis :[22] "Jabotinsky is in unqualified control of the Congress," he wrote on September 7. "No striking personalities have exhibited themselves so far, but may develop in the sessions." Four days later he gave a vivid picture of how the *Nessiut* [Presidency] of the Organization was formed by Jabotinsky: "Jabotinsky was boss in naming his slate to the steering committee, and used it as a channel for demanding an *en bloc* acceptance of his list. The men themselves are far from notable, and excepting one representative of the orthodox (group) all belong to the Revisionist guard. There was objection to [S.] Jacobi, who is rather unknown. . . . Of the group, Schechtman was the most popular, but there was also some objection to him. A few names like [Dr. Jacob] Hoffman were submitted to Jabotinsky by the permanent or steering committee, but he turned them down with bitter condemnation."

The objections to Jacobi and to this writer were indeed strong. In the belief that the withdrawal of our candidature would simplify the formation of the *Nessiut*, we asked Jabotinsky to drop our names from his list. His reaction was almost violent: "Are those grumblers and malcontents going to tell me with whom or without whom I have to work? They want me to take the responsibility for conducting the affairs of the movement and at the same time they are trying to deny me the cooperation of men whom I consider essential for the success of my mission. That will not do! I am going to teach them a salutary lesson and I expect you to cooperate. I want the two of you to state quietly and firmly that, in view of the expressed objections, you have decided not to join the *Nessiut*. I, in turn, will just as quietly and firmly state that without these two gentlemen I refuse to form my Cabinet. Then all the grumblers will come to you and beg you to reconsider your decision. Do me a favor and don't agree. Keep them in suspense for hours, and only then grudgingly accept. I will highly enjoy this performance."

The "two gentlemen" heartily disliked the assignment and begged Jabotinsky not to make them a party to this "educational venture," as he chose to call it. But he was adamant, insisting that he was staging it not for their sake, but for highly essential organizational reasons. "If you don't cooperate, I will in all seriousness refuse to form a *Nessiut* under my Presidency," he warned. There was no other way than to comply. The "performance" worked out exactly as he predicted. The steering committee was relieved when Jacobi and Schechtman finally said "yes."

Jabotinsky had his way. But the Congress took revenge for the disregard of its objection. When it finally came to elections, De Haas reported, "Jabotinsky was elected President [*Nassi*] with great enthu-

283

siasm, but his Executive [*Nessiut*] received only eighty-eight votes [from the approximately two hundred delegates present at the last nightly session], four opposing, and the rest refusing to vote." [23]

Another significant aspect of the Vienna Congress—so far as Jabotinsky was concerned—was his revolutionary new definition of the ultimate aim of Zionism.

For years, Jabotinsky's Zionist equation was : Zionism equals Jewish State in the whole of Palestine with a Jewish majority of population. In Vienna and during all the post-Vienna years, he drastically revised this formula, putting the emphasis, primarily, on "the humanitarian aspect of the movement rather than on its purely nationalistic aspirations. . . . The Jewish State is not the ultimate aim : it is merely the first step in the process of implementing Greater Zionism. Then will come the second step : the return of the Jewish People to its Homeland, *Shivath Zion,* the exodus, the solution of the Jewish problem. . . . Exodus is the real meaning which the Jews today read into the term 'Zionism.' . . . Even the demand for a Jewish majority in Palestine (which was long assumed to represent Zionist 'extremism,' but which means, after all, only the admission of a million more Jewish immigrants) sounds sadly inadequate in the face of the acute land hunger dominating probably not less than half the race. The meaning of Zionism is . . . the liquidation of the enforced Dispersion, the gradual repatriation of 'all those Jews who want it.' " [24]

In the spirit of this new Jabotinsky concept, the Vienna Congress instructed the *Nessiut* to prepare a Ten-Year Plan for transferring to, and settling in the whole of Palestine, within a period of ten years, approximately 1,500,000 new Jewish immigrants.

4. *The Sacred Treasures of Jewish Tradition*

One more essential component of the Zionist concept which Jabotinsky presented in Vienna, was its religious aspect.

Jabotinsky was never religious in the ordinary, immediate sense of the term. In his spiritual budget there was simple no place for God as supreme celestial being who had created the universe and had ever since directed the course of world events and presided over human destinies. A child of a rationalistic and secular-minded nineteenth century, Jabotinsky well remembered Laplace's remark to Napoleon that, in writing his *Mécanique Céleste,* he found no need to assume the existence of God. He did not attend religious services and did not observe the Sabbath and the Jewish dietary laws.

Yet he had an innate and strong respect, sympathy and even affection for those in whose life religion and religious tradition is playing a predominant role. The innermost source of such an attitude was his genuine respect for every honest human belief, as contrasted with spiritual emptiness and cynicism With regard to Jewish religion, one more powerful factor undoubtedly influenced his attitude. He was fully aware of the tremendous role religion and tradition had played in the preservation of Jewish national individuality throughout the centuries of dispersion. He also admired the oneness of religious Jewry, its fervent devotion to Zion, and its unshakable faith in the redemption of the Jewish people.

On the other hand, he had no understanding and no sympathy for any specifically religious concept of Zionism, to be served by a distinct faction within the Zionist movement. To Dr. Wolfgang von Weisl, who had been conducting negotiations with Orthodox groups, he insistently recommended "caution" : [25] "Our Party as such will never swallow even the slightest touch of traditionalism; this might be regrettable, but it is a fact. And any half-commitment in this field will be repudiated. An autonomous religious wing within Revisionism will be highly welcome, but not the tinging of the Party in its entirety."

This was for years Jabotinsky's stand in matters pertaining to religion and orthodoxy. He respected and admired a Jew imbued with sincere religious faith and was intent on manifesting his consideration in a tactful, unobtrusive way. At the same time, he never failed to stress his personal aloofness in all religious matters.

Signs of a change in this pattern of respectful indifference appeared simultaneously with the emergence of his revolutionary concept of the New Zionist Organization as the embodiment of the totality of the Jewish People. As he saw it, a party (like the Revisionist Union) or a combine of parties (like the World Zionist Organization) could well afford to have no attitude toward Jewish religious tradition and to consider religion the private affair of the individual Jew. But for a body aspiring to become the incarnation of the Jewish national renaissance, it would be absurd to ignore "a factor of such magnitude as thirty centuries of religious inspiration and thought." Succinctily formulating his stand in the above quoted memorandum to the British Colonial Office, he wrote : "Religion can, and should, be treated as

285

a 'private affair' in so far as the individual's personal attitude is concerned; he may believe or not, practice or not, preach orthodoxy or atheism in full liberty. But the question as to whether the vast treasury of spiritual values called Judaism should be cultivated or abandoned by the Jewish nation as a whole is the 'affair' of the nation as a whole. The New Zionist Organization deliberately and explicitly desires it to be cultivated by the nation, without prejudice to the individual citizen's freedom of conscience and speech."

It was along these lines that he introduced in his inaugural address before the Vienna Congress the "religious plank" of the NZO Constitution :[26]

When you approach a problem of this kind, you have to speak in a personal way. A wide section of the intelligentsia of my generation was brought up under the magic spell of the nineteenth century, the century of freedom, and its liberal ideas. Indifferent tolerance set the fashion for our attitude to religion. Our slogans were: religion is the private concern of the individual; separation of the State from church or community, and separation of the synagogue from the nation. . . . My entire generation went through it. We started by eliminating clericalism and wound up by eliminating Godhead. And this is something quite different. We now see into what human nature can degenerate if deprived of Godhead. We see it in many fields. The value of a man is no longer determined by the substance of his conscience, but by his class or race origin. Men of my generation are still faithful to the tradition of freedom. But we are beginning to ask ourselves whether the interpretation of the nineties of the past century is still valid in the twentieth century. Of course, religion is a personal matter as far as my own feelings are concerned—whether I have faith or not, whether I accept or reject religion; and I must never be made to suffer or be punished for that. It is, however, not just a matter of private concern whether or not in this world of ours, there are going to be churches or synagogues. It is of concern to the State whether religious holidays can be celebrated, whether candles can be lighted in churches and synagogues, and whether the voices of the prophets can still remain a living force in the life of the society, or be relegated—like mummies—to museums and kept in showcases.

In Jabotinsky's view, there could be no "neutrality" in the contest between those who believed in eternal spiritual values and those who did not: "The value of a man lies in his heart. 'You are as you believe.' This is probably the whole truth and the final result of the whole of human philosophy. There is a link between human nature and great mystery; a longing to know what there is in life that cannot be dissected or eliminated, nor hidden." He therefore greeted "with a particular feeling those of our brethren who came [to that Congress] to represent this eternal truth and longing." "I greet you," he said to the orthodox wing of the Congress, "not only as brothers, but—in spite of all the differences of opinion—also as comrades in the search for truth. Life has created a mountain of stone and granite between our two camps. A tunnel must be dug through this mountain. Such a tunnel is now being bored from two sides—by me from this side, by you from the other. No one knows when we are going to meet, when —in a few days or in a few months—the wall between us will disappear. It will take time, but we shall work together."

The offer to "build a tunnel" was addressed to the "Religious Block" of the Congress. The twenty delegates from Poland, where the independent religious list received sixty-five thousand votes (out of a total of about five hundred thousand) constituted its nucleus. They were joined by about forty delegates from other countries. The spokesmen of the "Block" were fully satisfied with Jabotinsky's stand. Some went even farther and insisted that he was mistaken in believing that there was a "mountain" to be penetrated between him and the religious camp; such a "mountain" did not exist, they claimed.

There was, however, also a vocal, though numerically small, opposition to Jabotinsky's attempt to introduce religion and tradition into the basic fabric of the movement's ideology. The most influential spokesmen for it were Jacob De Haas and Professor Alexander Kulischer; but several representatives of the movement's intelligentsia (Adolf Gurevitch, Mordehai Katz, Arye Dissentchik) were not less outspoken in rejecting this "intrusion." Not that they would not fully and wholeheartedly subscribe to any resolution in favor of far-reaching guarantees of the rights of the Jewish religion and tradition in the Jewish State-to-be. Their opposition was directed exclusively against the incorporation of the principle of "implanting in Jewish life the sacred treasures of Jewish tradition" into the very definition of the aim of Zionism, as formulated in the Constitution of the N.Z.O. In addition to purely ideological considerations, the speakers expressed apprehension as to the maintenance of freedom of conscience under the new "religious clause."

Jabotinsky firmly defended this clause, making abundant use of the *argumentum ad hominem*:[27] "I was born in reactionary Russia

287

and I am a fervent partisan of freedom of thought and speech. You may rely on my liberalism, and trust me never to permit any violation of freedom of conscience. May my right arm wither if I should ever be party to anything that smacks of obscurantism. If there is ever an attempt to limit freedom of conscience, I will have nothing in common with such a movement. . . . It is still difficult to ascertain which has a stronger appeal : nationalism or religion. But we will try to find a synthesis. In the meantime, each one of us must have respect for what is holy to the other, must have understanding for his brother's blindness."

Some of the *Betar* speakers claimed that by introducing new definitions Jabotinsky was "deviating from the fundamental principle of Zionist monism." "I deny it," he answered. "Our goal is the Jewish State. But we cannot remain indifferent to problems which are directly connected with statehood. We want to create a laboratory for great ideas of social justice, which would have world-wide significance. We want to revive our ancestral language. Are we turning aside from our monistic course when we are trying to incorporate these problems into the definition of our final aim? Certainly not. Then, why should we shy from taking cognizance of a fire that had been burning in our people for thousands of years?

"You may confidently rely on me, my Revisionist friends and comrades. I am at least as good a Democrat as all of you are. I would lose the very *raison d'être* of my life and work if I would not be able to live in freedom."

Jabotinsky had his way. The Congress overwhelmingly endorsed the Constitution with its religious clause. But Jabotinsky knew very well that a substantial section of the Congress, including several of his closest collaborators, did it halfheartedly, without real understanding of and sympathy for the innovation he so much insisted upon. Some just acquiesced in this Jabotinsky-sponsored new departure; some said, "he knows better"; others simply did not ascribe too much importance to the entire matter. It was not so much the open opposition, which found expression in speeches from the rostrum, as the silent aloofness of those who did not speak, that troubled Jabotinsky. But he was firmly convinced of the justness of the Constitution as a whole that he made the Congress endorse. "As far as I am concerned : I uphold every letter of it," he wrote to his son Eri on September 14.

This letter is in more than one respect a valuable and revealing human document. The Congress ended in the small hours of September 12. Two days later Jabotinsky got up at six a.m. "to pour out his heart" to his son who, he knew, was far from being in sympathy with any pro-religious tendencies : "I wonder what you think of it. . . ."

He categorically discarded the possible allegation that this proposal was "the result of a *Kuhhandel*" [horse-trading deal] with the orthodox circles to obtain their support. It was, he insisted, "a result of thoughts I had been nurturing for the last five years, and even longer."

I don't need to explain that I am now, as ever, for the freedom of thought, etc. and that I see no holiness in the [religious] ritual. The issue is much deeper: "the implanting in Jewish life of the sacred treasures of Jewish tradition." Everybody agrees that there are in the Torah "sacred" principles, and "really sacred" ones. It is worthwhile implanting them. On the other hand, however, these sacred things can be incorporated into a system of ethics, which any atheist would support as such. Then why implant them under the label of religion? Here lies the *main controversy*. It is quite possible to construct a moral system without any connection with the *Shekhina* [divine spirit]; I have been doing this all my life. Nevertheless, I am now convinced that it is *sounder to treat these ethical fundamentals as connected with a superhuman mystery.* And this not only out of "courtesy:" the Bible is indeed our primary source, so why should we hide it? Why is it permissible to proclaim Zionist principles in Herzl's name (while it is quite possible to uphold them without reference to Herzl) . . . and why have we to be ashamed of quoting the Torah? It is, in fact, but a kind of snobbishness, a shrinking from something associated with "jargon," plebeian clothes, etc. But it was, not only this, not only the revolt against "shrinking" and the desire to restore to decent society the Bible and God Almighty, that decided me— I go much farther: *we need religious pathos as such.* I am not sure that we will succeed in reviving it in the souls [of our generation]—maybe nowadays it is but an innate quality given only to a few, like being musically gifted. But I would be happy if it were possible to create a generation of believers.

There was abundant speculation as to the true motives of Jabotinsky's advocacy of "the sacred treasures of Jewish tradition." Even among his own family there is still a tendency to ascribe it to considerations of sheer expediency : it is claimed that it was in the hope of attracting the religious masses that he used the "religious gimmicks." This interpretation is anything but fair and convincing. Like every political leader, Jabotinsky was undoubtedly mindful of the necessity to make masses join his movement. But his whole life record speaks against any suspicion of hypocritical and cynical trifling with the holiest feelings of the people. If anything, he rather could have been accused of disregarding popular slogans and thus often harming the interests of his party. The roots of his longing to implant "religious pathos as such" must be sought largely in the profound impression made on him by the courageous stand taken by the leaders of religious Jewry (first and foremost by Chief Rabbi Kook) during the Stavsky affair. This stand was to him a revealing testimony of the great intrinsic moral force which is organically connected with the "religious pathos" and which cannot be easily swept by current political passions. Jabotinsky felt that secular impulses alone were insufficient to generate and maintain moral integrity in a nation. He was looking for spiritual inspiration of a nature as yet not clear to himself, but whose lofty creativeness he wanted to release and implant. Throughout the last years of his life, his interest in the problems of religion and tradition continued unabated.

THE LONDON ERA

1. *The British Partner*

THE VIENNA CONFERENCE decided to transfer the headquarters of the *Nessiut* to London. Early in 1936, a large house was rented on Finchley Road—a London edition of the Rue Pontoise—which housed all the institutions of the movement.

Jabotinsky left Paris for London with considerable reluctance. His late brother-in-law, Eliahu M. Galperin, told this writer of the last hour they had spent in a small and quiet French restaurant at the corner of Avenue d'Orleans and Rue d'Alesia. Jabotinsky spoke nostalgically of the charm of the city which had been his abode for more than a decade and which he was now exchanging for the cold British capital. Before the arrival of his wife, he stayed in the London flat of Y. Machover, with whom he remained friends despite the Kattowitz split. When Mrs. Jabotinsky arrived, they lived in one room of a quiet and clean old-fashioned hotel (12 Belsize Grove), about fifteen minutes' walk from the N.Z.O. office. The room served as bedroom, dining room and study. The telephone was in the corridor.[1] In July, 1936, Jabotinsky signed a contract and made an advance payment on a house in Hampstead Garden; the rest of the purchase price was to be paid off in twenty-one yearly installments. "The house is wonderful," he wrote to his son: "two floors and a huge attic; there is also a garden with a brook half-a-meter wide." Mrs. Jabotinsky went to Paris to see to the transportation of the furniture, and they expected the house to be ready for occupancy in September.[2] Jabotinsky's young collaborators were already making plans to buy him a small car to be driven by a *Betari* who would live in the same house.[3]

All these beautiful plans never materialized. There was no money to pay the second installment: whatever Jabotinsky earned was devoured by pressing party needs. Three months later, we read in a letter from Warsaw:[4] "Tonight I will have to decide to wire Ania either 'a house at all costs' or 'no house.' . . . I am afraid that I will have to agree with Ania's arguments and cancel the house. It's a pity." The "dream house" remained wishful thinking, and the hotel room—a reality. His mood, however, remained cheerful, and his younger collaborators gratefully recall how, after a fourteen-hour day, he used to entertain them until after midnight, occasionally seasoning his conversation with amusing advice on how to behave in London: "Here, if you want to kiss a girl you first have to marry her so as not to get entagled in a breach-of-promise suit."

Jabotinsky plunged headlong into political activities. The press published detailed reports of his conference with the Secretary of State for the Colonies [J. H. Thomas] and leading members of Parliament. His statement against the establishment of the Legislative Council in Palestine appeared in a number of influential English newspapers. A mass meeting against the Council, which he addressed, attracted a large and enthusiastic audience. The editor of the *Haolam* (the Hebrew official organ of the Zionist Executive) complained that with Jabotinsky's arrival in London, N.Z.O. "dangerousness" had increased considerably.

Then, as later, there was much comment on the fact that the Jabotinsky movement, after a lapse of three years during which its headquarters were in Paris, had again established its world center in the capital of the Mandatory Power.

Strong and consistent criticism, to which Jabotinsky had been subjecting the British Mandatory regime in Palestine since 1923, and his demands for a determined and unyielding Zionist political offensive against this regime, earned him, in many circles, the reputation of an "anti-British firebrand." A restrospective analysis of his political record not only disproves this allegation: it shows, on the contrary, that one of the fundamentals of Jabotinsky's political concept was deep faith in England, admiration for the English national character, and almost excessive loyalty to Jewish-English partnership. Of all Zionist political leaders, he was essentially the most staunchly "pro-British." The very outspokenness of his criticism was rooted in his lofty concept of Britain as a great nation which had respect for, and is responsive to a truly just and forcefully presented demand, however critical it might be of Britain's actual policy. He was organically incapable of accepting the argument that criticism might "offend" Britain; that "asking too much" might alienate British sympathy and support for Zionism; and that since the Jews possessed no physical force, all attempts to bring about a radical change of the British policy in Palestine were futile. Jabotinsky believed in the irresistible force of concerted moral pressure and he believed in England. Deviations from this course, which will be recorded in this chapter, were shortlived.

What could be described as Jabotinsky's basic "philosophy" of Anglo-Jewish relationship was best formulated in a penetrating essay "The Englishman" (1929).[5] Its subject was the faults and the virtues of the type of "educated Englishmen of the governing class," with whom Zionist Jewry had been dealing ("and I hope shall be dealing for many years to come") in Palestine and London. The well-balanced presentation culminated in a carefully-worded but firm conclusion that, in spite of his many and heavy shortcomings, this Englishman, if properly dealt with, is world Jewry's most suitable partner in the great Palestine venture : he is neither a "super-gentleman" who would run after you to pay off a contracted obligation, nor a callous deceiver, who is determined not to live up to his promise. He is conservative and slow, and his normal reaction is to say "no" to each demand calling for an effort. But if you do not take this "no" for an answer, and if you persist in reiterating your demand, and if your demand is a just and reasonable one, "after the seventh 'no' comes 'yes.' With an Englishman one has not got to be afraid of bothering him again, and again and again, or perhaps even of making a 'row.' " This does not mean, of course, that :

anyone who has a demand that he wants to make England agree to, must resort to violence, smash windows, prove his nuisance value. That is a very childish interpretation of a "strong" policy. . . . Strength is essentially polite and soft-spoken. But it is infinitely stubborn, absolutely impervious to rebuffs, unshakable in its conviction, with its Decalogue reduced to one sentence: the last word will be MINE, provided, of course, the cause that strength is fighting for is a good one . . . [the Englishman] has one virture, which overtops all his faults: in his own heart he has a Court of Appeal that is open to those who are not afraid to appeal; and he respects those who fight and never acknowledge defeat, who on the morrow of a failure begin a new attack.

293

We have seen (Chapter Seven) that this belief in England as world Jewry's "most suitable partner" was not shaken by the tragic events of August, 1929, and the subsequent developments. Swimming against the rising current of anti-British feeling, Jabotinsky insisted on a policy of the "last experiment," the prerequisite of which was a courageous and consistent Zionist policy. Before such an experiment had been carried out in all sincerity and to the very end, no hasty "away from England" conclusions must be drawn.

It was not easy to persist in this assertive view in the face of the continued and intensified anti-Zionist policy of the Mandatory Power. In June, 1931, Jabotinsky felt compelled to admit that "our relations with the Mandatory Power have reached a very dangerous stage." Two years ago, one might perhaps have still believed that it was merely the local Palestine Administration which was militantly pro-Arab and anti-Zionist, and that the Imperial Government in London was not aware of the true state of affairs: "Now, it has become clear that the London Government, and particularly the Colonial Office, knows very well what is going on in Palestine, and is in full sympathy with it." Jabotinsky's reasoning was: if this enmity to Zionism was in accordance with British Imperial interests, any attempt to fight it would be hopeless; if, however, anti-Zionism did not correspond to British interests, counter-action was possible and its success was dependent mainly on Zionist energy and political skill. He urged the immediate launching of such a counter-action, which would "very soon demonstrate whether it pays to continue the experiment with Britain." [6] Four months later, on the eve of the fourteenth anniversary of the Balfour Declaration, he frankly expressed his doubts as to whether England, whose might had considerably declined, was any longer able or willing to make the great effort needed to implement the Declaration honestly and in full: "By the time the Balfour Declaration is fifteen years old, we will have to know whether or not our paths coincide." [7]

For a time, Jabotinsky himself yielded to the "rise of strong anti-English feeling," which he predicted in a letter published in the London *Times* of January 26, 1932. Three months later, addressing the second national Revisionist Convention in France, he, for the first time, declared that "England's presence in Palestine is now a hindrance to our [Zionist] cause; her tactics are a menace to the *Yishuv's* very existence." [8] He called for a "change of orientation."

Anticipating the question as to who should take England's place, he said: "We refuse to answer this. The policy of a nation is not made by such declarations. All nations of the world have been—and still are—looking for allies, but they don't shout about their plans at every crossroad."

Speculation was rife at the time that Jabotinsky in fact was seriously considering the idea of "offering" the Mandate over Palestine to Mussolini's Italy. His personal correspondence gives a realistic insight into his actual attitude to this problem. He was supposed to address an Italian Revisionist Conference scheduled for February 7, 1932. Leone Carpi, the leader of the Revisionist Party in Italy, intended to arrange audience for him with leading Italian statesmen. The London Revisionist headquarters advised him to forego the entire trip to Italy. Commenting on this suggestion, Jabotinsky wrote:[9]

I am perfectly sure that there will be no "audiences" right now, when Italy is flirting so obviously with England . . . so the whole question is theory. But, before we advise Carpi to cancel the requests already made, I should like to understand the reasons. It has been understood since long before [the Fourth Revisionist World Conference in] Prague, that we have the right to acquaint *massgebende politische Faktoren* [determining political factors] with our point of view. Why is Mussolini an exception? Nobody is suggesting that we should offer him the Mandate; but if we could tell him that we are dissatisfied it would only be natural. The only reason for your fears, I gather, is that it might arouse suspicion in England. I have always understood that the more apprehensive the government becomes about Jewish allegiances, the better for us. . . . Granted, we do not say *los von England*, but we do most urgently need to show that we have connections, and the more influential the better.

It can be assumed that Jabotinsky never seriously considered "offering" Italy the Mandate. Righly or wrongly, he believed, however, that by making the British Government "apprehensive about Jewish allegiances" he would be able to make it more receptive to Zionist demands. (As he predicted, the audiences did not materialize, and "the whole thing" remained theoretical.)

This constituted but a passing episode in Jabotinsky's political thinking. He soon reverted to his fundamental concept of a world-wide Jewish political offensive, of which England would be simultaneously the object and the addressee: the petition movement, which he launched in 1933-34, was an indictment of the British anti-Zionist policy, but of its four addressees one was the British Parliament and the other the King of Great Britain. Jabotinsky's faith in Britain as a "Court of Appeal open to those not afraid to appeal" remained unshaken.

Speaking at the Sixth Revisionist World Conference (Cracow, January, 1935) before 178 delegates from 25 countries, he subjected the anti-colonization regime of the Mandatory Power to devastating criticism. He made it, however, perfectly clear that this criticism must not be interpreted as a *negation* of the Mandatory.[10]

British statesmen, and perhaps some of our own hot-heads too, should get one thing absolutely clear. We are mercilessly critical with regard to the Mandatory's *present* policy in Palestine, and we demand a switch to a better policy, more appropriate to the interests of Zionism. But since it is to England that we put such demands, it means that we want her to stay on in Palestine, and to go on ruling Palestine. For you cannot say to a person, "go away—and help me into the saddle." If you want England to help you into the saddle, you don't want England to go away: on the contrary, the implication is that you believe she can be persuaded to help you. What is more: Israel is no beggar asking for services that she does not intend to repay. Since you demand a historical service from England, you imply that, if that service is rendered, Jewish Palestine will be ready to repay it, loyally and durably, by service to the Empire. This triad: "Criticism of the present—Trust in the good will of England— Future Partnership"—is the essence of our attitude towards the Mandatory Power and must form the *leitmotif* of Revisionist policy.

He was more than ever convinced that the interests of Great Britain and Zionism coincided, and was eager to prove that, far from being "anti-British," he and his movement were willing to be and capable of being faithful and useful allies in time of need.

In the spring of 1935, the political situation in Europe, and in the Mediterranean in particular, became tense and explosive. Hitler decreed conscription on March 16; the unanimous protest of the Council of the League of Nations (April 15-17) was hautily disregarded; Mussolini's intentions toward Abyssinia were beginning to take shape. There was much speculation about England's next move. It was against this background that one must view the letter, marked "confidential," which Jabotinsky sent to Leopold Amery from Paris on April 24, 1935.

The letter began with a characteristic introductory sentence to the effect that, unless his memory deceived him, Amery was not a man to be surprised if he, Jabotinsky, stated his business without preamble. He then went on to say that, should a situation arise where England would require additional-man-power, he could guarantee a considerable response from among the Jewish youth of many countries. It would be futile to try to give exact figures, he wrote, but his estimate was in the neighborhood of one hundred thousand men for any Eastern field of action; if for Europe, about one-third that number. A large proportion would be trained men, in the sense of having previously done military service, although mainly under peace conditions. He explained that he was referring to men from outside Palestine, as those in Palestine would probably be available without any help from him, especially for the Orient. He asked that, in gauging the reliability of his estimates, it should be taken into consideration that "the mentality of Jewish youth today is very different from that which caused us so many disappointments in 1917." The Jewish Legion had become a cherished legend and an inspiring precedent. And in the deepest parts of the Ghetto, at least among that section of young Jewry with which he was in constant contact, military training had become extremely popular.

Jabotinsky went on to say that he did not know whether those in authority were anticipating any such complications, nor whether England was likely to want additional contingents, nor whether this kind of human material would be considered desirable, but if . . . he would like to have some idea in advance as to what he would have to do when the need arose. He was not looking for propaganda. What he meant was that, during the War, it took them two years to get the consent of the authorities to form the Legion, and in the meantime all enthusiasm was lost. This time (though, he added, they all hoped there would be no "this time") things would be likely to move much faster. That is why he considered it necessary to know beforehand whether the offer would be acceptable. He apologized for troubling Amery, explaining that he knew no one at the War Office, nor had anyone there heard of him, except perhaps in connection with his alleged "anti-Britishness." He expressed the hope that Amery needed no assurances from him that, "critical as I am and shall probably have to remain, for me—so long as the Balfour Declaration stands—it is England, right or wrong," adding that those who were of his way of thinking shared this attitude.

297

Jabotinsky sent a copy of this letter to political associates in London, with the comment: "I did not refer to Italy, because I did not want to complicate the matter. . . . What is important is to break down the myth of our anti-Britishness. . . . Don't be scared by my 'England, right or wrong.' Amery will believe it, and as far as I personally am concerned, it is true." Nevertheless, he added, "there are fifteen chances that Amery will not reply, seventy chances that he will refuse to forward my offer." [11]

Amery did reply, and he did not refuse to act. He wrote:

Dear Mr. J.

I was very much interested to get your letter and very much appreciated and understood the generous spirit of your offer. Nor do I in the least undervalue the help that any body of friends could give England in a crisis. But you and I both know how officialdom can hesitate and delay and so lose opportunities.

I do not myself believe that there is any real danger in the offing in the near future. But one can never tell. As soon as I get back to town I will try and sound the W.O. I don't expect them to take up your project with open arms. But it may be well to prepare their minds for it. It is the new ideas that are always the most suspicious!

Yours very truly,

L.A.

Amery's scepticism as to the reaction of the War Office proved to be correct. Four months later, Jabotinsky acknowledged that "the offer conveyed through Amery was turned down." [12]

This latter letter was written shortly after a tripartite conference between England, France and Italy (August 15-18, 1935) had ended in Paris without having reached any agreement on the Abyssinian problem. The probability of a British-Italian armed conflict seemed to have become stronger. Urged to react to this emergency, Jabotinsky advised against precipitate action. "The Abyssinian matter is of course very important," he wrote, "but I shouldn't hurry. . . . Nobody knows, least of all H.M. Government, whether England will really go on frowning (as for 'fighting,' there is no fear of that at all) or will soon find some formula to enable them to kiss and be friends again. In any case, there is time." Recalling that the British had turned down the offer conveyed through Amery in April, he did not think that it "would do to repeat it [the offer] at once."

Less than three weeks later, a new development made Jabotinsky

298

change his timing. He learned from a reliable source that a representative of the British War Office had approached Ben Gurion "on the question of a Jewish Contingent for the defense of Palestine in case of trouble. . . . B. G., according to the report, assured the representative of Jewish unanimity with regard to Palestine defense ('there will be a united front from left to right,' etc.)." Two considerations perturbed Jabotinsky in this idyllic picture. The first was that, according to his informant, the gentleman from the War Office hinted at the possibility of a mixed Arab-Jewish garrison. Jabotinsky did not know Ben Gurion's reaction to this eventuality, but believed that "there may be quite a section in the *Histadrut* who would prefer *Irgun Meshuttaf* [common organization with the Arabs] to associating with us [Revisionists]." The second perturbing thought was that "should trouble arise, some damaging Red influence might creep in, in which case B. G.'s crowd would be unreliable even if B. G. himself would stick to the 'united front.' " Jabotinsky believed that:[13]

under these conditions *our* [Revisionist] offer should be formally repeated. I do not believe there will be any complications, but that is of no importance. The concrete proposal now can only take one form: certificates. We would undertake to bring in well trained people from 21 to 27 up to 20 thousand in numbers. This seems to be the only sensible method of action at this moment. Should the Government people suspect that this is merely a trick to get certificates, tell them what you think of them and walk out.

Jabotinsky also stressed that "this time the offer must be confined to the defense of Palestine and operations strictly connected with that."

Jabotinsky's earlier scepticism as to the seriousness of His Majesty's Government's "frowning" at Italy's action in Abyssinia proved to be correct. Economic sanctions proposed by a Committee of the League of Nations were never imposed, and no country was willing to consider the imposition of military sanctions. A deal with Italy proposed by Britain's Sir Samuel Hoare and France's Pierre Laval, and approved by the British Government was, it is true, abandoned under the pressure of adverse public opinion in Britain. But in this atmosphere of "kiss and be friends," the British War Office showed little interest in any offer of a Jewish military contingent.

2. *Unheeded Warning*

In the early spring of 1936, tension in Palestine was high. The Arab nationalist leaders were insensed by the strong opposition to the project of a Legislative Council, which had found expression in the House of Lords (in February) and in the House of Commons (in March). They felt that Great Britain was "betraying them to the Jews." On the other hand, the Italo-Ethiopian War, then drawing to a close, had seriously impaired English prestige throughout the Middle East. The conflict with Egypt was assuming violent form. The Arabs thought that the time was propitious for applying strong pressure on Great Britain. Communist agents were busily contributing their share to the growing uneasiness.

Jabotinsky was watching these developments closely, both on the international and the local Palestine scene. He was also acutely aware of the appalling inadequacy of the British defense forces in the country; he knew that the still not legalized Jewish self-defense was incapable of coping with an organized Arab onslaught. There was no doubt in his mind that grave disturbances were imminent. Arab violence—unprecedented alike in duration and ferocity—that started in the second half of April, was foreseen by him with forceful accuracy, and the authorities forewarned.

On April 5, a fortnight before the event, Jabotinsky cabled to the High Commissioner in Jerusalem : [14]

Compelled to inform your Excellenty of alarming reports from Palestine voicing acutest apprehension of anti-Jewish outbreaks stop Reports affirm agitation furthered by circles hoping to force Zionists [and] pro-Zionists accept Legislative Council stop Authorization specific Arab manifestations unprecedented scale appears being exploited to revive ominous battlecry *Eddowleh Maana** stop World Jewry similarly alarmed stop Experience shows such developments inevitably result bloodshed especially considering scarcity imperial troops inefficient police recently confirmed by inspector general Spicer and absence legalised Jewish Self-Defense stop Consider my duty convey this information to your excellency as responsible administrator [and] soldier whom I personally heard [a] year ago asserting Palestine's unshakable security stop. Together with all Jews I respectfully await denial of danger or decisive action stop. Essence of this cable communicated home government and parliamentary friends.

* "The Government is with us."

300

The next day, on April 6, a copy of this cable was forwarded to the Colonial Office in London. There was no reaction from Jerusalem or from London. On April 20, Jabotinsky wrote to J. H. Thomas, then Secretary of State for the Colonies, pressing for a reply. On April 23, the Colonial Office answered that it "was unable to accept the suggestion as to the inadequacy of the Forces at the disposal of the High Commissioner." [15]

Disturbances started exactly two weeks after Jabotinsky's warning telegram. Both this warning and the Government's reaction to it were discussed at the Thirty-Second (Extraordinary) Session of the League of Nations Permanent Mandates Commission.[16] On August 7, 1936, Baron von Asbeck (Netherlands) referred to "a telegram sent to the High Commissioner before the outbreak by Mr. Jabotinsky, which was such as to arouse apprehension of an outbreak." He asked the accredited representatives of Great Britain "whether the telegram in question was received, and what importance was attached to the warning." The Chairman of the Commission, Mr. Orts, stressed that this telegram "was interesting because it seemed to indicate that, while the Administration had not foreseen the troubles, other persons, in particular the sender of the telegram, had expected them."

J. Hathorn Hall (former Chief Secretary to the Government of Palestine) replied that the Jabotinsky telegram allegedly "had been sent in connection with the Nebi Musa festival, when Arabs from all over Palestine were gathered together, and presumably Mr. Jabotinsky had some reason to think that the Nebi Musa festival would lead to serious outbreaks." But, since the festival "actually passed off quite quietly . . . Mr. Jabotinsky's specific warning proved to be ill-founded."

As can be seen from the text of Jabotinsky's telegram, it contained no mention whatsoever of the Nebi Musa festival, and drew the administration's attention to the entire dangerous situation in Palestine. The warning was disregarded in its entirety.

When the riots broke out, Jabotinsky appealed to the Prime Minister (Stanley Baldwin), to the Foreign Secretary (Anthony Eden), the Secretary for War (Duff Cooper), and the Colonial Secretary (J. H. Thomas). On April 27, he (together with Colonel Patterson and this writer) addressed a mass meeting in the East End of London. On May 21, he told a Conference of the English and Jewish Press that he had warned the British Administration before the troubles broke out and that these warnings were not heeded. Speaking in Warsaw on June 13, he openly demanded the resignation of Sir Arthur Wauchope, who for years had been highly praised by Zionist leaders, but whose policy was directly responsible for the bloodshed and anarchy in Palestine. "This demand," he said, "is not an act of revenge, but a logical consequence of the circumstances. The High Commissioner is like a Viceroy, and if his policy is a failure, he must quit." But, instead of dismissing Wauchope, the British began to talk of stopping Jewish immigration for the next two months. "As the Jews have been waiting for redemption for two thousand years, they can surely wait another few months."[17]

The British reaction, coupled with a marked shift of naval power in the Near and Middle East, again revived Jabotinsky's doubts as to whether Britain was a suitable partner in world Jewry's struggle for statehood. "Until some nine months ago," he said, "we honestly believed that England was the strongest country on the seas and in the colonial world; that she was the most reliable partner. But recently public feeling has changed. . . . England is now by far not the strongest power in the Mediterranean, where she has a powerful rival—Italy." He pointedly mentioned the prospect of "revising the distribution of Mandates" and the problem emerging for Jews from this new situation: "Who will be the rulers of Palestine, who will control the country, and under what laws shall we have to live?"[18]

This time, his renewed scepticism in regard to England as Mandatory Power was not a passing mood. In a letter to his son he wrote:[19] "Politically we are rolling downhill. There is no force capable of stopping the trend. We will have to descend to the very bottom before we will again see light. Not only we, but all the nations and states that have hitched their fate to England. England is trying to get rid of all her commitments and to follow the line of least resistance. The era initiated on November 2, 1917, has ended. What will follow, I still do not see clearly." His correspondence of that period with Jacob De Haas bears witness to his uncertainty, and his tense search for an answer.[20] Late in July, 1936, in reply to De Haas' plea to clarify and define a "way out" from the impasse in Jewish-British relations, Jabotinsky openly acknowledged his inability to give a clear and adequate answer: "The situation is rapidly changing around us, so rapidly that it is almost impossible at any given moment to realize what kind of a world it is we are living in today. I frankly admit that for the moment I have lost sight of the little trail which may bring us back to the big main road. It is the first time in my life that such a thing has happened to me : ever since the Young Turkish revolution, thirty years ago, in all the cataclysms we have lived through, I always had the impression, or the illusion, that I could see quite clearly that particular little track winding its way through bogs and boulders for the special benefit of the Zionist cause. But I cannot boast this now. The main asset in all our Zionist venture, England as we knew her up to yesterday, has disappeared. Sometimes I feel like Sinbad the Sailor (or what was that hero of the "Arabian Nights?") must have felt when he established his 'national home' on a little island, and the island proved to be a whale—and *adieu.* . . . I fervently hope that my blindness is temporary, but that does not matter. Somebody, if not I, is sure to rediscover the trail. For the present I want to indulge in the luxury of silence for a month : not to speak, not to write, not to think." The month he asked for went by, but on August 31 he was still struggling with himself for clarity : "The 'orientation' question is still not clear to me, and . . . I don't feel ashamed at all. The solution no longer depends on the 'attitude' of England (or the Arabs) only as it did before : now it is a question, above all, of England's objective value in the Mediterranean and European markets after the present cataclysms (Abyssinia), and also after the Spanish Civil War, the outcome of which is still in the balance. How can that value be gauged before the new situation has crystallized? I am getting a bit angry under the constant friendly bombardment to which I am being subjected these last months : 'Please give us a directive, Revisionism has always been accustomed to follow clear directives.' In so far as *I* was responsible for those 'directives,' they were clear *only* because I always took care, before formulating a program, to get a distinct view of the situation; and as long as the Earth's surface is still wriggling, I can't get it, and feel no shame in admitting it."

Shame or no shame, he could not evade the compelling necessity of analyzing the possible solutions to the agonizing dilemma, and two weeks later he introduced De Haas into the very laboratory of his tense reasoning. He reluctantly endorsed the thesis that "the British phase of Zionism is virtually over; even if certain demands and complaints will, for some time to come, still have to be addressed to England (Government and/or nation), it will have to be stated clearly that in our opinion England can no longer be expected to fill the role and that the Jews must start looking for some *Ersatz* (substitute). . . . We went into partnership with a Rockefeller, but now he has become second-rate, can he fulfill the expectations? Even worse: a pledge given by Don Quixote—can it be carried out by Sancho Panza?" Yet when it came to the fateful question of finding a substitute, for that "second-rate" partner, Jabotinsky was at a loss to name it:

Logically, the *Ersatz* could be either Italy, or some condominium of less anti-Semitic States interested in Jewish immigration, or a direct Geneva [League of Nations] Mandate, or a fourth alternative which I'll touch upon later.

Before June 30—July 15 I sounded alternative no 1. Result: not yet ripe, not by a long shot.

Alternative no. 2: sounding it now. There are possibilities (though a long way off). But the Jews will be frightened, will say it means condoning anti-Semitism. There is already a storm about it.

Alternative no. 3: vague, no precedent, no instrumentality; would, in fact, mean same as no. 4.

No. 4 would be: back to Charter, mandate in Jewish hands. England agrees to formation of a Jewish garrison and withdraws (. . . When planning always imagine that the policeman agrees to your plan). It sounds bold and fantastic, but perhaps is the only plan that would sound plausible and concrete to a good *goyish kopp*.

"Alternative No. 4" can be considered as the embryonic stage of the later *Irgun Zvai Leumi* concept of getting rid of British tutelage and establishing a Jewish administration of the country. But in 1936, this sounded indeed like an utterly "bold and fantastic" idea. There was no prospect of "the policeman" withdrawing voluntarily, and there was as yet no body of public opinion which would be ripe for even envisaging any attempt to drive out the British by force of arms. All the four alternatives he could think of proved unable to stand up to his own sober analysis. And on October 1, Jabotinsky reluctantly admitted to De Haas: "Our *Los von England* tendency cannot, for the present, go farther than something like this: a big last attempt to get what we need from *this* partner; and, if it fails, then. . . ." The "then" remained suspended in the air.

3. *The Battle of the Royal Commission*

Two and a half months after the outbreak of the Arab riots, the British Government appointed a Royal Commission to "investigate causes of unrest and alleged grievances either of Arabs or of Jews." Jabotinsky was outspoken in his apprehension regarding the purpose and prospects of this body. Quoting the British Government's previous abortive and shortlived attempts at devising some improvised "solution" to the Palestine crisis, he wrote: "If I had ready cash at my disposal, I would bet a hundred dollars that nothing will come of this Commission as well." Yet he realized that a Royal Commission was "no plaything" and "a far more official matter than the Inquiry Commissions that had been sent heretofore to Palestine. Its prestige is greater, its powers are wider, the choice of personnel is more deliberate, and generally there is a tradition that a 'Royal Commission' results in greater, more profound or even historic consequences." [21] He was therefore opposed to Jacob De Haas' suggestion to boycott this body: "I am all for denying the authority of the Royal Commission, but not for boycotting it. I think it might be very useful, for propaganda purposes, to come before it and give it a piece of our mind, blaming the inept Government both in London and Jerusalem and perhaps also the Jewish Agency." [22] His warning that "the present Jewish Agency will not be able to represent the Zionist case" [23] was backed by a considerable part of Jewish public opinion in Palestine. In a statement to the press, Colonel Wedgwood suggested that Jabotinsky be given the opportunity to testify before the Commission. He expected him to make a strong indictment of the Palestine Administration.[24]

The *Nessiut* of the New Zionist Organization accepted this suggestion and made a written request that Jabotinsky be allowed to testify in public session; the Royal Commission was expected to instruct the Immigration Department of the Palestine Government to issue an entry visa. An Anglo-Jewish journalist, who was then in Palestine, later wrote:[25] "Who of those that saw it can forget the suspense, the excitement in the streets of Palestine, the gesticulating groups who left work and business in order to give vent to their joy—when one of the newspapers published an item to the effect that Jabotinsky might possibly be coming to give evidence before the Royal Commission. Electricity seemed to fill the air. Nothing else mattered."

But the jubilation proved to be premature. While agreeing to hear Jabotinsky, the Commission announced that it was not prepared to intervene in the matter of the visa; and a letter from the Immigration Department over the signature of its Assistant Director, Edwin Samuel (a Jew, son of the first High Commissioner, Sir Herbert Samuel), stated that since Jabotinsky had been refused entry into Palestine under Par. 3 (1) of the Immigration Regulations, no visa could be issued to him.

This refusal provoked indignation both in Jewish and Gentile circles. Colonel Wedgwood, Lord Strabolgi and Colonel Patterson energetically intervened with the London Government. In a letter to Patterson, the Secretary for the Colonies said that he was sorry, and that the Commission would hear Jabotinsky in London.[26]

The hearing took place on February 11, 1937, in a small room (one hundred and twenty seats) of the House of Lords. The next day, the London press reported that "hundreds of Jews queued up outside the House of Lords" (*Daily Herald*), and "long before the sitting opened a queue of people waited in the Committee corridor, but there were more people turned away than could be admitted . . . the room was crowded with people" (*The Times*). Most of those present were Jews, among them Mrs. Vera Weizmann and the late Nachum Sokolov's daughter, Celina. But several distinguished non-Jewish personalities also attended: the new Secretary of State for the Colonies, William Ormsby-Gore; Lady Blanche Dugdale [Lord Balfour's niece], Colonel Patterson, as well as the well-known pro-Arab and anti-Zionist politician and writer, Miss Newton.[27]

Jabotinsky was well pleased with his testimony before the Royal Commission: "It was the best speech I ever made," he told S. Salzman.[28] In this he hardly exaggerated. Even now, over two decades later, the stenographic minutes of the evidence make fascinating reading as a closely reasoned, perfectly ordered and impressively delivered presentation of the case for "Greater Zionism," as Jabotinsky used to define his Zionist creed. The introductory statement took about an hour and a half; cross-examination by the members of the Commission lasted for about forty minutes. The entire English press carried extensive reports on Jabotinsky's evidence.[29]

Some of the reports contained the assertion that "striking the table before him with his fist, Mr. Jabotinsky exclaimed: You [the British] have promised a pound of flesh, pay a pound of flesh." This attempt to picture Jabotinsky in the role of a political Shylock was completely unwarranted. According to the official minutes, Jabotinsky said:[30]

When I am asked, when any Jew is asked: "What, are the Jews going to pin us [the British] down to the promise [of the Balfour Declaration] and to say—you have promised the pound of flesh, pay us the pound of flesh," Gentlemen, here I answer you in the name of the most extreme of Zionist parties: "No!" If Great Britain really is unable to do it (not unwilling, but unable), we will bow to her decision, but we then shall expect Great Britain to act as any Mandatory who feels he cannot carry out the Mandate: give back the Mandate.

All this is obviously just the opposite of a Shylock claim, and the *Evening Standard* was perfectly correct in saying that "in his evidence he [Jabotinsky] quoted Shylock, but only to dissociate himself from the Jew of Venice."

Having stated that if England feels unable to implement the Mandate, she should give it back, Jabotinsky immediately added: "I hope that time will never come. I am fully convinced that it will not be necessary. I believe in England just as I believed in England twenty years ago." "But," he stressed, "if Great Britain really cannot live up to the Mandate . . . we will sit down together and think what can be done." Asked by Sir Laurie Hammond (one of the members of the Commission) to whom he thought the Mandate could be turned over, he answered: "I think I could nominate several others powers, whom I, as a European, would trust to carry out this Mandate as honestly as England would. Is there anybody here who doubts that there are other civilized peoples as conscientious? . . ."

While speaking "in the name of the most extreme of the Zionist parties" and forcefully presenting its views, Jabotinsky was deliberately restrained and calm in his manner of speaking. He appealed not to sentiment but to logic. Only once—when dealing with the 1929 pogrom—did he speak with some heat; and he immediately restrained himself: "I am sorry if I am getting excited, and I apologize to the Commission and hope they understand the reason for it; but I do not think I have overstepped the boundaries of logic in submitting to this Royal Commission my case." When Sir Horace Rumbold, another member of the Commission, tried to dismiss Jabotinsky's contention as an *"ex parte* statement," the retort was: "Would you call it an *ex parte* statement if a person comes here and pleads in the name

of need? . . . It is not *parte*. I simply represent distress. I speak in
the name of the distressed. You may dismiss me and say it is impossible, but do not call it *ex parte*." While painstakingly avoiding any
criticism of a personal nature, he could not help putting an accusing
finger at the High Commissioner of Palestine, who happened to arrive
in London on the same day. Without calling him by name, he insisted
that the question of who was responsible for the bloody events in
Palestine must be investigated:

> Because I claim somebody is guilty. . . . With this famous theory of
> the "man on the spot," I want the man on the spot to stand before a
> Royal Commission, before a Judicial Commission, and I want him to
> answer for his errors. Sometimes even a humble man like myself has the
> right to say the words "*J'accuse*." They are guilty. They are guilty of
> commission, omission, neglect of duty. . . . I believe it is guilt and I
> believe that the person guilty should be punished, and that is what I
> humbly demand.

The reaction of the official Zionist press to Jabotinsky's evidence
was anything but friendly.

The London *New Judea* halfheartedly admitted that "Mr. Jabotinsky in the greater part of his evidence gave an able exposition of the
Jewish case"; the paper claimed that he was "unable to add much
either in substance or in detail to the Jewish case as presented by
the Jewish Agency," but acknowledged that "the vigor of his form
added interest to his statement." The organ of the Zionist Executive
was more critical, referring to Jabotinsky's "irrelevant criticism of
the Jewish Agency: his attempt to weaken the authority of the
Jewish Agency was as futile as in bad taste." [31] The New York *New
Palestine* also blamed Jabotinsky for "his denunciation of the Jewish
Agency," which "will be condemned by all Zionist and Jewish circles
as being unpardonable disloyalty to Jewish interests." [32] *Jewish Frontier,* the organ of the *Poalei Zion* party in America, branded Jabotinsky's utterances as "dangerous and treasonable" and was outraged
that he was "clamoring for a Jewish State . . . bellowing about a
Jewish Legion." [33]

An unsigned editorial ("Comments of the Week") in Johannesburg's *The* 11*th Hour*, which is known to have been written by
Jabotinsky, insisted that: [34]

308

the reproach should be addressed not to the New [Zionist Organization], but to the Old [Zionist Organization] crew: it was they, the Executive of the Jewish Agency, who made the first step in parading the Jewish split before the Royal Commission. As early as November 20, 1936, Dr. Weizmann, on behalf of the Agency, submitted to that Commission a bulky printed memorandum containing, *inter alia*, the following passage, on page 100: His (Mr. Jabotinsky's) views were unacceptable to the more moderate body of opinion which predominated in the Zionist movement. At the Eighteenth Congress (Prague, 1933) his group occupied only 45 seats out of 318. This was the last Congress which he and his followers attended. In 1935 the Revisionists seceded and formed an independent organization of their own. Its membership is not precisely known, but is estimated at approximately one hundred fifty thousand. The number of registered adherents (Shekel-payers) represented at the last Zionist Congress (Lucerne, 1935) was 1,216,030. These facts are mentioned in order that there may be no misapprehensions as to the status of the Revisionists.

This attack by the Jewish Agency against another Jewish body was thus launched nearly three months before Jabotinsky, in his evidence (February 11, 1937), stated that "the Jewish Agency represented 'neither the whole nor even the majority of Zionist Jewry.' Moreover, the Jewish Agency's attack on Revisionism was entirely spontaneous . . . whereas Jabotinsky never mentioned the split until directly asked about it by the chairman of the Royal Commission."

The Royal Commission minutes fully bear out this reference to Jabotinsky's reluctance to display before the Commission internal Zionist differences. He completely omitted them in his evidence and curtly answered "yes" to the initial question of Lord Peel as to whether the New Zionist Organization he represented "differs in certain material aspects in its views from the general Zionist Organization." Later, when asked whether his organization and "the more Orthodox Zionists agree on a great many points," he cautiously replied that "it is for them to decide." Lord Peel, the chairman of the Commission, insisted: "Your attitude is so judicial I am almost afraid of putting the question to you. I was going to ask what is the main line of policy in which you differ from what I may call the Orthodox Zionists." Jabotinsky again tried to avoid the argument: "Will you allow me just as a matter of personal favor to forego this question because it would lead me into criticism of another Jewish body which is really something I should like to avoid." Without going

309

into an ideological discussion, he merely mentioned two basic aspects of divergence: "We [N.Z.O.] insist that the Jewish Agency, the Jewish representation, should be based upon the universal suffrage principle, while the Zionist Organization bases it on a fee called the Shekel, a paid franchise." The second aspect was: "I think the same reproach applies to them [the Zionist Organization] as I tried to apply to the Colonial Office: no 'blue print.' They have no plan, they never had any plan of what they meant by colonizing Palestine or carrying out the Zionist program. . . . The first attempt at drawing up such a plan was the Revisionist program." Answering Lord Peel's question: "You mean you are more definite in your scheme of planning?"— he said: "Not that we are more definite; we are definite, they are not." The last reference to the Jewish Agency was the refutation of the latter's statement (by Moshe Shertok) that "the distribution of certificates between adherents and non-adherents of the Zionist Movement was done without any discrimination." "There is discrimination," Jabotinsky reported, "against at least one section—the *Brit Trumpeldor*—and that discrimination has been ordered in black upon white by the Jewish Agency for the only reason that the *Brit Trumpeldor* had left the Zionist Organization."

Three days after Jabotinsky's evidence before the Royal Commission, an impressive "Jewish Legion Dinner" took place in the Hotel Commodore to commemorate the twentieth anniversary of the founding of the Jewish Battalions in the British Army.[35] The invitations to the dinner were signed by Leopold S. Amery (former Secretary of State for the Colonies), Herbert Sidebotham (one of the editors of *The Times*, known under his pen-name "Scrutator"), Lieutenant-Colonel Fitzgerald Scott (Commander of the Fortieth Battalion), and others. At the main table with the initiators sat Field Marshal Sir Philip Chestwood, Colonel John Henry Patterson, Colonel Josiah Wedgwood, Lady Dugdale, and representatives of the diplomatic corps (France, Poland, Czechoslovakia, Rumania, Latvia, Estonia). Not a single leader of the Zionist Organization could be seen among the two hundred guests. Dr. Chaim Weizmann sent a letter stating that he was "compelled to leave for Paris" just that day. His colleagues of the Great Russell Street (the seat of the Zionist Executive) were conspicuous by their absence.

Sidebotham paid a glowing tribute to Jabotinsky, whom he had known for some twenty years and "found him the most delightful

310

of companions, the most faithful of friends, the gentlest of men, and one of the best friends of the British Empire that he had ever known." Patterson eulogized Jabotinsky's courage and determination. Amery, Wedgwood, Chestwood, and Scott strongly advocated the urgency of restoring the Jewish Legion. Sidebotham expressed in his address the hope that the two camps of the Zionist movement, the Zionist Organization and the New Zionist Organization, would unite : "Jews must close their ranks."

Replying to the toast, "The Jewish Legion," Jabotinsky referred to Sidebotham's appeal for unity : that appeal, he said, had deeply stirred him and he was sure it moved the hearts of every Jew present. "On my part, Mr. Sidebotham, you may tell your friends that we are ready for that old English way of establishing peace—Round Table Conference. The offer still stands." He drew his speech to a close by rising and proclaiming the final toast of the evening : "I believe in Freedom and the ultimate triumph of freedom. I believe in England, and the brotherhood between England and Israel."

SEVENTEEN

THE ANTI-PARTITION CRUSADE

1. *Two More Safaris*

Two WEEKS after his evidence before the Royal Commission, Jabotinsky left on the *Dunraven Castle* for South Africa, landing in Capetown on March 15.

This second South African "safari" was long and carefully planned. Because of lack of organization, his 1930 visit to that country was only a partial success. He left behind a largely "unfinished business," which looked, however, very promising. In order properly to capitalize on this second visit, Jabotinsky persuaded a young and dynamic Revisionist couple, Nahum and Herzlia Levin, to precede him and to remain in South Africa for at least one year after his departure. And this time he came not alone, but together with S. Jacobi, whose cooperation he valued highly.

Rabbi M. C. Weiler, Chief Minister of the United Jewish Reform Congregation of Johannesburg and a non-Revisionist, recalls that when Jabotinsky "visited this country in 1937, he was bitterly attacked and denied platforms by the official Zionist Organization and its spokesmen." [1] * Although "a consistent adherent of the *Histadrut*," Dr. Weiler felt impelled to protest against this intolerance. He wrote in the non-Revisionist *South African Jewish Times*: "The hostile attitude adopted by some official Jewish bodies will fail to receive the sympathy of any liberal and right-thinking man. Surely one should listen to Mr. Jabotinsky and show him all the courtesy possible and not attempt to intimidate a gullible public into not attending his meetings." [2]

* The Propaganda and Organization Department of the South African Zionist Federation issued a special pamphlet *The Truth About Jabotinsky and the Revisionists,* which accused him of every possible crime against Zionism.

In fact, South African Jews appeared to be not at all "intimidated" by official Zionist pressure and proved it by mass attendance at his lectures. Nahum Levin, who was responsible for the organization of Jabotinsky's tour, recalls that there was a lively discussion among leading Revisionists about admission to Jabotinsky's first address in Johannesburg. Many believed that it had to be gratuitous, others, though advocating payment, insisted on low prices, not exceeding the cost of movie tickets: from one to three shillings. Levin decided differently and announced prices up to one pound (five dollars). When Revisionist leaders, who went to Capetown to meet Jabotinsky, learned of this, they wired him: "Immediately reduce prices, otherwise lecture hall will be empty." Levin wired back: "Can't reduce, all seats sold out."[3] During the three and a half months of his sojourn in South Africa, Jabotinsky always spoke to packed halls, and was greeted with respect by Jews and Gentiles alike. In the capital, Pretoria, the N.Z.O. delegation (Jabotinsky, Jacobi, Levin) was officially received by the Mayor and members of the City Council. Welcoming them, the Mayor, H. W. Dely, said that the name of Jabotinsky was "a household word among the Jews, especially among the younger generation."[4] At a crowded meeting, Ivan Solomon, chairman of the Keren ha'Yessod Council, who presided, explained his reasons for assuming the chairmanship of the meeting:[5]

... I think that any man with a record such as Mr. Jabotinsky has, is entitled to the opportunity of stating his case and should be given a fair hearing. ... Mr. Jabotinsky has proved himself too great and true a Jew for anyone to doubt his motives. I, in common with millions of others, believe him to be utterly sincere in his zeal for Zionism. ... The ultimate decision of what is the correct policy still remains an individual one for each of us. ...

Jabotinsky was, however, uncompromisingly opposed to converting the delegation's appearances into an exclusive personal performance by him. When he saw, in Capetown, the advertisement of his first meeting, in which only his name was mentioned, he wired to Levin: "Protest omission of Jacobi's name." Advertisement of the second meeting already carried both names; but this, too, was not satisfactory to him; he insisted that his and Jacobi's names be set in the same size of type.[6] He was no less loyal to the young organizer of his tour, Nahum Levin, and unquestionably fell in with all his arrangements.

313

The only disagreement arose when he refused to fly to the town of East London to deliver a lecture, arguing that the journey was too long and exacting and that lamentably few people would come to listen to him anyway. When Levin tried to explain that all preparations had already been made, Jabotinsky exploded: "Who is supposed to speak in East London?" "You." "I will not speak, and that's final!" Levin heatedly retorted: "Who is the manager of your tour?" "You." "And I resign." They parted sullenly. But next morning Jabotinsky dutifully appeared at the airport and boarded the plane for East London together with Levin. On the way, engine trouble developed, and word got around that the plane might have to turn back. There was considerable excitement among the passengers, but Jabotinsky remained completely cool and went on writing the chapter of his *Autobiography* that he was working on. The meeting in East London proved to be very successful. More than four hundred people, Jews and non-Jews, filled the hall, among them many from distant small Jewish communities, three hundred to four hundred miles away. The financial results were also good. On the return journey, Jabotinsky meekly admitted: "You were right. You certainly are a better manager than I am." [7]

There were three main themes in Jabotinsky's South African lecture campaign. He forcefully put before his audiences the urgency of immediate evacuation of Jews inhabiting the belt of *Judennot* in the Eastern part of Europe, where they were regarded as "unwanted refuse" by the nations among whom they lived. They were desperately in need of outlets for mass emigration; but there were none. To dramatize this situation, Jabotinsky called it a "frozen stampede": "Imagine that a fire breaks out in a crowded movie house; people begin a frantic stampede to get out, but all doors and windows are hermetically closed."

The second main topic was the then already ripening plan for partitioning Palestine. Marshalling a wide range of political, economic, and demographic arguments, Jabotinsky devastatingly denounced Dr. Weizmann's willingness to sacrifice nine-tenths of Jewish national territory. He expressed the hope that "the dark clouds [of partition] on the Zionist horizon will disperse," but warned that "if the path of true Zionism is not followed—and especially if a new Uganda arises—then we shall fight, and that fight will be felt in South Africa as well." This course would inevitably affect the

314

unity of the Zionist movement, and unity, of course, was "a good thing." "But God's name is not unity. God's name is truth." [8]

It was in order to establish "unity based on truth" that Jabotinsky stressed the third major element of his campaign: the demand for a Round Table Conference. This demand enjoyed considerable sympathy even in the ranks of South Africa's official Zionist Organization. Aware of this sympathy, and in an attempt to counteract it, Professor Selig Brodetsky of the London Zionist Executive wrote to Nicolai Kirshner, President of the South African Zionist Federation, and tried to convey the impression that there had already been, between himself and Jabotinsky, some kind of preliminary negotiation about the Round Table Conference, but these had broken down because of the latter's excessive demands.[9] In an editorial published in *The 11th Hour* (No. 3), Jabotinsky branded this attempt as "a regrettable trick, as there had never been any such talks with Brodetsky; and an absurd trick, too, for the essence of a 'Round Table Conference' is not to formulate any demands but is to sit around that table with minds absolutely open." The editorial stressed further that "there is in that unfortunate letter a remark that deserves to be noted. Referring to the visit of the N.Z.O. delegation to South Africa, Mr. Brodetsky expresses the hope that nothing will be done by the South African Federation which might create the impression that this pro-Round-Table campaign enjoys their support, *or even their toleration.*"

We have seen that, at least at the beginning, the Federation's leaders tried to abide by this instruction "not to tolerate." They were, however, unable to ignore the popular appeal of the Round Table idea, and on April 5, under the chairmanship of Kirshner, a joint meeting of the Federation leadership with the N.Z.O. delegation (Jabotinsky-Jacobi-Levin) took place, at which the issue was discussed frankly and thoroughly. Jabotinsky's attitude was succinctly expressed in his answer to Kirshner's question as to what his conditions were for participating in a Round Table Conference: "There are no conditions. We are prepared to put everything in the melting pot." The further developments, to which this meeting led, belong to a different chapter (see Chapter Nineteen).

During his 1937 "safari" to South Africa, which also included short visits to Rhodesia and Kenya, Jabotinsky spoke to a wide variety of audiences. Some of them deserve special mention.

The non-denominational Rotary Club invited him to address a

luncheon-meeting attended by five hundred to six hundred Rotarians. Nahum Levin, who accompanied Jabotinsky, recalls: "After consulting the rich menu, I decided on roast duck. But it was Jabotinsky whom the waiter approached first and his short order was 'A piece of Matzah': this being *Hol-ha-Moed Pessach,* I could not order differently." Within the allotted twenty minutes, Jabotinsky gave a forceful presentation of the Jewish people's case for a country of its own. When he had finished, the usually cool and restrained Anglo-Saxon audience spontaneously jumped to their feet, applauding and cheering. After the prescribed vote of thanks for the speaker by one of the members, the chairman rose to say that, though it was contrary to the Rotarian tradition to pass judgment on the contents of an address delivered before them, in this case both the speech and the personality of the speaker leave him no other choice than to wish the speaker the fullest possible success in his struggle for Jewish statehood.

Another audience which deserves to be singled out was the Jewish Reform Congregation of Johannesburg. True to his conviction that "one should listen to Jabotinsky," this congregation's young Rabbi, Dr. M. C. Weiler, invited him to address a Friday evening service. "There was, of course," Rabbi Weiler later recalled, "passionate opposition to his appearance in our synagogue." Among those opposed were some strong adherents of the old Zionist Organization, while other members feared that Jabotinsky's appearance would do harm to their synagogue, which had only been in existence for four years and was still an insecure institution in the Jewish community. Disregarding this opposition, Rabbi Weiler announced in the Jewish and non-Jewish press that on June 18 at eight-fifteen p.m. Jabotinsky would deliver an address at Temple Israel on "The Crisis of the Proletariat." The large Temple was overcrowded, and hundreds of people had to be turned away. "But, unfortunately, there was no Jabotinsky. Advice had come from Skukuza, in the Game Reserve, that he was unable to keep his [speaking] appointment because of car trouble." This announcement provoked considerable comment. It was known that several leading Revisionists had advised against the acceptance of Rabbi Weiler's invitation. They argued that the Reform Synagogue was still very unpopular in the community, and that Jabotinsky's appearance there would unnecessarily complicate his already difficult task of preaching an unpopular idea. It was only natural that it should immediately be rumored that this [car trouble] was just a diplomatic excuse—that on account of pressure from his own ranks he had decided not to come. Rabbi Weiler's announcement that Jabotinsky would deliver his address the following Friday evening was received with scepticism.

But Jabotinsky did deliver the address on June 25, and it was a magnificent one, Rabbi Weiler later recalled.[10] What he did not know at that time, was that Jabotinsky's determination to appear before a Reform Congregation was dictated by a much deeper consideration than merely an understandable desire to keep a promise. Aware of Revisionist opposition to it, he wrote on June 15 a long letter to Nahum Levin on the subject, asking him "to circulate these remarks among our friends." He emphatically refused to exclude the Reform movement in Judaism from the national and Zionist camp:

There was a time when the Reform was anti-Zionist. Had it so remained, I should refuse any contact with its adherents. But this changed long ago. In America, the main country of the Reform movement, many Reform Rabbis are staunch Zionists and their temples are fortresses of Zionism; some support the N.Z.O. movement, as for instance Rabbi Louis Newman of New York. . . .

I absolutely refuse to treat it [Rabbi Weiler's congregation] as something to be shunned. The question has nothing to do with my own views on orthodoxy or reform; *this* I would only consider if I were invited to participate in any religious function. But to refuse the hospitality of a Jewish roof for giving a lecture—simply because it belongs to a community striving to revise the ritual—this would mean that boycott of non-conformists, which I consider unhealthy and reactionary. Whether I agree or not that such a revision is necessary or opportune is perfectly immaterial in this connection: as long as that revision is not tainted by assimilationist tendencies, I will never agree to treat it as something sinful or criminal or "untouchable." . . .

I very emphatically urge our friends to take a more serious view of such principles as freedom of conscience and freedom of thought. I, for one, am not prepared to support the mania of banning spiritual quest, so long as it does not imply blasphemy against the basic principles of liberty, equality and nationality.

During his stay in South Africa, Jabotinsky (together with S. Jacobi) was received by the Prime Minister, General Herzog. Among the guests at a luncheon in his honor were the Minister of Native

Affairs, P. G. W. Grobler, General J. C. Kemp, Minister of Lands; Dr. Bodenstein, Permanent Secretary for External Affairs; Mr. Hoogenhout, Secretary for the Interior, as well as seven Members of Parliament and the Commissioner of the South African Union for Palestine. Under-Secretary of State for External Affairs, Grobler, greeted Jabotinsky, who answered by an informal speech.

The highly successful South African tour was interrupted by urgent developments on the Zionist political front. Persistent reports that the Royal Commission was veering toward a "geographical" solution —partition or cantonization—had begun to appear in the British press by April, 1937, long before the Commission's report was published. In May, Eliahu Ben Horin, member of the N.Z.O. Presidency, flew in from London to join Jabotinsky on his campaign tour, and brought the definite news that the Royal Commission was about to propose partition. It was "in a very gloomy tone" that he conveyed this news; but after having asked for more detail and meditated for a few minutes, Jabotinsky turned to him and said smilingly : "Cheer up, the whole thing will never materialize, even if the Commission suggests it, and even if the [British] Parliament approves it." He then went on to explain that the partition proposal simply did not stand to reason; it would solve none of the many problems involved in the Palestine issue. He was therefore confident that it could be combatted successfully.[11]

It was high time to return to Europe for a supreme effort to head off the "partition craze," as he called it. But he felt very strongly that this time, even more than in 1930, he was leaving a highly promising "unfinished business" in South Africa, and in March, 1938, when the pressure of political events seemed to have eased somewhat, he yielded to the insistent requests of the South African leadership to come again for at least a short visit. Pressed for time, he made the trip not by boat as before, but by plane.

This visit was apparently not welcome to certain elements in South Africa. On March 9, 1938, F. G. Erasmus, the Nationalist Member of the Union Parliament, asked the Minister of the Interior whether "in the interests of the population of the Union the Government would take the necessary steps to prevent Mr. Jabotinsky from entering the Union." The Minister's reply was that the Government did not consider that Jabotinsky's visit, which would not exceed one month and was for the purpose of furthering the interests of the New Zionist

Organization, would be harmful to the welfare of the Union, and in the circumstances it was not proposed to prevent his temporary entry.[12]

Jabotinsky arrived, as scheduled, on March 22. The flight from London to Johannesburg proved to be an event in itself. Jabotinsky's plane was supposed to stop in Lorenzo Marques and then in Durban, from where he was to take a plane to Johannesburg. At the last moment, South African friends found out that there was no immediate connection from Durban to Johannesburg and that he would have to spend a night in Durban waiting for a plane. They therefore sent a message to Lorenzo Marques informing him that from there he could immediately board a direct plane for Johannesburg. Hundreds of people, among them one hundred uniformed *Betarim,* assembled at the Johannesburg airport to meet the plane from Lorenzo Marques. The plane arrived, but there was no Jabotinsky. From other passengers they learned that he apparently had not received the message and had continued to Durban. This was a minor calamity for the organizers of the tour. It meant that he would arrive with a delay of twenty-four hours, and miss the scheduled press conference and a series of important appointments. They decided to charter a special plane, which would fly to Durban, pick Jabotinsky up and bring him to Johannesburg the same night.[13] The entire press was full of reports about this adventurous night flight, which, as *The Star* put it, "made air history in South Africa"; it was the first occasion on which a machine left for the Natal coast after dark and returned the same night over the Drakensberg within a few hours.[14]

This third visit to South Africa was shorter than the two previous ones: from March 22 until May 13. At a meeting with the press, Jabotinsky said he had come "to explain our [New Zionist] demands to the Jews and non-Jews of the Union." The three main demands that he formulated were:[15]

1. That an international conference of friendly Governments be convened to study and solve the problem of Jewish migration. 2. That this conference consider the "Ten-Year Plan" of the New Zionist Organization—a scheme to settle 1,500,000 Jews in Palestine within the next ten years. 3. That a world Jewish National Assembly, elected by universal Jewish suffrage, be convened.

Explaining the urgency of these demands, Jabotinsky stressed that:

the situation for Jews in practically three-quarters of Europe is tragic in the extreme, and the prospects for the future are even more hopeless than they are today. All kinds of international problems face Europe today, but whatever happens anywhere, the greatest sufferers will be the Jews—no matter who is right or wrong. Any act of violence or catastrophe will be paid for mainly by Jewish suffering, hunger, and humiliation. The problem directly affects six or seven million Jews, most of whom are either homeless or virtually in that condition. Their main preoccupation is where to go, and no country is actually open to them except Palestine.

The fifty-two days Jabotinsky spent on this third—and last—South African safari were crowded with countless meetings, conferences, and appointments. He was dead tired on the eve of his departure; but he was satisfied with the fruits of his labor.* "This time, the success is even greater than last year. It is clear that the resistance of the old [Zionist] guard has become considerably more porous. I believe that in a year's time all controlling positions in this country will be ours. . . . To achieve these results, I would have to stay here until fall, which is impossible. However, my absence will affect only the tempo. South Africa is our main field." [16] "Being a stubborn fellow," he wrote to S. Jacobi, "I still regret that you brought me here last year; but as this has already been done, there is no denying that the Columbusses discovered America on their way to India." [17]

The seventeen days aboard the *R. M. S. Edinburgh Castle* were a most welcome rest. These he spent "for a change, in almost unbroken silence; did quite a lot of work and read a few books less trashy than my usual diet." [18]

2. *Nisht Geshtoigen Nisht Gefloigen*

July 7, 1937, the day scheduled for the publication of the Recommendations of the Royal Commission, found Jabotinsky in Alexandria (Egypt), where he had stopped for two days on his way from South

---

* *The Story of South African Zionism*, written and published on behalf of the official Zionist Federation of South Africa, reluctantly admits that "when Jabotinsky paid his third visit to S. A. in April, 1938, he received a larger measure of support than at any other time. . . . Certain Jews in S. A. . . . saw no ground for hoping that Palestine under present conditions could ever provide a solution to the Jewish problem, and they were only too ready to lend ear to the assertions of the Revisionists that the unfortunate position in Palestine was largely a result of the Jewish Agency's policy." (Marcia Gitlin. *The Vision Amazing: The Story of South African Zionism*. Johannesburg, 1950, p. 342.)

Africa to London. A mass meeting in the Alhambra Theater, the largest hall in Alexandria, was scheduled for the same evening. A local Revisionist newspaperman, Albert Starasselsky, used his journalistic connections for obtaining from the Reuter Press Agency an advanced copy of the document, and deliverd it to Jabotinsky one hour before the beginning of the meeting. Jabotinsky read it carefully and asked for a pencil, a sheet of paper, and a map of Palestine; he then traced the contours of the "Jewish State" as proposed by the Commission; it looked like a clumsy point of exclamation. Turning to Starasselsky, he said: "You see this nightmarish and ridiculous configuration? Is it a symbol of irony or of despair? And I am telling you—*nisht geshtoigen nisht gefloigen* (an untranslatable Yiddish expression, meaning approximately: it has no head or tail).* [19] Speaking immediately afterward at a meeting attended by six thousand people, Jabotinsky followed the same line: he was relieved, he said, when he learned the details of the Commission's plan; it was so absurd that there was no danger of the Zionist Congress falling into the trap of accepting this kind of solution. The scheme was not workable and would never be applied: it could only be characterized by an Italian word *chiuchiuchiachia,* meaning roughly "drivel." On the other hand, he welcomed the only constructive innovation of the plan: the clearly worded endorsement of the Jewish State idea. That, Jabotinsky said, would be the only thing that would remain of the whole Report. [20]

When the Jews of Palestine learned that, for the first time since December, 1929, Jabotinsky was "within speaking distance" of their and his country, and, appropriately enough, at a historic moment, enabling him to reply to the Royal Commission proposals almost on the spot and immediately after they were made, excitement ran high. The correspondent of the Johannesburg Revisionist weekly *The 11th Hour* wrote: "Jerusalem was full of excitement that Wednesday night, and the cramped offices of the Jewish Telegraphic Agency in Jerusalem were filled with people who had heard that Jabotinsky would say his word . . . ." Barred from entering the country, he made his powerful anti-partition statement by telephone from Alexandria to

* Jabotinsky was inexhaustible in inventing derisive comparisons in connection with the partition scheme. Once he said to this writer: "You know, it is like the Latin verb *aio,* which is a grammatical monster meaning 'I say:' it is present, it is imperfect, and it has no future." Another time, he compared the scheme with the wahoo bird which, according to popular folklore, flies in ever-decreasing circles until it swallows itself in utter confusion.

321

the Jewish Telegraphic Agency in Jerusalem, and a crowd of willing helpers assisted the journalist "to get Jabotinsky's statement down correctly, with every comma in place." [21]

To a delegation representing the Palestinian *Betar,* New Zionist Organization, and the *Irgun Zvai Leumi,* Jabotinsky firmly stated that he was dead sure that the partition scheme would never be implemented. Dr. Shimshon Yunitchman, one of the *Betar* delegates, informed him of the determination of the entire *Betar,* and above all of the *Betar* work-groups in Upper Galilee, to rise in open revolt if the British tried to impose partition—even if this uprising was doomed in advance to have the same fate as Massada.* To this Jabotinsky said : "If you ask me to give the order to revolt, I shall do so, but only if I'm together with you in it. For that you will have to land me at Machnaim [small airport in Upper Galilee, in the vicinity of the colony Rosh Pinah, which was then the center of the *Betar* work-groups], so that we can fight together, go together to prison, and, if need be, die together. But I don't think that the British will ever try to implement this fantastic scheme." [22]

The British Government officially endorsed the Royal Commission's plan the very day of its publication [23] and tried to rush it through the British Parliament and the League of Nations' Permanent Mandates Commission within a few weeks. Jabotinsky hurried to London. On July 13, he addressed a group of M.P.'s in the House of Parliament, with Sir John Haslam, Conservative M.P., in the Chair.[24] On July 23, he spoke at a well-attended meeting of the Palestine Parliamentary Committee in the House of Commons. His arguments against partition, as proposed by the Commission, were not of a romantic-sentimentalist or legalistic nature. There was no reference to national feelings hurt by the proposed violation of the internationally recognized historic connection of the Jewish people with the whole of Palestine. Nor did he refer to British promises and obligations under the Balfour Declaration and the Mandate. He dismissed the partition scheme primarily on the grounds of its utter impracticability.**

---

* Massada was the fortress where, nineteen hundred years ago, the Zealots and Eliezer Ben Yair held out to the end against the Romans, preferring death to surrender.

** In Eliahu Golomb's record of his conversations with Jabotinsky in July, 1938, there is an episode, the accuracy of which is difficult to ascertain. When Jabotinsky indignantly spoke of Dr. Weizmann's fervent advocacy of a Jewish State in partitioned Palestine, and branded it as a "renunciation of Eretz Israel," Golomb said: "A fortnight ago you yourself told me that you were prepared to revise your attitude on this subject if you

When the partition scheme came up for debate in the House of Lords (July 20 and 21) [25] and in the House of Commons (July 21), [26] it was subjected to devastating criticism. In the House of Commons, the Labor Party demanded a Joint Select Committee to study the partition plan. Even Churchill announced that he could not support his Conservative Government in this matter. The Government was forced to accept Churchill's compromise motion authorizing it to seek League of Nations approval as a necessary preliminary to the drafting of a definite plan for submission to the House of Commons. A resolution on these lines was adopted. It "left Parliament entirely unpledged to even the principle of a divided Palestine," commented Professor Paul L. Hanna. [27] "Without undue pride," Jabotinsky asserted: "I can say that the defeat of the partition scheme in the House of Commons was to a considerable extent assisted by our own work. This is not my opinion only." [28]

It was not a boastful exaggeration. Churchill's powerful intervention was indubitably largely based on the arguments and factual material of Jabotinsky's anti-partition memorandum. They also met for an hour-long conversation in the House of Commons, two hours before the meeting with the Parliamentarians. When Jabotinsky returned to the N.Z.O. office, late that evening, he did not expect much from the M.P.'s, but said that Churchill "might help if he wished, and gives the impression of wanting to." Churchill did indeed help. An analysis of essential extracts from Jabotinsky's memorandum in juxtaposition to selected quotations from Churchill's speech in the House of Commons, as well as from Churchill's article " Palestine Partition," reveals the scope of Jabotinsky's influence on Churchill's thinking in the Partition matter.* Churchill also endorsed Jabotinsky's proposal of delaying action on the British Government's scheme, and a motion to this effect carried the day.

could only believe in it [in the emergence of the partitioned Jewish State]." To this, according to Golomb's report, Jabotinsky replied: "I still maintain that if partition becomes a fact, I shall have to adjust myself to it. But to make it [partition] a matter of [Zionist] propaganda is something entirely different." Later he ironically charged that for "Weizmann and Co." the Zionist Basle Program now reads as follows: *Der Zionismus erstrebt die Teilung Palestinas, unter Hingabe von 95% des Landes, einschliesslich seines Bibel-historischen Teiles, an die Araber.*" (Letter to Nahum Levin, June 26, 1939.)

* This analysis was supplied by Dr. Oskar K. Rabinowicz from the manuscript of the forthcoming second volume of his study *Winston Churchill on Jewish Problems.*

3. *The Arab Angle*

One of the features of the Commission's partition plan to which Jabotinsky was particularly averse, was the proposed evacuation of the Arab population from the area of the prospective Jewish State. He called this "evacuation prattle . . . worse than preposterous : it is, from the Jewish viewpoint, down right criminal. . . . What an instructive precedent indeed for Jew-baiters all over the world," he exclaimed. "Until now, in our Zionist and Revisionist propaganda, we always held steadfastly and religiously to the principle that nobody shall be driven out ! . . . We are striving to attain a majority, not to show the minority the door." [29]

This had always been Jabotinsky's basic approach to the Arab problem in Palestine. He was no Arabophile in the usual sense of this term. He was, first of all, no admirer of the picturesque Orient, to which a certain school of Zionist thought was longing to return. "We Jews are Europeans," he wrote in 1925, to Senator O. O. Grusenberg, "and we are not only pupils, but also co-creators of the European culture. What do we have in common with the 'Orient ?' And everything that is 'oriental' there [in the Near and Middle East area] is doomed : look how Kemal Pasha is imitating Peter [the Great, of Russia] by shearing beards on a drum. Until the Arabs [of Palestine] are shorn—in every respect—they will be no company for us." He was therefore "not in favor of an Arab-Jewish State." [30] He also did not believe that Arabs would ever consent to any Zionist proposal of a *modus vivendi*, nor felt that their opposition could be overcome by such elaborate and artificial face-saving formulas as "bi-national State." His own recipe was realistic and stern : the establishment of a Jewish majority in Palestine will have to be achieved *against the wish* of the country's present Arab majority; an "iron wall" of a Jewish armed force would have to protect the process of achieving a majority; after that goal was reached, the Arabs would have no choice but to adapt themselves to the new state of affairs; then, and only then, a *modus vivendi* would be worked out, always on the basis of the premise that two peoples, Jews and Arabs, were going to live and work in that country.[31] However, Jabotinsky's firm opposition to any scheme calling for a compulsory transfer of Arabs from Palestine by no means precluded a sympathetic understanding for the prospect of their voluntary and organized migration to one of the Arab countries. The late

Edward A. Norman, an outstanding American Jewish philanthropist who, in 1937, conceived the idea of the transfer of Palestine Arabs to Iraq and started negotiations to this effect with the Iraqi Government, recorded in his unpublished diary (an excerpt from which he put at this writer's disposal) a conversation he had with Jabotinsky in London on December 2, 1937:

> He [Jabotinsky] had already read the copy of my Iraq paper. . . . He approved of the whole idea very much. He said that he felt, however, that the most difficult part would be to induce Arabs to leave Palestine. . . . Jabotinsky made the original suggestion that if the plan ever progressed to the point where Iraq was prepared to cooperate and proclaim an invitation to the Palestine Arabs to migrate to Iraq, it would be wise to have the Zionist Organization openly oppose Arab emigration from Palestine, and then the Arabs would be sure the scheme was not Jewish and that the Jews wanted them to stay in Palestine only to exploit them, and they would want very much to go away to Iraq. This sounds very Macchiavellian, but it may be very sound politics in dealing with such an ignorant and suspicious people as the Arabs.

Norman's Iraq scheme never went beyond the blueprint stage and it is impossible to judge to what extent Jabotinsky's "Macchiavellian" calculations would have proved to be "sound politics." But the evolution of the minority problem in pre-World-War-II Europe had, no doubt, considerably influenced his judgment in regard to the very idea of transferring minorities in cases when any other solution seemed to be impracticable.

On June 23, 1939, an agreement was signed between the Third Reich and Mussolini's Italy, providing for the voluntary transfer to the Reich of the 266,000 Germans from the Italian Southern Tirol. Of this number, 185,000 opted for the transfer.[32] Jabotinsky was strongly impressed by this move. It reminded him of a talk he had "one summer day, about 1916, at Preston, near London," with the noted Anglo-Jewish writer and thinker, Israel Zangwill. Zangwill, who was one of the earliest advocates of population transfers as a means of solving minority problems, saw in the evacuation of Arabs from Palestine the basic prerequisite for the implementation of Zionism.[33] In an article "A Talk With Zangwill," published late in July, 1939, Jabotinsky restated his objections to Zangwill's reasoning which, he admitted, might be logical, but was too far removed from his own conceptions. But the German-Italian transfer agreement seems to have made "one thing clear" to him : that "a precedent has been created here which the world will note and not forget,* and this precedent may perhaps be fated to play an important role in our Jewish history as well."[34] In his last book *The War and the Jew*, he fully endorsed the idea of a voluntary Arab transfer from Palestine, though still insisting that it was not mandatory since, objectively, "Palestine, astride the Jordan, has room for the million of Arabs, room for another million of their eventual progeny, for several million Jews, and for peace." [35]

4. On the Geneva Front

In the late summer of 1937, the center of gravity shifted from London to Geneva, where the Mandates Commission of the League of Nations had been called for an extraordinary session. For this stage of the anti-partition battle Jabotinsky mobilized a group of younger collaborators who had for some time been his political representatives in the Western and South-Eastern capitals, and had established valuable contacts there. Informing Haskel that he had been received by King Carol of Rumania during the latter's visit in London, he wrote on July 29 : "Keep this confidential, but he [the King] is ready to fight any scheme which threatens to curtail the area of the possibilities of Jewish expansion in Palestine. Only when talking to him did I realize what an enormous amount of educational work had been accomplished during the last six months by [Dr. B.] Akzin here [in London], by [Dr. Wolfgang von] Weisl in Rumania, by [Dr. J. B.] Schechtman in Poland.** I actually saw traces of our memoranda being circulated from Embassy to Embassy, Ministry to Ministry, Court to Court; actually heard quotations and figures and ideas

---

* In fact, the five years of World War II saw the transfer of nine hundred thousand persons belonging to fifty-five ethnic minority groups. In the first seven years of the postwar period (1944-1951) nearly twenty million persons were transferred. (Joseph B. Schechtman, "Postwar Population Transfers in Europe: A Survey." *The Review of Politics*, April, 1953, pp. 151-52.)

** Jabotinsky was very lavish in his praise for his younger collaborators. In an address delivered in Capetown in April, 1938, he, according to a *Jewish Herald* report, "paid a tribute to the able young diplomats of the New Zionist Organization, headed by Dr. Akzin and Dr. Schechtman, who have received full scope for their abilities after the break with the Old Zionist Organization. Successful contacts had been established with foreign Governments." (*The Jewish Herald*, April 14, 1938.)

repeated with full acknowledgment of N.Z.O. as their source." A week later he reported from Annemasse on the Swiss frontier : "Akzin, Schechtman, and Harry Levi have been in Geneva since July 30. . . . Our men have seen *all* the Members [of the Mandates Commission]." And again, two days later, he reported from Geneva : "Members of the Mandates Commission seem to be very safe as anti-partitionists —so far. Yesterday, for example, Schechtman and Akzin saw the Japanese [M] Sakenobe, who was most outspokenly against." [36]

The entire "legwork"—the direct contacts with members of the Mandates Commission and with representatives of Governments— was entrusted to younger colleagues. Jabotinsky limited himself largely to directing their activities and preparing the necessary background material : memoranda, documentation, letters, etc. Asked why he was so reluctant to meet the statesmen personally, he answered in his peculiar self-deprecating manner : "You know, I am no good at this kind of thing. I am like a hotwater faucet in a second-rate hotel : when you open it, you get cold water for the first ten minutes; then comes lukewarm water for the next ten minutes, and then only, if you are patient enough, it becomes really hot. That is the case with me : I am beginning to 'warm up' only after half an hour, while the 'Goy' I am speaking to has only half an hour to spare for me. No, *mes jeunes amis,* you are somehow much more direct and quicker than I am, and I fully rely on you." Dr. Harry Levi recalls that when it was suggested in London that not he but Jabotinsky should go to Brussels to present the anti-partition case to Orts, the Chairman of the Mandates Commission, Jabotinsky's reaction was : "I am no good for that purpose. My meeting with Orts will be a monologue, with me as the sole speaker, while what is needed is a dialogue, in which Orts must have a major share. Let Harry go."

These were, of course, some of the many disparaging legends Jabotinsky loved to spread about himself. More than once this writer had the privilege of being present at Jabotinsky's encounters with statesmen, and there never was even the slightest trace of "slowness" in his approach, or of monopolizing the conversation. After a twenty-minute conversation between Jabotinsky (who spoke for thirteen minutes only) and the Polish Foreign Minister, Colonel Beck, the latter told his Cabinet Chief, Count Michael Lubiensky, that during these thirteen minutes he learned about Zionism and Palestine "more than he could have learned from any other political leader in thirteen hours." "Mr. Jabotinsky," he added, "possesses an incomparable gift of clear and convincing presentation." [37]

He attached special importance to the attitude of the countries interested in Jewish emigration. On August 4, he related: [38] "Toward the end of August we shall have a team of three at Sinaia (Rumania) for the meeting of the Little Entente: the Czech Premier [Professor Kamil] Krofta [here Jabotinsky was in error: Krofta was Foreign Minister], who received Schechtman in June, and Rumanian Foreign Secretary [Gregor Gafencu] who has also been approached (and who will be, on September 10, *rapporteur* to the League's Council on Partition), will have to be seen for the finishing touches. So far they seem to be very firm; Krofta has really carried out his promise to Schechtman and sent out very stiff instructions against partition to his diplomats." At the end of the same month he again wrote to Haskel: [39] "I am sending you copies of a memorandum and a letter to our delegation at Sinaia—Schechtman [this writer was unable to go to Sinaia], Weisl, and Rabinowicz. At Sinaia, on the thirtieth, there will be a meeting of the foreign secretaries of Rumania, Czechoslovakia, and Yugoslavia. At that meeting they will fix their attitude toward the partition scheme."

The British Government's attempt to secure the approval of the Mandates Commission for its partition scheme met with little sympathy and cooperation. The Commission was obviously loath to commit itself. Prefacing its report with a suggestion that the Mandate might not have proved unworkable had Great Britain applied a firmer and more consistent policy, it grudgingly conceded that it would be desirable to examine a plan of partition; this vague assent was accompanied by a most intricate assortment of reservations. [40] Jabotinsky, however, considered even this moderate success of the British move as a defeat of the delegation he headed. In a letter to the prospective Sinaia delegation, he assessed the net result of the Permanent Mandates Commission's session as "a defeat of both the N.Z.O. and the Old Z.O. delegation in Geneva. We wanted the P.M.C. to reject partition *en toutes lettres,* and in this we lost." But "let me repeat again and again," he insisted, "that *the partition scheme is an impossibility,* and that nothing can save it from the inevitable 'naufrage,' and therefore every effort to push it forward can only result in sinking it deeper and deeper."

5. *On the Zurich Front*

Simultaneously with the Geneva session of the Mandates Commission, the Twentieth Zionist Congress was sitting in Zurich—the main item on its agenda was the attitude of the Zionist Organization toward the British partition scheme. Jabotinsky was, of course, fully aware of the influence which a positive or negative stand of the Congress would have on the Commission's decision, and on the further trend of events. He was therefore watching the developments in Zurich very carefully. He knew that many Congress delegates were opposed to any partition plan (by analogy with those who in 1903 had voted against the Uganda project, they were called *Neinsagers*) and that there was much speculation about their possible collaboration with him in a further struggle against partition. Though he was rather sceptical as to the steadfastness of these potential allies, he went out of his way and on a Friday afternoon slipped quietly into Zurich in order to meet a few leading opponents of partition, and slipped just as quietly away early on Sunday morning.[41] "Schechtman and I spent August 7 in Zurich," he reported to M. Haskel from Geneva. "Had a conference with [Rabbi Meir] Berlin and [Heshel] Farbstein of the *Mizrachi*, and Rabbi [Abba Hilel] Silver of the American *Neinsagers*. What we asked them was : Should their Congress pass a pro-partition resolution, will they, the *Neinsagers* within the old Zionist Organization, join us in openly fighting [partition] *nach aussen*? Their reply was, of course, not quite definite, but the tendency was rather favorable." Jabotinsky's own comment on this encounter was, however, still sceptical : "I should not rely very much on this tendency."[42]

A few days later, the Zionist Congress, by a majority of 300 to 158, empowered the Zionist Executive "to enter into negotiations [with the British Government] with a view to ascertaining the precise terms for the proposed establishment of a Jewish State."[43] In a strongly worded "Appeal to All," Jabotinsky branded the majority resolution as a "betrayal" and called on "all friends of integral Zionism, including those who belong to the Old Zionist Organization," to join in a common effort to convene a truly representative Jewish National Assembly, which would reassert the firm determination of the Jewish people not to give up the ideal of a Jewish State on both sides of the Jordan.[44]

6. *The Last Stages*

According to the League of Nations rule on procedure, the report of the Mandates Commission had to be submitted to the League Council which met in September. Jabotinsky expected that partition "will be strongly resisted there." [45] He was unable to leave London and delegated Dr. B. Akzin and this writer to Geneva, who continued the work along the lines laid down in August, maintaining close and active contact with Jabotinsky's London headquarters. The Council only partially granted Anthony Eden's request on behalf of his Government to authorize the preparation of a partition scheme : it agreed to an investigation of such a scheme but reserved full freedom of action to reject any plan which might be presented.[46]

Jabotinsky remained quietly confident that, notwithstanding the seeming "victories" of the partition idea in the Zionist Congress, the Mandates Commission, and the League's Council, the entire plan was irretrievably doomed. His personal letters for the period from September to December, 1937, are full of confidence : "There will be no partition of Palestine, and in general nobody is even thinking of it seriously except Dr. Weizmann and our Leftists. The [British] Government will, for some three months, go through the motions and obtain some harmless face-saving [League of Nations] resolutions in Geneva and then simply drop the entire matter. The question whether the *Yishuv* and other Jews want it or not, has no bearing on the matter, for the time being people think that all this is in earnest. They will soon begin to realize that it is as 'serious' as the dispatch of the British fleet to the Mediterranean two years ago. The depressing alternative the British are threatening us with, in case of non-partition, is also idle talk. If the Jews will use pressure, this will also disappear in two to three months." (Letter to Israel Rosov, September 8, 1937.) Three weeks later : "I feel confident, now even more than ever, that the partition scheme will be abandoned. Even what may seem to be steps in the direction of progress—for example the new Committee to be sent to Palestine—will result in pushing partition back and replacing it by some other scheme, probably based on a 'compromise between Jews and Arabs,' and probably as silly as partition. All this confusion, I think, will last a full year or so, and in the end will leave everyone sick to death of subterfuges and ready for

330

a straight clean line like our Ten-Year Plan : which Plan simply means 'stop this nonsense and carry out the Mandate in full.' " (Letter to M. Haskel, September 26, 1937.) And in mid-December : "Partition will soon be buried, the threatened bad alternatives will fizzle out, and by the end of the next summer the road will be open for true Zionism. All this optimism is difficult to substantiate—optimism always is— but I feel it in my bones and most of my colleagues concur." (Letter to Israel Brodie, December 19, 1937.)

Firmly convinced as he was that the "partition nonsense," as he called it, was doomed, Jabotinsky was not, however, prepared to wait fatalistically for its inevitable collapse. He intended to use the danger of partition as a point of departure for a world-wide political offensive in favor of the immediate creation of a viable Jewish State in the whole of Palestine, which would be able to satisfy the ever-growing need for mass emigration of East and Central European Jewry. One of the prerequisites for the successful launching of such an offensive was adequate financing. In this respect much was expected from a very rich and imaginative Jewish businessman in Paris, Simon S. Marcovici-Clejà. Without being an organized Zionist, he had ideas of his own in regard to several major problems facing Zionism and Palestine. He became interested in Jabotinsky's anti-partition crusade. In the spring of 1938, they met in Paris' *Circle des Nations* and frankly discussed all its aspects. "How much do you need to fight partition?" "Three million francs" [at that time about eighty-three thousand dollars]. "It's a deal, but I will personally handle the entire financing." "Sorry, this is not for sale." Clejà was not ready to cooperate on any other basis, and the deal was off. But he was deeply impressed by Jabotinsky and later said : "The only real gentleman I know in the Zionist Movement is Mr. Jabotinsky." [47] We will see in Chapter Twenty-three that this seemingly unsuccessful first meeting led to Clejà's substantial support of other activities, which were of profound interest to Jabotinsky.

Indeed, the "partition nonsense" proved to be shortlived. The Commission sent to Palestine to prepare a complete and workable plan of establishing a Jewish and an Arab State in divided Palestine presented a report to Parliament on November 9, 1938, to the effect that no plan of partition could be evolved which would offer much hope for successful application. [48] In a White Paper which accompanied the publication of the report, the Government admitted that "this solution of the problem is impracticable" and dropped it.[49] Jabotinsky's *nisht gestoigen nisht gefloigen* proved to be prophetic.

"Lost Without Trace" was the title of one of his most scathing articles on the partition scheme. The scheme remained lost without trace for a decade. But it left one immediate imprint on Jabotinsky's political thought and action : references to the possibility of replacing England by another Mandatory Power, which had been a frequent feature of his speeches and articles throughout the year 1936, disappeared from his political vocabulary. Moreover, he again started emphasizing the desirability of and necessity for the full implementation of the Mandate by the British Government.

This old-new trend was inevitably dictated by Jabotinsky's anti-partition stand. The Royal Commission's point of departure was the alleged "unworkability of the [Palestine] Mandate," the only alternative being the establishment of two separate States in parts of the mandated area. Since he negated partition, Jabotinsky was bound to assert the workability of the Mandate; at that time there was as yet no question of immediate Jewish sovereignty. And since he was not in a position to suggest any country to replace the present Mandatory Power, he had to insist on its continuing "in office," to drop any allusion to a "change of orientation," and to reaffirm his faith in England.

At the Eighth National Conference of the Revisionist organization in Poland (October 4, 1937), Jabotinsky, while sharply attacking the partition scheme and predicting that the British Government would withdraw it at the earliest opportunity, added : "We may have a number of grievances against England, but the English Government is and will be the Government of a well-disposed mother. We must have patience." [50] In the same month, October, he received from his son Eri, who was at that time the head of the Palestine *Betar,* a report about advances being made by someone connected with the Italian consulate. His reply was :[51] "I advise you most strongly to avoid contact of any kind with any individual or institution if you are not sure of two things : (1) that they are not against Zionism, and (2) that they are not against England. I am not writing this for the benefit of the [British] censor, but in full earnest. If there is even the slightest suspicion that the individual in question intends to stir up trouble, keep your distance and disregard any proposals of his."

This revival of the "English orientation" characterized the entire

332

period of Jabotinsky's anti-partition crusade. But even when the partition scheme was definitely abandoned (November, 1938), Jabotinsky was not ready to return to anti-British slogans. More than ever before, he believed that "the pressure of events—from without and from within—will very soon force England to agree to our 'Nordau Plan,' i.e., to the dumping in Palestine of about a million [Jewish] young men. . . . I earnestly believe that we, both of us, will witness [the emergence of] the Jewish State." [52] As late as February, 1939, he insisted that the question whether "we still have a partner, the great political partner of November, 1917 . . . must be approached calmly and cooly, without excitement and without stubbornness." Yet, he was again ready to put the "question whether this situation has not changed completely and fundamentally." [53]

He was still not prepared to answer this question in the affirmative. He envisaged, however, the possibility that the situation had changed, and felt that it was no longer "taboo" to deny the claim that "the Almighty Himself had tied us to them [the British Mandatory] for ever and ever, Amen." When the immediate threat of the British withdrawal because of the "unworkability of the Mandate" had receded, he was again in favor of saying to the British partner, simply and honestly: "As long as you want to carry on the partnership, we do too; but if you are tired—go in peace. There are other great democracies." The Jewish people, he warned, must be prepared for the eventuality that Britain was really "tired."[54]

THE EVACUATION TURMOIL

1. *The Time Factor*

A MONG THE Zionist leaders of his time, Jabotinsky was the only one to be acutely aware of the momentous significance of the *time factor* in Zionism. He was impatient with Time.

For more than a decade, the motive behind this "impatience" was of purely "Palestinian" nature : it originated in the stark demographic fact that, with a yearly Arab population increase of eighteen thousand, the current average Jewish immigration of fourteen thousand per year could not possibly lead to the establishment of a Jewish majority, which was to him the very essence of Zionism. He therefore, insisted that Zionism dare not allow itself the luxury of meticulously apportioned, piecemeal, slow-motion colonization, however "organic and practical" such a method may appear. He urged a greatly accelerated pace of Jewish settlement solely for the purpose of speedily converting Palestine into a Jewish State with a Jewish majority of population.

In the middle thirties, his concern regarding the time factor began to be diverted from Palestine to the Diaspora. He was increasingly haunted by the appalling awareness that time was running out on the Jewish communities in the areas he called the "Danger Zone" or "Zone of Jewish Distress," in Eastern, Central and South-Eastern Europe; that their position was deteriorating at a rate which was bound to lead to catastrophe; that they could be saved only by timely transfer to Palestine; and that Zionism must set the pace of its realization in accordance with the tempo of the impending calamity. For there was *periculum in mora* : time was imperilling the very existence of millions of European Jews and thus working against the constructive Zionist solution of the Jewish problem; it would start working in its favor only when made to do so. Dispatch was therefore mandatory, not as a manifestation of panicky haste or extremism, but as a dictate of harsh necessity. Jabotinsky was acutely aware that it was "later than you think," that time was of the essence, and that urgent, extraordinary action was a must. The over-riding aim was the rescue of millions of Jews from imminent doom.

Jabotinsky called this aim "humanitarian Zionism." He felt that this purpose, which should have had undisputed priority over any other consideration, was being largely neglected in Zionist thought and action and he often quoted an experience he had had when visiting one of the Zionist-controlled Hebrew schools. The teacher called on the brightest pupil of the class and asked: "What do you love and cherish above all?" *"Arzenu"* (our country—Palestine), answered the boy. The teacher beamed proudly. "And what else should one love and cherish above all?" asked Jabotinsky. The pupil had no answer, nor was the embarrassed teacher able to help him out. *"Amenu"* (our people), said Jabotinsky.

He was pathetically isolated in his agonizing appraisal of the time-table of the approaching calamity and of the ensuing mandatory pace of Zionist fulfillment. Jewish public opinion almost unanimously disregarded and condemned his diagnosis, which they called "alarmist," and his call for action, which they branded as "unrealistic." There was an abysmal discrepancy of timing between him and other Zionist leaders. One of ·them later disparagingly wrote: Jabotinsky "never lived in the regular time of day; he had his own time; when we Zionists saw the clock at six, he saw it at twelve." [1] Meant as a reproach, this formula offers a significant clue to Jabotinsky's unique personal mission in Jewish life: he "had his own time," and bitter experience has proved that he was prophetically right when he "saw the clock at twelve," and not at six as did the others. The symbolic difference of six hours roughly corresponds to the six millions of European Jews who perished in the holocaust.

2. *Anti-Semitism of Things*

The determining element in Jabotinsky's timetable was his conviction that alongside what can be described as the "anti-Semitism of Men": a subjective repulsion, strong enough and permanent enough to become anything from a hobby to a religion, as he later

335

characterized it—there also exists the "anti-Semitism of Things" : an objective state of affairs which tends to ostracize the Jew almost independently of whether his neighbors like or dislike him.[2] Germany offered a classical pattern of the first category : well-defined and easily recognizable. Less obvious and more complicated, but by no means less real and pernicious, was the second category, whose most typical focus was Poland. Its origin, as Jabotinsky saw it, lay in the bare statistical fact that the Jews constituted 10 per cent of the country's total population, and about one-third of its urban residents. From this state of affairs, the overwhelming majority of the Poles drew the conclusion that the application of full equality of opportunity to their Jewish minority was tantamount to (a) sharing with the Jews almost evenly mastery in the municipalities, and (b) giving the long-urbanized Jew the possibility of overtaking and beating his Polish competitor, the son of slow-witted peasants, in every branch of economy which requires some learning. This prevailing apprehension was poisoning the entire atmosphere of Poland's public life, quite irrespective of the attitude and policies of the changing Polish Governments. Jabotinsky did not overlook the responsibility of those Governments for the sore plight of Polish Jewry. But he insisted that the decisive factor to be acknowledged and reckoned with was not the guilt of men, but the tendencies of an elemental social process. And these tendencies were inexorably leading to a progressive deterioration of the Jewish situation, both economically and politically; the social evolution of Eastern Europe contained forces which were inherently undermining the very roots of the Jewish existence in this area. No Government supported by the majority of the Polish people could be expected to be able to reverse, or even substantially to stem, this process, deeply rooted as it was in the objective and inexorable setup of facts of life. It could be remedied or slowed down only by a radical and timely change of this very setup. In Jabotinsky's concept, such a change implied, first and foremost, the evacuation by a large section of Polish Jews of those economic positions which could not be maintained, and their mass immigration to Palestine.

An undertaking of that magnitude was, obviously, feasible only with the understanding and cooperation of that country's Government. Jabotinsky's point of departure was the belief that the Polish Government was not affected by the militant "Anti-Semitism of Men"; that its leaders loathed the prospect of anti-Jewish violence

336

and/or legal discrimination. Their attitude was of course motivated not by any fondness for the Jews, but by the awareness of the corrupting and degrading impact of such a course. But the Government had to face the increasing pressure of elemental forces within the country, clamoring for anti-Jewish legislation and occasionally breaking out into murderous rioting. In order to be able to counteract this mounting popular onslaught, the Government must be given a chance to offer a constructive alternative : to relieve the intensity of anti-Jewish pressure by sponsoring a Jewish-initiated scheme of large-scale orderly and voluntary evacuation. Such a joint Polish-Jewish scheme, as Jabotinsky saw it, was rooted in the community of interests of its two prospective partners. While their respective motives were necessarily different, even conflicting, the practical conclusion to which they were bound to come was fundamentally the same, making them collaborators and allies in a historic common undertaking of a grand-scale transfer of populations. Fully aware of the ominous meaning of the anti-Jewish storm which was raging in East-Central Europe, Jabotinsky insisted that "the storm in itself does not mean anything." He quoted the English poetess, Ella Wheeler Wilcox who, in a poem *The Winds of Fate,* written in the days of the sailing ships, when steam was unknown, wrote :

> One ship goes West, another goes East,
> In the selfsame wind that blows.
> It's the set of the sail, it's not the gale
> Which determines the way she goes.

Jabotinsky was therefore confident that while "this terrible storm can crush us, it can perhaps save us : this depends on the pilots, on the captains, on the set of our sails"; and among the black clouds he saw a "silver lining" on the horizon.[8]

This was, in a nutshell, Jabotinsky's concept of both "evacuation" and "policy of alliances," which, since 1936, had become the backbone of his political effort and the main target of his opponents.

In regard to this chapter of Jabotinsky's political struggle, this writer finds himself in a particularly privileged position. From 1936 to 1939 I was, in this field, Jabotinsky's main "troubleshooter," largely responsible for the formulation and implementation of the "policy of alliances," and the chairman of the section of the N.Z.O.

337

Nessiut, which was established in Warsaw, and which on June 13, 1936, Jabotinsky solemnly introduced to a mass meeting in the Polish capital, attended by more than four thousand people.[4]

The original, largely organizational, purpose of the Warsaw *Nessiut* was very soon overshadowed by predominantly political contacts with the Polish Governmental circles (and later with the Governments of other countries of the "danger zone"). Late in 1937, this writer was appointed the *Nessiut's* permanent political representative in Poland —a position I held until June, 1939. During the last three prewar years I reported regularly to London all important current political developments. Unlike many other political documents, an almost complete set of those reports survived the war turmoil and was available for the preparation of this chapter.[5]

3. *How the Hunt Started*

The concept of "evacuation" had been ripening in Jabotinsky's mind long before it became the storm center of Jewish public life. As early as August, 1932, he said at the Fifth Revisionist World Conference in Vienna : "Several million Jews must, in the nearest future, evacuate the main centers of Eastern Europe and create in Palestine a national Jewish State." [6] Three years later, at the Foundation Congress of the New Zionist Organization (September, 1935), he spoke of the "exodus" as the solution of the Jewish problem, and in June, 1936, at the above-mentioned mass meeting in Warsaw, he already openly spelled out *evacuation* as the only constructive solution of the Jewish problem.[7]

However, none of those pronouncements, made publicly and with Jabotinsky's usual clarity of emphasis, provoked strong, let alone violent, criticism and opposition. They were discussed in the Jewish multilingual press calmly, as a viewpoint which may be right or wrong, but is as "legitimate" as any other. It was not before September, 1936, that *the same* pronouncement suddenly aroused an almost unprecedented barrage of indignant denunciation as a heresy bordering on national treason. This writer and two other members of the N.Z.O. *Nessiut* in Warsaw (Dr. J. Damm and J. Spektor) were unwittingly instrumental in unleashing this storm.

Anxious to acquaint Polish public opinion with Jabotinsky's policy, we made arrangements with the editors of the Warsaw conservative daily *Czas*—one of the oldest and "cleanest" Polish papers, which had never indulged in anti-Jewish utterances—for a special four-page supplement devoted to a full exposé of the evacuation scheme. The supplement appeared on September 8, the day of Jabotinsky's arrival in Warsaw; it contained a reprint of his 1924 article: "The Favorable Storm," and articles by Dr. Jan Krakowsky (Dr. Jan Bader) and this writer, as well as an editorial, in which the *Czas* expressed its support for Jabotinsky's ideas. We made these arrangements on our own initiative and responsibility, without previous consultation with Jabotinsky. When he arrived and saw the paper, he did not seem to be very happy about it, but, with his usual loyalty to his collaborators, abstained from any unfavorable comment; he even congratulated us on a well-done job.

But it was exactly this *Czas* supplement that more than anything upset and enraged adverse Jewish public opinion in Poland and elsewhere. It was not so much the content of the articles as the fact of their publication in a non-Jewish paper, which produced the violent outburst of indignation and vituperation. As long as such views remained "within the Jewish community," argued the critics, they could be opposed, but tolerated; but to bring them into the open through the medium of the non-Jewish press was, in their eyes, the peak of irresponsibility, detrimental to the most vital interests of Polish Jewry. It was claimed that by speaking directly to the Poles, Jabotinsky was breaking Jewish national discipline and opening the way to Polish interference with "internal Jewish affairs"; that, by doing so, he was jeopardizing Jewish civic equality in the country; that he wrongly "exaggerated and dramatized" the Jewish need for mass emigration; and that by stressing both the necessity and desirability of cooperation with the Polish Government in order to secure possibilities for large-scale emigration to Palestine, he was exonerating "this anti-Semitic Government" from blame for the sore plight of its Jewish subjects.

The furor provoked by this first direct approach to Polish public opinion grew in intensity when the next day, September 9, Jabotinsky addressed a press conference, which was exceptionally well attended by correspondents of foreign, Polish, and Jewish newspapers. Speaking first in French and later, at the request of those present, in Russian, he lucidly presented his concept of evacuation as a matter of international concern, and as a solution to the Jewish problem in

Poland. Polish journalists displayed sympathetic interest; representatives of the Jewish press were both shocked and antagonistic.

They were quick to show their displeasure. The anti-Jabotinsky front was practically unanimous. Even the *Moment,* which had been Jabotinsky's mouthpiece since 1932, openly joined the opposition camp. The anti-Zionist elements on the paper's editorial staff utilized the situation : they had never before ventured to challenge Jabotinsky's dominant position, but now, with the mounting wave of popular hysteria against the "evacuation" slogan, they moved to the forefront and sharply attacked Jabotinsky's stand. When they learned that he sent in an article explaining his evacuation idea, they protested vehemently : "Blood will flow if evacuation propaganda be permitted in the *Moment.*" He found support on the part of several colleagues; a more moderate group, while opposing Jabotinsky's views, advised restraint in handling the situation : they feared to lose him for the *Moment* which, they argued, could not afford such a luxury. It was decided to invite Jabotinsky to a meeting of the entire staff of the paper and to discuss the issue. But, recalls a participant in this meeting, the discussion proved that there was no common language between Jabotinsky and his colleagues. The opinion of the extreme wing was clearly expressed by Noah Prilutzky, who stated : "Jabotinsky wants to evacuate from Poland a considerable part of her present Jewish population, and I would like to have here not three and a half but seven million Jews; this would increase our strength in fighting the anti-Semites." However, even among the "moderates," who were in the majority, no one endorsed or condoned the evacuation idea. They agreed, it is true, that Jabotinsky's article appeared in the *Moment,* but insisted on their right to publish articles criticizing his stand. Such an arrangement would create in *Moment* the same situation that existed in the *Haint* : Jabotinsky would contribute his articles to a paper opposing and combatting his ideas. He refused to accept. His statement was brief : "Dear colleagues, I am sorry that I have to say farewell to the *Moment*; and I regret that you do not see the dark clouds that are gathering over the heads of the Jews in Europe." [8]

Jabotinsky discontinued his collaboration in the *Moment.* He also severed his association with the Polish-language Zionist daily *Nasz Przeglàd,* for which he had been writing since 1935, and which took up a militant attitude toward the evacuation idea.

Besides depriving him of a very essential part of his journalistic income, this withdrawal made Jabotinsky all of a sudden "mute" in the Polish-Jewish press at a time when he was being subjected to an incessant barrage of vituperation.

One of the most vicious attacks was delivered by the famous Yiddish novelist, Sholom Asch, who was on a short visit to Warsaw at that time. Interviewed by the correspondent of the *Haint*, Asch declared that "what Jabotinsky is now doing in Poland goes beyond all limits. . . . One has to have a heart of stone, to be devoid of any feeling for human sufferings to be so brazen as to come to Poland with such proposals at such a terrible time. . . . Heaven help a people with such leaders!" * [9]

The anti-Jabotinsky campaign was not limited to Poland. It also provoked spirited discussion in Palestine and America. The Leftist *Davar,* Tel Aviv organ of the *Mapai,* ridiculed (on October 19) "the *Führer* Jabotinsky who all these years had been busily distorting every sound idea in Zionism." "We Jews," declared the paper, "will not let ourselves be expelled to Palestine with the help of Polish anti-Semites," and accused Jabotinsky of "having concluded a pact with the Polish Government to deport Jews from Poland in yearly installments." On the other hand, the organ of General Zionists, *Haboker,* published (on November 15) an article "Poland and Zionism" beginning with the sentence: "Jabotinsky was right." Several leaders of Zionist groups and local Palestine bodies, interviewed by the Revisionist daily *Hayarden,* firmly endorsed Jabotinsky's stand.

Not less contradictory was the reaction in America. At a conference called in New York in January, 1937, by the American Jewish Congress, to discuss the Jewish situation in Poland, Dr. Stephen S. Wise characterized as "apostates . . . Vladimir Jabotinsky and any other Jew who conduct negotiations with Colonel Beck and the Polish Government for the emigration of three million (!) Jews." [10] *New Palestine,* the official organ of the Zionist Organization of America, though reluctantly admitting that "logic may be with Mr. Jabotinsky," insisted that "there are moral protests that cannot be stilled

*After the outbreak of the war, Sholom Asch wrote to Jabotinsky acknowledging that the latter had been prophetically right in his policy of evacuation (*The Jewish Herald,* September 2, 1957). At a press conference in Jerusalem in 1952, Asch repentently said: "I deeply regret that I had fought against Jabotinsky's evacuation plan." (*Herut,* May 5, 1952.)

by casuistry." "It is evacuation under escort," the paper claimed expressing "surprise" that "there are some Jewish leaders who see nothing incongruous in sitting at the same table with Mr. Beck to discuss what should be done to facilitate the wholesale emigration of the victims of Polish oppression."[11] A different attitude was taken by the organ of *Poalei Zion-Zeirei Zion, Der Yiddischer Kempfer* (November 13, 1936), stating that Jabotinsky's policy was the inevitable result of the present Jewish position in the world: "It wasn't Jabotinsky who invented the problem. . . . The Polish Government did not have to wait for him to come and to arouse its appetite to get rid of the Jews. . . . If Jabotinsky has in this case committed a 'betrayal,' it is merely a reflection of the treacherous attitude which the world had assumed towards us."

The only remotely congenial voice was that of Lord Melchett. In the December, 1936, issue of *The Empire Review* appeared his outspoken article "Palistine and the Jews," in which he did not hesitate to state that "anti-Semitism is not invariably the result of malicious action by existing Governments . . . in the difficult and terrible circumstances with which the rulers of Poland are faced, there is only one way out of a situation steadily forcing millions of impoverished and persecuted Jews to the Left, and that is practical Zionism." Melchett insisted that if it were possible "to remove from Poland each year thirty-five thousand Jews, Polish Jewry would rapidly shrink to dimensions which would make its digestion within the country a relatively simple matter." He voiced similar views in the *Spectator* (November 13, 1936) and *Sunday Chronicle,* as well as in his thought-provoking book *Thy Neighbor.*

4. The Counter-Offensive

The attacks of the Jewish press, however, had very little effect on the attitude of the average Polish Jew. Among the masses of Polish Jewry, Jabotinsky enjoyed an exceptional status. There was hardly any exaggeration in the testimony of one of the leading Polish Revisionists, the late Samuel L. Katz, that whenever Jabotinsky came to Poland, Warsaw and other towns he visited "bedecked themselves in gala dress." Not only his party friends, but the entire Jewish populace "considered it an occasion for celebration." [12]

In the smaller towns, Jabotinsky would find the streets and houses decorated with flags and garlands. Women and children would scatter flowers in his path. One could sense the current of pride which ran through the Jewish masses, the feeling of increased security in an insecure world which gripped them as a result of his coming: here was that one man who could negotiate with statesmen for us on equal terms; here was that one Jew whose main concern we were, just because we were Jews.

The average Polish Jew remained faithful to his trust in and affection for Jabotinsky. Friends advised him to cancel a lecture he had to deliver in Warsaw's large *Novosci* Theater on November 13, at the very peak of the campaign against him : there were persistent rumors of an organized boycott and disturbances. He refused to yield. The lecture took place as scheduled, at noon, and a capacity audience filled the hall, received the speaker with thunderous applause, and repeatedly cheered the more impressive parts of the lecture; there was not a single attempt at obstruction.[13] A few hours later, the sport organization *Maccabi* bestowed on him the title of honorary member. More effective was the anti-Jabotinsky propaganda among the Jewish bourgeoisie and intelligentsia. The reception in the evening, arranged for him, attracted a much smaller number of participants than expected; many persons of wealth and influence who had previously accepted the invitation yielded to the prevailing animosity and did not appear.[14]

It was in these circles that a vigorous counter-offensive had to be launched. Jabotinsky accepted the invitation of the Warsaw Society of Jewish Physicians and Engineers to present his case.[15]

The major part of his address was devoted to a rebuttal of what, as he said, he might "out of politeness, describe as 'misunderstanding.'" These "misunderstandings" were many and manifold. The main one, and the one Jabotinsky resented most, was—"that I favor, or even only condone the curtailment of Jewish rights in order to assist evacuation."

I would call those who say so, liars, if they were not worse—simply fools. I am the chief author of the Helsingfors program, the highest expression of the demand for Jewish rights in the Diaspora. But there is one aspect of the situation which even those of shaky honesty and feeble mind ought to understand: we who want the Jewish nation to be powerful enough to "force" the hand of the Mandatory, to mobilize half the world and Geneva as our "allies," to overcome the Arabs' menace, etc., etc.—

343

how can it be suggested that we Revisionists, we of all people, can agree to reducing that nation to the status of a herd of cattle?

In Jabotinsky's estimate, the allegation that the evacuation scheme implied the transfer to Palestine of "all" the Jews from Poland and "all" the Jews from everywhere, all the sixteen or seventeen millions, belonged to the same category. "That is a stupid allegation," he said, and went on patiently to explain that "there is an area called the Diaspora, and another area called Palestine. Migration from the first into the second does not depend on what we Revisionists 'want': it will depend on the expulsive pressure of the Diaspora, and on Palestine's power of attraction and absorption. No one can foretell how many of us will, in the end, be ousted or partly ousted from the countries of the *Galut,* and attracted to or gather in by Palestine. But one thing we do know, all of us: if the channel of migration between the two areas is blocked while the pressure in the Diaspora is on the increase, then an alarm should be raised in the name of Justice to clear the channel."

The "channel of migration," Jabotinsky insisted, was, under certain conditions, a perfectly legitimate expression of the relationship between a State and its citizens.

It is perfectly beside the point to emphasize that we Jews in the Diaspora are there as of right and not on sufferance. Of course, as of right. I was born in Odessa, as of right; why, we Jews did more for building up Odessa and the whole of that Black Sea shore than the Russians ever did; which does not mean that I am obliged to stick to Odessa. I chose not to. I evacuated Odessa, despite the fact that I lived there as of right (and even loved, and still do love my beautiful city): simply because, following the call of my national conscience, I so found it necessary and so resolved and ruled.

If a people realizes that a certain position it holds in the world is untenable, economically and politically, it is its inalienable right and mandatory duty to evacuate it. "Evacuation of condemned positions is a free act of a nation's will: so it was when our ancestors left Egypt, not only without being 'forcibly expelled,' but even against the Pharaoh's will and decree." If the Jewish urge to emigrate is a legitimate one, then so is the endeavour of the Governments of the countries they intend to emigrate from, to "clear the channel" for them:

It is sheer political illiteracy to suggest that if a Government, whose citizens need outlets for emigration, intervenes on their behalf with another Government, that means it wants to get rid of those citizens. Prewar Italy—liberal Italy—never ceased to negotiate with the Governments of the United States, of the Argentine, of Brazil about privileges and facilities for Italian immigrants. This is one of the first duties of any decent Government.

Jabotinsky begged the Jewish intelligentsia not to let their "touchiness degenerate into an inferiority complex. Do not imply that a desire to emigrate, which is fully legitimate in an Italian, a Scandinavian, an Irishman, a Czech, is something to be ashamed of in a Jew; and that a Government should be praised if it defends the migratory interests of non-Jews, but if it does it for Jews it commits a crime."

Answering the challenge so often advanced, "Who gave you the authority" to discuss this vital problem of Polish Jewry with the Polish Government, Jabotinsky proudly asserted: "Polish Jewry itself gave us that power, in manifestations of unprecedented magnitude." He recalled that the Revisionist Petition to the Polish Government, launched in 1934, had been signed by 217,000 Polish Jews, who stated: "The only way of normalizing my existence is for me and my family to settle in Palestine. . . . I ask the Polish Government to intervene with the Mandatory Power so that the unjust immigration restrictions may be revised. . . ." And in 1935, when the Foundation Congress of the New Zionist Organization was called in the name of those very principles, four hundred fifty thousand Polish Jews went to the polls and endorsed this call. "No other Jewish party in Poland was ever backed by such a plurality; no one in Polish Jewry ever had such 'authority' to speak on their behalf as we have in this case."

Angrily referring to protests against his evacuation policy by American Jewish organizations, Jabotinsky said contemptuously:

I am not disposed to ask for any authority on behalf of those who (emigrants themselves, lucky chaps, who long ago "evacuated" the old Ghetto and now enjoy both security and prosperity of the Golden West) now raise their noble voices from soft armchairs in New York to protest against "evacuation." You who are still here, you who stood all the storms without running away, tell those heroes from afar to shut up. Day and night, they are blessing Destiny for having got them away; but as to you, they want you to stay, and whoever dreams of helping you to follow, or even to better, their example is to be decried as traitor. Theirs is the bravery of deserters. . . .

This address dispelled many, but by far not all "misunderstandings." Jabotinsky had again and again to refute both *bona fide* and malicious accusations.

One of the main points of criticism was the term "evacuation" which he used. In Poland, it revived painful reminiscences of the First World War, when the Czarist Government forcibly and cruelly "evacuated" hundreds of thousands of Jews from the north-west areas menaced by the German armies. Even some of Jabotinsky's party friends believed that he "should have avoided this unhappy word." He himself firmly defended the terminology he had chosen.

"Do not think," he wrote, "that I used this word lightly. For a long time I have been searching for a really appropriate term; I pondered over it, I weighed it a thousand times, and I found no better, no more appropriate word. I first thought of 'Exodus,' of a second 'Departure from Egypt.' But this will not do. We are engaged in politics, we must be able to approach other nations and demand the support of other States. And that being so, we cannot submit to them a term that is offensive, that recalls Pharaoh and the ten plagues. Besides, the word 'Exodus' evokes a terrible picture of horrors, the picture of a whole nation that—like a disorganised mob—flees panic stricken.

"Evacuation is something quite different," Jabotinsky patiently explained. What he had in mind when using this word was : a village lies at the foot of a volcano, menaced whenever there is an eruption; the Government of the country decides of its own will, in the interests of its own population, to evacuate the village. "We, too, who proclaim the 'Evacuation Plan' do so by virtue of our own national sovereignty, because we wish it, because we need it, because we want to save Jewry from the onrush of lava. Will anyone deny that there is this lava, and that it is coming nearer, and that we must find a means of defense?" Jabotinsky therefore insisted that "we shall not find a more appropriate word. And the man who says this has spent his whole life among dictionaries. Evacuation does not mean that others should evacuate us, but that we ourselves desire it; we, the Jewish people, want no *Galut*, but Freedom. In the Membership Certificate of the New Zionist Organization this idea, the Zionist aim, is formulated thus : *Shivat Zion lechol dorshe Zion, vesof lapizur*

(Return to Zion for all who want Zion, and an end to the Dispersion)." [16]

The two months (September 8 through November 10, 1936) spent in Poland under fire of the "evacuation" battle, constituted one of the most trying periods in Jabotinsky's life. Speaking in Warsaw before a gathering of members of free professions, he said sadly : "I must confess that while I used to come to Poland with great pleasure, I now feel uncomfortable among you. But I beg you to understand one thing : it is very easy to make a man to hold his tongue. The problem, however, does not lie there. What is at stake is a most vital Zionist issue which is, at the same time, a question of life or death for Polish Jewry. I am offering a solution for this question and I have devoted all my life to this solution." [17]

5. *In the Footsteps of Herzl and Nordau*

To those conversant with the classics of Zionist literature, there was little that one could take objection to in Jabotinsky's scheme : it merely represented a timely application of both Theodore Herzl's fundamental Zionist concept of 1896, and of the 1920 "Nordau Plan."

It was not in Jabotinsky's nature to hide behind the broad back of a recognized or sanctified Zionist spiritual authority, and he was reluctant to make his heatedly embattled ideas acceptable by quoting chapter and verse from Herzl's writings. Yet one evening he invited this writer to join him in, as he put it, "a brief excursion into Herzl's *Judenstaat,* just for our personal enlightenment and enjoyment." This was, however, by no means as improvised and casual an excursion as he wanted it to appear. The copy of Herzl's *Zionistische Schriften* he produced (a 1920 edition, published in Berlin by Dr. Kellner), was heavily marked and annotated, showing traces of previous diligent perusal; and we spent a full hour reading—and savoring—at least a dozen passages, in which the founder of modern Zionism expressed ideas, of which Jabotinsky's most "heretical" pronouncements were but a new and dramatic reincarnation. Some of those passages this writer has now easily identified in a recent English translation of the *Judenstaat.*[18]

Herzl's appraisal of the Jewish situation in the world:

. . . Is it not true that, in countries where we live in perceptible numbers, the position of Jewish lawyers, doctors, technicians, teachers, and employees of all descriptions becomes daily more intolerable? Is it not true that the Jewish middle classes are seriously threatened? Is it not true that the passions of the mob are incited against our wealthy people . . .?

Herzl's appraisal of anti-Semitism:

. . . I believe that I understand anti-Semitism, which is really a highly complex movement. I consider it from a Jewish standpoint, yet without fear or hatred. I believe that I can see what elements there are in it of vulgar sport, of common trade jealousy, of inherited prejudice, of religious intolerance, and also of pretended self-defense.

Herzl's question to his people:

. . . I shall now put the question in the briefest possible form: Are we to "get out" now and where to?

Or, may we remain? And how long?

Let us first settle the point of staying where we are. Can we hope for better days, can we possess our souls in patience, can we wait in pious resignation until the princes and peoples are more mercifully disposed towards us? I say that we cannot hope for a change in the current of feeling. And why not? Even if we were as near to the hearts of princes as are their other subjects, they could not protect us. They would only feed popular hatred by showing us too much favor. By "too much" I really mean less than is claimed as a right by every ordinary citizen, or by every race. The nations in whose midst Jews live are either covertly or openly anti-Semitic.

Herzl's advocacy of evacuation:

. . . The outgoing current will be gradual, without any disturbance, and its initial movement will put an end to anti-Semitism. The Jews will leave as honored friends, and if some of them return, they will receive the same favorable welcome and treatment at the hands of civilized nations as is accorded to all foreign visitors. Their exodus will have no resemblance to a flight, for it will be a well-regulated movement under control of public opinion. The movement will not only be inaugurated with absolute conformity to law, but it cannot even be carried out without the friendly cooperation of interested Governments, who would derive considerable benefits from it.

348

Herzl's advocacy of cooperation with the Governments:

... I imagine that Governments will, either voluntarily or under pressure from the anti-Semites, pay certain attention to this scheme, and they may perhaps actually receive it here and there with sympathy. . . . If we are not merely suffered, but actually assisted to do this, the movement will have a generally beneficial effect. . . .

Prayers will be offered up for the success of our work in temples and in churches also; for it will bring relief from an old burden, which all have suffered.

Herzl's answer to critics :

. . . Again, people will say that I am furnishing the anti-Semites with weapons. Why so? Because I admit the truth . . .?

Will not people say that I am showing our enemies the way to injure us? This I absolutely dispute. My proposal could only be carried out with the free consent of a majority of Jews.

There is striking similarity, not to say identity, between the *Judenstaat's* concept and terminology, and those of Jabotinsky's "evacuation" and "alliances" scheme.

Like Herzl, Jabotinsky had no prejudices or inhibitions in regard to the non-Jewish world. His attitude was unique in Jewish political thinking of his time.

Ghetto Jewry had two diametrically opposed attitudes to the "Goy" (Gentile). Those reared in the tradition of "chosen people" regarded the Gentile as an elemental, organically foreign and hostile force. This force had to be reckoned with, just as one had to reckon with an earthquake or a flood. But there was nothing to learn from it, let alone to find some community of interests leading to common action. On the other hand, assimilationist circles saw in the Gentile world the incarnation of all virtues the Jewish people lacked and looked up to it in unbounded admiration.

Both concepts were alien to Jabotinsky. He realized that the Jews had many weighty accounts to settle with the Gentile; but the Gentile was not a brute; nor was he an angel. Hatred and adulation are equally wrong and futile. Jabotinsky's own approach was formulated at the Second Revisionist World Conference held in Paris, in the close of December, 1926, where he forged the phrase: *Morenu ve'Rabenu, ha'goy* (our teacher and our mentor, the Gentile). In his concept, the non-Jewish world was a great and creative force, from which the Jewish national movement had a lot to learn

349

in the field of political thought and action. The Jewish problem must be integrated into the general framework of the problems the world is facing. The Jews must study the methods the Gentile had been applying to their solution; must learn the Gentile's way and look for avenues of mutually advantageous cooperation in the solution of the Jewish question. A fervent apostle of Jewish self-reliance, Jabotinsky was at the same time aware that in this complex world of ours no nation is capable of standing alone and solving its major problems on its own, without allies. Such allies must be sought not on the basis of sympathy or compassion, but solely on the basis of community of interests. His contention was that there exists a way of understanding and cooperation between the Jewish national movement and the Gentile world. The politically conscious Gentile is not necessarily an anti-Semite. For the sake of Jews, he would not swerve in the least from the course which he deems best to serve his interests, or even his foibles. But if the Jews come with a reasonable scheme which happens to coincide with his own aims, he may listen to it and even endorse it; he may become a partner in a common undertaking, not necessarily because of friendship, but because of well-understood self-interest. And this is the only thing that counts in the realm of real politics.

It was in this spirit that Jabotinsky approved of Herzl's negotiations with von Plehve in 1903, and that he himself, in 1921, concluded an agreement with Petliura's envoy, Professor M. A. Slavinsky (see Vol. I, Chapters One and Nine). There is a direct line connecting Herzl's and Jabotinsky's political thinking in this field.

A somewhat more complicated, though intrinsically similar ideological relationship can be established in regard to Max Nordau: the "Nordau Plan" became one of the cornerstones of Jabotinsky's "evacuation" crusade.

There has been much misunderstanding as to both the actual contents of the Nordau Plan and the time of its publication. Jabotinsky himself mistakenly traced its origin to the year 1919: in fact, Nordau presented it in ten articles, published in *Le Peuple Juif* of Paris, between September 14 and November 20, 1920. He urged the speedy transfer to Palestine of six hundred thousand Jews (not of five hundred thousand as Jabotinsky believed, and not of one million as Dr. Weizmann asserted in *Trial and Error*). Jabotinsky later frankly admitted that at that time he had failed to grasp the great revolutionary and constructive meaning of Nordau's plan: [19] "We all thought ourselves very clever in rejecting the idea then," he wrote repentently to a friend in November, 1938.

A partial explanation of this failure can be found in an article published in the spring of 1939 : "As with all my contemporaries, the Zionist belief of my youth was a belief in a long and slow evolution, which had to take a number of generations to be accomplished, the concrete fulfillment of which would be seen only by our children, and that in their old age; and even this was not quite certain." It is against this background that one must view Jabotinsky's early indifference towards Nordau's bold vision, which included all the basic ingredients of Greater Zionism : its main motivation was that "we must at any price become a majority in Palestine . . . otherwise our National Home would remain a delusion and a will-o-the-wisp." [20]

Nordau's bold and imaginative scheme failed to arouse a positive response in Jabotinsky, not only when it was first announced, but also for several years to come. It was not until the "evacuation" idea had taken shape in his mind that he fully endorsed the Nordau scheme as a concrete and timely proposition. At a press conference in Warsaw, held in September, 1936, he said : [21] "It appears that the time has now come to revive Max Nordau's plan," which must be viewed "in the light of our 15 years of experience." But his own "Ten-Year Plan" was in its original form only partly reminiscent of Nordau's revolutionary idea, the essence of which was a speedy one-time and short-term transfer operation. The "Plan," as approved by the N.Z.O. Convention in February, 1938, was based on an evolutionary concept of transferring a million and a half Jews in ten consecutive yearly installments : the installments were unprecedentedly large and the pace was an accelerated one, but fundamentally the scheme was a far cry from Nordau's dramatic and deliberately "unplanned" vision of abruptly "dumping" six hundred thousand Jews on Palestine's shore and placing the Jewish and non-Jewish world before an accomplished fact of historic significance.

However, this early discrepancy soon narrowed down. By the end of 1938, Jabotinsky already felt that [22] "the situation had so tremendously developed during the last few months that even a hundred thousand per-year plan sounds too slow for modern statesmanship." Those who are shaping the world's destinies "instinctively shrink from even considering plans which presuppose a longer period than *die absehbare Zeit* [foreseeable time] in the most literal sense of the

351

term. A plan which requires ten years or so before the Jews become a majority and the British are rid of the responsibility, would stand no chance in this psychological atmosphere. What is needed today is something which was considered madness in 1919, when Max Nordau urged that five hundred thousand Jews be dumped in six months on the shore of Palestine, and that the Jewish world take care of them there instead of Poland. . . . Today a Nordau plan is the only solution that *kommt in Betracht* [can be considered], only with a million instead of half a million."

"I am sure that elemental floods will soon break out all over East European Jewry, so terribly powerful that the German catastrophe will be eclipsed, that all twaddle about palliative charities will be swept away, all twaddle about Guiana [then suggested as territory for Jewish mass immigration], etc., dropped as inadequate, all Arab fury *in den Schatten gestellt* [overshadowed] as something infinitesimally puny; and then one thing will emerge as *consensus omnium*— 'a Jewish majority overnight.' "

"It may sound strange and silly," Jabotinsky admitted, "that a man snould pick just this time for being optimistic, but I feel more than optimistic—I am as sure of my forecast as I was of the failure of the partition twaddle. The only thing of which I am not sure is whether the Jews will prove able to play the role of *sage-femme* [midwife] properly in this elemental birth process, thus shortening the process and lessening the pain. They certainly won't if the Old Zionist Organization retains its predominance. But the march of events is so ordained by God Himself that it will end in the *Judenstaat* independently of what we Jews do or do not do."

This certainty of the predetermined ultimate triumph of the Nordau Plan, as he saw it, in no way impaired Jabotinsky's determination to play the role of *sage-femme*. His main efforts were directed at bringing the plan to the notice of the United States Government. Early in January, 1939, he wrote:[23] "For many months we have been making efforts to get Washington interested in what we call the Max Nordau Plan. Schechtman and I had long talks with [Francis Drexel] Biddle [United States Ambassador in Warsaw and a very sincere friend of our cause]. . . . Biddle assured me that every word of our talks had been reported to the White House." In an aide-memoire to the United States Ambassador in London, whom he had previously visited, Jabotinsky soberly acknowledged that he did "not

352

necessarily expect the Nordau Plan to become Washington's immediate platform of action. But for our purposes it will probably be enough if we impress Washington that, when the inter-Governmental conference is convened, some plan, concrete, tangible, and radically helpful, can be submitted for their consideration. The curse of Zionism has long been its vagueness : it never even claimed to present a quick remedy to violent outbreaks of *Judennot*." He therefore believed, he wrote, that "if we could only make ourselves heard above the noise that is going on in the world with the catchword—'the first million at once, the rest very soon'—public opinion might seriously and pragmatically turn to the only crew who know their own minds, and believe in their medicine. . . . I think Washington today is exactly in the mood where one is mortally sick of patchwork, and ready to snap at anyone who suggests more patchwork, but prepared to acclaim anyone who says the right word." [24]

As Jabotinsky saw it, the advantages of such a "right word" were many and far-reaching. "Its implementation would immediately ease the tension in Central and Eastern Europe : roughly about three hundred thousand could at once be evacuated from Germany and Austria, about five hundred thousand from Poland, one hundred thousand from Hungary and lesser States." But "still more important would be the promise, inherent in the very essence of a Jewish State, that further evacuations would follow." Even if, during the first years immediately after the landing of the initial million, immigration would have to be so trimmed down as not to interfere with its absorption,"the assurance that full steam would soon be resumed would help well-intentioned Governments to keep anti-Semitism within limits." He was confident that, faced with the phenomenon of a Jewish majority becoming a fact "almost overnight," Palestine Arabs would accept the *fait accompli* and "come to terms." Then, a democratically elected Parliament would form a Palestinian Government "and conclude with England, should she desire it, a treaty removing those features of the Mandate she considers burdensome. The actual burdensome or critical period involved in the fulfillment of the Mandate would thus be reduced to not more than three years, perhaps even less." [25]

6. The Policy of Alliances

Cooperation with the Governments of the countries directly interested in emigration outlets for their Jewish population, and utilization of their influence for securing possibilities for Jewish mass transfer to Palestine, constituted an essential component of Jabotinsky's evacuation concept. Poland was its major testing ground and field of operation. The years 1936 through 1939 were largely devoted to a sustained effort to establish a constructive working arrangement with Polish Government circles.

The immediate addressee was the Ministry of Foreign Affairs. Jabotinsky met the Foreign Minister, Colonel Joseph Beck, for the first time on June 9, 1936, immediately after the installation of part of the *Nessiut* in Warsaw; a second encounter took place early in July in Geneva during the session of the League of Nations. Beck's *chef-de-cabinet,* Count Michael Lubienski, told this writer that Jabotinsky "had made an exceptionally good impression on the Minister who has a very high opinion of him," * and volunteered to arrange an informal conference with the highest officials of those Ministries whose cooperation was particularly valuable for Jabotinsky's plans. "You see," he said, "Ministers come and go, but those officials are almost a permanent fixture of their respective Ministries, and their cooperation is often at least as essential as that of the Ministers themselves."

Such a gathering took place on September 9, in the form of a dinner at the Club of the Foreign Office officials. Among those present were representatives of the Foreign Office, the Ministry of the Interior, the Defense Ministry, and the Prime Minister's Office; Jabotinsky was accompanied by this writer and D. Mowszowicz, one of the leaders of the Revisionist movement in Poland. He was in excellent form. All those present spoke or understood Russian, and he was in his element. After dinner, we sat around the fireplace and talked until past midnight. The atmosphere was exceedingly congenial and stimulating. Our Polish hosts were men of high intelligence, and their questions and comments were both to the point and sympathetic. Summarizing

---

*Jabotinsky highly valued Count Lubienski's friendship and cooperation. This highly cultured and sensitive scion of the highest Polish aristocracy met Jabotinsky in the Fall of 1936, and remained from then on a confirmed admirer of his personality, and a staunch supporter of his policy. This writer, whose privilege it was for nearly three years to maintain almost daily contact with Count Lubienski, is glad to be able to testify that Jabotinsky held him in high esteem and fully reciprocated his personal regard.

the discussion, Lubienski said : "We will give a report of this evening's discussion to our respective Ministers and endeavor to bring about constructive cooperation with the N.Z.O., whose ideas and plans deserve the most far-reaching support from the Polish Government."[26]

The impression Jabotinsky had made on those present was best formulated by Lubienski when, sixteen days later, Jabotinsky and this writer visited him in the Foreign Office : "When you and your friends left and we Poles remained alone, we just looked at each other and said that only our Pilsudski was capable of grasping problems so deeply, and of considering imponderables in so penetrating a way. Your manner of presenting issues is very similar to that of Pilsudski, who very often expressed ideas and made proposals that seemed crazy even to his closest friends and confirmed admirers; later, in two to three months or in two to three years, we all had to realize how right he was."

Two days after the above mentioned gathering (September 11), Jabotinsky was received by the Prime Minister of Poland, General Felician Slawoy-Skladkowski. Jabotinsky's presentation of the Zionist case as he saw it culminated in the request that the Polish Government intervene on the international scene in the interests of Jewish mass immigration into Palestine. Since Jewish public opinion was inclined to identify such a step with the anti-Semitic tendency to get rid of the Jews, the Government should publish a declaration to the effect that, while striving to help the upbuilding of a Jewish national homeland through Jewish immigration to Palestine, it was determined to safeguard Jewish rights in Poland. The Prime Minister unhesitatingly admitted that the road chosen by Jabotinsky appeared to him and to the Polish Government to be the right one. Well aware of the violent opposition this idea had met with in Jewish circles, he added that it was "also the hardest road to follow," so that "even those close to you have alienated themselves from you : the same happened to Pilsudski, as well as to your savior Moses." He stressed that the Polish Government wanted to help the Zionist cause not because they were eager to be relieved of their Jews, but because they regarded Zionism as a noble and humanitarian ideal. He, however, did not commit himself with regard to the publication of the declaration suggested by Jabotinsky.*

* Efforts to obtain such a declaration continued for many months. There was no objection in principle in Government circles, but a series of irrelevant, though powerful,

355

Eager to convey his views to the widest possible Polish circles, Jabotinsky accepted an invitation to address a meeting on November 4, arranged by the Government-sponsored Institute for the Study of Minority Problems, whose members were recruited from among the Polish intellectual élite. Introduced by the former Minister of Foreign Affairs, Leon Waszilowski, he spoke on "Palestine and Emigration Problem of East-European Jewry." [28] Introducing himself to the predominantly Gentile audience, Jabotinsky did not mince words in defining where he stood on the crucial question of the relationship between emigration and civic equality:

I belong to that old-fashioned school who still believe that in every civilized community there must be some respect of man for man, class for class, race for race. I am convinced that even in such hard times as the present, everywhere men and women can be found who are capable of a sincere and pure sympathy with our Jewish woe and our Zionist ideal. I am convinced that those men and women, in pronouncing the word "Zionism," honestly interpret it exactly as I do: a return to Zion of all those—and those only—who freely express such a wish in the future. I am furthermore convinced that such men and women do not and cannot entertain any thought of forcible expulsion, or of depriving any citizen of his rights. To such men and women, and to such only, will I speak; and I need not remind them that two and two make four, and that a State where there is no equality is doomed to ruin. All this is the ABC of the language I use; and I know no other language, nor wish to.

The address was delivered (from notes) in Polish, which the audience found delightful; in his answer to questions, Jabotinsky spoke Russian.

After two months of intensive political activity, Jabotinsky left for London on November 10. Two days before his departure, Count Lubienski arranged a farewell dinner attended by high officials of several Ministries. Jabotinsky's presentation of "humanitarian Zionism" as a problem of international concern, found far-reaching understanding and sympathy.

---

circumstances prevented its publication. Jabotinsky felt very strongly about his failure in this field. He also deplored the recurrent excursions of the Polish Government circles into vague "territorialist schemes," which intermittently affected Polish pro-Zionist policy.

He returned to Poland in October, 1937. As reported by the *Zionews* press agency, he "renewed contact with important political personalities and continued the discussion on political problems, initiated by him during his previous visit and maintained under the guidance of Dr. Schechtman.* He was received by the Polish Foreign Minister Colonel Beck, and later, accompanied by Dr. Schechtman and Dr. Kahn, dined with a number of leading Polish statesmen and heads of departments." [29] However, the problem of correlation between the Polish Government's pro-Zionist attitude and the mounting wave of Government-condoned anti-Jewish outbursts weighed heavily on his mind. Addressing the Eighth Revisionist National Conference in Warsaw on October 3, he made a point of stressing that, while he and his movement "welcome the cooperation of the Polish Government for the achievement of Zionist aims," they also insist that "this movement of Jews to reestablish their healthy national existence cannot in the smallest degree justify any restriction of their rights of a national minority." [30] This was not casual and banal lip service to the principle of national equality. Jabotinsky was sincerely disturbed by the alarming rise of aggressive Polish anti-Semitism which, as he put it in a letter to S. Jacobi, was enjoying "official connivance" and spreading "precisely in Government circles." [31]

Having been promised an audience with the admittedly most powerful man in Poland, Marshal Rydz Smygly, he "decided to emphasize at that opportunity, quite clearly and forcibly, that all the efforts of Minister Beck regarding emigration, etc., are in danger of being frustrated, and Poland's position in Geneva made worse than awkward, unless the wave of brutality is stopped and a clear line against anti-Semitism adopted." This was a decision not easy to take. Jabotinsky knew that Rydz Smygly was prepared for a conversation along quite different lines, dealing mainly with practical help to the *Irgun Zvai Leumi* (arms, training facilities, etc.) and ready for far-reaching cooperation in this field; he also realized that by introducing the issue

---

* In his posthumous "Last Report" on the "Polish Policies 1926-1939," Colonel Beck related that he had "attempted to reach a certain cooperation with the heads of various Jewish groups in Palestine, with the leaders of international movements like Mr. Weizmann and Mr. Schechtman." A footnote to this latter sentence explained: "Mr. Chaim Weizmann is now President of the State of Israel; Mr. Schechtman represented Mr. Jabotinsky, President of the Zionist-Revisionists." (Colonel Joseph Beck. *Dernier Rapport. Politique Polonaise 1926-1939. Histoire et Société d'Aujourd'hui.* Editions de la Baconnière, Neuchâtel (undated), p. 140).

of Polish anti-Semitism, he was sidetracking the issue of such cooperation. Yet his mind was made up to take this risk. And in fact, the
major part of the one-hour encounter with the Marshal was devoted
to a courteous but firm indictment of the Polish Government's passive
attitude towards anti-Semitic excesses in the country. Both Jabotinsky
and the writer, who accompanied him, were outspoken in denouncing
this state of affairs.* Rydz Smygly was partly evasive and partly
apologetic. His knowledge of political matters was obviously scant and
he did not make the impression of a man used to taking criticism. The
discussion was rather desultory and inconclusive; no practical matters
were dealt with. On our way back, Jabotinsky wondered whether the
line we had taken was the right one and whether, for the sake of telling
a few bitter truths, it had been worthwhile losing the opportunity of
securing tangible help for the *Irgun*. Polish Government circles who
learned about the content and character of the audience, were, however, very much impressed with Jabotinsky's straightforwardness:
Count Lubienski told this writer that never during his term of office
had the Marshal met with such firm though respectful criticism. He
believed that in the long run the encounter would not fail to have
a salutary influence.

During the last year prior to World War II, Jabotinsky's most
cherished plan was to convene an unprecedented representative and
impressive *Rettungsparlament far dos Misrach-Europäische Juden-
tum* in Warsaw, which he alternatively also called "Parliament of
Jewish Misery," or more often *Zion-Sejm* ("Sejm" is the Polish term
for the lower chamber of Parliament). As he formulated it in a draft-
memorandum to the Polish Government, the main purpose of the
Zion-Sejm was:

---

*It is surprising to find in A. Remba's otherwise accurate report a highly incorrect
account (pp. 214-217) of this encounter with Rydz Smygly. As can be seen from the
above quoted letter, Jabotinsky had decided to broach the issue of anti-Semitism at
least six days before the audience took place and not, as Remba asserts, at the last moment,
on the way to the Marshal's audience, prompted by the recollection of Herzl's visit to
von Plehve (1903). It is also incorrect that Jabotinsky was alone while speaking with
Rydz Smygly, who allegedly demanded a *tete-a-tete* conversation: this writer was with
Jabotinsky throughout the entire audience and actively participated in the discussion.
The conversation was not conducted in French: our attempt to speak French embarrassed the Marshal whoes knowledge of French was very poor; he understood German,
but did not speak it fluently; nor did he know Russian. Finally we settled on a bi-lingual
conversation: we spoke German, and he answered in Polish.

A. To endorse the Nordau Plan.
B. To proclaim the convening of a World-Jewish National Assembly.
C. To announce the formation of a World-Jewish *Comite de Salut Public*, the nucleus of which should be constituted on the spot.
D. To appoint delegations to the Mandatory Power, to various Governments, and in particular to the United States.

"The *sine qua non* of the whole enterprise," the memorandum insisted, was :

an open attitude of good will on the part of the Polish Government. The Jews have obviously lost faith in the effectiveness of manifestations however big, but unsupported by any real *Machtfaktor*. On the contrary, they know from many recent examples that mass manifestations are considered a powerful help by governments, resolved to insist on a certain policy.

Without official backing, a call to *Zion-Sejm* elections would hardly arouse all the necessary attention. Backed by clear knowledge that the *Zion-Sejm* is to be an essential factor in the concerted policy of influential Governments, it will sweep Jewish multitudes as no other Jewish election has ever done.

In order to be effective, Jabotinsky explained, this backing "must be expressed in open official statements." He was confident that, provided the above conditions be met, "the *Zion-Sejm* elections will bring to the ballot-box the biggest mass of voters ever recorded."

At the outset, Polish Government circles, sounded out by Jabotinsky and this writer, were inclined to favor the *Zion-Sejm* idea and to be ready to give the green light to proceed with it. But this cooperative attitude began to change in 1939. The reasons for this change of heart were manifold, and their enumeration does not belong within the scope of this biography. In June, 1939, Jabotinsky arrived in Warsaw and made an energetic attempt to restore the original positive attitude of the Polish authorities. At his request, a special "conference" was convened at the Foreign Office, attended by four heads of Departments mainly concerned with the *Zion-Sejm* plan. "The outcome was," Jabotinsky reported, "all sympathy, but this is not the time. The Government cannot authorize any *big* manifestations while the present political weather lasts (they have forbidden the Fifth Assembly of overseas Poles due to take place this August) : and the whole sense of a *Zion-Sejm* is that it must be a big manifestation—big propaganda before the elections, big crowds around the election booths, and a very big assembly in Warsaw with many foreign delegates. All this would now be impossible. They advised us to postpone the show until after the trouble, which (in case there is no war) might mean early next year. Obviously, we had to take the hint. . . . Arguing would lead us nowhere." [32] Nor was there much interest and understanding for the *Zion-Sejm* idea among Jews, including even his closest collaborators.

Jabotinsky honestly tried to analyze the deeper causes for the fall-off in the understanding of, and sympathy for it among both Gentiles and Jews. One of the underlying factors he saw in the "undeniable drop in active anti-Semitism in Poland, Rumania, and Baltikum," which was largely caused by the general preoccupation with the world war menace. He was certain that this lull would prove as shortlived as it was undeniable and, as the fear of war receded, a violent revival of Jew-baiting was on the way. But for the moment there was a breathing space, and the Jews "are perfectly satisfied with today's mild weather and cannot worry about anything as distant as tomorrow." This mentality also affected Polish Government circles.

They have suddenly discovered that the Jewish question is "secondary." If pressed in conversation, they admit that it remains "primary," and will spring back into prominence as soon as there is a *détente*, and that rebound is going to take unpleasant forms, and you are right in saying that substantial measures should be taken before that happens etc., etc.—but in the meantime Jews, Jewish needs and all that, remain in the background; which, of course, can only encourage Jewish apathy.

In this atmosphere, which Jabotinsky described as the "chloroformed or lethargic state of the public mind," hardly anybody was very unhappy about the postponement of the *Zion-Sejm* idea. "The only man who regrets the delay is the undersigned," he wrote in a personal letter from Vals-les-Bains. "I foresee, after the present lull due to war talk, a sharp revival of street anti-Semitism all through East-Central Europe, which will now feed especially on the obvious collapse of all evacuation schemes symbolized by MacDonald's White Paper. What I wanted was to prepare, an hour before the sleeping dogs awake, a Jewish manifestation unprecedented in its magnitude, demanding an outlet for a mass emigration : not to convince or convert the hooligans, but to give those semi-friendly Governments some argument with which they could counteract the barking. I am sorry the attempt has failed, and the initiative of reviving Great Zionism will have to come from the anti-Semitic camp." [33]

While concentrating the bulk of his political activities on Poland, Jabotinsky did not neglect other political factors on the European scene, in the first place the countries of the "danger zone."

In the summer of 1937, King Carol II of Rumania, a country with the second-largest Jewish community in Europe (750,000), visited London and, after some hesitation, agreed to receive Jabotinsky. The audience took place on July 25. According to Jabotinsky's own account,[34] he was pleasantly surprised by the King's awareness of the problems facing Jewry and Zionism. Carol sympathized with his views and with the dynamism of the Revisionist Movement, in which he saw a movement of national liberation. The King frankly admitted that Rumania, together with Poland and Hungary—three countries with a big Jewish population—were under increasing Nazi pressure to institute anti-Jewish measures; his Government had so far resisted this pressure, but its position was a difficult one, and a radical and realistic solution of the Jewish problem was both mandatory and urgent. Jabotinsky drew Carol's attention to the overall destructive strategy of Nazi Germany: while attacking Jews, the Hitler regime was in fact aiming at undermining the entire existing social and political pattern of life, and preparing the ground for Germany's world-wide domination; by yielding to the Nazi propaganda, European Governments were unwittingly playing Hitler's game. A planned Jewish voluntary evacuation of positions which have become untenable offered the only constructive solution; the Rumanian Government, while fully maintaining Jewish equality in the country, must use its influence to secure open doors for Jewish immigration into Palestine. Carol expressed understanding for the idea of "restoration of Jewish Statehood in the historic homeland of the Jewish nation." "I personally would be glad to be among those who are helping to implement this great humanitarian idea, and to rectify the age-old injustice done to Jewish people," he added; he also favored Jabotinsky's suggestion of common action by countries with a dense Jewish population, with the aim of increasing the scope of Jewish immigration to Palestine, and expressed readiness "to fight any [partition] scheme which threatens to curtail the area of possible Jewish expansion in Palestine." [35]

Following up the Rumanian link, Jabotinsky, during a visit to Bucharest in October, 1938, went to see the Foreign Minister, Petresco-Comnen, and the Polish Ambassador, Count Roger Raczynski. However, reporting to the London *Nessiut,* he frankly admitted : "Can't call it complete success. Raczynski hadn't received any instructions yet (though Warsaw had promised to wire) . . . I rang Schechtman to get Lubienski send instructions to Raczynski. . . . As to Comnen, it was a mistake to visit him in such a hurry, before assuring myself that he had been properly approached by the Polish and the American Ambassadors." [36]

During the N.Z.O. Convention in Prague (February, 1938), Jabotinsky was granted an audience by Eduard Benes, President of Czechoslovakia. Reporting on it to the London *Nessiut,* he wrote : "Excellent. Support of the idea of an International Conference [on Jewish emigration] assured emphatically; even the possibility of taking the initiative in this direction would not seem to be out of the question. He will himself study the Ten-Year Plan. He listened to my criticism of partition, nodded assent and said : 'But I am glad to see that it has been dropped.' " "I didn't suggest it, *he* volunteered," added Jabotinsky. Equally satisfactory was the visit to E. Kamil Krofta, the Foreign Minister : "He [Krofta] was extremely attentive and sympathetic, and actually promised to support the idea of an International Conference. . . ." [37]

In December, 1938, V. Munters, then Foreign Minister of Latvia, visited London. Jabotinsky used this opportunity to see him in order to ensure Latvia's support for the projected "Congress of Jewish Distress" [*Zion-Sejm*]. A. Abrahams, who accompanied him on this visit, later recalled that Munters received them very pleasantly, and it was obvious that he had a very high regard for Jabotinsky. Aptly describing Jabotinsky's subtle diplomatic "technique," Abrahams wrote : [38]

Indeed, it was Munters rather than Jabotinsky who had to be put at his ease. And this Jabotinsky proceeded to do by suddenly fixing his gaze on a beautifully designed carpet that covered the floor of the audience chamber. Jabotinsky easily recognized it as of native Latvian manufacture, a product of Latvian cottage industry. It was obvious that Munters was relieved not to be jostled immediately into the subject of Jewish distress, emigration, and Palestine. Jabotinsky discussed the fine color scheme of the carpet, the texture, then proceeded to talk of cottage industry in general. This brought him to the work of Jewish artisans in Eastern Europe, their poverty despite their skill, and their ability to contribute to the establishment of a happy and prosperous Jewish State, if but allowed to do so. Slowly and almost imperceptibly the conversation came round to the subject of the projected Congress. Then, with typical directness, Jabotinsky half turned in his chair and said: "How strange this bright carpet looks against the dark November atmosphere outside." The Latvian Foreign Minister agreed with a smile. Before we left the audience chamber, all the matters we had come to discuss had been gone into, without too much formality, without stiffness, and without embarrassment to either side. The two had become friends. It seemed only natural that the audience should end with Munters helping Jabotinsky on with his coat, and seeming happy to do so.

In a letter to this writer, Jabotinsky described the results of this visit as "fairly satisfactory." Munters did not see any difficulty in enabling the Jews of Latvia to participate in the elections to the "Congress of Jewish Distress." [39]

Between May 1 and May 29, 1939, Jabotinsky delivered twenty-one lectures in Poland, Latvia, Lithuania, and Finland, followed by a series of meetings in Rumania, Yugoslavia, and Bulgaria. It was his dramatic final tour of Eastern and South-Eastern Europe before the outbreak of World War II. During this tour, he was received by the President of Lithuania, Antanas Smetona. In a letter to the *Nessiut* he reported: "Spent one and one-half hours with President Smetona (mostly general subjects), and twenty minutes with General [Jonas] Cernius, Prime Minister, to whom I spoke of the *Zion Sejm* and who said: 'If Poland and Rumania don't object, we certainly shan't be in your way.' " * [40]

---

* In January, 1938, Jabotinsky was received in Dublin by Eamon De Valera, the President of the Free Irish State, with whom he discussed the Jewish question in relation to Zionism. He was introduced by Robert Briscoe, the only Jewish member of the Irish Parliament (later Mayor of Dublin), who said: "Mr. President, many times during these years I had the privilege of introducing to you Jewish visitors, but it is the first time that I introduce to you a Jewish leader who speaks also for me." The official audience lasted for about an hour, but De Valera was not satisfied and asked Jabotinsky to come and see him again later in the evening. [41]

THE FATEFUL YEAR 1939

NOTWITHSTANDING THE gathering clouds—or perhaps largely because of them—Jabotinsky was more than ever firm in his conviction that the Jewish State was "just around the corner." In September, 1938, he assured his sister that after but a few years of "storms and horrors, probably still in your and my lifetime, will emerge a crowded Jewish Palestine on both sides [of the Jordan]. Whether it will be a very comfortable place to live in is another question, but it will come into being, and neither the Arabs nor the British will be able to do anything about it." [1] In another letter (to I. Rosov), written in November, he said: [2] "In the final analysis, and very soon, pressure of events, both from without and from within, will compel England to accept our 'Nordau Plan.' and dump into Palestine about a million lads at once. But until then we shall yet have a lot to swallow." And in the spring of 1939, he predicted in the article "This Night of Passover" : [3]

. . . The greater the catastrophe, the shorter the strip of Diaspora road along which we still have to drag ourselves. Shall I confess—or perhaps I have already confessed before—that I shall not consider it miraculous if this same pair of spectacles that today helps me see the black news daily in the newspapers more clearly, will yet see the fact of redemption? Is this senility, the dreams of age? Or is it perhaps only a healthy instinct, that lives and vibrates in harmony with a period in which the distance between London and Johannesburg is two days, the distance between independence and "protectorate" twelve hours [a reference to the Czechoslovak territories of Bohemia and Moravia, which were occupied by German troops on March 15, 1939, and proclaimed a Protectorate of the Reich the following day], and distances in general have become no more than jumps.

In the meantime, however, the political horizon was growing mena-cingly darker. On May 17, 1939, the British Colonial Secretary, Malcolm MacDonald, issued a White Paper providing for the gradual establishment of self-Government in Palestine, leading to Arab inde-pendence, and for the restriction of Jewish immigration and land purchases to keep the Jews in a state of permanent minority.[4] This document provoked an outcry of angry despair in all Zionist circles. Jabotinsky did not share this reaction. He refused to dramatize the White Paper's importance unduly, and explained his attitude in several interesting personal letters.[5]

"I don't think," he wrote from Warsaw on June 5, "that our people have yet realized the main thing about it: namely, that as a piece of *concrete* policy it is a total washout. I mean 'washout' independently of the question whether it is likely to stay: even if it stays for years it is a washout." Irrespective of whether the British Government really meant to enforce MacDonald's White Paper, Jabotinsky argued, there was not much to enforce in the *letter* of this document since almost all of it was *Zukunftsmusik*. He, however, admitted that "a really willful enemy could embroider quite a lot of tangible harm on the *spirit* of the document." In a later letter from Vals-les-Bains, he called this enemy by name: "The Jew-hatred of all British officials. Sup-pressed and pent-up for twenty years, it has now been morally unmuzzled. News from Palestine points to a most acute prospect in this regard: Palestine seems to be destined to become, in the very near future, the country of active, systematic, and poisonous official anti-Semitism par excellence."

He insisted, however, that, fundamentally, not the Palestine *Yishuv*, but Diaspora Jewry was going to be the real target and victim of the White Paper. By proclaiming that, with the exception of seventy-five thousand Jews to be admitted within the next five years, Pales-tine was to be closed for ever to further Jewish immigration, this document practically "converted the whole Zionist Movement into a 'subversive' movement in relation to England. Every Jew who dreams of immigrating, or who wants to help others to immigrate, is aspiring, henceforth, to something that is fundamentally prohibited by the laws of the Mandatory Government. Even the Jewish sigh 'Next year in Jerusalem' becomes anti-British. In a number of coun-tries, Government authorities may start considering the support of Zionism as 'an unfriendly act toward Britain.' "

This new situation, as he saw it, was likely to have far-reaching consequences in regard to the status of the Jewish communities in many parts of the world. As long as even the worst anti-Semites imagined that Jews would after all one day become a people with a State, with a country of their own, Jewish prestige grew: "From now onwards, this is shattered." Moreover: "In a sense, the position of East European Jewry may be compared to a mass of potential emigrants living at the coast waiting for a boat, at least this is how they appear to our enemies. Hitherto some, the better, of these enemies, have been able to hold back their own hotheads with the argument: 'Do not persecute them—their ship will be coming one day after all.' Now Britain has declared that the ship will never come." [6]

2. *The Great Mistake*

By the early spring of 1939 Europe was full of forebodings. Politically alert public opinion was overwhelmingly inclined to expect an impending armed conflict of unprecedented magnitude. Both in personal letters and in public appearances, Jabotinsky unreservedly contradicted this *communis opinio*.

On March 31 he assured his sister: "There will be no war; the German insolence will soon subside; Italy will make friends with the British; and the Arabs, together with their Kings, will lose even the little bit of market value they were supposed to have possessed until now because of alleged Italian support. . . . And in five years we will have a Jewish State." [7] A week later, in another letter, this time to S. Salzman: [8] "My prediction: a war—no; every other form of swinishness—yes. And in five to seven years—a Jewish State in the whole of Palestine, *if* there are still any Jews. I think that there will be." [8] He did not hesitate to voice this conviction publicly. In a lecture in Warsaw (shortly after the publication of MacDonald's White Paper) he said: [9] "I don't believe in the possibility of a war. The war jitters will disappear in two to three months." As late as the last week of August, he wrote from the little French village Pont d'Avon where he was vacationing: [10] "There is not the remotest chance of war; and I don't say it out of *akshanut* [stubbornness], but because it is so. . . . The world looks a peaceful place from Pont d'Avon, and I think Pont d'Avon is right." To Mrs. L. Strassman, who visited him and

366

expressed apprehension as to whether, in case of war, she would be able to return to her family in Warsaw, he said firmly:[11] "There will be no war. . . . Nobody wants it. . . . *On va se revoir* in a few days in Paris and *on fera la bombe* [we will go on a spree]."

He proved to be tragically wrong. World War II started just a few days after these confident statements. And he suffered greatly because of this, his first major blunder. To a friend who visited him in Paris shortly after the outbreak of the war, he said:[12] "I never believed in the possibility of war, perhaps my idealistic concept, my faith in the nobility of the spirit, is no longer in keeping with the prevailing fashion, not with the Jews and not with the Gentiles. I believed— and I was mistaken. . . . Of course, my opponents, who have been always trying to dismiss my political predictions, will now use this error of mine as proof that 'Jabotinsky was again wrong because he was never able to reckon with reality!' . . . This damned reality! And one *has* to reckon with it!" he added with a bitter smile.

The feeling of having been so greatly wrong in a question of such gravity, weighed heavily on Jabotinsky's mind. Late in September, in a letter to a friend who had asked for his appraisal of the present situation and of the post-war prospects, he admitted:[13] "I am singularly handicapped in writing this sketch of the situation: since I have proved wrong in believing that a war between really first-class powers is impossible, I feel reluctant about saying anything at all. So please remember in reading this that every word I write is written in great doubt." And early in February, 1940, he wrote to Mrs. Strassman, who had escaped from Poland to Trieste:[14] "I can't help remembering my conversation with you, what a fool I was then!"

For a time he felt entitled to use the face-saving argument that although the war did break out, it was not actually a "real" war. For approximately eight months (from September 3, 1939, until May 10, 1940) a strange, unbroken quiet reigned along the entire Western Front. The Maginot Line of the French and the Siegfried Line of the Germans stood face to face without a single major engagement. Newspapers and statesmen the world over nicknamed this peculiar situation "phony war." Jabotinsky tried to utilize this queer state of affairs for an at least partial self-justification. "I still don't believe in a genuine war," he wrote to Z. Lerner (Nahor); "this idyll between the Siegfried and Maginot Lines simply does not make sense."[15] And with this writer he argued:[16] "Plans we have many; the trouble is, however, that we, all of us, have been used to thinking in antediluvian categories, for instance—'war' and 'peace': in case of peace—Plan Number One; in case of war—Plan Number Two. But for a situation that is 'neither peace nor war' we have prepared no plan; and God Himself has apparently lost His wits." But in May, 1940, the "phony war" came to an end. Within a few weeks, the German armies overran the Netherlands, Belgium, and France. The whole of Continental Western Europe was in German hands. "Jabo is very downhearted," reported Colonel Patterson.[17] The late William B. Ziff, who saw much of Jabotinsky at that sad time, told this writer that "Jabo took it awfully hard and saw the immediate prospects of the gigantic struggle between Nazism and the Western democracies in a most gloomy light." [18]

2. The War Comes

Germany invaded Poland on the first of September. World War II was on. From Vals-les-Bains, where he had been vacationing, Jabotinsky rushed to Paris, where he stayed for two days. On September 3, he arrived in London

To a friend who visited him in Paris, he said:[19] "If you were to ask now what exactly my plans are, I could give you no articulate answer, for—in all frankness—I still don't know myself. But one thing seems clear to me: we shall have to consider, in all earnestness, the historic opportunities offered to us; how to use them constructively. . . . There is no doubt in my mind that the center of our national political activities has shifted to America. I shall now go to London, settle the most pressing matters there, and leave immediately for America. There is nothing to do in England. I do not belong to those optimists who believe that, under the pressure of war, Britain will change her anti-Zionist pro-Arab policy."

The projected mission to America did not materialize until March, 1940. Jabotinsky was held up in London for more than six months. These months were largely filled with unceasing efforts to put the Jewish problem "on the map," for Palestine and Zionism were being deliberately and systematically ignored by the Allied Governments. Anxious to demonstrate that the war they were waging against Hitler Germany was not a "Jewish war," those Governments studiously avoided any mention of its Jewish aspect. Jewry's plight had, as Jabotinsky put it, "no place at all among anybody's war aims, except Hitler's";[20] it became unmentionable. Repeated declarations of sympathy with the fate of suffering Jews did not go hand in hand with any provision of avenue for actual Jewish participation in a common war effort.

This attitude was largely conditioned by the disintegration of European Jewry and the enforced passivity of the Palestine *Yishuv*. In several letters written in September to October, 1939, Jabotinsky gave a penetrating analysis of the Jewish position and prospects at that early stage of World War II :[21]

The main feature of the new situation seems to be this: East European Jewry which was the mainstay of all Zionism, and particularly of *our* school of Zionism, has been smashed. Probably a third is to be swallowed by Russia, which probably means paralysis so far as the national movement is concerned. What will happen to the remainder is impossible to foretell, but it is safe to assume that as an *active* factor in Zionist policies they will hardly amount to much. . . .

Anglo-Jewry or French Jewry, even if the existence of anything answering those two descriptions could be proved, cannot be of any help in this respect: their whole *Einstellung* [attitude] is that of part and parcel of their respective master nations, their policy (if any) a function of Anglo-French policy without any additions: a sort of unpaid appendix, with nothing to sell and therefore unable to press for any extension of the Allies' war aim. The Palestine *Yishuv* is very much in the same position of impotence, though for other reasons. Palestine is not a front in this war, and it seems at least uncertain if she be likely to become one; and as long as that remains so, the *Yishuv* for the main part will be afraid of raising any questions about the future which might revive the quarrel with the Arabs and sadden the hearts of the Mandatory administration. . . . Should Palestine get nearer to the danger zone, a mixed militia will probably be raised composed of Jewish and Arab units—i.e. confirming the *status quo* muddle. The *Yishuv* might be a great factor in Zionism if its composition were not what it is; as it is, I fear, it is also not on the map.

In the long run, it was East European Jewry that was bound to become "an exceedingly powerful factor compelling the world to find room for an Exodus of unprecedented magnitude : whatever the shape and the constitution of Poland after this war, its paramount social problem will in all probability be evacuation of Jews; with analogous *Stimmungen* in all the neighboring countries. The only

369

people who doubt it are those who fear (or hope) that all this part of Europe will go Bolshie. . . . Whatever be the form under which the world will get about settling its unsettled problems after this crisis is over, and no matter *when* that moment occurs, this business of Jewish mass evacuation 'at once' will overshadow nearly everything else." [22]

Yet, these long-term prospects, however dramatic and powerful, did not offer any immediate means to overcome the dismal state of being "not on the map," an "evil which must be remedied at all imaginable costs." [23] He saw the most potent instrument for breaking the conspiracy of silence, and making the Jewish world problem topical, in the creation of a Jewish Army.

While still in Paris, Jabotinsky wrote to Anatole de Monzie, French Minister for Public Works, that his main project was to "recruit a large contingent for a 'Jewish Army.' " Already then he made a point of stressing that "this time, the purpose will be not the creation of a [Jewish] Legion destined for the Palestine front only, but rather of a task force ready to fight wherever necessary. . . . The rallying slogan shall be: 'All fronts on which our allies are fighting.' " [24] Elaborating later on the motives of this shift from "Legion" to "Army," he explained: [25] "Unless Italy joins the Germans, the Arabs are unlikely to change their good behaviour to bad, which means that the Levant may remain out of trouble and consequently out of the world's attention. This would bury all speculations connected with the Jewish Legion plans *à la 1917,* though not necessarily other similar plans not bound up with this particular theater. . . . I do not know whether the Allies will eventually agree to forming the Jewish units, but even if they do, it will be of no political significance. The situation has tremendously changed since 1917, when the formation of a Judean Regiment was such a revolutionary symbol: today a step of this kind will be unable to put us on the map."

The first thing he did after his return to London was to enlist the cooperation of the man who had commanded the Legion. "Within an hour of England's declaration of war on Germany on September 3, 1939," recalled Colonel Patterson, "I was rung up on the phone, and, answering the call, heard Jabotinsky's excited voice eagerly urging that we should once again cooperate as we had done almost a quarter of a century previously, and throw ourselves heart and soul into the creation, not of a Legion this time, but of a fully mechanized

Jewish Army, to fight side by side with the Allied forces. I willingly agreed to do everything in my power to help, and together we set the ball rolling." [26]

Jabotinsky realized that no human material for a Jewish Army was to be found in Europe. East European Jewry was no longer accessible and there was little to expect from "the Ghettoes of Mayfair and the Faubourg St. Honoré." This left as the only hope the Jews of the United States: [27] "*If* (I underline the 'if' as heavily as I can) there is a force that still can place the Jewish problem in the forefront and compel the Allies to treat us at least as they do Danish bacon (they pay for it!), that force can only come from within American Jewry." In an Aide-Memoire dated September 10, Jabotinsky accordingly outlined a plan for forming in the United States "an association of men of military age under the name of 'Jewish Army' which will enter into negotiations with the American Government on the one hand, with the Allied Governments on the other, for obtaining permission and help to join the Allied armies." The Jewish armed forces were to have no separate supreme command and fight on *all* fronts. The only condition was—"that the Jews are to be represented at the Peace Conference." The Aide-Memoire stressed that while from the point of view of legality, recruiting volunteers in neutral America for any of the existing belligerent armies was likely to be stopped as unlawful, the formation of a body describing itself as "Jewish Army" and proposing to negotiate with the Government for authority to join in the struggle, was in itself perfectly legal.

To work for the formation of a Jewish Army was the primary object of the Jabotinsky-led N.Z.O. delegation which was to proceed to the United States. The second object, which he particularly stressed in his approaches to the Allied Governments as organically connected with the first, was, as he put it in the Aide-Memoire, "to organize in suitable form, compatible with the law of neutrality, a campaign for America's intervention [on the side of the Allies]. . . . While direct interventionist propaganda may be very unpopular at first, so that newspapers may shrink from supporting it openly—the same argumentation under the cover of a 'Jewish Army' campaign will go down much easier, reaching at the same time wide circles outside of the Jewish community." There was, at this early stage of the war, hardly any body of men ready to undertake the ungrateful task of conducting an interventionist campaign in America: "That's why," Jabotinsky

371

frankly explained to de Monzie, "we had decided to risk this venture, which is unpleasant but necessary." [28]

The first six months of the war spent in London were overwhelmingly devoted to persistent attempts at punching even a tiny pinhole in the armor of aloofness with which the British Government had surrounded Jewish and Zionist affairs. In early spring of 1940, he prepared a ten-page "Memorandum on the Formation of a Jewish Army," which was submitted to the British Government by the *Nessiut* of the New Zionist Organization. The Memorandum—a masterpiece of closely knit, lucid, and sober presentation—defined world Jewry as "a natural associate" of the Allied Powers in this war. Referring to the functioning of Polish and Czech national armies or legions, Jabotinsky insisted that the Jewish Diaspora is in a more powerful position as an ally than the "States in Exile." The absence of a distinct and discernible Jewish share in the Allied military struggle was producing ominous effects in the countries fighting against Nazi Germany; this was also a feature inexplicable to neutral countries and an effective obstacle to the success of Allied propaganda in those countries. The establishment of a Jewish Army would produce in the United States a fuller faith in the moral value of the Allied cause. The Memorandum stated:

> We are aware that one of the chief arguments advanced against the proposal for the establishment of a Jewish Army is the fact that there exists, for the present, no urgent need of manpower. The restricted front, the limited fighting area, and the absence of more than a single avenue of approach to the enemy have created a state of mind which is prone to regard additional sources of manpower as of secondary importance. This, combined with the state of comparatively inactive war on land, has, without doubt, had a decisive effect on what appears to be the official attitude to offers of military cooperation from new quarters. . . . However, with possible emergence of new fighting fronts, the question of manpower must become one of progressive urgency, and every new source of manpower will necessarily be judged in the light of those conditions.

Jabotinsky drew up the Memorandum in March, 1940, when there was still one single fighting front. When it was submitted in April, the war had already extended to Scandinavia, and there were indications that other areas might be involved. "In the circumstances," added a *Nota Bene* to the main text, "all that has been said above applies with increased force."

The British Government was, however, impervious to arguments. In the spring of 1940, the shroud thrown over all Jewish and Zionist matters was as heavy as it had been in the fall of 1939. London was an unpromising and depressing place for Jabotinsky's dynamic efforts. Yet, he doggedly continued looking for ways to reactivate the movement's political effort.

Early in December, 1939, he put to this writer "a purely theoretical question" as to whether it would be worth its while to renew the latter's former connections with the Polish Government-in-Exile, which then had its seat at Angers in Western France: "Do you have acquaintances in the new setup? Would you personally be interested in any such an assignment?" [29]

Jabotinsky was well aware of the fact that many in his movement were unhappy about the unusually long absence of directives from him and the seeming inactivity of the leadership or, as he himself put it in a letter to a friend, had "the impression that we here [in London) have lost the compass and are not even dreaming of anything." This "impression" he categorically denied: "We do have quite definite outlines and, I think, interesting ones. But," he insisted, "we will announce them to the public at the proper moment; until that time we will keep silent and write articles about the weather. . . . Don't be afraid that we shall miss the bus. Should the Germans collapse tomorrow, the war will end without having started. But if the Germans do not collapse, the war will expand and become protracted, and on the global Allied area a place for us will gradually begin to shape as well. In this perspective, there is still much time ahead. We will not be too late. . . . I am looking ahead very cheerfully. The only thing that makes me sad is that our friends are bored, and losing courage. . . . I still hope to be able to cheer them up very soon." [30]

The last eight weeks he spent in London, waiting to leave for the States, were used largely for preparing his last *opus magnum—The Jewish War Front.* In its 255 pages, the book gave a bold and lucid analysis of the Jewish situation in Europe. It also offered a clear-cut blueprint for Jewish action during the war (world Jewry must take an active part in the struggle against Nazism through a Jewish Army) and after it (implementation of the Max Nordau Plan).

Though not prone to overestimate the intrinsic value of his own writings, Jabotinsky was convinced that "most of its [the book's] chapters would be of a durable value no matter who wins [the war]."

373

It appeared in June, 1940, much later than scheduled, and its price was more than double that originally intended: "This book certainly has the worst kind of luck any political book ever had," Jabotinsky complained in a letter written in New York on July 9, 1940. He was at that time working on a plan for rewriting it completely. He wanted to include in the new version "all those chapters whose contents are of durable interest," and, in addition, "to deal with many questions which interest any intelligent reader just now, for instance: Is it really true that democracy can never be efficient? Is it really true that the West has quarrelled with Germany for ever and ever and there is to be no *Versöhnung* (between 'Aryan' peoples)? In addition, I shall be able to give American Jews a piece of my mind." [31]

Jabotinsky believed that he could prepare such a new version "between now (July 9) and the middle of August . . . if free from all my everyday work"; "this," he added, "would mean a honorarium which I could not put below fifty dollars a week [a particularly meagre fee, indicative of his poor standard of living in New York], or two hundred and fifty dollars for the whole." The Alliance Book Corporation, to which the offer was made, was apparently in no hurry to reply; and on August 3, Jabotinsky was no more. The book was republished in New York in 1943 by the Jabotinsky Foundation under the title *The War And The Jew*. Even his political opponents were forced to admit that "the 'heretical' ideas which once earned for Jabotinsky only scorn and epithets, are today no longer heresy." [32]

3. *Unity Attempts*

The American journey which had been planned immediately after the outbreak of the war, and to which Jabotinsky attributed major importance, took months to materialize. Of the many obstacles— political, financial, and personal—one was particularly painful.

In a letter to Eri he explained: [33] "My absence from Europe may last a whole year. Obviously, I don't want to be away from mother for so long a time. I do not intend to tire her with innumerable little trips; but she can see both Americas without getting tired." However, the American Consulate in London refused to grant to Mrs. Jabotinsky a visitor's visa and let her accompany her husband on his trip to the States. Asking the Consul General to reconsider this ruling,

Jabotinsky gave his word that—"if alive—we shall, both of us, leave the States on or before the visa expires."

My reason for insisting is, frankly, my fear to leave a woman of fifty-five in delicate health all alone. My duties will take me, from the U.S.A., to the Argentine in May, and from there probably to South Africa in the fall, so that it looks rather like a year's trip at least. I really need not explain why I cannot leave her behind, at our age and in times like these.

The American Consul General refused to exercise his right of discretion in favor of granting this request. Jabotinsky had to leave London without his wife.

Shortly before his departure, he invited two members of the Jewish Agency Executive, Professor Zelig Brodetzky and Berl Locker, for dinner. In an after-dinner conversation on the prospects of restoring Zionist unity, he said that since the Old Z.O. represented 600,000 shekel payers and the N.Z.O.—713,000 voters to its Foundation Congress, such unity could be established on the basis of a fifty-fifty representation in the ruling bodies of the Zionist Movement. But he frankly admitted that the major motivation for this demand was not of an "arithmetical" nature: "I wouldn't demand parity if I had considered the Old Z.O. leadership to be still Zionists. But in my view you are no longer Zionists, and if I were to join as a minority an Executive dominated by your people, they would not only reject every proposal of mine, but would also continue their policy of Zionist self-liquidation—so that I would have once again to resign with a bang. This I am not prepared to do. That's why I need the minimum guarantee of parity." [34]

The conversation, as many others before, did not lead to any agreement. Its meaning and significance can be correctly understood and apprised only in the light of a long series of previous attempts to restore the unity of the Zionist movement.

Such attempts started very soon after the emergence of the independent New Zionist Organization. The intricate story of those attempts is still awaiting a chronicler, let alone historian, and does not belong within the scope of this biography. Yet many of them have been directly connected with Jabotinsky personally, and have to be dealt with at least summarily.

On May 28, 1936, Weizmann and Jabotinsky met in London in order, as the latter put it in a letter written the next day, "to ascertain whether a united front would prove feasible or workable"; it was agreed that the contact would be resumed in the second week of June, when they both returned from the Continent, and when David Ben Gurion was expected from Israel. Weizmann was supposed to invite Jabotinsky to a three-cornered discussion. However, while Ben Gurion did arrive in June, no such invitation was extended. The N.Z.O. Office wrote to Weizmann, reminding him of his undertaking, but no answer was received and no meeting arranged. At a session of the Zionist Actions Committee in Jerusalem (April, 1937), Ben Gurion reported that " actually Mr. Jabotinsky met Weizmann and, after a conversation, submitted in writing a proposal for the recognition of the N.Z.O. for the purpose of convening a Jewish Congress, thus abolishing the Zionist Organization. This absurd proposal terminated the negotiations." [35]

This presentation of Jabotinsky's letter to Weizmann is highly inaccurate. The available full text of this message (dated May 29, 1936) does not contain any proposal for "abolishing the Zionist Organization." Recapitulating the suggestions made the previous day during his conversation with Weizmann, Jabotinsky proposed the following agenda for unity:

1. A joint manifesto affirming the unity of Zionist views and Zionist action throughout world Jewry.

2. A provisional joint organ for concerted action pending the convocation of the National Assembly to be elected by universal suffrage without either fee or ideological declarations. The Assembly was to elect the entire Jewish Agency, examine and approve a "Ten-Year Plan," and launch a Jewish National Loan.

These suggestions could have been accepted or rejected, but their content hardly warranted to be called "absurd," to be left unanswered, and to be used as a reason for breaking off, in such a cavalier way, a discussion already initiated. M. Haskel, who was then eager to bring about cooperation between Jabotinsky and Weizmann, later recalled: [36] "I saw Weizmann in London and discussed the situation with him, appealing to him to consider an understanding with Mr. Jabotinsky. I assured him that Jabotinsky, with whom I had discussed the matter, would be willing to consider terms for an understanding. . . . I pleaded with him for nearly two hours to tell me what his terms for an understanding were, and I reiterated that Mr. Jabotinsky would accept reasonable terms. Weizmann's reply was very brief: 'I have no terms.' "

The problem of the relationship between the two Zionist organizations was left in abeyance. The subject was reopened with renewed vigor in the summer of 1937, when the attitude to the Royal Commission's partition plan became of major political importance. Aware that the leadership of the Old Zionist Organization was predominantly in favor of the scheme, Jabotinsky made an attempt to enlist the cooperation of the non-Zionist, extreme orthodox *Agudat Israel* for a joint demarche for the creation of an all-embracing Jewish national authority, competent to express adequately the will of the Jewish people. Proposed negotiations to this effect between the Jewish Agency, the N.Z.O., and the *Agudat Israel,* which were to take the form of a Round Table Conference, did not come about because the Agency did not agree to the appointment of a neutral chairman.[37] On July 22, 1937, Jabotinsky, as President of the New Zionist Organization, and J. Rosenheim, as President of the *Agudat Israel,* jointly addressed a letter to the President of the Jewish Agency stating that "apprehension is growing throughout the Jewish world that the proposals of the Royal Commission threaten to destroy the very sense and soul of the Jewish homeland movement": [38]

Whilst fully aware of the substantial differences of outlook between the undersigned organizations, we consider it nevertheless our common duty to put before the Zionist Organizations, the Jewish Agency, and the Jewish and non-Jewish world at large, our demand that the Jewish attitude regarding the future of Palestine be submitted to the decision of a special gathering, representative of all pro-Palestine world Jewry, regardless of their affiliations.

As a first step in this direction, we suggest that a Round Table Conference of our three Organizations be convened without delay, under a neutral chairman, in order that we may jointly decide on the ways and means of putting into effect the idea outlined in the preceding paragraph.

This appeal failed. The interest of the *Agudat Israel* in a united pro-Palestine front proved to be skin-deep, and shortlived. The issue remained, as before, between the two Zionist Organizations. Many well-meaning Zionists offered their services to bring about a reunification. One of them was a wealthy General Zionist of Warsaw, engineer Ryckwert—a good acquaintance and great admirer of Jabotinsky, who, when leaving for London, insistently enjoined this writer to "cultivate the contact with my friend Ryckwert." Being very keen on the matter of unity, the latter insisted on arranging a meeting in his house with one of the most influential younger leaders of Polish Zionism, Moshe Kleinbaum (later, under the name of "Sneh," he became one of the Communist leaders in Israel). The discussion centered on the basic Jabotinsky demand for abolition of the paid shekel, and for free franchise to the Zionist Congress. Dr. Kleinbaum stated that he was in agreement with this principle; he believed that it would be possible to have it accepted by the Zionist Actions Committee, if not *in toto*, then at least by way of reducing the price of the shekel to a token amount of ten *Groszen*. Then, he said, there would be no obstacle to the Revisionist participation in the then envisaged "extraordinary" Zionist Congress; such participation would imply the acceptance of the decisions of this Congress, elected on the N.Z.O. basis of free franchise. Should an understanding be achieved as to Revisionist participation in the Congress, a certain working agreement must be reached immediately regarding their actual cooperation in Zionist political affairs, which must be conducted "not by Weizmann alone but by Weizmann and Jabotinsky." Even before the Congress, at Ryckwert's insistence, both Kleinbaum and this writer undertook to contact their respective ruling bodies with a view of ascertaining their attitude toward the trend of their discussion.

In reply to a detailed report on "the Kleinbaum story," Jabotinsky wrote on December 5 : [39]

The truth about our participation in an extraordinary Congress of the Zionist Organization is, in my opinion, as follows: If such a Congress should take place, it would mean that history itself imposes exceptionally important decisions on this Congress, and there is no time to reform its electoral system. We would probably then have to participate in it, even if the Actions Committee does not lower the price of the shekel even by one single penny. If there is a hope to kill partition—we would have to go [to the Congress] in order to kill it; if it should so happen that England is firmly determined to override everybody and partition is inevitable—we would have to go [to the Congress] to fight for a place under the sun.

I would, therefore, in negotiations or conversations on this subject, not be very *insistent* on the demand that the Actions Committee immediately implement this reform. I underline "insistent": it does not pay to knock your head against the wall; but it is, of course, necessary to present this demand in order to get from the Actions Committee at least the recognition, in principle, of the idea of *kol-dichfin* [free franchise].

The question of discipline, as Kleinbaum rightly says, resolves itself automatically: *in so far* as the Congress of the Zionist Organization comes closer to the idea of a National Assembly, *to that extent* is the possibility of conducting any [political] negotiations over its head eliminated. . . .

All this, in my opinion, will prove to be theoretical, in the sense that I don't see any extraordinary Congress in the offing, and probably no one is prepared to worry now about what might happen at their ordinary Congress in 1939. . . . I consider it important, however, under any conditions, to spin the thread of those negotiations; *ergo*—go ahead.

Spurred on by this encouragement, this writer "went ahead"—and went apparently too far. On December 20, a "protocol" was signed by him, Kleinbaum, and Ryckwert, in which the first two undertook to work in their respective organizations for Revisionist participation in the Twenty-first Zionist Congress on the basis of a reduced shekel and proper representation in all ruling bodies of the Zionist Movement. When he learned of the contents of this document, Jabotinsky was very upset; following his lead, the N.Z.O. *Nessiut* disavowed and censured this writer, who, however, contended that he had acted in full accordance with Jabotinsky's instructions.

This disagreement was largely instrumental in sharpening the latent differences within the Jabotinsky Movement in regard to its relations with the Zionist Organization. On January 15, 1938, Dr. B. Akzin, Dr. Harry Levi, and this writer visited Jabotinsky in Paris, and for three and a half hours discussed the prospects of some compromise solution. He was more adamant than ever—perhaps deliberately exaggerating his inflexible attitude in order to impress upon us the utter hopelessness of our appeal. I recorded some of his statements immediately after we left him: "I shall never submit to any outside authority. I shall go along with you only when I head a unified World Zionist Organization with an Executive made up in such a way that even should I and four other Revisionist members depart for America, we would still hold a majority. I shall agree to no other kind of coalition." Asked what his position would be if in a genuine National Assembly, elected by unpaid universal suffrage, we would still remain a minority, he answered: "I would step aside. The Revisionist Party may submit, but I personally will never do so. It is my inalienable right to go home."

It was in this frame of mind that he opened the Prague Convention of the New Zionist Organization on January 31, which was attended by one hundred thirty delegates. At the beginning, he was confident that "the Convention's mood is all right" and reported that there were "not more than two or three partisans of a returning to the Old Z.O.—and even those are not very firm." [40] He was no less cheerful the following day: [41] "So far—really wonderful"; the first stages of the general debate also seemed highly satisfactory to him. But a post-scriptum to the same letter already sounded a different note: "After I wrote this letter, the atmosphere changed for the worse. The monkey wrench was the question of relations with the Z.O. I am surprised to see that there are about fifteen people or more who applaud speeches that aim to prove that the N.Z.O. is a failure. . . . There is a feeling that the wonderful *aliyat-ha-ruah* [the uplifted spirit] of Tuesday night has been lowered. . . . Never mind, it will all be healed after we disperse," he optimistically concluded.

In the summer of 1938, Rabbi Ze'ev Gold, one of the leaders of World *Mizrahi,* suggested a united front of his party, the Group B. of the General Zionists, and the Revisionists (N.Z.O.), which would make a concerted effort to "capture" the forthcoming Twenty-first Zionist Congress when the partition scheme would be submitted for approval. Jabotinsky was rather sceptical as to the chances that such a scheme would materialize. He was, however, ready "to discuss all its aspects at a serious conference if officially approached": [42] But he insisted on a cautious prior investigation of the identity and strength of the prospective allies, of the common program ("anti-partition only is obviously not enough"), and above all of the crucial question: "What would be their attitude in case our joint enterprise fails?" Jabotinsky admitted that should the results of all these queries be satisfactory, he might be strongly tempted to give it a good try, although he still doubted whether such an earnest preliminary conference would ever be held. And, in fact, it never came about.

While always ready—though not eager—to explore every possibility of restoring Zionist unity through a suitable combination of forces, Jabotinsky was adamant in refusing even to consider any suggestion of simply returning to the Zionist Organization. In August, 1938, B. Akzin wrote to him about "the contingency of our [Revisionist] deciding to go to the next Congress, and there to merge once more with the Old Z.O." The answer was that such a contingency "is absolutely and hermetically *ausgeschlossen* as long as I have any say in the Revisionist Movement."[43] He was, however, aware that there continued to exist in the movement tendencies which he branded as defeatist. The session of the Revisionist World *Parteirat* [Party Council], held in Warsaw late in 1938, was in this respect most unsatisfactory to him. He sadly described "the curious spirit and undertone" of this session : "Something has suddenly gone out of the *Hazohar*. I call it the *Hazohar* pride. All round defeatism." He consoled himself with the observation that "there was no trace of it at the *Kinnus* [rally] of the *Betar*," which was held simultaneously.[44]

Jabotinsky was in a restive mood before and during the *Parteirat*. When one of his younger collaborators, Yehuda Benari, showed him a voluminous file of drafts of the party statutes, and of resolutions to be submitted to the session, he roundly declined even to consider them; "Please, burn all that stuff ! I have enough of all such pre-cooked ingredients. Let the movement itself spell out what they really want. The only thing I hear from them is eternal grumbling." When told that without some plan prepared in advance by the leadership no conference can be productive, he refused to listen : "No, I will just get up, declare the session open and—*basta*. And perhaps I will simply resign, settle somewhere near London, and write novels. It's about time the movement stood on its own legs. The boys are old enough to do so." When, in the general debate, several speakers criticized certain features of his program and activities, he reacted with unusual impatience, advising all those who had no faith in his policy to "commit suicide" : interrupting Menachem Begin, Yeremiahu Halperin, Y. Benari, and M. Szeskin, he suggested in what specific manner each of them should perform this act. During the interval in the debate, all "beneficiaries" of this advice decided to form a "Suicide Club" with an eighteen-point constitution, insignia, and motto of its own, and submitted it all to Jabotinsky "for ratification." After reading it with mock seriousness, he asked for a red pencil and wrote in the margin : "So be it. Vladimir the First." Later he told Jacobi that this episode somehow changed his entire mood. Around two A.M. he met Benari in the corridor and whispered : "There will be no resignation, you ass. . . ."[45]

After the final abandonment of the partition scheme, Arab and Zionist representatives were invited to London to confer with the British Government on some schemes of an agreed settlement of the

Palestine problem. The conference (in which the N.Z.O. did not participate) lasted from February 7 to March 17, 1939—and brought no results. During this period, the demand grew insistent for effective unity in the *Yishuv* and in Zionism. Telegrams and resolutions poured in on the members of the *Vaad Leumi* present in London, urging them, and in particular Pinchas Rutenberg, to exert their influence in this direction. Rutenberg contacted Jabotinsky, and two informal conversations of inconclusive nature took place.

As usual, Jabotinsky was rather sceptical as to the seriousness and value of this kind of contact. On March 2, he apprised this writer: "Should you hear rumors to the effect that here in London 'negotiations are being conducted' between us and the Old Zionist Organization, don't believe them. There is nothing, except some private attempts at . . . [an unprintable Russian expression], and even these are half-hearted. Nobody is interested in all this; and as for myself, *vous savez*. . . . " Nevertheless, he made an attempt to bring the vague private approaches to a head. In a letter to Rutenberg he stressed that "the extreme gravity of the present crisis really demands a united front." Reiterating the conditions likely to form a basis for cooperation, he added that "should other proposals be submitted, we would be prepared to give them close consideration." In his view, there was a "quite sufficient basis for actually starting formal negotiations, provided there really is a mutual desire to treat the matter as urgent." Should the *Vaad Leumi* representatives desire to discuss—independently of the Jewish Agency—"some specifically Palestine aspects," he was also ready to meet them "provided that what is intended is not another private talk but a meeting of a fully official character." [46] For a time, this direct approach remained unanswered, and on March 9 Jabotinsky wrote to Haskel: "There are no negotiations between us and the Agency, nor between us here and the *Vaad Leumi* delegation. Please discredit all rumors to the contrary. It is true that the *Vaad Leumi* cabled its delegates to get in touch with us and that Rutenberg has taken great pains to promote negotiations; but *nothing* has come of all their efforts, and we have not even been approached by any of these bodies. Nor do I expect them to do so, even when their bankruptcy is final: for it would mean suicide, and that *svolotch* [Russian word meaning "rascals" or "rabble"] is not patriotic enough to commit *harakiri*." Three days later, an abortive meeting with Palestinians took place, and matters of Palestinian interest (coordination and security) were discussed. But no decision was reached.

No earnest attempt to break the deadlock was made during the first six months of the war. The inconclusive talk with Brodetzky and Locker was Jabotinsky's farewell gesture on the European Continent.

TWENTY

THE LAST BATTLE FOR AMERICA

1. *Conquering the Press*

JABOTINSKY arrived in New York on March 13, on the *S.S. Samaria*. His visit was sponsored by a representative "Jabotinsky Lecture Committee," among whose members were Congressman Emanuel Celler, Commander of the Jewish War Veterans J. Matbees, Horace Kallen, Rabbi Louis I. Newman, Mrs. Jacob De Haas, Mrs. John Gunther, Pincus Churgin, and Irving Bunim. Accepting the Committee's invitation to come to the United States, Jabotinsky wrote: "It is not with any political purpose in mind that I come to the United States. Your President [Franklin D. Roosevelt] has pointed the way for us Jews. If a large section of American official and public opinion believes that a haven should be found for refugees, then it is our duty to throw the doors of our Jewish National Homeland wide open to the persecuted of our own race, even though we may need force of arms to open our own frontiers."

The purpose of his visit was to enlist the sympathy and support of American public opinion for the ideas he was fighting for. The attitude of the press was obviously of paramount importance. This attitude largely depended on the impression he would make on newspapermen assigned to cover his arrival. Jabotinsky's first encounter with the representatives of the New York press is vividly described by Arthur M. Brandel, who was his public relations adviser during his stay in America.[1] When the liner was entering the New York harbor, a cutter went down the bay to meet her.

On board were a group of newspapermen, men whose lives are spent in seeking out people of interest aboard ships coming into the harbor, and interviewing them on any and all topics. Rough, tough, and nasty they are. Interested in a good story, and leading rather a monotonous life since most of the important people are stuffed shirts who act very condescending to the "ink-stained wretches," with whom they must speak. . . .

They met Jabotinsky and they were completely charmed. There was a man who asked them for information. Here was a man who spoke frankly and unhesitatingly about the subject that was nearest his heart. Jabotinsky took them into his confidence. Without evading any issues he told them why he was arriving in America. He told them why he was fighting for a Jewish State and they liked it, and they believed in him.

This writer spoke with several of the reporters later. All agreed that here was a Man. They compared him with every great leader in the world. He met with their approval.

Jabotinsky had several special interviews with feature writers of different papers. "Every one of those men," Brandel testifies, "were to become his ardent followers, and cause stirs in the city rooms of their newspapers by expounding the beliefs they had encountered." One of them, Ernest L. Meyer of the New York *Post* (a non-Jew), wrote:[2] "I was deeply impressed by his intelligence, his vigor, his unrhetorical eloquence, and by his unremitting battle on behalf of his group." Asked what his opinion of Jabotinsky was, one reporter said to him: "Mr. Jabotinsky was good news copy; he made a good story. But most of all he assumed that the reporters who interviewed him had intelligence, and therefore they liked him. In other words, said the reporter, he treated us as men, and not as mice."

Two days after landing, recalls Brandel,[3] Jabotinsky was the guest of honor at a cocktail party given by Mr. and Mrs. John Gunther at their home. To this party came some of the most important people in the newspaper world: Elmer Davis, Ernest Meyer, Harry Elmer Barnes, Quincy Howe, and L. F. Parton were among the guests.

All intellectuals, all sophisticated, and all as hard as nails. Again the guests at the home of the Gunthers were ready to do everything in their power to assist Mr. Jabotinsky in his work in America. Lemuel Parton had a cocktail party himself in honor of Jabotinsky. He invited other guests. These people, liberal, intelligent, and hardboiled, listened and were charmed. Not charmed as a bird by a snake, but charmed by a great personality, a great figure.

A strong impression was made at the press conference held soon after his arrival. Almost every paper gave whole columns to his introductory address and to the answers to questions put to him by the journalists. The N.Z.O. office in New York which collected the cuttings, filled a whole book with them. The attitude of the Yiddish press was a pleasant surprise, which one of Jabotinsky's younger colleagues described as "very sweetish, almost friendly." At an informal gathering of Yiddish newspapermen, on the editorial staff of the *Day, Morning Journal,* and the *Forward,* presided by Jacob Fishman of the *Morning Journal,* Dr. S. Margoshes of the *Day* "delivered an enthusiastic speech and so did the others. The whole atmosphere was more than friendly; Jabotinsky's address moved the whole audience."[4]

2. *The Spark That Ignites*

Jabotinsky found the United States, including its Jewish community, completely unmindful of the world crisis. "People here," he wrote three weeks after his arrival, "have simply stopped taking the war seriously; war news appears on the second page of the newspapers. Accordingly, the Jewish mood is also not at all 'on the eve.' "[5] The Jewish attitude to his wider plans which involved a departure from official neutrality was one of fearful restraint: "Jews are still shy of saying any decisive word less they be charged with warmongering (I have never seen American Jewry so scared of local anti-Semitism as they are now that the danger seems really tangible and widespread)." But he was by no means downhearted: "The wind seems to be blowing in our direction. . . . Soon it will become safe to speak more openly. If some kind of nucleus of attraction is born, for instance in Canada, wonders could be accomplished within a few months. But I would not attempt to make bricks without straw." [6] He did not doubt that America would eventually come into the war. But he predicted that it would be none too soon. On May 17, he wrote to Sir Archibald Sinclair, British Secretary of State for Air: [7]

This big blind America has suddenly awakened, but is still unable to realize that what she really longs for is to fight at once. Some of the magnetic centers dominating this peculiar public mentality are still asleep.

Perhaps you remember the offer outlined to you last autumn: to try and set in motion here a trail of electricity which, starting from Jews, will reach the Gentile bulk. I cabled Mr. Churchill repeating it the other day. The focal idea is to form a nucleus called "The Jewish Army." Now more than ever I am sure of success. Please help; please fight the suicidal tendency of neglecting "small" things which may look small but are pivotal. . . . This is the moment when just those whom I can influence probably better than anyone else are in a position once again to play the Jews' traditional role—of the spark that ignites.

Jabotinsky's first public appearance was on March 19 at New York's Manhattan Center before an audience of five thousand. Trouble was anticipated at this lecture because a Nazi gathering was scheduled to take place simultaneously in another part of the building. At the request of the management, the Germans moved their rally to another hall, and the lecture passed off without incident. Outraged by the necessity to yield to a Jewish meeting, delegates of the United German Societies lodged *post factum* protests with Mayor La Guardia, Governor Lehman, and President Roosevelt. Introduced by Dr. B. Akzin as "not a Chamberlain Jew" but a real representative of the Jewish nation, and by Rabbi Louis I. Newman as a man from whom Jewry expects "a decisive, dramatic stroke for the Jewish cause," [8] Jabotinsky spoke for two hours presenting an incisive analysis of the situation and offering a clear-cut program of action.

The attitude of official Zionist circles in America to this Jabotinsky program was a curious mixture of reluctant recognition and resentful disappointment. *New Palestine* wrote editorially:[9] "Mr. Jabotinsky made an interesting and valuable contribution to the discussion of the Jewish problem. . . . The setting on the stage was Revisionist in color and tone, but there was a general Zionist audience in the hall, and Mr. Jabotinsky's address could have been delivered without causing the slightest ripple of dissent in a meeting under official Zionist auspices. We are glad to note, Mr. Jabotinsky was vigorous and free in utterance, apt and resourceful in illustration, and showed no trace of the truculence of recent years. In fact, his public appearance was suggestive of the Jabotinsky of the early years whom we all admired and loved. . . . There were many in the audience who were interested to know . . . what it is that keeps Mr. Jabotinsky and his party out of the Zionist Organization, and what makes their return to the Zionist Organization impossible." Yet, two weeks later, the same paper complained editorially that Jabotinsky "studiously avoided a discussion of the program of the Revisionist party [and] . . .preferred to sacrifice the splendid opportunities he had for making the Revisionist program known and understood in order to win the favor of persons who would not be attracted by attacks and controversies. . . . This is indeed strange conduct for the leader of a militant, aggressive party," sourly commented the *New Palestine*.[10]

Thoughtful Gentiles saw in Jabotinsky's propaganda for the Jewish army a potent weapon against the disquieting growth of anti-Jewish feelings. Claire Boothe Luce,* who toured Europe in the spring of 1940, reported that "anti-Semitism was on the increase everywhere" and that the most popular quip in Paris was at that time : "The Jews ! Invincible in Peace and Invisible in War !"; this quip was accompanied by the comment : "The trouble with the damned Jews is that they won't make a stand anywhere." In an attempt to counter this vicious slander, Clare Boothe Luce quoted Jabotinsky as saying in his speech at the Manhattan Center : "I challenge the Jews, wherever they are still free, to demand the right of fighting the giant rattlesnake not just under British or French or Polish labels, but as a Jewish Army. Some shout that we only want others to fight, some whimper that a Jew only makes a good soldier when squeezed in between Gentile comrades. I challenge the Jewish youth to give them the lie." Though a Jewish Army was not raised, Clare Boothe Luce insisted that there was "no reason to look askance at Jews for this. . . . Perhaps the Jews will yet be allowed to make a last stand, and it would be fitting and proper if they made their last stand where they made their first one— in Palestine." [11]

3. *Touch and Go*

Official Zionist sourness in no way reflected the prevailing attitude of American public opinion which was definitely favorable toward Jabotinsky's political crusade. In a report to London, one of his associates wrote on June 11 : "Not a single word has appeared publicly in the Jewish press against the Army idea, and a surprising amount of sympathy is beginning to crystallize. But the main point is that whomever we approach among the Gentiles is extremely favorably disposed. Democrats and Republicans, liberals and conservatives are all tremendously impressed by the fact that Jews themselves will go out and fight for something that concerns them more than anyone else.

* Later, a U.S. Ambassador to Rome.

Our meeting of the nineteenth will therefore have some of the big names of Gentiles of America."

The meeting referred to was a mass rally to be held at the Manhattan Center in New York. It was conceived as an impressive demonstration of the community of interests between world Jewry and the Anglo-Saxon democracies in a joint armed struggle against Nazi barbarianism. Jabotinsky considered it of paramount importance to enlist for that purpose the sympathy and cooperation of the British Ambassador in Washington, Lord Lothian who, as Philip Henry Kerr had known him from the days of the campaign for the Jewish Legion. At Jabotinsky's request, Colonel Patterson went to Washington on June 7 to see Lord Lothian. According to Patterson's report, the latter fully agreed that the Jewish Army ought to be started as soon as possible and that, aside from its purely military value, its emergence would have a splendid effect on American opinion. Lord Lothian also "began to understand that Weizmann may be just a Jewish edition of a Chamberlainite and an appeaser and that it is no use relying on him for formation of the [Jewish] Army." [12] The Embassy cabled to the British Cabinet in London advocating an immediate authorization for the creation of a Jewish Army—of one hundred thousand men, as well as for an Air Force Squadron. The cable requested that a reply be given in time for the meeting of the nineteenth.[13] A week before the meeting, Lord Lothian received Jabotinsky in New York, expressed active sympathy and promised to cable again to London urging the acceptance of the Jewish Army scheme before that date.[14] The next day, F. R. Hoyer Millar, Secretary of the Embassy, informed the N.Z.O. delegation, on behalf of Lord Lothian, that His Majesty's Consulate General in New York had been instructed to be represented at the Manhattan Center rally. Lord Lothian, the letter continued, "has asked me to make it clear that he has as yet no information from London as to how the authorities view as a practical matter the proposal that the Jewish contribution to the Allied cause should take the form of a separate unit. This does not detract from his wish that there should be a British representative at your meeting to show his sincere appreciation of the Jews' desire to help at this crisis."

Then came the official counter-move. A delegation representing the "Emergency Committee for Zionist Affairs," headed by Rabbi Stephen S. Wise (other members were Louis Lipsky, Eliezer Kaplan, and Dr. S. Goldman) went to see the British Ambassador in Washington and declared that "responsible Zionist quarters disassociated themselves from Jabotinsky's adventurous scheme."*[15] Reluctant to alienate the sympathy of influential Jewish leaders in the United States, Lord Lothian felt compelled to withdraw his promise to the sponsors of the Manhattan Center rally and until his death, in December, 1940, practiced a policy of strict "non-intervention" in the matter that was provoking so strong a controversy among Jewish leadership.**

Notwithstanding this setback, the Manhattan Center meeting, addressed by Jabotinsky and Patterson, proved to be a great success. In a report to London, a member of the N.Z.O. delegation wrote:[16] "The hall was packed despite the season, which is most unfavorable to mass gatherings because of the proverbial New York heat. The relatively high admission fees (fifty cents to a dollar-fifty) did not act as a deterrent either. Even the counteraction of the Old Z.O. did not help them very much. They tried to prevent people from coming, they distributed leaflets at the entrance calling us names and saying that we are Mussolini's 'buddies' and cannot therefore fight him now; they also called a mass meeting in the hope of thus enticing a few hundred people away from our meeting. But all this failed. Our rally was a political event whereas their 'mass' meeting turned out to be a mess: the hall with a capacity of eleven hundred was about three-quarters empty."

Appealing for wholehearted Jewish cooperation with Great Britain in a common struggle against the Nazi onslaught, Jabotinsky said: "Our appeal does not mean that our grievances against the Mandatory Power are forgotten. But first of all the swiftly-moving Nazi rattlesnake must be disposed of,—and afterward our rights in Palestine and elsewhere will be reestablished." Forceful and impressive was his appeal for Anglo-American unity:

* When informed in London on July 5, by Robert Briscoe and Joseph Sagal of this anti-Jabotinsky demarche by the Jewish Agency representatives in the United States, Dr. Weizmann "expressed surprise." He undertook to cable the Zionist Organization of America that he was fundamentally in agreement with the Jewish Army project and to advise them to stop their opposition to it. (Report by Robert Briscoe. Minutes of the Meeting of the Administrative Committee of the New Zionist Organization, July 5, 1940). There is no no evidence that such a cable was ever sent.

** After Jabotinsky's death, Lord Lothian wrote to the N.Z.O. delegation in America: "Though Vladimir Jabotinsky and the British Government have been in constant disagreement for the past twenty years, one could not but admire his personal qualities and the uncompromising tenacity with which he fought for what he believed in. Nor can one forget the services which he rendered to Great Britain during the World War or his recent eloquent speeches in her favor."

Nine-tenths of all spiritual grass and forest harvest growing in America comes from English seed, and America knows it. Not one but a million "Mayflowers" have crossed the ocean, bringing nine-tenths of all that made America great. Now, the keepers of the original seed in England fight alone for survival, yet I hear youngsters with poisoned minds shouting "The Yanks are not coming:" As an old reporter, trained to read foreign peoples' mood, I send this message: "Mr. Churchill, they are coming, they will come, fists foremost, or will be dragged in, feet foremost. While others are losing courage in adversity, the 4,000-years-old nation remains unimpressed: no capitulation is conceivable, only fight to final victory."

The response of the American press was both widespread and sympathetic: the clipping office collected over a thousand clippings from all over the country. From all parts of United States inquiries poured in from people in all walks of life, among them a fair proportion of highly-trained men with considerable fighting experience; a good number were pilots and aviators, and more especially radio-operators.[17] Nevertheless, the official Zionist *New Palestine* continued its violent opposition. In an editorial "A Misleading Slogan," the paper wrote on June 21: "Responsibility for the press campaign of Mr. Jabotinsky for a 'Jewish Army' is disavowed by any responsible Zionist body in America. The proposal he is making runs contrary to the policies of the Jewish Agency." Stating that the Jewish Agency wants "only four divisions of Jewish soldiers in Palestine for the defense of Palestine and the Near East, plus eventually recruits from neutral lands who are living as refugees in those lands," *New Palestine* concluded: "This is the only kind of Jewish Army official Zionists are speaking about. All other forms of Jewish military cooperation are made up of ideas obsolete in our present-day thinking and mischievous in their effect upon the status of American Jews."

4. *Last Unity Attempts*

In the midst of raging controversy, Jabotinsky's ever-present concern remained the problem of Jewish unity, the necessity to secure something in the nature of a Jewish National Committee. He felt acutely that it was the absence of such a body which largely stood in the way of an irresistibly powerful campaign for a Jewish Army. He was therefore ready and willing to make all imaginable concessions, to sink all differences: he almost religiously believed that once Jewish leaders

391

stood shoulder to shoulder in the common struggle for the Jewish Army, all else would follow. Dr. S. Margoshes of *Der Tog,* who had been seeing much of him during this time, later recalled that the Jewish Army plan was foremost in Jabotinsky's mind:[18] "He felt that the World Zionist Organization should get behind this plan and carry it to fruition. To this end he was willing to abandon his old line of isolation. . . . [Yet] his efforts to move the World Zionist Organization proved completely fruitless. His proffered hand was rejected. I know because I tried to mediate between Jabotinsky and the World Zionist leaders. Stepehn S. Wise would not hear of any conversation with the Revisionist leader, nor would Chaim Weizmann."

Two months after Jabotinsky's arrival in the United States, German armies overran the Netherlands and the disastrous Battle of Flanders was in full swing. As though sensing tragedy and possibilities at the same time, Jabotinsky cabled (on May 18) to Dr. Weizmann, Ben Gurion, and Pinhas Rutenberg: "Propose to you joining efforts to establish united Jewish front for policy and relief; urge immediate consultation between ourselves or deputies." There was no reaction whatsoever to this appeal. A few weeks later, Eliezer Kaplan, member of the Jewish Agency Executive, then on a visit in New York, took the initiative of meeting Jabotinsky and explained that Dr. Weizmann had asked him to elucidate more thoroughly the scope of the suggestion made in Jabotinsky's cable. After a lengthy discussion, Kaplan promised to contact Jabotinsky again, but did not. His failure to do so strengthened Jabotinsky's original impression that this encounter was merely another attempt at further procrastination.[19] The direct transoceanic approach had failed. It was followed by an attempt at "mediation" in London.

In midsummer, 1940, the brothers Salomon and Joseph Sagall—non-Revisionist admirers of Jabotinsky with extensive connections both in leading official Zionist circles and among non-Jewish friends of the Zionist cause—made an attempt to bring about the unification of the Zionist effort, firstly with regard to the creation of the Jewish Army. On their initiative, a luncheon was arranged on July 2; among the guests (apart from Jewish personalities including Weizmann and Israel Zief) were Sir Gothbert Haslam, M.P. (former Chairman of the Conservative Party), Colonel Charles Ponsonby (Permanent Parliamentary Secretary to the then Foreign Minister, Anthony Eden), Sir Maurice Bonham (prominent leader of the Liberal Party), and Sir

Hugh Seely (wartime Under Secretary for Air). Asked about his attitude toward the idea of the Jewish Army and toward Jabotinsky's action in this field, Dr. Weizmann explained that he, too, was in favor of the Jewish Army. There were, of course, he said, essential differences between Jabotinsky and himself in internal Zionist matters: he was a man who believed in slow methods, in Jewish immigration into Palestine at a rate of several thousands a year, while Jabotinsky wanted a Jewish State immediately, on both sides of the Jordan. But cooperation with Jabotinsky on the Jewish Army issue, he thought, was not impossible; he planned to go to America soon and there he would get in touch with Jabotinsky. In the wake of this luncheon, a meeting was arranged on July 5 by Zief between Weizmann and Robert Briscoe, member of the N.Z.O. *Nessiut* and the only Jewish deputy of the Irish Parliament (in 1956-57 he was Lord Mayor of Dublin), at which Sagall was also present. According to Briscoe's account of this conversation, Weizmann declared that he had meant what he said at the luncheon about his "full sympathy with the Jewish Army project," and reiterated his willingness to meet Jabotinsky in New York immediately after his own arrival. There, it was agreed that Briscoe would draft the text of a cable to be sent by him to the N.Z.O. delegation in New York apprising them of the basic understanding reached with Weizmann. To avoid any possible mistake, the draft was to be shown to Weizmann the same afternoon for initialling. It was indeed submitted as agreed, but Weizmann expressed the wish to keep it for further thought and to return it the next day duly initialed; the next day, he indicated that he would like to submit it to his colleagues on the Jewish Agency Executive and that it would be initialed not later than July 8. Neither on that date, nor during the two and a half weeks that followed, was any reply from Dr. Weizmann forthcoming.[20] Instead, as can be seen from a letter addressed to him on July 24 by Joseph Sagall, he decided "not to proceed any further in the talks." "It is with immense regret that I had to learn of your decision," Sagall wrote, adding on behalf of his brother and himself: "It occurs to us that, in the absence of a direct cable from you to Jabotinsky, a complete breach could perhaps still be avoided by your agreeing to our cabling Jabotinsky as follows: 'We understand from Dr. Weizmann that he hopes to visit the U.S.A. toward end of August and will contact you.' " Such a cable was actually sent three days later, but in the meantime Weizmann unequivocally reversed his earlier stand in the matter. Informed by A. Abrahams, Political Secretary of the N.Z.O. *Nessiut,* of conversations which had taken place and of the regrettable lack of further action, Colonel Amery, an old friend of Jabotinsky, wrote to Weizmann expressing his concern. The answer he received was:[21] "I am sorry that you should have been worried by Mr. Abrahams—and in a matter of so little importance. I did not promise that I would send a cable to Mr. Jabotinsky in support of his scheme, since I know nothing whatever about such a scheme. Nor would I care to be mixed up in any of his activities, in America or elsewhere." The N.Z.O. organ *The Jewish Standard* regretfully announced the breakdown of the attempts to reach an agreement,[22] and Jabotinsky answered the brothers Sagall that while appreciating their friendly efforts, he was "compelled to consider the Agency's failure to answer direct as conclusively discouraging any positive anticipation; whatever further initiative shall be left entirely to the Agency."[23]

5. *Death*

After his arrival in New York, Jabotinsky for some time occupied a two-room suite in the penthouse of Hotel Kimberley (Broadway and 74th Street). But he very soon decided that these lodgings were "too expensive" and moved to the ground floor of a dingy brownstone house at 10 West 74th Street, where he lived in one room (partitioned by a curtain) with a kitchenette. He lived modestly, almost in poverty.[24]

His mood was anything but cheerful. The immediate political prospects, as he saw them, were depressing. Those who met him in the summer of 1940, are unanimous in stressing the gloominess of his general outlook. "I still see him walking the floor," recalls Israel B. Brodie, "indulging in what was almost a soliloquy, with profound sadness in his voice and in his whole posture, and saying: 'The Europe I knew is lost. I will not see the same Europe any more. I do not believe that it will ever recover the old spirit and I believe it will decay economically.' "[25] He was also increasingly plagued by mounting personal loneliness, by a feeling of guilt for having left his wife alone in besieged London. He said once to a younger associate:[26] "I have been preaching *hadar* to our youth for years. But I did not live up to this moral precept. Was it *hadar* to abandon Anna Markovna in London, under the German *blitz*?" For months his efforts to obtain an American visa for her remained unsuccessful. In desperation he cabled to London that should Mrs. Jabotinsky be unable to join him in America, he would return to Europe.[27] It was not before July 28, six days before his death, that he was able to inform his son:[28] "Mother is to receive her visa (as an immigrant within the Russian quota) early in August. As far as I know, her berth on the steamer has been kept reserved from week to week, so that I expect her to sail at once. May God keep her while sailing." He was also deeply concerned by the plight of his son, held by the British in the Acre prison, and threatened with losing his Palestinian citizenship. On top of his political troubles and cares, these gnawing personal anxieties were undermining his health. During the last weeks of his life, he looked worn out; his face was thin, ash-grey, and pinched; his eyes were sunken and seemed to have lost their lustre; he had visibly aged. Yet, until the very last few days, nobody suspected that he was dangerously ill. Colonel Patterson, who only a day or so before his death spent a very pleasant day with him, testified:[29] "He had never hinted to me that he had a weak heart."

It is not known when and where Jabotinsky contracted the heart ailment (*angina pectoris*) of which he was to die. On the whole, he enjoyed an exceptionally healthy and resilient constitution. His family doctor, the late Jacques Segal, who was also the house doctor of President Doumergue, used to say: "God is merciful and kind for He granted our leader a healthy body; I hope he will live long." From time to time Jabotinsky complained in his letters of utter weariness, bordering on exhaustion. In 1932, Dr. Segal discovered a "terrific percentage" of sugar in his blood; he was also considerably overweight.[30] Dr. Segal put him on a rigorous diet. For two months, his main food consisted of boiled spinach, and for almost a year he had to avoid bread and fats. He succeeded in losing twenty-two pounds and was extremely proud of this achievement: "I feel rejuvenated," he wrote to his sister, "I can run up three flights of stairs without getting out of breath, sleep like a baby, and I have forgotten what it is to be tired."[31] There was, of course, a good deal of comforting *bravado* in this report to his sister, who, he knew, was always concerned about his health. In August, 1936, he yielded to the pleas of his friend, S. D. Salzman, and came for a rest and cure to the famous Czechoslovakian health resort of Marienbad. He looked tired and depressed. Salzman urged him to consult a physician, and, after persistent press-

ing, he agreed to see Dr. Alexander Gottesman, a young enthusiastic
follower and admirer of his. The first visit was a long one, but Jabotinsky returned in a good mood : the doctor had found nothing wrong.

Five years after Jabotinsky's death, in a letter to Salzman, Dr.
Gottesman gave a detailed account of Jabotinsky's state of health in
1936. According to his report, the sugar content in Jabotinsky's blood
was above normal. But the main trouble was his deep fatigue, resulting
from overwork. Any physical effort left him out of breath. Dr. Gottesman had warned him that though, at the time, he had not found
any serious disease besides a neglected diabetes, he felt that further
overwork and the resulting exhaustion might well lead to serious
complications, and in particular might affect his heart. Before Jabotinsky's departure from Marienbad, Dr. Gottesman told him that the
main thing was to give his body some rest. Jabotinsky listened
patiently and politely and promised to obey in everything, but as
to the last point : "I cannot change my way of life." [82]

And he did not change it. The Marienbad cure resulted in but a
temporary improvement. Very soon, symptoms of weariness and
fatigue returned. His letters abound in brief references to increasing
lassitude : "I am very tired, and there is no possibility to take a rest;
people, good and bad, are devouring me, and there is no rest." He
looked bad, his hair became grayer; he grew increasingly impatient,
jumpy, irritable.

Nevertheless, there was no indication whatsoever of any heart ailment. When he left for the United States, his wife did not suspect
that anything might be wrong with his heart. In New York, he often
looked worn out and complained of utter weariness, but never mentioned—even to his closest collaborators—that his heart was affected.
It was not before Thursday, August 1, that he suddenly told Eliahu
Ben Horin : "My main worry for the moment is my heart. . . . I
think that I have *angina pectoris.*" Asked, "What makes you think
so ? Have you seen a doctor?" he answered in the negative, and agreed
to consult a physician only if he promised "not to tell a living soul
about the whole matter." Dr. S. Hirshorn, a staunch Revisionist, came
next morning. After the visit, both he and Jabotinsky assured Ben
Horin that the fears were unfounded; the trouble was caused merely
by extreme fatigue and overwork. After Jabotinsky's death, Dr. Hirshorn admitted that he had suspected a full-fledged *angina pectoris*
at the time, but, upon the patient's insistence, was compelled to

396

pledge his word as a physician and a Revisionist not to disclose his tentative findings to anyone. Since the exact degree of damage could not be established without a cardiogram and at that time there were as yet no portable cardiographs, he arranged for Jabotinsky to come to his office the following Monday. He therefore permitted the patient to spend the weekend at the *Betar* camp at Hunter, New York, some one hundred thirty miles from the city.[33]

This was Jabotinsky's second trip to the camp. His first visit, on July 13, had been an extremely enjoyable one. He went there by car and told stories and joked with his companions (Dr. and Mrs. D. Sheket and A. Hanin) all the way. When he arrived, long lines of uniformed *Betarim* met him in perfect formation : he slowly walked past the ranks, inspected the deportment and the face of each boy and girl, listened attentively to their evening prayer. In spite of weariness, he spent several hours that night with *Betarim* who gathered in the large dining room. There were no speeches. The evening was devoted to songs he had written for the *Betar*. The following morning he inspected the camp, going into every detail of camp life, watched the daily activities, gossiped idly and walked around with *Betarim*, sat with them on the grass, picked berries and flowers, went with them to the swimming pool where he launched a paper boat for the benefit of the youngsters. The camp was located at the top of a hill, high in the mountains, and in the afternoon he took a group of friends for some mountain climbing several miles away from the camp. "He walked in front, searching for the most difficult and inaccessible spots, jumping over bushes, leaping over brooks, and returned to camp worn out but happy. . . . All day he was on the go, never resting for a moment." [34] A. Gurvitch, who was with him, recalls that, walking briskly, they had lost sight of other members of the party. "Jabotinsky then suddenly interrupted our conversation and asked me to look for the missing friends, 'I will wait for you,' he said. Only after his passing did I realize that he must have had trouble with his heart and sent me away in order not to show it, and give himself time to recover." He was sorry when the time came to go back to New York, and promised to return soon and stay longer. On the return trip, the car was rather crowded, but the mood was excellent; they sang all the way, and Jabotinsky treated them to a solo performance of his old Italian favorite *Sorrento*. In a letter to his son he described the camp as "a most delightful place, standing all alone on the road, twenty acres with a cluster of buildings and a pool for swimming, and meadows and woodland." [35]

Permitted by the physician to keep his promise to revisit the camp, Jabotinsky was in a gay mood during most of the journey. D. S. Sheket, who drove him in his car, recalls, however, that when they stopped half-way for refreshments, he noticed that Jabotinsky discreetly swallowed some pills and that when they resumed the journey he asked A. Kopelowicz, who was with them, to sing the Kol-Nidre prayer for him: "Since it is written in Aramaic and not in Hebrew, I had never known it properly." Kopelowicz, a Yeshiva graduate, obliged, and Jabotinsky repeated the prayer word for word: this was but two hours before his death.

Shortly before reaching the camp, he showed signs of utter exhaustion. Met again by a *Betar* guard of honour, he alighted from the car with great difficulty: "Is this all really necessary?" he asked. Briefly reviewing the guard of honor, he began to walk toward the main building. There, he slowly mounted the stairs to his room on the upper floor. He was obviously in great pain. To the hastily summoned resident doctor (a competent Austrian refugee physician) he said: "Don't worry, doctor, I know that I have *angina pectoris.*" To A. Kopelowicz, who was helping him to undress, he muttered: "I am so tired, I am so tired." These were actually his last words. A second physician, Dr. Rodier, was summoned from neighboring Hunter; oxygen equipment was also brought. But the heart attack developed unabated. "He does not respond to the injections . . . the end is drawing near," announced Dr. Rodier. The end came at ten forty-five p.m.[36]

"He looked most peaceful in death—just as if he was asleep," wrote his faithful friend Colonel Patterson a few days later.[37] He was laid to rest in the New Montefiore Cemetery in Farmingdale, Long Island, New York. Thousands lined the route of the funeral cortege. There were no orations or eulogies either at the funeral services or at the burial; a chorus of one hundred and fifty cantors took part in the funeral rites.

Even a most summary recapitulation of the reaction to Jabotinsky's death in the Jewish communities of the free world would demand several dozen pages, and would hardly add anything of significance to his biography. It seems, however, worthwhile to record a few scattered reports from the Jewish communities in the Nazi- and Communist-dominated areas.

In the Warsaw ghetto, Jews refused to believe the terse dispatch on Jabotinsky's death published in the German press in the first half of 1940: "they suspected it was one of Goebbels' tricks calculated to confuse the Jewish masses and to drive them into a state of even greater despondency," recalls one of the survivors, Dr. David Wdowinsky. It was not before the second winter of the war that the message was definitely confirmed. A group of Revisionist leaders decided that the second anniversary of Jabotinsky's passing must be "solemnly observed, regardless of difficulties and dangers" in the Great Synagogue, and that a special issue of an underground paper be published, containing only one article in Hebrew, "After Two Years." The ghetto inmates could not, of course, be publicly informed of the planned memorial meeting. By word of mouth only his closest circle of friends as well as several prominent Zionist leaders in Warsaw were reached. Nevertheless, the Great Synagogue was crowded to capacity.[38]

A man who was in Vilno, Lithuania, when the news of Jabotinsky's death reached the Jews in that town, recalled:[39] "Vilno was then already under Communist control; the name of Jabotinsky was counter-revolution; the news of his death spread like wild-fire, and despite the obvious danger, men, women and children flocked to the synagogues and wept bitterly over their loss. 'Now that Jabotinsky is dead what can we hope for?' was their reaction."

In the cell No. 19 of the Soviet Lukishki Prison in Vilno, the news of Jabotinsky's death reached M. Szeskin, his devoted follower, in February, 1941. He fainted. When he recovered, he put on his hat, faced the wall and started saying Kaddish. When he came to the word "Amen," he heard a chorus of voices repeating the word: the eighteen Gentile Poles—professors of the Vilno and Cracow Universities, lawyers, army officers—who were his fellow-inmates—had put on their hats or caps, formed a semi-circle behind him and participated in the prayer. The first anniversary of Jabotinsky's death Szeskin spent in the hospital of a Soviet labor camp beyond the Arctic Circle, on the banks of the Petchora River. All the Jews in the ward gathered around his bed: "We speak in whispers, Hebrew mingled with Yiddish; when the evening falls, we all cover our heads and recite Kaddish. . . . We exchange reminiscences, and before parting

399

we swear a solemn oath that whoever survives this exile and returns to the free world, will take with him a handful of earth from this forlorn region and, across continents and oceans, bring it to Jabotinsky's grave in New York." [40]

A young man who returned from Siberia early in 1946, and had the rare opportunity of observing life among Jewish internees and evacuees there, related that the name of Jabotinsky had become a kind of watchword in many of those camps and that he himself had seen on walls and boarding inscriptions reading: "Long live Jabotinsky" and "Remember Jabotinsky." There are numerous touching reports of *Betarim,* Revisionists, and non-party men, who, at the risk of their lives, carried the picture of Jabotinsky in their pockets through all the years of horror and suffering; many actually perished with his photograph in their hands, and his memory in their hearts. [41]

For Churchill's eightieth birthday, England's Poet Laureate John Masefield wrote a quatrain, the first three lines of which succinctly formulate the service both Churchill and Jabotinsky had rendered to their respective nations: [42]

> This Man, in darkness, saw; in doubtings, led;
> In danger, did; in uttermost despair,
> Shone, with a Hope that made the midnight fair,

But the concluding line of the quatrain, "The world he saved calls blessings on his head," is even now only partly applicable to Jabotinsky. His death was lamented by friend and foe, and the recognition of his stature and of his life's record has now become universal in Jewry. Nevertheless, his dearest hope—to be buried in the free and sovereign Jewish State—had not materialized. In his last will he wrote that he wanted to be buried

just wherever I happen to die; and my remains (should I be buried outside of Palestine) may *not* be transferred to Palestine unless by order of that country's eventual Jewish Government.

Such an order has not been given during the first decade of the existence of the State of Israel. Quoting the above paragraph of Jabotinsky's testament and stressing that his query was being made "in a purely personal capacity, not as a party man but as Jabotinsky's biographer," this writer, in the early fall of 1956, took the liberty of approaching the Prime Minister of Israel with a direct question: "Why does the Government of Israel, of which you are the head, not give such an order?"[43] To this Ben Gurion replied, on October 3, 1956, that the question was a proper one, but that in his view only the remains of Theodore Herzl and of Baron Edmond de Rothschild ought to be reburied in Israel; as for all others—Israel "needs live Jews, not dead ones."

6

FORCES HE FATHERED

THE FATHER OF BETAR*

1. The "Benjamin" of the Family

A s TIME went on, the members of Jabotinsky's political family multiplied. Along with the Revisionist party (*Hatzohar*) and the youth organization *Brit Trumpeldor* (*Betar*), there came into being the *Brit Hachayal* (Ex-Servicemen's League), the movement of the Religious Revisionists (*Brit Yeshurun*—later *Achdut Israel*), the various organizations of the academic youth; in 1935, the New Zionist Organization was established; and last but not least—the *Irgun Zvai Leumi*. Jabotinsky was a devoted *pater familias* to all these groups, and each one acclaimed him as its beloved and undisputed leader.

However, the family member dearest and closest to Jabotinsky's heart was the *Betar*. He never made any secret about it and affectionately referred to the *Betar* as his "Benjamin," although, chronologically speaking, it was born simultaneously with the Revisionist party. "I love the *Hatzohar*, I love the *Brit Hachayal*, and the young *Brit Yeshurun*," he said at *Betar's* Second World Convention in 1934, "but above all I love *Betar*. The *Hatzohar* is the branches of the tree, *Betar* is the roots from which the entire tree receives its nourishment." [1] This love was fully reciprocated. The "romance" between Jabotinsky and *Betar* was deeper and more meaningful than the usual relationship between a "President" of a movement and his followers. It was a fascinating, almost mystical, association and it bore great fruit in the struggle for Jewish national liberation.

That Jabotinsky should have turned his attention to the creation of a youth movement of his own in 1923-24, was entirely logical and

* This chapter was contributed by Mordehai Katz, Secretary General of the *Shilton Betar* from 1936 and until Jabotinsky's passing.

natural in view of his past experiences. What was surprising was rather the fact that the idea had not occurred to him earlier.

2. *The Background*

By 1923-24, though only in his early forties, Jabotinsky was already an almost legendary world-wide Jewish figure and "steeped in triumphs." Yet he felt frustrated: somehow every triumph ended in defeat; there was no solid foundation on which his achievements could be added, like bricks, to one another and made to last; he felt that he was building on sand. And it was not the objective difficulties, the external forces that discouraged him and even caused him to contemplate retirement from public life in the prime of life and in the full bloom of his extraordinary energies. To use the analogy with his *Samson* novel, it was never the strength and cunning of the "Philistines," but the mentality and attitude of his own "tribes," of the Jewish people, that saddened him and often filled him with despair.

Looking back on his life at that point, Jabotinsky could not help reflecting on his bitter experience, on at least two crucial occasions, when Jewish public opinion first acclaimed him and then, immediately afterward, reneged and deserted him. The first to default was his own "tribe"—the Russian Zionists. Prior to World War I, he was their universal darling, the brightest star in the sky of Russian Zionism. Then war broke out and Turkey joined the Central Powers. Perceiving clearly the historic opportunities that this development offered the Zionist cause, Jabotinsky forcefully put forward the idea of the Jewish Legion. He met with almost universal disavowal on the part of the World Zionist movement. But the sharpest rebuff was administered to him by his Russian kinsmen. When he visited Russia in the summer of 1915, he saw that

after twelve years of national activity I was suddenly anathemized and treated like an outcast. In Odessa, my hometown, where not long before I had—quite undeservedly—been carried shoulder-high, I was now, on Sabbaths and Festivals, called a traitor from the pulpit of the Zionist synagogue *Yavneh*.[2]

Jabotinsky took the blow in his stride and carried to a victorious end his struggle for the Jewish Legion, in whose ranks he fought for the liberation of Palestine. He was universally hailed as the "Father of the Jewish Legion." As creator and first commander of the *Haganah*, defender of Jerusalem and "prisoner of Acre," he became an almost legendary figure throughout the Jewish world.[3]

Yet, when, in the early twenties, he unerringly realized that England had embarked on a course of reneging her promises to the Jewish people, and started urging an activist Zionist policy to combat this course, he again found himself pathetically isolated among both the leadership and the masses. For the second time, a generation he had for years been teaching, inspiring, and leading to victories, had turned its back on him when called upon for a great fighting effort.

It became unmistakably clear to Jabotinsky that if he was to continue his mission, he could not rely on "ready-made" Zionists, raised in the standard Zionist mentality, to carry on the type of battle which, he knew, would have to be fought in the years to come. He could not risk a third defection. And this meant that he would have to create a new generation in his own image, to educate and train it from early youth; to inspire it with his spirit, so as to have this new psychological formation to stand by him and his ideas in fair weather and foul, in triumph and adversity; they would do so because they would be imbued by his brand of Zionism and religiously believe that this was the only brand capable of achieving ultimate victory for the cause of Jewish national liberation.

Nor were the personal lessons of the recent past the only considerations for creating a new youth movement. The picture of the present offered an even more powerful factor. This picture was indeed not a pretty one, and it could not but arouse concern and anxiety in the heart of a Zionist patriot.

In the wake of World War I and the ensuing upheavals, three powerful social and political "enthusiasms" swept the world, especially Europe : one was the idea of national self-determination; the other— Socialism and Communism; the third was pacifism. These three tidal waves flowed parallel to each other and sometimes crossed and furiously battled one another. The Jewish youth, too, did not escape their impact. It became a hotly disputed battleground for conflicting ideas and umpulses.

Zionism was a natural integral part of the first "enthusiasm." But, with the Zionist idea reduced, as it were, to a small-scale colonizing enterprise, with immigration to Palestine limited to a few thousand certificated per annum, with the glamor of the statehood idea gone, the Jewish youth could hardly be blamed for deserting the Zionist movement in favor of more immediate, more universal and exciting "isms."

The official Zionist leadership reacted to this defeatist trend in a most self-defeating way. They neither took up the struggle for full-blooded State Zionism, nor followed the path of what is nowadays being described as imposed "coexistence," in the hope that better times would come. Instead, they picked up a third, the worst possible alternative: making virtue out of necessity, they gradually evolved a concept denying that a Jewish State had ever been the aim of Zionism; asserting that this aim was basically spiritual and cultural; and that a well-selected and trained Zionist élite in Palestine, not necessarily a majority of the population, was quite sufficient for the realization of that aim.

In the same spirit of yielding to defeat, of canonizing alien ideologies, Zionism "married into" Socialism and pacifism. To some, it was a love-match: considerable segments of the Zionist movement genuinely believed that those two universal ideas were the salvation for all nations and countries without exception. To others, it was a marriage of convenience: their belief was that such a blend would bring to the drab tents of Zionism some of the glamorous popular appeal of Socialism and pacifism and thus induce the Jewish youth to "stay home." But this synthetically concocted brand of Zionism, as was to be expected, did not "deliver the goods." Those who were thirsty for integral national liberation, could not quench their thirst with a Zionism that had renounced both Jewish statehood and Jewish majority in Palestine; and those who hankered for integral Socialism, knew where to look for the real thing.

Moreover, the strange bedfellowship of Zionism with other "isms," transposed into the realities of Palestine's upbuilding, generated a number of extraneous and explosive issues. At least two of them directly affected the thought and action of the Zionist pioneering youth.

Regardless of the merits or demerits of the Socialist system and of the class struggle in a normal country, both had no place in Palestine, where there was as yet nothing to "socialize" and everything to build. The process of building was bound to be a common venture of Jewish labor and Jewish capital, with the latter coming from Jewish businessmen abroad. Socialism and class struggle were therefore not merely a bad proposition economically; they were morally intolerable as well. In a different connotation, this also applied to the lofty idea of pacifism. It was common knowledge that the Arabs in Palestine were determined to obstruct and, at the first opportunity, destroy Jewish upbuilding work. In the face of such realities, it was obviously impossible to follow Gandhi's teachings. But the official Zionist line was that it was the duty of the British Mandatory Power, i.e., of the British soldier, to protect the peace-loving Jewish population against Arab attacks. Legally unassailable, this contention was, however, politically self-defeating and morally—a fraud. In plain words, it meant: Let the British soldier do the dirty job of shooting, while we, shielded by British bayonets, will be sanctimoniously extolling the virtues of pacifism.

3. The Creation of Betar

It was against this background that Jabotinsky, in 1923, created the youth movement of *Brit Trumpeldor,* or *Betar,* which was destined to serve as the main instrument in the molding of a new Jewish generation.

In the technical sense, Jabotinsky actually did not have to "create" the *Betar,* for it was already in existence in embryonic form, only it did not know it. Several young high school students in Riga, Latvia, headed by Aaron Zvi Propes, had, somewhat earlier, organized a local group named *Histadrut Trumpeldor.* The Group was formed as a tribute to the memory of Captain Joseph Trumpeldor, who died heroically in Tel-Hai in 1920, together with six other comrades, defending their settlement in Upper Galilee against an Arab attack. The organization had no program otherwise.

Jabotinsky affectionately recalled at the second World Convention of the *Betar* that when he visited Riga in November, 1923, Aaron Propes,* Dr. Jacob Hoffman, and Benno Lubotzky came to see him and endorsed his ideas: "I did not understand where these young people drew the will to swim against the current; they realized that something was wrong and aspired to do something better. Our move-

* Jabotinsky gratefully remembered this fateful encounter and never missed the opportunity to pay affectionate tribute to Aaron Propes, "the first *Betari* in the world," for the services he was rendering the *Betar* throughout the years in Latvia, Poland, Czechoslovakia, Rumania, and the United States.

ment was organized." Jabotinsky was favorably impressed by the young men who had the vision and the good sense to see in Trumpeldor an inspiring symbol for the Jewish youth. He was himself a great admirer of his old comrade-in-arms from the days of the Jewish Legion, who, as he put it in the *Story of the Jewish Legion,* "had been for many years a vegetarian, a Socialist, and a pacifist, but not one of those pacifists who sit tight, letting others fight and die."

Jabotinsky also attached great importance to Trumpeldor's conception of *Chalutziut* (Pioneerdom), as distinct from the meaning which was given to it by the Zionist-Socialist parties. On this subject Jabotinsky quotes Trumpeldor as having told him :[4]

. . . My conception is much broader. They must be workers as well, but not only that. We shall require people who are "everything," everything that Palestine will need. A worker has his workers' interests, a soldier has ideas about caste, a doctor or an engineer his habits. But among us there must arise a generation which has neither interests nor habits. A piece of iron without a crystallized form. Iron, from which everything that the national machine requires should be made. Does it require a wheel? Here I am. A nail, a screw, a girder? Here I am. Police? Doctors? Actors? Lawyers? Water carriers? Here I am. I have no features, no feelings, no psychology, no name of my own. I am a servant of Zion, prepared for everything, bound to nothing, having one imperative: Build!

This conception of *Chalutziut* later became the basis of *Betar's Plugot Hagius* (Mobilization Groups). Every *Betari* on arrival in Palestine was obliged to join such a group for a period of at least two years and serve the country in whatever capacity and locality the *Plugots'* command might decide, in accordance with the best interests of the Zionist objective.

Jabotinsky was thus glad to have come upon a *Histadrut Trumpeldor* in Riga. He was eager to see the memory of Joseph Trumpeldor, the soldier and the *chalutz,* become a source of inspiration to the Jewish youth. He decided then and there to use the Riga group as the nucleus of the world movement of *Brit Yosef Trumpeldor,* or *Betar* for short. The word *Betar* has a double meaning in Hebrew : it is an abbreviation of the full name of the organization, and it is also the name of the last stronghold of the heroic resistance against the Romans during the revolt of Bar Kochba. The new name was supplied by Jabotinsky himself, as was indeed most of the nomenclature later used in the movement, like *Rosh Betar* (Head of World *Betar*),

Shilton Betar (World Leadership of Betar), *Netziv Betar* (Chief of *Betar* in a country), etc. The originality and the aptness of the names are a tribute not only to Jabotinsky's sense of language but also to his extraordinary talent for detail.

4. *"Give Us An Ideal!"*

Through the *Betar* Jabotinsky set out to offer the Jewish youth a creative and powerful alternative to the confused, contradictory, uninspiring, and misleading conceptions described above.

A young man who welcomed Jabotinsky at a youth rally at that period, put the situation in a nutshell when he turned to the guest and said: "Our life is dull and our hearts are empty, for there is no God in our midst; give us a God, sir, worthy of dedication and sacrifice, and you will see what we can do." By "God," the somewhat over-dramatic speaker meant a great, lofty, all-consuming ideal. Jabotinsky met that request. He gave the Jewish youth an all-consuming ideal and thus saved it for Zionism. It was Menachem Ussishkin, no follower of Jabotinsky, who in the course of his speech at the Seventeenth Zionist Congress in Basle turned to Jabotinsky and the Revisionist benches and said: "To you I wish to express my thanks for having given the youth new hope in our political future." [5]

The first commandment in *Betar's* ideology was, of course, Jewish Statehood in all its original Herzlian inspiring simplicity, to which was added an aura of glory and majesty unsurpassed in all earlier concepts. It was not just with the notion of Statehood that Jabotinsky endeavoured to imbue the youth of *Betar,* but *Malchut Yisrael*—the Kingdom of Israel—with all the historic, spiritual, and poetic connotations that the term implied, though monarchy, of course, was not one of them. He mercilessly tore to shreds the spiderweb theories of official Zionism, the theories about "spiritual," "territorial," and "bi-national" centers, which in the last analysis amounted to the creation in Palestine of a new "Hebrew" Ghetto. He told the youth instead that they—the poor, persecuted, miserable, underprivileged boys and girls of the Jewish ghettos in Poland, Rumania, Lithuania —were the heirs to the Kingdom of David, to the spiritual values of the prophets and to the proud, heroic tradition of the Maccabees and Bar Kochba. He told them that history had assigned to their generation the unparalleled honor, as well as the unprecedented

411

responsibility, of resurrecting the Jewish State and that they dare not divest themselves of their destiny and responsibility. They did not.

The *Betar* absorbed this message into its heart and blood and carried it stubbornly, persistently, and successfully to the rest of the Jewish world.

Another precious article of faith was "Monism"—the belief in one ideal, as opposed to the synthetic concoction of Zionist Socialism or Socialist Zionism. Personally, Jabotinsky rejected Socialism as a method of achieving social justice in human society. But he did not attempt to draw the Jewish youth into a crusade against it, or any other "ism" as such; he combatted it merely in context with the Zionist task. The Zionist objective—the upbuilding of the Jewish State and the redemption of the Jewish people—was so great, so lofty, and at the same time so difficult and complicated an undertaking, Jabotinsky taught, that it required and deserved the full and unreserved dedication of the Jewish youth; Zionism could not tolerate "rivalry" from any other ideal, be it right or wrong, good or bad in itself. Reviving the biblical injunction against *shaatnez* (wearing garments made of a mixture of wool and cotton), he called on the youth to ban *shaatnez* from their ideological garments.[6] He did not mind mixing his metaphors in preaching this fundamental tenet of *Betar,* if this helped to implant it in the hearts of the youth. The other metaphor was a telling and beautiful stanza of one of Chaim Nachman Bialik's Hebrew poems, which runs thus:

> One sun in the sky,
> And one faith in the heart—and no other:

When Shlomo Ben Yosef of Rosh Pinah went to the gallows in Acre, in 1938, chanting the National Anthem and conquering death itself, he did so with that "one faith" in his heart; so did Dov Gruner and the other heroes of the underground, who followed later in the path of Ben Yosef.

5. *Iron and a King*

Yet the most powerful magic that Jabotinsky breathed into *Betar's* spiritual world, the force that made *Betar* a prime instrument in the great revolutionary upheaval which led directly to the establishment of the State of Israel, was something else. This "magic" has been called many different names at different times, good and bad ones: legionism, self-defense, resistance, military preparedness, militarism, underground army of liberation, terrorism, etc. All of these descriptions are indubitably related to the subject, but somehow none of them, singly or combined, adequately express its meaning.

Perhaps the genuine flavor of the "magic" is best expressed in Jabotinsky's *Samson* novel. There, the subjugated, divided, and demoralized tribes of Dan, Benjamin, Judah, Ephraim, etc., might be taken to represent the Jewish people of Jabotinsky's day; the Philistines—the external world, the adversaries of the Jewish people; Samson reflects much of the author's thinking, and Samson's band of faithful followers, the "Jackals," might be regarded as representing the youth.

From experience and keen observation, Samson came to the conclusion that the Philistines, though spiritually and morally inferior to the tribes of Israel, managed to gain the upper hand over them because of two reasons: first, they were wise enough to appreciate the importance of iron for the maintenance of power and took possession of almost all the available supplies in the region, together with the blacksmiths who knew how to convert the iron into weapons; and second—they knew the art of order and discipline, of acting like one man in cases of danger and emergency. In a final message sent to his people from captivity in Philistia through his faithful "Jackal" Hermesh, Samson said:[7]

"Tell them two things in my name—two words: the first word is iron. They must get iron. They must give everything they have for iron—their silver and wheat, oil and wine and flocks, even their wives and daughters. All for iron! There is nothing in the world more valuable than iron. Will you tell them that?"

"I will. They will understand that," answered Hermesh.

"The second word they will not understand yet, but they must learn to understand it, and that soon. The second word is this: a King! A man will give them the signal and all of a sudden thousands will lift up their hands. So it is with the Philistines, and therefore the Philistines are the lords of Canaan. Say it from Zorah to Hebron and Sechem, and farther even to Endor and Laish: a King!"

"I will say it," said Hermesh.

"Go now," said Samson.

413

Jabotinsky's call for iron and a King was certainly motivated primarily by the elementary logic of the situation. Logic was a prime force with Jabotinsky in all his thoughts and actions. Since the Arabs had made attacks on the *Yishuv* in the past, and since every child knew that they would attempt to do so in the future, what else could the Jews do but defend themselves? The only alternative was to rely on British bayonets, an alternative which was both morally untenable —for it was tantamount to a return to the infamous *Schutzjuden* system of the Middle Ages—and politically suicidal—for it was obvious that the British had no intention whatsoever to use their bayonets to defend the Jewish National Home.

Yet the purely logical and political necessity to learn the grim art of managing iron and obeying "King's" discipline, neither exhausted Jabotinsky's "military concept" of *Betar* nor explained its magic impact, conscious as well as subconscious, on the masses of the Jewish youth. There was another element to it, perhaps less perceptible, but not less potent. The Jewish youth in Europe, subjected to humiliation, discrimination, and persecution, might have been inclined to seek solace and refuge in Socialism, pacifism and other "isms"; but deep down in their hearts there lived an intense yearning for strength and power, for honor and dignity, for pride, and for such implements that would make it possible to achieve all those coveted things—i.e., for "iron" and for a "King."

"This was," testified Colonel George Henry Patterson, a faithful friend and confidant of the creator of "Samson," "the idea behind the *Brit Trumpeldor* movement, which he loved and cherished more than any other of his creations. In these *Betar* youngsters he was hoping to arouse the great longing for 'Iron and King,' for military preparedness, organization, self-respect, and discipline—all those elements of nationhood which he so badly missed in Jewish life and which, he knew, were the indispensable foundations for the rebirth of Jewish Statehood." [8]

The longing Jabotinsky was so intent to implant in the Jewish youth, had been ripening ever since the mid-twenties; it grew in strength and intensity as time went on. The ascendancy of Hitlerism did not extinguish this almost elemental yearning for strength and dignity; on the contrary, it made the youth more determined than ever to wage a "conquer or die" battle—which it ultimately did, in Zion, and conquered! Jabotinsky, through the *Betar*, was responsible for both the discovery and the release of these powerful pent-up yearnings and longings of the Jewish youth, as well as for molding them into a dynamic factor of Jewish national liberation.

Heroism and sacrifice, military prowess and magnificent exploits of the fighting Jewish youth, both in the underground forces and later in the Army of Israel, are now a source of universal pride in world Jewry. Events have fully vindicated the Jabotinsky-inspired "militarist" feature of *Betar's* program and education. The abuse and vilification Jabotinsky and the *Betar* suffered for their "militarism" only two or three decades ago, now appear almost incredible. They were accused of having driven a pernicious "military *dibbuk*" into the hearts and minds of the Jewish youth. Zionist leaders—among them some present leaders of Israel who are more militaristic today than Jabotinsky ever was—denounced the modest and reasonable demands for military preparedness as irresponsible "playing with wooden swords," and urging all good Zionists to exorcise the "evil spirits."

They did not succeed in this fanatical crusade. The Jabotinskian "*dibbuk*" not only survived, but fathered great and glorious forces. In the last years of the British Mandate, it took the form of fierce underground struggle, led by *Rosh Betar's* faithful and formidable disciple, Menachem Begin. In 1948-49, it inspired the soldiers of the victorious "War of Liberation." The "*dibbuk's*" latest appearance was in November, 1956, during the brilliant Sinai campaign. The historic truth is that every soldier who fought in Sinai had in his heart, whether he knew it or not, a spark of Jabotinsky's spirit—a spark that had been carried over a whole generation by the youth of *Betar*.

6. "Hadar"—a Philosophy of Life

Jabotinsky was above all an esthete. But unlike most esthetes who run away from the tumult of public life to a quiet and solitary corner in literature, music or art, to enjoy their lofty conception of beauty, he made his esthetics the cornerstone of his national and political struggle. It was natural and, indeed, inevitable that he should have given the *Betar* the concept of *Hadar* (i.e., "shine"): outward polish, reflecting inner warmth, a concept aimed at the creation of a new type of Jew, outwardly as well as inwardly, and of a new way of life based on what is true and beautiful.

415

Rosh Betar himself defined *Hadar* thus :[9]

Hadar is a Hebrew word which is with difficulty translated into another language: it combines various conceptions such as outward beauty, respect, self-esteem, politeness, faithfulness. . . . *Hadar* consists of a thousand trifles, which collectively form everyday life. . . . More important by far is the moral *Hadar*: you must be generous if no question of principle is involved. Every word of yours must be a word of honor, and the latter is mightier than steel. A time should eventually arrive when a Jew, desiring to express his highest appreciation of human honesty, courtesy, and esteem, will not say, as now, "He is a real gentleman," but "He is a real *Betari*."

He was eager to implant this lofty concept of knightliness in the *Betar* generation he was endeavoring to mold. When a Jewish Naval School was established by the *Betar* in Civitavecchia, Italy, he wrote to the pupils insisting on the strictest observance of the minutest rules of behavior and good manners :[10]

Be tactful, be noble . . . do not grab the first bench, even if it is given to you. Learn the Italian language well . . . learn to speak quietly in school, in the street, at your meetings. . . . Personal cleanliness of your clothing should be a commandment to you every moment of your life. You must shave every morning. . . . Every morning you must check whether your nails are clean. When you work, your face, hands, ears and your whole body must be clean.

Jabotinsky always conceived of *Betar* as a movement with both short- and long-range tasks. Even when the military aspect of its education had already become all-pervading, he kept on reminding the *Betar* leaders of farther horizons. In 1937-38, considerable friction developed between *Betar* and *Irgun Zvai Leumi*. While ideologically and politically the relationship between these two was the same as between the candle and the flame, there arose some misunderstandings. The senior leaders of *Betar* often complained to *Rosh Betar*, who was the head of both organizations, that the organizational activities of the *Irgun* in the diaspora were undermining the *Betar*. Jabotinsky's characteristic and invariable reply to these complaints was : "Don't worry, remember that the *Irgun*, no matter how important, is only a temporary thing, but *Betar* is for ever !"

There is little doubt that Jabotinsky envisaged the future mission of *Betar* in the free and independent Jewish State as that leading to development and crystallization of the concept of *Hadar* as a new way of life, affecting all facets of life, public as well as private. It remains to be seen whether *Betar* has completely spent itself in fulfilling its "short-range" tasks, or whether it will yet find the strength and inspiration to embark on the "long-range" mission, as dreamed of by Jabotinsky.

7. *The Generation That Stood Fast*

As far back as 1931, during the sessions of the First World Conference of *Betar* in Danzig, when the movement was still young and making its first steps, Jabotinsky, intervening in the debate, started by saying that this very morning he had written to his wife: "I am sitting at the Conference, listening, and having *nachat* (satisfaction) from my children."

Actually, the real *nachat* came later. The years 1933-34 provided two impressive demonstrations that Jabotinsky was no longer, as had been the case in the past, a lone wolf when it came to a serious crisis. In the early spring of 1933 the Kattowitz Affair exploded, which is described in another chapter. Whichever way one looks at 'Kattowitz" politically, its immediate result was that most of the adult leadership which had for years been associated with Jabotinsky in the movement, deserted him in that crisis. But not *Betar*.

In fact, most of the senior *Betar* leaders were opposed to Jabotinsky's line of leaving the Zionist Organization. But they realized that what really mattered was the great salutary revolution Jabotinsky was creating slowly in Zionist thought and action, and that *Betar* must therefore stick with him, Zionist Organization or no Zionist Organization. Though conjecture is not part of this biography, it is hard to resist the thought that had *Betar* deserted Jabotinsky in 1933, he would probably have retired from public life in despair. *Betar*, in turn, would have died of consumption, and the seeds of the great revolt which began with the "illegal" immigration into Palestine, continued with the glorious underground struggle against the British occupation, and ended with the War of Liberation and the establishment of Israel, would have never been sown.

The second demonstration came soon after, during the Arlosoroff blood-libel. This affair, too, belongs to a different part of the book. Here let it merely be said that the formidable onslaught was aimed

417

chiefly to destroy both Jabotinsky and his movement. He fought the great lie and triumphed in the end. The blood-libel wounded him deeply, but it also provided a source of deep satisfaction : *Betarim* everywhere, often boys and girls in their teens, stood by him and with him like rocks amid the incredible sound and fury. The Arlosoroff affair divided Jewish families in Eastern Europe and in Palestine into hostile camps; young boys and girls were often subjected to tremendous pressure by parents, brothers, and sisters to leave the "assassins'" camp. But *Betarim* never wavered. The ordeal merely made the bonds of love and faith between them and their *Rosh Betar* stronger than ever.

He was to them the embodiment of everything great, noble, and inspiring. Jacob De Haas, a keen and penetrating observer, who visited Poland in the fall of 1935, wrote (October 30) to Justice Louis D. Brandeis: "Jabotinsky created a youth movement . . . its code is *noblesse oblige,* and it is ready to go to the stake. . . . The *Betarim* are the nuclei of the new movement, the children carried the mesage to their homes. . . . This mass is bleeding itself white for Jewish causes, and these empty-bellied *Betarim* pay their dues when they can." The mass of "these empty-bellied *Betarim*" was to Jabotinsky a most cherished treasure. In 1936, the head of the *Betar* in Hungary tried to convince him that at least in that country the emphasis must be laid on quality rather than on the quantity of membership : a small circle of highly trained and qualified *Betar* leaders, he argued, was more valuable than many hundreds of "just *Betarim.*" Jabotinsky listened attentively, and then said: "You can establish a new body along the lines you are suggesting, and I personally am ready to become its honorary chairman. But *Betar* is and remains a mass organization." * [11]

The truly stunning demonstration of the Jabotinskian "iron" in *Betar's* blood came, however, in 1938, when the young *Betari* from Rosh Pinah died with Jabotinsky's name on his lips. The youth's unrivalled heroism, the olympic calm and *hadar* with which he conducted himself from the beginning of the trial and up to the very moment of his death, announced to the world that the new Jewish generation had arisen; it also sanctified forever the bonds between Jabotinsky and his spiritual children—a relationship without precedent in modern Jewish history.

* In 1938, the *Betar* numbered seventy-eight thousand members in twenty-six countries.

8. Rosh Betar—A Many-Splendored Title

The youth of *Betar* loved its *Rosh Betar* with a great love that stemmed from the innermost depths of its soul; it frankly worshipped him, was utterly dedicated to him. When he died, thousands of *Betarim* all over the world wept unashamedly, for they felt that to them life without Jabotinsky would never be the same again.

What inspired this love and devotion? His teachings?—Certainly. The fact that he raised them—as runs the *Betar* Anthem—"from the pit of dust and decay" to "a race—proud, generous, and fierce?" No doubt. But above all it was due to the personal example he set for the *Betarim*. He not merely practiced what he preached in the sense that he gave himself completely and unreservedly to the struggle for Jewish national redemption: he was also the living embodiment of the new type of Jew he was molding. *Rosh Betar,* a word which was —and still is—spoken with love and reverence by *Betarim* throughout the world, came to mean many things: father, commander, teacher, and leader. It was natural for a World Convention of *Betar,* after his death, to decide that no other person should ever be given the many-splendored title of *Rosh Betar.*

In an epoch in human history, when a Hitler, a Stalin, a Mussolini have desecrated the meaning of the word "leader," it was perhaps inevitable that to some confused and shallow minds the Jabotinsky-*Betar* phenomenon should appear as a reflection of a political trend, for which *Rosh Betar* had nothing but contempt. Leadership, of course, was a great and honorable mission long before the Hitlers and the Stalins arrived on the world scene and will remain here long after the last remnants of their poisonous heritage will be eradicated from human life. Leadership, and even cult of personality, which comes from a free choice by free men, prompted by faith in and admiration for fellow men endowed by Providence with great minds and valiant hearts, such leadership will always be a blessing, indeed a dire necessity, for human progress.

Colonel Patterson gave a moving expression to the relationship between Jabotinsky and the *Betarim* when he described the circumstances of *Rosh Betar's* death in the following words:[12]

Vladimir Jabotinsky's last walk on earth was between the lines of young *Betarim* who awaited his arrival in Camp Betar in Hunter, New York. They stood in military formation for his inspection. Although suffering from acute pain, Jabotinsky carried out the inspection and went straight to his room and died—a martyr to duty even unto death.

I was not with him during the last hours of his life. But when I heard of it, I could not help saying to myself that if Jabotinsky were to choose the setting for his death, it would have been something after this manner. The inspection of a *Betar* as his last deed in this world was highly symbolic.

THE FATHER OF " ILLEGAL IMMIGRATION "

1. *"On Adventurism": 1932*

IN MARCH, 1932, Jabotinsky published in the Yiddish press a challenging and widely commented on article "On Adventurism." [1] It was the first bold attempt to give moral and political sanction to the early tentative ventures of the so-called "illegal immigration" to Palestine and openly encourage them. At that time, the "illegality" was but a relative one. Jews, intent on settling in Palestine and unable to secure immigration certificates, would obtain a tourist visa and then remain in the country after their permit expired. According to the report of the Royal Commission, 22,400 such "unauthorized immigrants" were registered in Palestine in 1932 and 1933; the report of the Palestine Administration for 1938 gave the number of "tourists" who had overstayed their permits during the period from September, 1933 to 1938, as 10,094. Polish Revisionists actively participated in the organization of this "tourist traffic."

Yet, writing about "adventurism," Jabotinsky had in mind a different, more direct form of "illicit immigration": entering Palestine without any visa at all, evading British frontier patrols. He makes a young man or girl, who have for years set their hearts on going to Palestine and are preparing themselves for that eventuality, ask their father: "What shall I do?" They realize that "the rulers of Eretz Israel will never condone a large immigration" and that their chances of obtaining a certificate are worse than poor. And they ask, searchingly and persistently: "What shall I do, father?"

Should I submit to the British restrictions, bow my head and say: Good, I will be obedient. So long as I do not receive legal permission, I will be a good child and sit at home and possibly help you, father, sell potatoes at your stall. There is a danger, however, that I will not be able to bear it, and drift along other paths that do not lead to Zion, but lead to no good... On the other hand, I might attempt a totally different method—that of adventurism. Where is it written that one may enter a country only with a visa?

Jabotinsky earnestly advised every father to be careful in answering this pathetic query, not to discourage the young people by enumerating all the difficulties of this course; by doing so he would only deprive them of their last illusion and drive them into "paths which do not lead to Zion"—into Communist ranks. And he also advised against exaggerating the obstacles:

I know the borders of Eretz Israel well—and not all that is difficult is impossible. I do not wish to enter into details, but this adventure is not worse than many other adventures. It has the chances both of failure and of success.

One thing, however, must be clearly understood: a nation, particularly its youth, should not bow its head and say with a sigh: "In view of the fact that the police have forbidden our redemption, we should all resign ourselves and remain sitting at home obediently." We must continue to fight for our freedom. . . .

Where is it written, where does it say that adventurism may not be used as one of the methods of our struggle? Consider the lessons of history and you will discover that often even adventures that failed proved to be a means of struggle, particularly if it was not an individual adventure but a collective one. . . .

If I were young I would laugh at their visas and their restrictions. Impossible? Tell that to your grandmother, not to me, I would say: It is difficult; in fact, very difficult. But it is precisely this which constitutes that spirit of adventure which climbs mountains and not merely hillocks. . . . If I were young I would launch a new phase in propaganda betokened by a new symbol—a whistle, an ordinary tin whistle costing a few pence. And the slogan for this propaganda campaign would be— whistle at their laws and restrictions!

It took time for this spirited appeal to ripen into action. Smaller groups of "illegals" were already "stealing across the border" via Syria at that time, but it was not before the summer of 1934 that the two-thousand-ton Greek ship *Vellos*, chartered by *Hechalutz* leaders in Poland, succeeded in landing the first three hundred "illegals" on the Palestine shore. But the second trip of the *Vellos* proved to be a complete failure. Even more harmful to the further progress of the venture was the attitude of the official Zionist leaders. Jon and David Kimche, the authors of the semi-official history of *The "Illegal" Migration of a People,* admit that "the protagonists of this illegal immigration had to overcome the determined opposition of a large and influential section of the Zionist leadership headed at that time by Ben Gurion himself. . . . Such veteran leaders as Ussishkin, Ben Gurion and even the secretary of the *Hechalutz,* Eliahu Dobkin, contended that this was no way to gain their objective"; they hoped to obtain a substantial increase of the immigration quota instead.[2]

Jabotinsky's attitude was different. On August 18, and again on September 9, 1934, he wrote to S. Jacobi that "the most urgent matter for us is unauthorized *Aliyah.* . . . Now, it is being conducted by the Left parties for their own people, but it is *our* people who are helping them to land (Nathania is the center of our workers). . . . I ascribe *tremendous* importance to this task—especially politically: failures and arrests can be made much of in England and generate a lot of sympathy on the part of everybody except the officials of the Colonial Office. It would be the best demonstration of craving for Palestine one could imagine: a 'personified petition'. . . . We decided to release *one of our best men* from all other duties (I don't want to name him in a letter) and let him handle the matter."

In 1935, two leading Viennese Revisionists, Ernest Reifer and Max Schwarz, were approached by a Revisionist emissary from Palestine, by the name of Galili, with a concrete project for organizing systematic "illegal" immigration, with Vienna as a center. They declined to do anything without having consulted Jabotinsky and came to Paris to see him. Jabotinsky found the plan "reasonable and desirable." But while sending Reifer to London to present it to the *Nessiut* of the New Zionist Organization, he very carefully analyzed single points of the proposed scheme in a letter dated January 6, 1936. The London members of the *Nessiut,* Reifer later explained to this writer, "were for the plan in principle, but officially they were not ready to sanction it. Jabotinsky saw me the next day in Paris and gave me his blessing to go ahead. . . . It was, I believe, the first organized illegal *Aliyah.*"

"Illegal" immigration (it was also called *Aliyah Bet*—"Second Immigration"—and/or *Af-Al-Pi*—"In Spite of Everything") was conducted on a much larger scale also by the Polish Revisionists. Acting on Jabotinsky's instructions, this writer was able to secure effective cooperation on the part of the Polish authorities; the Rumanian Ambassador to Warsaw, Richard Franasovici, to whom he had been introduced by the Polish Foreign Ministry, made available to the "illegals" Rumanian transit visas (the Rumanian port of Constanza served as point of embarkation) without demanding visas for their country of destination.

Jabotinsky was likewise actively interested in the extensive *Aliyah Bet* conducted by the Revisionists in Czechoslovakia. On November 29, 1938, he asked Dr. Oskar K. Rabinowicz to give "full and detailed information" on this operation to his emissary Joseph Katznelson: "The Prague experiment is our first attempt to organize this branch of our activities on a well-regulated businesslike basis. Whatever you have achieved in this field, as well as any error that might have been committed, is of great importance for our future work."[3]

In 1938, the *Irgun Zvai Leumi* assumed the responsibility for the safe landing of the "illegals" while the *Betar* took care of the organization of their transports and of bringing them to the ports of embarkation. Jabotinsky sanctioned this division of work in two separate orders to the *Betar* and the *Irgun,* dated November 3, 1938.[4] The arrangement, though often challenged by both partners, proved to be efficient. A "most secret" British Intelligence "Report on the Organization of the Illegal Immigration" compiled by the Jerusalem C.I.D. (Criminal Investigation Department) on May 11, 1939,* mentioned the Revisionists in the first place among the organizers of the "illegal" transports and added that of all bodies involved in this operation "the Revisionists are at present organizing it on by far the biggest scale and making great political and financial profit thereby." An introductory note to the report gloomily stated that "the dangers of illegal immigration being used as a political weapon with the sympathy and resources of World Jewry behind it cannot be too strongly stressed."[5] A subsequent Intelligence report, composed during World War II, and based on the C.I.D. files, estimated that "as many as fifty thousand illegal immigrants probably reached Palestine since the formation of *Irgun* in 1937. There is no way of calculating the percentage of those who entered the country under the *Irgun* auspices, although it may be presumed that the society was responsible for a substantial share of the total."[6]

* This writer is indebted to Mr. Yehuda Slutzky of the Editorial Board of the *History of the Haganah* for putting at his disposal the Report.

2. *"National Sport": 1939*

By the end of 1938, more than a thousand "illegals" were entering Palestine monthly, and hardly a week passed without a secret night landing somewhere along the coast. In the spring of 1939, Jabotinsky published a stirring article—a matured sequence to his 1932 call for "adventurism"—in which he "heartily recommended to the Jewish Youth" to make "free immigration" the major "Jewish national sport." [7] "It is without a doubt the noblest of all the sports in the world. . . . It has a noble aim such as no other sport can show."

The Jewish national sport is helping to break through a barrier which stands in the way of millions of hungry souls; it is helping to win a country for a homeless rabble and to make the rabble a nation. Other sports are, after all, not more than just a game; our sport is sacredly serious. . . .

The as yet brief history of the first stages of our national sport already contains many chapters on how one gives the last drop of water to a girl, how one stands cramped in a corner all night so that a sick person may have a little more room to sleep.

Continuing on a personal note, Jabotinsky reminded Jewish parents that ever since he first took up a pen he had followed but one vocation : "I have spoiled your children, taught them to break discipline (and sometimes even windows), tried to persuade them that the true translation of 'komatz alef-o' is not 'learn to read' but 'learn to shoot.' I have always done this and I have a suspicion that so far it has not done the children much harm. I therefore hope that fate will not deprive me of the strength, and the honor, of pursuing the same system to the end of my publicistic career. . . . For I consider that the highest achievement, the highest degree of manliness as well as godliness that man can attain as he sets off on the road of life, all find expression in the wonderful, magic word, *shaigetz*—'scamp.' "

If I were now at the blessed age where it is possible to be a "scamp," I know what I should do. How big were the boats in which the Zaporozhe Cossacks used to cross the Black Sea and shoot at the Sultan in Constantinople? . . . Who thought of "tonnage" or even heard about it in those days? . . . If I were a boy today, I would first sit down to study what is needed for our national sport, how big it must be in order to permit me and a dozen friends, scamps like myself, to make the jump.

425

Can it be done on fifty tons? Or perhaps thirty? I remember Greek cargo boats that used to bring figs and oil and other good things from the islands in the Aegean Sea to the port of Odessa forty years ago, and these boats were certainly not more than a few score tons. Of course, you must also learn to be a sailor; and even such a boat costs money. So I, together with the other scamps, would get down to learning to be good sailors; and together with the other twelve scamps, I would begin to save the pennies, to buy the old boat. Then the boat can be bought only somewhere on the sea, while I might be in some inland town; but when you want to, you can find a way.

There is, of course, no way of ascertaining whether this call for openly breaking the "iron wall' around Palestine was reported to the British Secretary of the Colonies by his press service. However, it could hardly have been sheer coincidence that just a few weeks later (on June 6), Malcolm MacDonald indignantly told the House of Commons that the British Government was now dealing with a "large-scale attempt to flout the law" on immigration to Palestine; he repeated this statement twice—on July 12 and 20.[8] It must also have been perfectly clear to him who the main "culprits" were: on July 12, Colonel Wedgwood told the House that of the fifteen thousand "illegal" immigrants who had landed in Palestine during the previous six months, Jabotinsky's New Zionist Organization was responsible for seven thousand (46.6 per cent), the official Zionist Organization for forty-five hundred (30 per cent), and "independent contractors" for thirty-five hundred (23.3 per cent).[9]

Wedgwood had been all along an ardent advocate of Jabotinsky's "national sport." Shortly after the publication of this article, he told a meeting of the Anglo-Palestine club that Palestine Jews would not be doing their duty unless they "make illegal immigration possible and in the end make it legal."[10] On April 8, 1939, he addressed a letter "To Whom It May Concern," in which he fully and unreservedly identified himself with the effort of Jabotinsky. This courageous letter read:

I know how Mr. Jabotinsky and his friends have been helping the refugees, I approve of all schemes which get the Jews into Palestine, and have myself assisted this work financially. I am satisfied that this work injures no man, and assists the cause of humanity and justice. It has no connection whatever with any internal party dissensions in the Zionist movement, and all similar schemes will have my approval.

426

Those who wish can send the money to me, but the money can be handed over direct to Mr. Jabotinsky or his friends.

Colonel the Rt. Hon. Josiah C. WEDGWOOD,

P.C., D.S.O., M.P.

After Jabotinsky's death, Wedgwood said at the memorial meeting:[11]

"I think all the illegal immigrants in Palestine owe him [Jabotinsky] their lives and present liberties. Others would not have dared [to conduct 'illegal' immigration] had he not led the way."

The historian of *Af-Al-Pi* stresses that Jabotinsky saw in it "a powerful means of political pressure, whose function was to break down the restrictions imposed by the anti-Zionist regime in Palestine. He intended to bring into Palestine, within the shortest time possible, at least one hundred thousand Jews and thus put before the British the question: 'And what now?' "[12] But in his view, *Aliya Bet* was not a party venture, not even merely a method of political pressure: it was above all a means of saving Jews from the impending European catastrophe and bringing them to their homeland. Every Jew was entitled to be saved in this way.

Jabotinsky took a lively and active interest in all aspects of the "national sport," whose history records numerous instances of his personal concern for the fate of the "illegal" boats. When the vessel *Katina* with six hundred "illegals" from Czechoslovakia was not heard of for weeks, he was very anxious about the ship and her plight: every day he phoned Paris and later Bucharest, asking for details of the ship's peregrinations. "He has taken to his bed because of this anxiety." He actively intervened in the conflict between his two emissaries in the case of the boat *Draga*. When the *Draga* got stuck on her way, he took "profound interest in each detail, receiving reports, giving advice."[13]

When, in 1940, Dr. Reuben Hecht, one of the most devoted organizers of the illegal immigration, advanced part of the funds entrusted to him for business purposes by his wealthy family in Basle for this purpose, and ran into trouble, being accused of mismanaging family property, Jabotinsky wrote to him that he personally, and the entire Revisionist movement were ready to back him both morally and financially.

Jabotinsky did not hesitate to plead the case of the "national sport" before the statesmen of Europe. In April, 1939, he made the

427

round of the French ministers, asking for their active cooperation in facilitating the dispatch of "illegal" ships with Jewish refugees from the French ports. Reporting on his visit to Albert Sarraut, Minister of the Interior, he described the latter's reaction as "50 per cent sympathetic and 50 per cent non-committal" but "not averse to considering it [the request for cooperation] a reasonable request." When Sarraut asked, "Where will they [the refugees] go?" Jabotinsky answered: "Do you really want to know? They will have visas to exotic countries, but . . ." Anatole de Monzie, Minister of Public Works and an old friend, was "very friendly, furious with the [Jewish] Agency . . . and promised unreserved help." However, both Sarraut and de Monzie told Jabotinsky: "Go talk to Mandel, he is your man." Georges Mandel, Minister for the Colonies, was generally regarded as the "strong man" of France, the "man of the future"; many compared him with Georges Clemenceau. Though of Jewish descent, he was little conversant with, and interested in Jewish affairs and was rather reluctant to receive Jabotinsky. It was de Monzie who, at the latter's request, secured for him an audience with Mandel. Yet this encounter proved to be rather inconclusive. The Jew Mandel was courteous, listened attentively, but evinced little interest or sympathy.[14]

In Jabotinsky's lifetime, Revisionist efforts in the field of illegal immigration were not only opposed, but also repeatedly reviled by leaders of the official Zionist Organization. Ben Gurion, and later Professor Norman Bentwich (during his visit to South Africa) found it proper to assert publicly that "Revisionist boats" were bringing prostitutes into Palestine. Jabotinsky was deeply shocked by these insinuations. In a meeting with Ben Gurion, he bitterly protested against this blackening of the reputation of Jewish girls who were risking anything to get out of Eastern Europe and into the land of Israel: "You seem quite sure that they were prostitutes. How do you know?" he asked with biting irony.* [15]

Baron Robert de Rothschild, not a Zionist himself, but a friend and supporter of "illegal" immigration irrespective of which party was conducting it, suggested the unification of the Revisionist and

* When in October, 1939, Robert Briscoe came to South Africa to raise money for *Aliyah Bet*, the *South African Zionist Review* wrote that immigrants brought by Revisionist "coffin ships" are "dumped into Palestine without regard for their usefulness for the country; no screening or selection is attempted; some of them are Viennese prostitutes" (Robert Briscoe, *For The Life of Me*, Boston-Toronto, 1958, p. 278.)

official Zionist fund-raising, and of eventual practical work, in this field. In the summer of 1939, negotiations to this effect were initiated under his auspices, with the participation of Israel Sieff, S. Jacobi, and Jeremia Halperin. Not only the latter two, who represented Jabotinsky, but also Sieff, a Weizmann man, favored an agreement, and pressed for it; at a certain stage, Dr. Weizmann seems to have been ready to accept a settlement providing for 30 per cent as the Revisionist share in the joint drive.[16] Informed of these negotiations, Jabotinsky, on June 6, cabled his agreement. He however realized that "of course, there are all sorts of breakers ahead—even if everything is arranged, Ben Bouillon [mock name for Ben Gurion] will intervene to spoil it at the last moment." And in fact, the negotiations somehow started to peter out. A few days later, in a letter to the London Nessiut, Jabotinsky wrote that he assumed that neither Weizmann, nor [Berl] Locker [member of the Jewish Agency Executive] were to be found. "What is happening is probably this: they are using the interval to poison R[obert] de R[othschild] against us, so that he should withdraw his demand for negotiations. The only way, if I am right, is for us at once to raise a big noise—with R. de R— about their dodging agreement."[17] No final settlement was reached. In his talks with Eliahu Golomb (July 9, 1939), Jabotinsky inquired whether Golomb had been informed of these negotiations. The answer was that he had been indeed consulted by the London Zionist headquarters about Rothschild's idea and had expressed himself "against any projected merger or agreement as long as they [the Revisionists and the Irgun] remain outside Zionist and the Yishuv's discipline." "We must not," he said, "be responsible for any effort to bring into Palestine people who will increase anarchy and commit actions that we consider to be dangerous." [18] This attitude, of course, precluded any unification or coordination even in the limited field of bringing Jews to Palestine.

3. The Struggle for the "Sakaria": 1940

"National sport" continued unabated even after the outbreak of the war. On October 4, Malcolm MacDonald reported in the House of Commons that between August 1 and September 30, 4,892 Jews had entered Palestine without certificates. This movement had been powerfully stimulated by the dire need of thousands of refugees from Hitler-dominated countries. A highly dramatic situation was created in the fall and winter of 1939 in the Rumanian waters of the Danube where more than two thousand refugees from Greater Germany were stranded on four small steamers and barges. They were starving, freezing, and desperate. Accompanied by one of his younger colleagues, Y. Benari, Jabotinsky went to see the head of the Colonial Office in the House of Commons and pleaded that those refugees be allowed to proceed to Palestine with the proviso that two thousand certificates would be deducted from the next "quota." MacDonald sternly refused: "Should they try to land in Palestine, they will be arrested." After that statement, the following exchange of barbed remarks developed:[19]

Jabotinsky: "Then, I shall ask Mr. Benari to hand over to you the full list of names of the 'illegals' whom we have brought to Palestine during the last two years. You may arrest them as well."

MacDonald: "How many are they?"

Benari: "Seventy thousand."

MacDonald: (Silence.)

Benari: "When shall I send in the lists?"

MacDonald: "My secretary will advise you."

The "advice," of course, never came, and the lists were not submitted. But the plight and the sufferings of the unhappy escapees haunted Jabotinsky. On January 24, 1940, he cabled to Rabbi Louis I. Newman in New York that he had initiated in the press and in influential circles a campaign for allowing the marooned Danube refugees to proceed to Palestine. This campaign aroused considerable sympathy. As first tangible result, he quoted an editorial in the *Daily Herald* under the heading "Jews Dying on Frozen River Report Terrible Conditions"; the paper demanded that special treatment be granted to this group and that they be allowed to enter Palestine. He also approached the Joint Distribution Committee for funds which would "enable us to help the refugees on the spot and to shift them to their destination. . . . While we are helpless to save millions of unescaped, at least let us save the two thousand who escaped the Nazi hell," Jabotinsky concluded. Simultaneously he made an eloquent appeal to all members of the British Parliament "to intervene to save" those whose lives were indescribable agony. "Now that a German move into the Balkans is expected, they will not even be able to escape." Should they try to proceed to Palestine, "shipowners are threatened with confiscation of steamers and imprisonment for masters and crew, if captured near the Palestine shores." [20]

It would be cruelly futile to argue whether these refugees were "right" or "wrong" in trying to escape from hell. They HAVE tried in the only direction they (or you, or anybody) could think of. Today they must be saved, and as Rumania will not allow them to land, the only way to save them on the brink of a hideous hecatomb is to lift, for them at least, the Palestine ban.

No argument of "policy" can be invoked in the face of such misery, where only the argument of humanity has the right to be heard.

The appeal met with widespread understanding and support. But MacDonald refused to be influenced. Jabotinsky's son Eri, who was in charge of the New Zionist Organization's refugee work in Rumania and was directly affected by all the difficulties of the situation, kept in close contact with his father. On January 25, Jabotinsky cabled him in Bucharest that he was "making widespread efforts" to remedy the situation, adding a moving personal encouraging note : "I remember how I felt in 1915 [during the struggle for the Legion] when friends, maddened by misery, held me responsible for the weather, for *force majeure* and for everything; but I trust you are firm and I shall stand by you to win or lose together. Bless you."

Finally, the Turkish-owned steamer *Sakaria* was chartered to carry the refugees to Palestine; on February 1 it left the port of Sulina with twenty-four hundred passengers on board. Having passed the Dardanelles, the *Sakaria* was boarded by British Navy officers and directed to proceed under escort to Haifa. There, on February 14, the passengers were ordered to land and later released. But Eri Jabotinsky was arrested and sent to a War Prisoners Camp. "This is revenge for having accompanied Danubian refugees to Palestine," Jabotinsky wired to Colonel Wedgwood. "Disturbing feature is War Prisoners Camp, he being naturalized Palestinian. Could you ask the Colonial Secretary why Prisoners Camp and what are the Palestinian Government's intentions regarding him ?" Wedgwood demanded in the House of Commons that Eri should be tried before a court, but trial was not allowed, and a sentence of one year's detention in the prison of Acre was passed by the Palestine Administration under the "Prevention of Crime Ordinance" promulgated several years before. No charge was stated publicly, but a Colonial Office letter to Wedgwood explained that "the Secretary of State has reasons to suspect that he

[Eri Jabotinsky] has been concerned in organizing illegal immigration into Palestine."

In an "Aide-Memoire," circulated as a private document among Members of Parliament, Jabotinsky subjected this "explanation" to devastating legal and moral criticism :

The allegation that my son is concerned in organizing the "illegal" immigration of Jewish refugees into Palestine is an honor, and it is not for me to rebut it; but it so happens that in this particular case all the twenty-four hundred came to the Danube estuary either without even informing him or (in the case of one group of over five hundred) against his direct veto, the veto being due to the fact that there was at the time no steamer to take them farther. I have in my possession a letter with over five hundred signatures apologizing for that breach of discipline and explaining why those people had no choice but to start at once upon their journey down the Danube. Thus the business of taking them out of the frozen estuary became not a case of "organizing" immigration legal or otherwise, but rather a case of organizing the rescue of people in dire distress.

Though the *legal* aspect of the case is obviously of secondary importance, it is characteristic that the Government shrank from a trial though there is a perfectly rainproof Palestinian law against aiding "illegal" immigration. The reason is obvious: no court would convict a man under circumstances such as these. The ship was arrested hundreds of miles away from Palestine's territorial waters, was brought to Haifa under escort, and the passengers were ordered to land. In the eyes of the law, immigrants entering a country under such conditions are not "illegal" entrants. Nor would any court listen to the contention that the accused, while in Rumania, had "intended" to take these people to Palestine: courts of one country do not try people for intentions conceived abroad and, as explained just above, frustrated in the bud by the fact that the Government itself has subsequently done exactly what they are supposed to have intended.

The crucial issue, however, is not the *legal* but the *moral* one—an issue of public decency, and I only raise it because it has a general bearing on one of the most painful aspects of this wartime:

Is it decent to prosecute a man for saving fugitives, in a crisis like the present one, from No Man's Land or no Man's Water?

Is it decent to do so when the British Government themselves obviously admit that there was nowhere else to take them but to Palestine: for, having arrested the ship near the Dardanelles, they did not even attempt to unload it anywhere else—not even in British Cyprus—but took it straight to Haifa? In other words: is it decent to prosecute a man for having done the only thing that was possible, in the Government's own opinion, if these people were to be rescued at all?

Shortly after Eri's imprisonment, Jabotinsky left for the United States. Speaking, upon arrival, with American journalists, he said: "I am a fervent sympathizer with the smuggling of refugees into Palestine, though I am not a leader in it." When asked whether the estimate of twenty-six thousand refugees smuggled into the Holy Land in the last few months was accurate, he replied: "I don't know, but I hope it's low." [21]

THE FATHER OF JEWISH RESISTANCE

1. *Blessing the "Zealots"*

FROM 1930, a number of Revisionist youths in Palestine, mostly members of the *Betar,* had been openly defying the anti-Zionist policy of the British Administration. They were known as *Brit Ha' Biryonim* (Union of Zealots), an illegal organization whose existence, however, was well known to the police. The *Biryonim* took *à la lettre* Jabotinsky's denunciation of the census of the Palestine population announced in 1931 by the Mandatory Administration; he saw in it a "statistical prelude" to the Administration's attempt to introduce a Parliament with an Arab majority among its elected members. Wrote Jabotinsky: "Nothing can be easier than to sabotage this census—if several thousand people refuse to be 'counted,' the census would lose its authoritativeness, and it would be impossible to refer to it. Some say that this is punishable by three months of imprisonment. But every Jew in Palestine would pay a much higher price if the census were to succeed." [1] The *Biryonim* strictly followed the advice implicit in this article. They refused "to be counted" and tried to persuade others to do the same. They also booed Dr. Drummond Shiels, the anti-Zionist Undersecretary for the Colonies in the Labor Government, when he came to Tel Aviv, and Herbert Bentwich, former Attorney-General of the Palestine Government, known for his appeasement policy toward the Arabs, when he lectured at the Hebrew University. They combatted the appearance of non-Jewish policemen in the all-Jewish city of Tel Aviv, and removed the Swastica banners from the balcony of the German Consulates in Jerusalem and Jaffa. For these exploits, the group—whose spiritual leader was Dr. Abba Achimeir—earned in official Zionist circles the reputation of "irresponsible adventurers"; some of them—most often Achimeir himself—had clashes with the police and were repeatedly imprisoned (one hundred twenty-three were arrested in connection with the anti-census campaign).[2]

Jabotinsky's attitude to this significant trend among his youthful followers was that of a father: he blessed it, and curbed it, and supported its protagonists.

In March, 1932, he devoted to this new phenomenon a thought-provoking article "On Adventurism." [3] As can be seen in the previous chapter, it dealt primarily with "illegal" immigration as one of the means of breaking the British restrictions of Jewish immigration. But there was much more in this article than advocacy of one specific way of challenging the Mandatory Power. It contained a spirited "philosophy of adventurism," applicable to every possible pattern of combatting the anti-Zionist British regime. Jabotinsky ridiculed the prevailing concept that Zionist policy must always be "statesmanlike," never taking chances, without any trace of daring: "All serious-minded people called Herzl an 'adventurer.' I want to defend adventurism," he stated. "Where is it written, where is it said that adventurism may not be used as one of the methods of our struggle? . . ." To him it was "a totally normal reaction for abnormal conditions" that "was to be defended primarily because it is now unavoidable. . . . A state of silence can no longer exist for us simply because we Jews are not a dead nation, but a living one. . . . We must therefore investigate and consider whether it is perhaps not healthier to sanction the application of adventurism to our political situation." He realized that there were "as yet few in Eretz Israel who are ready for adventurism . . . but their numbers will grow with their achievements." He knew that their defiance of the authorities was bound to lead them to prison. But, he assured them:

prison is not a tragedy—for those who sit in prison. I read a most enjoyable description in one of the Tel Aviv newspapers, *Masuot*, cheerful portrayal of how the young men of Rosh Pinah who had been sent to Acre for propagating a boycott against the national census, were arrested. It was a real pleasure to read these lines in these days of bowed heads and obedient protests.

A knock at the door: "Will you submit to the national census?"

"No!—with a capital N!"

"Are you then the gentleman who did propaganda against the census?"

435

"Yes, and how!"

The vibrant pulse of youth, like a breath of wind, is felt in this sort of description. When they and their friends were forced to clean the steps of the prison, they dressed in their best clothes and wore white collars in order to carry out this menial job. Each bit of dirt which they unearthed was a stain on the uniforms of their guards and judges. Two girls, Shoshana Simonowitz and Raya Berman, refused to work since that might have been interpreted as cooperation. They were deported to Bethlehem. . . .

Prison is really not a tragedy—for those who sit in prison. It is a tragedy for those who send honest men to prison. . . .

The English regime in Eretz Israel is today bereft of all justice. God forbid that we should allow any opportunity to pass to break, or obstruct, this regime.

Even in the Revisionist ranks, and even in Palestine itself, there were at times strong misgivings in regard to single "excesses of zeal" on the part of Achimeir and his followers. In several letters to colleagues who had given expression to such apprehensions, Jabotinsky, always alert to undercurrents in his movement, argued against condemning the zealots. On February 3, 1931, after a lecture tour in Poland, he wrote to Dr. E. Soskin: "Let's confess, we have disappointed our party by passivity and loyalism; that's why pent-up vapors are breaking through here and there and, of course, not always in a desirable form; in particular, the Palestine [Organization] is manifesting their radicalism in a feuilletonistic manner; and we are sermonizing them without offering anything instead." Simultaneously, we read in a letter to B. Weinstein: "Notwithstanding the undeniable growth of Revisionism, I have seen everywhere the same internal dissatisfaction—the feeling that Revisionism did not live up [to its purpose], that we missed the bus, that we not only did not 'say the word,' but did not say anything at all. People are dissatisfied not only with Grossman, but even more with myself. There is no sense in arguing now who is right; but there *is* such a mood; I personally believe that it is three-quarters justified. . . . Don't indulge in the illusion that meek behavior would attract many well-to-do and solid people. They are even in time of elections not such fat prey. Just for the elections mobile and easily excitable elements are much more useful. The main thing is, however, that our future is connected with these elements and not with the sedate and well-to-do ones. We will have to correct their shortcomings, but they are still the foundation. We should not repel them." And in another letter to the same addressee, dated May 26, 1932 : "It would be simple blindness to underestimate the tremendous moral influence of the 'Achimeir spirit' in the Diaspora countries. Being close [to the Achimeir camp's deeds] you notice all the mistakes and failures. But for our youth here [in the Diaspora] this is the only redeeming feature of recent years. And we all feel that in Palestine there is a *need* for 'such' plans of an 'incorrect' character. It is of course a pity that they are sometimes implemented not in the proper way, and that an ideology opposing well-ironed pants is being created. But I would not advise the disbanding of this camp because of this, even if we were able to do it."

2. . . . and Curbing Them

In this spirited defense of "adventurism," Jabotinsky referred to its main promoter, Abba Achimeir, who had become a frequent resident of the British prisons in Palestine, as "my teacher and mentor." This title of distinction was widely interpreted as unqualified endorsement of Achimeir's views and tactics. Many *Betarim* and young Revisionists, both in Palestine and in the countries of the Diaspora, started disparaging the value of any legal political action and putting their hopes mainly, often even exclusively, in extra-legal activities.

Jabotinsky made a determined attempt to stem this trend. Explaining in *Rasswyet* "The Meaning of Adventurism," he said that he was, of course, ready to repeat the honorable title of "teacher and mentor" he had bestowed on "the young Palestinian who, defending his beliefs, was not afraid to be jailed, and even to get into a brawl with a policeman."

But I must forwarn both the mentors and their followers: up to this point—and stop, and not one single step further. From the fact that Ivan or Piotr must be acknowledged as our teachers in selfsacrifice, it does not at all follow that they can be recognized as teachers in the field of program and ideology. On the contrary: I categorically and firmly deny the ideology of *sansculotism*: it is no good, and if "adventurism" might sometimes be of use, it does not mean that "adventurism" is everything, or the main thing. Not at all. It is neither everything, nor the most essential thing.

Jabotinsky was particularly anxious to make his point clear to the *Betar* in Palestine. In a letter to Dr. Julius Freulich, head (*Natziv*) of that organization, he took note of the fact that in its ranks a lively discussion had been going on as to whether *Betar's* program was necessary and useful and whether it would not be advisable to abandon it and devote all forces to "extra-legal forms of political struggle." Answering this question, he acknowledged that "in certain times and under certain circumstances, extra-legal forms of political struggle undoubtedly become both inevitable and necessary. Such actions must not, of course, be contrary to moral law, in particular to the principle of the sanctity of human life, unless in self-defense." He even went farther, admitting that "a contingency may arise when an organization, which is itself a legal body, might be morally compelled, or even morally obliged, to declare openly its sympathy for acts of extra-legal nature." But he refused to give a wholesale endorsement of the trend advocated by Achimeir.[4]

At the Fifth Revisionist World Conference in Vienna (August, 1932), Achimeir headed a "Club of Revisionist-Maximalists," about twenty-five delegates strong. He demanded that the democratic structure of the Revisionist movement be abandoned; youth must be organized, on dictatorial lines, into a militant unit—similar to an exclusive Order—fighting for the establishment of the Jewish State. Jabotinsky forcefully refuted and combatted this "philosophy" of Revisionism, both during the Conference and afterward.[5] But he consistently supported the *Biryonim* in every one of their actual conflicts with the Palestine Administration. He openly acknowledged that their campaign against the census had been directly ordered by the Revisionist World Executive; there was no such order in regard to their other actions, but, he wrote, "I approve of them." [6] A brief outline of the *Brit Habiryonim* activities, published by the Jabotinsky Institute in Tel Aviv, gratefully acknowledges: "Jabotinsky endorsed, with his blessings, every deed of the *Brit*." [7]

3. . . . and Supporting Them

On July 22, 1933, Abba Achimeir and nineteen of his friends were arrested by the British police. Thirteen were released within a month. Of the remaining seven, five were charged with belonging to an "illegal terroristic organization," and two (Achimeir and Zvi Rosenblatt)—with complicity with Abraham Stavsky in the assassination of Dr. Chaim Arlosoroff : Rosenblatt as the actual killer, and Achimeir as the "spiritual instigator" of the plot (see Chapter Ten).

Jabotinsky unhesitatingly embraced the cause of the accused. Not even for a moment did he doubt their innocence. Twenty-four hours after their arrest, he wrote to Michael Haskel :[8] "Stavsky I never saw in my life; these men I know, and as sure as I am about my son, I am sure that they cannot be connected with murder. This is an obvious political crusade against an inconvenient party, initiated by the Zionist Left but now evidently taken up with great gusto by some elements of the Mandatory Administration. I shall not be surprised if attempts will be made to drag me in, too."

The attempt to involve the *Biryonim* in the Arlosoroff murder affair failed. On May 16, 1934, Achimeir was acquitted by the Court, and so was Rosenblatt on June 8. But the original charge of belonging to a terroristic organization remained. On June 19, Achimeir was sentenced by the Jaffa District Court to twenty-one months' imprisonment with hard labor, and his three co-defendants to three, nine and fifteen months.[9] A statement published by Jabotinsky stigmatized this verdict as an "act of revenge" on the part of the Palestine Administration, and conveyed to the condemned *Biryonim* "heartfelt greetings and appreciation on the part of the [Revisionist] movement." [10]

In the winter months of 1933, the Palestine Administration drastically reduced the number of certificates granted to Jewish immigrants, and started hunting Jewish tourists who had "illegally" overstayed their temporary visas. After a mass protest meeting organized on December 9 by the Revisionist Organization of Tel Aviv, thousands of Jews staged a street demonstration which ended in violent clashes with the police and hastily summoned military reinforcements. Several demonstrators were injured, others were arrested. When reports of this demonstration reached Paris, Jabotinsky cabled to Meir Dizengoff, the Mayor of Tel Aviv :[11]

Please convey to the demonstrators the following: Your righteous outburst of protest and your exalted sacrifice will remain in Jewish history as the birthday of a decisive offensive, which is now being inaugurated by world Jewry [referring to the petition movement which was being launched by Revisionist headquarters]. This offensive will break the rule of the enemies of Zion in Eretz Israel and will bring about the dawn of Jewish statehood.

When the seventeen arrested demonstrators had been sentenced to terms of imprisonment ranging from one to six months, Jabotinsky cabled: "Your imprisonment is an honor for our people and a shame for the [British] regime." [12]

Anxious to dramatize the Palestine protests and to secure the widest possible repercussions in the Diaspora, Jabotinsky called on this writer to phone the Revisionist headquarters of six countries, conveying to them a two-word directive in Hebrew: *Lishbor Khalonot* [break windows]: "They are smart enough to understand that you mean the windows of the British Embassies or Consulates. Our key men in those countries know you personally and will not ask unnecessary questions. Should some of them do so, please answer with another Hebrew formula—*Naasse ve'Nishma* [do and listen]. That will be sufficient. But please, make the calls from your own home, so that they should not be traced to our central office here in Paris."

The calls were made. There was no necessity to use the second formula, and within ten days windows had been shattered in the British Embassies of Warsaw, Riga, Kaunas, Prague, and Bucharest.

In the summer of 1934, Arab nationalistic youth organizations started forming "volunteer squads," which actively cooperated with the Mandatory Administration in hunting Jewish "illegal immigrants." This led to repeated clashes with Jewish youth groups and created an explosive situation in the country. In a letter addressed to the British Colonial Office on August 7, 1934, Jabotinsky took up the case for the youth and drew the attention of the Mandatory Power to the far-reaching complications which were likely to arise from this state of affairs.[13]

While backing any specific action of open defiance of the anti-Zionist regime in Palestine—which incidentally was not always organized by the *Biryonim* alone—Jabotinsky persisted in opposing any organized attempt to impart the views of the *Biryonim* on the Revisionist movement as such. He wrote in a letter to his sister:[14] "It is necessary to distinguish between a *Stimmung* [frame of mind] and *organization*. Maximalist *tendencies* in our ranks are inevitable and legitimate (with the proviso that there should be no exaggeration —for instance, the attempt to cancel Achimeir's naturalization should not be considered to be as terrible as the attempt to hang Stavsky:

the first is meanness, the second—horror, and they are not the same and should not be reacted to in the same way). But I will never agree to any *organized* forms of maximalism in our midst, not even in the form of 'cells.' The entire value of [maximalist] tendencies (just as that of 'adventurism') is that they are impulsive, that they erupt spontaneously; to convert them into a statute with paragraphs would make them ridiculous. . . . And one more thing: the [Revisionist] party as such, and its organs (for instance the Central Committee) must remain completely unconnected with maximalism. In its official manifestations, Revisionism must remain a constitutional movement; otherwise it would be impossible to conduct the petition action, to negotiate with Governments, etc."

THE FATHER OF JEWISH ARMED
RESISTANCE I

1. *The Haganah*

JABOTINSKY'S attitude toward organized self-defense of the *Yishuv* underwent a significant evolution from the early spring of 1920, when he had become the founder and the first commander of the *Haganah*. He had every reason to be proud of this body's—and his own—record. But those who have read the first volume of this biography will recollect that for years afterward he was highly sceptical, and often critical in regard to the *Haganah's* actual value as effective defender of Palestine Jewry in case of serious Arab trouble. For several years he fervently advocated the unconditional primacy of a Jewish military unit (as a part of the British garrison) over a voluntary civilian body of the *Haganah* type; when the prospects for such a military formation began to fade, he, without abandoning the Legion demand, concentrated his argumentation on stressing that the *Haganah's* extra-legal status was impairing its effectiveness as a defense force.

The Arab onslaught in August, 1929, served as the acid test of *Haganah's* record and achievement. It revealed both its merits and its shortcomings. In Jabotinsky's estimate, the balance was fundamentally positive. On August 29, when the pogrom was still raging in Palestine, he addressed a mass meeting in Paris and paid unqualified tribute to the *Haganah's* achievements:[1] "All of you know what saved the *Yishuv*, left by the [British] Government without armed defense. We must salute all members of the Self-Defense, those who perished and those who are alive; they saved the *Yishuv* during the four terrible days until the British troops arrived. . . . We need a Jewish Self-Defense Force in Palestine." Seven years later, after the new outbreak of Arab violence in Palestine, he wrote to Jacob De Haas:[2] "In fairness to the *Haganah,* nobody should be allowed to forget that it does exist and that it is immensely useful. The fact that so few colonies have been attacked is due to the Arabs' knowledge of the existence and the efficiency of the *Haganah.* Its enforced supineness is most depressing to all concerned and to the Diaspora Jew, but its presence has certainly saved the *Yishuv.*"

For years he insisted on the legalization of the *Haganah.* In a "Memorandum on Defense of Palestine," submitted to the members of the British Parliament in February, 1930, he argued that an extralegal defense organization, "run on the lines of a purely private concern, presents many inevitable defects." Smuggled arms were bound to be inferior both in quality and quantity; secret training could not be but very poor and was unable to guarantee the necessary moderation in defensive actions. "Legalization seems to be the only reasonable way of dealing with the problem. . . . The legalized Self-Defense should take the form of a permanent Special Constabulary whose instructors and commanders should be selected or approved by the Government." The existence of such a legally constituted force would in itself exert a certain prophylactic influence in discouraging attack.[3]

No progress was made in the attempt to obtain *Haganah's* legalization in 1930, nor in the following years. Reluctantly, but realistically, Jabotinsky had to reckon with this state of affairs. He felt that a Jewish self-defense body, however imperfect, was better than none, and deserved every support. This attitude was considerably strengthened by significant developments in the *Haganah* ranks.

A semi-official history of the *Haganah,* published in 1949 by the *Keren ha'Yessod* Youth Department, admitted that the 1929 events had "revealed dangerous defects not only in the system of defense as such but also in the practices of rural and urban settlements."[4] Valuable improvement was achieved in *Haganah's* technical and numerical expansion. But there was much resentment against the onesided character of *Haganah's* leadership. The source quoted asserted that after the pogrom, "a *Haganah* staff acceptable and answerable to almost all sections of the *Yishuv* was now set up."[5] This is, however, inaccurate. Many *Haganah* members and wide circles of the *Yishuv* complained that this organization had become

443

practically a branch of the leftist *Histadrut;* they insisted that the defense of the Jewish community in Palestine must be entrusted to an independent body, controlled not by one party, but by the community as such.

This brought about a split in the *Haganah* ranks. In 1931-32, an independent "second" *Haganah* (*Haganah Bet*), which even then was often called *Irgun Zvai Leumi* (National Military Organization), was created. It was organized on a purely military basis; its civilian backing was provided by a Board consisting of representatives of all non-socialist parties in the *Yishuv* (the General Zionists, *Mizrachi,* Revisionists, *Agudat Israel,* Jewish State Party). The rank and file of the *Haganah Bet* consisted overwhelmingly of *Betarim* and young Revisionists; its commander was also a Revisionist, Abraham Tehomi (his underground alias was "Gideon"). But the Revisionist movement as such had no decisive influence over this body, nor was Jabotinsky in any direct way connected with it. It was not before December 5, 1936, that a written "agreement between Z. Jabotinsky and A. Tehomi" was signed in Paris, the first paragraph of which stated that Tehomi had been "appointed the Commander of the *Irgun* (*Haganah Bet*) by the President of the New Zionist Organization, and will conduct it in the spirit of the latter's instructions." The agreement endorsed in principle the idea of the unification of the two existing *Haganah* organizations, stressing, however, that a vital condition for such a merger was the creation of "a united Zion and united *Yishuv*" and that a "round-table conference" of all constituent bodies must take place first of all.*

By that time, Jabotinsky's interest in the *Haganah* was considerably intensified. He was then, as before, still convinced that only a legally-constituted Jewish military unit was capable of coping adequately with the *Yishuv's* security problem. However, in the face of the growing Arab campaign of violence, which had started in April, 1936, he was fully aware of the urgent necessity for even an illegal Jewish defense force. He regarded the providing of properly trained cadres for this vital task as the primary duty of the Jewish youth in the Diaspora.

It was in this spirit that he wrote the article "Oif'n Pripetchek" (On the Hearth), which played a revolutionary role in the molding

* The author is indebted to Yehuda Slutzky of the Editorial Board of the *History of the Haganah* for putting at his disposal the text of the agreement.

of a new mentality among a large section of Jewish youth; it made them realise the paramount importance of military preparedness. Its main theme, "Young men, learn to shoot," has since become a household word in wide circles of the younger generation. "Oif'n Pripetchek" was read and reread in hundreds of gatherings, and reprinted as a separate pamphlet in several languages.[6]

As a point of departure, Jabotinsky took the"wonderful immortal song"of the Yiddish-American poet Warshawsky—"a song which may well be deeper and richer than all national anthems in the world" :

A fire is burning on the hearth and an old Rabbi is teaching little children the Alef-Beth. He begins with a "groan and a sigh laden with four thousand years of pain and loneliness." But as he continues the lesson, he conveys to the children the sublime truth that "one has to be strong to survive all that we have borne," and that "consolation may only be found in strength . . . there is no other consolation than one's own strength." Since "every generation has its own Alef-Beth," the Alef-Beth of the generation now growing "is very plain and simple : 'Young men, learn to shoot!' " Irrespective of whether one likes this ABC of shooting or not, everyone must realize that "of all the necessities of national rebirth, shooting is the most important. . . . We are forced to learn to shoot and it is futile to argue against the compulsion of a historical reality."

Jabotinsky realized the practical limitations of his precept: "Of perhaps a hundred who may be thinking of learning the new ABC, ninety may not be in a position to do so, with the best will in the world. There is no money, there is no time, or perhaps the Gentiles won't allow it." But "it does not matter," he insisted. Because "a nation in our position must know the ABC and acquire the psychology of shooting and the longing after it." And he concluded the article with the last stanza of Warshawsky's song: "Learn, my children, with great diligence, for that is what I say to you : 'He who will first learn his ABC, will get a flag.' "

But the very identity of this "flag" had in the meantime become doubtful. It transpired that Tehomi was planning the unification of the *Haganah Bet* with the "official" *Haganah,* without any of the safeguards stipulated in his agreement with Jabotinsky. Early in 1937, official Zionist leadership became convinced that partition of Palestine was inevitable and the establishment of a sovereign Jewish State in a part of the country close at hand. In eager anticipation of this event, they summoned representatives of all Zionist parties, and, waving before them the prospect of a regular Jewish Army, insisted on the immediate merger of *Haganah Bet* with the leftist *Haganah*. All parties represented in the Board of the *Haganah Bet* were for the merger; Tehomi also strongly advocated this course. It was, however, clear to everybody that without Jabotinsky's consent this operation had little chance of being carried through fully and painlessly. Moshe Rosenberg, one of Tehomi's closest collaborators and a faithful *Betari,* told him bluntly : "As long as Jabotinsky does not give us the 'green light' for such a merger, we will not move; and should you, as our local commander, order us to do so, we will revolt." [7] At a meeting of the civilian Board, to which Rosenberg and the head of the Palestine *Betar,* Benno Lubotsky, were invited, the latter said bluntly that among those present was missing the one man whose order the *Betarim* would obey—Jabotinsky; no vote of the Board could influence their attitude. [8]

In the hope of obtaining Jabotinsky's consent, several leaders of the *Yishuv* wrote and wired him; Rabbi Meir Berlin met him in South Africa with the same purpose in mind. Some influential Revisionist leaders in Palestine also approved of the merger scheme, and considerable pressure was applied to sway Jabotinsky in its favor. Colonel Patterson, who was at that time in the country and, as a soldier, appreciated the purely military advantages of unification, cabled him to Johannesburg, imploring him, in the name of "common sense," to confirm the agreement with the official *Haganah.*[9]

Jabotinsky saw things from a different angle. His approach was, as in all other matters, a political *par excellence.* The most vital problem then facing Zionism was the partition plan submitted by the Royal Commission. The Jabotinsky movement was unanimous in opposing this scheme; the parties backing the *Haganah Bet* were also mildly opposed to it; the Jewish Agency, under whose authority the leftist *Haganah* functioned, endorsed partition and fought for it enthusiastically. Should the two bodies merge, there would remain in Palestine no truly independent armed force to counteract the implementation of the partition scheme. Another major consideration was the attitude toward the official Zionist policy of *havlaga* (self-restraint), which prescribed purely defensive tactics and barred any attempt at retaliation for the wanton murder of Jews. The official *Haganah* strictly observed this policy. Disregarding growing discontent among

446

several younger commanders and many of the rank and file, *Haganah Bet* was actually following the same line; isolated acts of retaliation were severely condemned by Tehomi, and their perpetrators brought before the organization's Military Court. Jabotinsky himself was not ready to advocate retaliation as a system during the first half of 1936. The main difficulty, as he then saw it, was that the Jewish defense problem was connected not so much with the Arabs as with the British : [10]

The Jews would have defended themselves from the first moment, were it not clear that in that eventuality the [British] police and soldiers would be turned against them, against the defenders, and the situation would assume an entirely different aspect. . . . We are confronted with the dilemma either to fight with British military forces or to be content with the role of cowards and to suffer the consequences.

For a time, Jabotinsky was not prepared for an open military conflict with the British. But he anticipated the contingency of breaking the *havlaga* and having recourse to retaliation, and it was clear to him that a merger with the official *Haganah* was tantamount to precluding the very possibility of such a course. He therefore refused to consent to the merger.

But Tehomi, who had already come to terms with the leftist *Haganah* in the early spring of 1937, was by that time too much involved to go back on his commitments. He went ahead with the implementation of the merger scheme. However, he underestimated the impact of Jabotinsky's negative attitude. The majority of *Haganah Bet's* younger commanders revolted. On April 10, they issued a statement expelling Tehomi and his followers from the organization, and asserting its independence as *Irgun Zvai Leumi* [National Military Organization]; the overwhelming majority of the *Haganah Bet's* membership sided with them.[11] A plebiscite carried out in local units produced eloquent testimony of the rank and file's allegiance to Jabotinsky: in Ramat Gan, for instance, of three hundred fifty members only one followed Tehomi's call.[12] Eliahu Golomb, commander of the official *Haganah,* asserted that of the three thousand members of the *Haganah Bet,* about fifteen hundred joined together with Tehomi, "and later some left." [13] This estimate seems, however, to be highly exaggerated. According to other sources, not more than a few hundred went with Tehomi, and the percentage of those who subsequently reconsidered their action and left the *Haganah* was very high.[14] Tehomi proved to be not much of an asset and his position in the *Haganah* turned out to be a subordinate one. Two years later, he was "very anxious to be received" by Jabotinsky who, however, decided that such an encounter "would be as yet premature." As to the rank and file of Tehomi's boys who were still in the *Haganah*, Jabotinsky was informed that they constituted "in fact nothing but a collective Wallenrod [Konrad Wallenrod, Polish hero of Adam Mickiewicz's poem, who joined the Prussian camp with the purpose of bringing in a Trojan horse] and a fifth column." [15]

2. *The Irgun*

In the *Irgun Zvai Leumi*—as previously in the *Haganah Bet*—Jabotinsky held no official position of authority. Nevertheless, when its new leadership selected Robert Bitker as its first commander, they deemed it but natural to submit this nomination for Jabotinsky's approval, thus practically establishing Jabotinsky's supreme moral authority in all major *Irgun* matters. Later, this factual state of affairs was formulated as follows: Jabotinsky was the supreme commander of the *Irgun Zvai Leumi*; his orders were to be obeyed in questions of major policy; the *Irgun's* commander in Palestine was to be appointed by him; on the other hand, residing outside of Palestine, he was not to interfere in any matters of the *Irgun's* daily activities and in the appointment or promotion of officers. It was also agreed that this authority belonged to Jabotinsky personally; it was not to be extended to, and exercised by, the *Nessiut* of the New Zionist Organization he headed. It was a purely personal link between Jabotinsky and the *Irgun* (by the end of 1937, it was agreed that Jabotinsky was entitled to delegate his authority, again on a personal level, to S. Jacobi).[16]

Robert Bitker, the husky former head of the Jewish self-defense force in Shanghai, did not last long as the first *Irgun* commander. In October, 1937, Shmuel Katz arrived in Warsaw as the emissary of the *Irgun* and the Palestine Revisionist Party, to report to Jabotinsky on the complications that had arisen in consequence of Bitker's leadership and to submit to him the request for the latter's removal. The reasons for this request are not within the scope of this biography. What is, however, of biographical interest, is the manner in which

Jabotinsky dealt with this delicate matter. Katz found him in his hotel room, busily packing in preparation for a short trip, and was invited to tell what he had to say on the train:[17]

When he had heard what I had to report about Bitker, he put to me some searching queries and questioned the propriety of going over Bitker's head, since after all Bitker was in the position of a military commander. . . . He returned to the matter a few days later, when we came back to Warsaw. In the meantime, Bitker arrived there and came to report. When I was leaving him, Jabotinsky said: "Bitker is in the next room. You be careful as you go out. He's bigger than you and can easily give you a licking." (Bitker in the next room said to me: "I know what you're here for. Is the 'old man' very angry?").

Two days later Jabotinsky gave me verbal (and later written) instructions for Eretz Israel—including the retirement of Bitker. He said: "Until I saw Bitker I had to be his counsel. That was why I cross-examined you and criticized you in the train. As soon as Bitker came, I had to tell him some hard things and took the opposite stand. He thinks he acted correctly. But what I am proud of is that there wasn't the slightest factual discrepancy in the two stories I heard."

On the recommendation of the *Irgun's* High Command and the leadership of the Revisionist Organization in Palestine, Jabotinsky appointed in Bitker's place Moshe Rosenberg, Bitker's chief of staff; late in 1937, he replaced him with David Raziel, Rosenberg's aide. All these nominations were accepted without hesitation.

Jabotinsky's first direct contact with the *Irgun* High Command took place in July, 1937, in Alexandria (Egypt), where he met with Bitker and his lieutenants, Moshe Rosenberg and Abraham Stern, as well as with the delegations of the Palestine New Zionist Organization and of the *Betar*. At this conference, the question of breaking the policy of self-restraint (*havlaga*) and inaugurating a series of retaliation actions against the Arab terror was discussed at length. The necessity and inevitability of such a course appeared obvious. But for Jabotinsky it was in more than one respect a difficult decision to make. Though recognizing the bitter political justification for retaliation, he had grave doubts as to the moral aspect of such a course, which was bound to affect not only Arab terrorists, but also such Arabs—men, women and children—who were not directly responsible for indiscriminate killing of Jewish men, women and children. M. Rosenberg remembers him saying: "I can't see much heroism and public good in shooting from the rear an Arab peasant on a donkey, carrying vegetables for sale in Tel Aviv." *

On the other hand, Jabotinsky felt uneasy about authorizing the *Irgun* to undertake actions in which their freedom and their very lives would be in jeopardy, while he himself would be sitting safely in Europe.

It was finally decided to start preparations for retaliation; but actual large scale action was to be taken only when the *Irgun* received a wire from Jabotinsky signed "Mendelson" (his code name as the head of the *Irgun*) and saying "The deal is concluded." Jabotinsky had had a hard struggle with himself when faced with such a decision. Aron Kope [Kopeliowicz], one of his colleagues in the Presidency of the N.Z.O., told this writer that one evening, while in Paris, Jabotinsky seemed to have decided to do so. He wrote the text agreed upon and went to the post office to dispatch it; but at the last moment he tore up the telegram. In reply to Kope's astonished question "why?" he said: "I just couldn't. If I were with them, sharing all their dangers, I would not hesitate even for a moment. We would all have been in the same boat. But from this safe distance, no!" Later, in London, he gave one of his younger collaborators, Y. Benari, the fateful telegram at least four times, asking him to go to Calais in France to dispatch it from there to Palestine, and each time he cancelled the assignment.[18]

In letters to Jacob De Haas, Jabotinsky admitted that for a time he considered the *havlaga* "most useful as an argument in favor of [the reestablishment of the Jewish] Legion"; but later "it became obviously dangerous."

For years to come, Jabotinsky was extremely cautious about officially

---

* He also did not approve of individual political terror. In the autumn of 1937, the Mufti of Jerusalem fled from Palestine to Bludan in Lebanon, from where he continued to direct anti-Jewish terroristic activities. One day, a veteran foreign correspondent in Jerusalem, who had very close contacts with Arabs of all classes, told Shmuel Katz that an Arab friend of his, ostensibly a Mufti follower, offered to have the Mufti assassinated for the sum of two hundred pounds ($800 at that time); the payment was to be made only after the deed was accomplished. "Two hundred pounds was a substantial sum in those days," Shmuel Katz told this writer, "but I could have accepted the offer on the spot and found the money. Yet the implications of the proposal were clearly far-reaching. Using a private code, I sent a query to Jabotinsky through the late S. Jacobi. For some two months I heard nothing. Then came a message from Jacobi: 'Jabotinsky says no. Would you like to see the Arabs bumping off Weizmann or Shertok'?" (Interview with Shmuel Katz, Tel Aviv.)

associating himself with the policies and activities of the *Irgun*. On September 2, 1937, he wrote to S. Jacobi from Zurich: "Yesterday Novomeyski [Director of the Dead Sea concession] phoned me from St. Moritz, exhorting me that we give orders to observe the *havlaga*. I assured him that we don't know anything at all [of this matter], etc." Opening the First World Assembly of the New Zionist Organization in Prague on January 31, 1938, he welcomed the fact that "Palestine Jewry had finally abandoned that passive toleration of banditry and terror, which was called *havlaga*." He stressed, however, that "it was a spontaneous outbreak of the outraged feelings of the nation, and must never be ascribed to one party only." While the Palestine Government "saw fit to arrest, in this connection, numerous leading New Zionists and members of the *Betar* and imprison them in Acre jail," Jabotinsky described this action only "as an expression of the [Government's] appreciation of our [Revisionist] strength and of the direction of our spiritual influence." It is in this limited sense that he sent the prisoners of Acre "cordial greetings on behalf of this Assembly." [20] When, during the Assembly, Menachem Begin, then a young *Betar* leader, mentioned the *Irgun* and asked for directives, the answer was: *"Men fregt nit dem Taten"* (one shouldn't ask one's father's permission).[21] In July of the same year, in a conversation with Eliahu Golomb in London, he refused to say or to do anything which "could be interpreted as if I was taking upon myself the responsibility for what had been done [by the *Irgun*] and as if things that are being done now are in accordance with my orders." [22] And when, three months later, the Revisionist World Council, sitting in Warsaw, was urged to express its stand in regard to the *Irgun's* activities, Jabotinsky was strongly opposed to any discussion of this question.[23] Moreover, he even affirmed that, in fact, he was not in a position to issue any orders determining the character of the *Irgun's* activities since there was no certainty that such directives would be followed. When Golomb urged him to stop *Irgun's* independent actions, he asked: "Do you think that those who are engaged in such actions would accept my orders? . . . Would you give orders that will not be obeyed?" Golomb assured him: "I know you and your men. I know that your opinion is decisive for them." Jabotinsky remained unconvinced: "I am not competent to give orders in such matters." [24]

This cautious attitude was undoubtedly largely motivated by

Jabotinsky's rather special position. He was not only the supreme commander of the *Irgun*—a clandestine and outlawed military organization—but also, and primarily, the *Nassi* of the New Zionist Organization, President of the Revisionist World Union, and *Rosh* (head) of the *Brit Trumpeldor*; all legal bodies, and intending to remain so. This, he believed, obliged him to preserve at least the semblance of legality, avoiding any direct connection with openly illegal acts of "terrorism." But, in addition to this consideration, for some time there had been no real meeting of minds between Jabotinsky and the *Irgun* leadership in regard to some essential aspects of the *Irgun's* activities and political line.

The *Irgun* began its retaliation action a few months after the Alexandria conference. When, early in September, 1937, Arab terrorists murdered three Jews, the *Irgun's* counter-attack cost the lives of thirteen Arabs. Further outbreaks of Arab violence remained for a time unanswered. The *Irgun's* High Command decided on a "month of *Havlaga*" which was observed even when the Arabs attacked the *Betar's* most cherished *Plugat ha'Kotel*, a shock troop whose task was to protect Jews praying at the Wailing Wall. All attempts to induce the *Irgun* Command to counter-attack failed. Then a small group of *Betar* militants from the colony Rosh Pinah, organized by Dr. Shimshan Yunitchman, decided to act on their own. They succeeded in smuggling arms—and themselves—into Jerusalem and were preparing to take independent action. Anxious to prevent a partisan defiance of the *Irgun's* discipline, David Raziel, after much heated debate and soul-searching, yielded and, disregarding his own Command's previous decision, himself undertook to carry out the retaliation; the mutinous group was sent home.[25] The spectacular "black Friday" (November 14) in Jerusalem was a lightning answer to Arab provocation.[26] The Jewish Agency denounced these reprisals as "marring the moral record of Palestine Jewry, hampering the political struggle and undermining security." Jabotinsky's comment was, of course, different. When, after the Jerusalem operation, twenty Revisionists, including his son Eri, were arrested and interned in the concentration camp at Acre, his reaction was: "The tendency of the Jews to hit back cannot be stopped by arrests and imprisonments; I personally feel very proud that my son is among the arrested."

At the N.Z.O. Convention in Prague (February, 1938), the *Irgun* High Command put the case of the Rosh Pinah group before

Jabotinsky—in his double capacity as the head of the *Irgun* and of the *Betar*—accusing them of "partisan activities" which had forced the hand of the High Command and thus undermined the unity of action. Abraham Stern presented a forceful indictment. Defending the group's action, Dr. Yunitchman recalled the episode narrated by Jabotinsky in his "Story of the Jewish Legion." When, in 1915, Jabotinsky broke the discipline of the Zionist Organization and his mother heard from M. M. Ussishkin that her son should be hanged for that, she answered her son's query as to whether he should continue his work with the clear and simple advice: "If you are sure that you are right, go ahead." This reference won the day: the Rosh Pinah group was not only acquitted but also commended by the *Shilton Betar*.[27]

However, Jabotinsky for a long time continued to have grave doubts about the moral aspect of the reprisals which cost the lives of Arabs who were not directly connected with the Arab terror. A typical nineteenth century liberal, he considered human life as sacrosanct and was deeply upset by the fact that the Arabs who paid with their lives were not always those who took Jewish lives. Following a series of bloody reprisals by the *Irgun,* he called in the *Irgun's officier de liaison* in Europe and, in the presence of this writer, told him: "How can your *Irgun* people throw bombs in Arab quarters at random, indiscriminately killing women and children? You must at least warn the Arabs in time to evacuate the sections where you are going to retaliate."[28] Yaacov Meridor recalls that a wire was then received from Jabotinsky with a direct, stern injunction that "this should never happen again." David Raziel, the *Irgun's* commander, was flabbergasted: "Jabotinsky obviously does not realize what he is asking us to do. Would he perhaps advise us to inform the Arabs in advance of the exact time and place of our impending attack, or even give them the names and addresses of the attackers?"[29] * Jabotinsky was, of course, aware that his injunction made the task of the fighting underground even harder than it was, but, as he told Golomb two years later (June 19, 1939), "he had been struggling . . . with his conscience against hurting innocents."[30]

Even more far-reaching was the cleavage in regard to the character

---

* In later years, the *Irgun* made it its policy, whenever possible without directly jeopardizing its operations, to warn civilians, Arab, and British alike, of the impending attack. (Interview with Menachem Begin, Tel Aviv.)

and scope of the *Irgun's* role in the overall struggle for Jewish national redemption.

The very essence of Jabotinsky's credo had always been the belief that the Jewish problem can be solved and the Zionist aim achieved by world-wide political action. To him, *Judennot* was a most powerful dynamic force, bound to enlist the understanding and cooperation of the nations of the world for the Zionist solution. A sustained and concerted political offensive along these lines was the indicated method of Zionist struggle. Within its framework, *Irgun* was destined to play an important, but necessarily subordinate role, as an organic part of the overall effort. It was therefore expected to coordinate its strategy with the general scheme of action.

Some *Irgun* leaders felt differently. They had lost faith in "diplomacy" in purely political methods. Their contention was that in the world of 1937-38, after the practically unopposed annexation of Abyssinia by Mussolini's Italy, and after the cynical pact concluded with Mussolini by France's Pierre Laval and Britain's Samuel Hoare, it would be naive to believe in international conscience and to appeal for international cooperation; the only realities the world was ready to reckon with, were those created by military force. They therefore insisted that as a national military organization, the *Irgun* was destined to play a major role in the realization of Zionism, both militarily and politically. They accordingly resented the even remote dependence arising from the very fact that Jabotinsky was simultaneously their supreme authority and the head of the N.Z.O. and of the *Betar*. In this position, he was bound to insist on a certain balance of forces between the various components of his wide frontline, restraining one from interfering with the other. Some emissaries sent by the *Irgun* High Command to the Diaspora countries for the practical purpose of fundraising, training the youth, and securing the supply of arms, refused to accept this state of affairs and utilized their mission for purposes far beyond their assignment.

Among them was one of the most talented and dynamic young *Irgun* commanders, Abraham Stern, who read Homer in the original and wrote Hebrew poetry (his underground name was "Yair"). He arrived in Warsaw with a short and most generously worded letter of introduction from Jabotinsky to this writer, who had been the accredited political representative of the New Zionist Organization to the Polish Government since 1936. The letter read: "Do for the bearer of this message whatever you would have done for me." Stern was accordingly introduced to several leading officials in the Foreign, War, and Internal Affairs Ministries. He made an excellent impression and succeeded in securing a promise to put at *Irgun's* disposal a sizeable amount of arms and ammunition; part of it was an outright gift, the rest had to be paid for either in cash or in easy installments. Stern regarded this as an achievement of the *Irgun* as such. However, when, in the late spring of 1939, the first shipment had to be delivered, the Poles demanded that Jabotinsky personally authorize and confirm the deal. Jeopardizing his studied "aloofness," Jabotinsky, then in London, unhesitatingly cabled the required endorsement.[31] On a subsequent visit to Poland, on May 12, 1939, he addressed a letter to A. Zarychta, the head of the Emigration Department of the Polish Foreign Ministry, thanking him for his successful cooperation in "realizing an important transaction, which represents the [monetary] value of two hundred twelve thousand Zlotys [approximately forty-two thousand dollars, at that time a very considerable amount] :"*

I am convinced that the results of this useful and honorable operation will be appreciated by everybody.

I wish at the same time to confirm, in the name of my friends as well as in my own name, that we consider the credit extended to us as a debt of honor and that we will do everything in our power to redeem it in the nearest future.

Simultaneously with his efforts to secure arms for the *Irgun,* Stern started organizing special "cells" in the Polish *Betar,* whose members had to give an oath of allegiance to the *Irgun* as such, to obey *Irgun's* orders exclusively, and to comply with the orders of the *Betar* commanders only with the permission of their *Irgun* superiors. This venture created a problem of double loyalty, particularly painful in a youth movement; it also undermined the authority of the hierarchy of the *Betar,* which had always been Jabotinsky's most beloved child. Similar groups were later established among adult Revisionists and Revisionist proselytes. Capitalizing on the *Irgun's* great popularity and the halo of its fighting deeds and sacrifices, Stern was able to create a strong and efficient body of men and women who had no

---

* This writer is indebted to W. T. Drymmer, former senior official of the Polish Foreign Ministry, for making available to him the text of the letter, the original of which is preserved in the Ministry's files.

allegiance to any of the organizations headed by Jabotinsky; all their loyalty and enthusiasm belonged to the *Irgun*. Stern also did his very best to undermine—subtly and deliberately—the personal authority of Jabotinsky, in whom he saw the main obstacle to his efforts to establish the *Irgun* as an independent and dominating force in the struggle for national liberation. An *Irgun*-controlled Yiddish daily (*Di Tat*) was launched in Warsaw, followed by a Polish weekly (*Jerozolima Wyzwolona*); independent political contacts were established. *Betar* and Revisionist bodies responsible to Jabotinsky were deliberately and even contemptuously bypassed: *Oni i tak zdechne* (they will die out anyway), Stern said once to Henryk Strassman. Jabotinsky's influence was being insidiously undermined. In private conversation Stern derogatively referred to Jabotinsky as "Hindenburg," meaning a hero of former times who had become both obsolete and senile. When Eri once mentioned this remark in a letter to his father, the latter goodnaturedly signed his reply: "Yours faithfully—Hindenburg." [32]

Stern deliberately spoke of Jabotinsky as "your leader" (not his). He and his associates defiantly disparaged the value of any Zionist ideology, of political thought and action: a nation and a homeland cannot be redeemed through writing books and articles, holding speeches or evolving political schemes they argued; *action directe*—a gun and a bomb—is the sole efficient instrument of a nation's struggle for liberation. This "military Zionism" was developing into a determined opposition not only to the "cultural Zionism" of Achad Haam and the minimalistic Zionism of Weizmann, but also to the political Greater Zionism of Jabotinsky.

It could not be said that in these activities Stern represented the attitude and views of the *Irgun* High Command in Palestine, headed by David Raziel, which repeatedly and truthfully reasserted its allegiance to Jabotinsky. He was even less representative of the feelings of the *Irgun* rank and file, to whom Jabotinsky was the embodiment of the new fighting spirit in Jewry. Yaakov Meridor, then District Commander of the *Irgun* forces, emphatically assured this writer that the average *Irgun* soldier was completely unaware of the separatist activities of some of the emissaries, and responsible *Irgun* leadership would under no circumstances have agreed to be a party to any attempt at undermining the authority of the man whom they considered the greatest Jew of the generation. It was a source of profound regret to them that Jabotinsky did not as yet fully endorse their attitude and did not go the whole way with the *Irgun*. Yet they were unshakable in their faith that Jabotinsky was their natural ally and that, given time, they would join forces. But Stern deliberately disregarded this official stand and conducted a policy of his own, creating facts and situations without even informing Jabotinsky. When, with the active cooperation of the Polish Government, courses for *Irgun* instructors were established at Andzychow (Podkarpacie), Warsaw, Zofiow, Poddebie, etc., and Count Lubiensky congratulated Jabotinsky on their fine record, Jabotinsky felt deeply embarrassed: he did not even know of their existence. He later angrily asked Menachem Begin, who was at that time the head of the Polish *Betar*: *Hem mishelanu?* [are they (the *Irgun*) our people?].[33] To Mrs. Lubinsky he once said: "What kind of people are they? I know them very little. Their plans, their innermost thoughts just don't reach me." [34]

Jabotinsky was also opposed to the *Irgun's* exclusive reliance on armed force. At a private gathering in Warsaw, he once heatedly said: "In fact, their [*Irgun's*] philosophy is Weizmannism in reverse. Weizmann and his followers believe but in 'practical constructive work': one more dunam, one more cow, one more house. . . . To them, 'only thus' can Zionism be fulfilled. The *Irgun* leaders, too, have made 'only thus' their motto, substituting a rifle for the dunam—cow—house package. Both approaches are narrow-minded and wrong, because both are a-political. I stick to my own version of the first sentence of the Book of Genesis: *B'reshit Bara Elohim et ha-politica* (In the beginning God created—politics)." [35]

It would be undoubtedly wrong and misleading to dramatize unduly those similar displays of Jabotinsky's displeasure with certain aspects of the *Irgun's* activities and its slogans. They always occurred *in camera,* in a restricted circle of closest associates, and they certainly did not affect his general attitude toward the *Irgun*. But differences of outlook and emphasis did exist and could not fail to generate, here and there, misunderstandings and friction.

One source of friction was the *Aliya Bet* ("illegal" immigration), which, in 1937-39, had become a major activity of the Jabotinsky movement. The *Irgun,* which actively participated in its organization, insisted on playing the dominant role in this field. Jabotinsky determinedly opposed this claim. In his view, the *Irgun* was but "a landing agency" at the receiving end; its function was to take the immigrants off the boats on the shores of Palestine and to direct them to the settlements indicated by the *Betar* and the Revisionist party; he insisted that the entire organization of *Aliya Bet* in the Diaspora countries must remain in the hands of the *Betar,* and would not agree to any other arrangement. The *Irgun* leadership strongly resented this approach. They, in turn, insisted that they were sending to Palestine trained military cadres with the "illegal" boats, and these were of tremendous importance for their struggle; the *Irgun* thus had a direct and vital stake of its own in the entire operation. Stern and some of his colleagues went even farther and said that all Jabotinsky wanted was to utilize the *Irgun* for the aggrandizement of the *Betar* and of the Revisionist party; he would give them a letter of introduction to some influential Jew or Gentile and help them to get some money, but he would never permit them to become an independent powerful factor in Zionist policy.

By November, 1938, Jabotinsky was ready for a showdown. He wrote to the High Command of the *Irgun* in Palestine demanding that internal propaganda in the *Betar* be stopped and that their emissaries conducting "illegal" immigration be instructed to work exclusively through the *Aliya* Department of the *Shilton* [High Command] of the *Betar.* He also announced that he would shortly call a conference of representatives of the *Irgun, Betar,* and the N.Z.O. in order to establish a unified youth organization.[36] The conference took place in Paris in February, 1939. At Jabotinsky's insistence, David Raziel, overcoming great difficulties, came from Palestine. He strongly impressed Jabotinsky with his straightforward earnestness and quiet self-confidence, coupled with deep respect for his supreme commander. Their first conversation, as reported by an eye-witness, was as follows: "Are you a *Betari*?" "By birth." "Are you prepared to accept any decision we come to?" "Unreservedly." "I have been waiting for such a man for the last fifteen years," was Jabotinsky's comment.[37]

The conference gave little comfort to Jabotinsky. No agreed formula for the relationship between *Irgun* and *Betar* could be found. The discussion was tense and unpleasant. The *Irgun* delegation—with the exception of Raziel—was anything but cooperative, and Jabotinsky somewhat dejectedly observed that Raziel in fact did not seem to have full control of his own colleagues. At one of the sessions, in the middle of an acrimonious debate, Jabotinsky, who presided, sent a most unexpected note to this writer, who attended the meetings as one of the representatives of the New Zionist Organization: "Do you know that Aviva [the bride of his son Eri], who is a zoologist, is now working on cross-breeding, with a view to producing a new species of animal—a 'kosher pig,' cloven-footed and cud-chewing. Isn't this fascinating?" The note was accompanied by a drawing of a very fat pig labelled *kosher*. Replying to this puckish sally, this writer scribbled an amazed inquiry: "How can you think of such things in the middle of all this nasty strife?" Jabotinsky wrote back: "Thinking of 'such things' in this atmosphere is the best outlet for my present mood."

After a few days, the conference ran into a complete deadlock. Jabotinsky, who had to leave for a short visit to Belgium, told the participants: "Try to reach agreement in my absence; should you not succeed, I will dictate to you my formula after my return, and you will have to accept it as dictated." And so it turned out. A sub-committee appointed to work out a compromise solution failed to reach an agreement. Then, as one of the participants put it, he "took a 'night off,' " as happened so often before, and held a "round table conference" between the *Rosh Betar,* the Commander-in-Chief of the *Irgun,* and the President of the New Zionist Organization [he held all three offices]. The result of this palaver was a draft of an agreement, which was accepted by all parties without further discussion.[38] Since this is not the history of the *Irgun* or the *Betar,* the terms of this formula are not reproduced in this biography. This episode is told here merely as an illustration of the problems and difficulties Jabotinsky had to face.* He himself was far from happy about the entire "climate" of the Paris Conference. He felt, as he put it, that this Conference was no longer a "family gathering," but a meeting of "business partners," at which each party was struggling for its very own interests, to be written into a formal agreement.[39]

As could be easily foreseen, this agreement proved to be unworkable. The problems it was purported to solve remained as acute as before. The *Irgun's* representatives in Europe continued to act independently in the political field, defiantly disregarding the "Paris formula."

* The British Intelligence did not remain uninformed of the Paris Conference. A "most secret" C.I.D. Report on the Organization of the Illegal Immigration (May 11, 1939) gives a brief but essentially accurate survey of its proceedings and decisions; less correct is the list of participants.

In March, 1939, the editors of the *Irgun*-controlled *Jerozolima Wyzwolona* arranged a press conference, at which statements of far-reaching political nature were made. Jabotinsky was referred to as "ex-activist and extreme Jewish political thinker who now conducts a policy that seems to us to be a policy of complacency in Zionist affairs, while we are determined to take matters into our own hands." [40] Informed of this press conference, Jabotinsky disregarded the disparaging reference to himself,* but strongly objected to the "circumstances of the press conference—and the statements made at that occasion," which were "obviously calculated to convey the idea that they were made in the name of the *Irgun,* and covering essential fields of policy, not only military but also (even mainly) political." He insisted that "the *Irgun* as such can only act in Palestine" and that "there has never been any *Taccanon* (statute) recognizing the *Irgun* as a political movement, or as a body entitled to spread its direct command outside of Palestine. Even if our Warsaw friends thought that the *Irgun* has the right to act outside of Palestine, and that there was a need for a political statement on their behalf, even só they should have remembered that the chief [supreme commander of the *Irgun*] lives in Europe, that politics are his special field, for which the *Nessiut* is responsible, and that a permanent political delegate of the *Nessiut* lives in Warsaw. The editor of *Jerozolima* would consider it wrong if Dr. Schechtman were to make a statement on the policy of *Irgun* without consulting the proper representative. Does he think it is right to make statements on political questions without consulting Dr. Schechtman? . . . Any continuation of such a state of affairs would mean foolish disorder and absolute anarchy." [41]

3. The Danger of Civil War

On October 12, 1937, Jabotinsky wrote from Warsaw to S. Jacobi that he had been informed of a new attempt by the *Haganah* to enforce *Irgun's* observance of the *havlaga* and its submission to the "discipline of the national institutions." Dr. Arye Altman, who then headed the New Zionist Organization in Palestine, had been invited

* He was, however, fully aware of the fact that his personal prestige was rather low among the *Tat* and *Jerozolima Wyzwolona* people: "You know, they think and speak of me in the same way, in which we used to speak of Nachum Sokolov," he once said to Joseph Klarman.

to the *Vaad Leumi* where Eliahu Golomb demanded unification with the *Haganah,* threatening, in case of refusal, to "take other measures." Though Golomb did not specify the threat, Jabotinsky interpreted it as "either *messira* [denunciation] *en masse* or physical *rasprava* [Russian word meaning 'chastisement'] : the reason for this new pressure is, of course, that the Government have been taunting the Agency that it had no control over the *Yishuv* in the *havlaga* question." Taking notice of the *Irgun* leaders' opposition to yielding to the threat, he agreed with those who argued that "there is much less reason to accept the pressure now than ever before." He therefore sent a directive to Palestine, whose gist was : "*Ihud* [unification]— please, but on conditions which *they* will not accept, just because these conditions are perfectly logical."

But "what if they carry out the threat?" Jabotinsky asked. His answer was : "If they try violence there [in Palestine], it would evoke quite a forcible echo here [in the countries of the Diaspora]—the numerical proportion being almost reversed. . . . Were I in London now, I would propose to the *Nessiut* to warn Agency circles and outsiders of the type of [Herbert] Sidebotham [veteran English pro-Zionist], [Sir John] Haslam [pro-Zionist English politician], [Harry] Snell [later Lord, Labor M.P., and pro-Zionist member of the Shaw Commission], that the Agency are playing with Spanish fire, and not only in Palestine but also in the Diaspora."

The dire prospect of physical violence as a means of forcing the *Irgun* to stop its reprisal tactics and to "obey the discipline of the *Yishuv*" was frankly discussed in a long talk Jabotinsky had with Golomb in London on July 10, 1938. As recorded by Golomb, he told Jabotinsky : "Had we intended to use force, we could have prevented your friends from doing what they have done"; but since "this would have meant civil war," he asked Jabotinsky to "do everything in his power to prevent these happenings, so that we shall not have to resort to force." Jabotinsky flared up : "So you say that you will start terrorizing my friends? Do you believe that this will be restricted to Eretz Israel only?" Golomb denied that the *Haganah* was "prepared for a civil war"; but he clearly implied that an agreement between *Irgun* and *Haganah* along the lines he proposed was the sole means of preventing the "possibility of civil war ever occurring."

Fully realizing the ominous meaning of this statement, Jabotinsky, five weeks later, devoted a special press conference to the danger of civil war in Jewry. Speaking in Warsaw on August 16 to representatives of Jewish, Polish, European and American papers, he referred to the recent dispatch of the *New York Times* Jerusalem correspondent, who reported that "civil war among Jews," in the form of an armed pogrom of the Left parties against the Revisionists, was impending, and said: "This danger is unfortunately real. Already at the beginning of July I heard the same threat from a man who is very close to the security service of the Jewish Agency [Golomb]; he made it perfectly clear to me that, should they not succeed in achieving unity on the *havlaga* question, the elements who are under the influence of the Agency would use their arms against the Revisionists. At about the same time the same threat was repeated in Tel Aviv by another authoritative personality to a representative of the New Zionist Organization." "We would be closing our eyes to facts if we considered such threats as empty phrases," warned Jabotinsky. Quoting several instances from the recent past, he stressed that "the tradition of physical violence against ideological opponents is of long standing in Leftist circles." It must be clear, he insisted, that "such an attempt at an internal Jewish pogrom will result in an internal Jewish self-defense . . . should such a misfortune befall Palestine, it will not be limited to Palestine alone. On the contrary . . . it will, in a very serious form, be transplanted to the Diaspora countries." [42]

In the meantime, the situation in Palestine was growing increasingly tense. The Leftist groups intensified their hunting down of *Irgun* members and their sympathizers. By that time, in the Sarafend detention camp alone, hundreds of *Betarim* were held, besides many more in prisons of Jerusalem, Acre, Haifa, Tel Aviv, and other places.[43] On August 22, Jabotinsky wrote to a friend: "The Left there [in Palestine] had mobilized many hundreds of their *canaille* for spying. They know everybody's faces and even a disguise is not always safe. All the loopholes are being more and more hermetically corked up." On the other hand, he was reluctantly coming to the conclusion that his contention that Revisionist youth in the Diaspora was able to repay in kind any use of force in Palestine, was hardly realistic: when a group of Revisionist youngsters tried to disturb a *Poalei Zion* meeting in Warsaw, they were decisively beaten by their adversaries. "Our human material is simply physically inadequate. The *Brit Hachayal,* which once had in its ranks many broadshouldered fellows, has long since thinned out. . . . That means that clashes *there* [in Palestine], are not very likely to reverberate impressively here, and our adversaries know it. And if this is true, it means that we are cornered and there is little sense in going on making gestures. We will have to state it plainly to those concerned. . . . *Voilà,* this is what I am breaking my half-broken head about." [44]

"Those concerned"—the leadership of the *Irgun*—were accordingly informed. They themselves apparently felt at bay, weakened as they were by numerous arrests, and were looking for a respite. They therefore entered upon negotiations with the *Haganah.* These negotiations were carried on throughout the summer months, and a tentative agreement was initiated in the small hours of September 20, 1938, at the home of Israel Rokach, Mayor of Tel Aviv. The gist of it was that any reprisals would have to be agreed upon by a Commission of four in which the *Haganah* and the *Irgun* would be equally represented. The *Irgun* was to have a share in the legal forces under the Government (supernumerary police) and to be represented by autonomous units in all local self-defense bodies; self-defense in several places was to be fully entrusted to the *Irgun.* Each defense body would remain autonomous in its ideology, structure, hierarchy, etc.

When initialling the draft agreement, Eliahu Golomb emphatically stressed that their side would consider the pact as fully valid only after it was confirmed by the Executive Committee of the *Histadrut* ("I will resign if I remain in the minority," he firmly declared) and approved by Jabotinsky. Chaim Lubinski, who signed on behalf of the *Irgun,* answered: "If Jabotinsky approves the agreement, we will keep it, and you may be sure that he will see to it that we do." The same morning, at six A.M., Golomb arranged a seat for Lubinski on the plane for Warsaw, where a Revisionist World Party Council, headed by Jabotinsky, was in session. Jabotinsky reported the contents of the agreement to a small gathering of Revisionist leaders. [45] A lively discussion ensued, arguments pro and contra ratification were exchanged. Jabotinsky listened intently and then rose, saying: "Thank you, gentlemen. Now, Mendelson will think the matter over, and Mendelson will decide." When one of his colleagues continued to argue and tried to stop him at the door, he snapped: "Mendelson does not hear you, Mendelson does not see you, please let me pass." Later, in a private conversation, another younger colleague smilingly ventured: "In fact, Mendelson had already made his decision, hadn't he?" "You bet he had!" [46]

The decision was in the affirmative. In a conversation with Dr. Arye Altman, Jabotinsky said:[47] "If the *Irgun* people in Palestine consider this arrangement good and necessary, who am I to say 'no' and thus possibly endanger their lives, while I myself am not involved?" Golomb reported to the meeting of the Central Committee of the *Mapai* Party that "Revisionist emissaries have returned from abroad and told us that the agreement has been endorsed by Jabotinsky. . . . They read us a letter from Jabotinsky welcoming the agreement and expresing the hope that his friends will abide by it with honor and dignity, and stubbornly watch over their independence."[48]

Informing a friend that "just yesterday I gave my consent to a draft agreement between the two *Haganah* organizations in Palestine," Jabotinsky cautiously added:[49] "Of course, it may be rejected by the Left just as happened in 1935" [with the agreement he reached with Ben Gurion].

This apprehension proved to be prophetically true. The agreement was deliberately wrecked by Ben Gurion, who was at that time in London. His correspondence with Golomb was intercepted by the *Irgun* intelligence and published in full when, after months of delay, it became clear that the leaders of the *Mapai* were determined not to implement the unification of Jewish defense forces in Palestine— along the lines agreed upon in the pact of September 20. The correspondence revealed that on September 13, Ben Gurion had already wired to Golomb: "Absolutely opposed negotiations and proposals of agreements." When the Jewish Telegraphic Agency, on September 20, announced that the agreement was signed, Ben Gurion wired that he saw in this a "grave breach of discipline," and on September 23 ordered: "If [the agreement is] not signed, don't [sign it]: if signed, annul signature."[50]

Ben Gurion's uncompromising "no" was obviously prompted by the very features of the agreement that prompted Jabotinsky to welcome it. In a letter to the Secretariat of the *Mapai* Party in Palestine, he indignantly stressed that the agreement "does not repudiate the Revisionist anti-terror [actions], against which we have been fighting; on the contrary, it accepts the principle that such actions are permissible. . . . They only need the approval of a Commission in which there would be represented, on a parity basis, the *Yishuv* and the

Jewish Agency Executive on the one side, and delegates of the Revisionist *Biryonim* on the other side." [51] Neither the principle, nor its organizational implementation was acceptable to Ben Gurion. He was also not interested in an arrangement with the *Irgun* as such, which was necessarily limited to defense only. What he aspired at, was an overall political understanding with Jabotinsky, involving the disappearance of an independent New Zionist Organization and its absorption by the Zionist Organization. In his London talk with Golomb in July, 1938, Jabotinsky, too, argued that the question of common policy and common action of the *Haganah* and the *Irgun* could not be treated and solved as an isolated issue : only a full-fledged agreement between the Zionist Organization and the New Zionist Organization would be able to reestablish real unity in all fields of the Zionist effort. But in his view this agreement had to be achieved by a Round Table Conference between the two Zionist parent bodies, while Ben Gurion insisted on their merger as a prerequisite of any global settlement. He therefore did his very best to wreck the *Irgun-Haganah* pact and fully succeeded in his efforts.

Thus the conflict between the *Haganah* and the *Irgun* was revived and grew deeper and more tense. In the early summer of 1939, an attempt to effect a measure of collaboration was made by Simon Marcovici-Clejà, whose interest in the *Irgun* dated back to his first meeting with Jabotinsky in the spring of 1938, and who, during the second part of 1938, practically covered the *Irgun's* entire monthly budget. But Clejà nursed the hope of uniting the *Haganah* and the *Irgun,* and of overcoming their strife through unified financing. In May, he delegated his young friend, Benjamin Payn, to Palestine, providing him with a letter of credit on Barclay's Bank for one hundred thousand pounds (about five hundred thousand dollars). Dr. Payn's instructions were to make available this substantial amount to a special trust fund, if both Dr. Weizmann's Zionist Organization and Jabotinsky's New Zionist Organization agreed to use this fund for no other purpose than the acquisition of arms for both the *Haganah* and the *Irgun.* M. Grossman, who, in Clejà's view, held a "neutral" position in regard to the two camps, was to function as trustee; his task was to supervise the distribution of funds in accordance with the donor's intention. However, when Payn reported this offer to Weizmann, who received him in Rehovot, the answer was that Clejà's contribution was, of course, welcome and appreciated, but his conditions were unacceptable; no obligations in regard to the use of money could be assumed. The attempt failed.[52]

The tension continued unabated, and the dire prospect of civil war increasingly haunted Jabotinsky's mind. In the same month of May he instructed Eri, who was then in Palestine, to get in touch with Golomb and to give him the following message: "Father fears we are drifting to civil war within the *Yishuv;* if you can get full powers, father would like to meet you somewhere in Europe to see if there is any possibility of averting the clash." [53] The meeting took place two months later, on July 8 and 9, 1939. Jabotinsky's first question was: 'Is there, in Golomb's view, a danger of civil war in Palestine?' The latter, who at their encounter in July, 1938, was affirmative on this subject by implication only, stated this time quite outspokenly: "If the present situation continues, internal strife must start." [54] There was also one more substantial difference in the content of this meeting as compared with that of 1938. At that time, it was Jabotinsky who insisted that the question of the *Haganah-Irgun* relationship could be constructively solved only within the broader framework of the relationship between the Old and the New Zionist Organization. Golomb, according to his own record, then answered that he "intended to limit this talk to one subject only and not touch upon all the problems of Zionist' politics." Though a desultory discussion on these wider issues did take place, it proved inconclusive, and Golomb later commented upon it in a most uncomplimentary way: "My personal opinion is that Jabotinsky hopes to force the Zionist Organization to accept his organizational and political proposals through actions we consider to be dangerous." [55]

But this time, one year later, it was Golomb who asked: "Did he [Jabotinsky] think that under the present circumstances there should be a unified leadership of the Zionist Organization" and "a single command that would decide on whatever action should take place in Palestine?" Jabotinsky concurred, stating that it was "obvious that no partial agreement, covering defense questions only, could have any durable value as long as there is no common major policy." "I explained to him," reported Jabotinsky in letters to his party friends that:[56]

there was no other way of establishing a common [Zionist] authority but through an Assembly (call it Congress or Convention or whatever you like) elected by universal suffrage without fee. To my astonishment, he seemed never to have realized that *that* was what we [Revisionists] were after. . . . But during the second talk [July 9] . . . he undertook to fly home and try to bring back such samples of his crew as Ben Gurion, Berl Katznelson, [Itzhak] Tabenkin . . . to meet [our] friends somewhere near the place I am going to for my cure. . . . He [Golomb] is going to tell them that a *heskem* [agreement] on major policy is possible on the following terms (to make sure, he repeated them to me twice).

(*a*) A single "Assembly or Congress or Parliament" elected without any payment connected with the right to vote;

(*b*) He asked whether we would agree to demand some declaration from every voter. I asked: "Something simple like this— I demand a Jewish Palestine?"—He said yes. I said yes;

(*c*) As result of such Assembly—a single [Zionist] World Organization;

(*d*) In such an Organization, minorities would naturally have to submit, i.e. enter a coalition or be satisfied with opposing. But he said that his own party would reserve the right to rebel in an exceptional case; to which I replied: "I think we [Revisionists] should be fully prepared to pledge discipline to such an Assembly on exactly the same terms and with the same limitations as you." He agreed.

He [Golomb] thinks that the overwhelming majority among his leading crowd desire an agreement with us, "although we realize that that would weaken our power over the [Zionist] movement and the Yishuv. . . ." The [proposed] meeting should take place before their [Twentieth Zionist] Congress, so that the plan of a wider Assembly could eventually be submitted to the Congress.

Jabotinsky was rather dubious as to the practical outcome of these seemingly promising talks: "My own appreciation of this new departure: 80 per cent—no go." He proved to be right. On July 15 he wrote to Haskel: "Since then [the departure of Golomb to Palestine] I have heard nothing. In my *Schätzung* [estimate], nothing will be heard in future either. Nor will this question play any important role at their Congress; the few cranks who may raise it will soon be silenced. All the vested interests represented at their Congress (except the cranks who have no vested interests and no pull) would be bound to lose heavily in case of any agreement with us—at least so they fear— and no attempt to persuade them to commit suicide will therefore succeed." Of course, he added, we "will honestly do all in our power to promote the united front idea, and should my forecast prove wrong and the present leadership of the Old Zionist Organization be really willing to accept universal suffrage—we will honestly help and honestly rejoice that a Jewish organization, criminally guilty of many betrayals as it is, has been saved from collapse. But I doubt it." [57]

In December, 1939, the scheme worked out in the course of the Jabotinsky-Golomb encounter, was again tentatively revived in New York. The American representatives of the New Zionist Organization reported to Jabotinsky, who was still in London, about "Golomb's idea" of conducting activities of the N.Z.O., "under the management of the Jewish Agency." In his answer to this report, Jabotinsky bluntly said that all this was, of course, "bunkum."

"I assume," he wrote on January 1, 1940, to Rabbi Louis I. Newman and B. Akzin, "that what he [Golomb] honestly means is management under some kind of reconstructed Agency in which we too should be represented; I have the impression that he personally, and perhaps a couple of friends, are rather keen on such a reconstruction and even ready to make far-reaching concessions. Their trouble is that they have no influence whatsoever in all these matters, and even discussing such things [with them] is a waste of time. I warn you about this just for your personal illumination, not (God forbid) to entice you into being undiplomatic in your talks with those charming people."

This time, too, he proved to be right. Nothing tangible resulted from the New York talks.

4. The Ben Yosef Drama

On April 21, 1938, three young members of the *Betar* group in the colony of Rosh Pinah, Abraham Shein, Shalom Zurabin and Shlomo Ben Yosef (his name in Poland was Shlomo Tabacznik), outraged by a recent Arab attack on a Jewish bus on the Safed-Rosh Pinah route, during which fourteen Jews were killed and four Jewish women raped, decided to retaliate against an Arab bus carrying passengers to the neighboring village of Jaouni, from which the Arab terrorists originated. The attack miscarried; none of the Arab bus passengers was injured. Nevertheless, the British Military Court in Haifa on June 3 sentenced Zurabin to be placed under medical observation; Abraham Shein and Shlomo Ben Yosef were to "hang by the neck until they were dead."

Jabotinsky considered this sentence an outrage, both politically and morally. At a mass meeting in London, he said: [58] "For two years a handful of young [Arab] hooligans had been terrorizing the country of Jewish hopes. The Arabs went about freely, while humiliating the Jews and saying to them, in effect: 'You are dirt, you must not move about this country freely.' And then two youngsters, of seventeen and nineteen, went out and fired a volley, as it happened killing no one, and they were arrested, tried, and sentenced to death by a Government that was either unable or unwilling to do something which any other Government in its place would have done with a couple of battalions in a couple of weeks. . . . I would say to the Mandatory: 'It is no use sentencing Jews to death. You have either to stop it [the Arab terror] yourself or allow our youth in Palestine to stop it. Don't let two boys pay the penalty for something which you have done or omitted to do.' I don't know what is going to happen to them, but from this place I send them my blessings, and I let the judges there know that if anything irreparable happens to them, tens of thousands of children will sit *shiva,* and their names will remain in the nation's memory as names of martyrs and giants."

Jabotinsky spared no efforts to marshall all possible forces in English public opinion to save the youths' lives. Appeals for reprieve came from the Jewish national organizations, from the Chief Rabbi of the British Empire, from two Anglican Bishops, from the *Manchester Guardian,* from the Polish Government, from Chief Rabbi Herzog of Palestine, from British M.P.'s and newspaper editors, from churches and synagogues.[59] Jabotinsky approached the Secretary of War, Leslie Hore Belisha; at his request, Dulanti, Ireland's High Commissioner in London,* went to see the new Secretary for the Colonies, Malcolm MacDonald, who vaguely promised "to see what he can do."[59]

All this was of no avail. On June 18, Shein's sentence was commuted to life imprisonment, but Ben Yosef's was upheld. Six days later, Major-General Robert H. Haining, General Officer Commanding British forces in Palestine, confirmed the death sentence. The execution date was fixed for June 29. The remaining few days were packed with redoubled efforts, particularly the last day. In a cable to Ben Yosef's mother, Jabotinsky assured her: "We are making every effort and knocking at all the doors until early morning in order to save your son." This was no exaggeration.[60] The execution was fixed for June 29, eight A.M. (six A.M. London time). At two P.M., June 28, influential Conservative British M.P.s, Vivian Adams and Sir John

* In January, 1938, Jabotinsky was twice received in Dublin by President De Valera and succeeded in establishing very favorable contacts with Irish Government circles.

469

Haslam, in answer to Jabotinsky's plea, went to see MacDonald; their mission was unsuccessful. At 4 P.M. it was Jabotinsky's turn to be received by the Colonial Secretary. The audience lasted thirty-five minutes. MacDonald was polite but unyielding. Though only a few years ago he himself fought for the abolishment of capital punishment, he now insisted that the "unruly elements must be taught a lesson which would be severe enough to intimidate them and keep them quiet." Jabotinsky argued that he knew his own nation better: they would not be scared, on the contrary, the hanging of Ben Yosef was bound to arouse strong repercussions among the Jewish youth of Palestine; it would lead to acts which the British Government would have every reason to regret. MacDonald confidently replied that he was certain that the official Zionist bodies were in full control of the Jewish youth; should a few hotheads try to break this control, they would be effectively opposed by the entire *Yishuv* and its official representation. The attempt failed. At 6 P.M. the Irish High Commissioner again came to see MacDonald, who told him that he had seen Jabotinsky two hours before and stated his position firmly, and that in the meantime he had received a cable from Haining which only strengthened his stand.

At about nine P.M. Jabotinsky received a phone call from Tel Aviv: Dr. Philipp Joseph, the attorney for the condemned youth, excitedly reported that he had found a precedent dating back to 1901, when during the Anglo-Boer war, an appeal to the Privy Council against a Court Martial verdict had been allowed: "You will find the record on page . . . of the book. . . . Try and get a stay of execution for a few days in order to prepare an appeal." This new chance of saving the boy's life precipitated a series of frantic efforts. Jabotinsky hastened to Major Nathan, an M.P. and an experienced solicitor, who immediately arranged for a conference with MacDonald, the Attorney General for the British Isles, Sir Donald Sommerville, and the legal adviser of the Colonial Office, asking for a stay of execution. The conference was to take place in one of the rooms of the House of Commons, which was then in session. Simultaneously Colonel Wedgwood was alerted. He asked the Librarian of the House of Commons to enable Jabotinsky, despite the late hour, to look for the required legal source. Jabotinsky came with two younger collaborators, and a frantic search started in the library. The record of the South African case was not found. Jabotinsky was downcast. The House of

Commons in the meantime adjourned. The lobby became deserted. Jabotinsky and his colleagues did not leave the House. At one A.M. they were still waiting for the results of Nathan's conference with MacDonald. Finally, Nathan emerged from the conference room: the plea was refused. At this moment, Robert Briscoe, the only Jewish member of the Irish Dail (Parliament of Ireland) and a devoted follower of Jabotinsky, who had joined them, recalled a similar case: in 1920, an Irish "terrorist" was also sentenced to death, but they succeeded in obtaining a stay of execution and later a reprieve. Nathan rushed to the House of Commons Library, hoping to trace the record of this Irish case. After some time he returned: he could not find it. Nor could the lawyer who had handled the case be traced. Briscoe's reaction was "Don't you know the English way of dealing with national revolutionary movements? First, they just ignore you, then they ridicule you, then they start arresting and hanging, and then they sit down with you at a Round Table conference. You have already reached the penultimate stage of hanging, bear this ordeal with firmness." But Jabotinsky paid no heed to this comforting philosophy. He was fully absorbed by the urge to save Ben Yosef's life. At two A.M. (four A.M. in Acre) he phoned another solicitor who eagerly agreed to make one more try. Thirty minutes later, they rang the bell at the door of the High Court. To the astonished Court Attendant, who lived in the building, they explained that it was a matter of life and death for a young man, and he uncomplainingly led them to the cellar where the 1920 records were kept. Candles were lit, and the search began. By half-past three they had found the record, and rushed to the Colonial Ministry. MacDonald's private secretary was very kind and considerate; he did not at all resent being awakened in the middle of the night. But he was sorry, he did not know where the Colonial Secretary was spending the night. . . . It was already five A.M. in London—seven A.M. in Acre: too late to prevent the hanging.

Jabotinsky went back to the office. Then he went home. His wife later told friends that he did not go to bed; for the first time in her life she saw him cry.

Afterward, reports appeared in the English press asserting that Chief Rabbi Herzog of Palestine had cabled Jabotinsky that the Palestine Government was ready to grant Ben Yosef's reprieve if the

Revisionists in Palestine would sign an appeal for *havlaga*. This was officially denied by the *Nessiut*. No such information had come from Rabbi Herzog, and "if Mr. Jabotinsky had received such a proposal, he would have dealt with it as with any other attempt at blackmail. Nor was such a suggestion made by Mr. MacDonald during Mr. Jabotinsky's interview with him." [61]

The day following the execution, Jabotinsky told a press conference that this senseless cruelty had created a completely new situation. The Jews had not always been satisfied with Great Britain by any means, and were most certainly not satisfied with the Palestine Administration. Nevertheless, up till now blood had been shed in Palestine only as the result of the Arab-Jewish conflict. Now, the British partner had shed Jewish blood. [62] This new aspect of Anglo-Jewish relations provoked a far-reaching reaction in Jabotinsky's mind, both morally and politically.

At a monster protest and memorial meeting in London, at which he spoke, together with Colonel Wedgwood, Professor A. S. Yehuda, Horace Samuel, and Mordehai Katz of the *Betar,* he said bitterly that Ben Yosef's execution was "wholly unconnected with justice. Not even Downing Street pretended otherwise." In the last few days he had had dealings with many influential Englishmen, but none of them claimed that the hanging was an act of justice; they could only excuse it on the ground of "expediency." He knew that in the discussion that went on privately before the execution, two viewpoints came to light : one, that the Jews were to be "taught a lesson" and intimidated into submission; the second, that such profound changes had occurred in Jewish life that the present generation of Jews would not be deterred by death or suffering. "Those in high quarters are weighing in their minds whether the Jewish youth are dirt or whether they are iron. Ben Yosef's hangmen think they are dirt. We shall see. . . . I say to the Englishmen : beware! The Jews are beginning to ask themselves whether Ben Yosef's way is not the best one. We know from history that martyrs become prophets and tombs become altars." [63] For the first time in his political career, Jabotinsky openly questioned the viability of the British-Jewish partnership. "I have been one of the most stubborn partisans of a pro-English orientation. I confess that I no longer can guarantee that the illusion of partnership would last." [64] Referring to Wedgwood's endorsement of Ben Yosef's act ("any Englishman in his place might have done the same"), he said : "I am compelled to doubt now whether [High Commissioner of Palestine] Wauchope and not Wedgwood is representative of Britain." [65] In a confidential talk he had on July 10 with Eliahu Golomb he said: "If I were a terrorist in Eretz Israel, I would have felt the urge, after Ben Yosef's trial, to do something against England—in this case the Arabs have not given any reason for action against them. I do not say that one had to do something, but there is some logic to it. . . . This [Ben Yosef's execution] had touched me so much that I am seriously considering a complete change in our orientation toward England."

To a friend who was with him the day before he was executed, Ben Yosef said: "Please tell Jabotinsky that I will die with his name on my lips." Jabotinsky was deeply moved by this—as he felt— undeserved faith in him. In a short personal letter to the youth's mother, written in Yiddish, he told her in deep humility: "I have not merited that a noble soul like your son should die with my name on his lips. But as long as it is my lot to live, his name will live in my heart; and *his* disciples, more than mine, will be the trailblazers of a generation." In the same spirit he wrote to Ben Yosef's comrades in Rosh Pinah, who had spoken of him as Ben Yosef's teacher: [66] "I do not agree that he had but one 'teacher,' a teacher in the singular form. When a person lives and grows up among others, he owes his education to the environment and not to the influence of one man only, for it is the environment that strengthens or blunts the influence of one individual. I have not educated Ben Yosef: he was educated by the *Betar*, first by the *Betar* in Luck and in the whole of Poland, and during the last year of his life by the *Betar* of Rosh Pinah and Eretz Israel." Mordehai Katz, speaking at the Ben Yosef memorial meeting, "on behalf of sixty thousand *Betarim,* and indeed on behalf of hundreds of thousands of other Jews, young and old," said: "This is their message to you tonight: We know that the Jewish nation has many leaders, some worthy, some less so, but only one with whose name on his lips a great son of Israel deemed it a privilege to die." The audience sprang to its feet and broke in tremendous applause. "Jabotinsky was visibly moved," Katz recalls. "A few moments later, he approached me and without uttering a word seized my hand and pressed it warmly." [67]

In a cable to Ben Yosef's bereaved mother he assured her that her son's "name will be engraved in Jewish history among the rest of the

473

heroes of Israel. . . . We mourn, but we are proud that we have a comrade strong in spirit and courageous like your son." [68]

What particularly impressed Jabotinsky—and filled him with pride —was Ben Yosef's behavior in the last hours of his life. At the *Betar* World Conference in Warsaw, he said: [69]

. . . One of my friends in England told me of a conversation he had with an English sergeant who was in charge of the death cell of the youth from Rosh Pinah, and who witnessed his last night. He asked the policeman: "What thing impressed you most at that event? After all, you probably have been a witness to more than one hanging, and it is said that Arabs have gone to the scaffold bravely too. Tell me, please: How was the boy from Rosh Pinah different from the others?" And the policeman's reply was: "The thing that surprised me most was the fact that up to the last minute of his life, he never neglected that which is called 'ceremony.' I have seen people going to the scaffold with head held high, but all of them, during the last hours of their lives, when they had lost all hope for life, dispensed with this 'ceremony.' What difference does it make which way I sit? The end has arrived anyway. But the boy from Rosh Pinah never forgot 'ceremony.' He thought—what to say; what to wear; and at seven o'clock in the morning, a few moments before his hanging, he cleaned his teeth. We had never seen such a thing before in our lives—a person who had not relinquished his nobility."

When Jabotinsky came to Poland late in July, one of his first errands was the trip to Luck to pay a visit to Ben Yosef's mother.[70] In 1939, overcoming his deep aversion to asking favors of Malcolm MacDonald, he approached him with the request to intercede with the Palestine Government so that "immigration certificates be granted to Rachel Tabacznik of Luck (Poland), together with members of her family as per list enclosed."

"M-me Tabacznick," he wrote, "is the widowed mother of Shlomo Ben Yosef, executed in the Acre prison on June 29 last year. A small house will be provided for her at Rosh Pinah where her son is buried, and the New Zionist Organization assumes full responsibility for her maintenance should the need arise.

"I assume that, whatever may be the official view regarding Ben Yosef's personality and act, the [British] Government fully respect the feelings of a mourning mother and sympathize with her wish to end her days near the place where her son worked and was laid to rest."

No answer to this moving plea was ever received.

TWENTY-FIVE

THE FATHER OF JEWISH ARMED RESISTANCE   II

1. *The Inner Struggle*

WHILE ARGUING—and often wrangling—with the *Irgun* about the place which armed struggle in Palestine had to occupy in the overall national effort, Jabotinsky was continuously arguing with himself on this crucial issue. For almost a year preceding the outbreak of World War II, he underwent a significant evolution in the direction of the *Irgun,* often fighting a rear-guard action, asking for time to make up his mind. A few stray episodes in this inner struggle deserve special attention.

In the early fall of 1938, pressed to define his attitude toward the *Irgun,* he pleaded : "Just give me another few months; I think that I am beginning to see the prospect of radically revising the line of my views and activities." [1] In October of the same year, two new plans of partition were to be submitted by the Woodhead Commission, both drastically reducing the size of the envisaged Jewish State; it was also rumored that the British Government was contemplating some arrangement with the Mufti-led "Arab Provisional Government," and imposing it on the Jews. Jabotinsky was deeply disturbed by these rumors. He felt that a definite militant stand should be openly taken with regard to such a scheme, which was tantamount to the liquidation of Zionism, and that any attempt to implement it must be resisted, if necessary by force of arms. He was, however, as yet not prepared to say so himself. He therefore authorised this writer to issue "in the

475

name of the *Nassi* [Jabotinsky] and the *Nessiut"* a statement, warning that, should Britain :

attempt to destroy Zionism by the present plans, the Palestine conflict must assume the form of an open-armed struggle. . . . If an attempt is made to establish an Arab Government in Palestine, there will be a bitter fight in all parts of this country, commencing with Jerusalem. Jews will surrender nothing peacefully. The fight will continue in every Jewish settlement, every colony, and wherever else possible. . . . Jews must not only proclaim their readiness for an armed struggle but must also prepare for it. Their immediate task calls not only for self-defense, but for the militarization of the whole Yishuv.

Publishing this statement, *The Jewish Herald* of Johannesburg editorially described "Dr. Schechtman's message as a clarion call to action." [2] This was, however, not this writer's personal message : it conveyed the well-considered judgment of Jabotinsky. Four months later, he was already prepared to utter it himself, declaring that "to obtain actual power over the *Yishuv* the Arabs would have to conquer with their blood every lane of every colony and every Jewish street of every city." [3]

Early in 1939, Count Michael Lubiensky, *chef de cabinet* of the Polish Ministry of Foreign Affairs, arranged an intimate dinner for Jabotinsky, to which he invited his good friend, Professor Orzensky (a staunch liberal and pacifist of the "old school") and this writer. In the course of a lively after-dinner discussion, the idealistically minded Professor objected to the *Irgun's* armed actions, insisting that "reason and not the sword must rule human destiny." Instead of arguing against this lofty philosophy of history, which in itself appealed strongly to his own inclinations, Jabotinsky said : "The brilliant early socialist thinker and leader, a Jew by birth, Ferdinand Lassalle, very impressively dealt with your argument in his drama *Franz von Sickingen*. Father Oekolampadius, a Lutheran chaplain in Sickingen's household, used exactly the same reasoning in a discussion with the great humanist of the sixteenth century, Ulrich von Hutten. The answer he recived was, I think, very forceful (Jabotinsky quoted it in the original German) [4] :

476

My worthy Sir! You ill acquainted are
With history. You're right—'tis Reason that
Its contents constitutes, its *form* is ever *Force*
. . . My worthy Sir! Think better of the sword!
A sword, for freedom swung on high, that, Sire,
The *Word Incarnate* is of which you preach.

Recalling that it was the sword that saved Greece from Xerxes, and liberated Jerusalem from the Saracenes; that "it was the sword that David, Samson, Gideon, labored with," von Hutten concluded:

Thus, long ago, as well as since, the *sword*
Achieved the glories told by history;
And all that's great, as yet to be achieved,
Owes, in the end, its triumph to the sword.

When Lubiensky suggested that perhaps a "compromise" might be found which would make armed struggle unnecessary, Jabotinsky again quoted Lassalle, this time it was the answer given by Franz von Sickingen to the Emperor Charles:

Oh, Sire! With Truth there's no compounding!
As well compound with th'overtopping fiery pillar
That marched before the hosts of Israel;
As well compound with th'arrowy mountain stream
That, certain of its course, is dashing on!

The publication of MacDonald's White Paper in May, 1939, accentuated Jabotinsky's growing appreciation of the role the *Irgun* was destined to play in the development of major Zionist policy. Predicting, in a personal letter, that as a result of this document Palestine was going to become "a country of active, systematic and poisonous official anti-Semitism *par excellence*," he added: "This means—at least I hope so—*mutual* trouble, of which it would be risky to predict the forms." He thought "highly unlikely" that the *Yishuv* as a whole, or the Agency circles, "will retaliate in any tangible way." "But," he recalled, "there is, as we know, a more active and more courageous minority; and lately considerable unrest in the same direction has been undeniably signalled in the ranks of the Left. To sum up: it is likely that before our relations with the partner get better, they will have to get much worse; which perhaps is quite sound medicine with this kind of partner."

477

He was even more explicit in the article "Consequences of the White Paper," noting with deep satisfaction that "the first reports from the Palestine front show what spirit and what courage burns again in the old-new soul of the ever-young people: people of Gideon and the Hasmoneans, of Bar Kochba and the Zealots, David Alroy and Shlomo Ben Yosef, and Shlomo Ben Yosef's brothers. My children in Palestine 'write' better than I do, more succinctly and more clearly. From afar, in the name of millions, filled with respect and love, I send my signature to what they are 'writing,' and my blessing to what they are doing." [5]

At a mass meeting in Warsaw, he identified his "children" by name: [6] "When the *Irgun* grows, your hope also grows; when the *Irgun* does not progress, your hope wanes. The *Irgun* is your salvation. Its existence is your promise. . . . It is the strongest form of protest. With their sacrifice they awaken the conscience of the entire youth in Eretz Israel. The *Irgun* must grow, reinforced by whole battalions of young Jews from the Diaspora, thus establishing a powerful Jewish Army."

Even in an official "Observations On the Palestine White Paper," submitted to the League of Nations Mandates Commission on behalf of the N.Z.O., Jabotinsky made it clear that the Mandatory Power was mistaken in the belief that by closing Jewish immigration within a period of ten years it would lessen its burden of maintaining order and peace in the country: "This period," the memorandum outspokenly predicted, "will certainly be one of no less conflict, difficulty, and bloodshed than the period that has gone before. Such an open betrayal of a solemn undertaking, on the basis of which Jews brought over three hundred thousand additional population and over four hundred eighty million dollars, will not be carried into effect except at the cost of ceaseless turmoil, conflict, and bloody disturbances."

There was no doubt in Jabotinsky's mind that the resistance to the White Paper policy, if honestly meant and implemented, was bound to take the form of an open and costly conflict with the British Administration. In an angry article "What Had Been Evacuated," he ridiculed the "nincompoops" of official Zionism who, while condemning *Irgun's* militant strategy, were talking of "passive resistance" to the White Paper policy. The very term "passive resistance" was an absurdity, he insisted. "Either such resistance remains ineffective and that is, its pinpricks are so weak that the Government can laugh at

478

them and will not even take steps against them, or, if it is really powerful and bites deep into the Government's flesh, the Government will bite back, and 'passive resistance' will become an active revolutionary movement." [7]

Midsummer, 1939, was for Jabotinsky a period of ever-deepening inner conflict over his personal position in the *Irgun's* struggle. One day, after a tense discussion with a strongly pro-*Irgun* couple, he exclaimed : "Well, so what do you want me to do? If you can explain to me exactly how you visualize the struggle, if you have a real plan for proceeding from now on—an all-embracing plan which can only fail because of insufficiency of forces but not because of faulty conception—if you convince me, I swear : I am all yours! I will drop everything; I will not touch my pen except for what the *Irgun* will ask me to write; I will not speak at meetings except at the *Irgun's* request and in accordance with their views. I am ready the moment I am convinced, and your people consider it right, to go illegally to Palestine on the day they tell me to do so, and to do there any job I am told to do." Mrs. Strassman-Lubinsky, who recapitulated for this writer that memorable conversation, said that she and her husband were "quite shaken : it was the only time we saw him in private at the height of such an oratoric outburst, which was at the same time movingly, desperately sincere and somehow histrionic, but magnificently so." [8]

Before leaving Warsaw in June, 1939, Jabotinsky drafted a "Call to the Jewish Youth," which began with the statement: "We have come to the conclusion that the only way to liberate our country is by the sword," and appealed to the youth to register "for any possible purpose" both in Palestine and in the Diaspora.[9] He intended to begin this action in Poland "at once, after preliminary sounding of *Shiltonot* [Polish authorities] : not to ask permission but to ward off interference"; the same applied to Lithuania. He did not believe that in this particular case it was proper to "as much as mention" the *Nessiut* of the New Zionist Organization : "I would prefer, in principle, to keep this enterprise as one for which *only* our *betaroid* branches are responsible—militaristic but a-political." [10] Characteristically enough, this move met with strong opposition on the part of *Irgun* circles in Poland. They argued that this mobilization slogan, though it could have been meant as a demonstration only, would certainly alienate the average Pole in the street and the Polish Government leaders who had to reckon with their relations with Britain. There were also considerable doubts among the members of the Polish Revisionist Central Committee. The "Call" was never made public.[11]

By that time, Jabotinsky was already prepared to abandon his studied position of allegedly not being in any way connected with the *Irgun*. He openly and fully endorsed the *Irgun's* policy of wholesale retaliation about which he himself had had considerable moral doubts at an earlier stage. Everybody, he wrote, would like retaliations, provided they were immediately and exclusively directed against the bandits and not against the Arab population, however hostile. But it must be realized that:

the choice is not between retaliating against the bandits or retaliating against the hostile population. The choice is between . . . retaliating against the hostile population or not retaliating at all. . . . When it is a question of war, you do not stand and ask questions as to what is better, whether to shoot or not to shoot. The only question it is permissible to ask in such circumstances is, on the contrary: what is worse, to let yourself be killed or enslaved without any resistance, or to undertake resistance with all its horrible consequences.

For there is no "better" at all. Everything connected with war is bad, and cannot be good. . . . If you start calculating as to what is better, the calculation is very simple: if you want to be good, let yourself be killed; and renounce everything you would like to defend: home, country, freedom, hope.

"To this," Jabotinsky concluded, "to the spilling of *ha'dam hamutar,* the permitted blood, on which there is no prohibition and for which nobody has to pay, an end had been put in Palestine. Amen." [12] By that time he fully realized, as he told Golomb in June, 1939, that "it was not only difficult to punish only the guilty ones, in most cases it was impossible." He insisted that the British were hardly entitled to be too much incensed by "indiscriminate" punitive actions because that was "exactly what the British had done to Karlsruhe at the end of the war : as reprisal against German [aerial] attacks [against London], they sent airplanes to Karlsruhe which strafed innocent German civilians."

While fully endorsing the *Irgun's* action, Jabotinsky was, however, willing and eager to explore all possible avenues for easing the state of open warfare between the *Irgun* and the Palestine Government. Early in June, he wrote to the *Nessiut* in London—in connection

480

with the mass arrests of Revisionists which, he insisted, were "no tragedy to the arrested but very awkward for the Party"—that he was "seriously thinking" of instructing his son Eri "by a cable in plain English" to demand an interview with the then Chief Secretary to the Government of Palestine, Sir William Denis Battershill, "in order to ask that gent, on my behalf, 'what are the conditions upon which the Government would be prepared to stop this persecution.' " Eri was also to ask—on Jabotinsky's behalf—[Israel] Rokach [Mayor of Tel Aviv], [Itzhak] Ben Zvi [Chairman of the *Vaad Leumi*] and [Eliahu] Golomb [Commander of the *Haganah*] "what would now be their proposal for cooperation." He expected Eri "to write it all down and report to me personally." Then, should he come to the conclusion that "all this is reasonable," he would "send a copy of that cable to MacDonald, together with a letter about the futility of all this nonsense [of persecution]." [13] A few weeks later, thinking along similar lines, he discussed in a letter to the *Nessiut* the idea of suggesting to Colonel R. Meinertzhagen, then senior official of the British War Office, to arrange a *sauf conduit* to Palestine for him : "Make plain to him that I am there not as a conductor, but I may have some moral influence; I don't promise anything—I will simply have a look to see whether I can do anything. . . . You must, of course, emphasize [to Meinertzhagen] : Don't imagine for a moment that he can, or even wishes to stop our crew from kicking as long as they are being kicked. But there may be chances of mutual appeasement, and he is prepared to see what can be done *if!*" Jabotinsky anticipated that this suggestion would certainly be refused, but he deemed it useful to have such a proposal "on record for further inevitable polemics, as well as for a big complaint to Geneva [League of Nations]." Should, however, Meinertzhagen be ready to grant the request, "I would highly appreciate this opportunity." Answering this writer's query, Colonel Meinertzhagen wrote : "I was never approached [in this matter]. If I had been, I should have done my best for Jabotinsky."

On August 6, he had a long talk at Vals-les-Bains with an *Irgun* delegation (Hillel Kook, Chaim Lubinsky, Alexander Rafaeli), which was sent by the *Irgun* to Geneva, where the Twenty-first Zionist Congress was to take place. Their task, as they explained to Jabotinsky, was to "take advantage of the gathering of Jews and foreign journalists to tell them (especially the journalists) everything about the *Telsher Yeshive* [code name for the *Irgun* then used in correspondence] and

481

incidentally rebut the attack on *Aliyah Bet* [illegal immigration]."
"A very good plan," Jabotinsky commented in a letter to the *Nessiut*;
"the only trouble is that they just informed me of their intention to
go [to Geneva] instead proposing it to the *Nessiut*." The delegation
was, however, diplomatic enough to add : "Of course, you can forbid
our going to Geneva and it will be off," so that, as Jabotinsky put it,
"there was no room for a quarrel, unless one wished to provoke one,
which I did not." Three weeks later, admitting that the bulletins and
other literature which the delegation was issuing, were "below standard," he hoped that his London colleagues "would not suggest that
the literary criterion is the only one or the main one to be applied in
judging this performance." He was no longer interested in questions
connected with the *Irgun's* "separatism" : "Now this *perud* [split]
business is *le bébé de mes soucis* (the baby of my worries), provided
that the *Nessiut* and *Shilton* don't forget that little facts are little and
big merits are big." After a very friendly and "*plus que* friendly" talks
with the *Irgun* delegation, he felt that there was "in their mentality
a mixture of superficial separtion and of real quest for some policy
more adequate to the [present] period. It begins to dawn upon them
[in Palestine, too] that 'their' policy is just as inadequate as 'ours.' . . .
I'll try to arrange a symposium." [14]

2. *The Call for Armed Revolt*

When, early in August, 1939, an *Irgun* emissary visited Jabotinsky
in Vals-les-Bain, the latter unexpectedly inquired : "Do you think that
the *Irgun* is in a position to launch an armed revolt in Palestine and,
at least for several hours, occupy Government House in Jerusalem?"
Asked why he was putting this question, he answered : "I am coming
round to the *Irgun's* way of thinking. After the White Paper and after
all that has happened, I feel that my line is your line, and I am determined to devote myself wholly to its implementation, if I live and
will have the time to do it. You will hear from me before you leave for
Palestine."

Later, in Geneva, the emissary received from Jabotinsky a thick
envelope with a covering letter asking him to deliver it to the High
Command of the *Irgun* immediately after his arrival in Palestine.
The letter was duly delivered; but when it was opened, it seemed to
make no sense at all. In a few days two more envelopes arrived, and

later three more. Only then the picture became clear. The six letters contained, together, a complete outline of a military rebellion in Palestine to be staged by the *Irgun*. Three of them contained a code based on an alleged plan for a soap factory, with detailed specification of the necessary machinery and raw materials; every part of the machinery, every ingredient of the raw materials, every brand of soap to be produced had a meaning, which made it possible to decipher the other three letters devoted to the scheme of the rebellion as such. The scheme, in a nutshell, was as follows:

By October, 1939, a boat carrying "illegal" immigrants would arrive and disembark its human cargo somewhere in the very heart of the country, if possible in Tel Aviv. Jabotinsky would be among these "illegals." The *Irgun* had to secure their landing, if necessary by force. At the same time, an open armed uprising had to take place, and as many Government buildings as possible—principally Government House in Jerusalem—had to be taken over and the Jewish flag raised. These positions had to be held, regardless of sacrifices involved, for at least twenty-four hours; his, Jabotinsky's eventual capture was also to be resisted for at least the same period of time. During the shortlived occupation of the key Government positions, a Provisional Government of the Jewish State would be simultaneously proclaimed in the capitals of Western Europe and the United States, which would subsequently function as a Government-in-Exile, the embodiment of Jewish sovereignty in Palestine.[15]

This bold plan by far transcended the guerilla tactics which had hitherto been applied by the *Irgun* against the Arab terror. Those tactics were, indeed, of inestimable political and education value. They freed the *Yishuv* from the humiliating status of British *Schutzjuden;* they taught the Arab terrorist bands a healthy lesson; and they generated a new spirit of militancy and self-sacrifice in the Jewish youth. But they proved to be inconclusive as a solution of the political impasse. Jabotinsky came to the conclusion that the real roadblock on the way to Jewish Statehood was the unholy alliance between Arab intransigence and the British Mandatory regime, the latter being the main obstacle. As long as this state of affairs continued, the Zionist cause could make no real progress. This stalemate had to be broken at any cost, and soon, because time was obviously working against the Jewish cause. Jabotinsky's idea was to stage an armed Jewish *coup d'état,* which, though bound to be suppressed, would leave in its wake an international *fait accompli* of proclaimed Jewish Statehood. The very fact that Jews were able, even for twenty-four hours, to occupy the country's administrative key positions would create a political reality that could never be erased. Jewish sovereignty—once proclaimed, and perpetuated by the symbol of a Jewish Government-in-Exile—would be worth all the sacrifices involved in an armed rebellion. As he was prepared to participate personally in this action and to risk his own life, Jabotinsky felt entitled to propose such a course to the *Irgun*. His only concern was whether the *Irgun* was able to stage such an uprising efficiently and impressively, so that it would not degenerate into an operetta performance.

The *Irgun* High Command was taken unawares by this Jabotinsky move. Never before had they thought on such lines, and they had many grave doubts as to the practicability of the scheme. They knew only too well that militarily that they were not yet ready for an enterprise of such magnitude, and that the attempt was bound to result in a heavy depletion of the *Irgun's* cadres. Some questioned the value of a Provisional Government, if there would no longer be an Irgun to back it. Others insisted that Jabotinsky must not personally lead the uprising since—should he perish in this attempt—a Provisional Government not headed by him would lose most of its authority. Notwithstanding all these considerations, the overwhelming majority were ready to go along : if Jabotinsky believed in the decisive political significance of the plan, it was worthwhile to try and pay the price; they had confidence in his political vision. What they appreciated most, was that this offer fully vindicated their faith in Jabotinsky, and proved that it had been worth their while to wait for his "conversion" to the *Irgun's* ways. The sole dissenting voice was that of Abraham Stern, who persisted in his distrust of Jabotinsky. The controversy was submitted to David Raziel, who was at that time interned by the British in the Sarafend detention camp. While the discussion was going on, World War II broke out.* The entire situation had changed.**

* Eri Jabotinsky later revealed that his father had told him of this plan much earlier, months before the outbreak of the war. But "he hesitated to implement it because of mother, who already at that time was suffering from *angina pectoris.* . . . It was because of considerations of familial nature that he postponed the plan and then it was too late." (Eri Jabotinsky, "Imi". *Herut*, January 20, 1950).

** In a memorial article "Arlosoroff Planned Revolt in 1932," published in *The Jerusalem Post* of June 11, 1958, Shraya Shapiro reveals that the late Chaim Arlosoroff,

3. When War Broke Out

On September 4, the day after Great Britain declared war on Germany, Jabotinsky wrote to the British Prime Minister, Neville Chamberlain, that for the duration of the conflict world Jewry was ready to forget all its grievances against the British Administration in Palestine and to cast its lot with the fighting democracies.

This generous gesture of goodwill did not meet with proper appreciation. The British Government acknowledged it as their due, and expected more. On September 14, Jabotinsky met Colonel Meinertzhagen, who confidently said : "The War Office believe that all's well in Palestine now, except for a few scattered remains of Arabs—and your men [the *Irgun*]." Then, according to Jabotinsky's brief memo on this encounter, the following dialogue developed : [16]

M.—How far goes your say with them?

J.—Eighty-five per cent. To be clearer: I could persuade them to ignore snipers, but not to ignore physical obstruction to [*Aliya*] *Bet* [illegal immigration]. Let me see those War Office people.

M.—They won't see you unless you guarantee good behavior [on the part of the *Irgun*].

J.—Not if there is threat to *Bet*.

M.—They can't agree to *Bet*.

since the autumn of 1931 Political Secretary of the Jewish Agency in Jerusalem, a year before his assassination had come to the unalterable conclusion that "under the British there was no possibility of achieving a Jewish majority in Palestine," and that "he had in mind a real *putsch* against the British." In a letter to Chaim Weizmann, dated June 30, 1932, Arlosoroff wrote: "Zionism cannot, in given circumstances, be turned into reality without a transition period of revolutionary rule by the Jewish minority. . . . There is no way to a Jewish majority, or even to an equilibrium between the two races [Arabs and Jews]—to be established by systematic immigration and colonization—without a period in which a nationalist minority Government would take over the state machinery, the administration, and military power in order to forestall the danger of our being swamped by [Arab] numbers and endangered by a [Arab] rising which we could not face without having the state machinery and military power at our disposal."

Anticipating that he would be charged with siding with Jabotinsky, Arlosoroff took pains to stress that his plan had nothing in common with Revisionism and that he continued to regard Jabotinsky's "tactics, politics, and educational tenets as downright folly." The similarity of Arlosoroff's 1932 scheme (he even closely studied Curzio Malaperte's book of the theory of insurrections in the twentieth century) and Jabotinsky's plan of 1939 is, however, striking. For the evaluation of their respective maturity, one must of course take into consideration the realities of the 1932 and 1939 situations, in particular—the plight of European Jewry, the strength of the *Yishuv*, and the preparedness of its military forces.

No agreement was reached at this meeting, not even a common approach to the problem. An entry in Colonel Meinertzhagen's unpublished voluminous diary (Vol. 45, p. 64), which he kindly made available to this writer, refers to the luncheon he had on that date at the Carlton Hotel with "Vladimir Jabotinsky, President of the Zionist Revisionist Organization, a restless revolutionary, an ardent Left-wing Zionist [the Colonel explained in a personal conversation that the term "Left-wing" was meant merely to define Jabotinsky's "radical" Zionist views], militant, ruthless, but able. . . . He told me that he only exercised control over about 80 per cent of his people in Palestine and he refused to give a guarantee for their good behavior for the period of the war, which created a bad impression on me. He seemed anxious to impress the loyalty of his sector to Britain, but was unprepared to have peace in Palestine. I told him that his action would prevent us [the British] from moving military units from Palestine at a moment we badly need them elsewhere. To this he turned a deaf ear." *

The British Government was not satisfied with Jabotinsky's loyalty declaration in his capacity as President of the New Zionist Organization. What they wanted was a similar official move on the part of the *Irgun*, of which he was the titular head. According to Jabotinsky, "a few days after the outbreak of the war, the *Irgun* had broadcast a declaration of loyalty to the Allies, of willingness to cooperate with the British Government for the defense of Palestine, and on any other front, in the struggle for democracy and for creation of a Jewish State in Palestine"; they were ready for a "cease fire" for the duration.[17] According to *Irgun* sources, no undertaking of good behavior was ever made by *Irgun's* High Command, which had refused any

---

* In spite of the mutually disappointing outcome of this encounter, Colonel Meinertzhagen made a point of stressing—when this writer visited him in London on May 13, 1957—that in his opinion "the Jewish State owes its creation to Jabotinsky more than to Weizmann. Weizmann was more of a diplomat, while Jabotinsky was essentially an Israeli long before the emergence of Israel. To him, the interests of the Jewish State-to-be were above everything. If Jabotinsky were alive in 1948, he would have been the natural first President of Israel and would have provided the badly needed dynamic leadership. Of course, what Jabotinsky wanted was fraught with danger and might have led to explosive complications. But he was a Zionist fighter. The British Government considered Jabotinsky a menace not because they thought of him as anti-British (they didn't), but because they believed that his Zionist extremism was endangering the *status quo* in Palestine and making the British position even more complicated."

Asked whether this statement of his was for publication, the Colonel firmly answered in the affirmative.

statement to this effect as long as they and their comrades were being kept in prisons and concentration camps: "We don't negotiate in captivity," was their well-considered reply. It is true that "terrorist activities" were actually discontinued. This was, however, not an agreed cease fire, but a factual state of affairs caused largely by the arrest of the leadership and the ensuing weakening of the organization, as well as by the general relaxation of the Arab-Jewish strife in the early months of the war. Yet there was no relaxation in the attitude of the British administration toward the "Jabotinsky men." On September 29, Jabotinsky bitterly complained in a letter to M. Haskel: "The attitude of the Palestine Government toward our friends shows no improvement. A few persons have been released from *Sarafend*, probably just to please Rutenberg: but that red tape set of second-raters are still incapable of a big gesture which would equal our friends' offer of friendship and cooperation. What is necessary is to go on hammering through all possible channels that *Sarafend* [concentration camps] must be totally evacuated of Jews; hammering always helps in *such* cases, and we have already started it and won't cease."

It was in this spirit that, on December 27, Jabotinsky wrote to Colonel Meinertzhagen that he was "greatly worried about the arrests and sentences of our self-defense people in Palestine; the last bunch, sentenced to ten and six years, consists of Revisionists, but includes several girls."

While I wrote about them to Malcolm MacDonald, the answer was that he did not see any justification for Jews in Palestine continuing to arm and drill illegally. I hope I need not comment on this answer in writing to a man of your experience—at least this is the assumption on which I am writing at all. I only wish to add that when my friends in Palestine, on their own initiative, decided at the outbreak of the war to contribute to the country's pacification, they did not expect this gesture to be rewarded by an attempt to paralyze the Jewish self-defense, so essential to our future security. Apart from all politics, there is something ethically awkward in all this.

It has unfortunately become a rule that no complaint in this climate is considered valid unless accompanied by some veiled threat establishing the claimant's nuisance value, e.g. something about American public opinion or such like. I claim no nuisance value and foretell no retaliation in case the wrong is not righted, but I tell you all this is utterly wrong and worse than wrong.

To this, Meinertzhagen, who had been for many years a staunch pro-Zionist and a friend of Jabotinsky, replied on December 29, in an unusually stern letter written on the stationery of the War Office:

Dear Jabotinsky:

Though I can quite appreciate the worry which the recent sentence on your people may have caused you, you know as well as I do, that all this illicit drilling is not a genuine desire to help the Allies in the present war but has other motives. The presence of bombs among the culprits exposes the whole motive of the drilling with which I have no sympathy.

I fear your claim to nuisance value is too well known to be denied; but I can assure you that so long as this country is fighting for its life in Europe, such a thing as nuisance value becomes a criminal offence.

I am sorry to be so unsympathetic. When this war is ended to our satisfaction, maybe my sympathy for your cause will revive.

Apparently referring to this exchange of letters, Jabotinsky wrote in his *The War and the Jew* that "the explanation elicited from the proper authority in London" in reply to an inquiry "put in formal writing . . . was to the effect that the competent authority is unable to admit that any justification exists for the illegal arming and military training of Jews in Palestine." Jabotinsky's bitter comment was:[18]

A curious attitude this, in the winter of 1939, after three years' experience had shown how little official protection can actually be given to Jewish settlements even in peace time; and less than ever is given now, when we are perhaps on the threshold of unpredictable complications. More than ever, preparedness for self-protection should be openly recognized as justifiable. In this attitude there is no logic, no justice, no elementary care for the safety of an exposed minority; but there is method—it is that of the White Paper policy, resentful of all things in any way reminiscent of the Jewish dream of Statehood.

Frankly admitting that the "truce" he had offered was frustrated by the British Mandatory, he meaningfully concluded: "It would be ridiculous Quixotry for the Jew, who would have been the lesser partner in the truce, had there been a truce, to play the silly game of *noblesse oblige* where there is obviously no truce. War or no war, the major partner has decided that the debate on Palestine's future shall continue, and we follow suit."

The unabated, often vicious hostility of the Palestine administration toward both the *Irgun* and the entire Jabotinsky brand of Zionism, was understandably an ever-growing source of frustrating anger to his followers in Palestine. He, however, insisted that they should not be carried away by their natural resentment. A few days before his death, he wrote to Arye Altman, who was then the head of the New Zionist Organization in Palestine:[19] "I dare say you must have many moments of bitter doubt: for the old ingrained peculiarities of the Colonial Office do not seem to have disappeared. I need not tell you to disregard them as long as humanly possible. When this crisis is over—happily and successfully over, I hope, all the atmosphere around us will be so different, all the contents of such terms as the League of Nations, Mandate, etc., will have so radically changed their implications, that hardly anything said or written during the crisis will have decisive value for the realities of the future. Other factors will decide this and other issues. It therefore seems to me that your best course is to help the British in the fight and to attach no undue importance to symbols or inferences."

In the meantime, internal trouble was brewing in the *Irgun* leadership. Its commander, David Raziel, who had been for months imprisoned together with other comrades, was suddenly brought to Jerusalem and released. He himself categorically asserted that he had made no promise to the British Administration that the *Irgun* would "behave," but his colleagues, who remained imprisoned, insisted that he had, and in a strongly worded letter protested against his alleged commitment. Raziel was indignant and announced that he would resign as Commander. He submitted his resignation on June 17, 1940, on the day after the release of the last *Irgun* prisoners. He refused to work with those of his comrades (among whom a leading role was played by Abraham Stern) who, he felt, were conducting a mudslinging campaign against him. "Blood—yes, but mud—no," he said, and, smashing a glass, added: "Just as it is impossible to restore the integrity of this glass, so it is impossible that I should ever resume my position."[20] This personal conflict considerably affected the *Irgun's* morale. The Palestine leadership of the New Zionist Organization pleaded with Raziel to return. However, Raziel was adamant in his refusal, and Stern persisted in his unyielding anti-Raziel stand.

An appeal to Jabotinsky's authority became inevitable. Apprised by Altman, via Turkey, about the alarming state of affairs, Jabotinsky unhesitatingly heeded the plea to restore Raziel's position. On July 28, six days before his passing, he cabled to "David Limersky" [at that time this was Raziel's underground alias] : "I reappoint you to functions hereto held with full powers to appoint and remove any collaborators within any branch of your department. Cable acceptance. Jabotinsky." Simultaneously, he cabled to "Yair Fein" [Abraham Stern] : "Reappointing David Limersky and formally ordering you to comply with these directives. I also personally trust you will spontaneously maintain harmony within our movement on eve of great ordeals. Jabotinsky." In another cable to David Limersky, who was both the commander of the *Irgun* and head [*Natziv*] of the Palestine *Betar,* Jabotinsky instructed him to publish the following appeal to the *Betarim* of all *Betar* branches : "Separated from you by many obstacles, hopefully fighting for our old Maccabaean dream, chiefly supported in my struggle by my faith in you, my sons and pupils, I appeal to you : don't let anything disrupt *Betar* unity, obey your *Natziv* whom I trust, and give me assurance that your and my life's best work, the *Betar,* stands strong and united, enabling me to continue my hopeful struggle for our old dream."

Stern, who had for a long time been opposed to Jabotinsky's hold over the *Irgun,* was not ready to heed the latter's order to submit, and his appeal to "maintain harmony." The conflict in the *Irgun* leadership continued unabated, and in September, 1940, a month after Jabotinsky's passing, led to an open split. Stern and a group of his followers left the *Irgun* and founded an independent body under the name of "Fighters for the Freedom of Israel." One of the many points of divergence between the Stern Group (as they came to be called) and its parent body was the difference in their attitude toward Jabotinsky. The Stern Group avoided any mention of his name in their literature and denied any ideological link with his movement. The *Irgun,* on the contrary, always considered themselves disciples and spiritual heirs of Jabotinsky, and made a point of stressing this allegiance. A. Gurvitch, who, in January, 1947, secretly met the then Irgun Commander, Menachem Begin, in Tel Aviv, recalls a significant episode related by the latter : many *Irgun* members who came from the ranks of the *Betar* had in their homes a picture of Jabotinsky which indicated to the police their political allegience; this often led to their arrest. Prompted by considerations of security, Begin ordered the removal of all such pictures; but, he said, this was the only order of his the Betarim simply would not carry out.[21]

The British fully realized the impression Jabotinsky had left on the *Irgun*-Revisionist uncompromising struggle against the anti-Zionist policy of the Mandatory Power. In 1945, seven exiled *Irgunist* and Revisionist leaders were brought for interrogation from the detention camp of Asmara to the fortress headquarters of the British Intelligence Service in Cairo. When all attempts to obtain information from them had failed, one of the detainees, Shimshon Yunitchman, was summoned by the Intelligence officer who had been interrogating him for weeks, for the last of the nightly "heart-to-heart talks." Freely admitting "complete failure" of their inquiry, the officer ascribed it to the fact that they were:

dealing with a different type of person—a type we are facing for the first time in our careers. . . . You conducted yourselves [during the investigation] as if "someone" were in the room, someone before whom you are on trial . . . who is no longer among the living, but who for you is still very much alive. He lives within you, this man we have never seen, but about whom we have read and learned so much (we had to! . . .) at first through duty and afterwards because of interest—this Vladimir Jabotinsky, this Jabo as you call him. . . . I see him now before my eyes . . . he is smiling at all the trouble you are causing a great Empire, as if he were saying: "Didn't I warn you that my sons knew how to write better than I? And wouldn't it have been better for you to have their friendship than their hatred?" . . . I see him as your idol. . . . That's what he was during his lifetime and that's what he has remained after his death. . . . He gave you a religion . . . you hardly feel distress, and you don't suffer when in prison. . . . I can't forget what you told me . . . that he broke your lives and your careers, but if you were able to be born again, you would have chosen the same way, *his* way, again.

"Right," was the answer.[22]

7

THE MAN

The Man

JABOTINSKY WAS a man of many and often contradictory facets and is not easily classifiable. He was simple and yet complex; natural, unostentatious, humble, and at the same time self-reliant and self-assured. Keen-minded, analytical, and craving for exactitude, he was also a poet and a visionary. Not all these facets of his personality were obvious or truly genuine. Some he deliberately hid or disguised; others, easily discernible, were actually not his own, but masks he chose to wear either deliberately or by artistic whim. The Jabotinsky the world knew—or believed it knew—scarcely resembled the man he was. Apparently easygoing and accessible, he was in many respects a close-mouthed man who seldom and sparingly allowed his inner thoughts and emotions to be exposed. With his charm and consummate acting ability, he successfully concealed his inner self from personal friends and closest associates who were often baffled by this reticence. Hardly one of them could claim ever to have had a full view of his personality, or to be able to draw a full-size portrait of him : not because he was a "human sphinx," but because of the complexity of his individuality. His biography could, of course, be conceived primarily as a history of his writings and speeches, ideas and deeds. But his thoughts and actions can be intelligently presented and elucidated only against the background of his personality and of his private life, in so far as he can be said to have had a private life. And to comprehend his personality one must try to understand the inner workings of his delicate and complex spiritual mechanism.

The following pages are a humble attempt at an admittedly imperfect silhouette of the man Jabotinsky, as the writer came to know him during three decades of association, supplemented by years of diligent and loving study of thousands of personal letters and other available sources.

THE TUNE OF THE TEAPOT

1. *Husband and Father*

THERE ARE, Jabotinsky wrote in *Fairy Vagabunda*, two kinds of music in human life which have never been recognized by any of the existing music schools : one is the melody of the train in motion, of the turning wheels; the other—the song of the teapot or of a samovar. The two are antipodal and have always competed for predominance in the human heart.[1] It so happened that the song of the wheels of the train, restless and stimulating, played a decisive role in Jabotinsky's life. He had to be almost perpetually on the move, to live a life of congresses, meetings, committees, debates, and dissensions, submitting to all the busy and dismaying machinery which a great idea inevitably generates. But he was always alive to the charm and warmth of the tune of the teapot, of the peaceful domestic delights, and came to long for them more and more. "We are sick and tired of the endless scurry, and our daydream is, in one word, repose," he wrote in *My Village.*[2]

The domain of the teapot is by definition a woman's domain. Yet in Jabotinsky's concept, a woman's kingdom was by no means limited merely to domestic matters. He was, in his own words, "an advanced feminist." In an after-dinner speech, in 1923, he unhesitatingly asserted that women are not only entitled to full equality with men, but that "in the business of statecraft a woman is more in place than a man. . . . The main place for statesmanship is not the [speaker's] platform but the desk. A good statesman is not a good debater but a good ruler." And in the art of ruling states, he found a higher percentage of "great" queens among queens, than of "great" kings among kings.[3] He repeated this *profession de foi* in his Russian feuilleton *A Woman's*

Mind (Babiy Um).[4] Addressing the Revisionist Woman Organization (*Brit Nashim Leumioth*) in Warsaw and Prague, he extolled the role the Jewish woman is destined to play in the national renaissance of her people.[5] And in the second part of his *Autobiography*, he plainly said that with the exception of heavy physical work where muscular strength plays a decisive role, there is no task in the world which he would not entrust to a woman rather than to a man. He was convinced that any average woman is in fact an "arelit" (mythical winged lioness of great strength and celestial origin).

"This attitude of mine," he explained in his autobiography (pp. 17-20), "is not a matter of calculation. It is an organic feeling that is beyond any discussion, like *cogito ergo sum*. . . . It probably stems from personal experience . . . that implanted in me the notion of a soul woven from threads of steel and silk. This notion's name is—'woman.' My beliefs are few. One of them is that your mother, your sister, your wife are princesses." This credo, he pointed out, was magnificently vindicated in the dramatic era of his lonely struggle for the Jewish Legion when his mother, sister, and wife were for him a tower of strength, without which he would have never been able to carry this struggle to a victorious end.

Jabotinsky's admiration for and devotion to his mother and sister were great and unwavering; the first volume of this biography (pp. 29-30, 391-98) deals in some detail with Jabotinsky the son and the brother. But his mother passed away in 1926, and after his exile from Palestine in 1930, he saw his sister only twice (1935 and 1937), and then only briefly. It was the immediate family—his wife and his son—that constituted his personal world. And this self-styled bohemian and vagabond deeply enjoyed and cherished his family life.

The human climate of this life was not the usual one. Its determining characteristic was—ritual. At the Third World Convention of the *Betar* in Warsaw (1938), Jabotinsky eloquently formulated his longstanding cult of "ceremony" in human behavior: "Ritual demonstrates man's superiority over the beast. What is the difference between a civilized man and a wild man? Ceremony. Everything in the world is ritual." He fully applied this credo in his own home, where he firmly implanted the conviction that life was a game to be played in accordance with unwritten but very definite patterns of conduct. One of these patterns was studied politeness in daily relationship. Family life was not permitted to slip into formless and slovenly familiarity. After almost thirty years of marriage, Jabotinsky treated his helpmeet with the same accentuated eighteenth century courtesy with which he would have approached any lady of his acquaintance. She, in turn, would never enter his study without knocking at the door and asking: "May I?" Even when all the members of the family were at home—which did not happen very often—privacy was scrupulously respected: each one was careful not to be in the other's way. Jabotinsky's own privacy was diligently observed: when he was working in his study, no domestic matters were permitted to interfere, Mrs. Jabotinsky was eager to spare him any unnecessary inconvenience, guarding his health carefully and tactfully. All this was done quietly and unobtrusively, which he particularly appreciated. He reciprocated by equally unobtrusive but unwavering attention to all her needs and moods.

Just like any other good husband, he was always concerned about his wife's health and contentment. His correspondence with personal friends carefully registers the ups and downs in both fields. Here are, at random, a few characteristic excerpts from his letters:[6] "Ania is trying to be cheerful, but she is absolutely at her wits' end. She has a terrible blood pressure ($17\frac{1}{2}$ instead of 12) and one kidney does not work at all; she has been put on a saltless diet, etc." And in another letter: "Ania feels better." And again in another: "I am dissatisfied with Ania. She gets easily tired and is highly nervous." "Ania is rather seedy, but much better the last couple of weeks."

When she fell ill in Paris while he was in London, he phoned every day to inquire about her health.

In all domestic affairs, Anna Markovna was undisputed boss. All the money intended for the family was at her disposal; no accounting was ever expected. A peculiar feature of the household was the studied reluctance to speak of financial matters; money was something "unmentionable," a somewhat embarrassing topic that had to be treated with the great restraint. For some time, one of Mrs. Jabotinsky's kinsmen was serving as Jabotinsky's private secretary: his salary was not discussed beforehand, and when Mrs. Jabotinsky paid him his monthly due, she did so almost furtively, slipping a sealed envelope with money into his hand.

Until 1933, Mrs. Jabotinsky never actively participated in her husband's Zionist activities; she even pointedly manifested her disinterestedness in all Zionist affairs. This attitude changed shortly after the Kattowitz crisis of 1933 (see Chapter Nine), which seems to have affected her very deeply. She became both angry at Jabotinsky's former colleagues (in particular Machover and Grossman) and eager to help him in the task he had undertaken. The field she chose for herself was the management of the *Tel Hai* Fund, the central financial institution of the Revisionist movement. She was appointed the Fund's managing director, with an office in the rue Pontoise, in Paris, and later in Finchley Road in London. This gave them the opportunity of being together not only at home, but also in a common Zionist effort. In this Jabotinsky was more fortunate than Herzl, whose Zionism undermined his personal life, whose wife never understood and increasingly resented his political activities; the last years of Herzl's life were marred by this estrangement.

Jabotinsky highly valued his wife's work : "Ania is very punctilious in her *Tel Hai* job"; she is "just what I have always been missing— a good administrator."[7] In 1936, when the headquarters were transferred to London, she stayed in Paris for several months; early in 1937, Jabotinsky wrote to his son :[8] *"Keren Tel Hai* has suffered a lot because of the geographical separation between Mother and the office in the last year, and she is very sorry about the decline of that institution—for *without any doubt* [underlined in the original] it would have become 'rich' by now but for this separation." He also had much confidence in his wife's common sense and feminine intuition and strongly relied on her judgment of people.

His helpmeet's understanding and encouragement meant a lot to Jabotinsky. Mentioning, in a personal letter to Mrs. Jacob De Haas (October 24, 1935), that her husband, who was then on a political mission in Poland, *"immensely* appreciates the wholehearted backing he got at home, this time, more than any time before," he added : "I can fully understand him : let anyone who likes call me *Pantoffel-Held,* but I shouldn't be able to do things without this kind of backing at home. A shower of cold water from that quarter usually stops me, and a hearty Godspeed from that quarter always trebles my zeal." In public, he studiously refrained from any expression of his feelings for his wife, and broke this restraint only once, in January, 1938, in his closing speech at the N.Z.O. Convention in Prague. Thanking all his co-workers, he said :[9] "There is in this hall somebody, to whom I should like to quote the words of the Prophet Jeremiah—'I remember thee the kindness of thy youth, the love of thine espousal, when

thou didst go after me in the wilderness, in a land that was not sown.' "
That was all—he did not even mention the name of that "somebody."

During his long absences from home, Jabotinsky wrote to his wife
almost daily from every part of the world. His letters resembled a
diary, recording interviews with the statesmen of the world, huge
mass meetings, closed conferences, reflecting his emotions, hopes and
disappointments. Some were written after lonely days in far corners
of the world, some after strolls in centers of culture, after theater performances, and others again contained just general impressions and
experiences.

The world will never know the contents of hundreds, possibly
thousands, of those letters. Most of that correspondence, extending
over a period of twelve years preceding Jabotinsky's death, were put
away for safe-keeping in the vault of a London storehouse. In December of 1940, a German bomb destroyed the building and the letters
were blown away by the winds, together with the smoke. Only a
small number of letters—the last of which Mrs. Jabotinsky received
just before her husband's death—were saved by her.

Jabotinsky liked and enjoyed female company, and there was much
guarded talk about his alleged "romances." But once, when asked
by a friend whether, on his numerous journeys, he had any romantic
adventures, he said : "You will not believe me, but—apart from all
other considerations—nothing of the kind is simply technically
possible. Wherever I come, I am met by large crowds and then
solemnly escorted to my hotel room. There, two uniformed *Betarim*
permanently keep guard outside my door. Visitors come and go uninterruptedly. My timetable is prepared in advance down to the
minutest detail. Every hour is taken up and accounted for. In such
circumstances, even Casanova himself would have been unable to
engage in a love affair, however fleeting. No, my young friend, for
better or for worse, there is just no opportunity of indulging in this
kind of diversion."

Whether because of "technical" difficulties so humorously
described, or because of "all other considerations" so deliberately
mentioned in passing only, there were apparently no "love affairs"
in Jabotinsky's married life. But there were strong friendships, the
kind of man-and-woman relationship for which the French have the
finely nuanced expression *amitié amoureuse*. In Jabotinsky's case,
the emphasis was definitely on the *amitié*. The adjective *amoureuse*

constituted the stimulating—and in any genuine man-and-woman friendship inevitable—accessory of varying and variable intensity. Some of these relationships were casual and shortlived; others ripened into sincere and lasting friendships, usually at a distance of many hundreds of miles, kept alive by intermittent correspondence. To maintain such correspondence was for Jabotinsky, with his heavy load of work and worries, by far not an easy undertaking, and he sometimes felt that he just could not live up to it. On March 9, 1934, he dejectedly wrote from Paris to a friend in Warsaw:

. . . I am apparently lost for everything that is personal. Partly, simply because of old age and tiredness, partly because I am too much submerged by work. My great devotion for you remains as it always was; but I am now inevitably neglecting all obligations arising from attachments. Just write me off and don't bear me ill-will.

But two days later he regretted this outburst:

I am dissatisfied with what I have written you. I do not at all want you to write me off. Probably my nerves are finally beginning to give way, so that my hand writes under the influence of impressions which evaporate by tomorrow. The birth certificate is beginning to tell; or maybe I have really had my fill. The Stavsky affair; the witholding of certificates from our youth; the daily beating-up of our people in Palestine; and a hundred of other worries, including a dozen personal worries. . . . Some day all this will end well; for the time being, please do not write me off and do not pay much attention to the *ink* content of my answers. My soul is much better than my ink.

Mrs. Jabotinsky knew of her husband's female friendships and took them lightly, sometimes jokingly referring to her "innumerable rivals." Jabotinsky appreciated this attitude: "Ania is an intelligent woman; she knows what is hers and what is not," he once commented.[10] And "hers" was a very big part of her husband's heart and mind.

The same applied to their son Eri. Jabotinsky was strongly impressed by the occasional references in Herzl's diaries to his children, Hans, Pauline, and Trude:[11] "As I read I felt that subdued tenderness that was in his eyes and so seldom on his lips. I remembered that as I read I felt what every public worker probably feels at times, though he will not admit it, that ultimately, no matter how sacred one's public work is, and how much joy it gives you, what is real in life, what is

501

most important is, after all, Hans and Pauline and Trude." One feels how personal that was, how Jabotinsky applied what he had read in Herzl to "every public worker." It is in that same article that he reminds us: "I am a father myself, and I know how it hurts."

He was an affectionate and proud father. It was with barely restrained pride that he informed his friends that "Eri has passed his second competition for the Ecole Centrale and has been admitted fifth." [12] When, in 1935, Eri finished the Ecole Centrale, he received a very advantageous offer to stay in France and to work in the field of aeronautics. But he himself wanted to go into Zionist politics in Palestine. Friends of the family and Mrs. Jabotinsky were opposed to this course. But Jabotinsky said to them: [13] "I share your view. But I have for years been urging our youth to volunteer for national service [gius] in Palestine, how can I advise my son to pursue a personal career?" Eri went to Palestine. His father was glad to learn that Eri intended to write "a series of articles or even a book on Revisionist problems" and added in his usual self-deprecating manner: "I have been praying for some years that somebody would write such a book; maybe I shall learn from it what the movement lacks beside a suitable leader." [14]

Eri's active interest and active participation in Revisionist work was for Jabotinsky a source of satisfaction and pride. After the Revisionist World Conference in Cracow (January, 1935) he reported to his sister: [15] "Yesterday Eri addressed the Conference in Hebrew; it was very sensible." Apparently refering to the boy's early speech difficulties (see Vol. I, pp. 394-396), he added: "And his voice sounded perfect. We have only to think and to recall our fears of twenty years ago! Ania saved him." [15]

In August, 1936, Jabotinsky appointed his son head of the *Betar* in Palestine. The following year Eri was arrested under the "Prevention of Crimes Ordinance" for "endangering the public peace," and spent eighty-four days in the prison of Acre. The British Labor M.P., Hopkins, an old friend and admirer of Jabotinsky, energetically intervened on his son's behalf. In a brief note to Hopkins, Jabotinsky wrote: [16] "I cannot express how grateful I am for the interest you take in my son's fate. But the matter has nothing to do with him. I am absolutely against any intervention on behalf of Eri. Let me be quite frank: unless you feel you can speak to Mr. [Ormsby] Gore [Colonial Minister] on the broader issue, drop the matter altogether."

Considering Eri to be "not much of a disciplinarian," Revisionist leaders in Palestine wanted Jabotinsky to replace him with somebody else as head of the *Betar* in the country. Shmuel Katz, who was entrusted with the job of conveying the unpleasant request to Jabotinsky, recalls that the latter "was visibly upset, said something about 'a Jewish failing,' inquired whether I was of the same opinion, and then asked me to leave him alone for a while. Afterward he had a long talk with Eri; and he acceded to the request to replace him." [17]

The father-and-son relationship was based on deep, almost unlimited respect for and confidence in the latter's views and reactions. Early in 1936, Eri, who was then in Palestine, expressed the wish to come to Paris. The parents were at a loss to understand this wish. Nevertheless, Jabotinsky's answer was that, "right or wrong," he was ready to agree. Eri took this answer as an attempt to humor him. "That is not true," Jabotinsky explained. "I have a feeling—so does mother—that the inner motive that compels you to come to Paris this time must be a very deep one, very serious and decisive . . . though mother and I probably do not understand you as we should. . . . In my younger days I left the Gymnasium about one year before matriculation, and nobody understood why; but I knew. I have never forgotten this experience. I think that in such cases, if my opinion is asked, I have to tell the truth, that is, 'I disagree'; but I shall back you up 'right or wrong' for I have confidence that in your eyes it is 'right.' " [18] He took the same attitude four years later, when Eri decided that it was his duty to embark on the *Sakaria,* together with twenty-four hundred "illegal" immigrants (see Chapter Twenty-two). "I was opposed to this intention of his and wired him to this effect, but the wire arrived after his departure," Jabotinsky explained to Aviva Kogan, Eri's fiancée. "Yet I understand him well. . . . In his place, I also would have decided: 'All right, if it is that hard, I will go through it with all of you.' It is nonsensical but, psychologically, in *his* opinion, inevitable. It is the same psychology that made me enlist then [in 1917] as a soldier. If I would have remained 'Mr. Correspondent'—at that time a journalist in London was a tremendous force—I could have continued my talks with generals as between equals, and this probably would have been better for the regiment. But Jews are not used [to the idea] that the commander *has* to sit far away from the frontline, and all the others have to stay under the shower of bullets. That's why I became a private, deprived of all rights. I often regretted it, but today I would have acted exactly the same way. And Eri is completely right." [19]

Eri was imprisoned for bringing the *Sakaria* immigrants to Palestine, and the British Administration was planning to revoke his Palestine citizenship. In strongly worded cables to Amery, Churchill, Lord Cecil, Colonel Wedgwood, Lord Snell, Lord Strabolgi, and several other British political leaders, Jabotinsky denounced this attempt as "vendetta for an act of humanity which every unbiased conscience approves."

Ten years ago the same Government excluded me, too, from Palestine, for which I fought in a regiment raised through my efforts. I can only wonder if Englishmen who remember my service when world Jewry cursed me for supporting the Tsar's ally, will stand this ingratitude, injustice and refined cruelty rendering my boy stateless like his father at wild times like these.

Eri was not denaturalized. But he was detained in the Acre jail—the same prison of which his father had been an inmate two decades before—until his father's death. Six days before his death, Jabotinsky wrote to him: "Tomorrow's Clipper is expected to take letters for Palestine, so perhaps this will reach you. . . . God bless you. I know you are brave and strong and don't fret or worry. . . . Yours lovingly —Father." [20]

Jabotinsky's last will is a typical example of dispositions made by a *bonus pater familias,* concerned with the future of the three human beings closest to his heart: his wife, his son, and his sister. He left "all property in every sense that may be implied in this term (belongings, rights, claims, etc.)" to his wife, without any limitations, "in the full sense of *jus utendi et abutendi.*" "But," he added "I shall be glad if after her death all the rights would pass to our son Eri Theodor Jabotinsky." The rights he owned in the Hebrew Geographical Atlas (see chapter One), he left in equal parts to his wife and sister. "I have no doubt, however," he concluded, "that the three persons mentioned in the will—my wife, my son, my sister—will always help and support each other in case of need, beyond any provision of this will."

2. *Plenty of Friends*

Within the iron framework of Jabotinsky's attitude toward public life flourished a highly sensitive, emotional nature. His political vision had the stern strength of the Puritan outlook, but none of its bleakness. He was fully alive to the countless lovely and tender things in life.

In private life he was warm, human, imaginative, and simple— good company, generous, argumentative, humorous—qualities that are little known and are almost exactly the opposite of the caricature of him that attained wide currency. He was not a difficult man to get along with, or to be friends with : unconstrained, genial, with a taste for witticisms which nothing escaped, neither the sublime and beautiful, nor the petty and mean, and certainly not himself; but his witticisms were merry and discreet, not malicious or ill-natured. At every period of his life he had friends in plenty, from the most varied circles. He belonged to the category of men of whom it could be said that the better one knew them, the more one liked them. And in fact, almost all those who became his friends stuck to him closely throughout his life, irrespective of all vicissitudes and trials.

In a world where personal loyalty is not the commonest of virtues, he showed a loyalty to his friends and associates which was as sincere as it was unwavering. He never tired of doing things to show his concern for their welfare. While meeting arduous campaign schedules, he would never neglect to see to it that those travelling with him were comfortable. In the midst of feverish activity, he would remember to send flowers and a personal note to the wife of the humblest associate on her birthday. Dr. Weizmann describes him as "warmhearted, generous, always ready to help a comrade in distress.[21] More than once his helpfulness took forms he had every reason to regret—but he didn't. In addition to services he himself rendered, he was inordinately lavish, even wasteful, with so-called "letters of introduction," the beneficiaries of which were often persons known to him only superficially, or even complete strangers. It was sufficient that a friend or acquaintance approached him with the request for an introduction for a protégé of his; he unquestioningly obliged. Sometimes the letters were addressed to a specific person from whom a favor was expected; in other instances it was a general recommendation "to whom it may concern." In both cases, Jabotinsky was as a rule extremely generous in

505

describing the protégé's qualities and most eloquent in pleading his or her case, whatever the case might be. More than once this indiscriminate generosity was badly abused by unscrupulous individuals for dubious purposes, causing him considerable trouble. Friends often remonstrated with him and insisted on his being more circumspect in such matters. He usually penitently admitted his guilt and—continued sinning. He was simply unable to resist the temptation of rendering a service to people who asked for it. Quoting a line from a popular German song *Die Mädels von Java, die sagen niemals nein* [the girls from Java never say "no"], he once said with a twinkle in his eye: "Blessed be the Almighty who did not make me a girl."

He had the quality of quiet friendliness that attracted people and impelled them to confide in him. Undemonstrative on the surface, he had unfathomed depths of tenderness and pity. There was in him nothing of the hardboiled politician, fully engrossed in the struggle for ideas and power, indifferent to the problems and sufferings of the individual. After Jabotinsky's death, Professor L. I. Rabinowitz, Chief Rabbi of South Africa, told a touching story of "A Letter From Jabotinsky" which saved a young man's life. The story is worth recording.[22]

During his 1937 visit to South Africa, Jabotinsky became acquainted with a Jewish family in Johannesburg; their son, a lad of twenty, was a student in the Witwaterstrand University. At that time, anti-Semitism, which was hardly known in the country before, started to raise its head and be felt in the University. The sensitive youth suffered greatly in mind and spirit. He felt that there was no sense and no dignity in living in such a world and that suicide was the only solution for him. But before putting this dread decision into practice, he wrote to Jabotinsky, who in the meantime left for London, pouring out his heart to him and acquainting him with his intention.

"Jabotinsky answered," commented Rabbi Rabinowitz. "Is there not in these two simple words themselves, irrespective of the contents of the letter, an insight into the greatness of the man? For the life of me I cannot imagine, let us say Weizmann, sitting down to write a personal letter to a boy of twenty, with whom his acquaintance was of the slightest, living seven thousand miles away."

The letter, marked "private," reads as follows:

London, Nov. 27, 1938

Dear . . .

Suicide is worse than cowardice; it is surrender. Try and analyse any great or small *Schweinerei* in history or in life; you will always detect that its root was or is somebody's surrender. Surrender is the dirtiest trick in creation; and suicide, being the symbol of all surrenders, is like a call for universal betrayal.

In the case of your generation, it would also be a silly bargain.

Your generation is destined to see miracles, and, collectively, perform miracles. Don't get downhearted because of butcheries going on; every-thing, all forces of life and death, are now converging toward one end, a Jewish State and a great Exodus to Palestine.

I think, on a very conservative estimate, that in the next ten years the Jewish State of Palestine will not only be proclaimed, but a reality; probably less than ten. It would be unspeakably cheap and foolish to forego all this because there are *Schweinereis* at your university.

"What to do?" Forgive me, but this question, always in my practice, really means: "Can't you suggest a way in which I, A. B., should at once become a general with a special mission of my own?" We need privates, doing drab commonplace jobs, and your age (whatever your gifts) is private's age. Go to H.Q. and ask for drab errands to run. We all did it.

Mon ami, I should be thrilled, every hour of my wake and dream, if I had the luck of being twenty today, on the threshold of redeemed Israel and, probably, a redeemed world to boot; no matter what butcheries it may cost.

Give my love to your family.

Yours sincerely,

V. J.

This letter, that bespeaks a deep interest in the soul of a highly strung Jewish youth, saved the youth's life.

3. *Money*

In practical matters Jabotinsky was anything but worldly-wise. To him money had no meaning in itself. It was there only to be used for a purpose, usually not for a personal purpose, and he was inordi-nately generous, even somewhat casual about it in everyday life. Those acquainted with his household affairs, testify that he never knew whether the family budget was balanced or his son's college fees paid. All this was the domain of Mrs. Jabotinsky, who was not too practical a housekeeper either. His personal needs were limited to cigarettes (he stopped smoking in 1935), buying detective stories, and—extravagantly high tips which he used to give the personnel of hotels at which he was staying, or to restaurant waiters; he somehow felt uneasy about being served by others and tried to compensate by an almost Oriental lavishness of *pourboires*. A colleague of his, who happened to be staying for a few weeks at the same hotel, recalls that on leaving, Jabotinsky borrowed ten pounds (about fifty dollars) from him. This happened on the seventh floor of the building. When they reached the lobby, not a penny remained in Jabotinsky's pocket: the entire amount was distributed between the elevator operators and the bell boys.[23]

Financial troubles were a chronic feature of Jabotinsky's existence, reaching a climax every Fall, when he had to pay the premium for his life insurance policy. The amount involved was relatively high and he never had it available. Weeks in advance, he usually started trying to mobilize the necessary means, asking for a short-term loan from well-to-do friends or for an advance from papers he worked for. In September, 1927, he wrote to his sister: "On October 1 I have to pay the life insurance premium, so that I am in a miserable mood." Two weeks later he reported: "Everything is under control. I have paid the premium so that I can again, for a year, be without worry for Ania, Eri, and you." [24]

In fact, there was no objective reason for having financial worries. Jabotinsky earned well both as journalist and as lecturer, and his small family of three could have lived quite comfortably on these earnings. But besides his immediate family, there was a wider circle largely dependent on his support: his sister, nephew in Palestine (for a time), his brother-in-law's family in Paris, and many others, distant relatives, friends, acquaintances, and just solicitors. To the latter he was very rarely capable of saying no: "It is so much pleasanter to *give* than to *refuse*," he used to say. He even felt guilty when unable to help out, and went out of his way to remedy this failure. Once, when a cousin of his, who often borrowed money from him, asked for a loan again, Jabotinsky apologetically confessed that he himself was utterly broke; however, the following day the cousin received a triumphant special delivery postcard: "I have got the money, come and get it." [25]

But the main drain on his budget was his movement. It is impos-

508

sible to estimate even approximately the amounts he contributed, one way or another, to the party's chronically deficient treasury: over the fifteen-year period 1925-40, they must have totaled a six-figure sum. Indicative of the size of his contributions are the entries in his note-book for 1930: "Advanced to the [Revisionist] Executive Committee in Paris and London, from August to December, 1930, £722 (3,600 dollars); paid to Zeluk [printers of the two party papers] for *Der Nayer Weg*, Frs. 54,980 (2,160 dollars) and for the *Rasswyet* Frs. 32,587 (1,210 dollars)." Sometimes it was an outright contribution or a "loan" (never to be repaid); in other instances, it was the income from a lecture tour, the lion's share going to the party or its insti-tutions. The party's financial troubles were a recurrent phenomenon in Jabotinsky's life. In August, 1930, he wrote to a friend that while planning "to proceed to Bad P." for a rest, he received a wire from Paris informing him that the printer of the *Rasswyet* and *Nayer Weg* "can't extend our credit. So, I dumped my bags in a third-class car-riage and went off to Paris. . . . Can't even say I was sorry: I am simply past feeling anything. Simply drowned in *tzoress*, personal and public. Sometimes I think I'm riding for a fall, including per-sonal bankruptcy. I wish I could get sick, something serious like typhus, which takes a man away for weeks and weeks and settles all problems." [26] Six months later he bitterly upbraided himself for the discrepancy between his financial possibilities and the task he had set himself:[27] "Personally I am dissatisfied. A *Kabtzan* [beggar] should not become important: he has to live in Lomza and not to meddle in anything, for he will achieve nothing anyway. Such feats as are demanded from me can be produced only if one has three secretaries, and I have none; I even have to lick the stamps myself. . . . Never-theless, I am still riding high, and trying to organize something." In February, 1933, he undertook a lecture tour of Central, Eastern, and South-Eastern Europe; his meetings were always crowded to capacity and all tickets were always sold out, but, in a letter (March 11) to A. Weinshal, he sadly confessed: "My lectures will hardly pay off one-half of the *Rasswyet's* old indebtedness." On May 11 he appealed to Weinshal: "I implore you on bended knees to send a generous check for the *Rasswyet*." Six days later, gratefully acknowledging the receipt of one hundred pounds, he added: "But this is not enough. Please help to the very best of your ability. Give until it hurts, as I do." In January, 1935, he wrote to S. Jacobi:[28] "Here in Paris [then the seat of the Revisionist World Executive] we are penniless. . . . I expect very shortly to get from New York my share of the Paramount's payment for the Samson scenario (see Chapter Twenty-seven), namely 666 dollars or £133. I will lend this sum to the Executive. I beg you, Dr. [S.] Klinger, Dr. [M.]Schwartzman and Mr. [S.] Landman to follow my example to the limit of your possibilities." After the Foundation Congress of the New Zionist Organization, he wired from Vienna :[29] "Cannot leave because of debts caused by Congress." A year later we read in a letter from Warsaw :[30]

Hm . . . I am beginning to fall into a lyric mood because of sheer pennilessness. I have broken off with the two local papers I was connected with [*Moment* and *Nasz Przeglad*], it happened because of considerations of prestige . . . On the horizon I see a hole and in the hole—darkness. My lecture manager was ruined this year—and he is not lying . . . But this is not so important, for I went lecturing with the understanding that all my earnings will go to the bottomless pit of the Executive, etc. My situation is catastrophic; it is true that *es hart mich afilu nit in der linker piate nit* (it does not affect me in the slightest). I am writing this effusion merely for effusion's sake—in that (God is my witness!) gay mood which overcomes me each time the last string of the violin snaps.

More than once Jabotinsky assumed heavy personal responsibility for the mismanagement in the conduct of "illegal" immigration by those in charge of such activities. In 1933, the Revisionist "Tourist Office" in Warsaw, headed by Engineer M. Zajczyk, showed a huge deficit of ninety thousand Zlotys (then about eighteen thousand dollars); it owed this amount to prospective tourists who had deposited money with it. Though in no way connected with, or responsible for this institution, Jabotinsky immediately decided, as he wrote to M. Haskel, "to take upon myself as much of the burden as only possible." He borrowed fifteen thousand francs (about six hundred dollars), and sent them to Warsaw; he allocated to the same purpose the proceeds of the filmed speech in Yiddish he was then preparing, and of a new five-month lecture tour.[31] A similar situation was created in 1935-36, when D. Bojko, the leader of the *Betar* in East Galicia, mismanaged considerable sums entrusted to him by prospective "illegal immigrants." This new calamity was largely instrumental in killing Jabotinsky's dream of a house of his own (see Chapter Sixteen). "But why do you feel accountable for Bojko's irregularities?" asked a friend.

The answer was: "Legally, I am of course not answerable; but morally I am responsible for everything connected with the *Betar*." [32]

Among contemporary Zionist leaders, Jabotinsky was about the poorest money raiser. In this respect he strongly resembled Herzl, whose biographer stresses that "he was oversensitive in money matters and did not understand how to engage the practical interests of the big givers." [33] Any attempt to mobilize funds for the movement was moral torture to Jabotinsky. More often than not, he was simply unable to muster the courage for such an attempt, and when he did so, he felt handicapped and embarrassed. He never succeeded in mastering the technique of soliciting, pleading, and bargaining, and even when he was not refused, he usually obtained a much smaller contribution than a man of lesser stature but better salesmanship would have squeezed out from the same source. With very few notable exceptions, he had no common language with Jewish money-bags, and his sporadic excursions into this field were usually poorly rewarded.

TWENTY-SEVEN

SPIRITUAL VERSATILITY

1. *Violin of Many Strings*

L EONARDO DA VINCI—probably the classical example of human
spiritual versatility: painter, sculptor, engineer, architect—was
an object of perpetual admiration to Jabotinsky. "A man's violin must
have many strings," he used to say. And there were, indeed, many
strings to his own violin.

When the Great Dispenser distributed talents among those destined
to make history, he seems to have given Jabotinsky not the Biblical
maximum of five, but rather five times five. And the youth so richly
endowed was not one to bury or to waste his natural abilities. Driven
by an insatiable intellectual curiosity supplemented by hard work,
he surpassed considerably, during his lifetime, the performance of the
good servants in the Biblical parable who merely doubled their
original endowment. In addition to his political record, there is hardly
a field he touched in which he could not have achieved an outstanding
and lasting reputation. The beauty of his poetry, the thoughtful bril-
liance of his novels, the lucidity and freshness of his literary and
sociological essays, his unusual capacity for perfect expression in
several languages, make it certain that he could have become a cele-
brity in his own right in the world of belles lettres, social science,
and linguistics.

These great possibilities were only partly brought to full fruition.
His dedication to the cause he chose to serve largely overshadowed
and pushed into the background artistic and scholarly inclinations.
At an early stage, he might have regarded Zionism merely as one of
the items on his life's agenda. But what he first believed to be a
pleasant avocation, soon became an inescapable vocation, an unre-

lenting taskmaster to whom he could deny nothing. The main record of his life was taken up by Zionism. All the rest—poetry, literature, languages—had to be squeezed somehow into marginal notes, dealt with during occasional brief interludes in the busy existence of a political leader, publicist, and orator.

But he never permitted those marginal notes to be completely obliterated. Whenever possible, he eagerly grasped the opportunity of taking a vacation from the hurly-burly of politics, of forgetting for a while the Zionist taskmaster, and of talking quietly about authors and books. In an article devoted to women authors, he spoke longingly of a novel whose author was, as he put it, "totally removed from any 'ism,' had probably never read a single article by Achad Haam, or one of Nordau's Zionist articles, and had probably never heard any discussion about the falseness of assimilation." [1] In that same article, he said, referring to Edna Ferber's book *Cimarron* : "As I read the book, green envy raged in the Zionist portion of my heart." And he unashamedly claimed the rights of the non-political portions of his heart : "People won't believe," he wrote, "that a man who is in political life can ever want to talk of something else, religion or literature or fools. They commit a terrible injustice. Aren't we human beings? Mustn't we for one moment shake off the dust of battle and of elections and pogroms, to bathe in the spring of abstract thought?"

It was the urge "to bathe in the spring of abstract thought" that must have had largely motivated Jabotinsky's joining the Masonic lodge "Etoile de Nord," a constituent of the "Grande Loge d'Orient." Established in 1924 by Russian political émigrés, "Etoile de Nord" counted among its members the élite of the Russian émigré intelligentsia; about 40 per cent were Jews. Jabotinsky was introduced by two non-Jews : his old friend and admirer, the noted Russian novelist M. A. Ossorgin, and by P. N. Pereversev, former Minister of Justice in the Revolutionary Cabinet of A. F. Kerensky. When asked at a preliminary interrogation what was prompting him to join the lodge, he answered : "The longing to breathe the pure mountain air." He enjoyed the lofty spiritual atmosphere prevailing at the lodge's meetings and at least during the first two years of his membership he frequently participated in its activities : delivered several addresses on general and Jewish topics and took part in the discussion following lectures delivered by other members. [2]

Freemasonry is, by definition, a secret society. With his customary loyalty, Jabotinsky never divulged even to his closest collaborators his association with the lodge. It was only after his death that this writer was able to establish the above scant facts.

The "pure mountain air," the "spring of abstract thought" that he longed to breathe, or bathe in, were poetic descriptions of an uncommonly wide and variegated range of interests, public and private, intellectual and emotional. In the world of ideas, very few things were alien to his mind, which seized with avidity upon scores of apparently unrelated fields of human creative knowledge. Pierre van Paassen who, shortly before Jabotinsky's death, took a stroll with him in Central Park, followed by a late dinner, recalls an amazing variety of topics touched upon during their after-dinner talk. Alongside with Jewish and Zionist problems, he spoke of the need not to confuse the historical moment with the trend of history, the phase with the permanent *Weltgefühl;* of the neo-pagan movement in the days of the Borgias and of the Italian Renaissance as proto-typical of the present Hauser School in Germany; of the atmosphere of the Dutch public schools which he thought so pleasant that it was almost inevitable that a love of learning should flourish in that country; of Martin Buber's book on the myth of Jews; of the University of Ghent as the center of the struggle for cultural autonomy in Flanders; of the Calvinist doctrine of predestination and the contrasting doctrine of man's free will; of the tendency of all socialistic revolutions to degenerate into etatism and tyranny. One of his favorite subjects was also the sixteenth century Wars of Religions in France: he avidly studied Calvin's *Institution* in the Huguenot library on rue des Saints Péres in Paris. Colonel Patterson once told van Paassen that "even among the instructors at the British Staff College, with the possible exception of Repington, there was not one who could match Jabotinsky in competently and expertly discussing any detail of military science: whether he dealt with Joshua or Xenophon, Alexander, Napoleon or Garibaldi, Jabotinsky could hold an audience spellbound while reviewing the underlying causes of any particular war, the merits of the great commanders, the faults in their strategy, as well as the causes of their triumphs and defeats." Recording all that rich array of topics that Jabotinsky loved to speak of, van Paassen stressed that it was "not a vainglorious display of his almost encyclopaedic knowledge and quiet wisdom and not an outpouring of a garrulous nature. He merely felt released from his most pressing cares for the moment. The breadth of his spirit took a wider sway in the freedom of the trees and meadows." [3]

On another occasion, he surprised his secretary, Tauber, by giving a detailed analysis of a very technical report on the amount of bread consumed by an average individual.[4] This was, however, by no means an improvisation: in his note-books for 1930 can be found abundant quotations and data from a study by R. W. Child. "Your Food and Your Farmers," published in the *Saturday Evening Post*. In a spirited literary discussion with a group of friends in Warsaw, he strongly attacked the prevailing view that the short story was essentially American in its origin and nature and challenged those present to identify "the first short story in world literature": "The story of Susanna in the Apocrypha (chapter thirteen of Daniel)," answered one of them. "Right. It is a Hebrew creation, though it came to us in the Greek version. And in fact, the whole Pentateuch is but a collection of epic short stories." [5] He had pronounced preferences in world literature. In 1937, after his return from South Africa, he exuberantly shared with this writer his joy:[6] "I have just received a present, something unique of its kind: the *Netzivut Betar* in Johannesburg has collected and bound for me four poems which I mentioned in my *Autobiography* as my favorites: [Edgar Allan Poe's] *The Raven*, [Edmond Rostand's] *Cyrano de Bergerac*, [Tegner's] *The Saga of Fritjoff*, and [Mickiewicz's] *Conrad Wallenrod*—all in the originals! I am in seventh Heaven. Surely even the Emperor of China himself did not possess such a book!" Among the French poets, he preferred the "Romantics" to the "Classics" and had a particular weakness for Rostand, from whose *Cyrano* and *L'Aiglon* he happily quoted entire speeches; he was even more fond of Baudelaire and Verlaine, reciting with fine nuances the latter's famous *Les sanglots longs des violons de l'automne....*"[7]

Jabotinsky was a fascinating conversationalist, always willing and eager to discuss (showering his companions with quotations from sources as varied as Pushkin, Omar Khayyam, Gandhi or Lincoln) not only highbrow intellectual or scientific topics: with as much gusto and knowledge he talked about much lighter and more *terre-à-terre* subjects. On one occasion, during a lunch at the Strassmans' country house near Warsaw, the conversation turned to a discussion of various types of food in different countries, and, as the hostess recalls, Jabotinsky "became really poetic when describing all the kinds of pasta prepared in Italy : even the best macaroni elsewhere was like shoe-laces, whereas the gravies prepared by the Italians and the absolutely perfect consistency they gave their dough, convey to this most pro-letarian of foods a taste of ambrosia and nectar." After lunch, the guests took a walk in the garden. Stopping before a big red dahlia, on which a beautiful yellow butterfly was perched, Jabotinsky asked Mrs. Strassman : "Do you remember in which language the butterfly has the most fitting name—I mean, to suit its slender gracefulness? A real name, not as ugly as butterfly, or the German *Schmetterling,* or the Russian *babochka,* or even the French *papillon* which is not so bad; in Hebrew it is also pretty, *parpar,* you know; but there is one other . . . so lovely—*mariposa* in Spanish. . . . Isn't it beautiful? *Ma-ri-poooo-sa.* . . . There is the saying of Calderon . . . and he began to quote in the original the great Spanish poet of the seventeenth century."[8]

He also liked to discuss with friends detective novels, of which he was uncommonly fond. These were a most welcome source of relaxa-tion to him, and he used to buy or borrow them in wholesale quan-tities. Once, in Paris, he paid a late visit to this writer who, he knew, was, like himself, an addict of this kind of literature, and somewhat apologetically explained : "On my way home from a meeting I suddenly realized that I had no mystery story to read in bed. It was quite a shock, believe me. So, I decided to call on a kindred spirit to rescue me from my predicament." Armed with a dozen French detective pocket-books, he left, grateful and happy. During his last stay in New York, he asked his secretary to buy the latest issues of American mystery magazines and avidly plunged into them : then, having started to read aloud a detective short story, he "proceeded to guess who committed the crime . . . his logical deductions were proven correct at the conclusion of the tale."[9]

He also loved mystery films, and rarely mised the opportunity of seeing one. He knew that friends were rather amused by this weakness of his and was always ready to provide them with additional material for comments. In the summer of 1929, when, on his way from Pales-tine to the Zionist Congress, he made a stop in Cairo, a young Revi-sionist met him at the Cinema Kléber, which was then showing a police movie picture : "I am so fond of detective stories," Jabotinsky jokingly explained, "that I had traveled all the way from Tel Aviv to admire and enjoy this exciting film."[10]

His fondness for the cinema was not limited to mysteries only. He was an all-around movie fan and, whenever he was able to sneak away from his innumerable duties, the movie house was his favorite hide-out. He used to say that the temptation to indulge in such an escapade was always particularly strong immediately before he had to appear on a public platform: "It would have been so much easier and pleasanter both for me and my prospective audience," he argued. Of all the existing types of films he unashamedly favored the commonest ones: the Western, with lots of horses and shooting; comedies, and the adventure pictures. It was difficult to find a more responsive and enthusiastic moviegoer: he unreservedly enjoyed most shows, and laughed easily and wholeheartedly. "The greatest luxury," he used to say, "would be to see two movies a day, but who can afford such an extravagance, unless on a particularly festive occasion?"

He was much less enthusiastic about the theater. In his youth, he was a great theater fan, and frequently reviewed foreign and Russian plays and operas for his papers. He even wrote two plays (*Krov* and *Ladno,* see Vol. I, chapter Three); but in later years the theater ceased to attract him.

His busy life also prevented him from savoring the art treasures of the European capitals: "I haven't as yet been to the Louvre," he confessed in February, 1933; "maybe because of lack of time, maybe because the desire is lacking."[11] But it was hardly "the lack of desire." Returning one rainy Paris night from a long and dreary party meeting, he remarked bitterly to this writer: "It is simply a shame not to have mustered the necessary minimum of mental leisure and peace of mind to pay at least one single visit to the Louvre. What an unreal, nonsensical existence we, all of us, are leading in this wonderful city, which is bursting with art and beauty." Generalizing, and largely overstating the case, he complained to a friend that overwork was even depriving him of the opportunity "to read and to learn: I would pay any price for a chance to read at least one hundred pages a week —'*es wachst fun mir an am 'haaretz* (I am growing to be an ignoramus)." [12]

Jabotinsky was anything but a stuffed shirt. He did not shrink from "light," frivolous, or even profane subjects and expressions. In striking contrast to his pronounced politeness and cult of etiquette, he practiced, with much gusto, the art of profane language. He did so predominantly in his native Russian, sometimes in Italian, the languages of his exuberant youth, and in the company of friends and colleagues with a Russian background : they were the only ones, he smilingly claimed, who were able to grasp and properly appreciate the marvelous richness and flavor of this mode of expression.

There was neither malice nor vulgarity in his cursing. Fundamentally it was just a way of letting off steam. In one of his early feuilletons in the *Odesskiya Novosti*, Jabotinsky argued that a man who, in moments of stress or delight, is incapable of uttering a whole-hearted, juicy, even blasphemous profanity, is not a human being, but just a jelly fish. He appreciated the art of "bad language" and enjoyed fencing with those whom he considered qualified enough to cross verbal swords with him. He usually triumphed in such tournaments. The only "knight of profanity," whose superiority he willingly acknowledged, was his school friend Alexander [Sasha] Poliakoff. Announcing on one occasion that he was going to spend his vacation in the French Vosges together with Poliakoff, he said : "Just imagine the delight of lying on the grass and abusing each other with the most terrible blasphemous Russian words, just so, without any particular reason; just like a nightingale sings, to relieve one's heart; and Sasha is the only man in Israel who can curse in Russian better than I."

He had little patience with fools in his entourage, particularly with Sholem Aleichem's "winter fools," the ponderous type of man who wears heavy, pretentious robes of solemnity, and has to "undress" before you realize that he is just a plain fool.[13] He was rather more lenient toward Sholem Aleichem's "summer fools," the obvious ones. About one of them he said goodnaturedly : "A wonderful man this X., he never misses the opportunity of uttering some first class stupidity. . . . "

2. *Orator and Publicist*

Jabotinsky lived in an age when Jewish public activity was largely centered on the rostrum; so, accordingly, was his public life.

It is hardly possible to assess, even approximately, the number of his appearances on the speaker's platform during his thirty-seven years of Zionist service, nor the number of cities and towns on four continents where he addressed Jewish audiences, and certainly not the number of people who heard him. It can, however, be safely claimed that no other Jewish leader exceeded his record in any of these categories. The range of his "rostrum communion" with the masses of the Jewish people, the scope of his person-to-person contact with them, is unsurpassed both in intensity and immediacy.

It is also unsurpassed in quality. Friends and foes alike have—wholeheartedly or reluctantly—paid homage to the unequalled excellence of Jabotinsky's oratory. His enemies usually coupled praise for the perfection of form with depreciation of the content of his speeches. Their contention was that his audiences were swayed rather by the brilliancy and forcefulness of his oratorical delivery, than by logic and factual soundness.

In fact, Jabotinsky did not at all belong to the category of torrential orators who move public gatherings more by gusts of emotion than by the play of reason and the flash of inspiration; he defied the prevailing tendency to put the cart of style before the horse of logic and vision. He was a deliberate speaker, with little sympathy for the conventional bag of demagogic tricks used by professional spellbinders. His ambition was not to arouse the emotions of the listeners but to convince them, and he refused to win over, through the emotions, those who failed to comprehend his closely reasoned arguments. He never burst into the hysterical shrieks of some of the world's popular orators; nor did he ever make extravagant gestures, scowl, or curse. He disdained the rabble-rousing "shock treatment" of the masses and had supreme faith in the rightmindedness of the people, provided they could be made to understand the issue at stake. He never doubted their resources of good sense, their power of comprehension when the facts were presented to them simply and honestly.

He not only possessed the gift of crystallizing their longings and aspirations and formulating them in unforgettable terms, but also believed in their intrinsic intelligence, trusted their judgement, respected their reactions. To Jabotinsky the masses of Jewry were not human dust and worse, as they often were to other Jewish leaders. Zionism had awakened in them long dormant forces of dignity and self-reliance, and he liked to retell the tale of the water carrier of Warsaw—a ragged, starved, unidentifiable victim of ghetto existence. All his life the water carrier was nobody; he did not count; he suffered in silence. But when the Zionist movement awakened him to the consciousness of belonging to a living people, with a destiny and national responsibilities of its own, that man stood up and bought a Shekel; he became a full-fledged citizen of the State that was "in the process of becoming." It was Jabotinsky's firm conviction that this elevating feeling of being a partner in a great national undertaking must be lovingly cultivated. The numerous water carriers must be considered and treated as "Their Majesty the People" and be spoken to not as immature adolescents but as adults, with due respect for their innate perceptiveness.

The task of a lecturer, as he saw it, was not to sway the emotions of his listeners, but to stimulate their thinking, to lead them, step by step, toward the ideas he was striving to convey to them. Every one of his speeches was, therefore, a carefully erected logical structure. Stripped of all excess verbiage, they were measured, disciplined, carrying all before them. Faithfully adhering to the Aristotelian maxim that rhetoric is "an offshoot from logic," he also followed the prospect of that great modern logician, Whately, who described it as the art of "argumentative composition." His addresses carefully guided the audience from one premise and conclusion to another premise and conclusion, organically connected with the previous ones. Marshalling a rich array of facts and arguments, he left no escape from the closely knit logic of his reasoning, no gap for mental evasion. Having accepted a seemingly elementary, indisputable premise, the listeners could not help following the speaker all the way to the final conclusion. And it was a deliberately gradual and long way. Jabotinsky needed abundant time and freedom to present the full, artistically forged chain of his argumentation, to display all the supporting factual material. His lectures usually lasted two to two and a half hours, and even more. Many connoisseurs of oratory wondered how it was possible to hold the unwavering attention of mass audiences for so long. Among them were partisans, opponents, and the indifferent; young and old people; sophisticated intellectuals and simple commoners; freethinkers and orthodox: each section of those motley crowds somehow felt that Jabotinsky was speaking to them in particular, and responded each in its own way. In his *Samson* novel we find a description of Samson addressing a Hebrew crowd:

Samson spoke without any strain, neither loudly nor quietly, or perhaps both quietly and loudly at the same time . . . . The voice reminded the farmers of their meadows; the sailors of the tides; the prophets of the raging storm in the hidden crags of the mountains; the shepherds of the cries of the ox; the mothers of the sweet cooing of their babes at the breast; every girl the voice of her beloved for whom she waited; all of them heard him not with their ears but with their innermosts and they were all fascinated and yielded before they even understood him.

Not all features of this poetic description apply to Jabotinsky's audiences. But hardly any other speaker was able to dominate his listeners in such a "total," all-embracing manner, so completely and for such long stretches of time. Arthur Koestler, who has heard many famous political orators, says that none of them "could cast a similar spell over his audience for three solid hours," as Jabotinsky did in the Kursaal, the largest concert hall in Vienna, "without ever resorting to cheap oratory. There was not a cliché in his speech, delivered in a German worthy of the traditions of the Imperial Burg Theater; its power rested in its transparent lucidity and logical beauty." [14] On another occasion, in Haifa, he saw Jabotinsky keeping an open air audience of several thousand spellbound for five hours. [15] A vivid picture of Jabotinsky's impact on his listeners is given by a thoughtful observer of a lecture delivered in Antwerp : [16]

From the start I was captivated by Jabotinsky's manner and deportment. There was an undeniable air of distinction about the man. He still had something of what I would call the old world courtesy, a certain suavity, a certain urbanity, a certain charm and polish—qualities which have since well-nigh vanished from the public platform and the pulpit, and not only in Antwerp. His speech was plain, direct, unornamented, and free from all faults of taste. There was cohesion in it and logical sequence. He spoke with force and vigor, without the slightest trace of artificiality. Though he made a few gestures, his presentation was vivid and lucid. When Jabotinsky spoke, men thought of the things he spoke of, and not of his oratory or his person. Though he seldom spoke less than two hours or two hours and a half, he never rambled or went off on tangents.

An intellectual par excellence, Jabotinsky was no intellectual snob. His lectures were classic patterns of studied simplicity, which put them within the intellectual reach of an average listener. There was no heavy philosophical scaffolding to obstruct the harmoniously proportioned structure of his argumentation, no deliberately complicated scientific terminology in his vocabulary, no foggy abstractions. To those used to the—predominantly German—cryptic, long-winded, and supposedly "deep" style of a Martin Buber or Robert Weltsch, Jabotinsky's lucid clarity often appeared to be "primitive" : "Of course, he is a magnificent speaker," said a leading German Zionist after one of his lectures in Berlin, "but any uneducated man can easily understand what he wants to say; where is the profundity, the high intellectual level of such a presentation? . . . "

What was the secret of Jabotinsky's oratorical power?

Its ingredients are hard to capture. There was, of course, the musical charm of his voice : rich, deep, vibrant, harmonious, with an infinite variety of inflections, a voice which held subtle depths, an arresting virility in its timbre, a subdued strength in its apparent calm. There was the electric desire to convey and convince, coupled with complete concentration on the matter at hand. There was the prodigious and indiscriminate knowledge, put at the service of a first-rate mind, and the almost uncanny ability to pick out key factors in a situation, to collate, interpret, and synthesize competing circumstances, to get at fundamentals. When delivering an address, he spoke in many moods : he could be severely sober and jocular, describe far horizons, hit hard. There was an undefinable, essentially masculine quality of reassuring firmness and confidence. There was the cumulative effect of bold ideas and original reflections, interspersed with an ironic phrase, a properly placed joke, even a quip : he possessed a quiet, wry humor that flashed only briefly in his predominantly earnest and gravely thoughtful public appearances. There was the unobtrusively elegant sequence of arguments, the meticulously chiseled sentences, whose meaning shone clear as crystal, with more than one note of tragedy. And then, there was the carefully measured gesture, the noble deportment, and the well calculated pauses between the sentences, which he controlled and manipulated with graceful ease and impressive effect : all these infused his diction with a distinctive, hard-muscled grace.

But behind all this display of rhetoric, craftsmanship and inspiration were the deep earnestness and dedication of purpose, and hard, diligent work of preparation. Jabotinsky had a message to convey to his heterogeneous audiences, a message in which he himself believed religiously and which he was intent on implanting in the mind and soul of every listener. To achieve this goal, he carefully and conscientiously constructed and polished both the content and the form of every lecture he delivered. Its inner consistency, the graceful shape of its structure, the scintillating elegance of the facile flow of lofty speech, all this was meticulously measured and calculated in advance. It is said of the great American statesman and orator Daniel Webster that he prepared his speeches carefully, but seldom wrote them out in a prepared text: "He could think out a speech sentence by sentence, correct the sentences in his mind without the use of a pencil, and then deliver it exactly as he thought it out." [17] This was Jabotinsky's method.

Nevertheless, his rhetoric did not taste "pre-cooked." The performance was never too labored to defeat its spontaneity. When on the platform—sometimes repeating the same address for the n'th time— he seemed to be handling the subject for the first time, thinking aloud, weighing the pros and cons, framing and uttering ideas conceived on the spot. Never so facile as to appear insignificant, his presentation possessed an amazing freshness and immediacy which endeared him to his listeners.

A widely acclaimed, and avidly listened-to speaker, Jabotinsky, however, disliked the rostrum. He became increasingly weary of always being expected to provide a "stirring address," to impress the audience by a "perfect performance." Surrounded by multitudes, he longed for solitude and silence. In a letter to a friend he wrote: "I am disgusted with journeys, disgusted with delivering lectures, disgusted with everything. It would be wonderful to sit home in Paris, to work for the *Rasswyet,* for the *Betar,* in general for something, only not in a train and not among people." [18] Dr. M. Schwarzman, who had known Jabotinsky ever since their early manhood, and was one of his closest personal friends, rightly observed: [19] "No stranger has ever known as we did how he hated to be in the limelight, how difficult it was for him to overcome some deeply-rooted inner inhibition each time he had to appear before a multitude, and how happy he was in solitude."

He was often accused of being an actor, of seeking after histrionic effects. In fact, there was a good deal of the actor in him, especially on the lecture platform, and he deliberately cultivated theatrical skill as a quality belonging to the political job he was doing: "A public figure is always on a stage," he used to say. But his histrionics were never cheap and he never permitted them to degenerate into *Selbstzweck.* They were servants, never masters of his oratorical art.

In his youth, in Russia, he was reputed and feared as a formidable antagonist in debate. Yet in his mature years he was, as a rule, reluctant to engage in public discussion with political opponents. He contended that he was not good at the quick, spontaneous reaction to the arguments of an opponent; he preferred a well-prepared, undisturbed exposition of his ideas. On the other hand, he used to say: why should he make available to an adversary his own mass audiences, which the latter would never have been able to attract?

Of the two main media of conveying ideas—the spoken and the written word—Jabotinsky unhesitatingly preferred the latter. If he had to choose between being a publicist or an orator, he would have chosen the former. He was often annoyed by the necessity to appear night after night on the platform; and was nervous, even irritable before every lecture. He never felt this way in regard to his journalistic work, which he liked and respected. It was to him an article of faith that "the world's ruling caste are the journalists," and, paraphrasing Disraeli's proud self-introduction, "I am a gentleman of the Press and have no other 'scutcheon,'" he used to say: "I am, by God's grace, a scribe and nothing else."

Jabotinsky rarely tired of writing. He felt at ease with his thoughts, his fountain pen (or typewriter), and a pile of paper. In this company, he was free to arrange his ideas as he saw fit, to rearrange them if necessary, to coin the proper expression. He wrote easily and quickly, was rarely at a loss in selecting topics for his articlies, and as a rule enjoyed his publicistic labor.

He had a highly distinctive publicistic style of his own. Even unsigned (or signed with a pen-name never previously used) articles of his could be almost unmistakably identified by most of his regular readers. They were unrivalled in the lucidity of their content, and the closely knit though seemingly nonchalant presentation, in the subtle turns of mind and flashing insights. With incredible frequency the reader came upon passages which concisely expressed ideas that lesser writers need volumes to treat, formulated with a consistency, depth, and beauty rarely excelled. He was the opposite of those who cannot see the wood for the trees: he saw the wood distinctly and made others see it. He made them see it in his own way, and time proved convincingly that a very good way it was—and still is. His writing was free of spiritual hiatuses or pedestrian prose. It stimulated the readers' minds and forced them to re-evaluate their entrenched concepts. Writing about Max Nordau, Jabotinsky said that "the genuine, the specific art of a 'publicist' is the power to reach, with the word, the deepest depths and the darkest corners of the reading public, to gain the attention of the most indifferent mind, to influence even a sleeply head, even a watery soul. . . ." [20] Both Nordau and Jabotinsky possessed this "specific art" to a degree hardly surpassed by any contemporary writer. André Gide's defiant *profession de foi*, "To disturb is my function," is largely applicable to Jabotinsky. He had been for decades the great disturber of prevalent complacency. But in the same vein he brought confidence to the troubled, courage to the timid. Many were grateful to him for his lesson of integral sincerity, for his stirring and straightforward message that those who know the truth must smite the infidel. He refused to believe that principles can ever be advanced by condoning those who deny those principles. He was one of the great modern Socratic midwives of thought in modern Jewry, urging his generation to make its own judgments and follow them to their conclusions.

In his article on Nordau, Jabotinsky sadly acknowledged that "a publicist, no matter how ingenious, steps off the stage when the period in which he was influential ends. Who now reads [Ludwig] Boerne? Who in France today reads the writings of Paul Louis Courie, who was a brilliant and profound publicist in the beginning of the last century? Or the Russian [Nicolas K.] Mikhailovsky, who, still in my youth, was called the Master of Thoughts by an entire generation?" Answering this agonizing query, Jabotinsky says that Nordau was saved from oblivion and survived in the spiritual memory of his people "because to us he was not a 'publicist,' but a reformer of our national life, one of the children of the prophets." This was also Jabotinsky's own case. Several of his articles were not merely "publicistic," but events of major, often revolutionary, national significance. "The Three Years of Sir Herbert Samuel," "The Political Offensive," "The Prospects of the Gvirocracie," "The Favorable Storm," "On Adventurism," "Cool and Steadfast," "Oif'n Pripetchek," "Our National Sport"—to name but a few—were in their time (and some still are) the source of dynamic and momentous developments in Jewish life; they still glow and still inspire.

There is a widespread notion that, exceptionally gifted as he was, Jabotinsky did not have to invest much work and diligence in his literary achievements: everything came to him easily and effortlessly. This is, of course, not so. He was a great worker, never relying on his talents, never choosing the easy way to creativeness. He craved

525

for exactitude and thoroughness, refusing to be satisfied with second-hand material, always looking for primary sources, studying them laboriously and searchingly. Books he used are heavily annotated. His voluminous note-books abound in references, quotations, dates, and figures. It was the light grace and simplicity of the finished products of his toil that created the impression of sparkling super-ficiality. Talent and quickness of perception were, of course, helpful. A less gifted man would have had to invest incomparably more time and effort, and would have never reached the same level of creative achievement. But it was the happy blend of talent and purposeful labor that molded Jabotinsky's spiritual personality.

His capacity for work was extraordinary, and he did not measure out his hours. Itamar Ben Avi recalls that many a time he found Jabotinsky in Jerusalem still at work in the very early hours after dawn when he himself was on his way to the offices of the *Doar Hayom*.[21] Like all people of very active mind and living under almost continued strain, he needed a great deal of sleep. But when necessary, he could go without, or with very little sleep for long stretches of time. What saved him from complete exhaustion was the precious faculty of being able to fall asleep whenever the opportunity presented itself and thus make up for lost hours; he was also able to store up reserves of sleep in anticipation of a strenuous time.

He possessed remarkable powers of concentration, which enabled him to devote himself to one subject for hours at a stretch, without ever allowing his mind to be distracted by errant thoughts. He was able to work under all circumstances: in the office, at home, on a trip, on vacation. While on the boat to South Africa (1937), he composed a preface to this writer's book on Trans Jordan, and the second part of his autobiography. In 1939, during a period of recuperation after an attack of influenza, he wrote his *Taryag Milim* (613 Hebrew words), an introduction to spoken Hebrew (in Latin characters) for adults. In the first tense months of World War II, he wrote his *Jewish War Front* (*The War and the Jew*).

3. Novelist

Jabotinsky once told his publisher that of his forty years of writing not more than five or six had given him any true satisfaction: the years he had been working on purely literary subjects—the translation into Russian of Bialik's poetry, the Hebrew Atlas, his *Samson* novel; the remaining thirty-five years he "wasted" on journalism.[22]

This is indubitably an overstatement. Jabotinsky hardly considered the years he devoted to journalistic work as "wasted." But he was quite sincere in his claim that it was in the field of belles-lettres that he felt unreservedly at ease and happy. When he received the first copy of his novel, *The Five,* in London, he wrote to his brother-in-law: "I was so happy that I spent the whole day going from one movie house to another." [23] And he was, as he put it in another letter, "very eager to write . . . there are several topics which inspire me—both fiction and serious ones . . . they are completely ready in my head." He specifically listed three novels that were taking shape in his mind: 1. "A Girl from Shunem"—"the maiden whom King David, when he became old, took into his bed . . . she is, my intuition tells me, the Shulamith of the 'Song of Songs' "; 2. "Rebecca's Son"—the story of Jacob; 3. "Mrs. Glemm"—an episode from the life of Edgar Allan Poe.[24] Two years later, he contemplated writing a further three novels: (a) on King David; (b) on contemporary Jewish life in Palestine; (c) a mystery story set among the Aztecs of old.[25] Shortly before his death, he said: "I have in my head a hundred books." [26] For a time, he also toyed with the idea of writing his autobiography in the style of a *biographie romantique.**[27]

As can be seen from the above, Jabotinsky was particularly attracted by Biblical subjects. As a rule, stories from the Bible are considered the most debilitated type of literature: whenever there appears to be a dearth of plot subjects, the quondam author turns his eyes toward some well-tested episode from the Bible; usually the

---

* In August, 1939, he prepared a synopsis entitled *Vivarais: A Best Seller,* whose hero conceived an abortive plan of making an independent Principality of the French Vivarais province. An earlier (unnamed) synopsis develops (in some detail) the rather unconvincing but amusing plot about young King Aladar, who is "bored with being King" and wants to marry a tomboy press reporter, whom he meets disguised as a barber's apprentice, instead of the beautiful princess Maritza who, in turn, is in love with a Republican. Aladar and Maritza cleverly arrange for a Republican victory at the elections: he is proclaimed President, and the two love marriages are made possible.

best that can be said of this kind of historical novel is that they sometimes serve as an incentive to turn to the source.

Jabotinsky felt differently. To him the Bible was an inexhaustible and wonderful source of inspiration. He dreamed of a trilogy: Jacob —Samson—David. Asked what was the trait linking these three vastly different characters, he answered: "In their lives the primary thing is love." He always regretted that only the middle part of the trilogy matured into a novel—*Samson the Nazarite*.

There are indications that the idea of the *Samson* novel started crystallizing in his mind as early as 1919: while in Jerusalem, he made extensive notes on the subject, and showed much interest in the names of the men and women of the period of the Judges.[28] His notebooks for 1923 contain a concise synopsis of a Samson novel. He actually started working on it in 1925, and it was first published in installments in his Russian weekly *Rasswyet* during the year 1926. The following year, the Russian publishing house "Slovo" in Berlin printed it in book form; in 1928, it appeared in German translation in Munich (Verlag Mayer und Yessen) under the title *Richter und Narr* [Judge and Fool].: the Russian edition was signed "V. Jabotinsky (Altalena)," the German—"Altalena." The English edition took time to materialize. The New York publishing house of Alfred Knopf refused the offer: "The novel is excellent, but our foreign department is overloaded." [29] *Samson* was published in 1930 by the Liveright Publishing Corporation under the title *Judge and Fool*. (It was republished in 1945 by Bernard Ackerman, Inc., under the unfortunate title *Prelude to Delilah*.)* Jabotinsky was very unhappy about the English version. He complained that the novel which he had written in the Russian original all in short words, staccato style, had been translated into English by somebody who "seemed to have searched for the longest words he could find, so that the whole spirit of the book was changed." [30] "Terribly dull," he wrote to friends. "I've managed to salvage bits of it for the London edition, but in America I consider it lost. . . . The translation is wooden. . . . I don't expect the book to be a success." [31]

---

* In 1935, Paramount acquired the film rights to *Samson* for the paltry sum of two thousand five hundred dollars, and shelved the manuscript for fourteen years. In 1949, Cecil B. de Mille used bits of it for the monumental film *Samson and Delilah*, in which Jabotinsky's creative concept was irretrievably buried under the heavy and splashy varnish of de Mille's elaborate production. It was painful to watch this well-intended mutilation of a great historical novel.

It was a success with the reviewers of most of the leading American periodicals: the *New York Herald Tribune*, the *New York Times*, Chicago *Sun, Book of the Month Club, Saturday Review of Literature, Boston Evening Transscript*. Their judgment was almost unanimously favorable. The book was compared to *Quo Vadis, The Robe, Ben Hur*, to the historical novels of Dmitry Merezhkovski, Sigrid Undset, Thomas Mann, and Lion Feuchtwanger. Others went so far as to warn against ascribing to Jabotinsky Balzacian or Tolstoian stature.

Not less laudatory was the earlier response to the Russian and German editions. Such exacting Russian writers and critics as M. Ossorgin (in *Posledniya Novosti*), J. Eichenwald (in *Rul*), M. Zeitlin (in *Sovremeniya Zapiski*) acclaimed the novel. Leading German papers (*Vossische Zeitung, Frankfurter Zeitung, Koelnische Volkszeitung, Koelnische Zeitung*) were unsparing in their praise.

Samson is indeed one of the century's most outstanding historical novels. Jabotinsky fashioned the Biblical story into a modern novel in a way that makes it an original work of art, rather than an adaptation of an ancient tale. His Samson is more human and alive, a fuller, more distinct, and dramatic personality than either the giant of the Book of Judges or the hero of Milton's great poem *Samson Agonistes*.

In a brief introductory note to the original Russian version Jabotinsky quoted Victor Hugo's proud statement that in the novel *Ruy Blas* (1838) there was—be it in regard to private or public life, setting, heraldry, etiquette, biography, topography, figures—"not one single detail which did not correspond to historical truth." "For my part," Jabotinsky commented, "I do not claim anything of the kind. This novel is completely free from both the framework of the Biblical tradition and archaeological data or conjectures." [32] This remark—at least in regard to "archaeological data or conjectures"—is incorrect. Jabotinsky did allow himself considerable liberty with the three chapters (14-16) of the Book of Judges dealing with the period of the interregnum and the forty years of Philistine rule; he freely embroidered on the bare Biblical outline and built it into a stirring full-sized novel. But the innumerable details of public and private life of that far-off age, the setting of the drama, the character, speech, and habit of thought of the main and minor people of the story, were based on extensive and diligent study of the available vast archaeological material, creatively embroidered into the easily flowing tale. In fact,

Samson is a truly learned work. Jabotinsky made abundant use of a vast array of scholarly studies (English and German) on the pre-historic culture of the Minoans, reputedly ancestors of the Philistines, and the earlier Hebrew civilization. The theories and "conjectures" of the scholars that he consulted may or may not always have been correct and defendable, as were also some of Jabotinsky's own inter-pretations. However, whether correct or not, they were not fanciful improvisations. The life of Samson's time in grim Dan and gay Philistia was recreated with painstaking care, after thorough research. The reader does not notice the dust of the workshop because its products have been woven into the story in a masterly unobtrusive way, without ever cluttering up the stage set for drama, as is so often the case in the use of such material. Jabotinsky created a fascinating tale not by pure imagination, roving irresponsibly over the Biblical subject, but by the exercise of a highly developed evocative power disciplined by scholarly erudition. The reviewer for the Chicago *Sun* described *Samson* as "the best type of historical novel, for it recreates vividly and truthfully that far-off age. . . . The author takes you into the villages and inns. You can almost smell them. You, for the time being, become a part of that society." History, plot, tragedy have been ingeniously and convincingly filled into the gaps left by the Biblical text, so that the reader cannot help forgetting that he is dealing with dust tier upon tier, millenium upon millenium, and finds himself passionately taking sides.

Jabotinsky's Samson has two distinct and seemingly clashing hypostases. In his Philistine hypostasis, he is a boisterous playboy de luxe, capable of drinking a bit more heavily than his Philistine asso-ciates, engaging somewhat more indecorously in amours, inexhaustible in jokes and pranks, laughing wholeheartedly and homerically. With his own people, he is a wise and stern judge, never touching strong drink, impervious to feminine charm, unbending and unsmiling. He was a "fool" in Timnath and a "judge" in Zorah.

The lusty giant was beloved by the Philistines because he under-stood them. He loved them, too. The sophisticated society of those reputed descendants of the island Minoans, with its refinements, feastings, and easy friendships, was an irresistible delight and lure for him. He unreservedly enjoyed their pleasures. Yet there was never any question of divided loyalties. Deep down, Samson was never faced with the dilemma of whether to join the charming Philistines with whom he had so much of the external in common, or to stay with his uncouth tribe of Dan whose mentality and looseness he detested, which often betrayed him, but of whom he was part and parcel. He had no illusions about Philistia. He saw clearly the utter superficiality of her civilization—a highly finished surface devoid of depth, without genuine hold on the land and its people. Philistia—the wise, the corrupt, the gay, the doomed—was an open book to him. He penetrated the very source of her power. Watching the spectacle of thousands of dancers harmoniously "obeying a single will, he caught a glimpse of the great secret of politically minded peoples." It was this essential quality of discipline that his people lacked, and mischievous Ahish put the finger on this great shortcoming: "There's no sign of agreement between you. There is no order among you and there never will be; every one wants to do things his own way, and you trample on each other's feet." Samson's answer to this contemptuous comment was his "Jackals," a commando-type group of raiders whom he taught iron discipline and coordinated action; and one of his three last messages to his people was—to choose a king who "will give them the signal and of a sudden thousands will lift up their hands."

He also learned another, more obvious secret of the Philistines' power: they had iron swords and his people had none. His second message to the Hebrew tribes was therefore: "Get iron." From this iron they were to forge swords; and they had to learn from their foes how to use them. "A man's strength," he told his Philistine hosts, "lies not in his arms and legs but in his head; a Philistine sword— we have no swords yet—causes so deep a wound not because iron is iron but because it has been forged by the smith and ground by the sharpener." He was confident that his people possessed a "head" and was able to provide smiths and sharpeners.

This was a goal not easy to achieve. The Hebrew tribes had apparently little in common. They quarreled among themselves, were distrustful of one another, stole from each other, and had not even a common faith or common desires. Yet, deep inside them they carried a vague but great vision. The Judean Joram told Samson: "Listen: people say you despise us all—Dan, Judah, and Ephraim—and perhaps you are right. . . . We are little people and paltry; we speak with unworthy lips, but our thought is a burning bush, a ladder from earth to heaven."

Jabotinsky repeatedly complained in his letters that his Samson novel, though very favorably received by reviewers, was generally considered a novel written à thèse, with a distinct political tendency : "Everybody begins with a remark that the author is a publicist, and of course . . . a shoemaker undertakes to bake a pie; and how amazing it is that the pie turns out to be eatable, etc." [33] And in another letter : "I am beginning to grow angry at all the Jewish reviewers who consider my novel tendentious. What twaddle! Living in those times, Samson could not help dreaming of iron and of a king, even if the author were a pacifist." [34]

Jabotinsky's denial of Samson's tendentiousness was indubitably sincere and correct. In any direct way, the novel has no specific and definite message, no deliberate appeal. It was not meant to be a vehicle for propaganda of any sort. Its meaning is not a concocted blend of philosophical maxims or political slogans. Nor is its hero a paragon of all virtues, embodying the author's dearest ideals. Samson is drawn with love but without varnish or whitewash. Jabotinsky had the courage to mold him as a great, struggling human soul, groping, throughout his double life, for some inner light. Samson is awake and alive—flesh and blood and breath; his weaknesses and failures, sins and defeats are related with painful sincerity. Like other characters in the novel, he possesses all those basic human qualities, both good and evil, that have not altered down the ages. Samson is first and foremost a novel; its wisdom is an integral part of an absorbing adventure story, of a stirring historical drama; and this wisdom is not an artificially uniform one—there are in the book several conflicting ideas and concepts, all of them related adequately and truthfully; the author's sympathy for Samson's views and deeds is obvious, but not blindly wholesale and not necessarily inviting total acceptance. He leaves it to the reader to draw his own conclusions. And many did. Colonel Patterson, who is probably second to none in his insight into Jabotinsky's personality, stressed that Jabotinsky "puts on Samson's lips a great deal of his political philosophy" and that "not until he read the Samson novel was he able to draw himself a full picture of Jabotinsky's make-up." In this novel "Jabotinsky gives expression to his political philosophy to a greater extent than in his many articles dealing with current problems. There, in the life of Samson, in the riddles which he used to pose to the Philistines, and in his wise aphorisms, Jabotinsky states his innermost dreams and longings. When I read this book years ago, I finally understood what it was that Jabotinsky searched for in the Jewish Legion, and what it was that made of this short episode a lasting imprint on his life."

Quoting Jabotinsky's message to his people—to get "Iron and a King," Patterson says:

In these two short words you can find everything: Jabotinsky's uncompromising revolt against the unorganized, formless Jewish dispersion with no state organization, no leadership, no discipline, and no national policy. And you can find in it, too, the foundations of his simple yet sound and constructive political program for the Jewish people. He wanted for the Jews what they lacked most: a united nation with a central leadership; a state with an army; "iron" for their defense in a hostile world, and a man who gives the signal and thousands lift up their hands . . . .

The youth proved to be particularly alert to the *Samson* message. By them the novel was received as Jabotinsky's *autobiographie romantique*. It was stressed that Samson was, like his creator, an activist, opposed to compromising with the enemy, preaching and practicing bold *action directe* as against the cautious diplomacy of the elders. Others commented that both Samson and Jabotinsky were not understood and not followed by their people. Like Samson, Jabotinsky looked for support from the younger generation, loved the informal gaiety of the student corps' revelries, their songs, jokes, and jibes; both liked caricatures and parodies. What is, however, more important—many of Jabotinsky's youthful followers have read into the novel specific, actual—and prophetic—political implications. The Philistines' rule was identified with the British rule in Palestine, and the peoples surrounding the Hebrew tribes—with the Arabs. Samson's message to "get iron" and to use it for liberation from the Philistine yoke, became the inspiration for the *Irgun* and the *Lechi* (Stern Group); it was asserted that various schemes, ruses, and exploits of the underground were largely influenced by the Samson tale. The massage to "get a King" as the symbol of an organized nation, became the source of the military—and later civic—hierarchy, which culminated in the creation of the State.

Of the "hundred books" Jabotinsky had "all ready in his head," only two crystallized into full-size novels: the *Samson* novel and *The Five (Piatero)*—the story of his beloved Odessa.

There is no similarity and there can be no comparison between the

533

two. They are completely different in their topic and epoch, and even more so in spiritual climate. Irrespective of whether Jabotinsky intended it or not, *Samson* had a message. *The Five* is a plain novel, largely autobiographical. There was no need of extensive research and documentation for writing it: Jabotinsky simply drew on the precious treasure house of personal memories of the happy "Altalena" years spent in this lively Black Sea harbor city, which he adored, yearned for, and was haunted by all his life: "I feel that I have once again recaptured all the nonsense, all the hopes and the entire 'swing' of that period," he wrote to a friend.[35] Yet, the autobiographical character of the novel does not convert it into a self-centered story. The "I" of the author appears in the background only, discreetly and rather incidentally, mostly in the role of a narrator, of a sympathetic connecting link between the *dramatis personae* of the story. He himself singled out the two central themes of the novel: "It is a pretty broad picture of our Odessa and, what is more important, of that last period of Russification in the middle strata of our venerable tribe.[36]

The story revolves around the Milgroms, a typical Jewish upper-middle-class family: its five children are the central characters of the novel. There is Seriozha—a highly talented and charming good-for-nothing, completely devoid of any ethical considerations, a card-sharper, a "male-kept mistress" of a mother-and-daughter liaison. There is Lika—a beautiful fanatical revolutionary, hating and despising almost the whole of humanity, who somehow slavishly falls in love with a Czarist agent-provocateur, while still spying on him on behalf of the Party. There is Marco—a scatter-brain lad, today an admirer of Nietzsche, tomorrow an ardent stamp collector, the next day a fighter for *kosher* food. There is Torik—the hope of the parents, capable, practical, well organized, always coming first in his class. And finally, there is Jabotinsky's favorite—Maroosia: vivacious and flirtatious, irresistibly enticing to the Odessa youth (though he himself never courted her), seemingly shallow but with a heart of gold, with unfathomed depths of love, courage, and self-sacrifice (many believe that Delilah in *Samson* is but another incarnation of Maroosia). They are all drawn with fine artistry, sometimes with a slight undertone of irony, but always with insight and warmth. They are not judged—praised or condemned: just depicted as Jabotinsky saw them and as he tried to understand them. Single chapters

534

("Decameron-like," "A Confession of Lanjeron," "Gomorrah"), dealing with deeply intimate, often risky subjects, are masterpieces of exquisitely sensitive artistic delicacy.

Tragedy overtakes the apparently happy and carefree Milgrom family : death, mutilation, utter moral debasement. Their lives are destroyed in a senselessly cruel fashion. The only one who escapes unscathed is the "model boy" Torik, who, to secure his career, embraces Christianity.

There is in the novel no attempt at rationalizing or moralizing. But behind the individual dramas of the Milgroms looms unmistakably the great collective tragedy of a generation in the last stages of assimilation. Odessa's Jewish middle class and intelligentsia have irretrievably lost their Jewish roots and have not acquired new ones. Their souls are pathetically empty. They are spiritually and morally "displaced persons." There is no inner stability, no sense and no promise in their lives. Their doom is preordained and inescapable.

The Five was completed and corrected in March, 1935, during a lecture tour in America. But Jabotinsky worked on the novel for several years : single chapters ("Marco," "Lika," and others) were published in the Warsaw *Haint* in 1931. Early in 1936, it appeared in Paris in book form (with excellent illustrations by the painter Mad) in the original Russian version, was well received by reviewers, but was never translated into a European language. In 1947, *The Five* was republished in New York, again in Russian, by the Jabotinsky Foundation. When a Hebrew translation was suggested, Jabotinsky was rather doubtful about its feasibility : stressing the specific *couleur locale* of the story and the abundant use of the peculiar Odessa slang, he wondered whether it would lend itself to translation at all. Besides, he argued, he had doubts about the very justification of a Hebrew version : "The older generation [in Palestine] is little familiar with Hebrew, and the young generation will anyway not understand the meaning and flavor of the story." A posthumous (1947) Hebrew edition convincingly refuted these apprehensions : the translation (by J. H. Yeivin and Chananya Reichman) is being considered a *chef d'oeuvre* of its kind, and is widely read and appreciated by the Israeli public.

4. *Linguist**

Itamar Ben Avi claims that Jabotinsky "knew nineteen languages almost as well as his native Russian and some other twenty sufficiently to enable him to follow the press of most of the countries of Europe, including Turkish, and some of the rest of the world's languages: Arabic, Maltese, Japanese, Malayan, etc. When he decided to go to South Africa on one of his celebrated propaganda tours, I found him studying the Hottentot language in his room, and on his way to India [Jabotinsky never went to India] he basked in the sunshine of the Bengalese of Rabindranath Tagore." [37]

There is an odd mixture of *Dichtung* and *Wahrheit* in this statement. It is, of course, not correct that Jabotinsky knew nineteen languages "almost as well as his native Russian." The number of languages he fully mastered—reading, speaking, and writing—did not exceed seven: Russian, Hebrew, Yiddish, English, Italian, French and German; he was also well versed in the literature of those languages. At different times, and to a different degree, he also had a fairly adequate working knowledge of at least a dozen other languages, some of which are mentioned by Ben Avi (but not Japanese, Arabic, or Bengalese). The term "adequate working knowledge" means that he was easily able to make himself understood, to read a newspaper, and (with a dictionary) a book, to quote from a poet who had caught his fancy, and prepare and deliver a speech or lecture.

It would, however, be misleading to try to define the range and character of Jabotinsky's linguistic personality by the number of tongues he knew. In his thought-provoking essay *Tristan da Runha* he describes the Finnish Pastor Aho as "a passionate lover of languages." [38] This characteristic is largely autobiographical. Jabotinsky was undoubtedly possessed by a powerful linguistic passion. He was keenly interested not merely in one or three or five specific languages, and not even in one or another linguistic group, but in languages as such. They fascinated him as a permanent spiritual challenge. As every true passion, this pursuit of linguistic conquest was fundamentally an unselfish one. The mastery of English, French, German, Yiddish,

---

* This writer is indebted to Serge Galperin and Adolophe Gourevitch for their generous cooperation in the preparation of this chapter. Both are distinguished linguists in their own right and were closely associated with Jabotinsky in his linguistic labor.

Mr. Gourevitch also contributed a special chapter on "Jabotinsky the Hebraist."

etc., had, of course, practical advantages as well: they were the tools of his métier as lecturer and journalist. But the immediate usefulness of a score of other tongues and dialects which attracted his attention, was scant, if any: he studied them for sheer personal delight; it was largely art for art's sake, one of the keystones of his spiritual self. Seemingly casual, but revealing deep insight, references to linguistic matters can be frequently found in the *History of the Jewish Legion, Samson, Tristan da Runha, The Five,* the short story *Diana,* not to speak of his *Ha' Mivta ha' Ivri* and *Taryag Milim.*

Jabotinsky possessed the precious ability to grasp the spirit of most languages very rapidly. But without being a professional philologist with a host of learned studies to his credit, he was also not a mere gifted amateur, picking up by ear, in a Levantine manner, smatterings of foreign languages and relying predominantly on an innate linguistic perception. At the celebration of his fiftieth anniversary in Warsaw, a speaker praised his "wonderful linguistic intuition." Referring to this compliment in his concluding remarks, Jabotinsky respectfully disagreed: "So far as I am concerned, I rely not on intuition but on grammar." [39] He always stressed that every language he knew he had acquired solely through a study of grammar: "without knowing the grammatical rules I have been unable either to absorb, or even to hear precisely the sounds of a foreign language. Even now, were it necessary, I could, by studying the grammar as an introduction, acquire any European language in a very short time;* it would be impossible for me without knowing the grammar." [40] He highly appreciated, and made extensive use of, the so-called "Metoula" (Methode Toussaint-Langenscheidt) grammars, dictionaries, and travel books with their excellent phonetic transcription.[41]

The range of his linguistic curiosity and ability was exceptionally wide, often surprisingly so, covering an amazing variety of languages and dialects: major, minor, and exotic ones.

In the summer of 1915, he spent about two months in the Scandinavian countries: after two weeks, he was able to read Stockholm papers and in about three months—easy stories. Later, he forgot

---

* Asked by Oscar Rabinowitz how long it took him to master a language, Jabotinsky said: "An eternity. In fact, I never 'master' a language. But I think I would be able to make intelligent conversation in any language I do not know now, within six to seven months."

Swedish.[42] Nevertheless, when he was in New York in 1921-22 and had dinner with a famous Scandinavian actress then visiting the United States, he surprised his table companions by quoting at length from ancient Norse Sagas in the original.[43]

In the spring of 1914, he visited the universities of Brussels, Louvain, and Ghent to study their organization and finances. On the return journey he stayed over in Berlin, where he met this writer and exhibited several books and periodicals in the Flemish language. In reply to a somewhat sceptical query, "Do you want me to believe that in the course of your two-week stay in Belgium you have really learned Flemish?" he smilingly said: "Of course I did. I now read Flemish easily, and if you insist I shall quote you some awkward sounding but charming bits of Flemish poetry." And indeed, in his version, even Flemish sounded melodious. This interest in the Flemish tongue was not of a passing nature. Eighteen years later, in the summer of 1932, he delivered a lecture "Flemish and Jewish Nationalism" in Antwerp's huge Salle Rubens. The war of languages in Belgium was then at its height. The Flemings fought hard to defend their language from the onslaught of the French culture. Most of the country's Jewish population opted for French as the language of instruction for their children: it was a universal language while Flemish was considered a regional, uncouth, peasant dialect. By doing so the Jews became unwitting tools in the hands of the French-dominated Belgian Government intent of denationalizing the Flemings; by the same token they became the enemies of the Flemish nationalist "activists." It was therefore both a revelation and a shock when, thanking the Burgomaster of Antwerp, Dr. Camile Huysmans, who was present, and the municipal authorities for their hospitality, Jabotinsky did so in Flemish. Pierre van Paassen, who was present at this lecture, recalls:[44]

With his opening words Jabotinsky stunned his audience into bewilderment. For an instant there was perplexed silence as if men doubted the evidence of their own ears. When they recovered, a storm of applause broke loose. Jabotinsky lifted the Flemish activists, who had come out in large numbers, into the seventh heaven by quoting one line from their poet-priest, Guido Gezelle, a sentence which summed up the whole plight of the Flemish people cut off from their Dutch motherland: "Must Flanders then forever wear the Walloon [French] straightjacket?" There was pandemonium in the Salle Rubens that night. Many wept. Thousands of voices intoned the national hymn, while

Jabotinsky stood stiffly to attention. For the first time a stranger, who was a man of international status and reputation, had taken notice of the Flemish national cause . . . . With one stroke he had that huge audience in his hand.

In March, 1928, he wrote to a friend in Warsaw confessing that, in spite of his promise to deliver a speech in Polish at his next visit, he had not as yet started working on the Polish language. "I shall do so a month before my journey to you; then," he added jokingly, "I will pass my exams at Leszno 19 [Revisionist headquarters in Warsaw], and if they will approve, I will make my appearance in the circus arena." [45] He did not appear in the "circus arena," but spoke on the Polish radio in 1930 and 1933 and delivered a lecture in Polish at the Institute for the Study of Minority Problems in 1936. In private conversation, he more than once delighted his friends by quoting by heart from the Polish classics. At an intimate dinner he and this writer had in 1937 in Warsaw with Count Michael Lubiensky and Professor Orzensky, he recited by heart, in the original, entire passages from Mickiewicz's *Pan Tadeusz* and *Konrad Wallenrod*. A few months later, after a stimulating drawing-room meeting at a private house, when everybody had left, he quoted the opening words of Wispiansky's *Wyzwolenie* [Liberation]—the words of a lonely actor on a deserted stage: *Sam ty na vielkiej pustej scenie* (you are alone on the big empty stage). . . . This piece of Polish literature is extremely highbrow and only those thoroughly conversant with Polish culture are familiar with it.[46]

In May, 1938, envisaging the prospect of a lecture tour in South America, Jabotinsky mentioned in passing that he "would be prepared to lecture in Spanish as well if that should be required." [47] Three months after the outbreak of the war, he reported that he was "now sweating over a Spanish primer (for my prospective trip to Argentina)." [48] And when this trip did not materialize, he complained: "Just imagine; I've already taken eighteen lessons in Spanish conversation and have already repeated to my teacher three times over the speech I intended to make in Buenos Aires." [49] He also wrote an introduction to the Spanish edition of his *History of the Jewish Legion,* published in Buenos Aires by Dr. Jose Mirelman; it was, of course, done with the help of an expert editor, but the original Spanish draft he prepared himself. Ten days before his death he dispatched to Dr. Mirelman a long, handwritten Spanish letter.[50]

One day, in 1934, this writer came to see Jabotinsky in his Paris study and found him surrounded by several volumes in some completely puzzling languages. Answering a mute query, Jabotinsky said: "This is the Bible in several Negro tongues and dialects of Central Africa. I don't know any of them, but I know the Biblical text and it is fascinating to compare the variations in the translation of the familiar sayings and sentences." He was fascinated by the sound of *Elohim* in Malgas (the language of the Madagascar natives): *Andria-manitra.*[51] Though he never "studied Hottentot," as Ben Avi claims, he might have had a vague notion of the language from the Hottentot translation of the Bible, a glance at the Metoula and a few searching questions asked during his three stays in South Africa (1930, 1937, and 1938).

It was also easy for him to branch out from any of "key" languages he knew thoroughly, to some of their linguistic kin: from Italian to Spanish, Ladino, Portuguese; or from Russian to Ukrainian, White Russian, Czech and Slovak, Bulgarian and Serbian. Yet he for some reason pretended that, in spite of its Latin roots, he did not know Rumanian at all: "Of all the languages of Latin origin, Rumanian is the only one I was absolutely incapable of learning."[52] There is, however, sufficient evidence to believe that this statement was slightly exaggerated. Among other European tongues, the Finno-Ugrian languages remained to him *terra incognita;* at best, he was able to quote a few lines from the Hungarian national poet Sandor Petöfi, and had probably picked up a snatch of Hungarian songs at the revelries of the Transylvanian student corps *Baryssia,* of which he was a *honoris causa* senior; his translations from Petöfi's poetry were made from a German version. But he highly appreciated the phonetic qualities, the very resonance of the Hungarian language. In a foreword to a collection of articles by the Hungarian Revisionist leader Denis Silagi (*Nevelés nemzeti forradalomra*—"Education for National Revolution"), published in 1939, he wrote that he greeted its appearance partly because he was "an admirer of beautiful, powerful languages, which never get muddled and do not disregard the sound of the words; they render honor to every letter and, so to speak, engrave each syllable in steel and copper, and make each double consonant resound like the blow of the hammer. The Hungarian language belongs to this category, so, too, did the Hebrew language of old and so will the Hebrew of the future."

During his séjour in Constantinople (1909-10) he must have acquired a smattering of Turkish, which he partly preserved by the use of Metoula. His knowledge of Arabic was practically nil. What little he may have known, he probably picked up in the Legion and post-Legion days (1918-20) in Palestine, plus the inevitable Metoula and, possibly, Arabic Bible in Latin transcription, altogether not much. He knew, however, an impressive assortment of Arabic curses and claimed that, next to Russian, Arabic was the best medium for profane self-expression.

Most of the languages he mastered in his youth he spoke practically without an accent. In later years, he found it more difficult to adapt his pronunciation to that of the native population. He himself believed that this defect was "very slight and only I myself can notice it." [53] But in fact, with the possible exception of Italian, he had a definite and noticeable, if slight, foreign accent, usually very charming, which he did not even attempt to hide, occasionally overdoing it. When it suited his fancy, he deliberately coined linguistic "Jabotinskyisms." He had a musical ear for languages, a keen sense of linguistic word-play, humor, paradox, and punning.

He was very proud of his linguistic achievements and rarely missed the opportunity of exhibiting his marvellous ability to move from language to language with seemingly effortless ease. At a public meeting in Paris, held in January, 1927, in connection with the Second Revisionist World Conference, he greeted every delegate in the language of his respective country, and enjoyed this performance greatly. On February 3, 1938, accompanied by Dr. Oscar K. Rabinowicz, he was received at the Hradcin Castle by the President of Czechoslovakia, Eduard Benes. Asked by Benes' secretary what language he wished to use in his conversation with the President, Jabotinsky answered smilingly: "Any European language the President may choose": in fact, French, English, and Russian were used in the course of the audience. At the opening of the N.Z.O. Convention in Prague, January 31, 1938, Jabotinsky began his address in French (for foreign diplomats who attended the gathering) and then spoke briefly in Czech, referring to the late Czechoslovak President Tomas Masaryk as the teacher of the youth in many lands. Well rehearsed, his pronunciation was perfect.[54]

He loathed the classical languages in school and later asserted that he knew, as Shakespeare put it, "little Latin and less Greek." But this is only partly true. In fact, his Latin was quite adequate, well above that of the average cultured writer who usually forgets what he has learned in high school. In addition to the remnants of school Latin, there was a substantial layer acquired by the study of Law in Rome (1897-1900). A. Gourevitch and S. Galperin remember discussing some fine points of Virgil's and Horace's poetry with him. He possessed a fair stock of medieval Latin quotations and kept them fresh by frequent contact with student corporations where Latin songs (*Gaudeamus* and others) were part of the ceremony. He knew a few liturgical hymns and often quoted strophes from *Dum Dianae vitrea, Confessio Archipoetae, Aestivali sub fervore,* and others.[55] His classical Greek was shaky. But he could, and did decipher it (although he strongly disliked the script), and understood Homer in the original without much difficulty, competently discussing Homeric prosody in relation to the Biblical and modern Hebrew poetry. His knowledge of modern Greek was possibly superior to his knowledge of ancient Greek. Odessa possessed a large and dynamic Greek colony, and in his youth he must have picked up some rudiments of the specific Odessa brand of spoken Greek; his general interest in the revival of "dead" languages probably prompted him to look into sources dealing with popular Greek; and during his visit to Salonica (1926) he showered local Revisionist leaders with questions pertaining to its use.

Languages which had been long "dormant" as acknowledged media of national culture and were struggling for revival and political recognition held a particular attraction for him: Flemish, Ukrainian, Norwegian, Gaelic (Irish); he saw in them parallels to the national and political renaissance of Hebrew.

He had a deep-seated aversion for what his wife called "Tartar" scripts of any kind: Hebrew, Sanscrit, Arabic. While he could easily and quickly grasp a line or a sentence written in Latin or Cyrillic, he experienced considerable difficulty in deciphering a text which was, as he used to complain, *napisano po Tatarsky* (written in Tartar). He insisted that this obstacle was easily removable and devoted considerable study to Maltese, a Semitic language of predominantly Arabic origin but with a strong admixture of Berber and Latin-Italian; spoken by native Catholic Maltese, it was written in Latin characters, and Jabotinsky considered it a useful example for Latinizing the Hebrew script. For the same reason, he was also interested in Kemalist Turkish.[56]

He was keenly interested in the so-called universal languages. In his library could be found the classic dictionary of Interlingua (*Vocabulario Commune*, 1915), by its originator, the Italian mathematician and linguist G. Peano, and he spoke enthusiastically of L. Couturat's and L. Leau's *Histoire de la Langue Universelle* (1903). From his early youth he was interested in Esperanto, not so much as a means of human intercourse, but as a linguistic curiosity; he felt, however, that it possessed literary power, beauty, precision and flexibility and liked to quote from the Esperanto hymn *La Stelo Verde* (The Green Star) and from the translation of the *Lorelei* into Esperanto.[57]

He claimed—half-humorously, half-seriously—that a born linguist feels a kind of "universal language," or at least a certain broad, geographically and climatically determined "substratum," of which the formal, historically determined tongues are but practical adaptations. This was not a definite linguistic theory of an alleged "common origin" or "common nature" of languages—in fact he denied the existence of such formal community, but an attitude, an instinctive perception. More definite seems to have been his belief in the existence of a certain "Mediterranean linguistic substratum" which in his view was at the bottom of all languages spoken "wherever garlic is used as a staple." [58]

He did not share the high-brow contempt for dialects and jargons. To his linguistic taste, "jargons were always more intimate and alive than the official idiom of books and lawyers; they suck life's atmosphere from the very source." In Italy, he learned to admire and to enjoy "all the twelve dialects of the Italian tongue"—from the urban Tuscan to the blunt Romanesco.[59] He loved the Odessan slang, claimed that it was his true and only native mother-tongue, praised its inherent dignity and sameness, and denied that it was "Russian"; the little poem *Lavrik* (in *The Five*), written in Odessite, he considered his masterpiece. In Paris, he liked to listen to the various nuances of French in different parts of the city, trying to determine their regional sources.

In several languages which he did not know, he was able to cite passages from poetry, passages which he remembered by heart, understood, and knew how to pronounce. He was always ready with an apt quotation, a sport that he enjoyed for its own sake. He used to cite from the Finnish national epic *Kalevala,* from E. Tegner's *Fritiofs Saga,* from Taras Shevchenko as well as from Kotliarevsky's

Ukrainian parody on Virgil's *Aeneid*. With particular pleasure he quoted from Frédéric Mistral's poem *Mireio,* which he read (and fragments of which he translated) in the original. He also liked and quoted troubadour poems by Jaufré Rudel, Bernard de Ventadour, and others.

There were, however, essential limitations to Jabotinsky's feeling for languages, which was fundamentally spiritual rather than intellectual. His grasp of languages ended where he was unable to reshape the established formal pattern of the tongue to his own instinct. This largely explains why he never fully and creatively mastered French, which is the most rigid literary language on earth, a spoken "classic," with no leeway for adaptation. Jabotinsky spoke it well enough, with frequent Anglicisms in his vocabulary, and a pronunciation which was extremely pleasing, even charming, but sounded quite un-French ("as if an aristocratic Prussian of the eighteenth century had come to life again—whose cultural mother tongue was French *but . . .*" wittily comments A. Gourevitch). He often apologized for his *français nègre,* and his speeches in French were never quite as inspiring as in other languages. He never attempted to write poetry in French, though he translated some into Russian and Hebrew. Explaining this phenomenon, he said: "I don't feel French prosody at all. There should be twelve syllables in an Alexandrin [the main measure in French poetry], with a 'césure' or stop in the middle; unless I count them on my fingers, I don't notice them." And indeed, he had no ear for this most striking French verse: he was attuned to *tonic* poetry only.[60]

Jabotinsky mastered fully and, in the main, brilliantly, five European languages. But his own language was none of them: it was the sixth—Russian. This he freely, though somewhat reluctantly, acknowledged. When Joseph Leftwich decided to include some of his writings in the anthology *Yisroel,* he asked "to be included in the Russian group, because that was where he belonged." [61] In an autobiographical account of his linguistic abilities, he stated:[62] "If I think in words, then the words are Russian, except on special occasions. . . . When I find myself in a new linguistic environment, I begin, after some time, to forget the other languages, except Russian. . . . I prevail only in the Russian language. Only through it can I express everything up to the last thought; but this does not mean that it is easier for me to speak or lecture in Russian. Perhaps on the contrary, just because of the extensive Russian vocabulary at my command I have difficulty in choosing the correct words. . . . My language of conversation is Russian."

His attitude to Yiddish was pragmatic and practical, not dogmatic or sentimental. "I do not love Yiddish," he wrote. "How can I love a language I first spoke at the age of thirty-five? But I do more than that: I respect it. And I showed my respect by learning it, and speaking it, and writing it." [63] He hardly ever felt "at home" with Yiddish, but he learned it because it was part of his job, a powerful instrument to spread his cause. And he acquired not just a smattering of this tongue but complete mastery. Yet it was in more than one respect a very personal, specifically Jabotinskian Yiddish. It had a structure and flavor of its own, but was at the same time somehow different. There was in it a clearly discernible charming, outlandish quality. Stalwart Yiddishists used to say that while they enjoyed Jabotinsky's writings and speeches in that tongue, they always felt their non-Yiddish essence.

TRUTH-SEEKER AND ZIONIST

1. *The Supreme Meaning of Truth*

JABOTINSKY was incapable of living without a central, dominating spiritual obsession—many irreverently called it a hobby-horse— on which he would concentrate all his energy and in the service of which he knew no moderation. By nature and temperament he was *a homo unius rei* and a *conquistador* in the world of political ideas, with all the unsatiable spiritual curiosity, the boldness, and the tenacity that are characteristic of that type of human being.

To him a great and true ideal was an integral whole, which could not be split without killing its very essence : half-truths are not partly true—they are all wrong, worse than outright falsehood; possessing as they do some external trimmings of veracity, they are likely to be accepted as truths and deceive the nation; they must therefore be unmasked and combatted even more ardently than obvious falsehoods.

But what is the supreme meaning of TRUTH as Jabotinsky saw it? In an attempt to give an answer to this question, Dr. J. H. Hertz, the Chief Rabbi of Great Britain and Ireland, said in a penetrating memorial address : [1]

The primary definition of Truth is the ability to see things as they are. This is a rare gift . . . . It took mankind millenia to learn to read the difficult language of facts . . . . [Yet] seeing things as they are is only half of the Truth. For, in addition, we must at the same time be able to see things as they ought to be, as they very easily might be, if human weakness, ignorance, and hatred did not confuse and darken the souls of men. Jabotinsky was one of those select mortals who was endowed with that fine double gift. He could see things as they are, and as they ought to be . . . as they might be, if Jews and non-Jews alike brought vision and truth, courage and humanity to the solution of this human problem.

Jabotinsky had both the courage to see things as they are and the vision to see them as they ought to and might be. Armed with this double sight, he exposed and combatted every attempt to seek solace in half-truths. But he was more than merely an iconoclast. He lived by inner light and believed that virtue consisted in making full truth prevail against any resistance. He possesed the disturbing quality of having faith in every word of what he himself preached, and in every letter of every word. He was intent on spelling out each idea fully and correctly, unabridged and unadulterated.

He paid dearly for this yearning for spiritual purity. No coin in circulation has ever been minted of pure gold, without an admixture of base metal. Moreover, the so-called Gresham law * holds good not only in the monetary field but also in the world of political ideas. Jabotinsky's full-truth approach was therefore bound to possess but a limited appeal for otherwise-disposed public opinion with its ideal of blandness and compromise and its suspiciousness of directness and spiritual courage. In a thoughtful foreword to President John F. Kennedy's challenging *Profiles in Courage,* Professor Allen Nevins aptly stresses that while "moral courage is great and admirable in itself," it is "a diamond with many facets, and it owes much to its setting. . . . It almost never appears except as part of that greater entity called character. A man without character may give fitful exhibitions of courage . . . but no man without character is consistently courageous, just as no man of real character is lacking in consistent courage. In short, moral courage is allied with the other traits which make up character: honesty, deep seriousness, a firm sense of principle, candor, resolution." [1a]

Jabotinsky's "consistent courage" can be fully viewed and rightly understood only as organic part of "that greater entity called character" with all its basic ingredients.

He was also incapable of keeping a truth "in cold storage" when he saw it. He just *had* to proclaim it, and start battling for its implementation. Zalman Schneur once said figuratively that when a new idea was taking shape in Jabotinsky's mind, red spots appeared on his face, like on the face of a pregnant woman. It never occurred to him to temporize, to let things take care of themselves, to wait until

---

* A theorem formulated four centuries ago by the English financier Sir Thomas Gresham, according to which coins having the least intrinsic value supplant in circulation coins having a higher intrinsic value.

an idea would ripen in the minds of his contemporaries and thus become easily palatable and digestible. He did not believe in time-tables for truth. At all times he did what he thought right and not what was expedient, comfortable, profitable or popular.

To him, the important thing was to be on the right side of a current issue, not on the popular side. He refused to be bound by every impulse of the public, to follow the tides of public sentiment: what counted, was the dictate of his deliberation and conscience.

In Ferdinand Lassalle's drama *Franz von Sickingen* (which Jabotinsky valued highly for its bold and challenging ideas and which he often quoted in private conversation) the great medieval humanist Ulrich von Hutten says: "I would rather wander from village to village like a hunted animal than keep silent and abandon my vocation for truth-telling":

> I cannot hold my peace; I cannot buy
> At price of silence, safety for myself;
> The spirit drives me on to testify:
> I cannot stanch the mighty stream within.

The burdensome vocation for truth-telling was part of Jabotinsky's fundamental spiritual setup.

Contrary to his reputation, he was not impetuous by nature. He refused to act on the impulse of the moment, to "shoot from the hip." A recurrent sentence in his letters is: "I will think it over and decide what to do." Occasional outbursts of temper were not at all typical of him, and were caused by the strain and pressure under which he lived. As a rule, every move of his was deliberate and based on careful planning.

2. *Jabotinsky's Zionism*

In modern terminology, one would call Jabotinsky a "natural" Zionist.

His road to Zionism was a singularly straight and simple one, even in comparison with that of Herzl. Before the Jewish State idea ripened in his mind, Herzl went through several delusions. In 1882, he believed in complete assimilation of Jewry; in 1893, he advocated mass baptism of Jewish children and/or socialism as solution for the Jewish problem. "It is fascinating to watch Herzl blundering around the logical issue of his views without actually coming through," says his biographer.

There were no similar "blunderings" in Jabotinsky's course. He made his first Zionist speech at the age of seventeen; after a five-year lapse, which was completely void of any specific Jewish content, he declared himself a Zionist and remained so for thirty-seven years, until his death. It was a very long "term of office," considering that only about seven years were given to Herzl the Zionist. It was also a full-time job. During these thirty-seven years, service to the Zionist cause was Jabotinsky's only occupation. He never permitted any other vocation to distract him from the main course. Journalism, lecturing, poetry, politics—everything was part and parcel of Zionism. Dr. Oskar K. Rabinowicz remembers him saying: "When I look at a lamp and talk of it, I do so 'Zionistically'; when I look at a house, a street, a ship, or talk of them, I do so 'Zionistically.' " [2] Zionism permeated his whole personality and existence.

The late Dr. M. Solieli (Soloveitchik), who had been close to Jabotinsky in the early years of their Zionist career, once said to this writer: "Jabotinsky was the first citizen of the Jewish State, long before its emergence. He felt and acted like one, with the calm assurance of a man who had already obtained his 'citizenship papers'; what was still missing was only the external attributes of statehood, but these, he was confident, our generation will fight out." It is therefore hardly surprising that of all the Zionist leaders Jabotinsky was the only one, many years before May, 1948, to call for the drafting of State legislation, for a ten-year plan of repatriation and settlement, for a Jewish Army project, and even for a Constitution. His faith was so firm that he wished the structure of the State to be ready for all eventualities; above all he felt that the structure should be determined not by the prospective State itself, but by the nation as a whole —that is by the Diaspora in concert with the Palestine *Yishuv*. And as long ago as 1929, Jabotinsky commissioned the late Professor Alexander M. Kulischer, a noted international lawyer and leading Revisionist, to draft a series of legislative and constitutional blueprints. A great deal of this material has been lost in the course of the war, although it is quite possible that some of it still remains in individual hands. A. Abrahams, who was personally associated with this work, recalls "the painstaking care which Jabotinsky lavished on it. He applied himself to it not as an orator, but as a statesman. . . . Everything to the smallest detail was foreseen by him as though the State was already in being. He wished to avoid unpreparedness, dangerous improvisation or the temptation of a new Government to consider immediate issues above the larger considerations." [3]

The same concern for the needs of the Jewish State motivated Jabotinsky's active interest in the first Jewish Marine School, which was established in 1934 by the *Betar* at Civitaveccija as an autonomous section of the Government-supervised Italian seaman's school: its subsidiary language was Hebrew, it enjoyed self-Government in its own barracks, had kosher food and Sabbath services. At that time Italy was still free from racialism. The school started with some thirty pupils from fifteen countries, led by Jeremiah Halpern; during the second and third year, above one hundred Jewish boys underwent training on the four-master Sara I. To Jabotinsky, the Civitaveccija school was the precursor of the Jewish navy. As such, it commanded his closest attention. In order to study its needs and problems, he visited it in November, 1935; his notebooks (November 9 to 11) contain twenty-seven pages of evidence collected from Captain Nicolas Fusco, the school's Gentile director, and from eighteen pupils. He devoted to the meaning and vicissitudes of the school a charming feuilleton "The 'Periple' of Sarah the First." [4] And when the Italian Government went Nazi and the school had to be closed, he continued pressing for its reestablishment in another country: "The State will need sailors," he insisted.

Reuben Hecht (Haifa) recalls that at the Founding Congress of the New Zionist Organization in Vienna (1935), he hesitatingly showed to Jabotinsky his draft sketches of the insignia for the future Jewish State, for its Army and Air Force, and selfconsciously described them as *Kindereien* (childish nonsense). Jabotinsky's answer was: "Oh no, these are no *Kindereien*—we will need all of them very soon." Dr. Hecht could not help comparing this reply with the reaction of Dr. Weizman, to whom he had spoken, at the Nineteenth Zionist Congress in Luzern, about the necessity of training Jewish youths as pilots for the future Jewish Air Force: "Jewish pilots? My dear young man, maybe my grandchildren—or your children—will live long enough to see them flying."

All his life long, he was an unhyphenated Zionist: not a Socialist Zionist or a religious Zionist, but a Zionist *tout court*. Ideological mixed marriages were alien and hostile to his mind. To him, two ideals, which simultaneously dominate one's mind and soul, were "an absurdity like two Gods, like two altars in one temple"; a soul which can absorb two ideals and remain satisfied is "one of small worth." For "a healthy soul can be only monistic . . . the word 'ideal' has in its essence no plurals. . . . If Zionism is an ideal, there remains no room for any other independent objective of equal right; and there can exist no partnership, no cartel and no combination." [5] He rejected Socialist or religious Zionism not because he was *in merito* opposed to Socialism or religion, but because they had no place within the temple of Zionism.

He did not believe in the shallow wisdom of the adage: "half-a-loaf is better than no loaf at all." In his concept, a man or a people must never demand a larger loaf than is vitally necessary for subsistence and normal development. The needs of a people must be honestly and realistically assessed and formulated. But after that, there can be no bargaining. It is a "loaf" that the people is in need of, and no fraction of it would do. Policies of a nation dare not follow the pattern of oriental market places where Levantine traders ask prices for their merchandise calculated to be halved or quartered by a skilled bargainer. The Zionist goal is *prix fix*.

It was Jabotinsky's contention that there was no extremism or maximalism in his concept of Zionism. He often quoted the case of Dickens' *Oliver Twist*: together with other boys in the workhouse, Oliver was for months "suffering the tortures of slow starvation," and finally, "desperate with hunger and reckless with misery," he, after a meager supper, summoned up the courage to say to Mr. Bumble, the master: "Please, I want some more." Everybody was horrified by this "temerity and impertinence." But, Jabotinsky argued, little Oliver Twist actually was not asking for more. He demanded just the barest minimum of food that his emaciated body desperately needed to survive and grow. The workhouse had been giving him "half-a-loaf" of this minimum, and all he was asking for was "a loaf." There was no impertinence and no extremism in the plea. He just could not compromise on less.

There was also no extremism in Jabotinsky's insistence on not concealing behind various vague and hair-splitting formulas the true scope of the primary Zionist demand for a Jewish majority in a Jewish State in the whole of Palestine. He opposed and combatted these verbal disguises on two counts: they did not deceive the non-Jewish world and they were demoralizing the Jews. During the long night when small-scale Zionism and faint-hearted appeasement dominated the Zionist scene, he kept alive and nurtured the spirit of Greater Zionism.

There was in Jabotinsky's complex personality an almost surprising directness—one is tempted to say primitiveness—of correlation between thought and action. He took ideas and ideals in earnest and brought to his political battles an uncommon singleness of purpose. It was self-evident to him that having conceived and proclaimed an idea, he had to live it; and if the idea called for action, it seemed but natural that he had to be the first one to "invest" himself in this effort. Then—and only then—he felt entitled to preach it. If a job had to be done, he did it without delay and in full. When, at the age of twenty-three, he felt that self-defense against pogroms was the right thing for Jewish youth, he came to the clandestine quarters of the self-defense organization, rolled up his sleeves and started hectograph-ing their first illegal leaflet and collecting money for arms. The crusade for Hebrew he initiated by learning Hebrew himself; to his son he spoke Hebrew only. He was the only one among the small group of promoters of the Legion idea who enlisted in the British Army as a private and particpated in the actual fighting in Palestine. When, shortly before World War II, he came to the conclusion that the armed struggle of the *Irgun Zvai Leumi* against the British rule in Palestine was the most potent factor in the realization of Zionism, he suggested to the *Irgun* High Command that he would land illegally on the shore of Palestine to head an armed uprising. He said what he thought, and acted as he spoke. To conceive an idea, to announce it, and to be in the forefront of its implementation, was to him Holy Trinity, an organically integrated entity: to split it, was blasphemy. He lived in accordance with the autobiographical formula of Ulysses S. Grant: "A verb is anything that signifies to be; to do; to suffer; I signify all three."

Dr. Weizmann stressed in his *Trial and Error* (p. 63) that "Jabotin-sky, the passionate Zionist, was utterly un-Jewish in manner, approach, and deportment." He reproached Herzl for the same reason.

In both cases he was indubitably right. As so many of the great master builders in Jewry in the tradition stretching from Moses to

552

Herzl, Jabotinsky was not part of the main stream of Jewish life; like them, he came to his people as a stranger when he reached manhood. He was cast in their great mold. His underlying contribution to the national redemption of Jewry was not extracted from the mines of the Jewish mode of life : its roots must be sought in the outside world. His Zionism was not nourished by the messianic emotional and mystical longing of the ghetto Jew. Herzl, Nordau, and Jabotinsky were all products of assimilation, so far removed from actual Jewish life, and yet, just because of it, so much more able than their predecessors to forge into a nation their dispersed and desperate people. Deeply steeped in the Western way of life, they had to discover their people in order to possess it, and find themselves. Like Herzl and Nordau, Jabotinsky had little in common with that brand of Jewishness which Arthur Koestler describes as "tradition-bound, jargon-bred" and which is largely typical of Weizmann's mentality. Weizmann was born in Motele, a hamlet deep in the Jewish Pale of Settlement, and reared in the spiritual climate of a Jewish small-town society. Jabotinsky grew up in Odessa, a harbour city of international importance, where, as he put it, "every corner of local life used somehow to get entangled with affairs and questions of world-wide range." Similarly, Herzl and Nordau grew up in cosmopolitan Budapest, Vienna, and Paris. Their upbringing was secular, their outlook worldly, their sense of values European. Their Zionism was built on modern ideas of national normalcy, on a virile, instinctive self-assertion in the face of a fundamentally hostile and often provocative non-Jewish world. It was but natural that their entire mentality and deportment should have appeared "utterly non-Jewish" to Dr. Weizmann, whose background was completely different; this background, with all its implications, remained for him the embodiment of Jewishness. Herzl, Nordau, and Jabotinsky came from a different world, and they always remained alien and inacceptable to Weizmann and to many other Zionist leaders whose background was similar to his.

Claiming (wrongly) that Jabotinsky "disliked Achad Haam who did not fit in his scheme of things," Weizmann says that "Nordau was much nearer to the spirit of Jabotinsky." In this last comment he is correct. There is a direct line leading from Herzl through Nordau to Jabotinsky. They all belong to that great dynasty of political Zionists, which ended with Jabotinsky. They form an organic and exclusive Trinity. No other Zionist leader of stature can be said to belong to it as of right. The formula "Herzl-Nordau-Jabotinsky" sounds natural; but it would sound false to say: "Herzl-Nordau-Weizmann," or for that matter "Herzl-Nordau-Sokolov-Ussishkin-Ben Gurion." Two widely divergent lines of succession to Herzl's leadership are easily discernible: the spiritually straight and legitimate one—through Nordau and Jabotinsky; and a collateral, essentially deviating one, as represented by Weizmann and the others. There is a deep ideological and psychological cleavage between them. It is therefore not at all incidental that large sections of Weizmann's *Trial and Error* are devoted to a strenuous attempt to depose Herzl and Nordau —and through them Jabotinsky—from the top place they occupy in Zionist history.

Jabotinsky used to say of himself that he had a *"goyishe Kop."* Referring to this expression, his old comrade-in-arms, Colonel Patterson, who knew and loved him as very few did, interpreted it as meaning that Jabotinsky's mentality was fundamentally that of a Gentile, "void of the peculiar inhibitions of a Jewish mind influenced and twisted by the abnormalities of centuries of life in dispersion," and added with amazing insight: "That was probably the main reason why his political philosophy was so healthy and simple, and why with all his tremendous popularity he never became the recognized leader of the Jewish people." [5a] A similar comment this writer heard from another Gentile admirer of Jabotinsky, Count Michael Lubiensky: "You know that I hold Jabotinsky in highest regard and that my opinion of Weizmann is trimmed accordingly. But as I see it, Dr. Weizmann has all the chances to retain the allegiance of the majority of the Jewish people. Because his entire mentality is identical with that of an average ghetto Jew, while the mentality of Jabotinsky is spiritually nearer to me, a Gentile. I understand him better; he evokes in me a kindred response. For a ghetto Jew he is, on the contrary, too simple, too direct. He will be listened to, applauded, but he will be followed only by those who have overcome the ghetto complex." And, in fact, the prevailing attitude toward Jabotinsky was the reverse of the traditional Jewish pledge "We shall do and listen" *(Naase we'nishma)*; in the majority of cases, it was "We shall not do but we shall listen."

A life so vigorous, a purpose so forthright and so uncompromisingly pursued, inevitably courted criticism and animosity. When Jabotinsky's ideas were first advanced, they were resisted with a ferocity almost bordering on panic. Now, several decades later and twenty years after his death, it is easy enough to express shocked surprise at the violence of the early antagonisms. But to do so is in effect tantamount to denying, or badly underestimating, the utter novelty and the revolutionary impact of those ideas; they constituted nothing less than a new mode of thought in Jewry and Zionism. It was therefore perhaps almost inevitable that Jabotinsky had met with a degree and ferocity of enmity and abuse hardly ever heaped upon any public figure. Jefferson wrote in 1800 to Uriah McGregory: "The floods of calumny have been opened upon me." Jabotinsky had every reason to repeat this complaint. His opponents fell upon him with a zest that was bound to cut his sensitive nature to the quick. "Dictator," "militarist," "Fascist," "comedian," "murderer," "irresponsible adventurer," "Duce," "Vladimir-Hitler,' are but a small selection of the epithets that have been thrown at him in word and print.

It may be assumed that a major part of the bitter opposition to Jabotinsky was due to the often subconscious resentment of his opponents at the fact that he actually believed that his ideas were right and sought to make them prevail; that he did not gracefully settle his differences with those who in his opinion were distorting the truth. He had a dogged courage on matters of principle and scorned the expediencies of day-to-day politics. Always keeping his eyes on the one paramount matter, time and again he stated openly what he believed in, even when what he had to say cost him valuable support. He did not possess the essential quality of a successful trader who offers only merchandise likely to please the customer. This quality also determines the success of a political leader: to gain power he has to go with the stream, to play on popular emotions, and not to tell the general public all that he knows and believes in, because much of it may be displeasing and unpalatable.

Jabotinsky was not made in this mold of immediate expediency. He followed Woodrow Wilson's precept: "I would rather fail in a cause which will ultimately triumph than triumph in a cause which will ultimately fail." For that he was accused of obstinacy, of fixedly pursuing undiluted and unpopular aims. Replying to one of these reproaches, he said in a private conversation: "It seems that our culture has changed a lot since the days when we were taught in school that for Columbus to urge his crew 'Sail on! Sail on!' while the vast majority clamored to turn back, was brave and fine, not stubborn and undemocratic."

It was not in his nature to shirk issues, and nimbly manoeuver in compromise. He was not out to appease opponents, to seek or expect public gratitude, but to serve a cause. He therefore accepted accusation and abuse without murmur, and with unfailing dignity. His was a life beset by troubles and disappointments that would have embittered many a man. But he took them in his stride, like a good sport. "Here's to Trouble," he wrote to a friend "Trouble is the only vital principle in life and history." [6] This philosophy and faith in what he was fighting for, made him rise above disappointments in a manner so composed and so genuine that it was almost painful to watch. There was about him a fidelity to his belief in what was best for his people, that transcended self.

He was not one to sit sulking in his tent, or to regret the strenuous record of his life. In a feuilleton written in 1933, he mentioned that at a party in his home somebody asked all those present : would they be prepared to relive their lives from the very beginning, exactly the same, without any alterations? Surprisingly many of the guests said "no"; some tried to "bargain" for the elimination of one or other unpleasant episode. "I am proud," Jabotinsky stressed, "that I was one of the few who immediately, without bargaining, without hesitation, answered yes." [7]

There was no boastful self-righteousness, no smug complacency in this firm "yes." Jabotinsky possessed the essential quality that sets apart a man of stature : dissatisfaction with himself, the Faustian quest which cannot be easily fulfilled in the here and now. Throughout his life he displayed the stern self-criticism that one finds in those who have set themselves lofty goals and are fully aware of both their capabilities and their limitations. No matter how imposing their achievements appear, no matter how dazzling their popularity, men of this stature are ever cognizant of the inadequacy of the attained when measured against the goal. Jabotinsky's unreserved "yes" was therefore uttered in the calm confidence that the life he was ready to live again was one of freely self-imposed service to a cause which was both great and beautiful, and with which he was deeply in love : there was nothing to regret or be ashamed of. Whatever he did for the cause was not sacrifice, but a delightful and exciting labor of love. He was happy in this labor. He lived a full and crowded life. In fact, he fitted several lives and careers into the span of his fifty-nine years.

Jabotinsky was often pictured as dogmatic and zealous, a willful and unbending visionary; a man who was both reluctant and unable to waver even one iota from a standpoint once adopted.

This is a onesided and therefore grossly distorted picture of the man. He was, it is true, as hard as a nail and as sharp as a dagger in matters of fundamental significance; here he would not yield an inch. Abraham Lincoln's wife once said about this great President: "None of us—no man nor woman—could rule him after he had made up his mind." This applies to Jabotinsky's major decisions. His numerous ideological and political battles he conducted with militant determination, without apologizing for what he believed right and fair, always willing to face critical audiences and to present to them a patient, well substantiated exposition of the issues and his own stand. He never dodged troublesome questions or tried to take refuge in equivocation.

But dogmatism and rigid orthodoxy were, from his early manhood, alien to his nature. In matters of political strategy he was openminded, willing to see the other's point of view, listening to the other's arguments, and accepting or rejecting them on their merits and not because of ready-made preconceptions. There was in him an engaging reasonableness that admitted the right to differ and accepted compromises of issues, not of principles. He was reluctant to close the door to compromise on method, and never claimed that his ideas could not be improved by amendment and experience.

He had little respect for "consistency at any price." He called such consistency a hobgoblin and liked to quote Gandhi, who once wrote: "My aim is not to be consistent with my previous statement on a given question, but to be consistent with the truth as it may present itself to me at a given moment. The result is that I have grown from truth to truth." To a friend who disapprovingly mentioned that in several important matters Gandhi had been "changing his views like gloves," Jabotinsky replied: "I see nothing wrong in doing so. In the winter one wears warm gloves, in the spring light ones, and in the summer—none. Only a pompous fool sticks to unseasonable gloves because of ill-conceived 'consistency.'" He had none of the dictator's yearning for infallibility and did not worry about "losing face" by admitting an error. When told that such an attitude might weaken his moral authority among his followers, he again retorted with a quotation from Gandhi: "Moral authority is never retained by attempting to hold on to it. It comes without seeking and is retained without effort."

Alive to the realities of political struggle, to its everchanging tides and trends, he was more than once prepared to admit himself wrong and adapt his views to new situations. To quote a few instances: he readily admitted that he was wrong and Trumpeldor was right in the attitude toward the Zion Mule Corps; he twice reversed his opinion of Sir Herbert Samuel; he left the Zionist Organization in 1915, during the struggle for the Legion, rejoined it in 1920, and became a member of the Zionist Executive; he left both the Executive and the Organization in 1923; however, from 1925 to 1933 he served as a delegate to five Zionist Congresses; he finally broke with the Organization in 1935. In 1937, he was dead set against the suggestion of the British Royal Commission for Palestine to transfer and exchange Arab and Jewish minorities in the envisaged Jewish and Arab states of Palestine; and in 1940 he advocated this scheme. He admitted his failure to grasp and endorse Nordau's vision of 1920, and made the Nordau Plan a mainstay of his entire scheme in 1936-39.

Far from being a "professional dissenter and secessionist," he strove, on the contrary, to find common ground and pave the way to cooperation with other groups in Jewry and Zionism. His record in this field is both distinguished and impressive. In 1920-21, he forcefully advocated a "Great Coalition" to head the Zionist movement. In 1933-35, he tried hard to come to terms with Grossman's splinter Jewish State Party. In 1934, he successfully negotiated with Ben Gurion the "labor agreement" which was later rejected by a *Histadrut* plebiscite. In 1937, he negotiated with the *Agudat Israel* about common action. He passed away in 1940, in the middle of a sustained effort to establish a united front of world Jewry.

In the commonly accepted sense of the term, Jabotinsky was hardly ambitious, or very slightly so. For a man active in political life this was a major deficiency, for ambition is to politics what the profit motive is to business. Jabotinsky did not belong to the category of leaders intent on having their name carved on a rock for the posterity. Even Herzl was not free from this yearning. We read in his literary testament (February 12, 1897): "What I was for the Jews, the future generations will judge better than the contemporaneous masses. . . . My name will grow after my death." [8] Not even the faintest hint of this kind can be found in Jabotinsky's writings, letters, or private conversations. He never dreamt of posthumous fame and was both critical and ironical in regard to fulsome praise. In 1936, his old friend and admirer, S. Gepstein, prepared for the forthcoming Hebrew edition of his works an expansively laudatory foreword which the publisher sent to Jabotinsky for approval; the reply was: [9] "Please embrace Gep[stein] and burn the article. . . . How can one write this kind of things about a pal who is still alive and who never slighted him in any way? The only thing that is missing is an epigraph by [the noted Russian actor] Duvan Tortzov about [the noted Jewish-Russian novelist Semion] Yushkevitch: 'While riding along the Krestchatik [Kiev's main street], choose a site for your monument.' "

He made light of this kind of ambition. But he certainly cherished a strong desire to attain goals truly worthwhile in life. His longing was to achieve something, not to become somebody. As he grew older, he felt that he had to hurry, that his time was running out. In 1933, he said to leading Lithuanian Revisionists who were urging him to postpone the decision to create an independent Zionist Organization for a year or two: "Look, among other things, I am no longer young; I have probably another five years or so of active life left and I want to accomplish something before I am done." [10]

3. *The Last Knight*

Georg Brandes called Garibaldi *"the last chevalier sans peur et sans reproche."* Many maintain that the last scion of that great knightly dynasty was Jabotinsky. This discussion is hardly enlightening. For there never existed in this imperfect world of ours such a human specimen as the sixteenth-century French "knight without fear or reproach," and Bayard's modern biographers have introduced some essential corrections to the idealized image of this medieval knight in shining armor. It would, however, hardly be an overstatement to say that Jabotinsky came as close to Bayard's formula as a human being can. He was certainly a knight, in either sense of this word: as a born crusader, always ready and eager to rise in defense of a cause he deemed good and noble, to serve it with the utmost devotion, traveling for its sake to the confines of the earth; and as a man of knightly behavior, whom even his strongest opponents described as a "gentleman par excellence." In his lifetime, this crusading spirit appeared foolish to many, and he was ridiculed as a modern Don Quixote. But Don Quixote's only fault was that he fought imaginary giants, and with obsolete arms. The forces of evil Jabotinsky fought against were, on the contrary, very real; and his weapons were very much up to date, although their efficiency was often jeopardized by the somewhat "oldfashioned" code of their knightly usage, to which he strictly adhered. In this combination, there was nothing wrong with the rôle of *chevalier errand,* and in this capacity Jabotinsky was fully vindicated long ago.

What remains poorly understood and appreciated, is the second aspect of his knightliness: respect for the inalienable rights of the individual; almost puritanic adherence to a strict code of honor and behavior; cult of gracefulness of form and manner; and love for ritual in human life. Dr. Weizmann characteristically reproached Jabotinsky with "a certain queer and irrelevant knightliness, which was not all Jewish." This reproach is hardly unexpected: to Weizmann's own brand of Jewishness, rooted as it was in a formless and slovenly ghetto pattern, Jabotinsky's cult of form and ritual in human relations appeared indeed alien and "queer."

Life to Jabotinsky was a game to be played to established rules. He displayed a pronounced eighteenth-century courtesy, making a point of cultivating consideration and obligingness in his relations with young and old, famous and humble, friends and acquaintances alike. He had a strong reluctance to troubling others, an almost aggressive eagerness to overload his own shoulders with burdens, however lowly, which others could well carry He was seen more than once running up and down the stairs of the Revisionist head office with papers in his hands in order to spare the typist's energy. Like Herzl, he attached great importance to outward appearance, to manners, dress, and deportment. Herzl's biographer describes him striding through the streets of Paris "erect, graceful, nonchalant, a vision of elegance in his faultless clothes." [11] Nature deprived Jabotinsky of Herlz's inborn physical advantages of noble stature and sculptural beauty of pronouncedly Semitic features. He had a massive head with rather Slavonic facial features, was slightly under medium height, and was conscious of that shortness. Mrs. M. Kahan recollects that during the sixteenth Zionist Congress at Zurich (1929) she once came to see Jabotinsky in his hotel room. On the threshold she heard a fragment of a discussion he was apparently carrying on with a few friends: "Napoleon probably also suffered from being undersized." When she entered, he immediately suggested: "Take off your shoes, let's go to the mirror; you see, without the high heels you are smaller than I am." [12] Though most of those whom he met towered over him in size, he never tried to appear taller than he was. Instead, those conversing with him were obliged to stoop a little, and thus seemed to be paying court to him.

He was always careful to carry himself erect, like a soldier, and dressed with studied, though unobtrusive elegance; the severe simplicity of his clothes only underlined their quality. Jack Tauber, an American *Betari* who was Jabotinsky's secretary during his stay in America in 1940, stresses that "no matter how indisposed he might have been, regardless of the weather or the amount of work that lay before him, he always took his morning shower. He dressed well and wore his clothes regally. . . . He kept all his effects in order . . . never permitted anyone to see him in an unpresentable state." [13]

4. *Democracy and Leadership*

Jabotinsky used to call himself "an old-fashioned nineteenth century liberal." There was deliberation in this label. The purpose was to stress that he believed unswervingly, and above all, in the basic goodness and dignity of the individual human being; that he had unlimited faith in public opinion and its ability to protect a just cause. Its meaning was also, as he put it, that he and his generation "grew up in the firm conviction that a regime based on general and equal suffrage to which the Government is responsible, is the best and the most complete answer to all political troubles." He personally, like many other Zionists, was "not quite sure" that such a regime would be able to cure anti-Semitism: it was hard to forget the Dreyfus affair in democratic France. But that was their only doubt: they were confident that democracy could put everything else right.

This faith lasted throughout the earlier postwar period. Then, hard facts of life began to convey an uneasy feeling that "all is not well with democracy." To Jabotinsky's generation this feeling was "like a slap in the face, or worse still, a stab in the heart." They saw that the great majority of the German people had freely voted for Hitler: was

561

the Hitler regime a democracy? It was not, and this meant that it was possible for "a democratic vote to bring about anti-democratic results." This was puzzling: "the whole world is topsy-turvy." On the other hand, in France, with "too much democracy," Parliament was "playing skittles with Governments" which were "allowed an average of three or four months before being dismissed."

Jabotinsky was not at all blind to all these—and many other—deviations from and distortions of the liberal-democratic creed. But he contended that what was required was not the rejection of the basic principle but timely revision of its application: "each law must have its brought up to date interpretation; what is sacred is the essence of the law, and to save those essentials it is sometimes necessary to revise the interpretation." "It is really a Revisionist world: Revisionism at every turn," he concluded.[14]

He was not ready to give up the liberal-democratic concept as such. With the passing of time, his faith in it grew rather than diminished. In December, 1938, he put a straight question to J. Bartlett, the editor of the great independent progressive London daily *News Chronicle* (circulation 1,500,000):[15]

Are you interested in the revival of Liberalism, the old-fashioned creed of the nineteenth century? I feel its time is coming; I think in about five years it will have enthusiastic crowds of youth to back it, and its catchwords will be repeated all the world over with the same hysteria as those of Communism used to be five years ago, those of Fascism today; only the effect will be deeper, as Liberalism has roots in human nature which all barrack room religions lack.

If you are interested, and perhaps know of some budding initiative to act in this direction and to sponsor the launching of a militant or crusading Liberalism, I should like to help.

It is hardly necessary to add that, in speaking of Liberalism, I do not mean any British party but simply that philosophy which, shared by men of many parties in many countries, made the nineteenth century great.

Since, as he put in the letter, "some Jewish opponents of my brand of Zionism pretend to suspect me of being pro-Fascist," * he found it necessary to say: "I am just the opposite: an instinctive hater of all

---

* In the Prague review *Das Neue Tagebuch* of March 3, 1934, a certain Ben Gavriel published an article "Die Braunhemden Zions," in which he wrote about Jabotinsky: "His role became tragically grotesque as he, financed by the rising Italian and in

kinds of *Polizei-Staat,* utterly sceptical of the value of discipline and power and punishment, etc., down to *economie dirigée.*

Jabotinsky's entire concept was indeed "just the opposite" of everything that Fascism stands for. An essential feature of Fascist ideology is the glorification of a totalitarian state fully dominating the thoughts and acts of its citizens. The searching essay "Revolt of the Elders," published in Russian in 1937, preaches, on the contrary, "a minimalistic State," which leaves the citizen free to fend for himself as long as he neither hurts his neighbor nor asks for help, a State which behaves "like a decent policeman intervening only when you call for him." [16] Another essential Fascist feature is the cult of a leader. "But what is a leader?" [17] Jabotinsky asked scornfully.

In the modern sense he is a man who has been given authority to do all the thinking for the whole movement, so that the rank and file no longer need to think; in fact, no longer may. Discussion, logic, argument, proof —all that has become unnecessary; the reply, always ready, is to the effect that the leader knows best. If what you object to were true, he would realize it himself; since he doesn't, it isn't. Just like that Arab conquerer who ordered the library of Alexandria to be burned, for if the books contained anything different from the Koran they were no good.

Things were different when I was young, and I am of the opinion that they were much better than they are now. It was our belief that nations or churches or movements consist of people who are all equal, each one a prince or king. When elections come, it is not individuals who are chosen, but programs. Those who are elected are only the instruments to carry out the program. We, the mass of people, listen to them and obey them not because they are leaders, but because we have elected them to do what we want done. And, since you have voluntarily appointed a number of stewards and told them to work for you, it is your duty either to assist them, or to depose them. This is the only sense of "discipline"; you do not obey their will, but your own will expressed in the election . . . .

Real leaders are born rarely, and often they are recognized by the fact that they have no desire, no claim to lead. Following them is not a matter of discipline. You follow them just as you follow raptly the singing of a wonderful voice. Because the melody expresses your own yearning. And there is one other point. A Herzl when he dies, even thirty years after and more, still remains our leader.

particular German Fascism, started to form in Jewry a Fascist party, or to be more precise a more extremely anti-labor and anti-Arab, though naturally not anti-Semitic, brand of Hitler party."

This rebuttal and denunciation of personal leadership was indubitably sincere. But no less undeniable was the fact that Jabotinsky was one of the few public figures in the modern world who molded and held together a great and complicated voluntary movement largely by force of his own personality. He was in full control of all the instruments of his movement, an unchallengeable source of ultimate authority. It was a case of an unprecedentedly wide personal union. He was the main symbol of unity between the various, often competitive branches of the "Jabotinsky movement" as it came to be called in its totality. This unity, which he diligently strove to preserve, was in more than one respect a synthetic one, and he often preferred to ignore internal controversies rather than face them, pretending that he presided over one harmonious and happy political family. He had little confidence in the wisdom and efficacy of formal statutory dispositions strictly dividing the spheres of competence among the various ramifications of the movement; in the opinion of some of his colleagues, he was unduly indulgent about their overlapping. A devoted Revisionist from East Galicia once told him that "he had a wonderful dream last night" : he saw a "round table conference" between the *Nassi* of the N.Z.O., the President of *Hazohar*, the *Rosh Betar*, the *Mazbi* of the *Brit Hachayal*, and the *Mefaked Rashi* of the *Irgun*, called to order to lay down a pattern for their interrelationship. "You have a vivid and optimistic imagination, indeed," smilingly said Jabotinsky : "in your lifetime and mine it is bound to remain a pipe dream." In fact, he had neither understanding nor respect for organization matters. When he once asked a leading Polish Revisionist whether there was ever going to be any order in the Revisionist movement, the answer was :[18] "Not as long as it continues to be headed by an Odessa anarchist."

Jabotinsky *was the movement*. There was in his entourage no one in whom the movement had an even remotely similar faith and on whom the leadership could devolve in case he disappeared.

This state of affairs was anything but reassuring and sound. Jabotinsky sincerely disliked the system of personal leadership and always insisted on the necessity of putting an end to it. Yet, strangely enough, he never gave any thought to the problem of succession, and evaded any attempt to discuss it. Some of his colleagues tried to argue that when he died, a dangerous power vacuum was bound to be created in the movement; as a *bonus pater familias* he was therefore duty bound to clear the decks in good time for a smooth transfer of power : since no man around him had the stature to succeed him, the thing to do was to select the best available team, train and groom them in the craft of leadership, introduce them to the movement as his collective heir apparent, and have them accepted in this capacity.

He was, however, evidently reluctant even to contemplate any such contingency. In his opinion, "all this talk about a power vacuum" was vain talk : should he pass away, "the movement will be sorry for a while, but will easily survive it; and qualified leadership will evolve naturally and organically."

There was a fundamental difference between Herzl's and Jabotinsky's attitude towards their associates.

In February, 1902, Herzl praised David Wolfson, who later became his successor, as "the prototype of the faithful and blindly obedient fellow," who himself declared that he would continue to follow Herzl even when he believed him to be in the wrong. To Joseph Cowen he wrote on June 4, 1903 : "I do not want the honors of a leader, all I want is that my wishes should be obeyed, or, let us say, that my requests be fulfilled." [19]

Jabotinsky's philosophy of collaboration was the opposite of Herzl's. He hated yes-men and always stressed his pride in the independence of those of his colleagues who did not hesitate to disagree with him when they deemed him in the wrong, and to oppose his views. In 1938, the New Zionist Club in Warsaw arranged a banquet for this writer, at which Jabotinsky was the main speaker. The banquet was held right in the midst of one of the acutest conflicts between the two of us, and one of our colleagues parenthetically referred to this state of affairs. Jabotinsky did not let this remark pass. At the end of his address he said : "If I were you, I would not worry. It is not the first time—and I pray not the last—that my closest associates and friends oppose my ideas and plans. I shall always argue with them and do my utmost to convince them to go along. But I am no end proud of their independence of mind and I am always grateful for their opposition. There is a wonderful French proverb : *on ne s'appuie qu'à ce qui resiste*—one can lean only on something that is capable of resisting. One cannot lean on a jellied substance that yields to the slightest pressure."

It was only in the later years of his life that Jabotinsky's willingness to take into consideration the views and advice of his colleagues and collaborators began to undergo noticeable change. The late M. Berchin, a man of deep and quiet insight and for years one of Jabotinsky's closest associates, testifies that in those later years Jabotinsky often "strongly resented the necessity to compromise and change his plans in order to placate his colleagues. I remember that once, at a secret meeting, when some of his co-workers insisted on a compromise, Jabotinsky exclaimed rather heatedly:[20] 'Well, I will do as you want me to, but I wouldn't advise you to force your opinion on me too often. If I stand for anything, it is the fact that I am straightforward and consistent.'"

This writer can confirm Berchin's observation. During the last few years of his life Jabotinsky undoubtedly grew increasingly impatient with those of his colleagues who persisted in opposing one or other of his views and plans, and preferred to listen to those who—wholeheartedly or not—concurred. He refused to sacrifice to friendship ideas and actions that he believed in. M. Berchin recalls that Jabotinsky was "deeply impressed" by the words of the French poet and philosopher Paul Valery, "do not hesitate to do things that would alienate half of your friends if this will double the devotion of the remainder."[21]

There was in fact a striking contradiction in Jabotinsky's attitude toward people. Its underlying characteristic was profound respect for, even glorification of, the individual: every human being is a prince by birthright. "Pan-Basilea" was the proud name of this concept. However, the very loftiness of the concept, its sweeping egalitarianism, largely vitiated its worth, precluding any appraisal of individual quality. Since *everybody* was a prince, there was no difference between them: no one was prince number one, two, seven or seventeen. There was no scale of values, no spiritual "table of ranks" in this "Pan-Basilea." Jabotinsky negated the very notion of qualitative selection and half-jokingly, half-seriously asserted that any average man was able to become Prime Minister of France or Governor of the Bank of England. M. Berchin wrote in a thoughtful memorial article:[22]

In reality, Jabotinsky, with but rare exceptions, had a highly critical attitude toward Jewish leaders. He considered most of them—and this applies to friends and opponents alike—weak and short-sighted, unable to rise above their daily petty interests, selfishness, and vanity. Some were better, some were worse, but the difference was only one of degree.

Among his collaborators, he esteemed those who, in his opinion, knew how to do things for which he himself had no talent. Orators, journalists, propagandists—their number was legion. Besides, he, Jabotinsky, took part in all these things, to an extent no smaller than anyone else. But practical work was another matter. Men who knew how to raise funds for the movement, to enlist members for the organization, to contact people useful to the cause, to organize meetings and mass demonstrations, those were in his eyes priceless magicians. This accounts for the somehow paradoxical fact that Jabotinsky often gave preference to collaborators who were intellectually and morally inferior to other men around him.

And in fact, beneath the unwavering cordiality and loyalty, which he so generously—and indiscriminately—extended to his fellow-workers, one failed to discern any genuine personal appraisal and evaluation. What determined his benevolent and considerate attitude toward them was an essentially pragmatic appraisal of their function in the movement. Casual remarks in his letters are highly revealing of this impersonal criterion : [23]

"I judge people not in accordance with the impression they make on me—something I am not good at—but simply : did this man build a house? If he did, he is an architect." Or : "We cannot demand of every man to be a Selfridge [department store in London] in miniature—with every kind of goods in stock." Or : "It is for me more convenient and more pleasant to consider those I am working with as decent and intelligent people; that's why I simply refuse to look in the direction of their shortcomings. I don't know whether this is the right system; but I am not going to change it, because this would be both inconvenient and unpleasant, so far as I am concerned." Or : "Believe me, you are mistaken if you think that 'talent' is everything. Among the equipment a man requires for rendering good public service talent is only one of a dozen items, and not always the most important one at that."

This "applied philosophy," with its loyal defense of "record" against "talent," made cooperation with Jabotinsky both easy and pleasant. But it actually eliminated any evaluation of individual intrinsic quality in his associates.

TRAGEDY AND GREATNESS

MORE OFTEN than not Jabotinsky was right in his political fore-casts, and the march of events time and time again proved the harshest and most vocal of his opponents to have been in the wrong. This empirical fact induced many among his followers to believe that he was singularly prescient, endowed with the gift of second sight, of prophetic clairvoyance.

This is, of course, a wrong belief. In Biblical terminology, Jabo-tinsky was "not a prophet and not a son of a prophet." And one can say so without detracting from the value of his political vision. There is little merit in being a prophet and being right. The prophet is sup-posed to derive his foreknowledge of the future from an unimpeach-able and omnipotent super-natural source that is the very force determining the shape of things to come. It is therefore only natural that a divinely-inspired seer is bound to be always right.

The source of Jabotinsky's vision was, however, not divine, and his forecasts were not due to any lightning flash of inspiration. Modern psychology is as yet unable to explain the origin and nature of the perception that guides a certain rare category of men to follow up a "something" that they feel to be significant, not so much as a thing in itself but as an indication of ripening trends of major significance. Jabotinsky himself—half-ironically, but with an undertone of pride —used to define this elusive gift of his as "my nose—an oddly sensitive instrument endowed with a keen ability to 'smell' things that are still invisible to the eye." Others, inclined to look for a less prosaic explana-tion, called this ability "intuition."

Jabotinsky was undoubtedly endowed with an acute intuitive power. But the striking perspicacity of most of his forecasts was rooted primarily in an unusual combination of strictly earthly ingredients: vast knowledge, exceptionally keen analytical mind, deep insight, moral courage, and readiness to face and handle every problem squarely. If was due to this unique blend of truly human qualities that Jabotinsky, without being a seer, was, as a rule, amazingly correct in foretelling events and developments. For the same reason he was also bound to be occasionally wrong.

He was right in his struggle for the hebraization of the Jewish schools; he proved to be right in his pro-Allied orientation and the demand for the creation of a Jewish Legion; he foresaw the 1920 pogrom in Jerusalem, the failure of the partition scheme in 1937-38, the holocaust of European Jewry in 1936-40. As against this, he was mistaken in his prediction that Czarist Russia would emerge victorious from World War I and become master of the Dardanelles; he erred in his noncommittal attitude toward Trumpeldor's Zion Mule Corps; he failed to grasp the great constructive value of the Nordau scheme when it was first announced; and in the summer months of 1939, he was tragically mistaken in asserting that no World War II would break out.

Jabotinsky's tragedy was a classic one of a thinker and statesman who was years ahead of his time and his contemporaries. Before him, this was the tragedy of Theodore Herzl. When Herzl died, Israel Zangwill said in a sonnet written in his honor:

> Farewell, O Prince, farewell, O sorely tried!
> You dreamed a dream, and you have paid the cost.
> To save a people, leaders must be lost;
> By foes and followers be crucified.

Like Herzl, Jabotinsky was born into Jewry decades too early and had to pay the usual price which History extracts from its precocious children. He could not gather around him the majority of his people because this majority was not ready for him.* When told that since

---

* It could be said of him in the words of Ch. N. Bialik's stern poem "*Go, Seer, Flee Thee Away*, which he translated into Russian in so masterful a manner:
> . . . hatchet-like doth fall my word . . .
> . . . No anvil hath my hammer met,
> My hatchet smote a rotten tree . . .
>   Eng. transl. H. (Kaltzkin).

it was so, he was duty-bound to accept the verdict of the majority and stop fighting it, he respectfully but firmly disagreed. Invoking the authority of the great Russian revolutionary thinker and sociologist, Nikolas K. Mihailovsky, he insisted that the duty of a true democrat is to serve not the current *opinions* of the people—which may be correct or mistaken, and are subject to changes—but its *interests* as he sees them. And all his life, he fervently argued with his own people, trying to implant ideas in the reluctant Jewish public and move them to deeds that ran counter to the entrenched pattern of their mentality. Hence ensued a long intermittent struggle between Jabotinsky and his people.

This was, however, a peculiar struggle. Georges Clemenceau, who had known Herzl intimately, once said to Pierre Van Paassen that Herzl's "fight with Israel," who "knew him not or did not rally to him with spontaneous impulse," reminded him of Delacroix' famous painting *Jacob Battling with the Angel* at St. Sulpice church : "It is a terrible combat that the artist presents here. A battle of Titans. . . . And the Angel is fully capable of overpowering Jacob, but does not do it. If you look long enough at the painting, you sense that there is infinite love between those two, in spite of the struggle." And beneath the rough·surface of a relentless, often fierce conflict, there was "infinite love" in Jabotinsky's lifelong struggle with his people.

The simplest, surest, and possibly the one true criterion of man's stature is the test of memorability. The superior human life is, simply, one which, when it recedes in time, leaves behind a residue of truth or beauty; one which proves to be worth remembering. Time possesses the exacting ability to separate the gold from the dross. The memory of many men who in their lifetime were considered great, begins to wane almost from the very day of their passing and eventually fades like the morning mist before sunrise. As the noted English orator and statesman John Bright once said, men are not great statesmen merely because they happen to have held great offices : they must present better title deeds to eminence, of which memorabilia is one.

Jabotinsky withstood the test of time victoriously. He belonged to the exclusive race of the "untimely" ones, to whom their own age pays little heed, but who prove to be the "timeless" ones when history gives its judgment. The lesson that he drummed so patiently and indefatigably to the often deaf ears of his generation, eventually sank in. It has been reviewed and vindicated in the supreme court of time, and today all thinking minds recognize its verity and its greatness.

They realize, as can be seen so often in the perspective of history, that the so-called visionary was in fact the true realist. Jabotinsky's passing revealed to many what he had been to his people: they learned from the feeling of emptiness created by his disappearance. The prevailing reaction can probably be most fittingly expressed by the first verse of Bialik's *When I am Dead (Akhrei Moty)*:

> There lived a man, and see, he is no more.
> Timeless to death he went
> And in the middle day,
> His song of life was rent.
> Ah! pity, for he had yet one song more,
> And now that song is lost, and lost for aye.

Jabotinsky had much more than "yet one song more" to convey when "timeless to death he went." Paradoxically as it might appear, the undying actuality and freshness of his ideas, which speak to us now with an immediacy that seems to surmount the barriers of time, can be at least partly ascribed to their non-acceptance by the majority of Jewry at the time when they were announced. Because a man who has a message, can often be liquidated by the success of his crusade, as much as by its failure. When the people agree, the people forget. The firebrand of yesterday dwindles to a meaningless commonplace. He may "go out" and stay "out"—just because his gospel was so smoothly and quickly accepted. He has nothing more to convey, to fight for.

Jabotinsky belongs to the rare category of men whose mature years were as charged with virile creative power as their formative years. He surrendered to time nothing of the stimulating fragrance of growth, of trial and error, of great demands upon himself, of combativeness, which are so engaging in the account of his early career.

Most of the notable figures in Jewish life have passed from the land of the living, spiritually childless. No Zionist leader after Herzl has left behind what could be called a political "family" of his own, a school of thought and action, which would proudly claim to be his spiritual heir, be eager to continue and develop his ideological tradition. There is in post-State Zionism—both in Israel and in the Diaspora—no "Weizmann school" or "Sokolov school." Recognizable traces of "Weizmannism" can be found in the mentality and policy of some *Mapai* leaders, and even more so among the Progressives;

these are, however, ossified remnants of the past rather than live and creative trends.

Jabotinsky enjoys the unique privilege of having remained, twenty years after his death, a living and vibrant spiritual force, whose memory has not been blotted out in the minds of men. In his lifetime, he often spoke of a "Revisionist race" which, in his concept, represented much more than an arithmetical sum total of men and women who had subscribed to his political program; he insisted that there was a deep, innate mental and spiritual kinship between all those who joined his movement, that they were intrinsically prone to think and feel the same and to react alike to events and developments. Even Jabotinsky's closest collaborators used to oppose this "racial theory" of his as artificial and unrealistic. However, it has been largely vindicated in the post-Jabotinsky era. Those whom he considered "racially akin" in spirit, continue to form a world-wide "Jabotinsky family," which, besides being a political movement, is also (perhaps even primarily) an ideologically conditioned school of thought. The image and tradition of Jabotinsky—the *Rosh Betar,* the *Nassi* of the New Zionist Organization, the Commander of the *Irgun Zvai Leumi* —still constitutes the strongest link between the *Herut* party in Israel and the Revisionist organizations in the Diaspora; it is still a most powerful unifying force, which overcomes the discrepancies arising from the difference of geographical and political surroundings. Even the former leaders of the "Stern group," who for years denied allegiance to Jabotinsky, are now coming back to the sources of his ideology and referring to him as their "Father and Teacher."

The "Jabotinsky family" is acutely aware of its common origin and intent on cultivating Jabotinsky's legacy. Whenever faced with an issue of national significance, both the leadership and the rank and file invariably ask themselves—though not necessarily in these words— "How would Jabotinsky approach and solve such a problem?" They realize that answers to such a query cannot be found ready-made in Jabotinsky's writings or his blueprints for a party program. His most recent *Torah she b'ktav* (written Torah) is twenty years old and was, of course, never meant to make life easy for dogmatically-minded party scholastics by always providing them with an appropriate quotation and enabling them to say *kach omar Jabotinsky* (so said Jabotinsky). Those looking for inspiration and guidance in Jabotinsky's spiritual legacy, which is anything but rigid, dogmatic, or sclerotic, have to study and apply not dead quotations but the *Jabotinsky method,* his unique way of viewing events and trends, appraising their significance, drawing conclusions. This is not an easy undertaking, and misinterpretations are unavoidable. Yet, it is the only correct and creative means of living up to the great Jabotinsky tradition.

APPENDIX

JABOTINSKY AND THE HEBREW
LANGUAGE

By ADOLPH GOUREVITCH (A. G. HORON)

IT IS hard enough to summarize in a few pages the many-sided contribution of Vladimir Jabotinsky to the development of Hebrew
as a modern language. The difficulty becomes more forbidding when
one has to carry out such a task in English. Indeed, it seems well-nigh
impossible to convey in a foreign tongue any adequate characteriza-
tion of this forceful Hebrew speaker, poet, and writer.

Nevertheless, when the author of the present biography, not being
a Hebraist himself, suggested that I should try my hand at such a
perilous chapter, I had no choice but to accept. I felt that somebody
should take the risk and start explaining to a non-Hebraic audience
the nature of Jabotinsky's linguistic personality, which was of no
lesser moment in the renaissance of the Jewish people than his personality as a statesman. Having had the privilege, especially in the
early Thirties, to observe at close range his influence on the shaping
of a new Hebrew language, I may perhaps be allowed to add my
testimony to the still very meager literature which exists on the
subject.*

* It can hardly be said to exist in English. The two short essays: "Ze'ev Jabotinsky,
the Hebraist" by *Meir Ben Horin* (*American Youth*, November, 1940), and "Jabotinsky
and the Hebrew language" by Professor *Joseph Klausner* (*The Jewish Herald*, July 6, 1956)
deal with cultural-political aspects rather than with those that are strictly linguistic.

Jabotinsky stood at the very center of the struggle for Hebraization in the Diaspora as well as in Palestine, since the first decade of the present century. This has been brought out in an earlier section of Dr. Schechtman's biography, insofar as Jabotinsky's social-organizational activities are concerned, both within and without the framework of Zionism.* In the present chapter, which deals chiefly with the later part of his life, we shall have occasion to add a few words on this topic. But our main task will be to recapture something of the essence of Jabotinsky as a creative writer, a linguistic reformer, a practical phonetician, and a poet of great stature in Hebrew.

A man of *word* was blended in Jabotinsky with the man of the sword. The old Aramaic description of "Scribe and Swordsman" (*safra' we-sayyafa'*) has been fittingly applied to him. He thus appears at one and the same time as the Mazzini as well as the Garibaldi of our own "Risorgimento." The international public knows him more or less as the political-ideological exponent or fountainhead of our modern national movement, and founder of the Jewish Legion which helped reconquer Palestine from the Turks. But the world at large as scarcely aware of his wider rôle as the Hebrew teacher of an entire generation.

His own followers judged him perhaps better. To them he was *navi* as much as *Nassi'* : a great prophet in the shape of a princely leader. Prophet in the Biblical and Hellenic sense : no soothsayer, but he who brings forth the ancient word of truth—which is logical in contents and therefore original in form, harmonious, and forceful in sound.

This true word and primeval meaning of *logos* contains the indivisible *logic* of Jabotinsky's entire mission : all the philosophy, the rationale, the esthetics of that revolution—both rhetorical and political —which he wrought in Jewish life.

"Jabotinsky's spirit was Jewish; his way of thinking was 'Goyish,' " writes one of those "Goys" who understood and loved him best, Colonel John Henry Patterson** And he adds : "Logic, the Greek art, was Jabotinsky's guide in political thinking." But this remark applies equally well to all of Jabotinsky's thinking and feeling, in every field. Especially in the field of language, and of Hebrew language.

* See *Rebel and Stateman*, p. 169 & ff.

** Foreword to the American edition of *The Story of the Jewish Legion*, New York, 1945, pp. 10 and 12.

The simple yet artful belief in a necessary connection between shape and substance, between outward appearance and inner structure, is a key to Jabotinskian theory and practice. It largely explains his private mannerisms and personal discipline and boldly-stated public doctrines.

These may have sounded rather un-Jewish not so long ago. But then Jabotinsky thought of himself as a "Hellene" : that sort of man who is less remote from ancient Mediterranean (and therefore Biblical) humanity than from the average type of contemporary Diaspora Jewry. We should not forget that he came from Odessa, from the strikingly un-Russian metropolis on the Black Sea, where Jew rubbed shoulders with Greek and Italian, and where even the local Slavonic vernacular took on the melody of a sunny south. He was well aware of his own personal Mediterranean background, which was his by choice and not merely by birth. Its pristine clarity and unity pervaded all his thoughts, his tastes, his deepest convictions, in matters esthetical as much as in ethics and politics. The Greek saying which he quoted most often was *kalós k'agathós* : "virtue goes with beauty," a good man ought also to look like a gentleman, and the national language must convey to the ear the style and dignity of a nation.

He lived up to such standards in each of his gestures and sentences; and he never tired of preaching this credo to his many audiences, including the political audiences, even where it might have seemed irrelevant to the unitiated, who believed that public affairs should be divorced from esthetics. When the mass-movement of national youth known as *Betar* * elected him as its leader (*Rosh-Betar*) and then followed him through thick and thin, he coined a one-word slogan for the rising generation—or rather he added glamor to an old Hebrew expression : *hadar,* which is really the equivalent of the Greek *kalós k'agathós* ideal.

Nowhere did he enjoy and enhance this pride of *hadar* more eagerly than in the various facets of a renascent Hebrew tongue, whose growth and improvement he fostered at home, in the street, in schools and conference-halls, in his own writings, published and unpublished—including a far-flung correspondence which provided him with one of his most subtle channels of expression, quite as effective as his fascinating informal talks with hundreds of lovers and practitioners of the language.

* See Chapter Twenty-one.

By the late Twenties of this century, Jabotinsky had gained world-wide recognition as a guiding spirit of Hebrew education in the Diaspora.* The *Tarbut* could now boast of a wide network of schools in Eastern Europe, where nearly one hundred thousand pupils were taught all the general as well as the specifically Jewish subjects in Hebrew, according to the principle which he himself had first established. Yet he was far from satisfied with this outstanding achievement. At the Danzig Conference of the *Tarbut* (July, 1928), the proceedings were opened by his speech wherein he drew attention to those many thousand people who knew Hebrew but failed to use it, in conversation, reading, etc. As Meir Ben Horin puts it,** Jabotinsky described them collectively as "the Hebrew *Golem,* in the sense of a huge figure awaiting redemption. The conquest of this Golem is what he demanded. . . ." He also accused the Zionist Organization, which had completely deserted the educational field, and he found "in this passive attitude the reason for the loss of strength in the Hebrew movements as well as for the lowering of the prestige of the Zionist Organization itself." Many leaders and delegates of *Tarbut* undoubtedly felt the same way and hastened to elect Jabotinsky as a member of the Conference's presidium.

A year later, Jabotinsky carried the fight to the Zionist Organization which he had criticized. One of the highlights of the Sixteenth Congress was a special session devoted to Hebrew cultural work in the Diaspora. Jabotinsky was among its six speakers. He reminded the Congress of that great struggle for Hebraization which had started sixteen years earlier.*** Although he fully realized the difficulties which stood in the way and the insufficiency of the results so far achieved, he would not renounce the ultimate goal nor accept any compromises. "Here I must admit," he exclaimed, "that I still believe with the same naïveté as in 1913 at Vienna, in the possibility of creating a Hebrew environment. This is merely a question of will-power; it depends solely on our own stubborness and organizing ability. It does not depend on the masses. Only the thoughts of individuals can convince and bring decisive action. Now as before, we must rely on oases in the desert : on individual houses or families where the Hebrew language is cultivated. It is the Hebrew-speaking mother who will largely deter-

* Cf. Vol. I, p. 182.
** *Meir Ben Horin,* op, cit., p. 121.
*** See Vol. I, pp. 175-184.

mine the issue. . . . All such people should wear a special badge, to mark that 'I speak Hebrew.' "

In a similar vein, Jabotinsky insisted once more* that the Hebrew University in Jerusalem should become the crowning achievement of a world-wide system of Hebrew education : "The Jerusalem University must be developed in such a way as to become an educational instrument satisfying the needs of its students. Today in Palestine, every parent believes that he ought to send his sons or daughters to a foreign university, simply because nobody knows how long they shall have to wait until there is a real Hebrew university for them."

In the early Thirties, Jabotinsky was growing increasingly disappointed with the old Zionist Organization—in matters not only of politics, but of culture as well. He therefore turned more and more to other audiences and sought other institutions as instruments for the furtherance of his projects in Hebraization. He found what he looked for among the youth of *Betar,* a movement of which he was the shaper as well as the leader.

In his mind, *Betar* had primarily an educational purpose : training in military self-defense, political and social instruction in the service of the nation, but also education in national culture—therefore in the usage of Hebrew as a living tongue. With its large membership of teen-agers (on the eve of World War II the movement counted nearly sixty thousand members in Poland alone), *Betar* became thus one of the important carriers of the Hebrew language in the Diaspora. It was Jabotinsky himself who coined the word to sum up this program of "Hebraization" : *ivrúr.* He devoted much of his time, talent, and enthusiasm to the task of building up *Betar* as an organization wherein Hebrew was a cornerstone not only in institutional theory, but in everyday practice. The administrative routines of the *Shilton Betar* (i.e., the general headquarters, in Paris, London, or elsewhere) and the work of most regional headquarters, provincial commands or local branches, were really conducted in Hebrew. The *kinnusim* (congresses) of *Betar*—contrary to the Zionist congresses—were also transacted to a large extent in Hebrew. The various terminologies, general and technical, used in *Betar,* as well as its official and unofficial songs and hymns, were likewise couched in Hebrew, or created in Hebrew. Selection and creation were largely the work of Jabotinsky himself,

* See Vol. I, pp. 185-194.

or at least the product of his advice and inspiration. At times, the *Shilton Betar* resembled a seminar of Hebrew studies. Members of the staff perfected their knowledge and their tastes under the guidance of the best tutors—a "commander-in-chief" who was a master in national culture as much as in national strategy.*

Needless to add, Jabotinsky would talk and write Hebrew, and only Hebrew—on principle, with infrequent mitigations whenever circumstances warranted—in the performance of his many duties as *Rosh-Betar*. He was giving thus a constant example of what a Hebrew "father" owed, in his opinion, to his many "children."

Such was his behaviour in public life, as a leader of the youth. But in private life, his attitude was no less consistent. In the narrow circle of his little family he spoke only Hebrew with his son Eri, as well as with the few youngsters (relatives or friends) who were steady visitors at the house. Thus Eri, although a mathematician rather than a linguist by bent and schooling, became one of the first men who might boast of a particularly elegant Hebrew as his mother-tongue. Or rather, his "father"-tongue. For indeed Mrs. Jabotinsky never managed to speak Hebrew, though she could understand it.

Hebrew, of course, was not a mother-language for Jabotinsky himself. In his days, at the turn of the century, it was nobody's mother-language. A few enthusiasts in Jerusalem, including the learned Eliezer Ben Yehuda, were just starting to revive it as a vernacular, by teaching their small children to babble nothing else, and ultimately to talk something which had not been heard in everyday life for perhaps fifteen hundred years.

Nor should one describe Hebrew, at this stage, as a "dead" language. It had never ceased to be used in written and even in spoken form,and cultivated throughout a long record of millennia, in a super-abundant literature, in scholarly discussions, in daily prayer. Since the nineteenth century, its literary revival was gathering momentum, especially in the south-western provinces of the Empire of the Tsars, thickly populated with Jews.

Yet this language was still only half-alive. In its prose, its poetry, its limited spoken usage, it remained somewhat stilted, as if stiff with age and scholarship. Writers were more concerned with showing off

* These remarks are based on the author's personal recollections, as a secretary to *Rosh-Betar*, and later a technical secretary to *Shilton-Betar* in the early Thirties.

their own learning than with fashioning a pliable, exact and exacting instrument of modern national expression. It seemed permissible to mix indiscriminately all the clashing inheritance of an exceptionally long past : from timeless Canaanite archaisms in the Bible to Aramaic colloquialisms in the Talmud, and from insipid arabesques found in medieval Hebrew to the preciosities of a latter-day *melitsa* ("rhetoric").

Worse than that : Hebrew, as pronounced in Central and Eastern Europe, had evolved into a peculiar dialect far removed from classical standards. It had become a so-called *Ashkenazic*,* thus named in contrast to the more faithfully Mediterranean (or "Spanish") *Sephardic*. While there was much weight in the contention of those who advocated the supremacy of the glorious national tongue over "Yiddish," the mostly Germanic jargon of East-European Jews, it seemed rather illogical to claim such distinction for the *Ashkenazic* variant of the old language, which did not sound so very different from a jargon.

Ben Yehuda and his friends, the Judaean revivalists of vernacular Hebrew, had adopted quite properly the *Sephardic* pronunciation and were rearing their children to its harmonious if somewhat monotonous sounds. However, the results could not be entirely up to expectations. The teachers themselves were mostly of *"Ashkenazite"* linguistic origin and passed on some of their habits of elocution to their pupils; the acknowledged bards of the age, Bialik, Shneour, and the others, and even the musical Chernikhovsky, continued unrepentedly to write in *Ashkenazic*. Despite its great merits, this poetry was so to say still-born : the younger people, those who were already native to the new spoken language, could hardly appreciate the "official" *Ashkenazie* verses as living poems; much less enjoy them, or be moved to original creativeness by their best intentions clothed in now alien phonetics.

It is here that Jabotinsky stepped into the breach, armed with his perfect taste and straightforward logic. Hebrew being our common heritage, it should be treated accordingly : not only written correctly, and used on all possible occasions in public and private life, as well as in the education of our children—but also pronounced with loving care, even fastidiously, so as to bring out its inherent nobility. The problem of diction, and therefore also of versification, was not for him

---

* From *Ashkenaz*, the Biblical form of the name of the barbaric Scythians, which would be used in Rabbinical literature to designate the Germano-Slavonic area of Europe.

a side-issue, an artistic luxury, but a matter of national *hadar*. He was never afraid of being thought of as "high-brow"; he wanted everybody to be high-brow in this respect; sloppiness in elocution seemed to him a sign of mental muddle and spiritual decay.

Toward the end of a lengthy career as a master of the Hebrew word, he wrote in his English introduction to *Spoken Hebrew for Beginners* :* "Spoken Hebrew has many elements of phonetic beauty, but that beauty needs careful 'tending,' and this is exactly what too many speakers of our language neglect. Even more than neglect: they are likely to laugh at one who correctly says *perati* . . . [i.e. "private" in three syllables] . . . instead of the slothful *prati* . . . to call his pronunciation affected or snobbish, and finally to mock him into renouncing most of the sonorous majesty hidden in Hebrew syllables. I earnestly advise my pupils who will inevitably meet with that attitude, not to give in. . . . Even if sometimes that obstinacy should single them out almost as a 'caste,' never mind; the English language has enormously profited by the influence of the harmonious speech 'affected' by those (also accused of being a 'caste') who value and cultivate spoken music."

Jabotinsky had no illusions about the idiom that went as *Sephardic* Hebrew in his own days. He warned ** . . . "that 'the Palestinian pronunciation' cannot always serve as a model. Even in Palestine, there is, as yet, no phonetic standard. The *Ashkenazi* immigrants import into their Hebrew all kinds of twangs—Yiddish, Russian, Polish, American, German—while the Yemenite spices it with Arabian gutturals which are equally out of place (for if it is true that Hebrew and Arabic are related languages, so are English and German—yet no one wants to talk English with a German accent, or vice versa). Under all these influences, the younger generation of the Palestinian *Sephardim* also begin to lose the beautiful diction of their fathers."

But in this linguistic domain as in all others, Jabotinsky's criticism remained constructive. By speaking and writing the language in his own matchless manner—elaborately unadorned and pleasurably musical—he opened the way toward its new style and prosody. Nor was he content with showing by his personal example what the

---

* *Taryag Millim*, Johannesburg, 1949, p. 6—Revised Israeli edition, Jerusalem, 1950 with foreword, by the author of the present chapter (under the pen-name of *A. G. Horon*)
** Ibid., p. 9.

Hebrew vernacular could and should become in true life as well as in belles-lettres. He also set out to define a novel "phonetic" theory which was the rational basis of his poetical taste.

His essay on "The Hebrew Pronunciation" * must be viewed as a landmark in the current improvement of our national tongue. It is a pity that this remarkable booklet was never translated from its Hebrew original; its slow but pervasive influence in Israel has materially helped in starting, at least, the trend toward a standard of cultured speech and disciplined versification.

The implications of Jabotinsky's phonetic preferences transcend the realm of pure linguistics : they amount to a statement of his *credo* as to the entire nature of Hebrewism—which to him appears as essentially Western, notably Mediterranean. I cannot hope to convey this instinctive yet well-reasoned philosophy in a more concise and better way than by translating here some of the relevant passages ** from the original :

It is not possible at present to divine what was exactly the sound of Hebrew speech in the days of our distant forefathers. One thing is clear, however: their pronunciation was distinguished by extraordinary precision. They did not speak with haste, nor swallow syllables, nor mistake one vowel for another. In short, they were far removed from that careless and sloppy idom which one hears nowadays on our streets. [V. J. then proceeds to prove his point by arguments pertaining to the traditional Hebrew orthography and vocalization] . . . . Our forefathers spoke a tongue that was rich in phonetic nuances. They kept apart the smallest shades of difference between sounds, and uttered with care each single syllable. They were obviously proud, or even "vain," about their pronunciation. It is a pity to spoil such a tongue . . . .

Language forms the kernel and basis of the national symphony. And just as the musical performer rehearses his piece before playing it in public, so everyone of us should work on the improvement of his own diction.

But where are we to find the rules and examples for the "right" pronunciation of each consonant and vowel?

Quite naturally, everybody tends to carry over into "his" Hebrew the phonetic peculiarities of that foreign language with which he happens to be familiar since childhood . . . . Such a "system" is no system at all.

* *Ha-mivta' ha-'ivri*, Tel Aviv 1930.
** Ibid., pp. 3-9.

Our very first concern must be to free ourselves from all these alien accents.

There are scholars who deem it necessary to bring the pronunciation of Hebrew closer to that of Arabic. This again is a fallacy. Hebrew and Arabic are Semitic tongues, but it does not follow that Hebrew ought to be spoken with an Arabic accent . . . . The sound of a language does not depend on its grammatical structure. It depends on the "musical" tastes of its speakers; it must adjust to what seems pleasant to the collective ear of the people concerned . . . .

In the days of the blossoming of our language in ancient Israel, we had almost no contacts with the Arabs. The name: "Arab" appears very seldom in the Bible. Arabic developed in a climate and natural environment which do not resemble in the least those of our fatherland: in a practically boundless space and not within the narrow stretch from Dan to Beersheba . . .; in the tropical heat of Arabia and not in cool Jerusalem; in the loneliness of the desert and not amid a crowded cross-road between Egypt and Assyria. The two races are also quite different. At the start of the period known as the "conquest of Canaan," this country was as full of races as a pomegranate is full of seeds: the Jebusite, the Hittite, the Amorite, the Philistine, and many more. Some of them were the remnants of European and Anatolian nations, others were of African origin. But toward the end of the time of Kings, these peoples of Canaan had already disappeared, or nearly so. In other words, they had for the most part assimilated with Israel and Judea. This is how the Hebrew type was formed: as a man of the Mediterranean, in whose soul and very blood are blended some of the trends and tastes of Northern as well as Western peoples . . . .

Thereafter Jabotinsky goes into technical details to show the phonetic incompatability of Hebrew and Arabic, and to describe certain peculiar properties * of classical Hebrew which resemble those of the gentlest idiom of Italy : Tuscan, the tongue of Dante.

I have insisted on these details because they provide an introduction, or transition, to that idea which follows unavoidably from all we have said before. If we have to turn to other tongues in order to find a starting point for determining the phonetic rules of modern Hebrew, then we should take our models not from Arabic but from among the languages of the West. Especially from among those which like Hebrew originated or developed on the shores of the Mediterranean Sea. I am convinced, for instance, that in general phonetic style, in "prosody" so to say, our

* Notably the functional spirantization of stops in postvocalic position; e.g. in Tuscan: *casa* (house) but *la hasa* (the house).

586

ancient Hebrew was much closer to the classical languages, Greek and Latin, than to Arabic . . . .

I am not ashamed to admit, or even to proclaim, that the "taste" which dictated the phonetic rules propounded in the present booklet is a European and not an "Oriental" taste . . . . The one according to which Italian is considered beautiful and Chinese ugly. If I have chosen this standard, it is first and foremost because we too happen to be Europeans, and our musical tastes are European; they are those of a Rubinstein, a Mendelssohn, a Bizet. But also if we look at the problem objectively, we must admit (because of all the reasons given above) that the diction defined in this booklet comes close enough to the "right" pronunciation: i.e. to the ancient sound of our language as spoken by our forebears. Much closer, no doubt, than any imitation of Arabic gutturals. To say nothing of that sloppy manner of talking, with neither trend nor law nor taste, which has debased our tongue—one of the finest and noblest on earth—and reduced it to a jargon, now in danger of becoming a mere noise devoid of style and structure.

Almost thirty years after this warning was first sounded, one may assert with some confidence that the Hebrew language is in the process of developing again in Israel a style, a propriety, a phonetic balance, at least among a minority of cultured speakers and authors. Its standard of excellence comes nearer to the Jabotinskian ideal than to any other. This is especially true of the Jabotinskian prosody, now prevalent among our younger poets, who are in this sense the pupils of Jabotinsky, either wittingly or unwittingly.

I do not wish to overstress the "personal" rôle of Jabotinsky in the growth of present-day Hebrew as a Mediterranean rather than an Oriental language. His influence in what is now the State of Israel was largely indirect, and often remained unconscious or unacknowledged even among those who followed his lead. Nor do I want to imply that the Western quality of modern Hebrew is the result of a great man's choice. Linguistic development is not a one-man job, not the work of a single genius. Language is perforce a collective rather than an individual creation. But the chief merit of Jabotinsky was to sense profoundly and to state clearly, logically, the permanent nature of our tongue and taste. Here, just as in his politics, he appears today more than ever as the Hebrew "prophet" of our century, he who is proven right in the end, he who remains true to an unfailing *logos*.

587

The direct impact of Jabotinsky's own Hebrew verses was perhaps greater than that of his linguistic theories. As he himself narrates in his autobiographical essay,* he took to the Muses since childhood. No sample of his earliest attempts has survived; but he was still in high school when he produced his first noteworthy poem : a Russian version of Poe's *Raven,* which after several revisions became a sort of classic in Russia's abundant translation-poetry. In Italy, in his late teens, he amused himself with Italian rhymes; but as far as I can see, only one sonnet has come down to us,** and its merits are slight. There was certanly the making of a real poet in this very young man, yet he matured more slowly in this field than in most others. He always remained strangely shy about his own poetic outpourings, which he often belittled or even discarded. Or, on the contrary, which he reworked time and again, before allowing their publication. Sometimes he reshaped his favorite pieces and themes until he could express them in more than one tongue : an amazing procedure, giving additional insight into the linguistic ambivalence of this exceptional polyglot. We should also remember that some of his most significant verses have circulated "unofficially" for years, often in several variants, before being published. Certain poems were "discovered" among his papers and have appeared posthumously*** and I am afraid that there are others which have been lost irretrievably.****

In his early twenties, Jabotinsky, when he felt so inclined, was capable of writing quite mature poetry in Russian, as original in form as in content. But he was much slower in his start as a Hebrew poet. He felt a healthy respect for the Biblical togue, which he studied, spoke, and wrote in prose for many years before daring to use it in rhyme. His earliest acknowledged Hebrew verses go back only to 1910, when he was thirty years old.

---

* *Sippur Yamay* (*The Story of My Life,* about his early days before the First World War), Tel Aviv, 1936, p. 29: ". . . I started to write when I was only ten years old. Verses, of course."

** See *Rebel and Statesman,* Vol. I, pp. 60-62.

*** Thus, a Hebrew version of Dante's *Inferno* XXXII-XXXIII, and of Verlaine's *Les sanglots longs des violons de l'automne* . . . . Cf. the Collected Works of V. J. published by Eri J.: *Ze' ev Jabotinsky, Shirim* (Vol. II of *Ketavim*), Jerusalem, 1947.

**** One example: V. J. used to hum an insignificant English tune about "A little Spanish town"; it inspired him to compose a sonorous Hebrew ditty, now apparently lost. I well remember its burden: *Bi-Sfarad, be-'ir 'al yam, le-or ha-kokhavim* . . . . which I may retranslate as "In Andalusia, by the light of the stars, in a city by the sea . . . ."

Typically, his first Hebrew poem destined for publication was the same old *Raven* by Edgar Allan Poe, whose Russian version had already earned Jabotinsky a high standing among contemporary poets. His choice of subject is rather striking for a "beginner." To render *The Raven* in Russian was hard enough; but to recreate in the language of the Bible this intricate piece of English verbal music seemed quite another matter. However, nothing was more congenial to Jabotinsky than overcoming obstacles. In 1914 the first Hebrew version of *The Raven* was published; in 1924 it appeared in a final form, complete to the last detail: the basic rhyme in *-or* ("Nevermore"), as postulated by Edgar Allan Poe himself.

In my humble opinion, *The Raven*, Poe's most famous achievement, is not his masterpiece. Perhaps Jabotinsky thought likewise. His best translation from the great American magician is a much simpler song: *Annabel Lee;* simpler in its prosodic structure and more convincing in its melody. Indeed, Jabotinsky's *Annabel* is a thing of breathtaking perfection. Those who know both English and Hebrew sufficiently well may readily agree that this small masterpiece of delicate melancholy has lost nothing, and gained much, by being rendered in what apparently must have been the original tongue in the seraphic "kingdom by the sea."

Other, gloomier kingdoms, "full of sound and fury," were awaiting Jabotinsky. His ripening as a statesman, the World War, the struggle for the Legion, and rebellion against the betrayal of the Mandate, left him little leisure to dally with belles-lettres. Yet it was precisely a politico-military event—the death of Trumpeldor in the defense of Tel-Hai near the sources of Jordan (early 1920)—that first stirred him into becoming an original Hebrew poet, no longer merely the translator of alien poetry. He had soon found himself in the fortress of Acre, a prisoner of the British, with time on his hands and an audience attuned to his grief and his longings. There he wrote his first major poem in Hebrew, the "Song of the Prisoners of Acre." *
A short song, on the sacrifice of Trumpeldor and his companions; and yet one of the grandest dirges ever recited since David bewailed the loss of Jonathan, the fall of Saul.

Here we find no longer *The Raven's* interplay of rhyme and rhythm, nor the dreamlike subtle music of *Annabel Lee*. Everything

---

* Better known as *Minni Dan. . .*, "From Dan (to Beersheba)," which are its opening words.

is uttered in the plainest and most direct language. It fired the hearts
of the youth "from Dan to Beersheba, from Gilead to the Sea" (in
the very words of the author). Later it became a favorite hymn of
Betar. The patriotic geography of its concluding lines remains timely
even today, and its elementary beats are like the footfalls of a nation
on the march :

> . . . *lánu, lánu, tihye lánu*
> *kéter ha-Hermón.* *

Cornered in the ancient prison of Acre, Jabotinsky was in no mood
for the lighter aspects of his often frivolous Muse. Once more he
began "translating" in Hebrew verses; but this time he selected Omar
Khayyam ("the Persian Ecclesiaste," as he called him**), and more
ambitiously—Dante Alighieri for his mentors.

Of course he knew no Persian, and had to Hebraize the quatrains
of Khayyam from Fitzgerald's brilliant (and so the Persians say—
unfaithful) English. Yet in the shape which Jabotinsky gave them they
are much more than poetical trifles. Simpler in style, graver in tone,
they recapture something of a genuine Oriental wisdom.

To tackle Dante was altogether a different matter. Here the translator could not get away with a mere *tour de force,* even though he
possessed a perfect knowledge of the Italian language. The *Divine
Comedy* is a universe by itself, which begins in the gloom of a nether-
world. And it is indeed in prison that Jabotinsky started his own extraordinary version of the *Inferno. Canti* I-IV, X and XIV were
published during the Twenties; *canti* XXXII-XXXIII, extant in
manuscript, appeared in print only posthumously, in 1947. All in
all, he had found occasion to render in Hebrew almost fourteen
hundred verses : one third of the *Inferno,* or about one ninth of the
grandiose and bulky *Divine Comedy.* In more normal circumstances
than those which surrounded his stormy life, he would have doubtless
accomplished this stupendous feat of recreation in its entirety.

As they are, the ten *canti* in Hebrew stand like a monument—
unparalleled in world-literature. Many are the tongues in which Dante
has been translated and unavoidably betrayed; *traduttore, traditore,*
say the Italians. Jabotinsky has succeeded to do full justice to the

* ". . . Ours, ours, you'll be ours,
  Crown of mount Hermon."

** *Qohéslat Paras,* according to the subtitle in *Targumim,* 1924.

greatest, most exacting poet of Italy, and perhaps of all Europe. The Hebrew rendering of the *Inferno* is amazing, first of all, in its technical precision : the entirely faithful meter, the mosaic-like texture of the difficult *terzine*-rhymes, the correspondence of nearly all sound-pictures and word-plays, testify to a power of transubstantiation from one idiom and culture into another, which seems well-nigh unique.

But the *Tófet** of Jabotinsky is much more than an excellent Hebraization of the Tuscan masterpiece. It amounts also to a metamorphosis of the entire Hebrew style of poetry. The point which Jabotinsky proved to himself and to others was that the Hebrew language can embrace the entire universal sphere and express it in all the most peculiar tones of Mediterranean civilization, medieval as well as ancient and modern. Here the Mantuan Virgil instructs his pupil, Francesca da Rimini whispers her lovely woes, Farinata rises with the passion of Florence, and Ugolino's curse descends upon Pisa —as if all Italians or Romans or Gauls of yore had never spoken but with the one tongue of the Bible. Occasionally, when Dante seems hasty in his panoramic descriptions, Jabotinsky adds his own magnificent touch, and one wonders how the Tuscan genius could have done without it. Thus for instance Semiramis, "empress of many races,"** becomes :

> Semiraniis, queen of the East, and mistress
> Of monats numerous beyond account.***

The language of *Tófet* is neither a modernistic nor an archaic Hebrew; it is Hebrew as it would have sounded if it were spoken by Tuscan poets of the *Trecento*. It came as a revelation to all true lovers of our national speech.

Despite that mock modesty which he affected, Jabotinsky knew full well the magnitude and historic resonance of his attempt. In the early Twenties he wrote the following ironic and prophetical lines :

---

* Hebr. for *Inferno*.

** ". . . imperatrice di molte favelle." *Inf.* V, 54.

*** *Shemiramit, malkat Mizrah, u-gvéret*
    'al geza'im harbé le-lo' sefor.

Tofet V, 53-54.

There once lived in Russia, a couple of centuries ago, a versifier named Trediakovsky. As a poet he lacked both gift and taste; in his days everybody poked fun at his verses, and they still seem laughable in our time. Yet Trediakovsky influenced Russian poetry in a quite decisive way. All poets before him . . . had written in the "syllabic" meter, which is alien to the spirit of the Russian language . . . . Trediakovsky was the first one to choose the more suitable "tonic" meter . . . . People laughed at his poetry, but his prosody won the day.

He who translated the poems which are collected in this booklet is not a poet himself. But he believes that the language of our modern poetry is *Sephardic* Hebrew; and though his rhymes be of slight value, his opinion shall prevail*.

And so it did. A slender collection of his shorter poems—recast from English, Italian and French originals which differ widely in worth, mood, tone, texture—was published in 1924 under the deceptively plain title of *Translations (Targumin)*, and prefaced with the remarks from which we have just quoted.** Perfected and polished by virtue of an unmistakably Jabotinskian touch, this string of poetic jewels reflected the versatile grace of a language that sounded more easy and conversational than the highly sophisticated style of the "medieval" *Tófet*. It probably gained a wider audience, and marked the turning point in Hebrew verse-writing. *Ashkenazic* stood now condemned, lingering on solely among the diehards of an older generation. Even some of the established bards found the courage of learning the lesson: thus the celebrated Yaacov Kahan, for example, who from then on wrote only in Sephardic. As to the younger poets, they hardly needed prodding. To them, the choice of "dialect" was self-evident. What Jabotinsky offered them, however, was a model of prosody, exact phraseology and verbal-musical refinement.

His last work of poetic transmutation (or "plagiarism," as he playfully called his own recastings of foreign song***) was again boldly borrowed from one of the grand masters: from Goethe. Some of the

---

* Foreword to *Targumim*, Berlin 1924.

** The collection had the following contents: from English—Poe's *Raven* and *Annabel Lee*, and seventeen quatrains from Fitzgerald's *Rubayyat* of Omar Khayyam; from French —a sonnet of Soulary and excerpts of Edmond Rostand's *Cyrano de Bergerac*; from Italian —a sonnet of Gabriele d'Annunzio.

*** He uses in fact the word *Plagiarisms* in the title of a collection of his Russian verses, to describe those that flow from an alien source.

opening scenes in the Jabotinskian *Faust*—approximately three hundred and fifty verses—conjured up a persuasively Hebrew Mephisto conversing wittily and wickedly with the learned Doctor, in the aboriginal tongue of all spirits and demons, alchemists and cabalists.*

Jabotinsky was certainly an alchemist of poetry, a " linguist of the spirit"—as he sometimes described himself : a soul able to penetrate behind the innermost barriers of formal diversity and to combine the hidden elements into new beings, fully alive yet secretly akin to their strange heterogenous forerunners. But was he also a creator himself? He had proven his ability as a Russian poet of considerable distinction. In Hebrew he had composed his unforgettable *Minni Dan* (*The Song of the Prisoners of Acre*). What could he add to this, that would not be a version but an original creation?

Only seven hymns, in addition to *Minni Dan*, constitute the entire known production of Jabotinsky in the later Twenties and the Thirties, as far as original Hebrew poetry is concerned.** All of them are political in purpose and inspiration; and not all seem remarkable from any other point of view. Yet two or three, at the very least, are quite outstanding even by the strictest standards of "art for art's sake"—to say nothing of the national bugle-call which they convey, and which still echoes in the minds of many thousands.

The latest among Jabotinsky's major compositions in Hebrew—the poem *She's all mine* (1938)***—has a quality of ringing challenge and grimness unsurpassed in patriotic hymnology. It renders in a partisan mood of collective assertiveness, and in sound-pictures of great magnificence, the overwhelming contempt of a true leader of men toward the worm-like inhumanity of his antagonists, the Cain-like pettiness of fellow-Zionists.

Another, earlier masterpiece, midway between *Minni Dan* and *Kulláh shellí*, is *The, Song of Betar*, written in 1932.**** It was conceived as the official hymn of this organization and it became in fact the Jabotinskian *Marseillaise* of our youth. Quite apart from its highly significant ideology, this song is characteristic of Jabotinsky's manner as a pure poet who owes something to a lifelong appreciation of

* Published first in 1936-37.

** Cf. *Shirim*, 1947, pp. 187-218 and the notes thereto, giving also some of the variants.

*** *Kulláh shellí.*

**** *Shir Betar.*

Edgar Allan Poe's workmanship. As I chanced to be on the spot* at the very inception of this hymn, I may as well take the reader behind the scene for a glimpse of how Jabotinsky was wont to build up a poem, logically and harmonically, from its most elementary verbal basis—irrespective of the particular idiom in which he happened to compose.

One day in Paris, in the spring of 1932, Jabotinsky had in my presence a half-jocular, half-earnest discussion with his son Eri, about the merits of mathematics versus poetry. I remember him quoting from Poe's *Philosophy of Composition* : "It is my design to render it manifest that no one point . . . is referable either to accident or intuition—that the work proceeded, step by step, to its completion with the precision and rigid consequence of a mathematical problem." Eri, who professed no feeling whatsoever for any kind of versification, was but mildly thrilled. As to myself, I would not have missed for all the world such an occasion to be admitted into the workshop of Jabotinsky's poetry. So I challenged him to give us a demonstration. He took the bet. Being very busy at the moment—as usual—he gave us an appointment much later that night in a café.

"Tonight I must write a new hymn for *Betar*," said Jabotinsky when he finally joined us. "Let's do it together, mathematically. Let's take the *-ar* of *Betár* as the dominant rhyme. It will serve the same purpose as the *-or* of Poe's *Nevermore*."

So "we" started. The debate was naturally in Hebrew. Jabotinsky wanted to express three main ideas : that of *Betar,* and of course that of *hadár,* and something else beside—less tame, less gentlemanly, more challenging and rebellious.

"Something mischievous, troublesome, scandalous. . . . Wait, I have it : *Betár—hadár—scandár* !"

Here Eri looked up in wonderment : "There isn't such a thing in any vocabulary ! What do you mean by *scandár* ?"

"You don't get it ?" replied Jabotinsky. "*Skandál* in Russian, the English 'Scandal,' or if you wish—Colonel Patterson's favorite toast : 'Here's to trouble !' No doubt we'll find the appropriate Hebrew word rhyming in *-ár*; no problem in that. But for the time being we mark

* Together with Eri Jabotinsky. The episode has been mentioned in a note to his edition of his father's verses (*Shirim* 1947, p. 306), but all too sketchily. Being the " friend " who was present at the sitting in the Café Acropole, I think it fit to recount this memorable incident more fully.

down *scandár* as a makeshift, a mere 'mathematical' formula. . . . "

A little while afterward, he turned to me : "We need a juicy, war-like equivalent of *scandár*, in Hebrew."

I had it already on the tip of my tongue : " *Tagár*" (i.e. "warfare").

"All right then, it will do," concluded Jabotinsky : "*Betár—hadár—tagár.*"

After a few more such exercises, we went home. We felt puzzled rather than persuaded by this bare skeleton of a future poem. Yet some days later Jabotinsky breathed into it a full spirit of life, and launched it on its career as a most beautiful Hebrew anthem.

This example (and I could adduce many more) shows how Jabotinsky's linguistic faculties transcended any one idiom, and how freely he would draw from any source that appealed to his fancy.

Yet he needed no personal flights of imagination to give adequate and forceful expression to his political philosophy. His patriotic verses remain striking and unforgettable even when they do not rank among his best from a purely poetic standpoint. Such is the case of his famous song on *The Left Bank of Jordan,* whose slogan-like directness impressed itself on the minds of our national youth, thus helping more than any amount of polemic literature to keep alive the yearning for "both sides of Jordan, the one which is ours—and the other which is *ours too.*"

Nevertheless (and however outspoken his assertion of our collective rights), Jabotinsky was anything but a chauvinist. The same Jordan-poem also stresses our duty to Moslems and Christians as well as to Jews : along the "sacred" stream, there shall be "happiness and plenty" for "the son of Arabia, the child of the Nazarene, and my own son."

The Hebrew prose of Jabotinsky was no less full-blooded and free-moving than his poetry. Unfortunately, his many duties and interests as a publicist, a statesman, or even as a fiction-writer, prevented him from developing his talent to the fullest extent in Hebrew. By far the bulk of his huge production was written originally in Russian, Yiddish, and other languages. Much of it was later translated into various tongues, including Hebrew; but some of these translations are, to say the least, indifferent, hasty, or quite inadequate.

The world-wide audience of Jabotinsky the prose-writer, mostly Jewish, was by the nature of the case "international" as far as language is concerned; it was attuned to the contents rather than to the form of his message. Appreciation of the extraordinary qualities displayed in his Hebrew prose remained perforce restricted, for a long time, to a limited public, in Palestine as well as in the Diaspora.

Even today in Israel, the need of collecting and thoroughly studying Jabotinsky's *original* works in Hebrew is not yet fully realized. I know so far of no attempt to reunite in a single volume (or series of volumes) the exclusively Hebrew heritage left by this great restorer and reformer of our language. Any judgement about his style, and the lessons we may learn from it, must therefore remain tentative and sketchy for the time being.

This much should be stressed even now : the Jabotinskian prose is fully as significant in the evolution of modern Hebrew as his verses and his "phonetic" theories. Its major characteristics are : concision, studied simplicity, a Latin-like clarity, avoidance of empty rhetoric or needless archaisms, coupled with a far-reaching boldness in the adaptation of Western phrasing and the coining of Semitic neologisms.

He thus helped create a new, highly versatile and vigorous Hebrew prose; not merely in the realm of belles-lettres, but also for the various purposes of practical life. Here we must be content with only a very few illustrations. Jabotinsky's Hebrew *Atlas** remains the first of its kind and is still valuable as a cornerstone of our modern geographic terminology. His Hebrew *Pocket-book for Schoolboys*** is likewise without precedent, and ranges from scholastic subjects to table-manners.*** And we have already mentioned some of his works specifically dedicated to the improvement of our national language.****

The longest piece of Hebrew prose which Jabotinsky happened to write—the autobiographic *Sippur Yamay* (some eighty pages in length)—is a model of elegance, directness, and pregnancy. I must confess that it was always a riddle for me why he did not compose in Hebrew his most powerful novel—or perhaps, really, his political testament—about *Samson*; it would have gained enormously, so it seems to me, by being written in original Hebrew.

It is perhaps quite artificial, in the case of Jabotinsky, to subdivide his production into "poetry" and "prose." Indeed, his prose is often

* *Z. Jabotinsky and Dr. Sh. Perlman, Atlas*, London-Leipzig 1925.

** *Kol-bo la-Talmid.*

*** For both these works, see Ch. I of the present volume.

**** Cf. *Ha-mivta' ha-'ivri; Taryag Millim.*

as poetical and always as melodious as his verses. He simply could not write otherwise. This peculiarity has been already alluded to, in the first volume of the present biography, in connection with his funeral eulogy of Trumpeldor and his companions. Let me quote one more instance, of a more trivial nature. In a feuilleton (which appeared in a Palestinian newspaper in the Twenties, if I don't err) Jabotinsky comments upon the amazingly fast growth of Tel Aviv: its town hall stands actually on what was a bare wind-swept dune only a few years before, on a spot which the author had visited and where he had lost his glasses. Jabotinsky tells about it quite unpretentiously and prosaically: "So that the town hall of Tel Aviv was built on a pair of broken glasses." But in Hebrew this plain sentence becomes a high-sounding distich of admirable harmony and eloquence, perhaps unconsciously so:

ki 'al zúg / mishqafáyim / shevurót
n i v n e t á / ' i r i y á t / T e l - A v i v . . . .

The whisper of the wind on the dune and the crunch of the broken glass give way suddenly to the ample majesty of the raising of a capital city.

The fact is that Jabotinsky was very much an orator, first and last: a mighty artist of the spoken word, even when he wrote—be it a poem, a news-item, a business-letter, or whatever. He did not write with his pen and typewriter, he spoke with them. Likewise, he did not read with his eyes, he listened with them.

Such is the reason why he was so fond of transcribing the Hebrew tongue in plain, easy-to-catch, unambiguous Latin characters. He started doing so in his youth;* later he wrote and tried to publish a complete text-book of "Romanized Hebrew."** He never ceased to advocate this method, or to practice and improve it, in the innermost circle of his friends and followers. Not that he lacked ability or tutoring in "square Hebrew." But he was all for a *Kemalistic* reform of this alphabet, for a way that would permit listening correctly to a Semitic (or any other) idiom in the universal notation-system of Western

---

* *Sippur Yamay*, p. 82. Cf. *Rebel and Stateman*, Vol. I, p. 170.

** *Taryag millim*; here is how Jabotinsky explains this title: "*Taryag millim*, in Hebrew, means '613 words.' I have chosen the figure 613 . . . because of its traditional associations which may make it sound attractive to those who remember that there are '613 commandments' . . . the pious Jew ought to observe." (Ibid. p. 5).

culture. Only thus, he believed, could Hebrew become a fully spoken tongue; a living yet stately vernacular.

Jabotinsky was not in the position of a *Kemal,* and he could not impose his reform on reluctant people. The first Palestinian enthusiasts of Romanization had not fared too well. Itamar Ben Avi, son of the celebrated Ben Yehuda, had attempted during the Twenties to publish Hebrew texts and periodicals in Latin transcription. They had met with the indifference of the general public and the opposition of the Rabbinate. One should add that Ben Avi's orthography was unduly complicated, often illegibly so, and had little to recommend itself. Jabotinsky took all this into account in developing his own system, which was distinguished by its simplicity, elegance, and typographical practicality. Even so, he did not publicly insist on the urgency of such a reform. For the time being he propounded it merely as an instrument for beginners.

He perfected his method from year to year, as an "introduction into spoken Hebrew, in Latin characters," * until it took shape as a conversational handbook, quite unique in form and function : not only helpful as a primer, but also excellent as an exposition of the Jabotinskian approach to Hebrew.** Last but not least, it makes very pleasant reading, because the author was a firm believer in the entertainment value of anything worth publishing . . . even a grammar.

For instance, while explaining the Hebrew personal pronouns, such as *ani* ("I"), *hu* ("he"), *hi* ("she"), Jabotinsky cannot refrain from "quoting here the angry comment of an English pupil: 'What a lingo! She is he, and he is who, and who is me, and me is Annie. . . .' From which you may learn again that 'who' is in Hebrew *mi.*" *** The reader laughs, but he has learned painlessly a set of important words which he is not likely to forget again.

Habent sua fata libelli : indeed, this charming booklet was pursued by ill-luck. In 1938-1939, an English original of *Taryag Millim* was being made ready, a German version had been prepared, a Polish at least planned. But each time the handbook was to appear in print— in Vienna, Prague, Warsaw—the Hitlerites promptly marched in. Finally, a first English edition appeared in 1949, in South Africa, posthumously.

* To quote the subtitle of *Taryag Millim.*
** Cf. the passages quoted above in this Chapter.
*** *Taryag Millim,* p. 25.

"The fact that Latin transcription only is used in the booklet," said Jabotinsky in his own preface, "has nothing to do with the question as to whether Latin characters should or should not be adopted generally for printing Hebrew books and newspapers. That question is an interesting one, but here it is quite beside the point. I use Latin characters simply to make the access to spoken Hebrew easier for Western beginners."*

As the editor of the handbook's revised edition (Jerusalem, 1950), the author of the present chapter felt that "these words of Vladimir Jabotinsky, written nearly twelve years ago . . . may sound rather too modest nowadays. Of course, *Taryag Millim* aims first and foremost at introducing the tourist and the immigrant into spoken Hebrew, as fast and painlessly as possible; it does so by removing, at least in the initial stage, the very serious obstacle of the traditional script, as well as the obstacle of a traditional grammar based largely upon this script. But Jabotinsky's method is also of interest to the ever-growing number of people who are no beginners in Hebrew and who feel the need for a modern standard rendering of this language, a rendering which would be adequate for nationals and foreigners alike. This is a problem which the official use of the 'square' alphabet, however improved, cannot possibly solve."**

Jabotinsky himself was of course aiming, ultimately, at a more ambitious goal: a renaissance of modern Hebrew through the Westernization of its script in normal everyday usage.

This is one phase of Jabotinskian linguistic reforms which has not prevailed so far. Yet I am convinced that it shall prevail one day, like other prophetic views held by this great teacher of our national language.

---

* Ibid., p. 5.
** *Taryag Millim*, Jerusalem edition, p. I.

ABBREVIATIONS

Periodicals

J.C.—The Jewish Chronicle, London

J.D.N.B.—The Jewish Daily News Bulletin, New York

J.H.—The Jewish Herald, Johannesburg

J.T.A.—The Jewish Telegraphic Agency Press Bulletin, New York

J.F.—The Jewish Frontier, New York

J.St.—The Jewish Standard, London

Information Bulletin : *Information and Press Bulletin* of the *Nessiut* of the New Zionist Organization, London

M.I.—Medina Ivrit, Prague

M.J.—Der Yiddisher Morgen Journal, New York

N.J.—The New Judea, London

N.P.—The New Palestine, New York

N.W.—Der Nayer Weg, Warsaw

R.—Rasswyet, Paris

U.W.—Unser Welt, Warsaw

Z.R.—The Zionist Record, Johannesburg

Books, Reports, Documents

Cmd—Great Britain. *Parliamentary Papers*

House of Commons—Parliamentary Debates, House of Commons, Official Report

House of Lords—Parliamentary Debates. House of Lords, Official Report

Litvinoff. *Ben Gurion*—Barnett Litvinoff. *Ben Gurion of Israel,* London, 1954

Protokoll, XIII, XIV, XV, etc.—Official *Protocols* of the Thirteenth, Fourteenth, Fifteenth, etc., Zionist Congresses

Aisik Remba, *Jabotinsky*—Aisik Remba. *Jabotinsky's Teg un Necht,* Paris, 1951

Sh. Schwarz. *Jabotinsky*—Sh. Schwarz. *Jabotinsky. Lochem ha'umah,* Jerusalem, 1943

Trial and Error—Trial and Error : *The Autobiography of Chaim Weizmann,* New York, 1949

Reports—Reports on Political Activities, regularly sent by J. Schechtman, N.Z.O. political representative in Warsaw, to the *Nessiut* in London

Report—Tetikeits-Baricht, presented by the Revisionist World Executive to the Sixth World Conference. Warsaw, 1935

Weltkonferenz—Protokoll der III Weltkonferenz der Union der Zionisten Revisionisten, Paris, 1929

NOTES

ONE

1. Letters to Mrs. T. E. Jabotinsky-Kopp, January 24 and 27, 1923.
2. Interview with Dr. S. Perlman, Tel Aviv.
3. Letter to Mrs. T. E. Jabotinsky-Kopp, September 12, 1923.
4. Shlomo Salzman, "My Reminiscences of Jabotinsky." *Hamashkif,* July 30, 1943.
5. Letter to Mrs. T. E. Jabotinsky-Kopp, October 27, 1923.
6. Letter to S. D. Salzman, May 6, 1925.
7. *N.P.,* January 5, 1926.
8. Letter to Mrs. T. E. Jabotinsky-Kopp, May 19, 1924.
9. Letter to Mrs. T. E. Jabotinsky-Kopp, July 5, 1924.
10. Letter to Mrs. T. E. Jabotinsky-Kopp, July 17, 1924.
11. Letter to Mrs. T. E. Jabotinsky-Kopp, March 30, 1935.
12. Dr. G. Karesky. "Why Has the Atlas Not Appeared Again?" *Histadrut Ovdim Editions,* 1951, pp. 40-43.
13. Interviews with D. Davissky, L. Czeskis, and Mrs. B. Czeskis-Gomelski, Tel Aviv.
14. Israel Zangwill. *Watchman, What of the Night,* New York, 1924, p. 23.
15. Communicated by Itzhak M. Levinson, Johannesburg.
16. V. Jabotinsky. "The Hasmonea of Riga," *R.* February 28 and March 7, 1926.
17. *Der Tog,* November 23, 1923.
18. Quoted in *R.,* January 16, 1924.
19. *R.,* March 2, 9, and 16, 1924 .
20. Letter to Dr. Jacob Hoffman, March 3, 1924.
21. Letter to Israel Trivus, April 11, 1924.
22. Letter to I. Klinov, December 20, 1923.
23. Letter to Dr. Jacob Hoffman, January 29, 1924.
24. Letter to Dr. Jacob Hoffman, May 9, 1924.
25. Arthur Koestler. *Arrow in the Blue—an Autobiography,* New York, 1952, pp. 117-18.
26. Interview with David S. Sheket, New York.
27. Letter to Yona M. Machover, March 7, 1925.
28. Interview with L. Czeskis, Tel Aviv.
29. N. Yevin. "Naissance du Sionisme Revisioniste"; and I. Frankel. "Trente Ans." *Notre Drapeau,* July, 1955.

30. "Zionist Revisionist Conference." *R.*, May 10, 1925.
31. V. Jabotinsky. "Political Tasks of the Conference." *R.*, April 19, 1925.
32. Letter to Joseph B. Schechtman, June 4, 1925.
33. Letter to Joseph B. Schechtman, July 13, 1925.
34. Letter to S. D. Salzman, June 30, 1925.
35. Lotta Levenson, "At Vienna," *N.P.*, September 11, 1925.
36. Hamabit. "From a Congress Notebook," *N.P.*, September 11, 1925.
37. Lotta Levenson, *op. cit.*
38. Louis Lipsky. "Vladimir Jabotinsky: Stormy Petrel." In *A Gallery of Zionist Profiles*, New York, 1936, p. 105.
39. Abraham Goldberg. "Congress in Retrospect," *N.P.*, October 2, 1925.
40. Ludvig Levisohn. "Jews in Council—Impressions of our Congress," *Ibid.*, September 18, 1925.
41. *Protokoll XIV*, p. 250.
42. Abraham Goldberg, *op. cit.*
42a. *Protokoll XIV*, pp. 231-32.
43. *Ibid.*, pp. 323-28.
44. *Ibid.*, pp. 467-79; *J.N.D.B.*, August 28, 1925.
45. *Protokoll XIV*, p. 545
46. Letter to S. D. Salzman, September 8, 1925.
47. *R.*, January 3 and February 27, 1926.
48. "Jabotinsky in Rumaenien," *Juedische Rundschau*, November 27, 1925.
49. Letter to S. L. Jacobi, December 2, 1925.

TWO

1. Letter to Dr. J. Hoffman, January 6, 1926.
2. Israel Posnansky. "January 1926—January 1935," *Our Voice*, January, 1935.
3. *J.D.N.B.*, January 28, 1926.
4. *Ibid.*, February 2, 1926.
5. Letter to E. M. Altschuler, May 15, 1926.
6. Letter to T. E. Jabotinsky-Kopp, February 21, 1926.
7. *Der Tog*, February 20, 1926.
8. Quoted in *R.*, March 3, 1926.
9. "Mr. Jabotinsky's Views" (editorial), *N.P.*, March 19, 1926.
10. *Ibid.*, March 19 and 26, 1926.
11. *J.D.N.B.*, March 19, 1926.
12. Interview with Elias Ginsburg (Gilner), New York. Also, Elias Ginsburg. "Elisha and the Dead Horse," *The Zionist*, November 5, 1926.
13. Bernard G. Richards. "Nathan Strauss: A Few Reminiscences," *The Zionist*, January 23, 1931.
14. *J.D.N.B.*, March 24, 1926.
15. *Ibid.*, April 11, 1926.
16. I. Posnansky, *loc. cit.*

17. *J.D.N.B.*, January 29, 1926; *R.*, February 21, May 16, 1926.
18. Revisionism in America," *R.*, July 18, 1926.
19. *N.P.*, April 1, 1926.
20. *J.D.N.B.*, April 26, 1926.
21. Letter to E. M. Altschul, May 15, 1926.
22. *J.D.N.B.*, April 9, 1926.
23. *"Revisionism in America,"* *R.*, July 18, 1926.
24. *J.D.N.B.*, June 22 and 23, 1926.
25. *Ibid.*, June 23, 1926.
26. *R.*, July 19, 1926.
27. *N.P.*, July 9, 1926.
28. *J.D.N.B.*, July 4, 1926.
29. *Der Tog,* July 3, 1926.
30. *Ibid.*, July 29, 1926.
31. Quoted in *R.*, August 8, 1926.
32. *N.P.*, July 23, 1926.
33. Letter to I. Klinov, July 17, 1926.

THREE

1. Letter to Mrs. T. E. Jabotinsky-Kopp, December 10, 1923.
2. Letter to Dr. Jacob Weinshal, August 11, 1926.
3. The Hebrew text of the script under the title *Gan'tsori* was published in Vol. VII, p. 219-67 in : Z. Jabotinsky. *Ketavim,* in a translation by Hananyah Reichman, Jerusalem, 1949.
4. The synopsis was published by Jack Tauber in "Off the Record"; *Hadar,* November, 1940.
5. Sh. Schwarz, *Jabotinsky,* p. 125.
6. Quoted in *R.*, October 24, 1926.
7. Sh. Schwarz, *Jabotinsky,* p. 116.
8. *R.*, October 24, 1926; *Hatzafon,* October 5, 1926.
9. *Palestine Weekly,* October 19, 1926.
10. Sh. Schwarz, *Jabotinsky,* pp. 120-26.
11. Nahum Levin. "Jabotinsky in Haifa," *J.S.*, July 18, 1941.
12. Interview with Nahum Levin, Tel Aviv.
13. Interview with Dr. Joseph Paamoni, Tel Aviv.
14. Nahum Levin, "Jabotinsky in Haifa," *loc. cit.*
15. *R.*, October 24 and 31, November 21, 1926.
16. *R.*, October 24, 1926.
17. *N.P.*, October 29, 1926.
18. Interview with Mrs. Mirra Weinshal, Jerusalem.
19. Communicated by Samuel Rosov, Haifa.
20. *Hatzafon,* October 8, 1926; Sh. Schwarz, *Jabotinsky,* p. 122; *R.*, October 24, 1926.
21. Sh. Schwarz, *Jabotinsky.* p. 126.

22. Yohanan Pograbinsky, "Achad Haam and Ze'ev Jabotinsky," *Hadoar,* May 30, 1941.
23. *Ibid.*
24. *Protokoll XVII,* p. 173

FOUR

1. *R.,* November 14, 1926.
2. Letter to T. E. Jabotinsky-Kopp, December 3, 1926.
3. "The Second Conference." *R.,* January 9, 1925.
4. V. Jabotinsky. " The Black Guest," *Ibid,* May 3, 1925.
5. V. Jabotinsky. "About Cassandra," *Ibid,* August 1, 1926.
6. V. Jabotinsky. "The White Guest," *Ibid,* December 26, 1926.
7. "The Second Conference," *Ibid.,* January 9, 1927; *J.D.N.B.,* December 27, 1926.
8. Letters to S. L. Jacobi, September 11 and October 21, 1925.
9. Letter to Abraham Recanati, December 4, 1925.
10. Letters to S. L. Jacobi, December 3, 1926; March 3 and May 8, 1927.
11. Letters to Dr. Jacob Hoffman, July 1 and 13, 1926.
12. Letter to Mrs. T. E. Jabotinsky-Kopp, July 27, 1927.
13. Letter to S. L. Jacobi, August 18, 1927.
14. *Protokoll XV,* pp. 120-28.
15. Letter to Mrs. T. E. Jabotinsky-Kopp, September 15, 1927.
16. Hamabit. "From a Congress Note-Book," *N.J.,* September 23, 1927.
17. Dr. S. Bernstein. "The Congress at Work," *N.P.,* September 9, 1927.
18. Letters to Y. M. Machover and S. L. Jacobi, September 13, 1927.
19. Letter to Mrs. T. E. Jabotinsky-Kopp, September 15, 1927.
20. *Protokoll XV,* p. 375.
21. V. Jabotinsky. "Cabinet of Curios," *R.,* September 9, 1930.
22. V. Jabotinsky. "My Particular Opinion," *R.,* May 9, 1925.
23. Letter to S. L. Jacobi, April 26, 1928.
24. *J.T.A.,* May 7, 1928.
25. Interview with Joseph Fraenkel, London.
26. Rabbi I. Z. Kantor. "Jabotinsky and the Student Corporations," *Hamashkif,* August 20, 1940.
27. *R.,* October 23, 1927.
28. Letter to Dr. Jacob Hoffman, October 30, 1927.
29. Letter to the Central Committee of the Revisionist Organization in Palestine, March 23, 1928.
30. Interview with Albert Stara (Starasselsky), Tel Aviv.
31. Interview with Joseph Klarman, Tel Aviv.

FIVE

1. Letter to S. L. Jacobi, June 1, 1927.
2. Letters to Mrs. Jabotinsky-Kopp, May 19, June 8, July 7 and 27, September 15, 1927.

3. Letters to Mrs. Jabotinsky-Kopp, August 16 and September 17, 1927.
4. *R.,* September 30, 1927.
5. Letter to S. L. Jacobi, October 3, 1928.
6. *R.,* December 21, 1928.
7. *House of Commons,* November 27, 1928; March 29, 1929.
8. Letter to I. Klinov, August 19, 1929.
9. Interview with Nahum Levin, Tel Aviv.
10. Arieh Ben Eliezer. "Un grand en Israel," *Notre Drapeau,* June-July, 1953.
11. Norman Bentwich. *Wanderer Between Two Worlds,* London, 1941, p. 145.
12. Baruch Weinstein. "Of Those Meetings," *Hamashkif,* August 6, 1948.
13. V. Jabotinsky. *Zionism and Palestine,* St. Petersburg, 1905, pp. 2 and 16.
14. V. Jabotinsky. "The Land of Love," *M.J.,* July 10, 1934.
15. Interview with A. Propes, Tel Aviv.
16. Interview with Uri Carin, Jerusalem.
17. Interview with Shalom Rosenfeld, Jerusalem.
18. Quoted in *R.,* December 2, 1928.
19. V. Jabotinsky. "Fleeting Observations," *R.,* May 26, 1929.
20. *R.,* November 25, December 9, 1928.
21. Interview with S. K. Gepstein, Tel Aviv.
22. Letter to A. Propes, September 22, 1933.
23. Eliahu Ben Horin. "With Jabo," *Hadar,* February-April, 1941.
24. *Ibid.*
25. Letter to J. B. Schechtman, December 5, 1928.
26. Minutes of the Revisionist World Executive, February 1, 1930.
27. Interview with S. K. Gepstein.
28. *J.D.N.B.,* July 23, 1930.
29. Altalena. "Utilization of Niagara," *R.,* July 25, 1926.
30. Vladimir Jabotinsky. "Secret of Successful Colonization : The Products of Jewish Palestine for World Jewry," *N.P.,* October 12, 1928.
31. Letter to J. B. Schechtman, December 29, 1928.
32. Interview with S. K. Gepstein.
33. Vladimir Jabotinsky, "Secret of Successful Colonization, *loc. cit.;* Altalena, "Utilization of Niagara," *loc. cit.*
34. V. Jabotinsky. "The Manufacturer and the Merchant," speech at the Manufacturers' Conference. *Palestine and Near East Economic Magazine,* July, 1929.
35. Letter to S. L. Jacobi, October 3, 1928.
36. Letters to Mrs. and Eri Jabotinsky, April 22, May 18 and 28, 1919.
37. Interview with Adolphe and Ada Gourevitch, New York.
38. Interview with Mrs. T. E. Jabotinsky-Kopp, Haifa.
39. Letters to S. L. Jacobi, November 3 and 16, 1929.
40. Letter to R. Rosov, December 26, 1929.
41. Interview with M. Rubin, Jerusalem.
42. V. Jabotinsky. "Fleeting Observations." *R.,* June 16, 1929.
43. Israel Rosov. "Who Needed It and What For?" *Haaretz,* Keshvan 14, 1928 (*R.,* November 18, 1928).

SIX

1. *Weltkonferenz, III.*
2. Letters to J. B. Schechtman (April 9, 1928) and S. L. Jacobi (April 26, 1928).
3. Letter to the Revisionist Central Committee in Palestine, June 12, 1928.
4. *J.D.N.B.,* August 16, 1928.
5. Letter to Eliahu Ginsberg, September 10, 1928.
6. I. Klinov. "After the Third Conference," *R.,* January 13, 1929.
7. Letter to S. Gepstein, December 31, 1928.
8. Col. Josiah Wedgwood. *The Seventh Dominion,* London, 1928.
9. Letter to Col. Wedgwood, March 5, 1928.
10. *Weltkonferenz III,* p. 94.
11. *J.D.N.B.,* May 21, 1929.
12. Letter to S. K. Gepstein, December 31, 1928.
13. *Weltkonferenz III,* p. 85.
13a. *J.D.N.B.,* July 7, 1929.
14. V. Jabotinsky. "My Typewriter Speaks," *M.J.,* December 4, 1932.
15. Letter to Mrs. M. Kahan, May 23, 1929.
16. V. Jabotinsky. "The Land of Love," *M.J.,* July 10, 1934.
17. I. Klinov. "Jabotinsky at the Sixteenth Congress (Letter from Zurich)," *R.,* August 11, 1929.
18. *Protokoll XVI,* pp. 113-23.
19. *N.P.,* August 23, 1929.
20. *Protokoll XVI,* pp. 142-43, 138, 216, 166, 155, 133, 240, 336-37.
21. Letter to I. Klinov, August 13, 1929.
22. Letter to A. Poliakoff, August 13, 1929.

SEVEN

1. *Cmd. 3530.*
2. Interview with M. Ginsburg, Tel Aviv.
3. *Palestine Commission on the Disturbances of August, 1929: Evidence,* Colonial. No. 48. Volume I, London, 1930, p. 28 (later referred to as "Colonial 48").
4. Letter to S. Horowitz, December 9, 1928.
5. *Colonial 48,* Vol. II, pp. 671-72.
6. *Ibid.,* pp. 588, 810, 666.
7. *Report of the Commission on the Palestine Disturbances of August, 1929.* Cmd. 3530, p. 155
8. *Doar Hayom,* January 7, 1930.
9. *Colonial 48,* Vol. I, p. 28; Vol. II, p. 659.
10. Letter to Max Seligman, October 24, 1929.
11. *J.D.N.B.,* February 6, 1930.
12. *Colonial 48,* Vol. I, p. 74.
13. *Ibid.,* p. 92.
14. V. Jabotinsky. "It Is Bad," *R.,* September 29, 1929.
15. B. Samueli. "Why Wasn't Jabotinsky Heard?" *R.,* January 3, 1930; also: I. Trivus. "The Struggle Around Jabotinsky," *Haint,* January 1, 1931.
16. The letter was published in *Doar Hayom,* January 15, 1930.
17. *Cmd. 5350,* p. 108.

18. *Ibid.*, pp. 108-10, 176.
19. *J.D.N.B.*, February 6, 1930.
20. Full text of the speech in *Doar Hayom*, December 24, 1929.
21. *R.*, March 23, 1930 (editorial).
22. *R.*, June 29, 1930 (editorial).
23. Letters to S. L. Jacobi (May 10, 1930) and S. K. Gepstein (June 4, 1930).
24. *J.D.N.B.*, September 12, 1929.
25. *House of Commons,* February 5, 1930.
26. Letter from L. S. Amery, February 7, 1930.
27. *House of Commons,* March 17, 1930.
28. *Yerusholaim,* June 29, 1930.
29. Letter to S. K. Gepstein, July 10, 1930.
30. Interview with Max Seligman, Tel Aviv.
31. *J.D.N.B.*, June 29, 1930
32. *Ibid.*, June 11, July 31, 1930.
33. *House of Commons,* September 11, 1931.
34. *J.D.N.B.*, December 19 and 21, 1933.
35. *Ibid.*, April 13, 1934.
36. *Al Jamia al Islamia,* August 15, 1934.
37. Aisik Remba. *Jabotinsky,* p. 182.
38. *R.*, October 13 and 20, 1929; December 1, 8, and 15, 1929; *Doar Hayom,* October 23, 1929.
39. *Cmd.3692.*
40. *R.*, August 17, 1930; *J.D.N.B.*, August 12, 1930.
41. Interview with Isaak Levinson, Johannesburg.
42. *R.*, March 3, 1930.
43. Letter to Kadmi-Cohen, February 17, 1930.
44. *R.*, April 13, 1930.
45. Marcia Gitlin. *The Vision Amazing: The Story of South African Zionism,* Johannesburg, 1956, p. 309.
46. Isaak Levinson. "When Jabotinsky Visited S. Africa," *Z.R.*, July 21, 1950.
47. Interview with Isaak Levinson, Johannesburg.
48. V. Jabotinsky. "In the Days of Kruger and Devet"; and "Boers," *Posledniva Novosti,* February 19 and June 21, 1931.
49. Letters to S. K. Gepstein, June 4, and S. L. Jacobi, October 3, 1930.

EIGHT

1. Minutes of the Session of the Revisionist World Executive, London, June 8-9, 1930.
2. Letter to S. L. Jacobi, October 31, 1930.
3. Altalena. "A Talk with the Devil," *R.*, October 17 and 27, 1926.
4. Letter to the Revisionist Central Committee in Palestine, March 22, 1928.
5. Letter to J. B. Schechtman, Decembber 5, 1928.
6. Letter to S. K. Gepstein, August 5, 1929.
7. Letter to S. L. Jacobi, January 20, 1930.

8. Letter to Abraham Weinshal, December 29, 1930.
9. Quoted in Gustav Krojanker. *Chaim Weizmann: Reden und Aufsaetze: 1901-1936,* Tel Aviv, 1937, p. 28.
10. Letter to Dr. E. Soskin, September 3, 1930.
11. Letter to the Executive Committee of the Revisionist World Union, November 2, 1930.
12. Letters to Y. M. Machover, January 25, March 31, 1931.
13. Letter to Richard Lichtheim and Y. M. Machover, March 26, 1931.
14. Letter to Y. M. Machover, September 6, 1931.
15. V. Jabotinsky. "The Meaning of the Congress Elections," *M.J.,* June 19, 1931.
16. *Protokoll XVII,* pp. 164-78.
17. The story of this interview was told in Jacob Landau. "Experiences and Encounters," *Der Tog,* October 3 and 20, 1951.
18. *Protokoll XVII,* p. 290.
19. *Ibid.,* p. 304.
20. *Ibid.,* pp. 385, 397.
21. *Trial and Error,* pp. 339-40.
22. Jacob Landau, *op. cit.*
23. Interview with Joseph Klarman, Tel Aviv.
24. Leonard Stein. "Eder as Zionist," In *David Eder,* London, 1945, p. 196.
25. *Protokoll XVII,* p. 397.
26. *Ibid.,* p. 398; *J.C.,* July 17, 1931.
27. Interview with Abraham Tulin, New York.
28. Interview with Dr. Ignaz Schwarzbard, New York.
29. Interview with M. Grossman, Herzlia.
30. *Trial and Error,* pp. 339-40.
31. Interview with Dr. Oscar Rabinowicz, New York.
32. *J.C.,* September 11, 1931.
33. Letter to Richard Lichtheim, August 7, 1931.
34. Letter to Israel Rosov, August 24, 1931.
35. Letter to Y. M. Machover, September 6, 1931.
36. Letter to Richard Lichtheim, August 17, 1931.
37. Letter to Israel Rosov, August 24, 1931.
38. *The Revisionist Bulletin,* September 3, 1931.
39. *Ibid.,* September 30, 1931.
40. V. Jabotinsky. "Calais," *R.,* November 22, 1931.
41. Letters to Eliahu Ben Horin, October 1 and 24, 1931.

NINE

1. *N.J.,* December, 1931—January, 1932.
2. *Ibid.,* April, 1932.
3. Letter to B. Weinstein, April 28, 1932.
4. Letter to R. Lichheim, July 3, 1932.
5. *R.,* September 11, 1932.
6. *N.J.,* August-September, 1932.

7. *R.,* September 11, 1932.
8. *Ibid.*
9. *Z.R.,* September 23, 1932.
10. V. Jabotinsky. "The Meaning of the Plebiscite," *R.,* April 23, 1933.
11. Robert Stricker. "Lost the Way," *N.W.,* April 28, 1933.
12. Jabotinsky. "The Meaning of the Plebiscite," *op. cit.*
13. *Z.R.,* September 23, 1933.
14. *R.,* September 18, 1933.
15. Haim Finkelstein, "Haint," In *Fun Noentn Ovar* [From a Recent Past], Vol. II, New York, 1956, p. 133.
16. *N.J.,* November, 1932, January and March, 1933.
17. V. Jabotinsky, "The Meaning of the Plebiscite," *loc. cit.*
18. Letter to Israel Rosov, December 24, 1932.
19. Letter to Mrs. M. Kahan, November 15, 1932.
20. Letter to B. Weinstein and H. Rosenblum, January 6, 1933.
21. Letter to A. Poliakoff, February 25, 1933.
22. Interview with Joseph Klarman, Tel Aviv.
23. *J.C.,* March 24, 1933.
24. *Ibid.,* March 31, 1933.
25. V. Jabotinsky. "The Meaning of the Plebiscite," *loc cit.*
26. Interview with Joseph Klarman.
27. *J.C.,* March 31, 1933.
28. *Z.R.,* April 14, 1933.
29. Interview with Joseph Klarman.
30. Letter to S. L. Jacobi, April 14, 1933.
30a. Letter to Dr. Max Bodenheimer, May 17, 1933.
31. Letter to A. Poliakoff, April 15, 1933.
32. M. Grossman. "The Political Realist," *Zionews,* September 1, 1942.
33. *Z.R.,* May 12, 1933.
34. Letter to S. L. Jacobi, April 17, 1933.
35. *Z.R.,* April 28, 1933.
36. *Report,* p. 7.
37. Letter to Dr. Max Bodenheimer, May 6, 1933.
38. Letter to A. Abrahams, August 2, 1933.
39. Letter to S. L. Jacobi, October 7, 1933.
40. Letters to S. L. Jacobi, May 27, June 10 and 13, 1933.
41. *J.C.,* March 31, 1933.
42. Letters to Dr. Max Bodenheimer, May 6 and 17, 1933.
43. *Protokoll XVIII,* p. 240.
44. Letter to A. Abrahams, August 2, 1933.
45. A. Remba. *Jabotinsky,* p. 86.
46. Joseph Fraenkel. "Robert Stricker," In *Robert Stricker,* London, 1950, p. 17.
47. Letter to the *Nessiut,* February 12, 1938.
48. A. Remba, *op. cit.,* p. 113.
49. *J. S.,* September 13, 1941.
50. M. Grossman's Letter to J. B. Schechtman, June 5, 1956.

TEN

1. *House of Commons.* June 23, 1933.
2. *Report by His Majesty's Government to the Council of the League of Nations on the Administration of Palestine and Trans Jordan, 1934.*
3. Quoted in *Our Voice,* July, 1934.
4. Quoted in *Di Welt,* November 16, 1933.
4a. Letter to B. Weinstein, June 28, 1933.
5. Letter to S. L. Jacobi, June 26, 1933.
6. Eliahu Glazer. "Two Episodes," *Herut Editions,* July, 1955, p. 15.
7. Mordehai Katz. "The Jewish Prometheus," *The Jewish World,* September, 1956.
8. V. Jabotinsky. "A Congress Program," *M.J.,* April 16, 1933.
9. V. Jabotinsky. "A Congress of Hope," *Ibid.,* July 23, 1933.
10. *Z.R.,* August 18, 1933.
11. *Protokoll XVIII,* pp. 125, 127-29.
12. *Ibid.,* p. 399-402.
13. *Z.R.,* September 15, 1933.
14. *Protokoll XVIII,* p. 397.
15. *Ibid.,* pp. 399-402.
16. *R.,* September 21, 1933. *J.D.N.B.,* August 27, 1933.
17. *Z.R.,* September 29, 1933.
18. Interview with Menachem Begin, Tel Aviv. Also: Menachem Begin. "Neither Rest Nor Respite," *J.H.,* July 1, 1955.
19. V. Jabotinsky. "Those Who Saved Stavsky," *R.,* August 31, 1934.
20. *Ibid.*
21. Letter to S. L. Jacobi, July 26, 1933.
22. Letters to S. L. Jacobi, January 21 and February 1, 1934.
23. *R.,* February 28, 1934; *Our Voice,* April, 1934.
24. Letter to M. Haskel, July 23, 1933.
25. Letters to A. Weinshal (August, 1933) and "Friends" (August 4, 1933).
26. V. Jabotinsky. "Those Who Saved Stavsky," *loc. cit.*
27. Letter to M. Haskel, July 23, 1933.
28. V. Jabotinsky. "The Jackals and the Clams," *R.,* February 28, 1934.
29. *House of Commons,* June 14, 1934.
30. Letter to A. Poliakoff, August 1, 1934.
31. *J.D.N.B.,* July 20, 1934.
32. Letters to S. L. Jacobi, August 8 and 22, 1934.
33. Letter to T. E. Jabotinsky-Kopp, September 27, 1934.
34. Letter to T. E. Jabotinsky-Kopp, January 7, 1935.

ELEVEN

1. *J.D.N.B.,* March 28, 1934.
2. *Report,* pp. 8, 10.
3. V. Jabotinsky. "Together," *U.W.,* February 16, 1934.
4. V. Jabotinsky. "Our Future," *Ibid.,* May 4, 1934.
5. *Ibid.*

6. V. Jabotinsky. "About Broken Discipline," *M.J.*, February 25, 1934.
7. *Report,* pp. 105-40.
8. V. Jabotinsky. "German-Jewish War," *R.*, April 23, 1933; *M.J.*, April 24, 1933.
9. Letter to Joel Pincus, May 5, 1938.
10. Letter to Dr. Joshua Yevin, May 14, 1933.
11. Letter from Dr. Abba Achimeir to J. B. Schechtman, July 23, 1956.
12. Letter to Dr. Hans Bloch, May 17, 1933.
13. *J.D.N.B.*, May 1, 1933.
14. Letter to Elias Ginsburg (Gilner), September 8, 1933.
15. "Jabotinsky Urges New Boycott Strategy," *J.D.N.B.*, December 24, 1933. Also: "Statement to the Press," London, November 15, 1933.
16. Letter to S. L. Jacobi, February 5, 1934.
17. *Ibid.*
18. Letter to S. L. Jacobi, January 28, 1934.
19. Letter to Dr. Jacob Hoffman, October 10, 1933.
20. Letter to Dr. Jacob Hoffman, November 13, 1933.
21. Letter to S. Meyerowitch, February 7, 1934.
22. Letter to G. Bonfeld, October 18, 1934.
23. Letter to S. L. Jacobi, August 10, 1934.
24. Letter to Mrs. M. Hoffman, February 6, 1934.
25. Dr. Shimshon Yunitchman. "When Jabotinsky Chose Menachem Begin," *J.H.*, Rosh-Hashana, 1917-1955.
26. Letter to T. E. Jabotinsky-Kopp, January 17, 1935.
27. *J.D.N.B.*, January 10, 13, 14, 1935.
28. *M.J.*, February 11, 1935.
29. Saul K. Padover. *Jefferson.* New York, 1953, p. 161.
30. *Ibid.*
31. Letter to S. L. Jacobi, December 30, 1935.

TWELVE

1. *Rebel and Statesman,* Vol. I, Chapter XIX.
2. Letter to Abraham Recanati, December 4, 1925.
3. V. Jabotinsky. "The Left," *R.*, January 25, 1925.
4. V. Jabotinsky. "Basta," *Ibid.*, June 28, 1925.
5. V. Jabotinsky. "The Enemy of Labor," *Ibid.*, August 2, 1925.
6. Letter to J. B. Schechtman, July 4, 1925.
7. V. Jabotinsky. *Keren Tel Hai* (from an unpublished manuscript).
8. V. Jabotinsky. "We, the Bourgeois," *R.*, April 17, 1927.
9. Letter to I. Klinov (undated).
10. Letter to J. B. Schechtman, May 30, 1929.
11. Letter to I. Klinov, August 19, 1929.
12. V. Jabotinsky. *Keren Tel Hai* and *The Ideology of Betar.*
13. Letter to S. K. Gepstein, October 18, 1929.
14. V. Jabotinsky, "We and the Workers," *R.*, September 10, 1929.

15. *J.D.N.B.,* August 15-16, 1930.
16. Letter to I. Klinov, December 16, 1930.
17. V. Jabotinsky. "A Second *Histadrut," R.,* May 29, 1932.
18. V. Jabotinsky. "The Red Hakenkreuz," *Ibid.,* October 23, 1932.
19. V. Jabotinsky. "Yes, To Break," *Haint,* November 4, 1932.
20. V. Jabotinsky. "The Organization of the Middle Class," *M.J.,* October 29, 1933.
21. V. Jabotinsky. "The Working People," *Ibid.,* December 11, 1932.
22. V. Jabotinsky. "Defenders and—Defenders," *Der Moment,* December 23, 1932.
23. V. Jabotinsky. "The Organization of the Middle Class," *loc. cit.*
24. *J.D.N.B.,* April 14, 1934.
25. Letter to G. Bonfeld, May 27, 1935.
26. V. Jabotinsky. "From a Diary," *M.J.,* February 4, 1934.
27. V. Jabotinsky. "A Chapter 'Truth From Palestine,' " *Ibid.,* February 11, 1934.

THIRTEEN

1. *Report,* pp. 64-65.
2. Letter to S. L. Jacobi, September 30, 1934.
3. Litvinoff. *Ben Gurion,* p. 105.
4. *Ibid.,* p. 107.
5. *Ibid.*
6. Interview with David Elpern, Tel Aviv.
7. Letter to J. B. Schechtman, October 12, 1934.
8. Litvinoff. *Ben Gurion,* p. 113.
9. Interview with I. Levinson, Johannesburg.
10. Litvinoff, *Ben Gurion,* p. 13.
11. Letter to D. Ben Gurion, October 29, 1934.
12. Full text of the agreement in *J.D.N.B.,* October 29, 1934.
13. *J.D.N.B.,* November 19 and 20, December 15, 1934.
14. *Report,* p. 85.
15. *J.D.N.B.,* November 19, 1951.
16. Litvinoff, *Ben Gurion,* p. 114.
17. S. Yunitchman. "When Jabotinsky Chose Menachem Begin," *J.H.,* Rosh-Hashana, 5716-1955.
18. *J.D.N.B.,* January 13, 1935.
19. *Ibid.,* February 13, 1935.
20. Letter to the *Shilton Betar,* March 19, 1935.
21. *J.D.N.B.,* March 26, 1935.
22. Litvinoff, *Ben Gurion,* p. 114.
23. *Ibid.,* pp. 114-15
24. *Ibid.,* p. 115.
25. Quoted by Aisik Remba, in *Jabotinsky,* pp. 129-30.

FOURTEEN

1. V. Jabotinsky. "L'Amérique à un Mètre," *Posledniya Novosti*, March 3, 1932.
2. *M.J.*, February 10 and March 17, 1935.
3. Letter to Mrs. T. E. Jabotinsky-Kopp, January 17, 1935.
4. *Our Voice*, March-April, 1935.
5. *J.D.N.B.*, January 28, 1935.
6. *Ibid.*, January 27, 1935.
7. *Avukah Bulletin*, November, 1934.
8. "The Heresy of Free Speech," *Our Voice*, June, 1935.
9. *N.P.*, March 1, 1935.
10. *The New York Times*, May 5, 1935.
11. *J.D.N.B.*, January 27, 1935.
12. *Ibid.*, February 3, 1935.
18. *N.P.*, March 15, 1935.
19. *Ibid.*, February 1, 1935.
20. *Ibid.*, March 15, 1935.
21. *Ibid.*
22. *Ibid.*, September 20, 1933.
23. *Ibid.*, March 15, 1935.
24. "Dr. Wise's Speech" (editorial), *Ibid.*
25. Quoted in *N.P.*, March 15, 1935.
26. *J.F.*, April, 1935.
27. *J.D.N.B.*, March 17, 1935.
28. Letter to S. L. Jacobi, February 18, 1935.
29. Letter to the Revisionist World Executive, April 21, 1935.
30. *J.D.N.B.*, April 21, 1935.
31. Letter from Rabbi Louis I. Newman to Jacob De Haas, July 21, 1935.
32. *J.D.N.B.*, April 11, 1935.

FIFTEEN

1. *J.D.N.B.*, February 14, 1935.
2. Letter to M. Haskel, March 25, 1935.
3. *J.D.N.B.*, March 26, 1935.
4. *Ibid.*, March 28, 1935.
5. *Ibid.*, April 8, 1935.
6. *Our Voice*, May, 1935.
7. Letter to Dr. M. Schwarzman, April 24, 1935.
8. Letter to S. D. Salzman, April 25, 1935.
9. Letter to S. L. Jacobi, May 12, 1935.
10. Letter to S. D. Salzman, June 15, 1935.
11. Letter to Jacob De Haas, June 15, 1935.
12. Letter to S. L. Jacobi, June 19, 1935.
13. *U.W.*, May 31, 1935.
14. Letter to S. D. Salzman, May 19, 1935.

15. V. Jabotinsky. "Why the Revisionists Left the Zionist Organization," *Z.R.*, August 8, 1935. Also: "How and Why We Left the Zionist Organization," Johannesburg, 1937.
16. M. Grossman, "The Political Realist," *Zionews,* September 1, 1942.
17. *Z.R.,* June 28, 1935.
18. Letters to S. L. Jacobi, May 12 and June 19, 1935.
19. Letter to J. Benyamini, July 12, 1935.
20. V. Jabotinsky. "One Million," *U.W.*, July 23, 1935.
21. Letter to S. L. Jacobi, August 31, 1935.
22. Letters of Jacob De Haas to Rabbi Louis I. Newman and Justice Louis D. Brandeis, September 7 and 11, 1935.
23. *Ibid.*
24. Jabotinsky's opening address at the Foundation Congress of the New Zionist Organization. *Kongress Zeitung der N.Z.O.,* September 8, 1935. Also: "New Zionist Organization: Its Structure and Aims," A Statement Submitted by the *Nessiut* to the British Colonial Office.
25. Letter to Dr. Wolfgang von Weisl, January 29, 1931.
26. *Kongress Zeitung der N.Z.O.,* September 8, 1935.
27. L. Radol. "The Religious Debate," *U.W.,* September 29, 1935.

SIXTEEN

1. A. Remba, *Jabotinsky,* p. 12-14.
2. Letters to Eri Jabotinsky and T. E. Jabotinsky-Kopp, July 19 and 30, 1936.
3. A. Remba, *Jabotinsky,* p. 13.
4. Letter to S. L. Jacobi, October 6, 1936.
5. V. Jabotinsky. "The Englishman," *Rasswyet,* December 1, 8, 15, 1929.
6. V. Jabotinsky. "England," *R.,* June 28, 1931.
7. V. Jabotinsky. "November Second," *Ibid.,* November 1, 1931.
8. *R.,* April 3, 1932.
9. Letters to the Revisionist Head Office, January 16 and 28, 1932.
10. Letter to the Editor of the *Jewish Chronicle,* January 18, 1932; *J.D.N.B.,* January 10 and 14, 1935.
11. Letter to S. L. Jacobi, April 25, 1935.
12. Letter to S. L. Jacobi, August 31, 1935.
13. Letter to S. L. Jacobi and Col. Patterson, September 10, 1935.
14. *"Evidence Submitted to the Palestine Royal Commission by Mr. V. Jabotinsky." New Zionist Publication No. 3,* London, 1936, p. 47.
15. Horace B. Samuel. *Revolt By Leave,* London, 1936, p. 48.
16. League of Nations. Permanent Mandates Commission. *Minutes of the Thirty-second (Extraordinary) Session,* Geneva, 1937, p. 107.
17. *Information Bulletin,* London, July 3, 1936.
18. *Ibid.*
19. Letter to Eri Jabotinsky, July 30, 1936.
20. Letters to Jacob De Haas, July 30, August 31, September 15, October 1, 1936.
21. V. Jabotinsky. "The Last Week," *World Jewry,* July-August, 1936.

22. Letter to Jacob De Haas, July 30, 1936.
23. V. Jabotinsky. "The Last Week," *loc. cit.*
24. Aisik Remba. *Jabotinsky,* pp. 183-94.
25. The Diarist. "By Way of Comment," *J.S.,* August 9, 1940.
26. Aisik Remba, *Jabotinsky,* p. 186.
27. *Ibid.,* pp. 186-88.
28. S. Salzman. *Min Ha'Ovar,* p. 265.
29. *News Chronicle, Daily News, The Times, Morning Post, Manchester Guardian,* February 12, 1937.
30. *"Evidence Submitted to the Palestine Royal Commission by Mr. V. Jabotinsky."*
31. "Jabotinsky's Evidence Before the Royal Commission," *N.J.,* February, 1937 (editorial).
32. "Mr. Jabotinsky Speaks Softly," *N.P.,* February, 1937 (editorial).
33. "Jabotinsky Outdoes Himself," *J.F.,*March, 1937 (editorial).
34. *The 11th Hour,* 1937, No. 6.
35. *J.C.,* July 19, 1937.

SEVENTEEN

1. Rabbi Dr. M. C. Weiler. "Only History Can Judge," *J.H.,* Rosh-Hashanah, 5711-1950.
2. Rabbi Dr. M. C. Weiler. "Revolutionaries—Saints of Tomorrow," *South African Jewish Times,* June 18, 1937.
3. Interview with Nahum Levin, Tel Aviv.
4. *Pretoria News,* April 1, 1937.
5. *The 11th Hour,* 1937, No. 3.
6. Interview with Nahum Levin.
7. *Ibid.*
8. Speech in Johannesburg, June 28, 1937, *J.H.,* July 21, 1950.
9. *M.I.,* April 16, 1937.
10. Rabbi Dr. M. C. Weiler. "Only History Can Judge," *loc. cit.*
11. Eliahu Ben Horin. "The Non-Obvious in Jabotinsky," *Zionews,* September 1, 1942.
12. *J.H.,* March 13, 1938.
13. Interview with Nahum Levin.
14. *The Star,* March 23, 1938.
15. *The Daily Express* and *The Daily Mail,* March 24, 1938.
16. Letter to G. Bonfeld, May 12, 1938.
17. Leter to S. L. Jacobi, May 9, 1938.
18. Letter (no addressee indicated), May 23, 1938.
19. Interview with Albert Starasselsky (Stara), Tel Aviv.
20. Eri Jabotinsky. "The Alexandria Conference," *Answer,* September 12, 1943.
21. "On the Spot in Palestine," *The 11th* Hour, July, 1937.
22. Interview with Dr. Shimshon Yunitchman, Tel Aviv.
23. *Cmd* 5479.

24. *The Threatened Partition of Palestine.* Address to Members of Parliament on Monday, July 13, 1937, by V. Jabotinsky, London, 1937 (mimeographed).
25. *House of Lords,* July 20 and 21, 1937.
26. *House of Commons,* July 21, 1937.
27. Paul L. Hanna. *British Policy in Palestine,* Washington D.C., 1942, p. 133.
28. Letters to M. Haskel, July 23 and 29, 1937.
29. V. Jabotinsky. "Lost Without Trace," *Palestine Flames,* September, 1937.
30. Letter to Senator O. O. Grusenberg, June 3, 1925.
31. V. Jabotinsky. "The Iron Wall" and "The Ethics of the Iron Wall," *R., Deutsches Heft,* Berlin, 1925, pp. 55-67.
32. Joseph B. Schechtman. *European Population Transfers 1939-1945,* New York, 1946, pp. 52, 58.
33. *League of Nations Journal.* Quoted in Israel Zangwill: *The Voice of Jerusalem,* New York, 1921, pp. 103-06.
34. V. Jabotinsky. "A Talk with Zangwill," *Der Moment,* July 29, 1939.
35. V. Jabotinsky. *The War and the Jew,* New York, 1942, pp. 218-22.
36. Letters to M. Haskel, August 6 and 8, 1937.
37. Interview with Joseph Klarman, Tel Aviv.
38. Letter to M. Haskel, August 4, 1937.
39. Letter to M. Haskel, August 27, 1937.
40. League of Nations. Permanent Mandates Commission. *Minutes of the Thirty-second (Extraordinary) Session,* Geneva, 1937, pp. 225-30.
41. "Zurich-Geneva" (From our special correspondent in Zurich), *The 11th Hour,* August 27, 1937.
42. Letter to M. Haskel, August 8, 1937.
43. *N.J.,* August-September, 1937.
44. "Jabotinsky's Appeal to All," *M.I.,* August 27, 1937.
45. Letters to M. Haskel, July 29, August 4 and 28, 1937.
46. League of Nations. *Official Journal,* Vol. XVIII (1937), pp. 885, 887, 899, 907 (Minutes of the Ninety-eighth Session of the Council).
47. Interview with Chaim Lubinsky, Tel Aviv.
48. *Cmd* 5854.
49. *Cmd* 5893.
50. *The 11th Hour,* October 29, 1937.
51. Letter to Eri Jabotinsky, October 10, 1937.
52. Letter to Israel Rosov, November 21, 1935.
53. V. Jabotinsky. "The Partner," *J.H.,* February 10, 1939.
54. *Ibid.*

EIGHTEEN

1. Louis Lipsky. "Vladimir Jabotinsky: Stormy Petrel" [In *A Gallery of Zionist Profiles*], p. 106.
2. Vladimir Jabotinsky. *The War and the Jew,* pp. 53-79.
3. From an address "Na'hamu Ami," delivered in Johannesburg in 1937. *J.H.,* July 21, 1950.
4. *Information Bulletin,* July 3, 1938.

5. *Reports* from Warsaw.
6. *R.*, September 11, 1952.
7. *Information Bulletin,* July 3, 1936.
8. Itzhak Bornstein: "The Meeting at Nalevki 38," *Der Nayer Moment* (Sao Paolo), July 30, 1954.
9. Full text of the interview in Aisik Remba. *Jabotinsky,* pp. 164-66.
10. *J.D.N.B.,* February 13, 1937.
11. "Jabotinsky Wants Evacuation" (editorial), *N.P.,* November 27, 1936; "The Problem of Poland" (editorial), *Ibid.,* January 15, 1937.
12. Samuel L. Katz. "Jabotinsky in Poland," *Zionews,* September 1, 1942.
13. *U.W.,* September 16, 1936.
14. *Reports* for the period September 11-15, 1936.
15. *U.W.,* September 30, 1936.
16. V. Jabotinsky. "Evacuation," *M.J.,* November 2, 1936.
17. V. Jabotinsky. "Self-Evacuation is the Solution," *M.I.,* October 7, 1936.
18. Theodor Herzl. *The Jewish State,* New York, 1946, pp. 85-86, 75, 86, 83, 149-50, 154.
19. Letter to Dr. Danziger, November 29, 1938.
20. V. Jabotinsky. "This Night of Passover," *J.H.,* April 21, 1939.
21. *Information Bulletin,* September 21, 1936.
22. Letter to Dr. Danziger, November 21, 1938.
23. Letter to Dr. B. Akzin, January 2, 1939.
24. Aide-Memoire for the United States Ambassador in London, December 1, 1938.
25. *Ibid.*
26. *Reports* for the period September 20-26, 1936.
27. *Ibid.*
28. *M.I.,* November 6 and 12, 1936.
29. *The 11th Hour,* November 19, 1937.
30. *U.W.,* October 8, 1937; *The 11th Hour,* October 10, 1937.
31. Letter to S. L. Jacobi, October 13, 1937.
32. Letter to M. Haskel, June 14, 1939.
33. Letters to M. Haskel, June 5 and 15, 1939.
34. Aisik Remba, *Jabotinsky,* pp. 197-201.
35. Letter to M. Haskel, July 29, 1937.
36. Letter to the *Nessiut,* October 14, 1938.
37. Letter to the *Nessiut,* February 2, 1938.
38. A. Abrahams. "Jabotinsky Visits a Foreign Minister," *J.S.,* July 27, 1945.
39. Letter to J. B. Schechtman, December 10, 1938.
40. Letter to the *Nessiut,* May 8, 1939.
41. *J.H.,* January 14 and 28, 1938; E. Ben Horin. "We Meet Robert Briscoe," *Ibid.,* October 27, 1939.

NINETEEN

1. Letter to T. E. Jabotinsky-Kopp, September 29, 1938.
2. Letter to I. Rosov, November 21, 1938.

3. Vladimir Jabotinsky. "This Night of Passover," *J.H.*, April 21, 1939.
4. *Cmd* 6019.
5. Letters to M. Haskel, June 5 and July 15, 1939.
6. Vladimir Jabotinsky. "Consequences of the White Paper," *J.H.*, June 9, 1939.
7. Letter to T. E. Jabotinsky-Kopp, March 31, 1939.
8. Letter to S. D. Salzman, April 6, 1939.
9. V. Jabotinsky. *Di Drei Geboten fun der Shoh* (The Three Commands of the Hour), published by the *Keren Tel Hai* in Latvia, Riga, 1939.
10. Letters to the *Nessiut,* August 25 and 26, 1939.
11. Interview with Mrs. L. Strassman-Lubinsky, Tel Aviv.
12. Interview with Dr. B. Weinstein, Tel Aviv.
13. Letter to M. Haskel, September 29, 1939.
14. Interview with Mrs. L. Strassman-Lubinsky.
15. Interview with Mr. Z. Lerner (Nahor), Tel Aviv.
16. Letter to J. B. Schechtman, December 3, 1939.
17. Letter by Col. J. H. Patterson to Dr. J. Damm, May 31, 1940.
18. Interview with William B. Ziff, New York.
19. Interview with Dr. B. Weinstein.
20. Letter to Dr. Louis I. Newman, October 22, 1939.
21. Letters to M. Haskel (September 29, 1939) and Dr. Louis D. Newman (October 18, 1939).
22. Letters to M. Haskel (September 29, 1939) and Dr. B. Akzin (September 18, 1939).
23. Letter to Dr. Louis I. Newman, October 22, 1939.
24. Letter to Anatole de Monzie, September 2, 1939.
25. Letters to Dr. B. Akzin (September 18, 1939) and Dr. Louis I. Newman (October 22, 1939).
26. Col. J. H. Patterson. "Some Memories of Jabotinsky," *Zionews,* January 9, 1942.
27. Letter to Dr. Louis I. Newman, October 22, 1939.
28. Letter to Anatole de Monzie, September 2, 1939.
29. Letter to J. B. Schechtman, December 3, 1939.
30. Letter to I. Rosov, February 3, 1940.
31. Letter to Henry C. Kappel, July 9, 1940.
32. C. A. "A Plan for the Future," *N.P.,* February 19, 1943.
33. Letter to Eri Jabotinsky, January 11, 1940.
34. Interview with Berl Locker, New York.
35. *N.P.,* April 30, 1937.
36. M. Haskel. "They Do Not Want Unity," *J.H.,* April 16, 1939.
37. *The 11th Hour,* July 30, 1937.
38. *Ibid.,* August 13, 1937.
39. Letter to J. B. Schechtman, December 5, 1937.
40. Letter to S. L. Jacobi, February 1, 1938.
41. Letter to the *Nessiut,* February 2, 1938.
42. Letter to M. Haskel, August 9, 1938.
43. Letter to Dr. B. Akzin, August 2, 1938.
44. Letter to the *Nessiut,* December 14, 1938.

45. Interview with Y. Benari, Tel Aviv.
46. Letter to Pinhas Rutenberg, March 3, 1939.

TWENTY

1. Arthur M. Brandel. "Vladimir Jabotinsky Meets the American Press," *Hadar*, November, 1940.
2. Ernest L. Meyer. "As the Crow Flies," *New York Post*, March 20, 1940.
3. Arthur M. Brandel, *op. cit.*
4. Letter of A. Kopelowicz to N. Levin, March 28, 1940.
5. Letter to A. Abrahams, April 4, 1940.
6. A. Abrahams. "Jabotinsky in America." *J.St.*, July 10, 1940.
7. Letter to Sir Archibald Sinclair, May 17, 1940.
8. Report by Dr. Georg Landauer to Moshe Shertok, March 25, 1940.
9. "Mr. Jabotinsky's Address" (editorial), *N.P.*, March 22, 1940.
10. "Jabotinsky's Strange Silence" (editorial), *Ibid.*, April 5, 1940.
11. Clare Booth. *Europe in Spring*, New York, 1940, p. 113.
12. Letters of Col. Patterson to Dr. J. Mirelman (June 8, 1940) and of Dr. B. Akzin to A. Abrahams (June 11, 1940).
13. Letter to Dr. B. Akzin, June 13, 1940.
14. Cable from A. Kopeliowicz to the *Nessiut*, June 15, 1940.
15. A. Kopeliowicz. "The War for a Jewish Army," *The Jewish Digest*, September, 1941.
16. Letter from A. Kopeliowicz to N. Levin, June 26, 1940.
17. Letter from A. Kopeliowicz to N. Levin, June 24, 1940.
18. Dr. S. Margoshes. "News and Views," *Der Tog*, June 15, 1950.
19. Letter from A. Kopeliowicz to N. Levin, June 24, 1940.
20. Reports by A. Abrahams and Robert Briscoe. Minutes of the Meeting of Administrative Committee of the New Zionist Organization, July 5, 1940.
21. Letter from Dr. Weizmann to Col. Amery, July 26, 1940.
22. *J.St.*, July 26, 1940.
23. Cable to J. Sagall, July 31, 1940.
24. Interview with D. S. Sheket, New York.
25. Interview with Israel B. Brodie, New York.
26. Interview with S. Merlin, Ramat Gan.
27. Jack Tauber. "Off the Record," *Hadar*, February-April, 1940.
28. Letter to Eri Jabotinsky, July 28, 1940.
29. Letter from Col. Patterson to Dr. J. Damm, August 7, 1940.
30. Letter to S. L. Jacobi, September 18, 1933.
31. Letters to T. E. Jabotinsky-Kopp, January 17 and September 18, 1933.
32. S. D. Salzman. "Jabotinsky's State of Health," *Hamashkif*, July 10, 1945.
33. E. Ben Horin. "With Jabo," *Hadar*, February-April, 1940; Interview with D. S. Sheket.

34. Yehuda Rosenman. "Jabotinsky in Camp *Betar*," *Hadar*, February-April, 1940; Maria Propes. "The Last Meeting," *Ibid*; "His First and Last," *Hadar*, November, 1940; Aaron Z. Propes. "Those Evenings and Nights," *Ibid.*; Aron Hanin. "The Two Week-Ends," *Tagar*, July 17, 1947.
35. Letter to Eri Jabotinsky, July 28, 1940.
36. Prof. B. Akzin. "The Kol-Nidre on the Last Day of Jabotinsky's Life," *Tribuna Sionista*, October 2, 1954; Interview with D. S. Sheket.
37. Letter from Col. Patterson to Dr. J. Damm, August 7, 1940.
38. Dr. David Wdowinsky. "Vladimir Jabotinsky and the Warsaw Ghetto," *Answer*, July 18, 1947.
39. Mordehai Katz. "European Jewry and Jabotinsky," *J.St.*, July 26, 1946.
40. Interview with M. Szeskin.
41. Mordehai Katz, *loc. cit.*
42. John Masefield. "On the Birthday of a Great Man," *The Times* (London), November 30th 1956.
43. J. B. Schechtman's letter to D. Ben Gurion, September 24, 1956.

TWENTY-ONE

1. Quoted in *Hadar*, November, 1940.
2. V. Jabotinsky. *The History of the Jewish Legion*, New York, 1945, p. 55.
3. *Rebel and Statesman*, Vol. I, pp. 322-65.
4. V. Jabotinsky. *The History . . .* , pp. 39, 89-90.
5. *Protokoll XVII*, p. 179.
6. V. Jabotinsky. "Sh'atnez Lo Ya'ale Alekha," *Hadar*, November, 1940.
7. V. Jabotinsky. *Prelude to Delilah*, New York, 1945, p. 330-31.
8. Col. J. H. Patterson. Foreword to Jabotinsky's *The History of the Jewish Legion*, pp. 13-14.
9. V. Jabotinsky. *The Ideology of Betar*, New York, 1941, pp. 8-9.
10. Letter to a Pluga of *Betarim* in Civittavechia, *J.H.*, July 27, 1950.
11. Interview with Denis Szilagy, Munich.
12. Col. J. H. Patterson, *loc. cit.*, p. 9.

TWENTY-TWO

1. V. Jabotinsky. "On Adventurism," *M.J.*, March 8, 1932.
2. Jon and David Kimche. *The Secret Roads: The "Illegal" Migration of a People, 1938-1940*, London, 1954, pp. 20-21, 23.
3. Letter to Dr. Oskar K. Rabinowicz, November 29, 1938.
4. Full text of the orders in Chaim Lazar, *Af-Al-Pi*, Tel Aviv, 1957, pp. 141-42.
5. This writer is indebted to Yehuda Slutzky of the Editorial Board of the *History of the Haganah* for putting at his disposal the Report.
6. Quoted in J. Borisov. *Palestine Underground: The Story of the Jewish Resistance*, New York, 1947, pp. 11-12.
7. V. Jabotinsky. "National Sport," *Der Moment*, April 28, 1939.
8. *House of Commons*, June 6, July 12 and 20, 1939.

9. *Ibid.*, July 12, 1939.
10. *J.D.N.B.*, June 11, 1939.
11. *J.St.*, August 9, 1940.
12. Chaim Lazar, *op. cit.*, p. 157.
13. *Ibid.*, p. 176.
14. Letters to the *Nessiut*, April 16, 1939, and to Anatol de Monzie, April 18, 1939.
15. A. Abrahams. "By Way of Comment," *J.H.*, March 25, 1955.
16. Interview with Dr. Benjamin Payn, New York.
17. Letter to Rabbi Louis I. Newman and Dr. B. Akzin, January 1, 1940.
18. Eliahu Golomb. *The Hidden Strength (Khevion Oz)*, Vol. II, p. 98.
19. Interview with Y. Benari, Tel Aviv.
20. *J.St.*, February 10, 1940.
21. The *New York Post*, March 13, 1940.

TWENTY-THREE

1. V. Jabotinsky. "Census," *R.*, October 4, 1931.
2. *Berit ha'Biryonim*, published by the Jabotinsky Institute, Tel Aviv, 1953, p. 7.
3. V. Jabotinsky. "On Adverturism," *M.J.*, March 8, 1932, *Khasit Ha'am,* March 11, 1932.
4. *R.*, July 24, August 21, 1932.
5. "The Fifth Revisionist World Conference," *Ibid.*, September 9, 1932.
6. V. Jabotinsky. "The Stavsky Affair," *Ibid*, October 22, 1933.
7. *Brit ha'Biryonim*, p. 9.
8. Letter to Michael Haskel, July 23, 1934.
9. *J.D.N.B.*, June 26, 1934.
10. *Report,* pp. 73-74.
11. *Ibid.*, p. 48.
12. *Ibid.*, p. 49.
13. *Ibid.*, pp. 59-60.
14. Letter to T. E. Jabotinsky-Kopp, January 17, 1935.

TWENTY-FOUR

1. *R.*, September 8, 1929.
2. Letters to Jacob De Haas, August 31, September 15, 1936.
3. Full text of the Memorandum in *J.D.N.B.*, February 7, 1930.
4. *Haganah Becomes An Army*, Tel Aviv, 1943, p. 22.
5. *Ibid.*, p. 24.
6. V. Jabotinsky. "On the Hearth," *Der Moment*, August 28, 1936 (reprint of an earlier article published in 1930).
7. Interview with Moshe Rosenberg, Tel Aviv.
8. Jabotinsky Institute. *David Raziel*, Tel Aviv, 1956, p. 16.
9. Interview with Chaim Lubinsky, Tel Aviv.
10. V. Jabotinsky. "The Last Week," *World Jewry*, July-August, 1936.
11. Interview with Chaim Lubinsky.

12. Interview with Aaron Heichman, Tel Aviv.
13. Eliahu Golomb's speech at the meeting of the Executive Committee of the *Histadrut. Khevion Oz,* Vol. II, Tel Aviv, 1953, p. 85.
14. Interview with Chaim Lubinsky.
15. Letter to the *Nessiut,* August 1, 1939.
16. Interview with Chaim Lubinsky.
17. Shmuel Katz. "Glimpses of Jabotinsky," *Jewish World,* March, 1956.
18. Interview with Y. Benari, Tel Aviv.
19. Letters to Jacob De Haas, August 31 and September 15, 1936.
20. *J.H.,* February 25, 1938.
21. Interview with Menachem Begin, Tel Aviv.
22. Protocol of Eliahu Golomb's conversation with Jabotinsky, July 10, 1938.
23. Interview with Jacob Armarnik, Tel Aviv.
24. Eliahu Golomb, *loc. cit.*
25. Interview with Dr. Shimshon Yunitchman, Tel Aviv.
26. Quoted in J. Borisov, *Palestine Underground,* New York, 1947, p. 11.
27. Interview with Dr. Shimshon Yunitchman.
28. Interview with Chaim Lubinsky.
29. Interview with Yaakov Meridor, Tel Aviv.
30. Protocol of Eliahu Golomb's conversation with Jabotinsky, June 8, 1939.
31. Interview with Chaim Lubinsky.
32. Interview with Chaim Lubinsky, Tel Aviv, and Mordehai Katz, New York.
33. Interview with Menachem Begin.
34. Interview with Mrs. L. Strassman-Lubinsky, Tel Aviv.
35. Interview with Dr. A. Altman, Jerusalem.
36. Letter to Aaron Propes, November 15, 1938.
37. The Jabotinsky Institute. *David Raziel,* p. 20.
38. Interviews with Chaim Lubinsky and Mordehai Katz.
39. Interview with Dr. A. Altman.
40. Interview with Mrs. L. Strassman-Lubinsky.
41. Letter to Dr. Henryk Strassman, July 17, 1939.
42. A full report on this press conference was published in the Prague *M.I.,* August 29, 1938.
43. *This is Betar,* New York, 1946, p. 59.
44. Letter to S. L. Jacobi, August 22, 1938.
45. Interview with Chaim Lubinsky.
46. Interview with Y. Benari.
47. Interview with Dr. A. Altman.
48. Eliahu Golomb. *Khevion Oz,* Vol. II, pp. 90-91.
49. Letter to M. Haskel, September 25, 1938.
50. *The Jewish Call,* December 22, 1938.
51. *M.I.,* 1938, No. 44.
52. Interview with Dr. Benjamin Payn, New York.
53. Letter to M. Haskel, July 15, 1939.
54. Protocol of Eliahu Golomb's conversation with Jabotinsky in London, July 8, 1939.

55. Protocol of Eliahu Golomb's conversation with Jabotinsky in Paris, June 10, 1938.
56. Letters to the *Nessiut* (July 10) and M. Haskel (July 15), 1939.
57. Letter to M. Haskel, July 15, 1939.
58. *J.H.,* July 1, 1938: *J.C.,* June 24, 1938.
59. Remba. *Jabotinsky,* p. 191.
60. The dramatic story of those tense last twenty-four hours has been reconstructed on the basis of the following sources: Remba. *Jabotinsky,* pp. 192-93; I. Giorin. "Drama of Shlomo Ben Yosef's Last Moments," *The Jewish Call,* December 22, 1938; Interview with Y. Benari.
61. *J.H.,* July 15, 1938.
62. *The Jewish Call,* December 22, 1938.
63. *J.C.,* July 15, 1938; *The Jewish Call,* September 23, 1938.
64. *M.I.,* July 15, 1938.
65. *J.H.,* July 8, 1938.
66. Letter to Dr. Shimshon Yunitchman and Shalom Rosenfeld, July 5, 1938.
67. Mordehai Katz. "The Jewish Prometheus," *Jewish World,* October, 1954.
68. *J.H.,* July 1, 1938.
69. *Ibid.,* August 5, 1938.
70. *J.C.,* July 15, 1938.

TWENTY-FIVE

1. Interview with Chaim Lubinsky, Tel Aviv.
2. *J.H.,* October 14, 1938.
3. *Ibid.,* March), 1939.
5. Vladimir Jabotinsky. "Consequences of the White Paper," *J.H.,* June 9, 1939.
6. *The Three Commandments of the Hour: Jabotinsky's Speech in Warsaw,* Riga, 1939 (Yiddish).
7. V. Jabotinsky. "What Had Been Evacuated," *J.H.,* August 1, 1939.
8. Interview with Mrs. L. Strassman-Lubinsky, Tel Aviv.
9. Interview with Menachem Begin, Tel Aviv.
10. Letters to the *Nessiut,* June 5 and 9, 1939.
11. Interview with Mrs. L. Strassman-Lubinsky and Menachem Begin.
12. V. Jabotinsky. "Amen," *Der Moment,* July 9, 1939.
13. Letters to the *Nessiut,* June 2 and 24, 1939.
14. Letters to the *Nessiut,* August 7, 22 and 26, 1939.
15. Interview with Chaim Lubinsky.
16. Aide-Memoire on the conversation with Colonel R. Meinerzhagen, submitted by Jabotinsky to the *Nessiut.*
17. V. Jabotinsky. *The War and The Jew,* New York, 1942, pp. 177-78.
18. V. Jabotinsky. *Ibid.,* pp. 179-80.
19. Letter to Dr. A. Altman, July 27, 1940.
20. Interview with Chaim Lubinsky.
21. Interview with A. Gurvitch, New York.
22. Interview with Dr. Shimshon Yunitchman, Tel Aviv.

TWENTY-SIX

1. V. Jabotinsky. "Fairy Vagabunda," *Causeries,* Paris, 1930, pp. 49,54.
2. V. Jabotinsky. "My Village," *Ibid.,* pp. 75-86.
3. V. Jabotinsky. "Of Cabbages and Kings" (unpublished manuscript).
4. V. Jabotinsky. *Causeries,* pp. 119-32.
5. *M.I.,* December 18, 1936; February 5, 1938.
6. Letters to S. Jacobi, May 28, October 13, 1928; April 26, 1928; November 3, 1929.
7. Letter to A. Poliakoff, August 1, 1934.
8. Letter to Eri Jabotinsky, February 25,1937.
9. Aisik Remba. *Jabotinsky,* p. 35.
10. Interview with Mrs. M. Kahan, Tel Aviv.
11. V. Jabotinsky. "His Children and Ours (On Herzl's Children)." Quoted from *Hadar,* February-April, 1941.
12. Letter to S. Jacobi, September 15, 1931.
13. Interview with Y. M. Machover, London.
14. Letter to Eri Jabotinsky, February 3, 1936.
15. Letter to Mrs. T. E. Jabotinsky-Kopp January 7, 1935.
16. Letter to "Dear Hopkins," November 15, 1937.
17. Interview with Shmuel Katz, Tel Aviv.
18. Letter to Eri Jabotinsky, February 3, 1936.
19. Letter to Aviva Kogon, February 18, 1940.
20. Letter to Eri Jabotinsky, July 28, 1940.
21. *Trial and Error,* p. 63.
22. Chief Rabbi, Prof. K. I. Rabinowitz. "A Letter from Jabotinsky," *J.H.,* July 25, 1947.
23. Eliahu Ben Horin. "The Non-Obvious in Jabotinsky," *Zionews,* September 1, 1942.
24. Letters to T. E. Jabotinsky-Kopp, September 25, October 5, 1927.
25. Interview with S. Cherniak, New York.
27. Letter to Mrs. M. Kahan, February 16, 1931.
28. Letter to S. L. Jacobi, January 25, 1935.
29. Wire to S. L. Jacobi, October 17, 1935.
30. Letter to S. L. Jacobi, October 3, 1936.
31. Letter and Memorandum to M. Haskel, November 30, 1933.
32. Interview with Y. M. Machover, London.
33. A. Bein. *Theodor Herzl: A Biography,* Philadelphia, 1945, p. 212.

TWENTY-SEVEN

1. Quoted in J. Leftwich. "Some Personal Reminiscences," *J.St.,* July 18, 1941.
2. Interview with A. S. Alperine, Paris.
3. Pierre van Paassen. "As I Remember Him," Foreword to V. Jabotinsky's *The War and the Jew,* New York, 1942, pp. 9-11. Also: Pierre van Paassen. "Vladimir Jabotinsky: A Reminiscence," *Midstream,* Winter, 1958.

NOTES

4. Jack Touber. "Off the record," *Hardar*, November, 1940.
5. Interview with Z. Lerner (Lahor), Tel Aviv.
6. Letter to J. B. Schechtman, December 12, 1937.
7. Interview with A. Stara, Tel Aviv.
8. Interview with Mrs. L. Strassman-Lubinski, Tel Aviv.
9. Jack Tauber, *op. cit.*
10. Interview with A. Stara.
11. Letter to Mrs. R. Levin, February 21, 1933.
12. Letter to Mrs. M. Kahan, March 29, 1928.
13. V. Jabotinsky. "About Fools," *Haint*, October 4, 1931.
14. Arthur Koestler. *Arrow in the Blue*, New York, 1952, p. 118.
15. Arthur Koestler. *Promise and Fulfilment*, New York, 1952, p. 302.
16. Pierre van Paassen. "Vladimir Jabotinsky: A Reminiscence," *loc. cit.*
17. Senator John F. Kennedy. *Profiles in Courage*, New York, 1956, p. 54.
18. Letter to S. Jacobi, October 30, 1930.
19. Dr. M. Schwarzman. "The Unyielding Jabotinsky," *J.St.*, July 25, 1941.
20. V. Jabotinsky. "The Other Max Nordau," *Hadar*, February-April, 1941.
21. Itamar Ben Avi. "Jabotinsky the Fearless," *The Bnei Zion Voice*, September, 1940.
22. S. D. Salzman. *From the Past (Min Haovar)*, Tel Aviv, 1943, p. 289.
23. Letter to I. Galperin, June 7, 1935.
24. Letter to S. D. Salzman, March, 19, 1935.
25. Letter to J. B. Schechtman, November 10, 1937.
26. Sh. Schwarz. *Jabotinsky*, p. 89.
27. Letter to S. D. Salzman, March 19, 1935.
28. Shlomo Salzman. "The Year 1919 in the Life of Jabotinsky," *The Leader of a Generation (Manhig ha'Dor)*, Tel Aviv, 1946, pp. 117-29.
29. Letter to S. L. Jacobi, April 26, 1928.
30. Joseph Leftwich. "Jabotinsky as I Knew Him," *J.St.*, September 20, 1940.
31. Letters to S. L. Jacobi, November 3, 1929, and February 7, 1930.
32. *R.*, January 31, 1926.
33. Letter to O. O. Grusenberg, February 25, 1928.
34. Letter to Mrs. M. Kahan, August 2, 1928.
35. Col. J. H. Patterson. Foreword to V. Jabotinsky: *The Story of the Jewish Legion*, pp. 10, 12, 13
36. Letter to S. D. Salzman, June 15, 1935.
37. Letter to S. D. Salzman, March 19, 1925.
38. Itamar Ben Avi. "Jabotinsky the Fearless," *loc. cit.*
39. V. Jabotinsky. "Tristan Da Runha," *A Pocket Edition of Several Stories, Mostly Reactionary*, Paris, 1925, p. 193.
40. Interview with Dr. J. Szofman, Tel Aviv.
41. Letter to Dr. Isaak Epstein, July 9, 1929. Reproduced in Sh. Schwarz, *Jabotinsky*, pp. 392-95
42. Interview with Serge Galperin, New York.
43. Letter to Dr. Isaak Epstein, *loc. cit.*
44. Interview with A. Tulin, New York.

45. Pierre Van Paassen. "Vladimir Jabotinsky: A Reminiscence," *loc. cit.*
46. Letter to Mrs. M. Kahan, March 19, 1928.
47. Interview with Mrs. L. Strassman-Lubinski, Tel Aviv.
48. Letter to Dr. J. Damm, May 14, 1938.
49. Letter to J. B. Schechtman, December 3, 1939.
50. Letter to Dr. J. Damm, April 16, 1940.
51. Letter to Dr. J. Mirelman, July 24, 1940.
52. Interview with Serge Galperin, New York.
53. Letter to G. Bonfeld, August 11, 1929.
54. Letter to Dr. Izaak Epstein, *loc. cit.*
55. Interview with Dr. Oskar K. Rabinowicz, New York.
56. Interview with Serge Galperin.
57. Interview with A. Gourevitch, New York.
58. Interview with Serge Galperin.
59. Interview with A. Gourevitch.
60. V. Jabotinsky. "Diana," *A Pocket Edition of Several Stories, Mostly Reactionary,* pp. 56, 63-64.
61. Interview with A. Gourevitch.
62. Joseph Leftwich. "Jabotinsky as I Knew Him," *J.St.,* September, 20, 1940.
63. Letter to Dr. Isaak Epstein, *loc. cit.*
64. Joseph Leftwich, *op. cit.*

TWENTY-EIGHT

1. "On Jabotinsky," by the Chief Rabbi Dr. J. H. Hertz. *J.St.,* August 30, 1940.
1a. Allan Nevins. Foreword to *Profiles in Courage* by Senator John F. Kennedy, New York, 1956, p. xvi.
2. Oscar K. Rabinowicz. "A Few Memories," In *Robert Stricker.* Edited by Joseph Fraenkel, London, 1950, p. 54.
3. A. Abrahams. "If Jabotinsky Were Premier," *J.S.,* August 6, 1948.
4. V. Jabotinsky. "The 'Periole' of Sarah the First," *J.H.,* April 14, 1938.
5. V. Jabotinsky. "Shaatnez Lo Ya'ale Alekha," *Hadar,* November, 1940.
5a. Col. J. H. Patterson. Foreword to *The Story of the Jewish Legion,* p. 10.
6. Letter to S. L. Jacobi, September 22, 1933.
7. Altalena. "At a Ball," *R.,* November 26, 1933.
8. Alex Bein. *Theodore Herzl,* p. 204.
9. Letter to S. D. Salzman, February 9, 1936.
10. Interview with Mordehai Katz, New York.
11. Alex Bein, *op. cit.,* p. 234.
12. Interview with Mrs. M. Kahan.
13. Jack Tauber, "Off the Record," *loc. cit.*
14. V. Jabotinsky. "Leadership" (1929), quoted from the English translation published in *J.St.,* August 10, 1945.
15. Letter to J. Bartlett, December 9, 1938.
16. V. Jabotinsky. "Revolt of the Elders," *Contemporary Annals* (russ.), LXIII, Paris, 1937.

17. V. Jabotinsky. "Leadership," *loc. cit.*
18. Interview with Dr. J. Szofman, Tel Aviv.
19. Alex Bein. *Theodore Herzl,* p. 432.
20. M. Berchin. "Alone," *Zionews,* September 1, 1942.
21. *Ibid.*
22. *Ibid.*
23. Eliahu Ben Horin. "The Non-Obvious in Jabotinsky," *Zionews,* September 1, 1942.
24. Letters to S. L. Jacobi, January 20, 1930, and March 22, 1927; letter to Mrs. T. E. Jabotinsky-Kopp, October 22, 1931; letter to David Raziel, November 18, 1939.

INDEX

INDEX

Abrahams, Abraham, 181, 362, 391, 549
Abyssinia, 296, 298, 299, 303, 454
Achad Haam, 67, 123, 456, 513, 553
Achimeir, Dr. Abba, 7, 96, 161, 185, 196, 201, 216, 251, 434-440
Acre, 502, 504
Actions Committee of the World Zionist Organization, 70, 77, 93, 144, 157, 166, 195, 196, 203, 271, 275, 276, 378
Adams, Vivian, 469
Af-Al-Pi, 181, 423, 427
Agronsky (Agron), Gershon, 94
Agudat Israel, 56, 377, 444, 558
Ahdut ha' Avoda, 230
Akzin, Dr. Benjamin, 326, 327, 330, 379, 380, 387, 468
Aleinikov, Michael S., 65
Alexandria, 320, 321
Al Hamishmar, 185
Aliyah, 281
Aliyah Bet, 427, 457, 458, 482, 485
Al Jamia al Islamia, 130
Allen, Isaak, 258
Allies, 370, 372
Al Parashat Drakhim, 68
Altalena, 140
Altman, Dr. Arye, 460, 463, 489
America, 46, 113
American Jewish Congress, 30
Amery, Leopold S., 87, 107, 126, 127, 296, 297, 298, 310, 311, 394, 504
Amnon, 59
Angel, A., 142, 145
Ani maamin, 150
Anti-Semitism, 124, 186, 216, 304, 365, 366, 386, 477, 561
Anti-Semitism of Things, 335, 336
Arab Executive Committee, 126
Arabian Nights, 303

Arabic Language, 541, 587
Arabs, 184, 303, 324, 325, 326, 353, 366, 408, 434, 447, 449, 450, 452, 453, 469, 473, 474, 485
Argentine, 345
Aristide, 157
Arlosoroff, Dr. Chaim, 104, 150, 158, 184, 186, 189, 199, 202, 203, 261, 417, 418, 439, 484, 485
Art epistolaire, 19, 226-229, 268
Asbeck, von, Baron, 301
Asch, Sholom, 341
Ashkenazi Jews and Hebrew pronunciation, 26, 583, 584, 592
Assefat ha' Nivcharim, 109, 158
Austria, 34, 36, 44, 180
Avukah, 261
Azmi, Dr. Mahmoud, 65, 66

Bader, Dr. Jan, 339
Baldwin, Stanley, 301
Balfour Declaration, 123, 124, 126, 144, 160, 294, 297, 307, 322
Balm of Gilead, 58, 59
Bar Giora, Student Corps, 79
Barissia, Student Corps, 36, 540
Bar Kochba, 79, 111, 410, 411
Bar Kochba, Student Corps, 79, 478
Bar Mitzvah, 58
Barnes, Harry Elmer, 385
Barondes, Joseph, 53
Bartlett, J., 562
Battershill, Sir William Denis, 481
Baudelaire, Charles, 515
Bayard, Pierre Terraie, 559
Beck, Col. Josef, 327, 341, 354, 357
Begin, Menachem, 7, 197, 251, 381, 415, 451, 453, 457, 490

631

INDEX

United Palestine Appeal, 51
United States of America, 52, 91, 256, 257, 264, 270, 345, 352, 353, 370, 384, 396, 432, 483, 538
Unser Welt, 82
Untermeyer, Samuel, 218
Ussishkin, Menachem, 137, 411, 423, 453

Vaad Leumi, 64, 65, 89, 93, 103, 106, 108, 116, 122, 123, 129, 382, 461
Valery, Paul, 566
Van Paassen, Pierre, 514, 538, 570
Vellos, 422
Ventadour, De, Bernard, 544
Verlaine, Paul 515, 588
Verne, Jules, 27
Vienna, 30, 34, 40, 44, 79, 105, 167, 280, 282, 510, 521, 550, 580
Vienna Congress of the New Zionist Organization, 282-288
Vilna, 399
Virgil, 542, 544
Voelkischer Beobachter, Der, 217
Voix Juive, La, 82

Wagner H. and Debes E., 29
Wailing Wall, 92, 116, 118, 119, 452
Wallenrod, Konrad, 448, 515, 539
Warburg, Felix, 39, 132
War Office, British, 297-299, 485, 488
Warsaw, 36, 82, 85, 105, 130, 131, 162, 292, 302, 347, 365, 366, 399, 460, 462, 478, 479, 497, 510, 565
Warshawsky, Mark M., 445
Wasssilovsky, Leon, 356
Waterman-Wise, James, 261
Waterman-Wise, Mrs. Louise, 266, 267
Wauchope, Sir Arthur, 129, 130, 131, 203, 302, 473
Wdowinsky, Dr. David, 399
Webster, Daniel, 523
Wedgwood, Colonel Joshua, 87, 107, 108, 109, 127, 129, 200, 202, 305, 306, 310-312, 316, 317, 426, 427, 431, 471-473, 504
Weiler, Rabbi M. C., 312, 316, 317
Weinshal, Dr. Abraham, 193, 196, 199, 509
Weinshal, Dr. Jacob, 37
Weinstein, Dr. Baruch, 436

Weisbrot, Aaron M., 262, 271
Weisgal, Mayer, 48
Weisl, von, Dr. Wolfgang, 121, 127, 161, 285, 326, 328
Weizmann, Dr. Chaim, 26, 36, 39-43, 61, 77, 92, 124, 132, 137, 144, 150-153, 230, 248, 309, 310, 314, 322, 323, 330, 350, 375-378, 389, 390, 392-394, 429, 450, 456, 465, 485, 505, 506, 550, 552-554, 560, 571
Weizmann, Mrs. Vera, 151, 306
Welfare State, 244
Wells, H. G., 21
Weltsch, Robert, 521
White Paper, The, 43, 132, 365, 366, 477, 478, 482, 488
White, Zalman, 94, 96, 97
Wilcox, Ella Wheeler, 337
Wilson, Woodrow, 555
Wise, Rabbi Stephen S., 151, 152, 260, 261, 265-270, 341, 392
Wolfson, David, 565
Wolfson, Leo, 8
Woodhead Commission, 475
Wyspiansky, Stanislas, 539

Xerxes, 477

Yeivin, Joshua H., 96, 216, 535
Yeivin, N., 36
Yehuda, Professor A. S., 472
Yerozolima Wyzwolona, 456, 460
Yerusholaim, 97, 129
Yevreyski Glas, 36
Yiddische Stimme, 63, 189
Yiddish language, 545, 583
Yiddishe Folk, Dos, 32, 48
Yiddisher Kempfer, Der, 342
Yishuv, 61, 63, 64, 67, 89, 91, 92, 113, 116, 121, 200, 201, 232, 236, 237, 294, 365, 369, 429, 442-444, 461, 466, 470, 476, 477, 485, 549
Yugoslavia, 328
Yunitchman, Dr. Shimshon, 225, 322, 452, 453, 491
Yushinsky, Andrei, 186
Yushkevitch, Semion, 559

Zajczyk, M., 510
Zangwill, Israel, 30, 33, 269, 325, 569